SolidWorks 2021
Step-By-Step Guide

CADFolks

© Copyright 2021 by **CADFolks**

This book may not be duplicated in any way without the express written consent of the publisher, except in the form of brief excerpts or quotations for the purpose of review. The information contained herein is for the personal use of the reader and may not be incorporated in any commercial programs, other books, database, or any kind of software without written consent of the publisher. Making copies of this book or any portion for purpose other than your own is a violation of copyright laws.

Limit of Liability/Disclaimer of Warranty:
The author and publisher make no representations or warranties with respect to the accuracy or completeness of the contents of this work and specifically disclaim all warranties, including without limitation warranties of fitness for a particular purpose. The advice and strategies contained herein may not be suitable for every situation. Neither the publisher nor the author shall be liable for damages arising here from.

Trademarks:
All brand names and product names used in this book are trademarks, registered trademarks, or trade names of their respective holders. The author and publisher are not associated with any product or vendor mentioned in this book.

For Technical Support, contact us at:

cadfolks@gmail.com, mail@cadfolks.com

For Resource files, please visit:

www.cadfolks.com

Contents

Introduction i

Topics covered in this book ii

Chapter No 1: Getting Started with SolidWorks 2021 1-1

Introduction to SolidWorks 2021 1-1

Environments in SolidWorks 2021 1-1

    Part Environment 1-1

    Assembly Environment 1-2

    Drawing Environment 1-2

Parametric Modeling in SolidWorks 1-2

Associativity in SolidWorks 1-3

File Types in SolidWorks 1-3

Starting SolidWorks 2021 1-3

SolidWorks User Interface 1-4

Quick Access Toolbar 1-5

    New 1-5

    Open 1-7

    Save 1-7

Menu Bar 1-8

View (Heads-Up) Toolbar 1-8

CommandManager 1-8

Part Environment 1-9

    Features CommandManager 1-9

    Sketch CommandManager 1-9

    Sheet Metal CommandManager 1-9

    Evaulate CommandManager 1-10

    DimXpert CommandManager 1-10

Assembly CommandManager 1-10

    Assembly CommandManager 1-10

Drawing Environment 1-11

    ViewLayout CommandManager 1-11

    Annotation CommandManager 1-11

FeaturesManager Design Tree 1-11

Changing Background Color 1-11

Mouse Functions 1-12

    Left Mouse button (LMB/MB1) 1-12

    Middle Mouse button (MMB/MB2) 1-13

    Right Mouse button (RMB/MB3) 1-13

Some of the Important Shortcuts in SolidWorks 1-14

Questions 1-16

Chapter No 2: Basic Sketching tools 2-1

Starting a New Document in SolidWorks 2021 2-1

    Sketching directly in the Part Environment 2-2

Draw Tools 2-3

    The Line tool 2-3

        Line Tool 2-3

        Centerline Tool 2-7

        Midpoint Tool 2-7

    The Circle tool 2-8

        Circle Tool 2-8

        Perimeter Circle Tool 2-9

    The Spline Tool 2-10

        Spline Tool 2-10

        Editing the Spline Tool 2-12

    The Rectangle Tool 2-13

        Corner Rectangle 2-13

        Center Rectangle 2-14

        3 Point Corner Rectangle 2-14

    3 Point Center Rectangle 2-15

    Parallelogram 2-15

  The Arc Tool 2-16

    Centerpoint Arc Tool 2-16

    Tangent Arc Tool 2-17

    3 Point Arc Tool 2-17

  The Ellipse tool 2-18

    Partial Ellipse Tool 2-19

    Parabola Tool 2-19

    Conic Tool 2-21

  The Slot Tool 2-22

    Straight Slot Tool 2-22

    Centerpoint Straight Slot Tool 2-23

    3 Point Arc Slot Tool 2-24

    Centerpoint Arc Slot Tool 2-25

  The Polygon tool 2-25

  The Point Tool 2-27

Dimensioning 2-28

  Applying Dimensions to the Sketch Using Smart Dimension Tool ....,,........................ 2-28

  Linear Dimension 2-30

  Radial & Diametric Dimension 2-31

  Angular Dimension 2-32

  Applying Diametric Dimension to the Sketch of Revolve Features 2-33

Examples 2-35

  Example 1 2-35

  Example 2 2-39

  Example 3 2-41

Questions 2-46

Exercises 2-46

  Exercise 1 2-46

iii

Exercise 2 2-47

Exercise 3 2-47

Chapter No 3: Advance Sketching & Editing tools 3-1

The Fillet tool 3-1

    Sketch Fillet Tool 3-1

    Sketch Chamfer Tool 3-3

        Angle-distance 3-3

        Distance-distance 3-4

Trim Entities Tool 3-6

    Power Trim 3-6

    Corner 3-7

    Trim Away Inside 3-8

    Trim Away Outside 3-8

    Trim to closest 3-9

Extend Entities Tool 3-9

Convert Entities Tool 3-10

Text Tool 3-11

Offset Entities Tool 3-13

Mirror Entities Tool 3-16

Creating Patterns 3-18

    Linear Sketch Pattern 3-18

    Circular Sketch Pattern 3-19

Editing Patterns 3-21

    Editing Linear Pattern 3-21

    Editing Circular Pattern 3-21

Editing Tools 3-22

    The Move Entities tool 3-22

    The Copy Entities tool 3-24

    The Rotate Entities tool 3-24

The Scale Entities tool	3-25
The Stretch Entities tool	3-27

Questions 3-28

Exercises 3-28

    Exercise 1 3-28

    Exercise 2 3-29

    Exercise 3 3-29

Chapter No 4: Applying Dimensions and Geometric Relations 4-1

Dimensioning 4-1

    Smart Dimensioning 4-1

    Horizontal Dimension 4-2

    Vertical Dimension 4-3

    Ordinate Dimension 4-4

    Horizontal Ordinate Dimension 4-4

    Vertical Ordinate Dimension 4-5

    Path Length Dimension 4-5

Geometric Relations 4-6

    Horizontal 4-6

    Vertical 4-7

    Collinear 4-8

    Perpendicular 4-8

    Parallel 4-8

    Equal 4-9

    Tangent 4-9

    Coincident 4-10

    Midpoint 4-11

    Concentric 4-11

    Intersection 4-11

    Cordial 4-12

Symmetric	4-12
Fix	4-12
Merge	4-13

Turn ON/OFF Dimensions and Relations 4-13

Examples 4-14

    Example 1 4-14

    Example 2 4-21

    Example 3 4-26

Questions 4-32

Chapter No 5: Solid Modeling Tools 5-1

Extruded Boss/Base Tool 5-1

Extruded Cut Tool 5-10

Revolved Boss/Base Tool 5-17

    Revolve the Sketch as Solid 5-17

    Revolve the sketch as Surface 5-18

Revolved Cut Tool 5-20

    Removing Material by using Revolved Cut Tool 5-20

Examples 5-22

    Example 1 5-22

    Example 2 5-24

Questions 5-31

Exercises 5-31

    Exercise 1 5-31

    Exercise 2 5-32

    Exercise 3 5-32

Chapter No 6: Reference Geometry and Curves 6-1

Reference Features 6-1

Default Plane 6-1

Uses of Reference Plane 6-2

Creating Reference Plane 6-2
    Creating An Offset Plane 6-2
    Creating Plane Through Selected Points 6-5
    Creating Plane At An Angle 6-6
    Creating Tangent Plane 6-7
    Creating Parallel Plane 6-8
Reference Axis 6-10
Uses of Reference Axis 6-10
Creating Reference Axis 6-11
    Two Planes 6-12
    Two Points/Vertices 6-12
    Cylindrical/Conical Face 6-12
    Point and Face/Plane 6-13
Reference Coordinate System 6-14
Creating Reference Point 6-15
    Arc Center 6-15
    Center of Face 6-16
    Intersection 6-17
    Projection 6-17
    On Point 6-17
    Along Curve Distance or multiple reference point 6-18
Center of Mass 6-18
Mass Properties 6-18
Questions 6-19

Chapter No 7: Hole Features and Pattern Geometry 7-1

Hole 7-1
    Creating Simple Hole 7-1
Hole Wizard 7-3
    Creating Counterbore Hole 7-4

Creating Countersink Hole	7-9
Creating Hole	7-9
Creating Counterbore Slot	7-10
Mirror	**7-11**
Mirror a Feature/Features of a model	7-11
Mirror the Whole model	7-12
Pattern Tools	**7-13**
Linear Pattern	7-13
Editing the Linear Pattern	7-14
Circular Pattern	7-15
Curve Driven Pattern	7-16
Sketch Driven Pattern	7-17
Questions	**7-18**
Exercises	**7-18**
Exercise 1	7-18
Exercise 2	7-19

Chapter No 8: Advance Solid Modeling Tools 8-1

Swept Boss/Base Tool	8-1
Sweep Feature with Guide Curve	8-3
Sweep Feature with Twist	8-4
Using the Swept Cut Tool for Removing Material	8-4
Swept Cut with Circular Profile radio button	8-5
Swept Cut with Solid Profile radio button	8-6
Lofted Boss/Base Tool	8-7
Loft Feature by Defining Start and End Constraint	8-9
Lofted Feature with Guide Curve	8-10
Lofted Cut Tool	8-12
Boundary Boss/Base Tool	8-12
Boundary Cut Tool	8-15

Examples 8-17
    Example 1 8-17
    Example 2 8-22
Questions 8-29
Exercises 8-29
    Exercise 1 8-29
    Exercise 2 8-30

Chapter No 9: Advanced Solid Modeling Tools -II 9-1

Rib Feature 9-1
    Create a Rib Feature 9-1
    Create a Rib Feature by Selecting asn Existing Sketch 9-2
Draft Feature 9-3
Shell Feature 9-5
    Shell with Multiple Thickness 9-6
Wrap Tool 9-7
Mirror Tool 9-9
    Mirror a Feature/features of a Model 9-9
    Mirror the Whole Model 9-11
Fillet Tool 9-11
    Constant Size Fillet 9-11
    Variable Size Fillet 9-13
    Face Fillet 9-15
    Full Round Fillet 9-15
FilletXpert 9-16
    Add Tab 9-17
    Change Tab 9-18
    Corner Tab 9-19
Chamfer Tool 9-20
    Angle Distance 9-20
    Distance Distance 9-20

Vertex	9-21
Offset Face	9-22
Face Face	9-23

Questions 9-25

Exercises 9-25

    Exercise 1 9-25

    Exercise 2 9-25

    Exercise 3 9-26

    Exercise 4 9-26

Chapter No 10: Creating Assemblies 10-1

Starting an Assembly 10-1

Assembly Environment 10-1

Inserting Components 10-2

Applying Mates 10-4

    Automatic Mate 10-4

    Coincident Mate 10-6

    Parallel Mate 10-6

    Perpendicular Mate 10-7

    Tangent Mate 10-7

    Concentric Mate 10-7

    Lock two Components Together 10-7

    Distance Mate 10-8

    Angle Mate 10-8

    Fix 10-8

Advanced Mates 10-9

    Profile Center 10-9

    Symmetric 10-10

    Width 10-10

    Path Mate 10-11

Linear/Linear Coupler	10-12
Distance	10-13
Angle	10-13
Mate Alignment	10-13
Exploded View	10-14
Example	10-16
Example 1	10-16
Example 2	10-24
Questions	10-38
Exercises	10-38
Exercise 1	10-38

Chapter No 11: Drawings and Views 11-1

Starting a Drawing in SolidWorks 2021	11-1
Drawing Sheet Selection	11-3
Edit Sheet Size	11-4
Creating a Drawing from any Opened Part or Assembly	11-5
Generating Standard Views	11-7
Generating model Views	11-8
Projected View	11-11
Auxiliary View	11-12
Section View	11-12
Detail View	11-13
Broken-out Section	11-14
Break	11-14
Generating the Drawing View of an Exploded Assembly	11-15
Generating Bill of Material	11-15
Adding Balloons	11-16
Adding Balloons Using Auto Balloon Tool	11-17
Customize the Title Block	11-18

Applying Dimensions to the Drawing View 11-20

    Generating Dimensions of the Drawing View 11-20

Examples 11-22

    Example 1 11-22

Questions 11-26

Exercises 11-26

    Exercise 1 11-26

    Exercise 2 11-27

Chapter No 12: Sheet Metal Design 12-1

Starting a Sheetmetal Part File 12-2

Convert to Sheet Metal 12-9

Lofted Bend 12-11

Edge Flange 12-13

Miter Flange 12-21

Hem 12-24

Jog 12-27

Sketched Bend 12-29

Cross-Break 12-30

Swept Flange 12-31

Corners 12-33

Sheet Metal Gusset 12-37

Tab and Slot 12-37

Extruded Cut 12-39

Simple Hole 12-40

Vent 12-41

Unfold Tool 12-43

Fold Tool 12-44

Flatten 12-45

Rip Tool 12-47

Insert Bend Tool	12-47
No Bends Tool	12-49
Questions	12-50

Chapter No 13: Surface Design 13-1

Extruded Surface	13-1
Revolved Surface	13-3
Swept Surface	13-4
Lofted Surface	13-5
Boundary Surface	13-6
Filled Surface	13-7
Freeform	13-9
Planar Surface	13-11
Offset Surface	13-12
Ruled Surface	13-12
Surface Flatten	13-16
Fillet	13-17
Surface Editing Tools	13-18
Delete Face	13-18
Replace Face	13-20
Extend Surface	13-21
Trim Surface	13-22
Untrim Surface	13-24
Knit Surface	13-25
Thicken Surface	13-26
Thicken Cut	13-27
Cut With Surface	13-27
Questions	13-29
Exercises	13-29
Exercise 1	13-29

INDEX I-1

Introduction

Welcome to the **SolidWorks 2021 Step-By-Step Guide** book. This book is written to assist students, designers, and engineering professionals. It covers the important features and functionalities of SolidWorks using relevant examples and exercises.

This book is written for new users, who can use it as a self-study resource to learn SolidWorks. In addition, it can also be used as a reference for experienced users. The focus of this book is part modeling, assembly modeling, drawings, sheet metal, and surface design.

Topics covered in this Book:

Chapter 1, "**Getting Started with SolidWorks 2021**", introduces SolidWorks. The user interface and terminology are discussed in this chapter.

Chapter 2, "**Basic Sketching tools**", explores the basic sketch tools in SolidWorks. You will also learn to create parametric sketches.

Chapter 3, "**Advance Sketching & Editing Tools**", teaches you advance sketch tools and various editing tools used while creating complex sketches in the Sketch Environment.

Chapter 4, "**Applying Dimensions & Geometric Relations**", teaches you to apply dimensions and geometric relations to the sketch or sketch entities.

Chapter 5, "**Solid Modeling Tools**", teaches you to create basic 3D geometry using the Extrude and Revolve tools.

Chapter 6, "**Reference Geometry and Curves**", explores the tools used to create reference planes, reference axes, reference coordinate systems, and reference point.

Chapter 7, "**Hole Features and Pattern Geometry**", explores the tools to create Holes, patterned and mirrored geometry.

Chapter 8, "**Advance Solid Modeling Tools**", teaches you to create basic and complex features by sweeping a profile along a path.

Chapter 9, "**Advance Solid Modeling Tools-II**", teaches you advanced features used while creating complex features.

Chapter 10, "**Creating Assemblies**", explains you to create assemblies using various assembly tools in the Assembly Environment.

Chapter 11, "**Drawings and Views**", covers how to create 2D drawings from 3D parts and assemblies in the Drawing Environment.

Chapter 12, "**Sheet Metal Design**", covers how to create sheet metal parts and flat patterns in the Sheetmetal Environment.

Chapter 13, "**Surface Design**", covers how to create complex shapes using surface design tools.

Chapter 01: Getting Started with SolidWorks 2021

Introduction to SolidWorks 2021

SolidWorks is a parametric and feature-based software that allows you to create 3D parts, assemblies, and 2D drawings. The design process in SolidWorks is shown below. If you are a new user of this software, then the time you spend on learning this software will be a wise investment. If you have used previous versions of SolidWorks, you will be able to learn the new enhancements. I welcome you to learn SolidWorks using this book as it provides step-by-step examples to learn various tools and techniques.

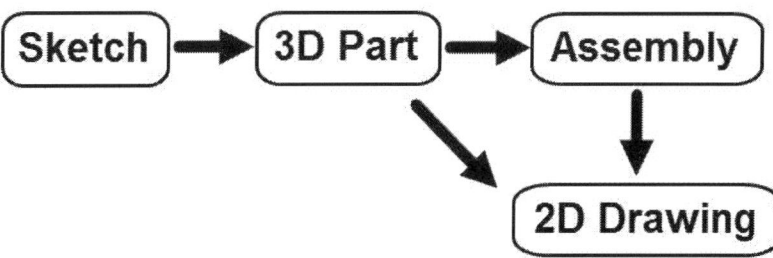

Environments in SolidWorks 2021

SolidWorks offers various types of environments to perform different types of operations. For Example, SolidWorks provides you with the Part Environment to design a part, Assembly environment to perform assemblies, similarly there are many other environments to perform advance operations such as, manufacturing process, process diagrams, drawings, and so on. However, in this book we cover basic environments like Part, Assembly, Drawing, Sheet Metal, and Surfacing. A brief introduction to these environments is given next.

Part Environment

The **Part** environment provides you the tools to create parametric solid models. You can start a document in this environment by clicking the **New** icon and then double-clicking on the **Part** button from the **New SOLIDWORKS Document** dialog box, as shown.

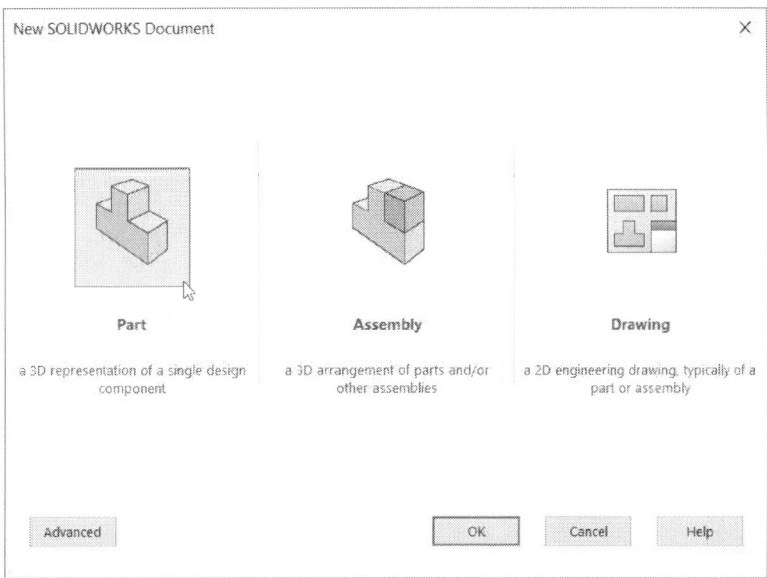

To create solid models, you must draw parametric sketches in the **Sketch** environment and then convert them into solid model, as shown.

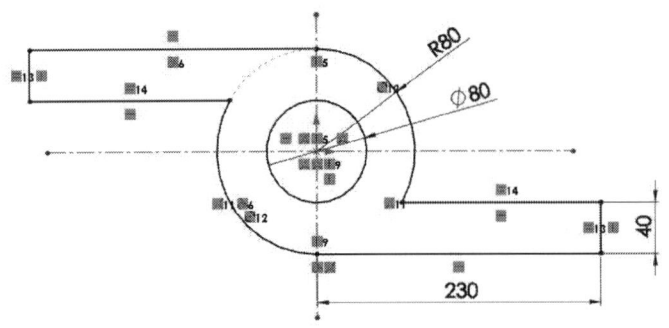
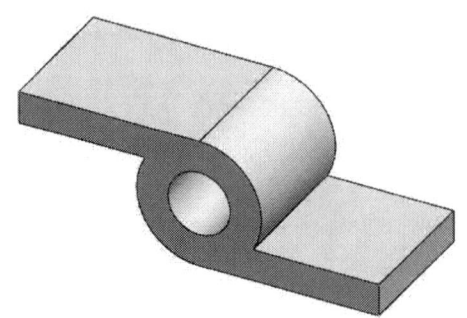

However, you can add some additional features to the solid model, which do not require sketches like hole, fillet, chamfer and so on, as shown.

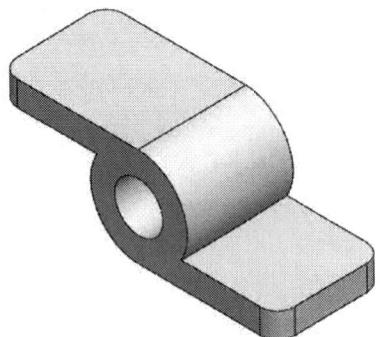
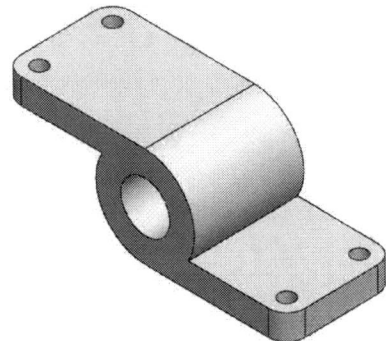

Assembly Environment
The Assembly environment (click on the **Assembly** button from the **New SOLIDWORKS Document** dialog box) has tools to combine individual parts in an assembly. There are two ways to create an assembly. The first way is to create individual parts and assemble them in the Assembly environment, known as **Bottom-up assembly design**. The second way is to start an assembly file and create individual parts in it, known as **Top-down assembly design**.

Drawing Environment
The **Drawing** environment (click on the **Drawing** button from the **New SOLIDWORKS Document** dialog box) has tools to create 2D drawings, which can be used for the manufacturing process. There are two methods to create drawings. The first method is to generate the standard views of a 3D component or assembly. The second method is to sketch the drawing manually.

Parametric Modeling in SolidWorks
In SolidWorks, parameters, dimensions, or constraints control everything. For example, if you want to change the position of the hole shown in figure, you need to change the dimension and constraint that controls its position.

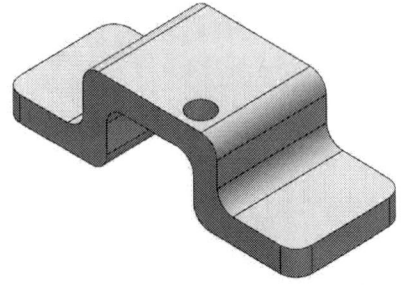
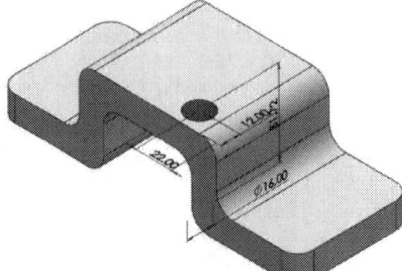
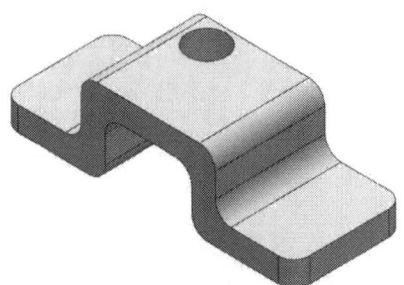

Similarly, if you want to change the radius of the fillet feature applied to the below given model, you can simply double-click over any filled corner and then click over the radius value displayed and enter the required values in the edit box, as shown. Note that you need to click on **Rebuild** button from the **Quick Access toolbar** to apply changes.

Alternatively, you can directly edit the respective feature from the **FeatureManager design tree** located on the left of the screen, which will be discussed further in this book.

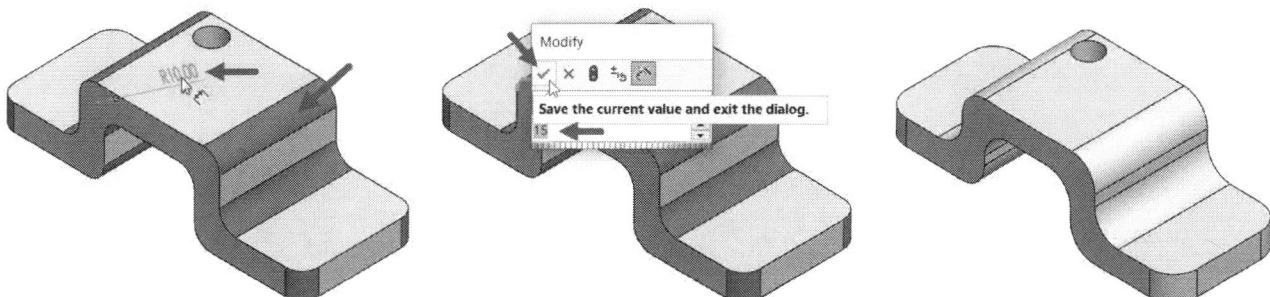

Associativity in SolidWorks

The other big advantage of SolidWorks is the associativity between parts, assemblies, and drawing. When you make changes to a part, the changes will take place in in any assembly that it is a part of, as shown. In addition, the 2D drawing will update automatically.

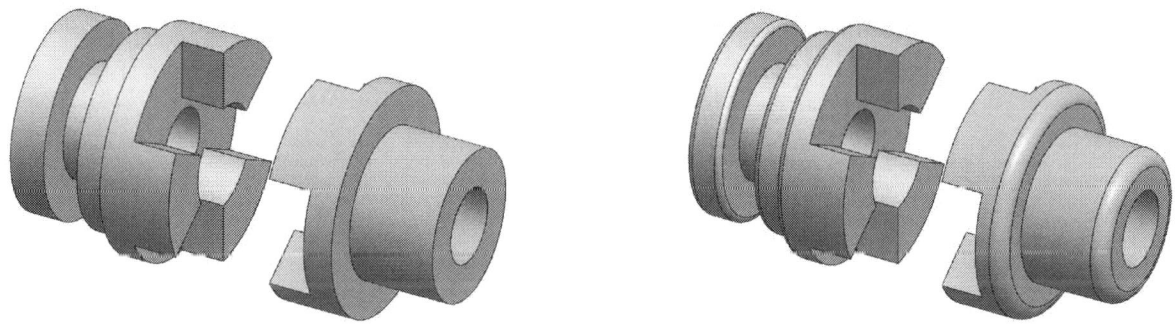

File Types in SolidWorks

Creo Parametric offers three main file types:

(*.prt;*.sldprt): This type of file has a geometry of individual part. The files created in Part environment. Sheetmetal environments will have this extension.

(*.asm; *.sldasm): This type of file is an assembly of one or more parts. In fact, it is a link of one or more parts.

.drw: The files created in the drawing environment have this extension.

Starting SolidWorks 2021

To start **SolidWorks 2021**, double-click on the **SolidWorks 2021** icon on your desktop. Alternatively, click **Start** > **SolidWorks 2021** > **SolidWorks 2021**, as shown.

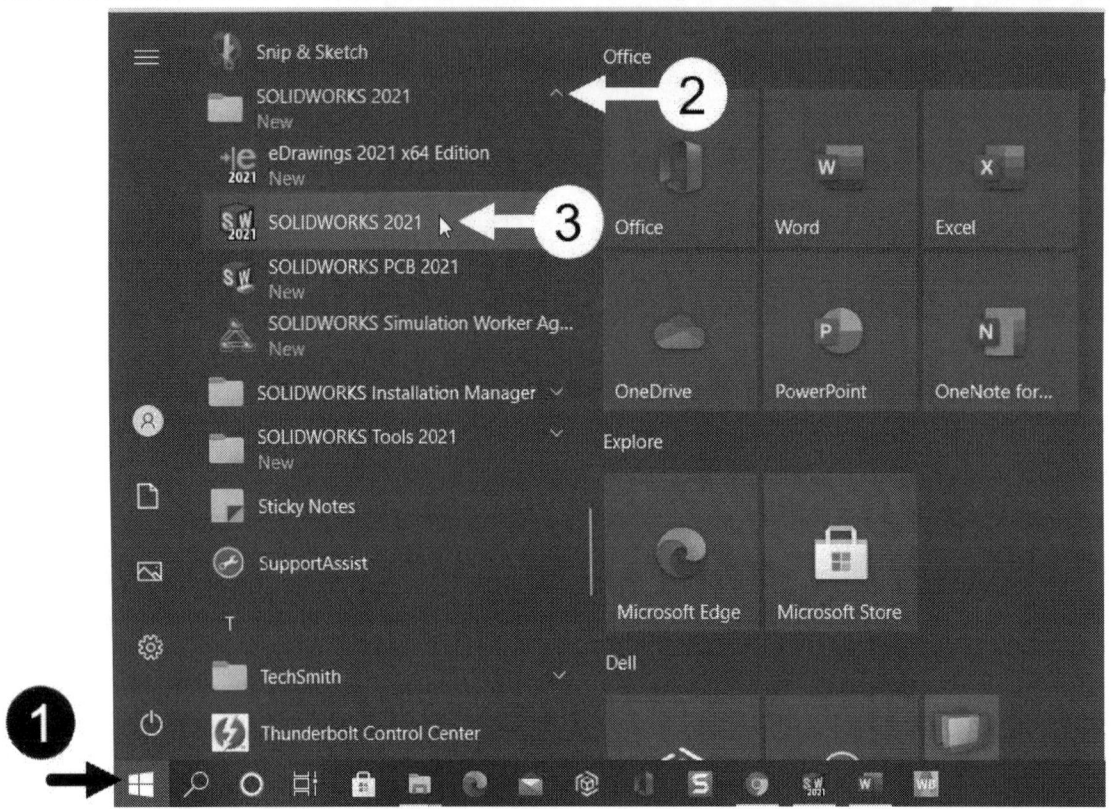

SolidWorks User interface

While starting SolidWorks for the first time, the SolidWorks screen with **Welcome – SolidWorks 2021** dialog box by default get displayed, as shown.

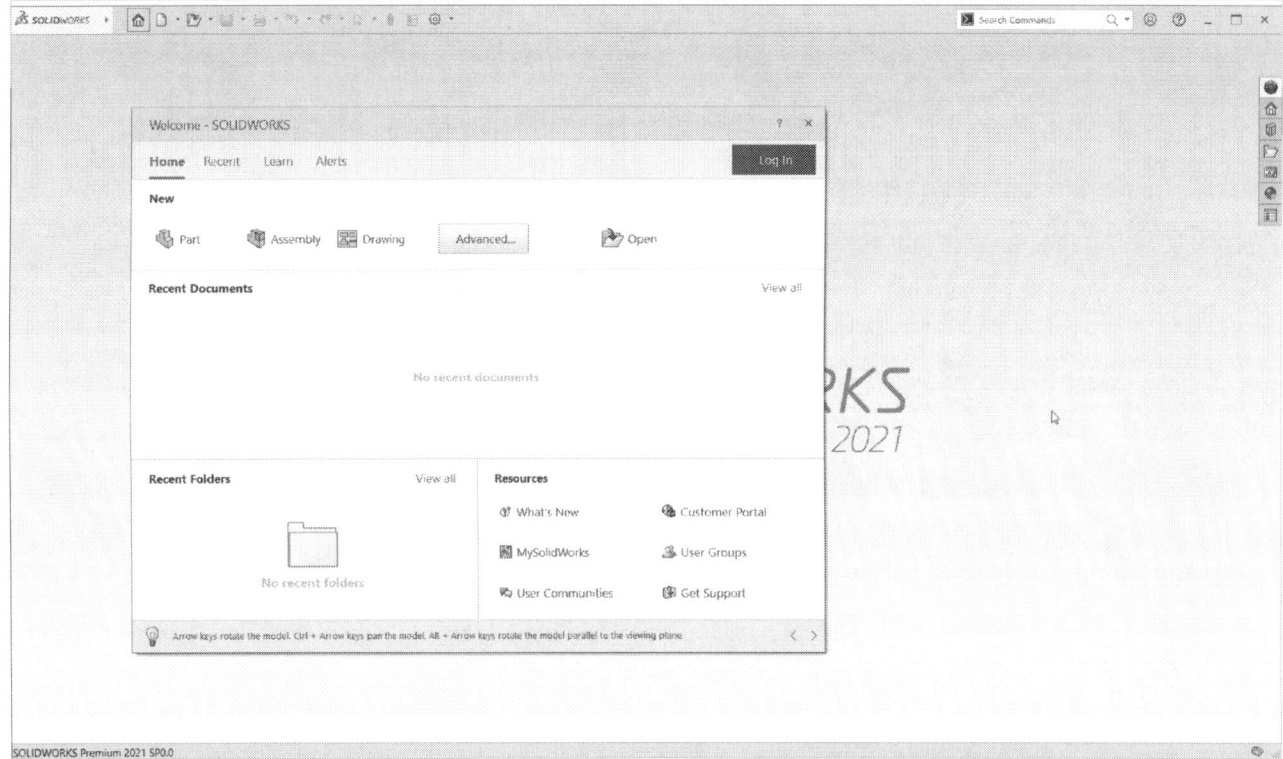

To enter in the Part environment, click on the **Part** button from the **Welcome – SolidWorks 2021** dialog box displayed by default, as shown.

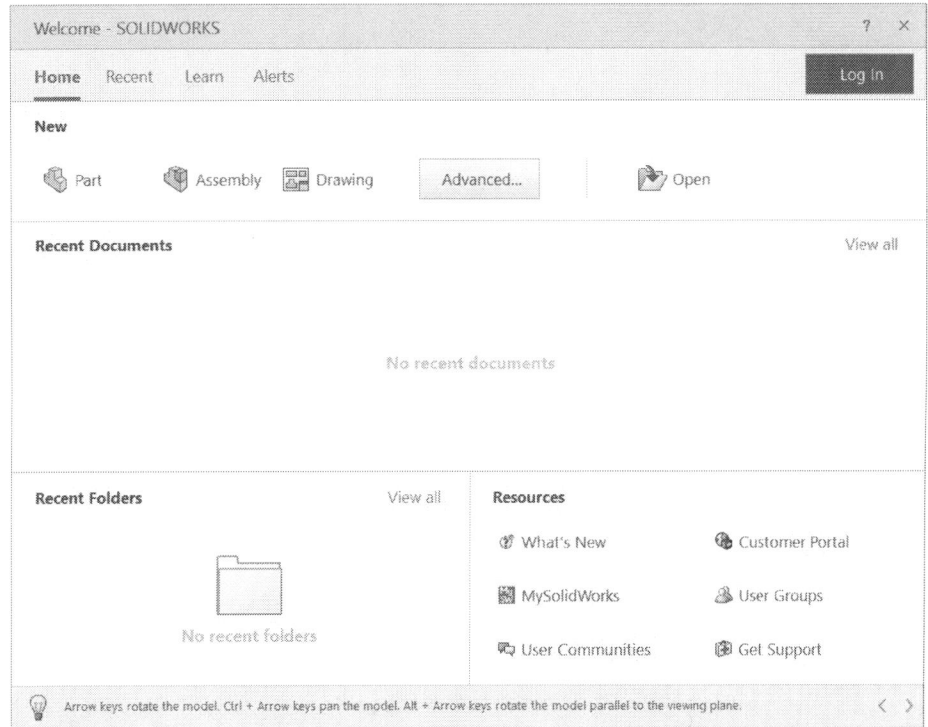

You can also click on the **New** button from the **Quick Access Toolbar** to display **New SOLIDWORKS Document**, as shown.

Various components of the user interface are:

Quick Access Toolbar
The **Quick Access Toolbar** is located at the top of the **SolidWorks** or above CommandManager. It provides quick access to some commonly used tools such as **Home, New, Open, Save, Print, Undo, Select, Rebuild**, and so on, as shown.

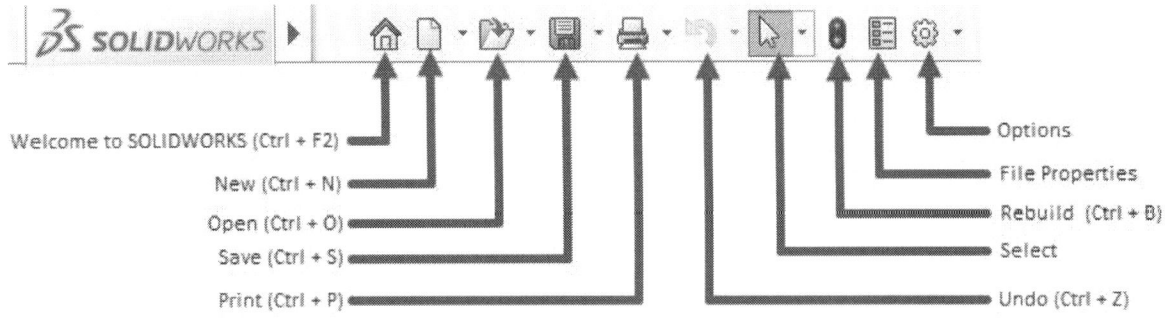

Some of the commonly used tools in **Quick Access Toolbar** are discussed next.

New
The **New** tool is used to display **New SOLIDWORKS Document** dialog box with **Part, Assembly**, and **Drawing** buttons used to enter their respective environments of SolidWorks.

> Click on the **New** button from the **Quick Access Toolbar** to display **New SOLIDWORKS Document** dialog box, as shown.
> Next double-click on the **Part** button to enter in the Part Environment, as shown.

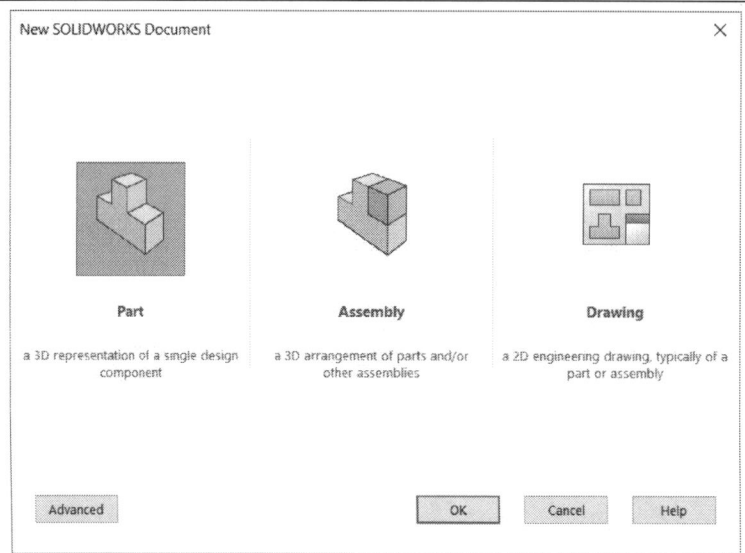

Note that if you are using SolidWorks for the first time on your system, the **Units and Dimension Standard** dialog box get displayed on your screen, as shown. Select the unit system as **MMGS (millimetre, gram, second)** and dimension standard as **ISO**, as shown.

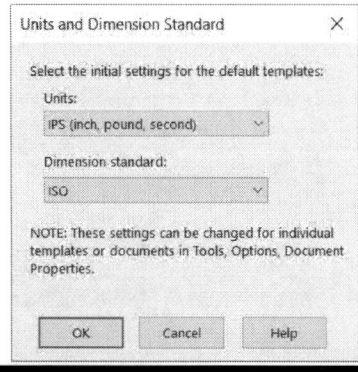 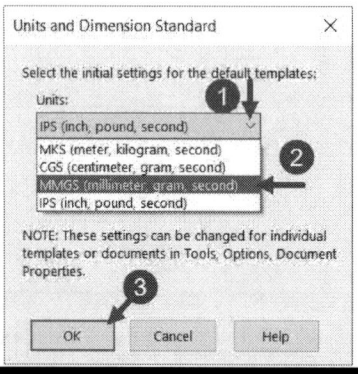 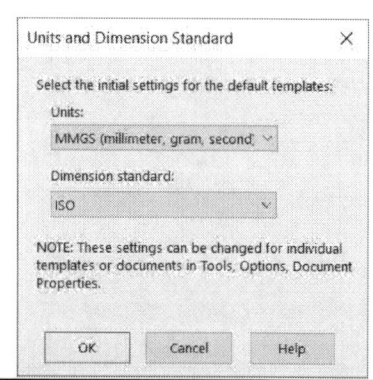

Open

The **Open** button is used to display **Open** dialog box to open existing SolidWorks files in the system.

➢ Click on the **Open** button from the **Quick Access Toolbar** to display **Open** dialog box, as shown.

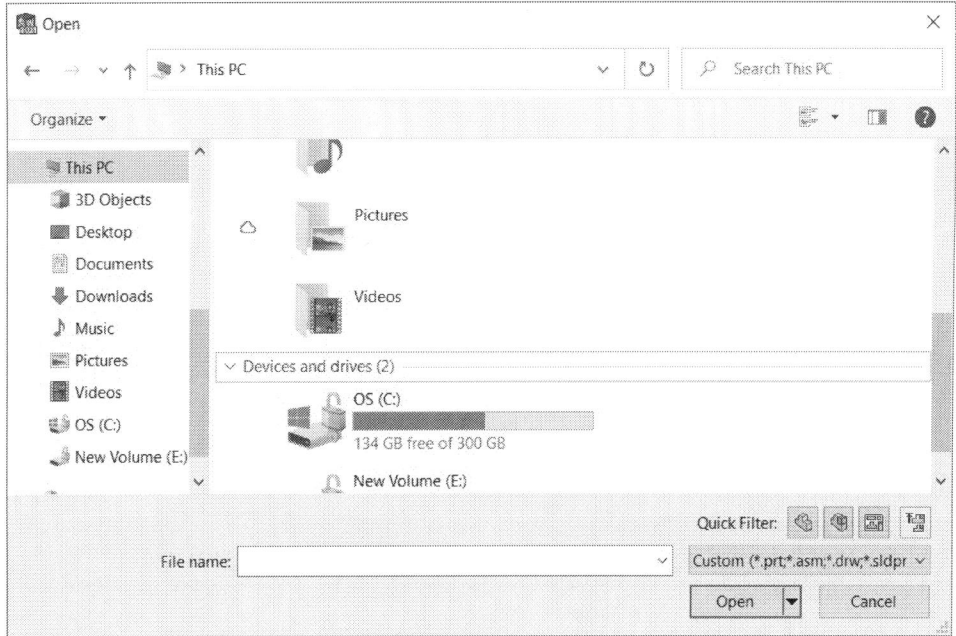

➢ Next browse to the required object file in the required folder in **Open** dialog box, as shown.
➢ Select the required file and click on the **Open** button to open it, as shown.

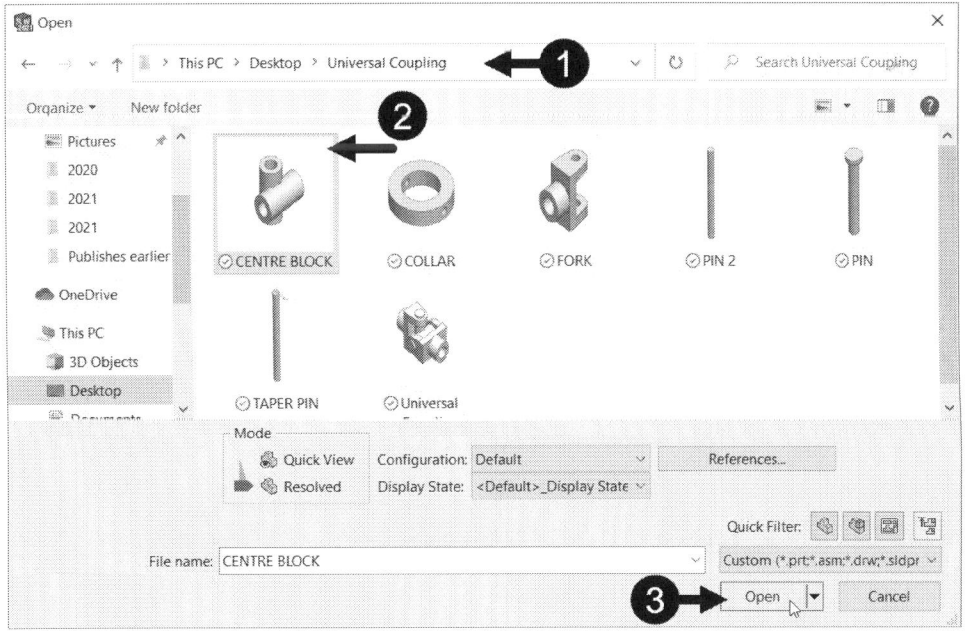

Save

The **Save** button is used to save the model created in various SolidWorks environments, in the desired folder.

➢ After creating any model, click on the **Save** button to display the **Save As** dialog box, as shown.
➢ Browse to the desired folder and enter the desired name in the **File name** edit box, if required.
➢ Next, click on the **Save** button to save the file in the selected folder, as shown.

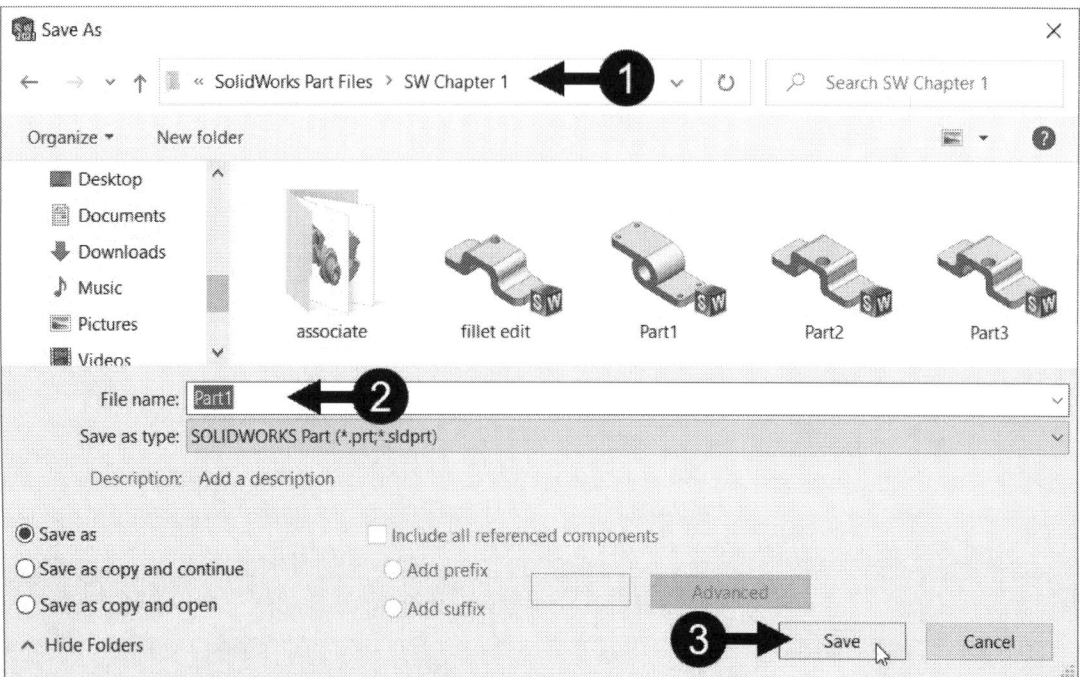

Note: When you click on the **Save** button, the **Save As** dialog box with the previously selected folder get displayed. If you click on the **Save** button the object gets saved in that folder. You can browse to any other folder/location and save the object there, if required.

Menu Bar

To display the Menu bar:

> Move the cursor over ▶ arrow at top left corner of the SolidWorks window, as shown.
> Next, click on the 📌 icon to pin the menu bar, as shown.

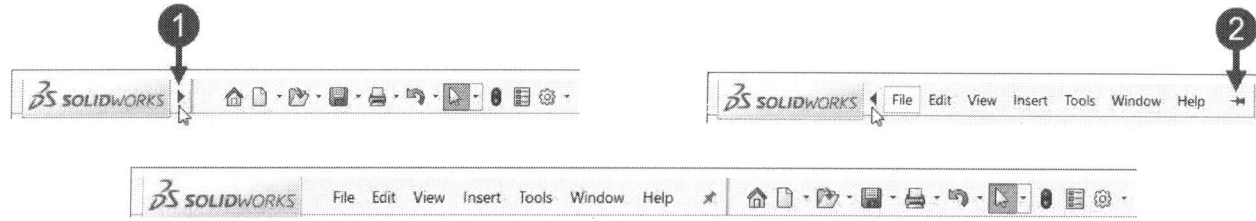

View (Heads-Up) Toolbar

This toolbar is located at the top of the drawing/graphic area. In this toolbar, the tools used to modify display are grouped in it, shown.

CommandManager

CommandManager is located at the top of the window and below the Menu Bar, as shown. It contains tools organized in the set of various CommandManager tabs. On each tab, the related tools/buttons are grouped. When you click on a tab, various groups appear. These groups have different tools, as shown.

Various CommandManager available in different environments are discussed next.

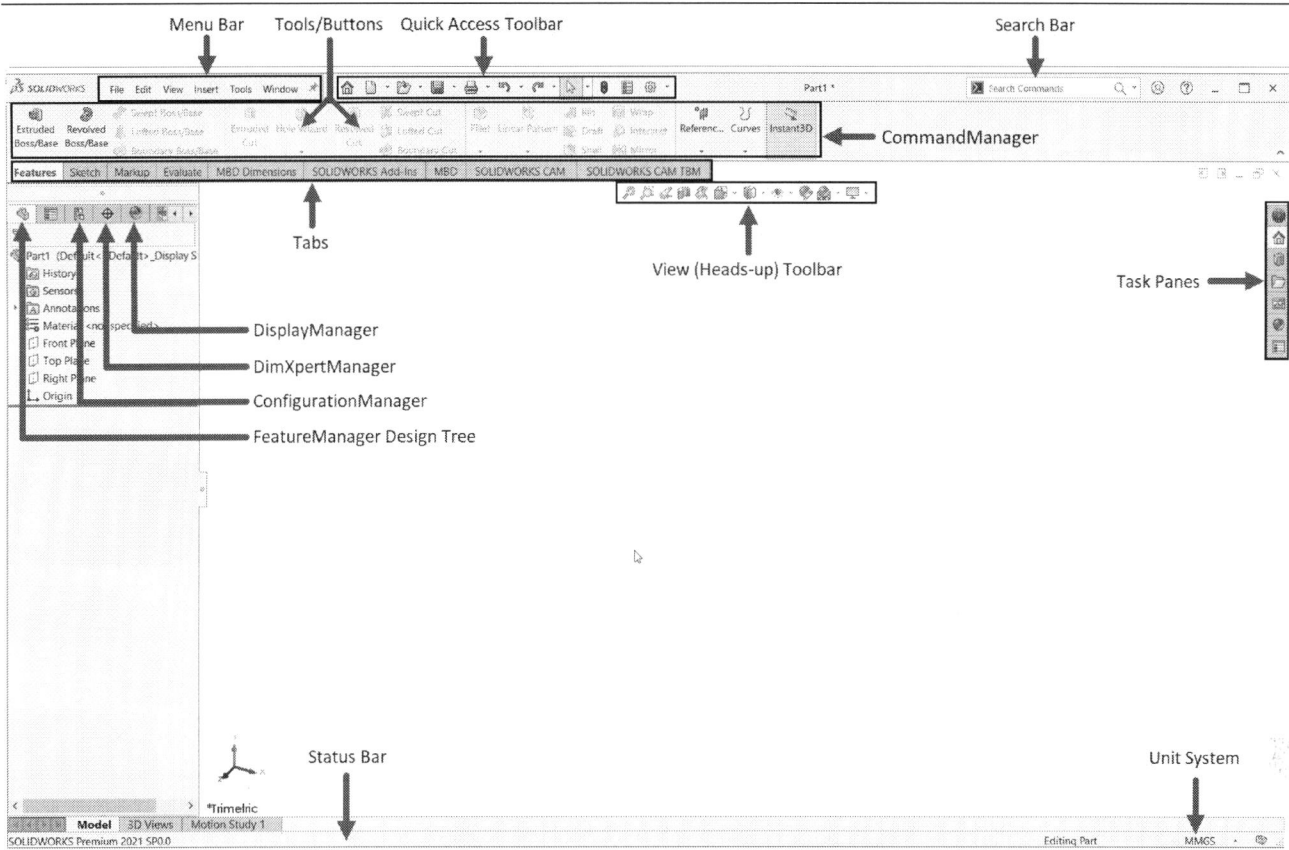

Part Environment
The Part environment consists of various CommandManager tabs with different tools used for creating different part files. Below is the initial screen of the SolidWorks with Part environment.

Features CommandManager
This CommandManager tab has various solid modelling tools used to convert sketches in solid models.

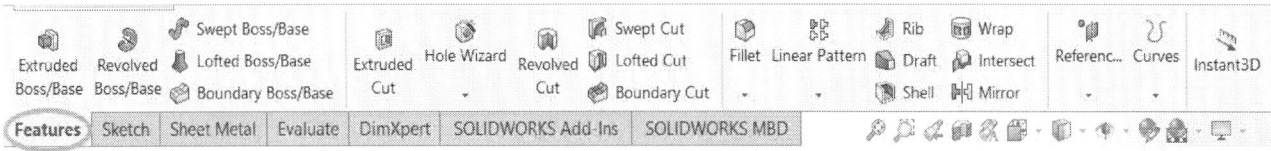

Sketch CommandManager
This CommandManager has various sketching tools, used for drawing 2D and 3D sketches.

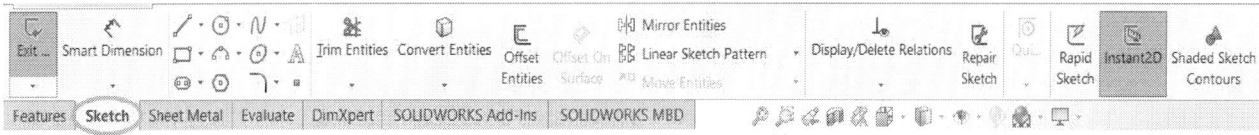

Sheet Metal CommandManager
This CommandManager has tools to create sheet metal components.

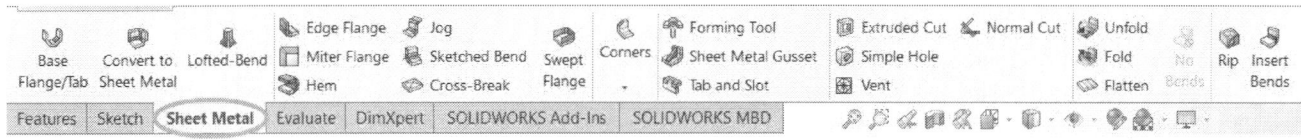

- Right click over any CommandManager tab to display the shortcut menu, as shown.
- Click on the **Sheet Metal** option to make it visible, as shown.
- Similarly, you can display other tabs also.

Note that the Sheet Metal tab is not visible by default and to display it:

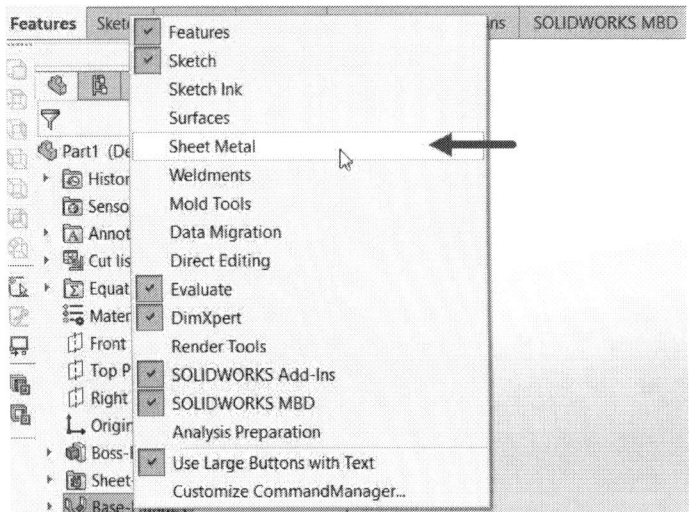

Evaluate CommandManager
This CommandManager contains the tools to measure various dimensions i.e. distance, angle, and radius in sketches, 3D models, assembly and drawings. Also contain tool to calculate the mass properties of a solid model.

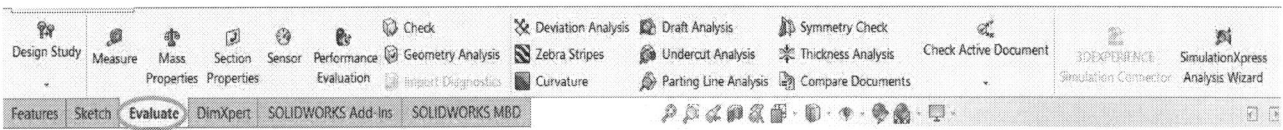

DimXpert CommandManager
This CommandManager contains the tools used to add dimensions and tolerances to the part features.

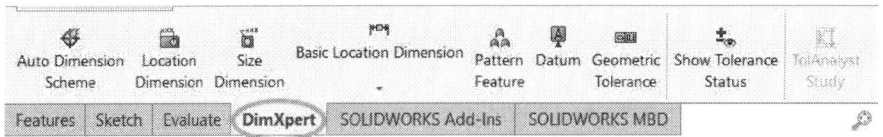

Assembly Environment
The **Assembly** tab has tools to create components or insert existing components into an assembly. There are various CommandManagers in the assembly environment, discussed next.

Assembly CommandManager
This CommandManager contains the tools used to insert the previously created components and assemble them by applying various mates.

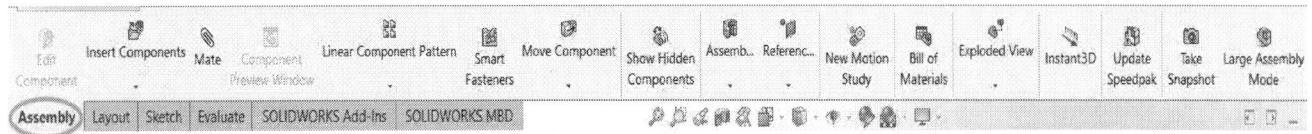

Drawing Environment
The Drawing environment consists of various tabs with different tools used for generating various drawing views of a solid model.

View Layout CommandManager
This CommandManager contains the tools used to generate standard views, model views, projected views, and so on, of a solid model.

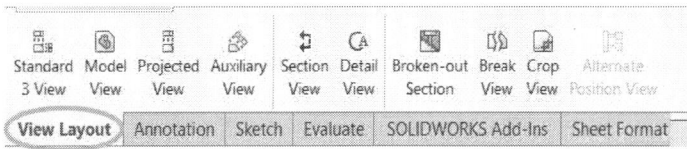

Annotation CommandManager
This CommandManager contains the tools to add dimension, notes, balloons, geometric tolerance and so on, to the drawing views, as shown.

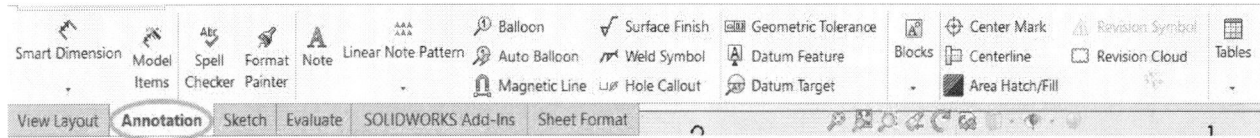

FeatureManager Design Tree
The **FeatureManager Design Tree** is a type of Navigator window that stores and display all the features/operations in a sequence that you have done while working in any file. It also contains details of planes, materials, appearances, lights and other features, added to the model. By default, it displays on the left side of different environments in SolidWorks (in part model, assembly, drawing, and so on). To edit/modify any feature, you can select the respective option from the shortcut menu display after right clicking over any respective feature, as shown.

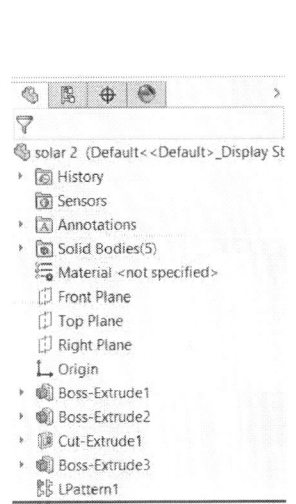
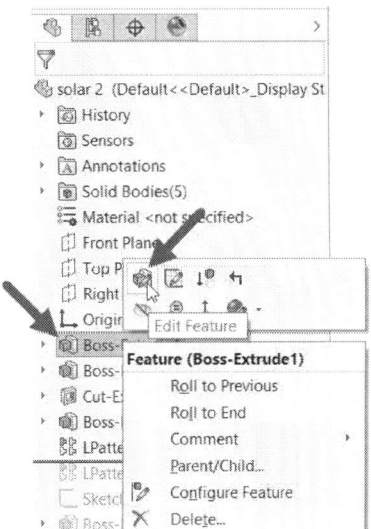
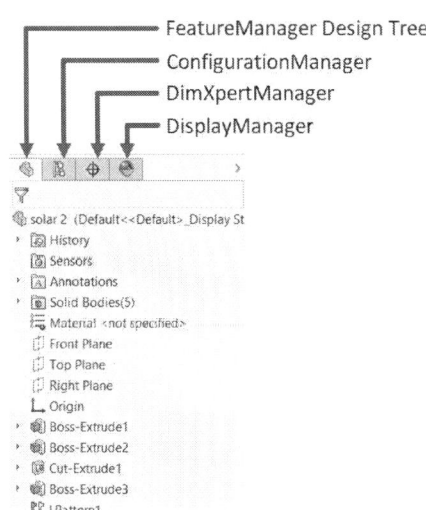

Changing Background Color
To change background color of SolidWorks graphic window.

> Click on the **Options** button from the **Quick Access Toolbar** to display the **System Options** dialog box, as shown.

- Click on the **Colors** option from the left of the dialog box to display options related to color scheme.
- Select the **Plain** radio button under **Background appearance** area of dialog box, as shown.
- Next choose the required color and click on the **OK** button of **Color** dialog box to exit it, as shown.
- Now click on the **OK** button of **System Options** dialog box to apply the color selected and exit it.

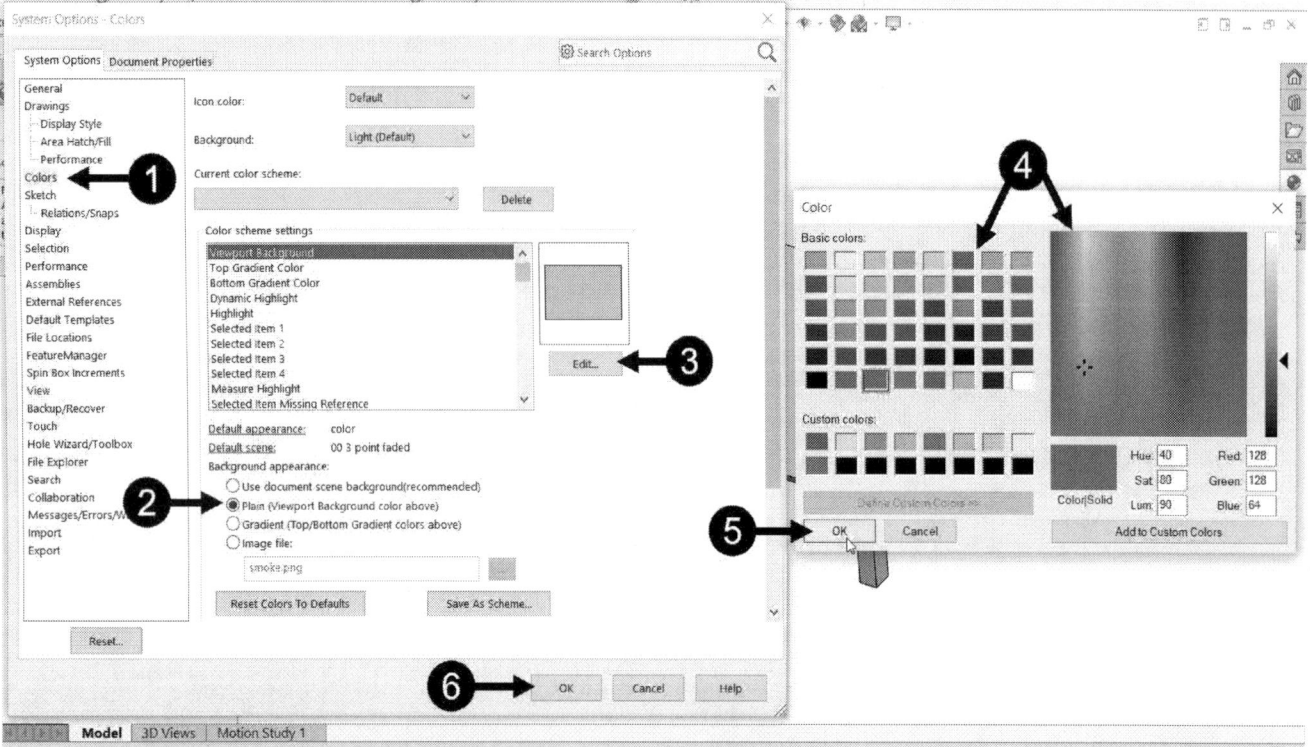

Note: After selecting the required color, you can save the color scheme by clicking on the **Save As Scheme** button of the **System Options** dialog box and then enter the required name in the **Color Scheme Name** dialog box, as shown.

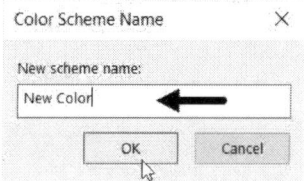

To change color of icons, you can select the required option from the **Background** dropdown list below the **Icon color** dropdown list of the **System Options** dialog box, as shown.

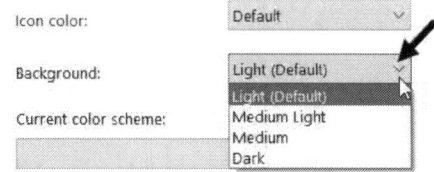

Mouse Functions
Various functions of the mouse buttons are:

Left Mouse button / Mouse Button 1 (LMB / MB1)
The **LMB** can be used to select any tool, button, and option. Also, you can double-click **LMB** on a model, to display its dimension, as shown. Using this detail, you can edit the parameters of the objects.

1. Double-click on the object to display its dimensions, as shown.

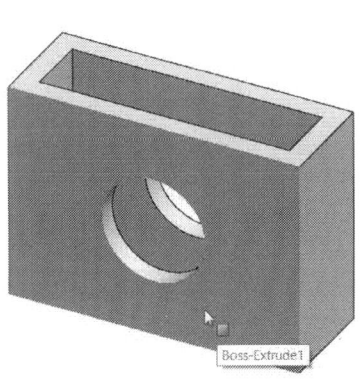 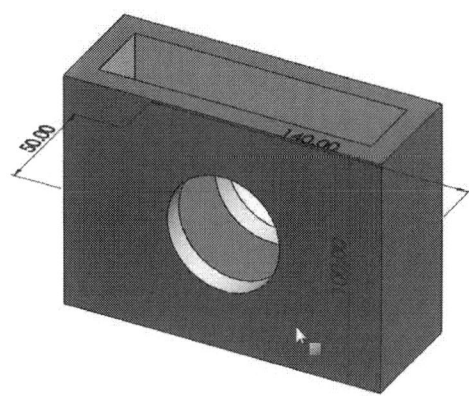

2. Double-click on any dimension value to display **Modify** dialog box with dimension, as shown
3. Enter new dimension value in it and click on the [button] button to apply change.
4. Next click on the button to exit it and click the **LMB** anywhere in drawing area to display the model with applied changes, as shown.

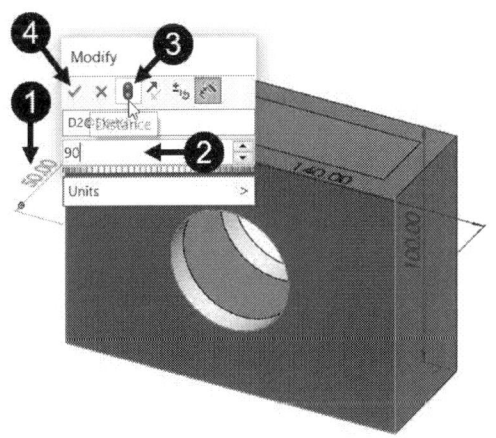 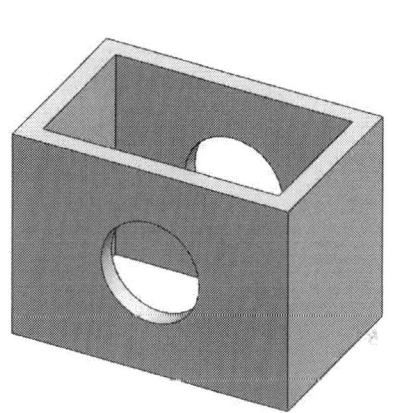

Middle Mouse button / Mouse Button 2 (MMB / MB2)

❖ Press and hold the **Ctrl** key and the **MMB** (middle mouse button) and drag the mouse to pan/move the view.
❖ Press and hold the **Shift** key and **MMB** (middle mouse button) and drag the mouse in upward and downward direction to **Zoom In/Zoom Out** the view.
❖ Press and hold the **MMB** to use it as **Rotate** tool to rotate the model.

Right Mouse button / Mouse Button 3 (RMB / MB3)

❖ By clicking this button; the shortcut menu gets displayed with respect to the object/feature selected.
❖ To display the mouse gestures, press and hold the RMB and move the mouse up to some distance; the mouse gestures get displayed, as shown.

Note that you can also customize the mouse gesture and add tools in it, as per your requirements.

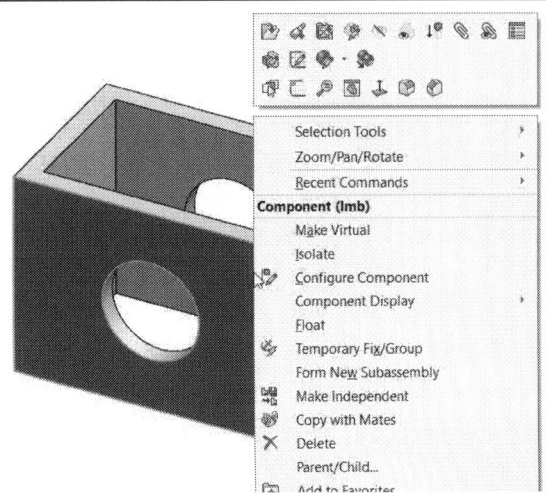
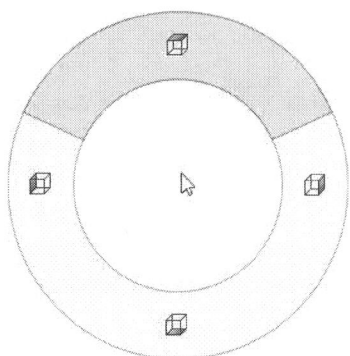

Some of the Important Shortcut keys In SolidWorks

SOLIDWORKS SHORTCUTS	
FILE	
Ctrl+ N	New
Ctrl+ O	Open
Ctrl+ A	Select All
Ctrl+ S	Save
Ctrl+ P	Print
EDIT	
Ctrl+ Z	Undo
Ctrl+ X	Cut
Ctrl+ C	Copy
Ctrl+ V	Paste
DELETE	Delete
Ctrl + Q	Rebuild
Ctrl + B	Rebuild

VIEW	
Arrow Keys	Rotate the model
Ctrl + Arrow Keys	Pan the Model
Shift + Arrow Keys	Rotate the model 90º
Alt + Arrow Keys	Rotate the model CW or CCW
Z	Zoom Out One Step
Shift	Zoom In One Step
F	Zoom to Fit Screen
SPACE	Orientation

OTHERS	
Ctrl + 1	Front
Ctrl + 2	Back
Ctrl + 3	Left
Ctrl + 4	Right
Ctrl + 5	Top
Ctrl + 6	Bottom
Ctrl + 7	Iso
Ctrl + 8	Normal to
F1	Help
Ctrl + Tab	Cycle between documents
L	Line
F5	Toggle Selection Filter Toolbar
Arrow Keys	Move model Up, Down, Left, Right

Questions:

1. Where is **Quick Access Toolbar** available in the drawing area?
2. What is the **FeatureManager design tree** and where is it located?
3. How can you change the background color of the drawing area?
4. Which mouse button is used to display the mouse gestures?
5. Which shortcut is used to for **Rebuild**?

Chapter 02: Basic Sketching tools

This chapter covers the methods and tools to create sketches used in the part environment. The tools and methods are discussed in context to the part environment. In SolidWorks, you can create sketches in Sketch environment. You will learn to create sketches in this environment.

In SolidWorks, you create a rough sketch, and then apply dimensions and constrains that define its shape and size. The dimensions define the length, size, and angle of a sketch element, whereas constrains define the relations between sketch elements.

The topics covered in this chapter are:

- ❖ Starting a new document in SolidWorks
- ❖ Learn sketching tools
- ❖ Editing Spline tool
- ❖ Dimensioning the sketch

Starting a New Document in SolidWorks 2021

To start a new document in SolidWorks 2021:

➤ Select the **New** button from the menu bar to display the **New SOLIDWORKS Document** dialog box, as shown.
➤ Next click on the **Part** button of the dialog box, if it is not selected by default, as shown
➤ Now click on the **OK** button; the part environment will be displayed, as shown.

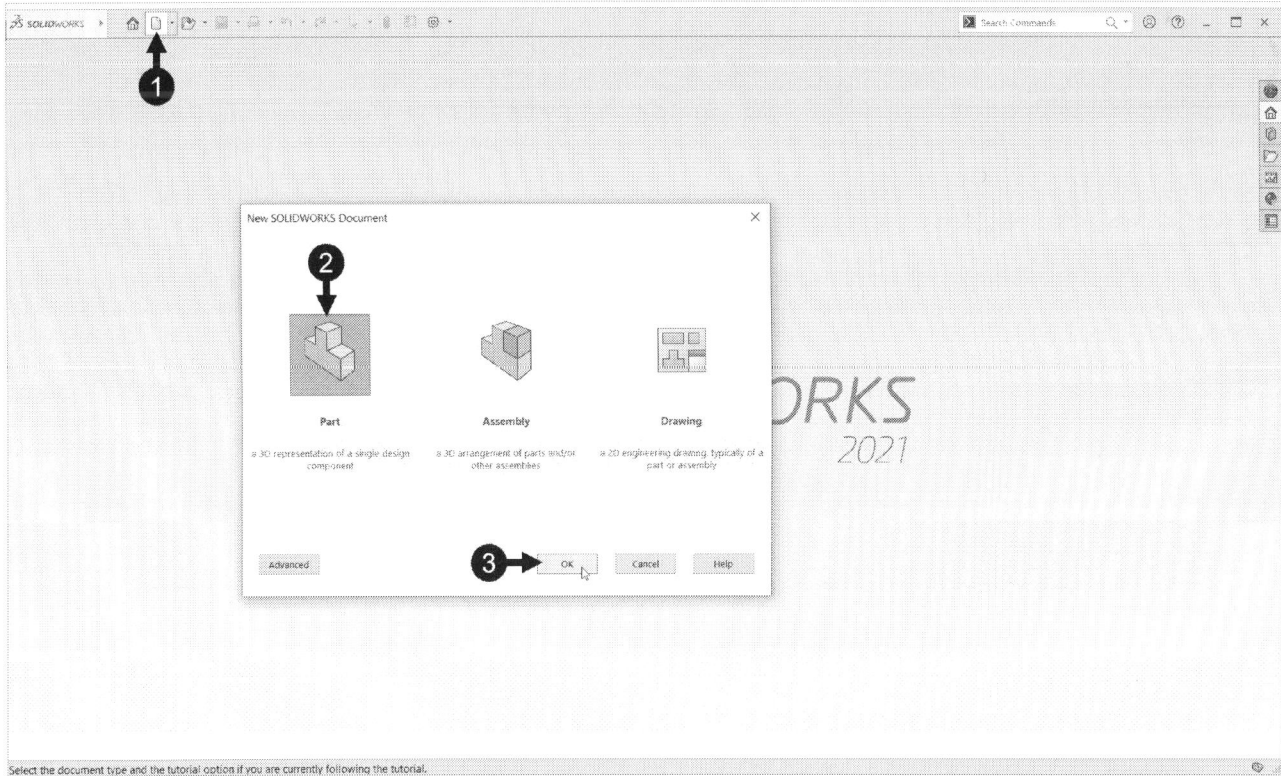

Note that you need to click on the **Sketch** tab to enter in the Sketching Environment, if any other tab is selected by default, as shown.

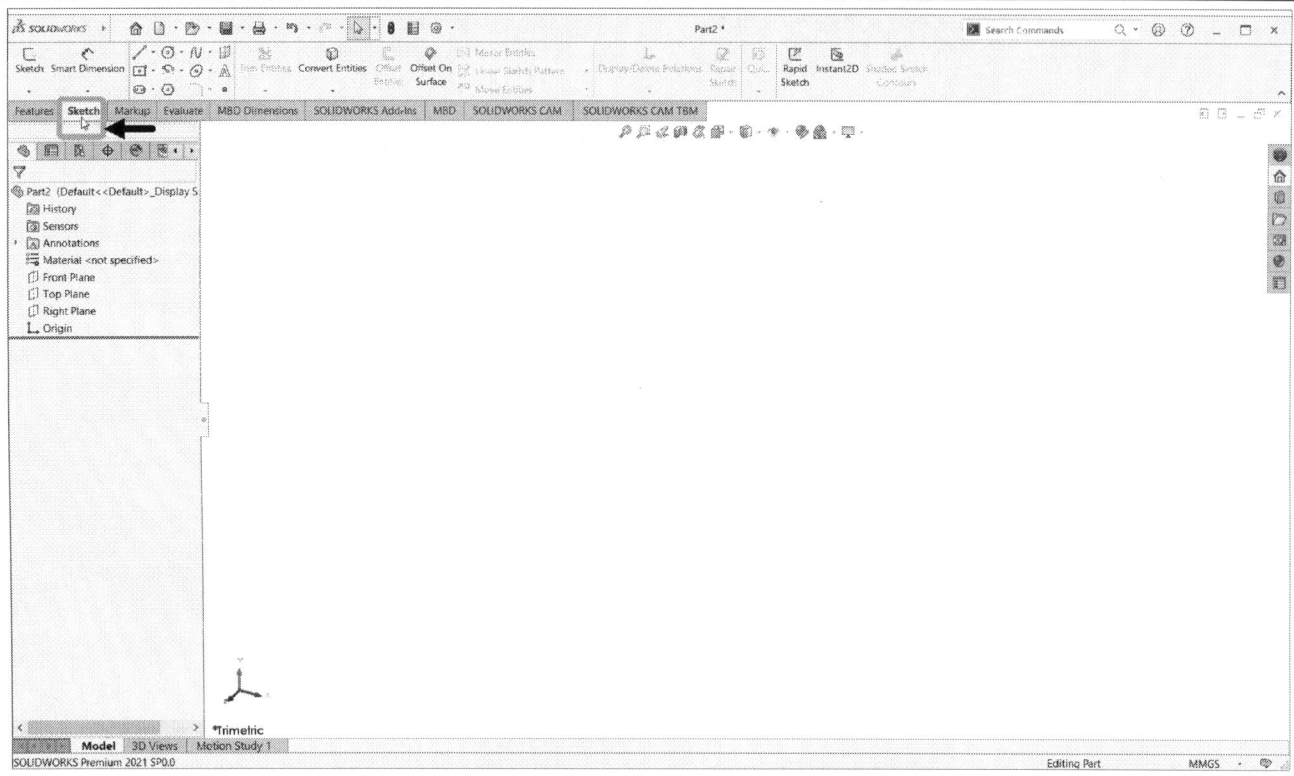

Sketching directly in the Part environment

Creating sketches in SolidWorks Part environment is very easy. You have to activate the **Sketch** tool first and then define a plane on which you want to create the sketch. To do this, click on the **Sketch** button from the **Sketch CommandManager**, the planes get displayed. Now you have to select any of the required plane in which you want to draw the sketch, as shown.

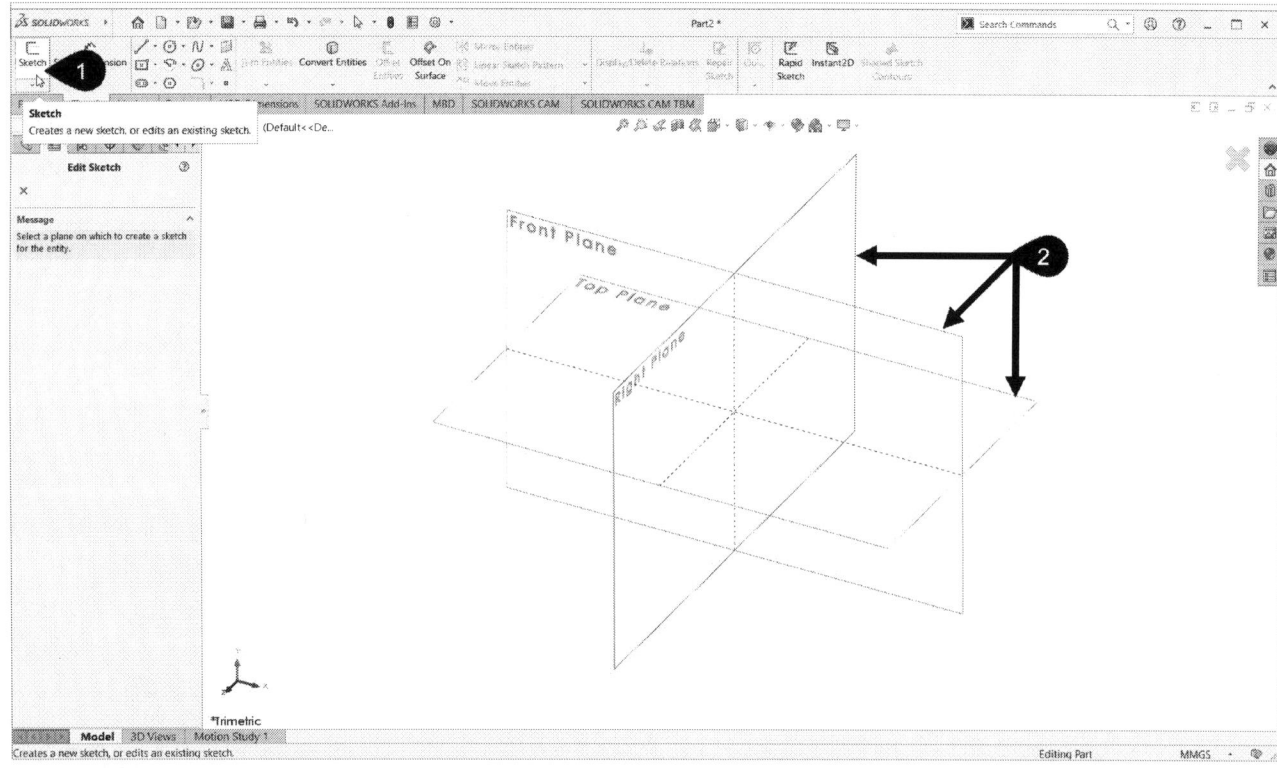

Next, the Sketching environment will be displayed after selecting any of the required plane, as shown. You can now draw the desired sketch over it, using various sketching tools discussed next.

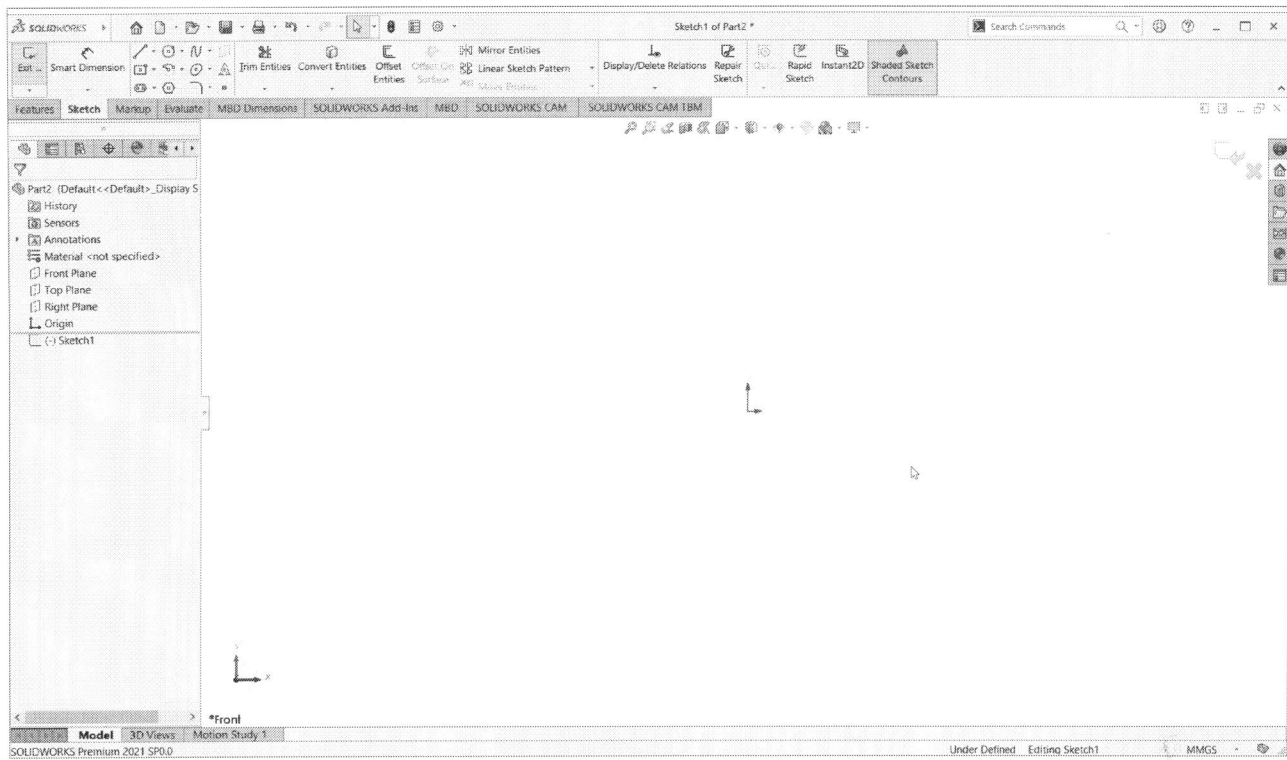

The tools in **Sketch CommandManager**, used in sketch environment in drawing sketches are discussed next:

Draw Tools

SolidWorks provides you with a set of tools to create sketches. These commands are located on the **Sketch CommandManager**. These tools are discussed next.

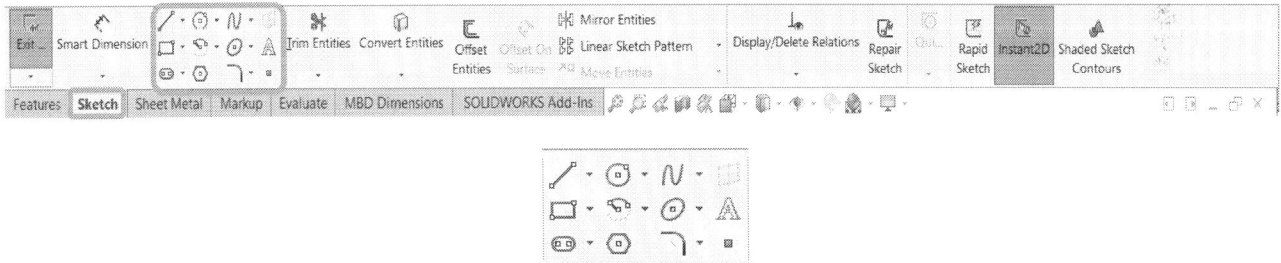

The Line Tool

This is the most commonly tool used for creating a sketch. In SolidWorks, there are three types of tools used for drawing lines, as discussed below:

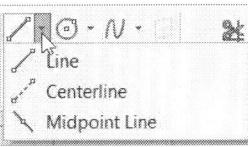

Line Tool

This tool is used to draw a line while creating sketches. The steps to draw a line using this tool are.

➤ Click on the **Line** button from the **Sketch CommandManager** to activate the **Line** tool, as shown above.
  Alternatively, you can activate the **Line** tool by pressing the "**L**" key from the keyboard.

TIP: To activate **Line** tool, you can click **Tools > Sketch Entities > Line** from the SolidWorks menu. You can also select the **Line** tool from the **Sketch** toolbar or press the "L" key.

- The **Insert Line PropertyManager** will get displayed, as shown.
- Click in the drawing area to define the start and endpoints of the line, as shown.

Note: While drawing sketch lines, the length and angle value will get displayed along with relation symbol, as shown.

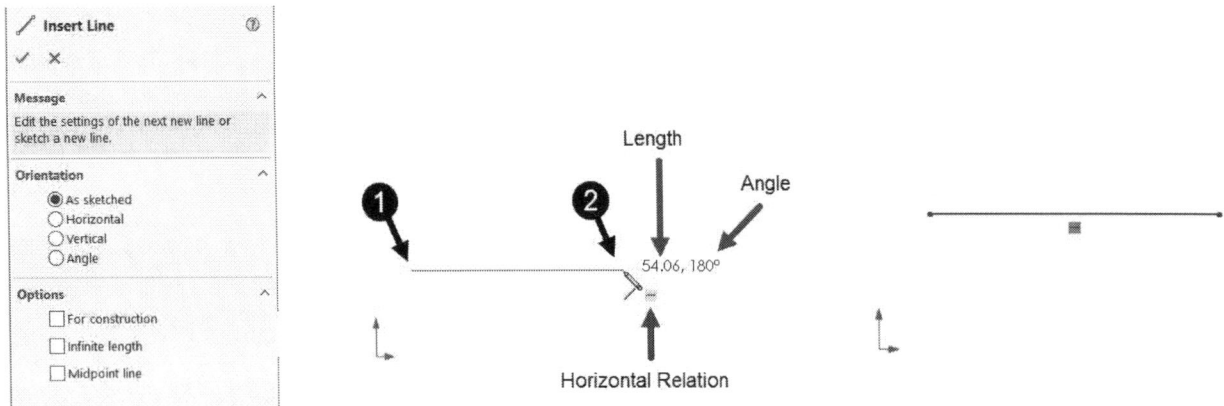

- If you draw a horizontal and vertical line, the respective symbol of the line gets displayed with it, as shown.

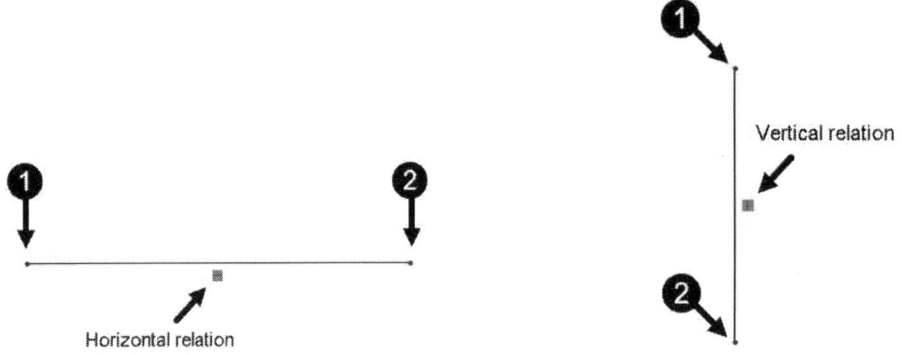

- Press the **Esc** key from the keyboard to deactivate the **Line** tool.

The options in the **Orientation** rollout of the **Insert Line PropertyManager** are discussed next:

As sketched
The **As sketched** radio button is selected by default which helps you in drawing the line in any direction, until you release the pointer.

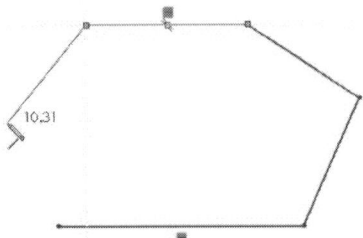

Horizontal
This radio button is selected to draw the line horizontally.

Vertical
This radio button is selected to draw the line vertically.

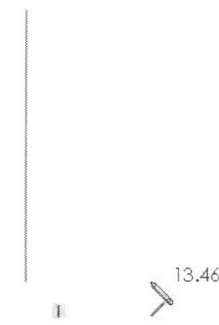

Note: While selecting the **Horizontal** or **Vertical** radio button, you can draw the line in their relative directions only.

Angle
This radio button is selected to draw the line at an angle, relatively with the horizontal line.

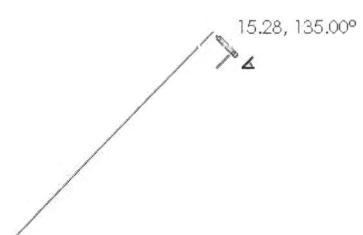

The options in the **Options** rollout of the **Insert Line PropertyManager** are discussed next:

For construction
This radio button is selected to draw a construction line, as shown.

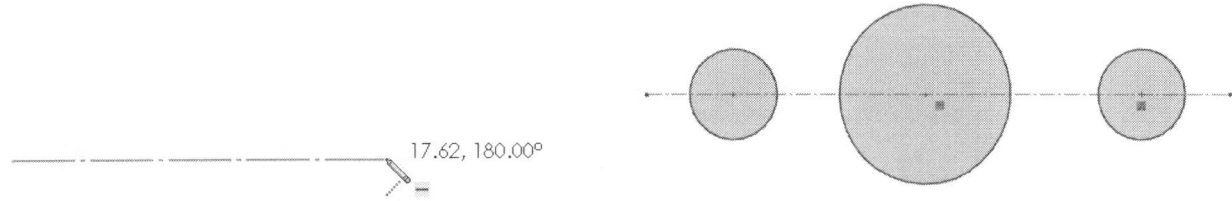

The drawing of construction lines will be discussed further in this chapter.

Infinite length

This radio button is selected to draw a line with infinite length, as shown.

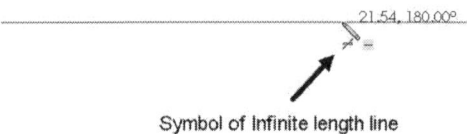

Symbol of Infinite length line

Midpoint line

This radio button is selected to draw a line, symmetrical from the midpoint of the line.

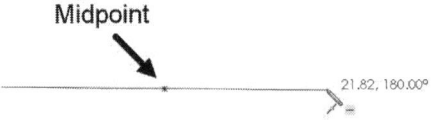

> **TIP:** If you select **Horizontal, Vertical** or **Angle** radio button; the **Parameters** rollout with **Length** and **Angle** edit box will get displayed in the **Insert Line PropertyManager**, as shown. These edit boxes can be used to draw a line with required length, angle or both.

Toggle between Line and Arc Tools

After drawing the line entity, you can switch between the **Line** and **Arc** tools, which helps you in drawing normal or tangent arc to the previous line.

- To switch between **Line** and **Arc** tool, after drawing lines right-click to highlight the shortcut menu and select "**Switch to arc (A)** "option from it; the **Line** tool get changed to **Arc** tool.

  Alternatively, you can toggle between the **Arc** and **Line** tool by pressing the "**A**" key.

- Move the cursor towards left to define the second point of the arc, as shown.

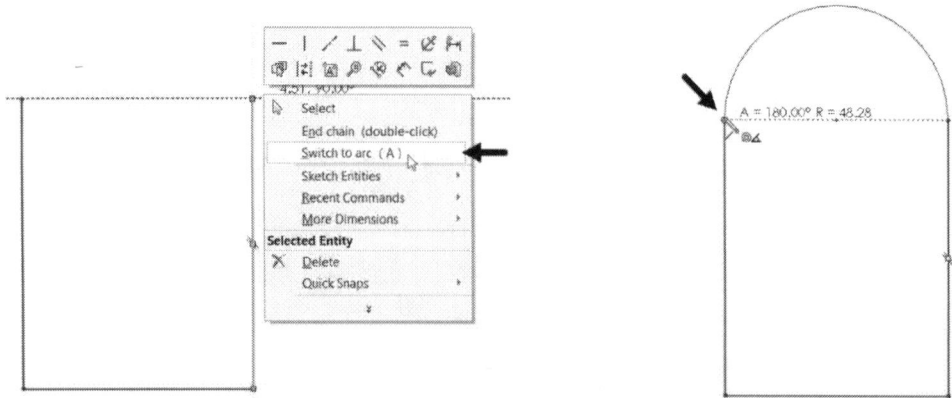

> **Note:** After drawing the line entity, the **Line** tool remains active, so you can activate or toggle with **Arc** tool by moving the cursor over previously defined point.
>
> Also, to toggle between directions of arc, you need to do the same.

Basic Sketching Tools

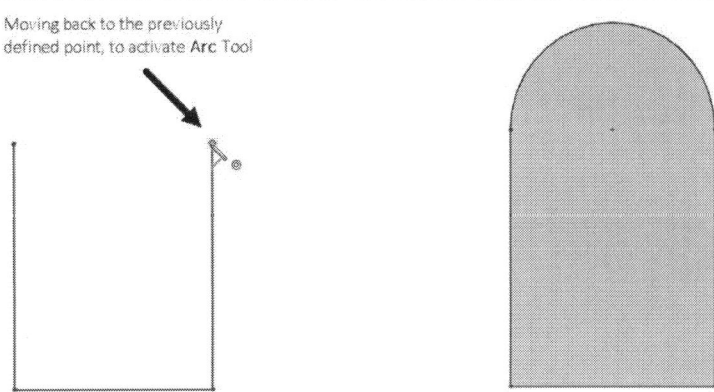

The Centerline Tool

This is the most commonly tool used for creating centreline or construction lines or axis of rotation. The steps to draw a line using this tool are:

- Select **Line > Centerline** from the **Sketch CommandManager** to activate **Centerline** tool.
- Click in the drawing area to define start and end point of the center line, as shown.
- Press **Esc** button from the keyboard to deactivate the **Centerline** tool.

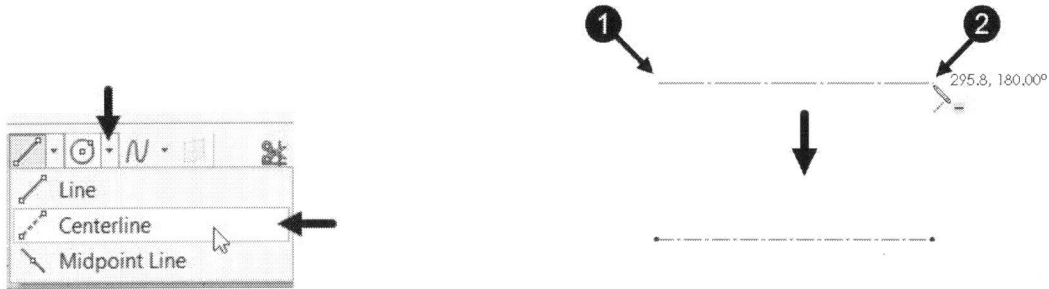

You can also draw the centerline or construction line, using the **Line** tool by selecting **For construction** check box from the **Insert Line PropertyManager**, as discussed earlier. The options in the **Insert Line PropertyManager** are same, as discussed earlier

The Midpoint Line Tool

The **Midpoint Line** tool is used to draw the line that will be symmetrical from the midpoint of the line. To draw a line using this tool, you need to define midpoint and end point in the drawing area.

- Activate this tool by selecting **Line > Midpoint Line** tool from the **Sketch CommandManager**, in the Sketch environment.
- Click in the drawing area to define midpoint of the line entity.
- Move the cursor slightly right; the line get increased symmetrically.
- Click again at the required distance to define endpoint of the line entity, as shown.

You can also draw this line, using the **Line** tool by selecting **Midpoint line** check box from the **Insert Line PropertyManager**, as discussed earlier.

Basic Sketching Tools

TIP: To display the dimension, edit box along with entities while creating, select the **Enable on screen numeric input on entity creation** checkbox from the **System Options** tab of the **System Options**, as shown. Next you can enter the required dimension values in it, as shown.

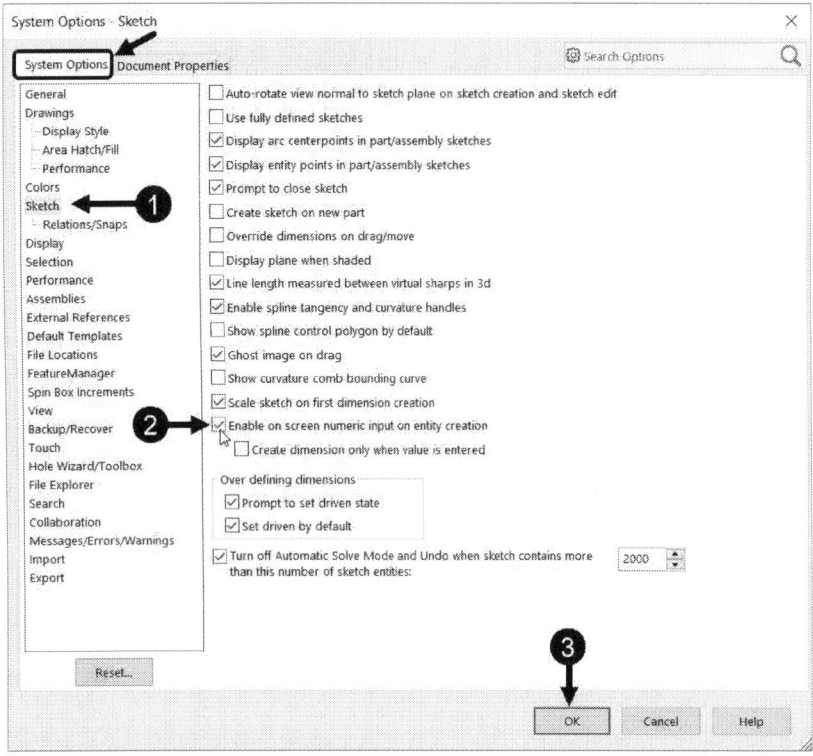

The Circle Tool

This tool is used to draw a circle during drawing a sketch. There are two options available in the **Circle** flyout for creating circles: **Circle**, **Perimeter Circle**, as shown. The use of these tools is discussed next.

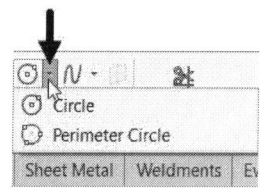

Circle Tool

This is the most common and easiest way to draw a circle.

➤ Select **Circle > Circle** option from the **Sketch CommandManager** to activate it and display the **Circle PropertyManager**.

Alternately, you can click on the **Circle** tool directly, if it is selected by default.

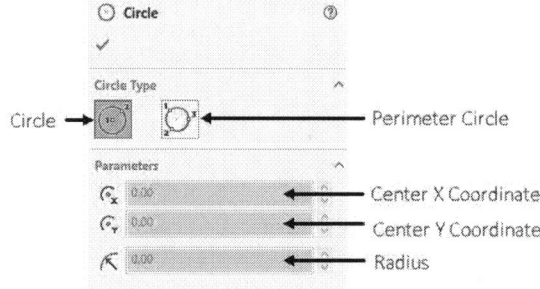

Basic Sketching Tools

2-8

- Click to define the center point of the circle.
- Move the cursor upto some distance and click to define the radius of the circle.

- Press the **Esc** key from the keyboard to deactivate the Circle tool.

 Perimeter Circle Tool

This tool is used to create a circle by using three points.

- Click **Circle > Perimeter Circle** from the **Sketch CommandManager**, as shown above.

  You can also toggle between **Circle** and **Perimeter Circle** tool from the **Circle Type** rollout of the **Circle PropertyManager**, as shown above.

- Click and define three points in the drawing area, as shown.

  The first two points define the location of the circle and the third point defines its radius.

- After drawing circle using tools in the **Circle** flyout, the **Circle PropertyManager** get replaced with new **Circle PropertyManager**, as shown.

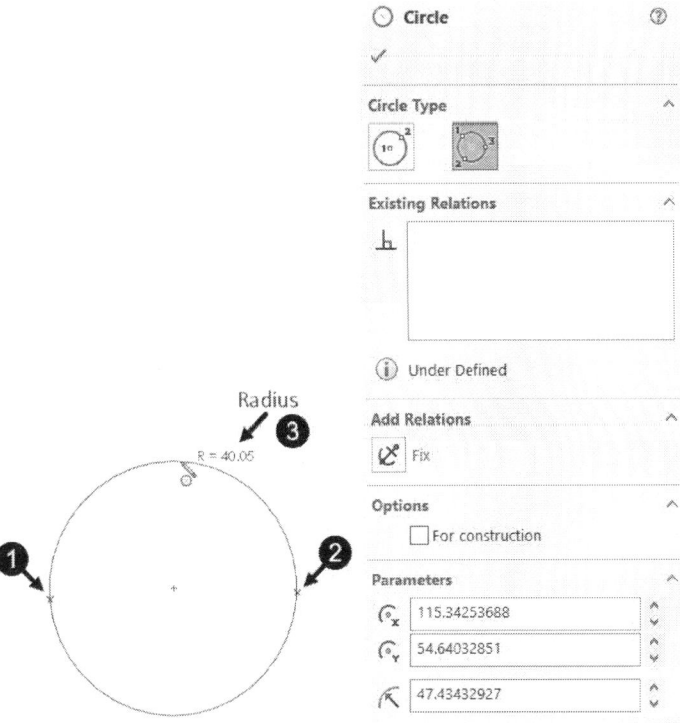

The options in the **Parameters** rollout in the **Circle PropertyManager** helps in modifying radius and coordinates of the center point of the circle. You can also draw a construction circle by selecting the **For construction** check box in the **Options** rollout, after drawing a circle. The circle will get converted into construction circle.

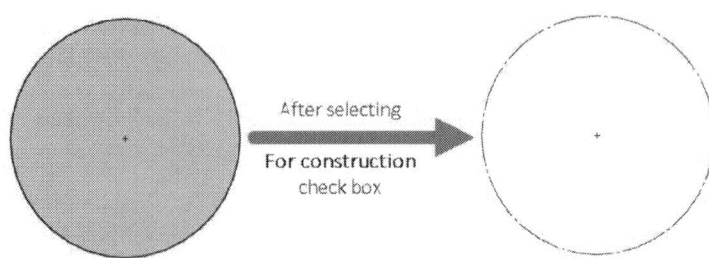

TIP: While creating any closed loop, it gets display shaded. To toggle between the shaded close loop and non-shaded close loop, you can select the **Shaded Sketch Contours** button (**Ribbon > Sketch > Shaded Sketch Contours**) as shown below.

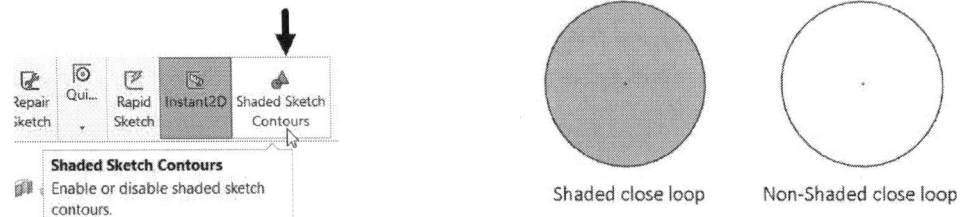

The Spline Tool

This tool is used to create a smooth spline curve passing through the defined points by clicking in the drawing area. There are four different tools available in the **Spline** flyout to create splines in four different types, as discussed one by one.

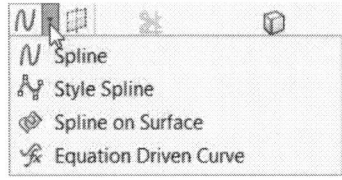

Spline Tool

This tool is used to create a smooth spline curve passing through the defined points by clicking in the drawing area.

➢ Select the **Spline** tool (select **Sketch > Spline**).
➢ Click to define start points for the spline in the graphics window.
➢ Similarly, click to define the other points for creating spline, as shown.

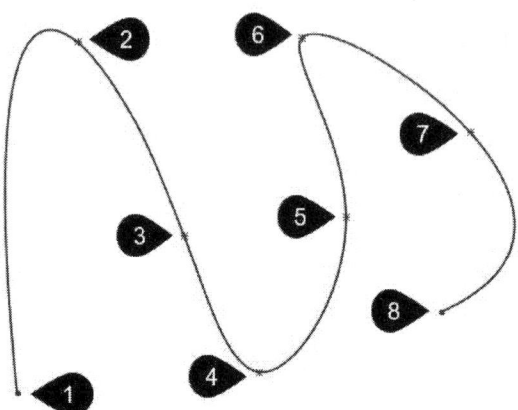

Basic Sketching Tools

- Now, press the right mouse button (**RMB**) to display the shortcut menu, as shown.
- Click on the **Select** option to exit this tool and display the spline created, as shown.

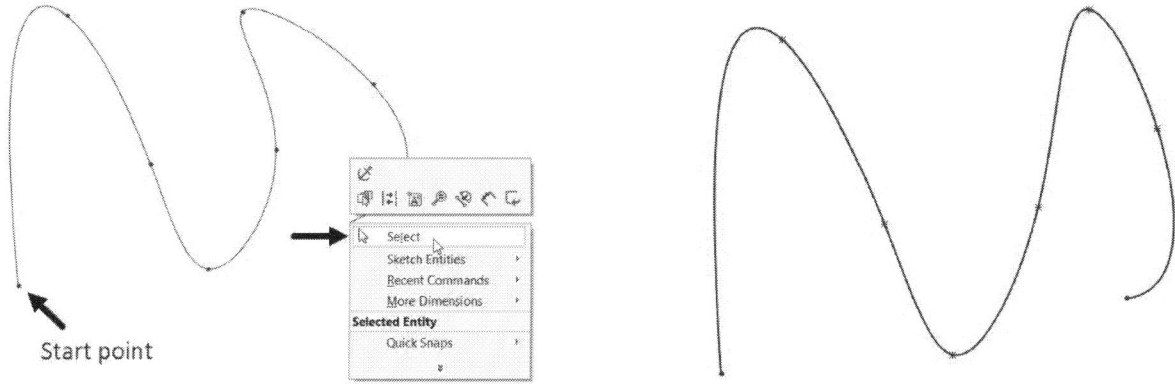

- To add more points on spline, right-click over spline to display the shortcut menu, as shown.
- Next select the **Insert Spline Point** option from it and click on spline to define points, as shown.

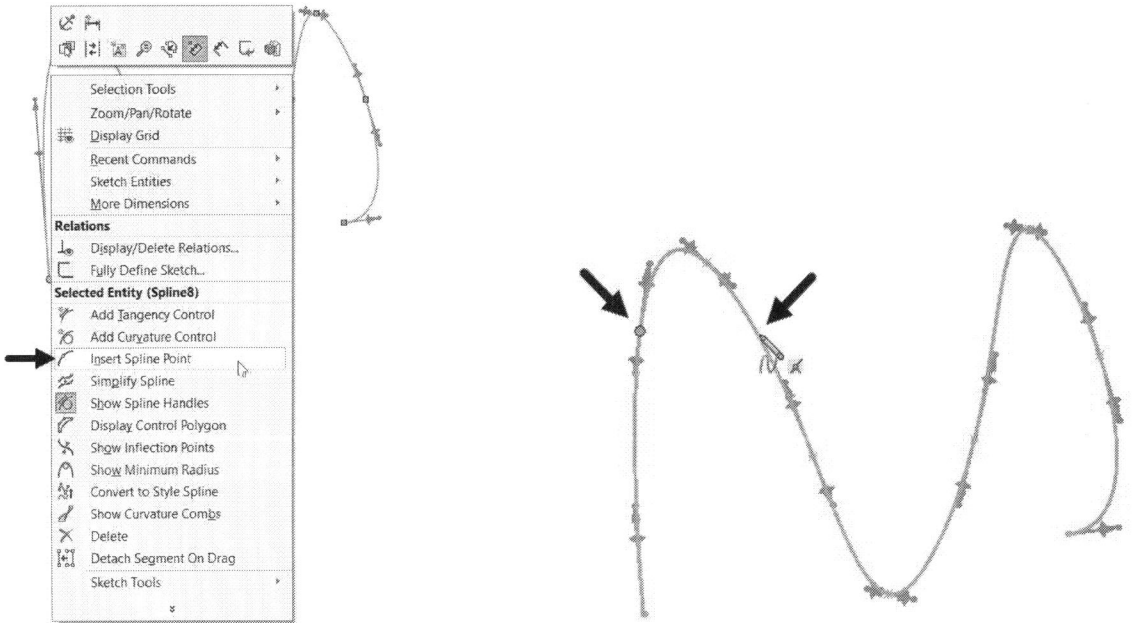

Similarly, you can define other points as per your requirements and again.

- Again, right click to display the shortcut menu and click on the **Select** option to exit it and display the spline with newly added points.

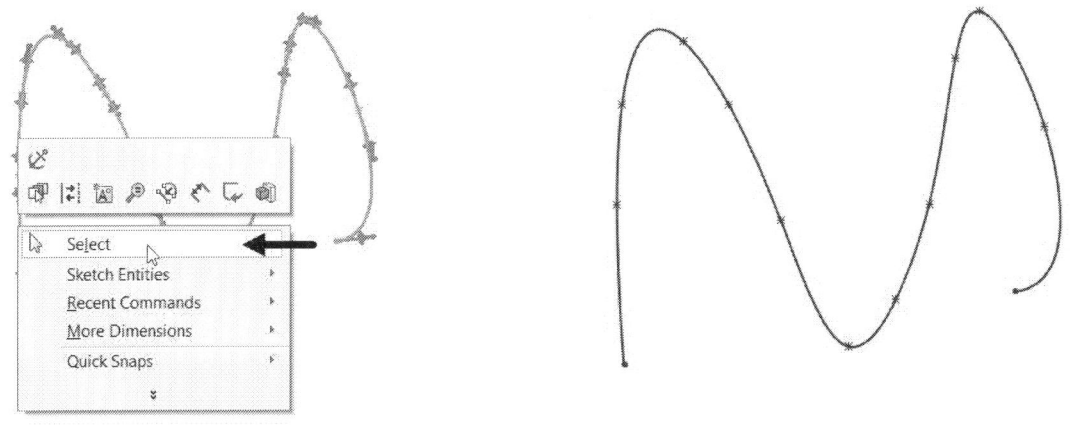

Basic Sketching Tools

Editing the Spline Tool

To edit any spline, follow the steps:

➤ Press and hold the left mouse button (**LMB**) on any point of the spline, as shown.
➤ Move/drag the cursor up to some distance, as shown.

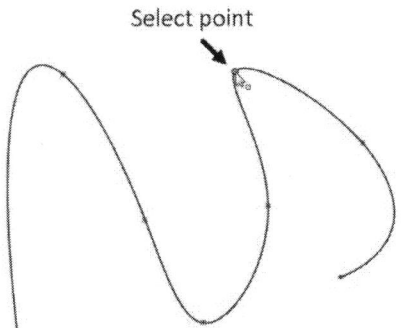
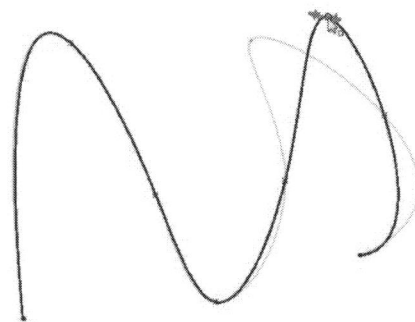

You can also edit the spline by selecting it to display the handles on every point, as shown. Next, select and drag the handle up to the required distance, as shown.

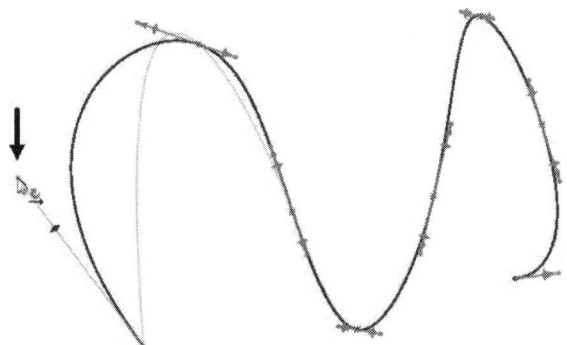

To edit the spline points from the **Spline PropertyManager** follow the steps:

➤ Click on the spline to display the **Spline PropertyManager**, as discussed above.
➤ The first point is selected in the **Spline Point Number** spinner under **Parameters** rollout of PropertyManager, as shown.
➤ You can use **X Coordinate** and **Y Coordinate** spinner to edit and change location of selected point, as shown.

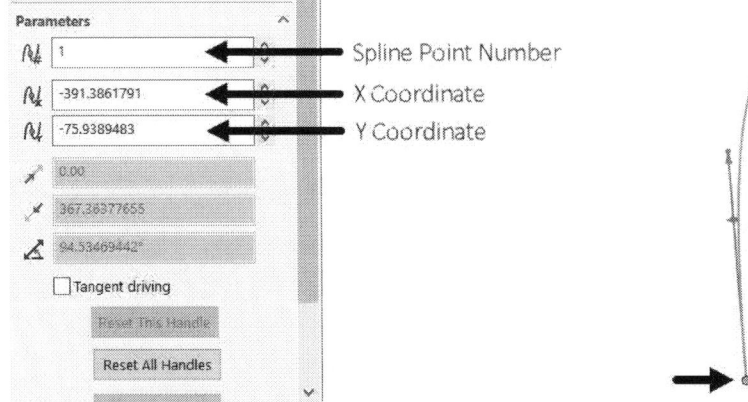
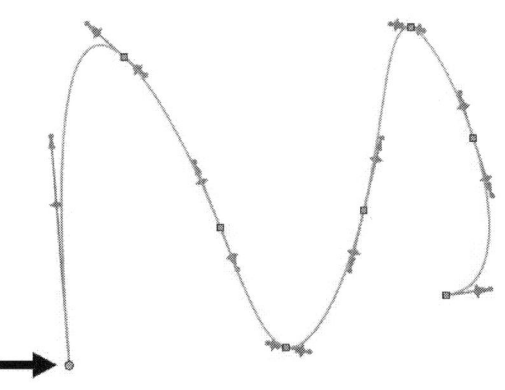

Similarly, you can edit other points one by one after selecting in the **Spline Point Number** spinner of PropertyManager.

Basic Sketching Tools

The Rectangle Tool

The **Rectangle** tool is used to create rectangle which is the combination of four lines. There are five different tools available in the **Rectangle** flyout to create five types of rectangles, as discussed one by one.

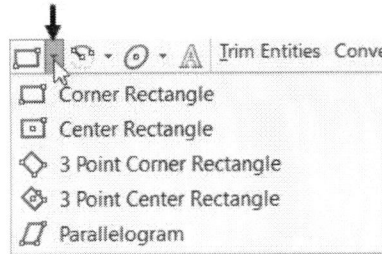

Corner Rectangle

This tool is used to create a rectangle by defining its corners diagonally.

- Click on the **Corner Rectangle** tool from the **Rectangle** flyout to display **Rectangle PropertyManager**, as shown.
- Click in the drawing area to define the first corner of the rectangle, as shown.
- Drag the cursor diagonally and click to define the second corner of the rectangle, as shown.
- The X & Y measures the length and width of the rectangle.

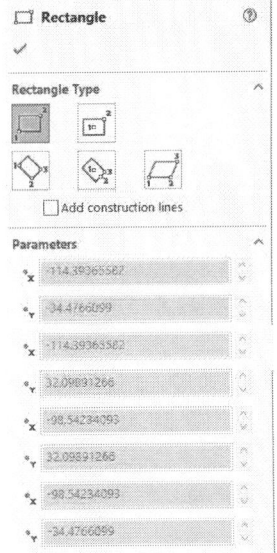
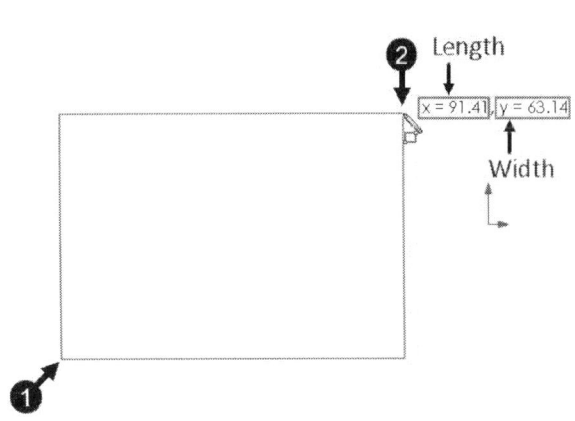

To create a rectangle with construction lines, select the **Add construction lines** check box from the **Rectangle PropertyManager**. Next, you can select the required radio buttons under it – **For Corners** & **From Midpoints**, as shown.

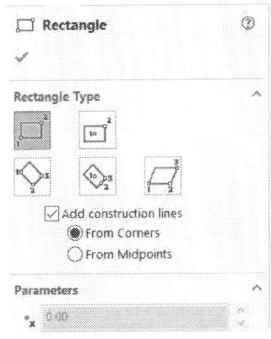
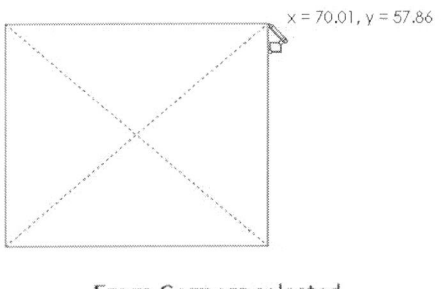
From Corners selected
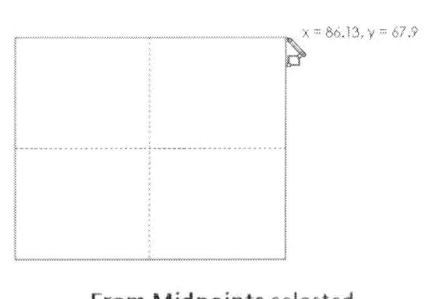
From Midpoints selected

Basic Sketching Tools

TIP: You can use the **Tab** button from keyboard to toggle between length and width dimensions while creating rectangle, as shown.

If **Enable on screen numeric input on entity creation** checkbox is selected in the **System Options** tab of the **System Options** box, as discussed earlier.

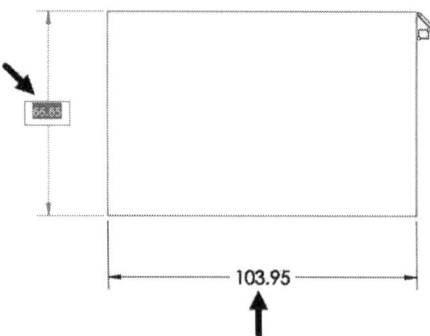

You can also switch to other types of rectangles from the **Rectangle PropertyManager**, by selecting the required buttons available under **Rectangle Type** rollout, as shown.

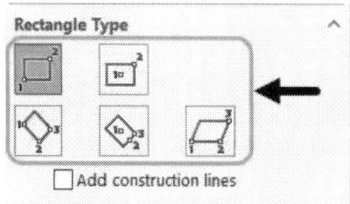

Center Rectangle

This tool is used to create rectangle by defining two points: center point and one of the corners.

- Click on the **Center Rectangle** tool from the **Rectangle** flyout.
- Click anywhere in the drawing area to define points 1 as the center point of the rectangle, as shown.
- Move the cursor up to some distance and click to define point 2 as the length/width of the rectangle.
- All corners of this rectangle have equal length from the centre.

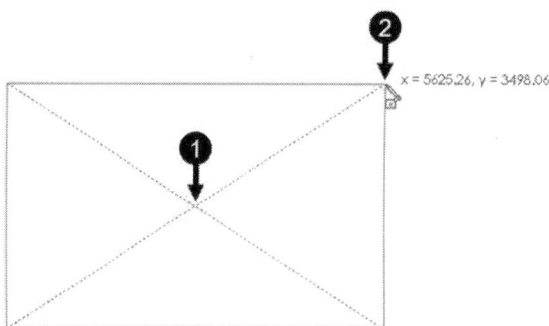

3 Point Corner Rectangle

This tool is used to create a rectangle at a selected angle, by defining three points: center of the rectangle and its corner.

- Click on the **3 Point Corner Rectangle** tool from the **Rectangle** flyout.
- Click anywhere in the drawing area to define point 1 as the start point of the rectangle, as shown.
- Move the cursor and click to define point 2 as the endpoint of the base line, as shown.

➢ Again, move the cursor and click to define point 3 as the width of the rectangle, as shown.

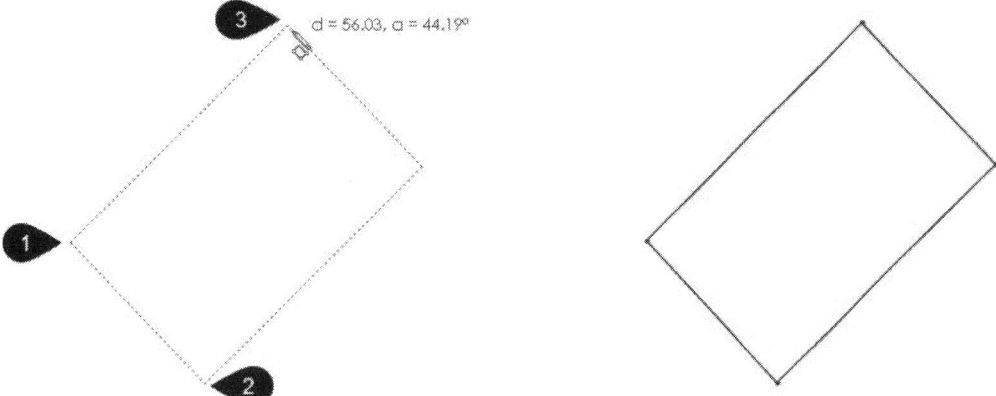

3 Point Center Rectangle

This tool is used to create a rectangle with center point at an angle,

➢ Click on the **3 Point Center Rectangle** tool from the **Rectangle** flyout.
➢ Click anywhere in the drawing area to define point 1 as the center point of the rectangle, as shown.
➢ Move the cursor and click to define point 2 at the distance half to the length of rectangle, as shown.
➢ Again, move the cursor and click to define point 3 as the width of the rectangle, as shown.

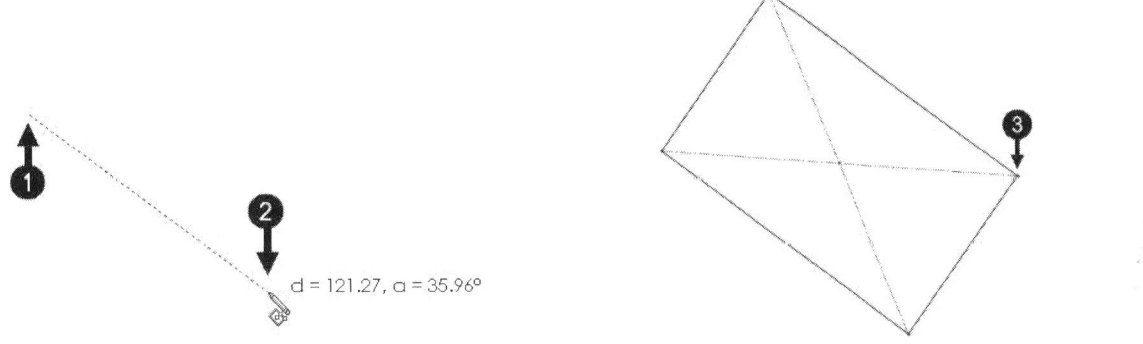

Parallelogram

This command creates a parallelogram by using three points that you specify.

➢ Choose the **Parallelogram** tool from the **Rectangle** flyout.
➢ Click in the drawing area and define start and end point of the length of the base line of the parallelogram, as shown.
➢ Move the cursor and click anywhere to define the height/width of the parallelogram, as shown.

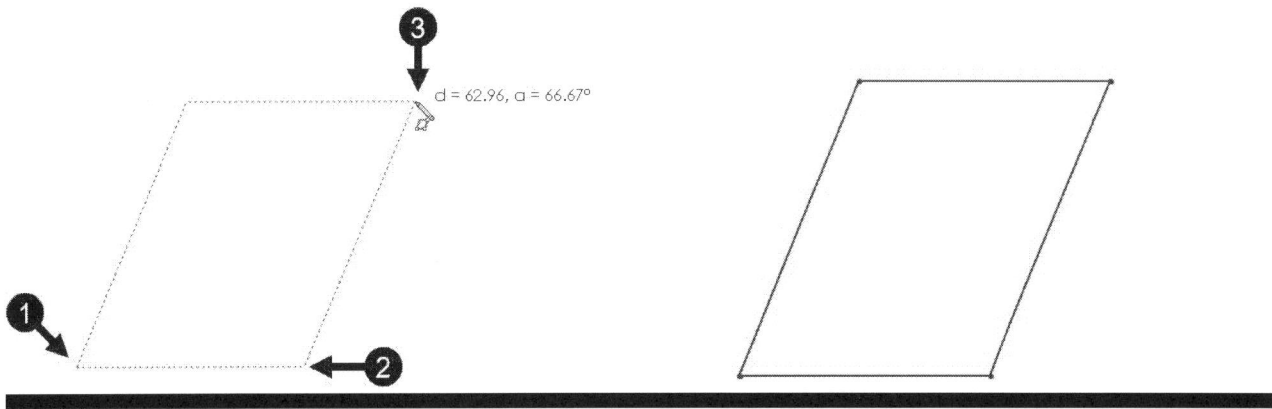

Basic Sketching Tools

The Arc Tool

This tool is the used to draw an arc during drawing a sketch. There are three different tools available in the **Arc** flyout to create three different types of arcs, as discussed below.

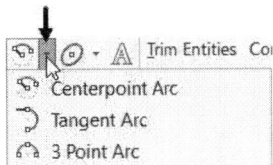

 ## Centerpoint Arc Tool

This tool is used to draw an arc by defining center point, start point and end point.

➢ Select **Arc > Centerpoint Arc** from the **Sketch CommandManager** to activate it and display the **Arc PropertyManager**, as shown.

Alternately, you can click on the **Centerpoint Arc** tool directly, if it is selected by default.

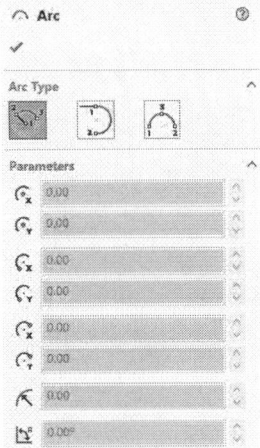

➢ Click in the drawing area to define center point (1) for the arc, as shown.
➢ Move the cursor upto some distance towards left and click to define start point (2) of the arc.
➢ Move the cursor upwards and click to define third or end point (3) of the arc.
➢ Press the **Esc** key from the keyboard to exit the tool and display arc created.

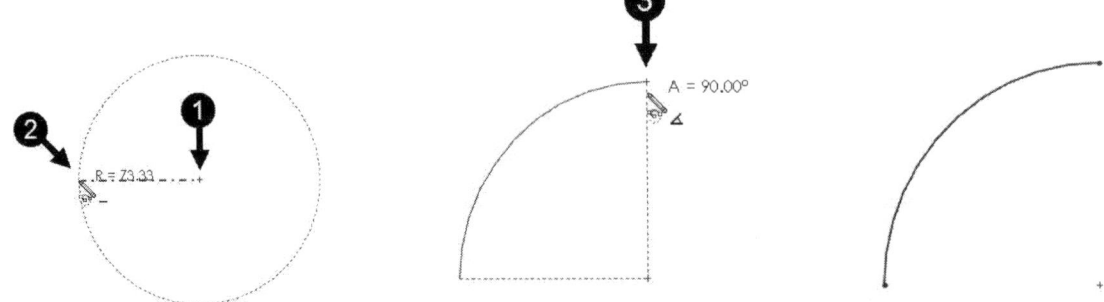

You can also switch to other types of arc from the **Arc PropertyManager**, by selecting the required buttons available under **Arc Type** rollout, as shown.

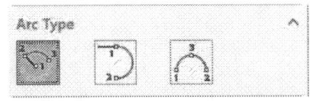

Tangent Arc Tool

This tool is used to draw arc tangent to an existing entity.

> Select **Arc > Tangent Arc** from the **Sketch CommandManager** to activate it.

Alternatively, you can also select **Tangent Arc** tool from the **Arc Type** rollout of the **Arc PropertyManager**, as shown above.

> Click on the end point of the left line entity to define start point (1) of the arc, as shown
> Move the cursor slightly right and click on the end point of right line entity to define end point (2) of Arc, as shown.
> Press the **Esc** key twice from the keyboard to exit the tool and display arc created, as shown.

 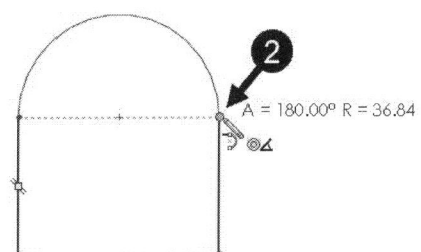 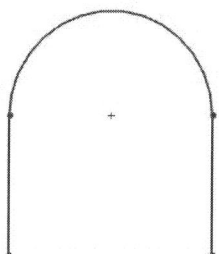

 3 Point Arc

This tool is used to create an arc by defining its two endpoints, and a radius.

> Select **Arc > 3 Point Arc** from the **Sketch CommandManager** to activate it.
> Click in the drawing area to define start point (1) and end point (2) of the arc, as shown.
> Move the cursor upto some distance and click to define third or end point (3) of the arc, as shown.

The third point defines radius of arc, as shown.

> Press the **Esc** key to exit the tool and display arc created, as shown.

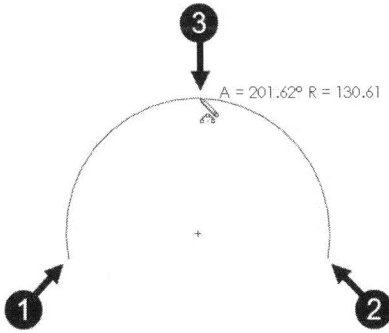

 The Ellipse Tool

The **Ellipse** tool is used to draw an ellipse while drawing a sketch. The tools available in the **Ellipse** flyout are used to create an Ellipse, Partial Ellipse, Parabola, and Conic, as discussed below one-by-one.

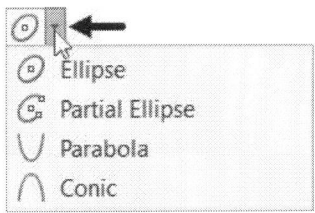

Ellipse Tool

This tool is used to draw an ellipse by defining center point and end points for major and minor axis.

- Click on the **Ellipse** tool from the **Sketch CommandManager** to activate it.
- Click in the drawing area to define point (1) as the center point of ellipse, as shown.
- Move the cursor horizontally and click to define point (2) as the radius along major axis, as shown.
- Now, move the cursor vertically and click to define point (3) as the radius along minor axis, as shown.

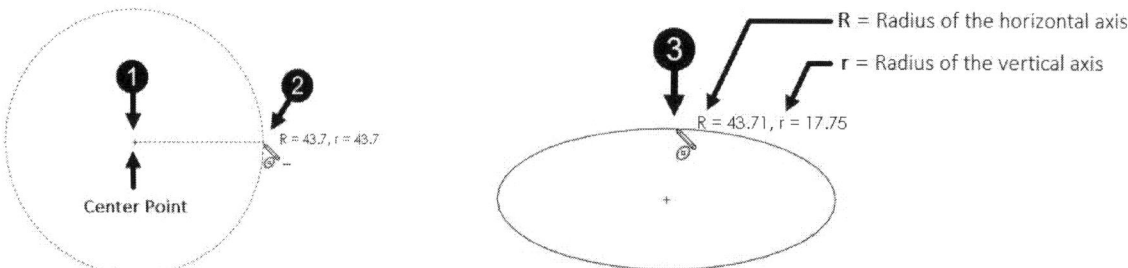

- The preview of ellipse with major and minor axis along with **Ellipse PropertyManager** gets visible, as shown.

  You can enter the required values for major or minor axis in their respective spinners in **Ellipse PropertyManager**, as shown.

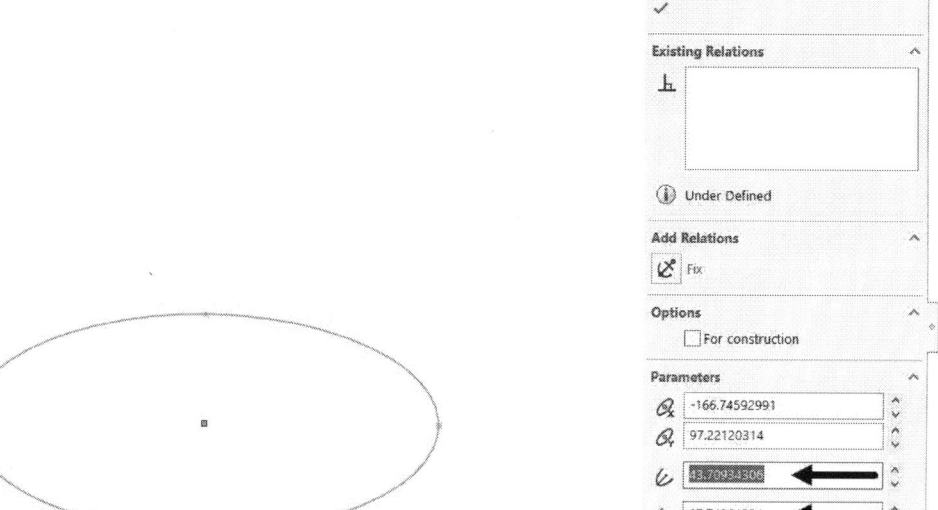

- Click on the ✓ button from the PropertyManager to exit the tool and display the ellipse, as shown.

TIP: The **For construction** check box in the **Ellipse PropertyManager** is selected to display construction ellipse, as shown.

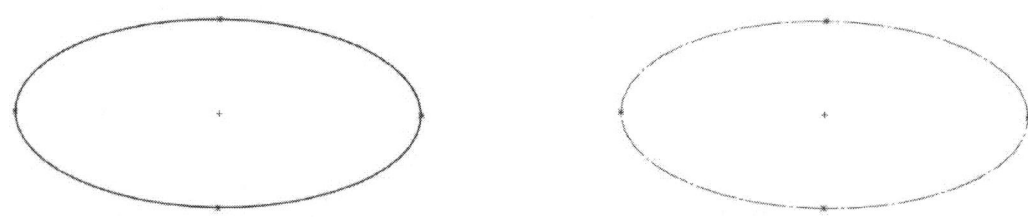

Basic Sketching Tools

Partial Ellipse Tool

This tool is used to create a partial ellipse in the sketch environment.

- Select **Ellipse > Partial Ellipse** tool from the **Sketch CommandManager**, as shown above.
- Move the cursor horizontally and click to define point (1) as the center of ellipse, as shown.
- Move the cursor vertically and click to define point (2) for the radius along major axis, as shown.
- Next, click to define point (3) for the radius along minor axis and start point of ellipse, as shown.

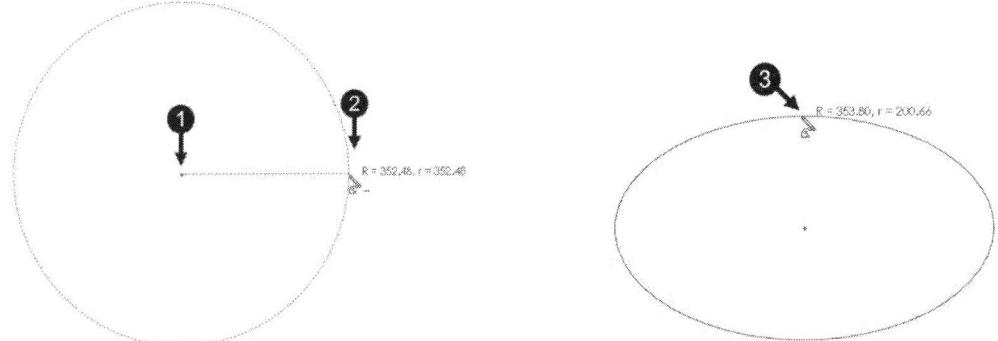

- Now click to define point (4) as the end point of the ellipse and display the preview of partial ellipse, as shown.

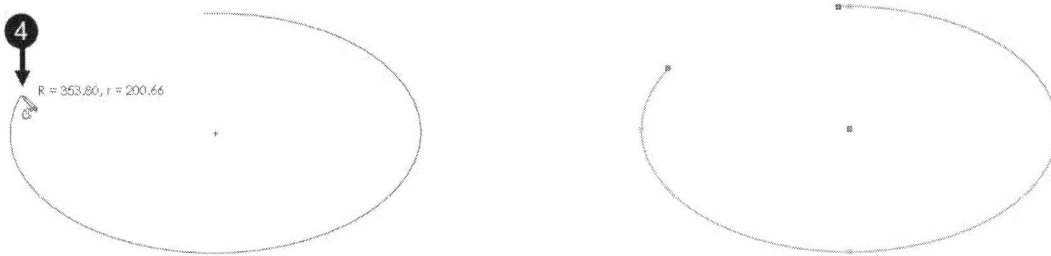

- Next, you can enter the required values in the respective edit boxes available under **Parameters** rollout of **Ellipse Property Manager** if required, as shown.
- Click on the ✓ button from the PropertyManager to exit it and display the ellipse, as shown.

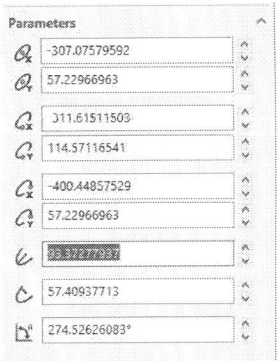
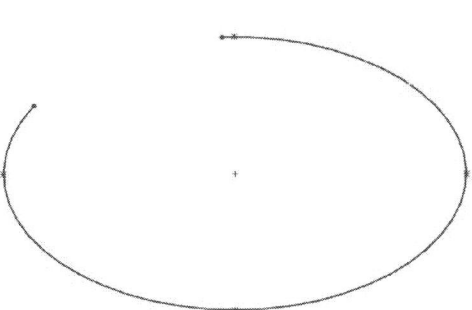

Parabola Tool

This tool is used to create a parabolic curve in the sketch environment.

- Select **Ellipse > Parabola** tool from the **Sketch CommandManager**, as shown above.
- Click to define point (1) as the focal point of parabola, as shown.

Basic Sketching Tools

- Move the cursor vertically downwards and click to define point (2) as the apex point of parabolic curve and display the reference parabolic curve, as shown.

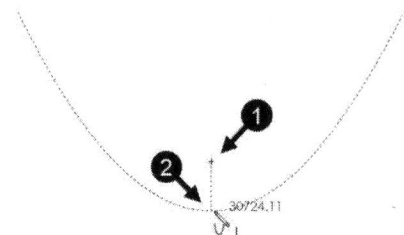

- Next, click to define point (3) & point (4) as start point and end point of parabolic curve and display the parabolic curve, as shown.

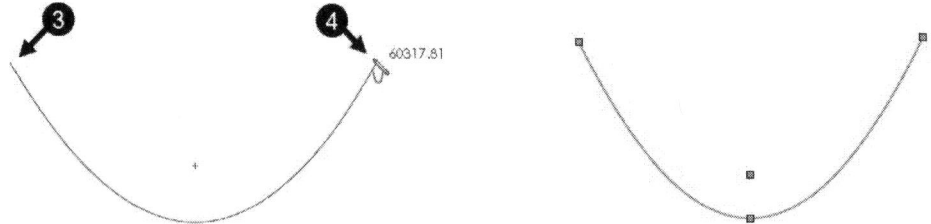

- After parabolic curve get displayed, the **Parabola PropertyManager** with active edit boxes under **Parameters** rollout get displayed, as shown.
- Next, you can modify the properties of parabolic curve by entering the required values in these edit boxes, if required.

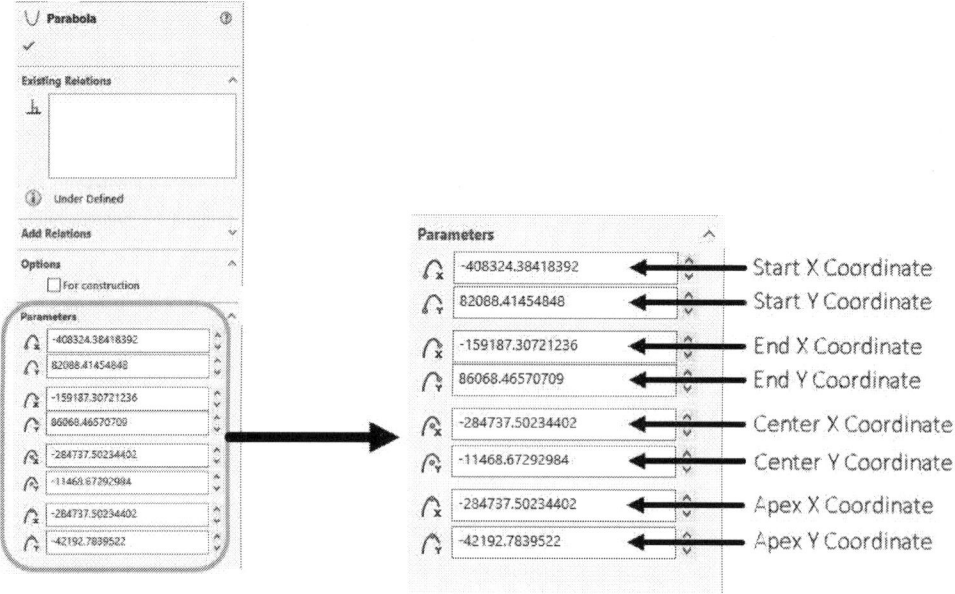

- Now click on the ✓ button from the **PropertyManager** to exit it and click anywhere in the drawing area to display the parabolic curve, as shown.

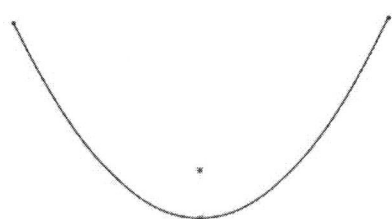

Conic Tool

This tool is used to create a conic curve in the sketch environment.

- Select **Ellipse > Conic** tool from the **Sketch CommandManager**, as shown above.
- Click to define point (1) and point (2) as the start and end point of conic curve, as shown.
- Move the cursor and click to define point (3) as the vertex of conic curve, as shown.

- Again, move the cursor and click to define point (4) at the location related to the required **Rho** value and display the conic curve, as shown.

- After conic curve get displayed, **Conic PropertyManager** with active edit boxes under **Parameters** rollout get displayed, as shown.
- Next, you can modify the properties of conic curve by entering the required values in these edit boxes, if required.

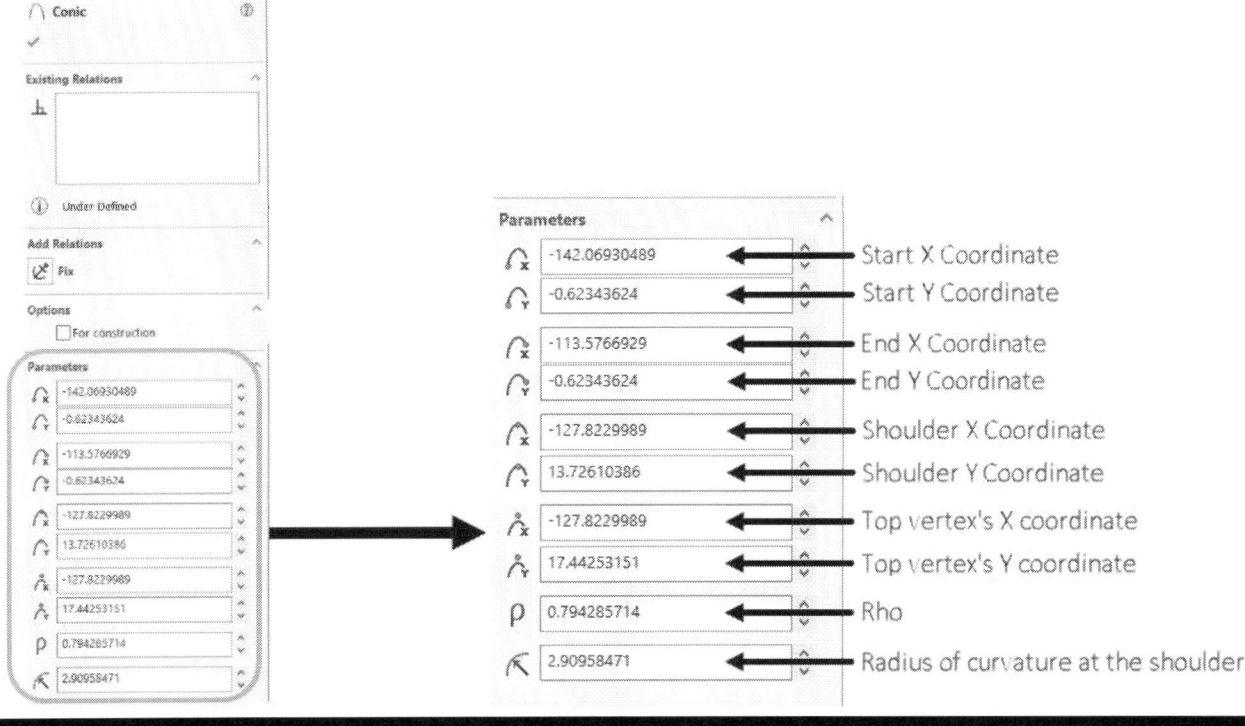

Basic Sketching Tools

> Now click on the ✓ button from the **PropertyManager** to exit it and click anywhere in the drawing area to display the conic curve, as shown.

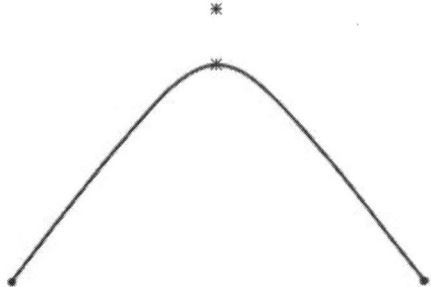

The Slot Tool

These tools are used to create slots. There are four different type of tool in the **Slot** flyout to create slots, as shown.

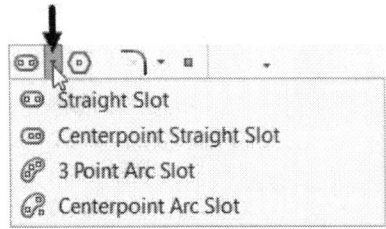

Straight Slot Tool

This tool is used to create a straight slot by defining three points – first end/start point, second end point, and third point that defines its width.

> Click on **Slot > Straight Slot** tool from the **Sketch CommandManager** to activate it, as shown above.
> Click in the drawing area to define the point (1) as first end/start point of the straight slot, as shown.
> Move the cursor up to some distance and click to define point (2) as second end point of the slot to display the preview of slot, as shown.
> Again, move the cursor up to some distance and click to define point (3) for width of Straight Slot, as shown.

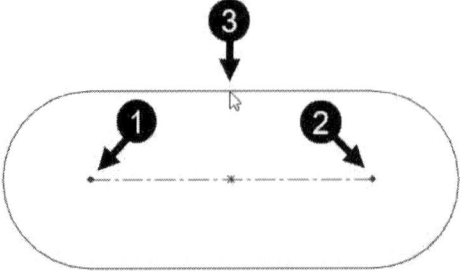

> After Straight Slot get displayed, the **Slot PropertyManager** with active edit boxes under **Parameters** rollout get displayed, as shown.
> Next, you can modify the slot by entering required values in their respective edit boxes if required, as shown.

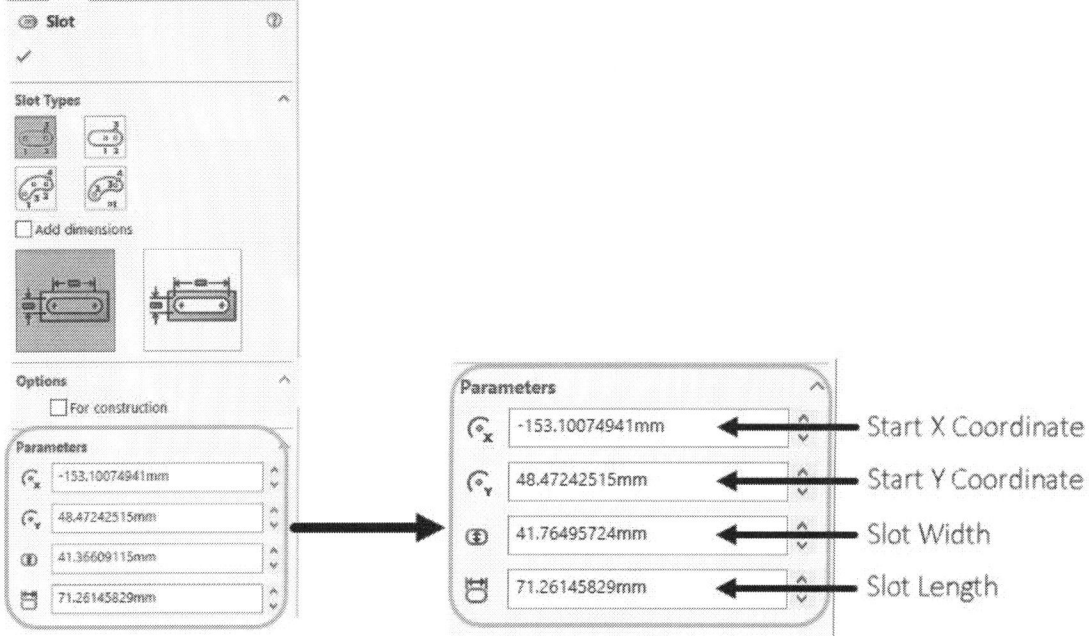

> Now click on the ✓ button from the **Slot PropertyManager** to exit it and click in the drawing area to display the straight slot, as shown.

Alternatively, you can select the **ESC** key from keyboard.

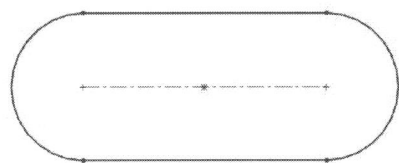

TIP: You can switch to any type of slot by clicking on the required slot type under the **Slot Types** rollout of the **Slot PropertyManager**, as shown above.

Centerpoint Straight Slot Tool

This tool is used to create a slot by defining three points - center point, endpoint, and point for width.

> Click on **Slot > Centerpoint Straight Slot** tool from the **Sketch CommandManager** to activate it, as shown above.
> Click in the drawing area to define the point (1) as center point of the Centerpoint Straight Slot, as shown.
> Move the cursor up to some distance and click to define point (2) as end point of the slot and display the preview of slot, as shown.
> Again, move the cursor up to some distance and click to define point (3) for width of Centerpoint Straight Slot and display the preview of slot, as shown.

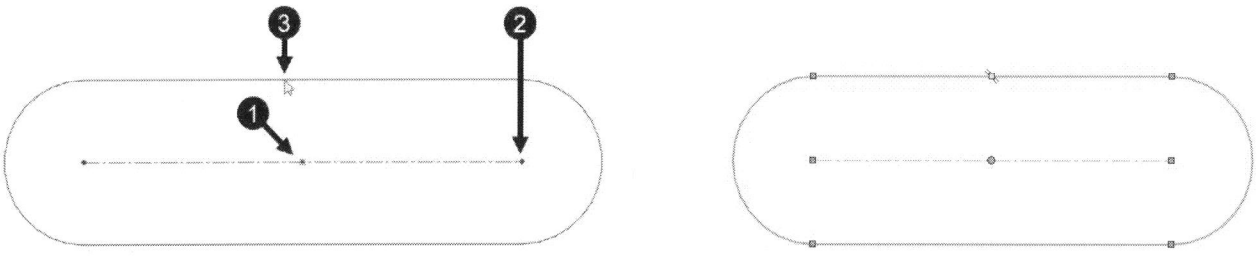

Basic Sketching Tools

- After Centerpoint Straight Slot get visible, the **Slot PropertyManager** with active edit boxes under **Parameters** rollout get displayed, as shown above.
- You can modify the properties of slot by entering the required values in their respective edit boxes under **Parameters** rollout of **Slot PropertyManager** if required, as shown.
- Now select the **ESC** key from keyboard to exit PropertyManager and display the Centerpoint Straight Slot, as shown.

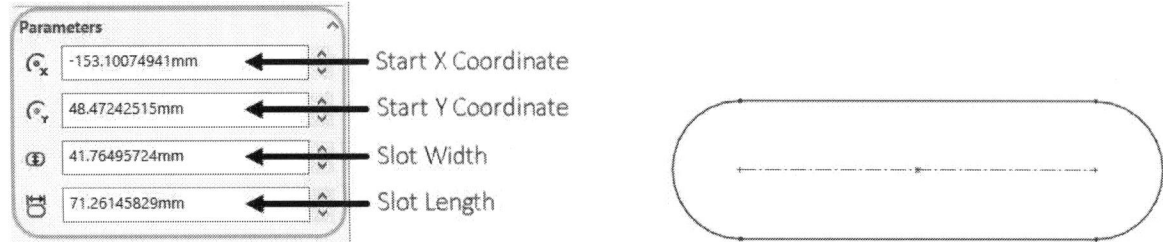

 ## 3 Point Arc Slot Tool

This tool is used to create a 3 Point Arc Slot by defining four points.

- Click on **Slot > 3 Point Arc Slot** tool from the **Sketch CommandManager** to activate it, as shown above.
- Click in the drawing area to define the point (1) as start point of the 3 Point Arc Slot, as shown.
- Move the cursor upto some distance and click to define point (2) as end point of the slot and display the preview of slot, as shown.
- Again, move the cursor upto some distance and click to define point (3) and radius of Slot, as shown.
- Now, move the cursor upto some distance and click to define point (4) for width of Slot and display the slot, as shown.

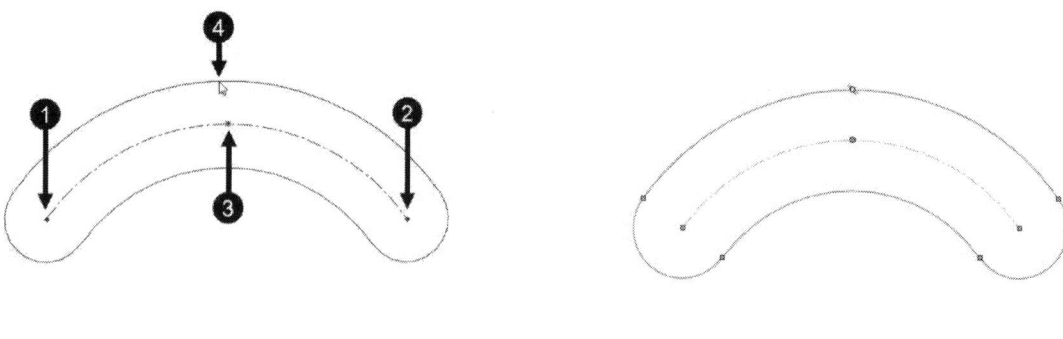

- Next, you can modify the properties of slot by entering required values in the active respective edit boxes under **Parameters** rollout of the **Slot PropertyManager**, if required, as shown.
- Now select the **ESC** key from keyboard to exit PropertyManager and display the 3 Point Arc Slot, as shown.

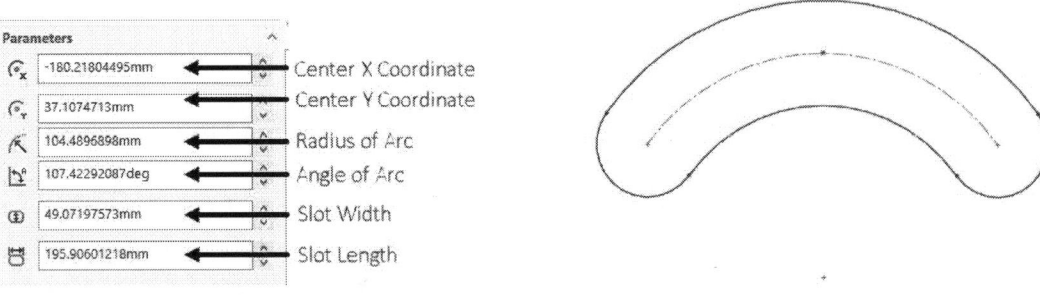

Basic Sketching Tools

Centerpoint Arc Slot Tool

This tool is used to create a straight slot.

- Click on **Slot > Centerpoint Arc Slot** tool from the **Sketch CommandManager** to activate it, as shown above.
- Click in the drawing area to define the point (1) as center point of the Centerpoint Arc Slot, as shown.
- Move the cursor upto some distance and click to define point (2) as start point of the slot, as shown.
- Move the cursor upto some distance and click to define point (3) as end point of the slot and display the preview of slot, as shown.
- Again, move the cursor upto some distance and click to define point (4) for width of Slot to display preview of the slot, as shown below.

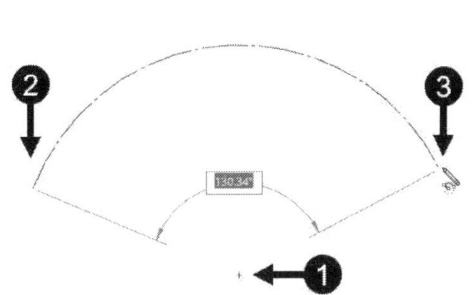 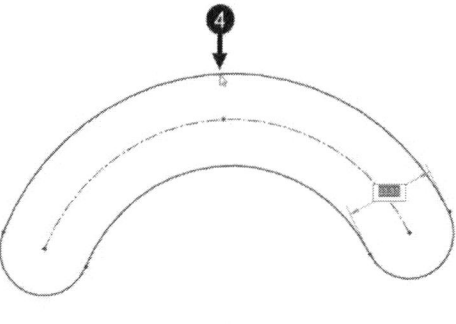

- Next, you can modify the properties of slot by entering required values in the active edit boxes under **Parameters** rollout of the **Slot PropertyManager**, as shown above.
- Now select the **ESC** key from keyboard to exit PropertyManager and display the Centerpoint Arc Slot, as shown.

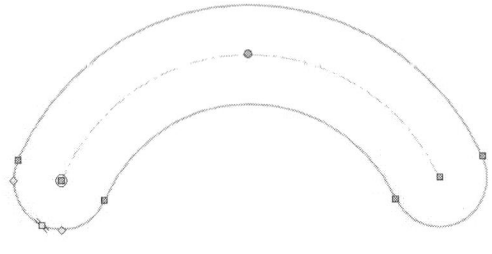 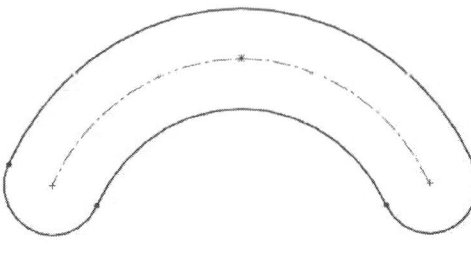

The Polygon Tool

This tool is used to create a polygon. A polygon is a single object having multiple sides and all sides equilateral and equiangular with each other. In SolidWorks, you can draw a polygon with 3 to 40 sides. The polygon is displayed inside or outside the construction circle.

- Click on **Polygon** tool from the **Sketch CommandManager** to activate it and display the **Polygon PropertyManager**, as shown.
- Enter the required number of sides of polygon in the **Number of sides** edit box under **Parameter** rollout, as shown.
- Select the **Inscribed circle** radio button if it is not selected, as shown.

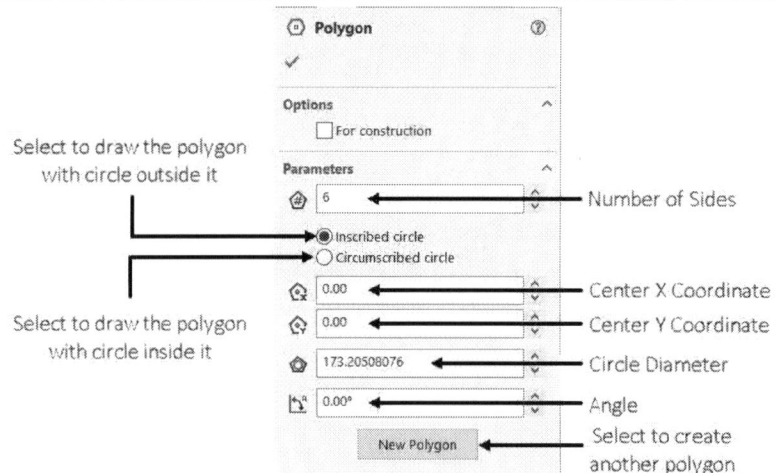

- Click in the drawing area to define the point (1) as center point of the construction circle of polygon, as shown.
- Move the cursor upto some distance and click to define point (2) for radius of construction circle of polygon, as shown.
- Now click on the **Close Dialog** ✓ button from the PropertyManager to display the polygon with construction circle inside it, as shown.

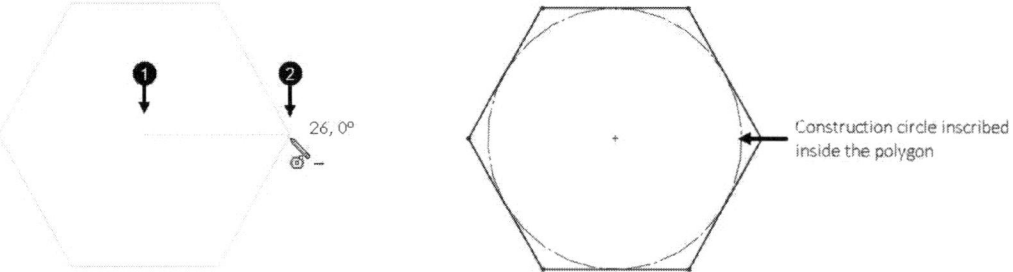

Similarly, by selecting the **Circumscribed circle** radio button from the **Polygon PropertyManager**, you can create a polygon with construction circle outside it, as shown.

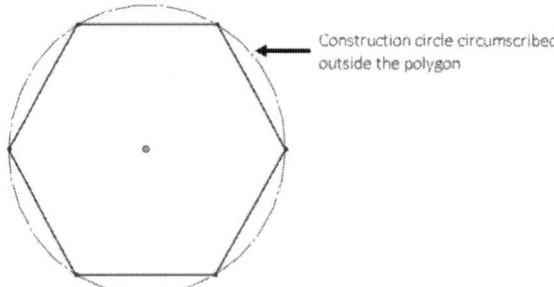

Note that the dimensions of polygon depend upon the diameter of construction circle, as shown. To change it, you can simply edit or change it, discussed later in this book.

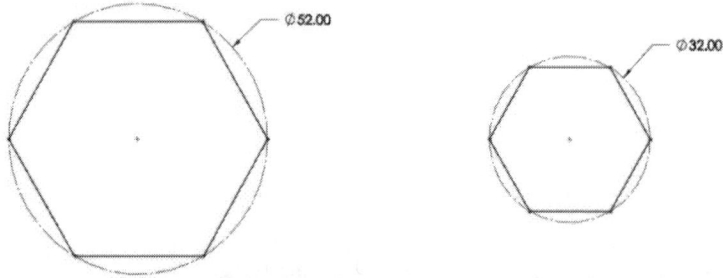

To draw a polygon with construction lines, you can select the **For Construction** check box from the PropertyManager after creating polygon, as shown.

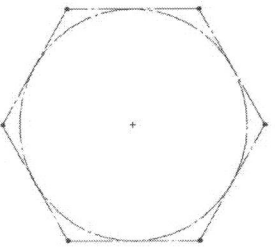 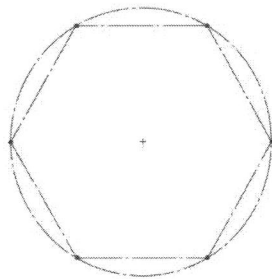

The Point Tool

This tool is used to place sketched point in the drawing area or on any sketch entity while drawing a sketch.

➢ Click on **Point** tool from the **Sketch CommandManager** to activate it
➢ Click anywhere in the drawing area to place Point and display the **Point PropertyManager**, as shown.
➢ Also, the coordinates of point at current location get displayed in the **X Coordinate** and **Y Coordinate** spinners, as shown.

You can enter the required coordinates in these spinners to change it location.

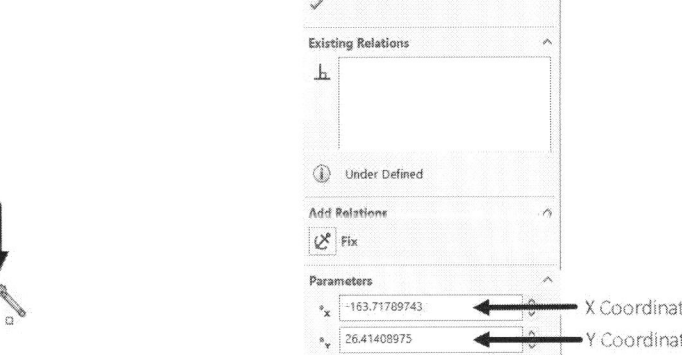

➢ Now click on the Click Dialog button from the PropertyManager to close it and display the point placed, as shown.

Similarly, you can place the point on other entities also, as shown.

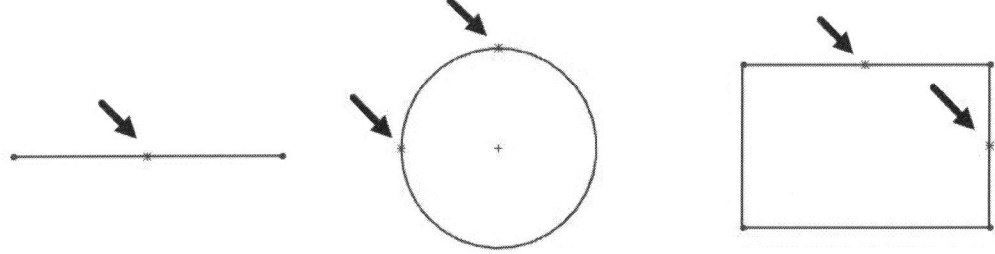

Dimensioning

In SolidWorks there are different types of tools for applying dimensions to the sketch. These options are available under **Smart Dimension** flyout, as shown below.

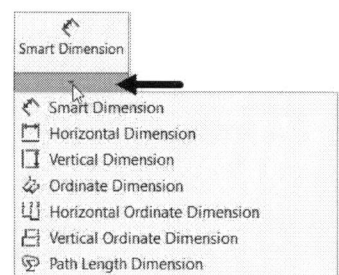

Applying Dimensions to the Sketch Using Smart Dimension Tool

In SolidWorks, in order to apply dimensions to the sketch drawn in the sketching environment, you can easily apply dimensions by selecting the **Smart Dimension** tool from the **Sketch CommandManager**. The applied dimension using this tool depends on the type of entity selected.

➢ Click on the **Smart Dimension** button from the **Sketch CommandManager**.
➢ Click on the vertical entity to display its dimension value, as shown.
➢ Move the cursor up to some distance and place the dimension by pressing the left mouse button (**LMB**), as shown.

➢ Also, the dimension of the selected entities gets displayed in the **Modify** edit box, as shown. You can enter the required dimension value in it, as per your requirements.
➢ Click on the ✓ button of the edit box to exit it and display dimension created, as shown.

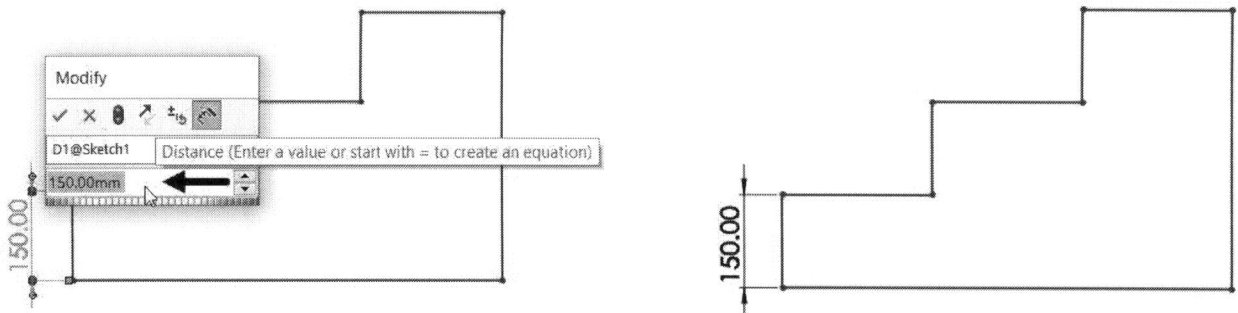

You can also generate vertical dimension by selecting two horizontal line entities or vice-versa, as shown.

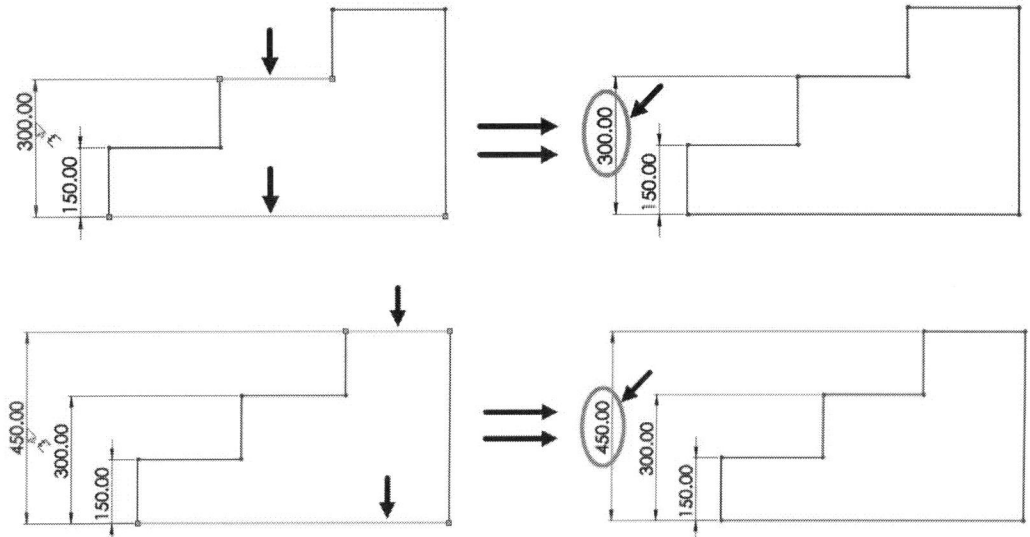

Similarly, you can generate horizontal dimensions by selecting two respective vertical line entities, as shown.

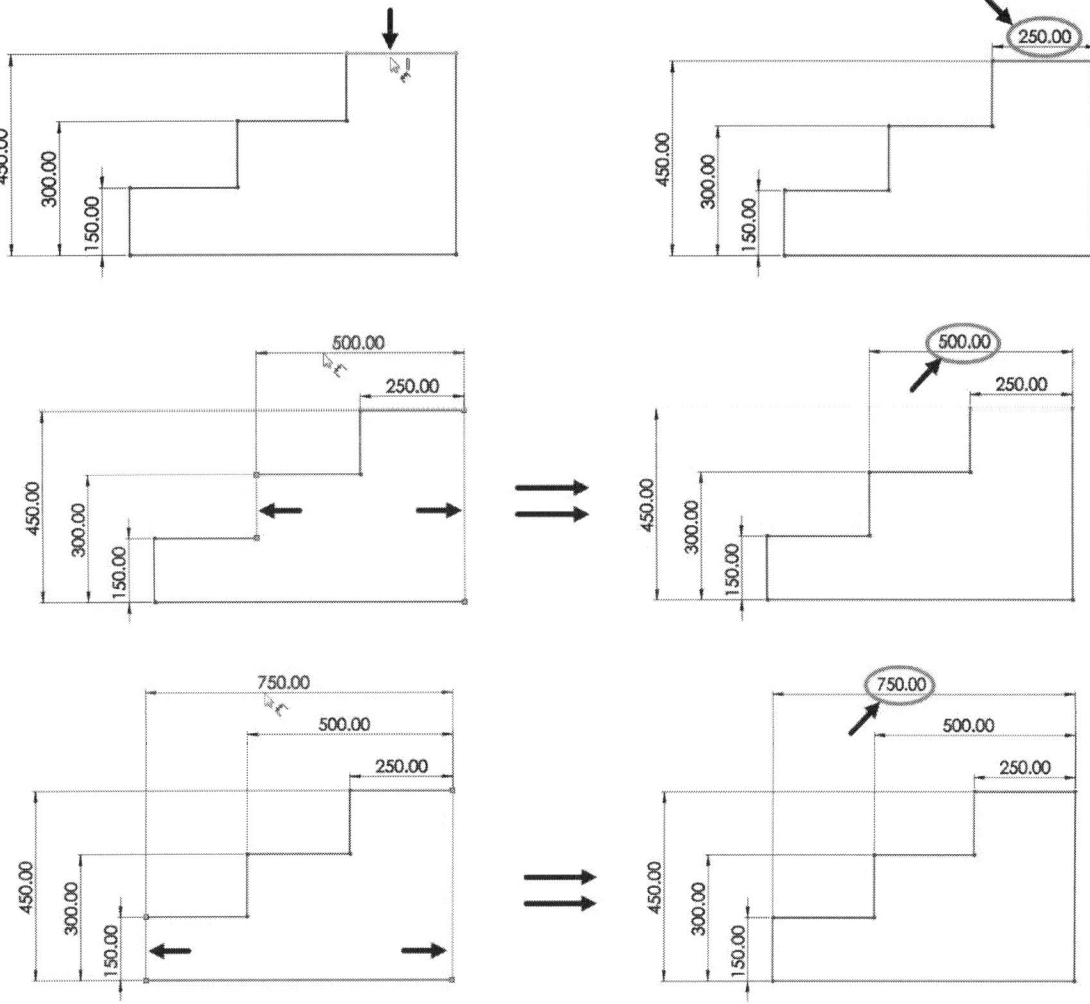

To move a placed dimension to a new location:

- Press and hold the **LMB** (Left Mouse Button) over the dimension to move, as shown.
- Drag it up to the required distance.
- Release the LMB to place the moved dimension at new location.

Basic Sketching Tools

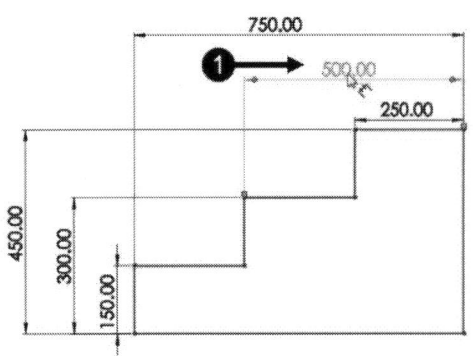 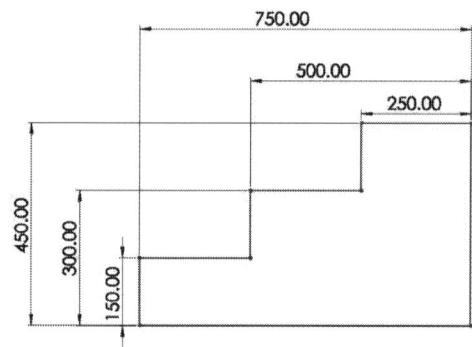

> Similarly, move & place other dimensions at their required locations also, as shown.

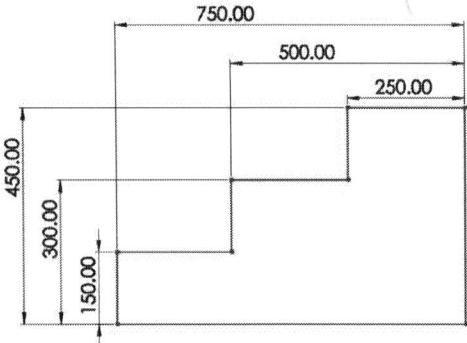

Note that to apply the horizonatal and vertical dimensions in the sketch, you can also use **Horizontal Dimension** and **Vertical Dimension** options available in the **Smart Dimension** flyout, as shown.

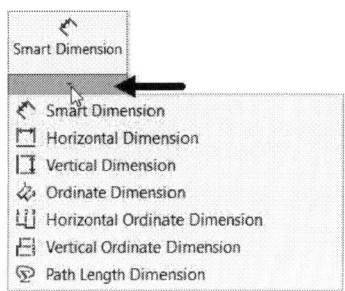

Different types of dimensions created in SolidWorks, using **Smart Dimension** tool are:

Linear Dimension

The steps for placing different types of linear dimensions are

> To apply an aligned dimension, activate the **Smart Dimension** tool and select the line entity, as shown.
> Move the cursor up to some distance and press the **LMB** (Left Mouse Button) to place the aligned dimension and display the **Modify** edit box, as shown.
> Enter the required dimension value in it, if required.
> Next, click on the ✓ button of the edit box to exit it and display dimension created, as shown.

Basic Sketching Tools

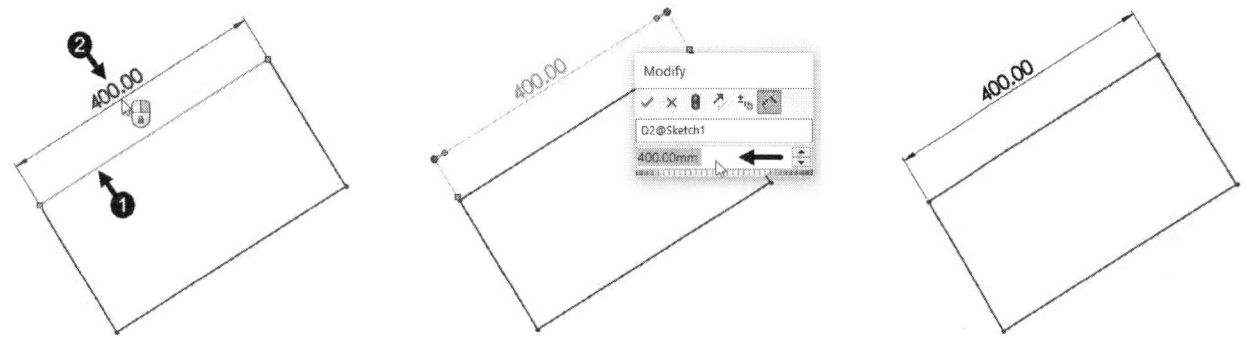

- To apply a vertical dimension, activate the **Smart Dimension** tool and select the vertical points one by one.
- Next you need to follow the same steps as discussed above to apply dimension, as shown.

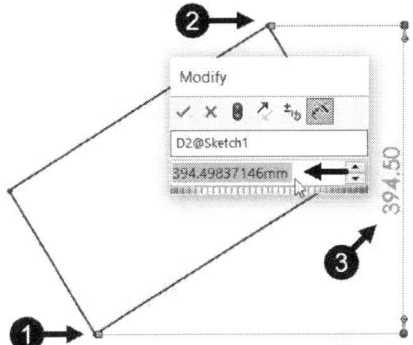 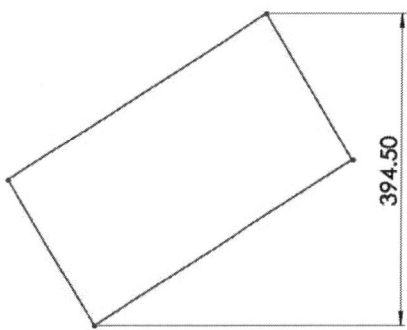

- To place a horizontal dimension, activate the **Smart Dimension** tool and select the horizontal points one by one.
- Next you need to follow the same steps as discussed above to apply dimension, as shown.

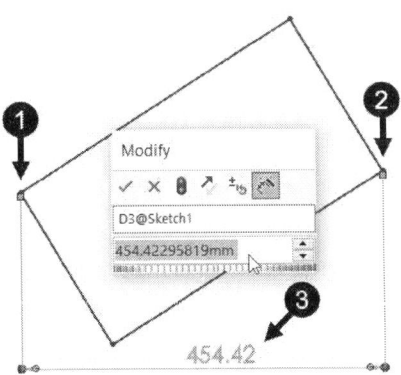 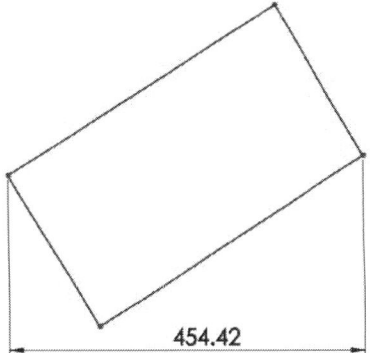

Radial & Diametric Dimension

The steps for applying radial and diametric dimensions are.

- Activate the **Smart Dimension** tool.
- Click on the circle entity to apply dimetric dimension and click on arc entity to apply radial dimension, as shown.
- Move the cursor up to some distance and press the **LMB** to place the dimension applied and display the **Modify** edit box, as shown.
- Enter the required dimension value in the **Modify** edit box, if required.
- Next, click on the ✓ button of the edit box to exit it and display dimension applied, as shown.

Basic Sketching Tools

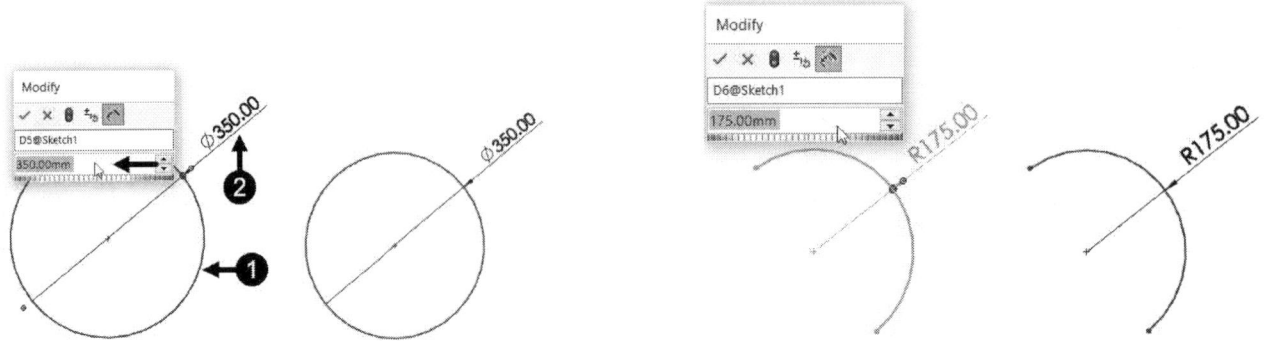

TIP: You can adjust the required dimension value by using the thumb wheel and spinner available in Modify edit box while applying dimensions, as shown.

You can also enter the required dimension value in it.

Angular Dimension

The steps for applying angular dimensions are

- Activate the **Smart Dimension** tool.
- Click on the points of arc entity one by one and then click on the arc entity to display the angular dimension, as shown.
- Move the cursor up to some distance and press the **LMB** to place the dimension applied and display the **Modify** edit box, as shown.
- Enter the required dimension value in the **Modify** edit box, if required.
- Next, click on the ✓ button of the edit box to exit it and display dimension applied, as shown.

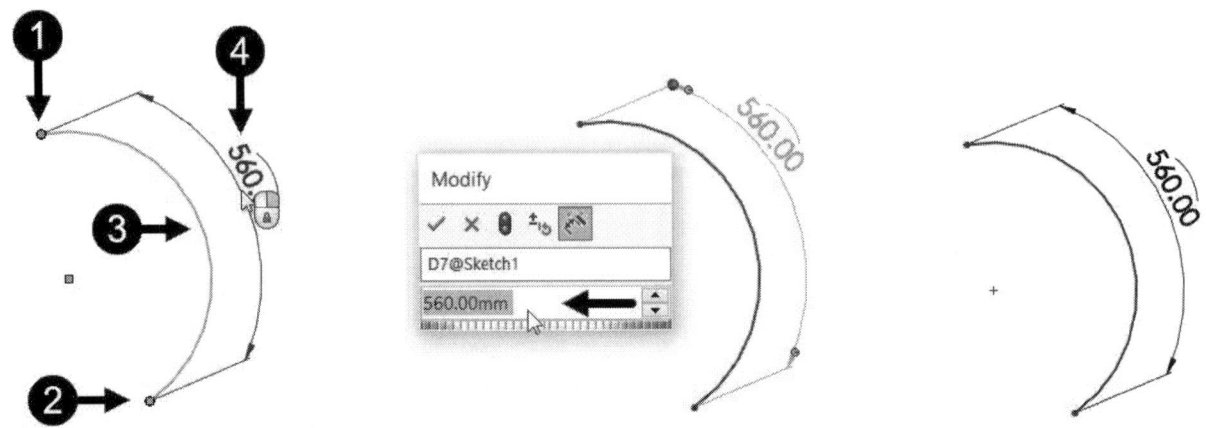

Basic Sketching Tools

Apply Diametric Dimensions to the Sketch of Revolve Features

The steps for applying diametric dimensions to a sketch of revolve features are.

- ➢ Activate the **Smart Dimension** tool.
- ➢ Select the centerline and then select the sketch entity to display its radial dimension.
- ➢ Now move the cursor up to some distance in downward direction and slightly left to display its diametric dimension, as shown.
- ➢ Click to place the dimension value and display the **Modify** edit box to modify or enter required dimension value in it, if required, as shown.

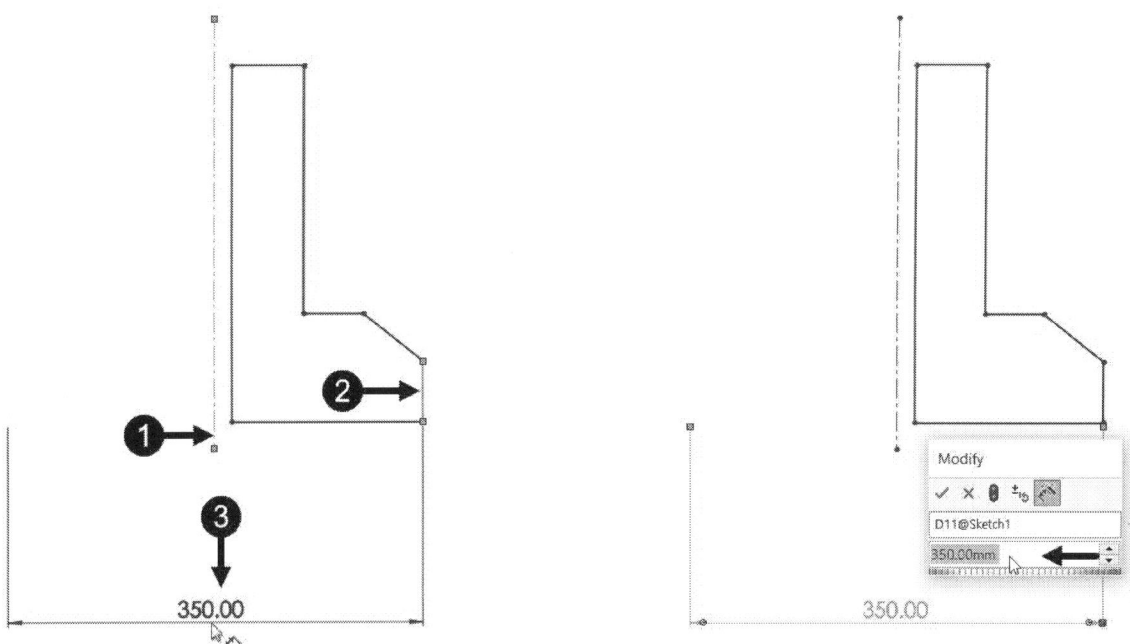

- ➢ Similarly apply other diametric dimensions, as shown.

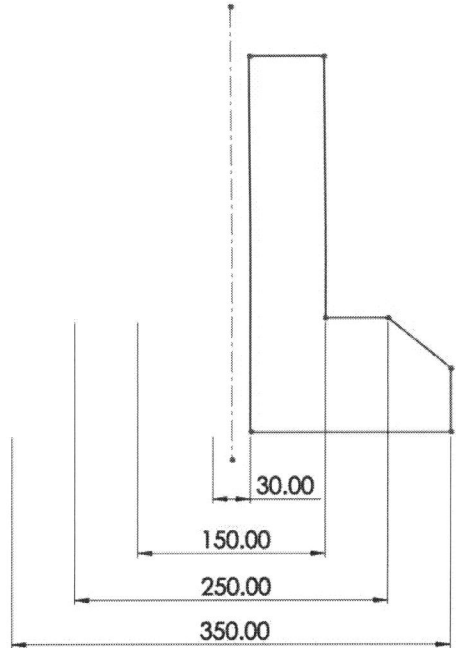

You can toggle between the visibility of dimensions by clicking on the **View Sketch Dimensions** button available under **Hide/Show** Items flyout of the **View (Heads-Up)** toolbar, as shown.

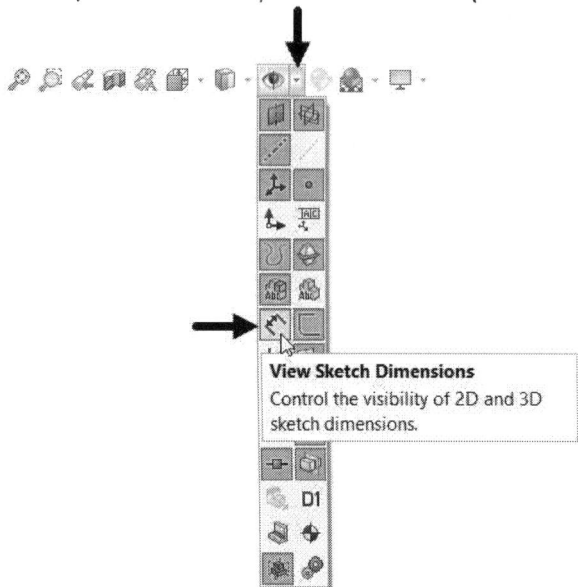

The options available in the **Smart Dimension** flyout are discussed in chapter 4 of this book.

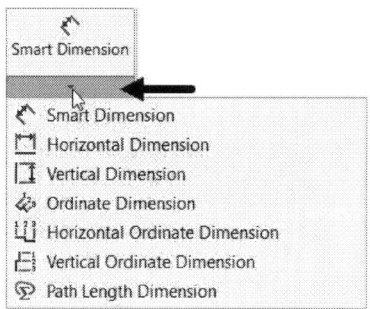

Examples:

Example 1 (Millimetres)

In this example, you will create the sketch for the part shown below.

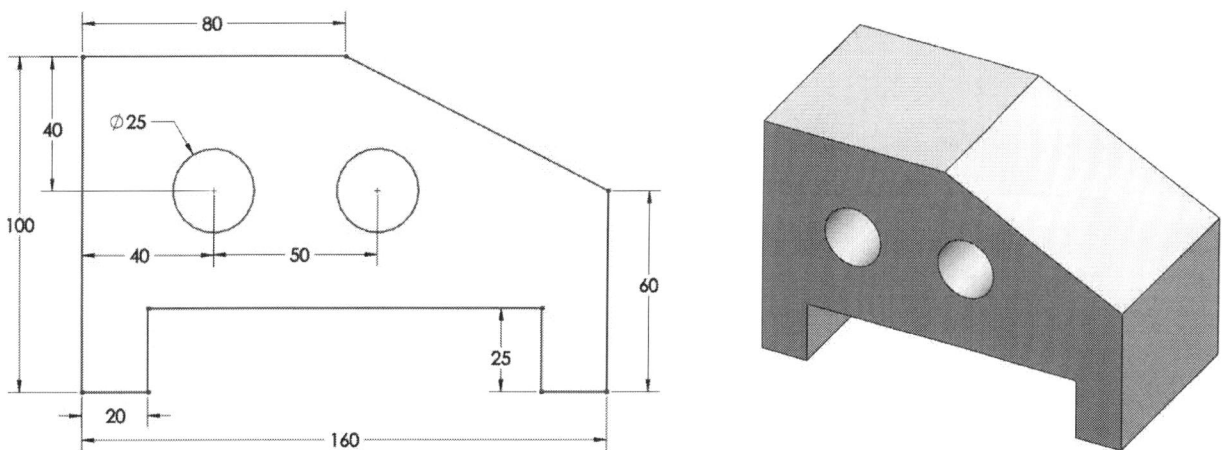

- Start SolidWorks 2021 by clicking **SOLIDWORKS 2021** icon on your desktop.
- Click on the **New** (📄) button from the Menu Bar to display the **New SOLIDWORKS Document** dialog box, as shown.

    Alternatively, press **Ctrl + N** key from the keyboard to display the **New SOLIDWORKS Document** dialog box.

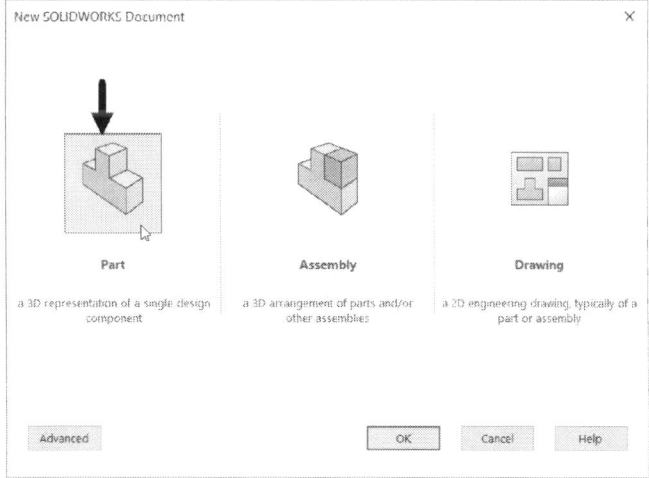

- Click on the **Part** button from the dialog box, if it is not selected by default and then click on **OK** button from dialog box to enter in the Sketching Environment.

    Alternatively, you can double click on the **Part** button to enter in the Sketching Environment.

- Click on the **Sketch** tab to display tools used in creating sketch, as shown.

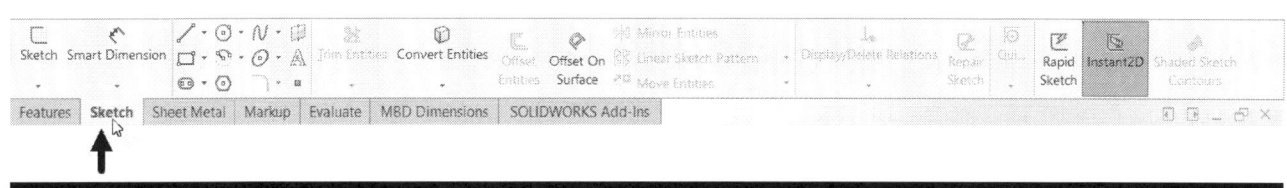

➤ Click on the **Sketch** button from the **Sketch CommandManager** and then click on the **Front** plane to make it parallel to the screen, as shown.

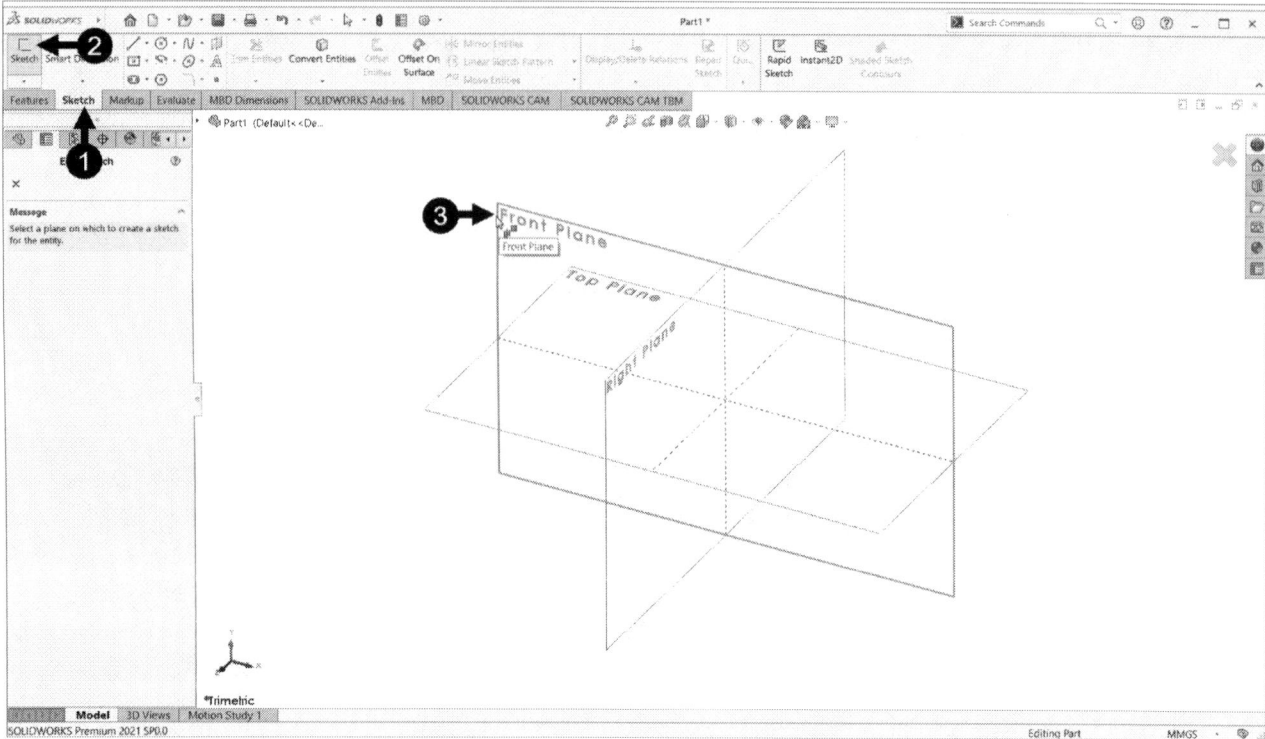

➤ Next for the better visibility of display, you can change background color to white:

- Click on the drop-down next to **Apply Scene** button from the **View (Heads-Up)** toolbar, as shown.
- Next, select the **Plain White** option to change background of drawing area to white, as shown.

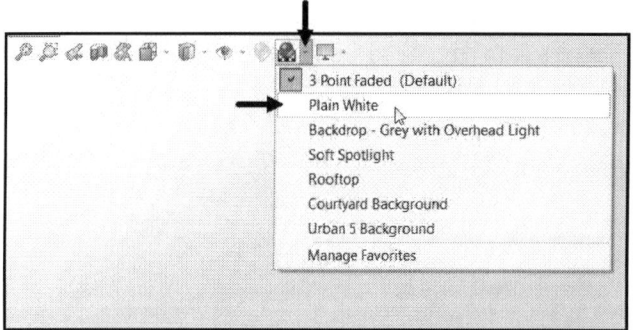 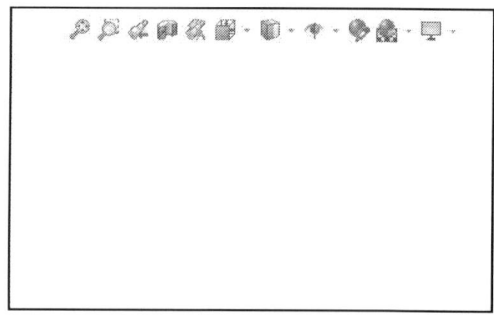

➤ Select the **Line** tool to display the Insert Line PropertyManager, as shown.

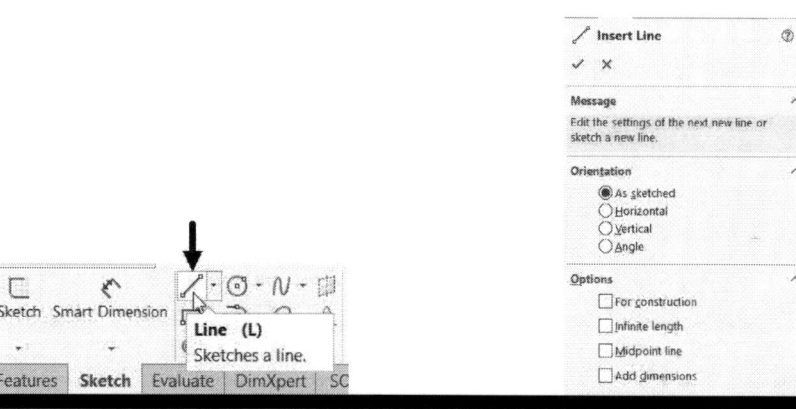

Basic Sketching Tools

2-36

- Draw the sketch, as shown.
- Now apply dimensions by using **Smart Dimensions** tool, as discussed above.

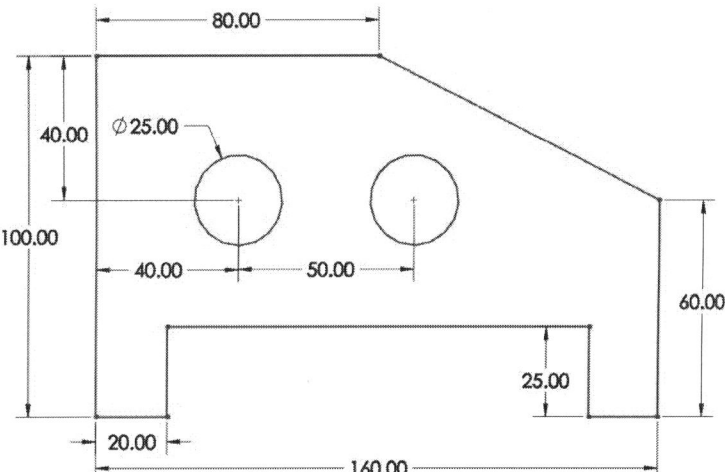

- To make change in any dimension, right click on any of the entity to display the **Dimension PropertyManager on** left, as shown.
- You can edit or enter new dimension value and change precision values in the PropertyManager, as shown.

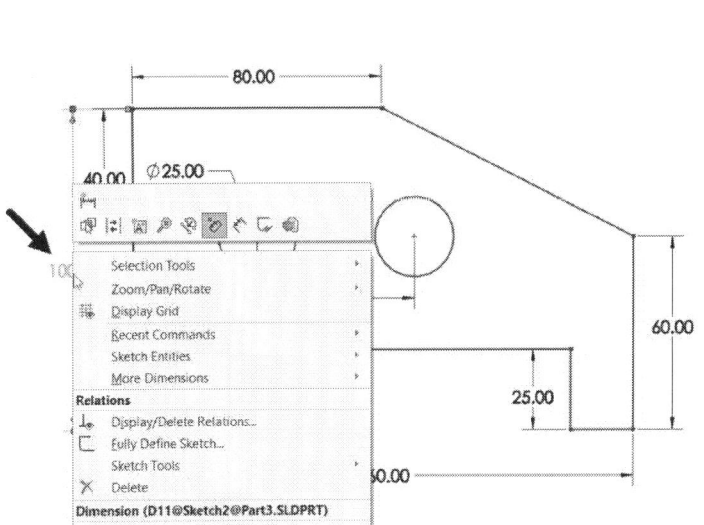

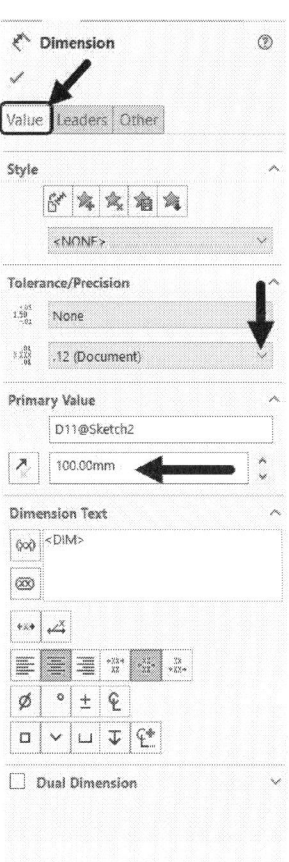

- Click on the **Unit Precision** drop-down and click on the **None** option to generate dimensions without precision, as shown.

Basic Sketching Tools

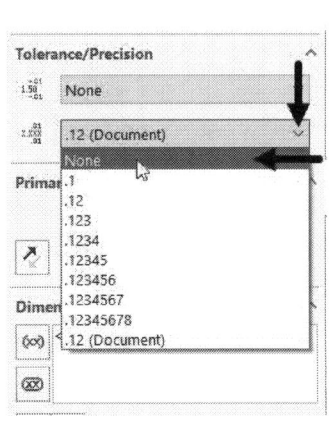 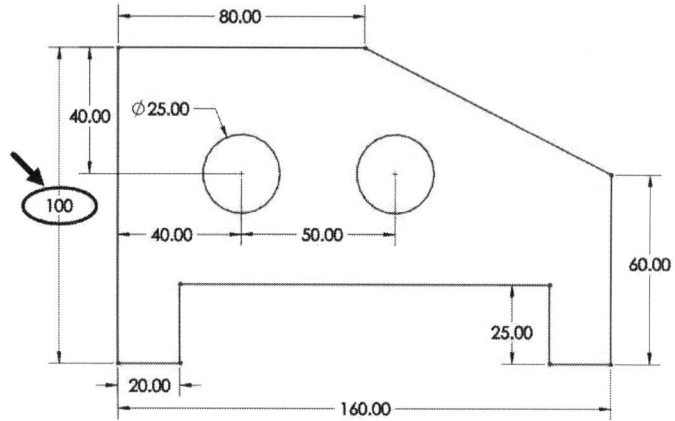

- Now to change size of dimension value, you can select the **Other** tab then deselect the **Use document font**, as shown.
- Next, click on the **Font** button to display the **Choose Font** dialog box, as shown
- Now you can change the Font Style and Text Height from the dialog box as per your requirements, as shown.

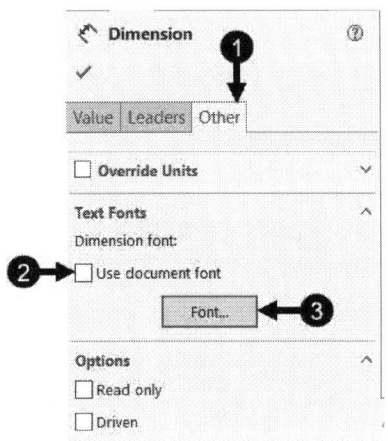 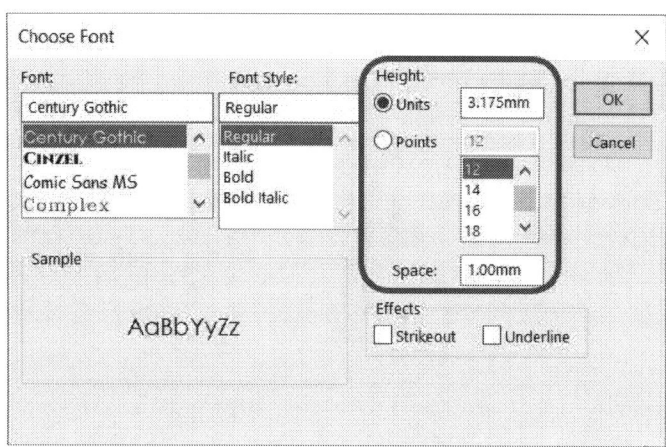

Similarly, you can change precision value and dimension size of other dimensions of the sketch also, as shown.

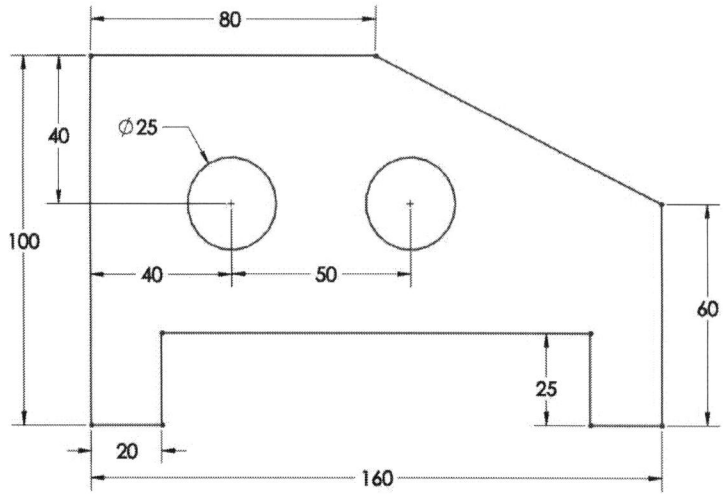

› The sketch is complete, click on the **Exit Sketch** button from the **Sketch CommandManager** to exit from the sketch environment and display the sketch created.

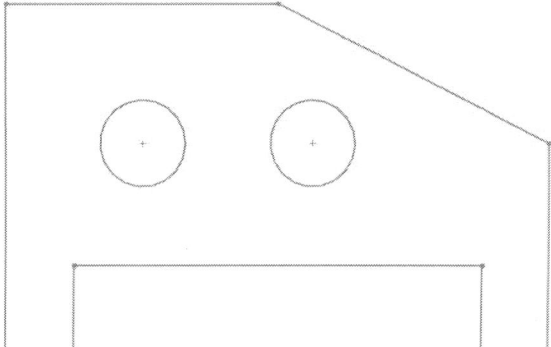

› Click on the **Save (Ctrl+S)** button from the **Menu Bar** to display the **Save As** dialog box.
› Next browse to the folder of **chapter 2** and enter name **Ch02-exam01** in the **File name** edit box.
› Click on the **Save** button from the dialog box to save the file.
› Now click on the **Close** button from the top right corner of the drawing area to close it.

Example 2

In this example, you will create the sketch shown below.

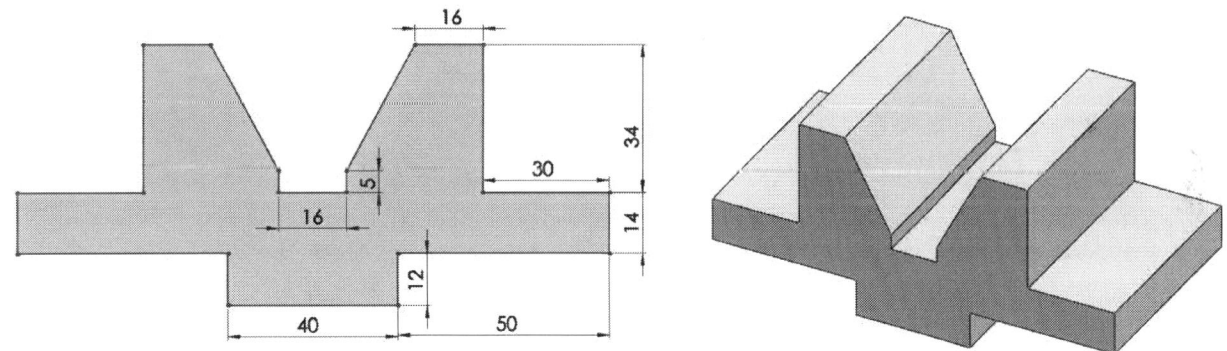

› Start SolidWorks 2021 by clicking **SOLIDWORKS 2021** icon on your desktop.
› Click on the **New** ( ) button from the Menu Bar to display the **New SOLIDWORKS Document** dialog box, as shown.

Alternatively, press **Ctrl + N** key from the keyboard to display the **New SOLIDWORKS Document** dialog box.

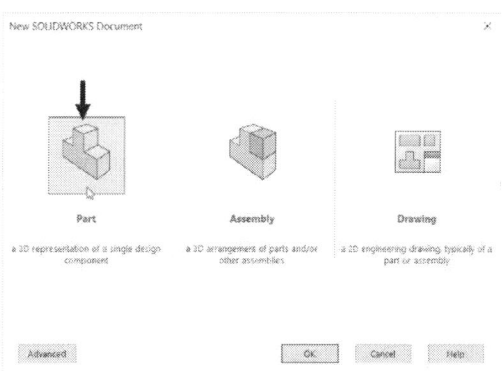

➢ Click on the **Part** button from the dialog box, if it is not selected by default and then click on **OK** button from dialog box to enter in the Sketching Environment.

Alternatively, you can double click on the **Part** button to enter in the Sketching Environment.

➢ Click on the **Sketch** tab to display tools used in creating sketch, as shown.

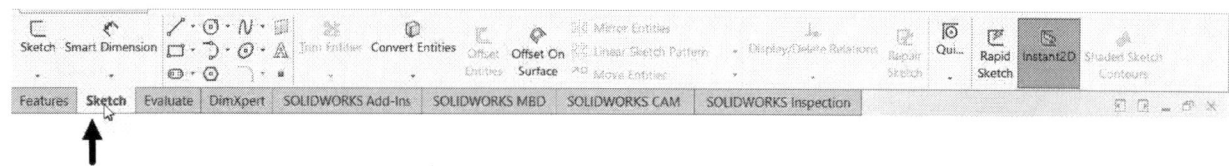

➢ Click on the **Sketch** button from the **Sketch CommandManager** and then click on the **Front** plane to make it parallel to the screen, as shown in previous example.

➢ Next for better visibility of display, change the background color to white, as discussed in previous example.

➢ Select the **Line** tool to activate it.

➢ Next, draw the sketch, and apply dimensions by using **Smart Dimensions** 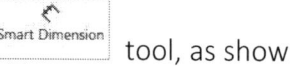 tool, as shown and as discussed earlier.

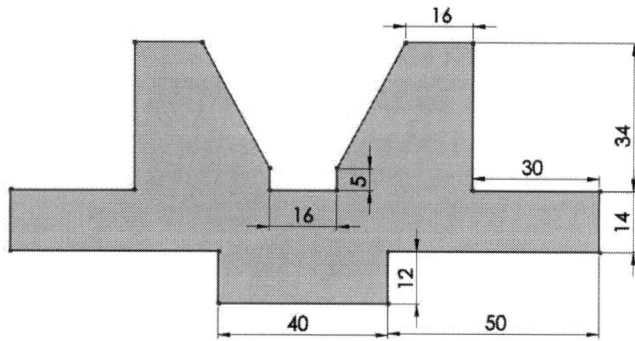

➢ The sketch is complete, click on the **Exit Sketch** button from the **Sketch CommandManager** to exit from the sketch environment and display the sketch created.

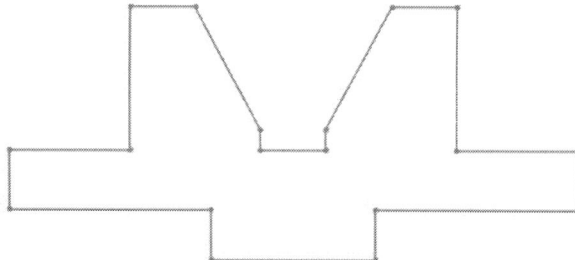

➢ Click on the **Save (Ctrl+S)** button from the Menu Bar to display the **Save As** dialog box.
➢ Next browse to the folder of chapter **2** and enter name **Ch02-exam02** in the **File name** edit box.
➢ Click on the **Save** button from the dialog box to save the file.
➢ Now enter the **Close** button from the upper right corner to close it.

Basic Sketching Tools 2-40

Example 3 (Millimetres)

In this example, you will create the sketch shown below.

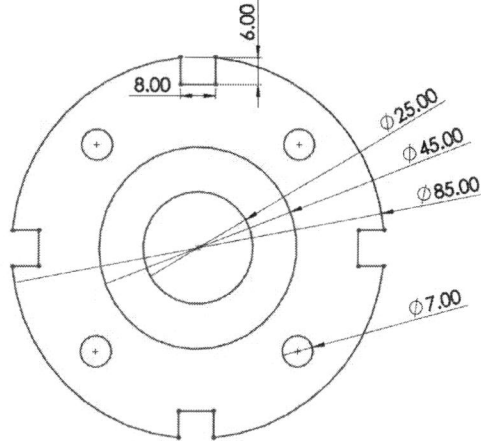

- Start SolidWorks 2021 by clicking **SOLIDWORKS 2021** icon on your desktop.
- Click on the **New** (▢) button from the **Menu Bar** to display the **New SOLIDWORKS Document** dialog box.

  Alternatively, press **Ctrl + N** key from the keyboard to display the **New SOLIDWORKS Document** dialog box.

- Click on the **Part** button from the dialog box, if it is not selected by default and then click on **OK** button from dialog box to enter in the Sketching Environment.

  Alternatively, you can double click on the **Part** button to enter in the Sketching Environment.

- Click on the **Sketch** tab to display tools used in creating sketch.
- Click on the **Sketch** button from the **Sketch CommandManager** and then click on the **Front** plane to make it parallel to the screen, as shown in previous example.
- Next for better visibility of display, change the background color to white, as discussed in previous example.
- Activate the **Circle** tool from the **Sketch CommandManager** to activate it and draw circle entities.
- Click in the drawing area to define the center point of the circle & move the cursor up to some distance and enter **25** as its diameter, as shown.
- Press the **ENTER** key from keyboard to display the circle with its diameter, as shown.

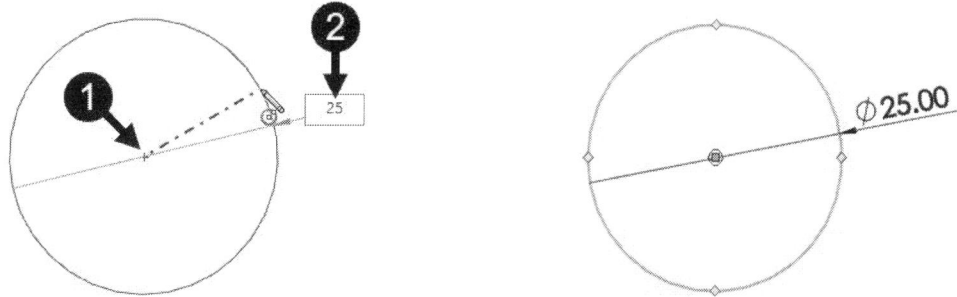

- As the **Circle** tool is still active, similarly draw two more circles, as shown.

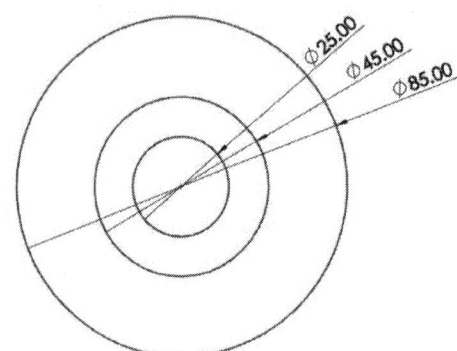

> Now to draw a construction circle, draw a circle of **65** dia and then select the **For construction** radio button from the dialog box, as shown.

> Click on the **Close Dialog** ✓ button from the dialog box to exit the **Circle** tool and display the construction circle creates, as shown.

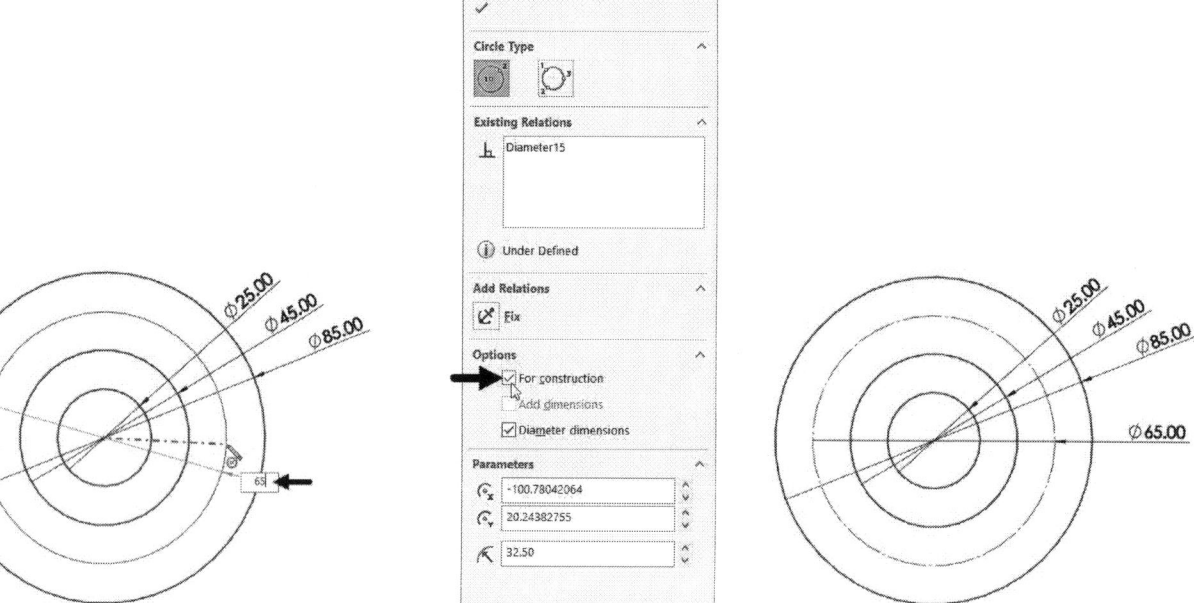

> Activate the **Centerline** (**Sketch > Line > Centerline**) tool and draw the centreline, as shown.

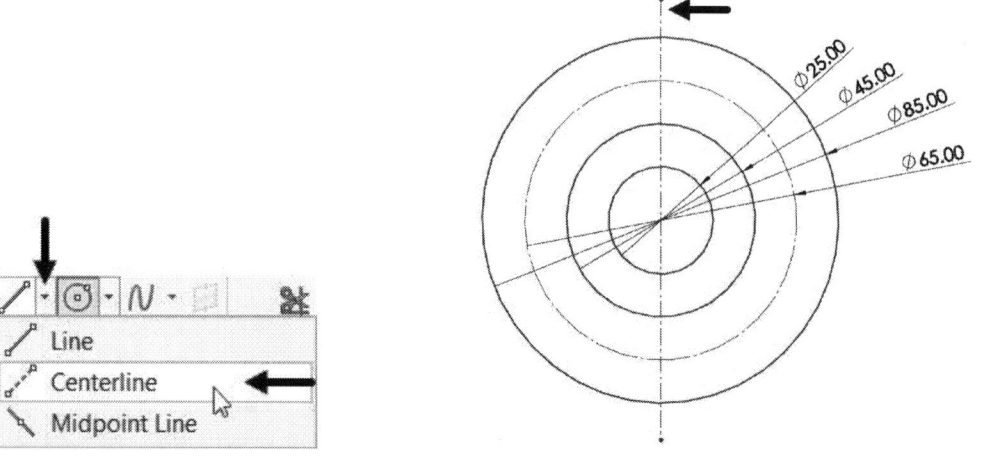

> Activate the **Line** tool and draw the sketch, as shown.

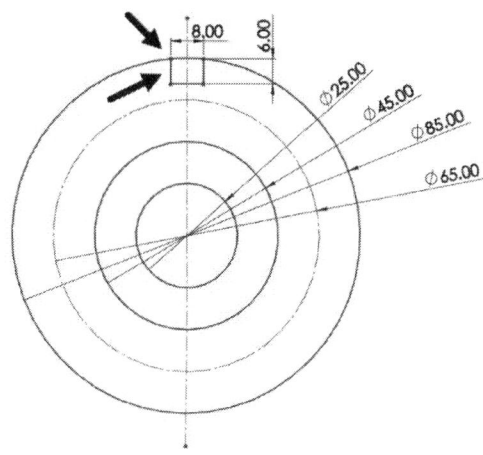

- Activate the **Trim Entities** tool and move the cursor over unwanted entities to remove, as shown.

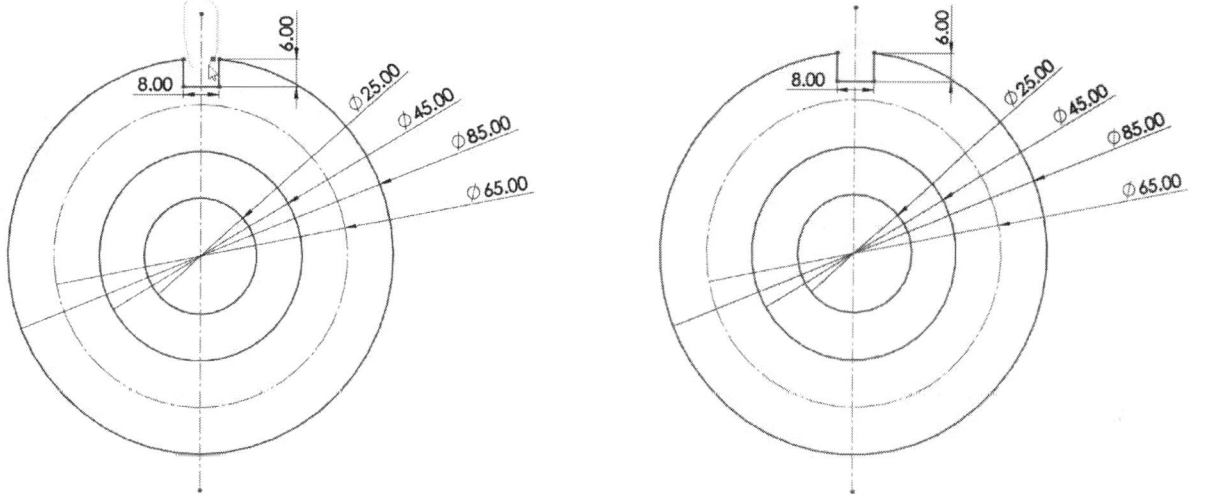

- Activate the **Centerline** tool and draw two centerlines at angle **45** degrees from the vertical line, as shown.
- Activate the **Circle** tool and draw a circle of radius **7** at the intersection of construction circle and construction point, as shown.
- Similarly draw another three circles of same radius, as shown.

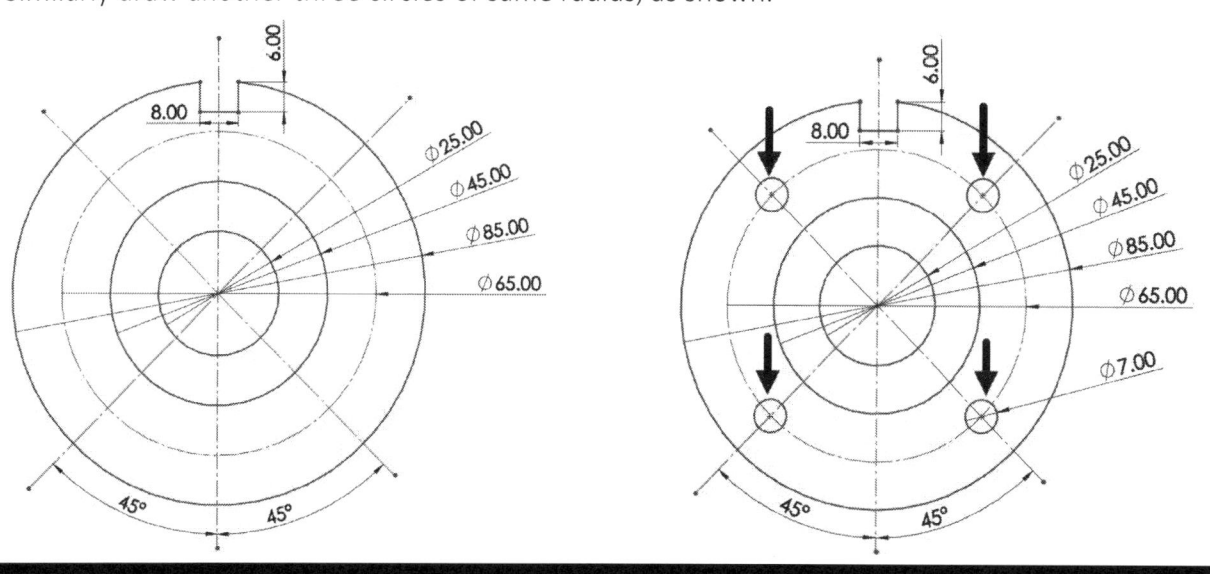

- Now, Select the **Mirror Entities** tool to activate it and display the **Mirror PropertyManager**, as shown.
- Select the entities to mirror and then click in the Mirror about area of the PropertyManager.
- Next, select the ceneterline to display the preview of mirror feature at 90-degree angle, as shown.

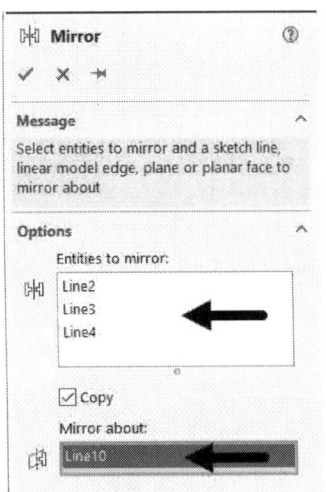
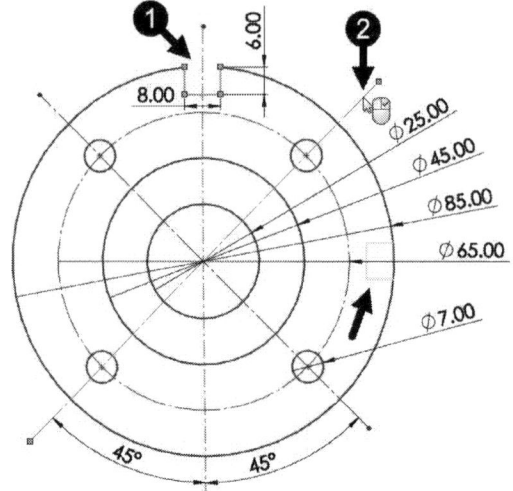

- Similarly create two more mirror features of the same.
- Again, activate the **Trim Entities** tool and move the cursor over unwanted entities to remove, as shown.

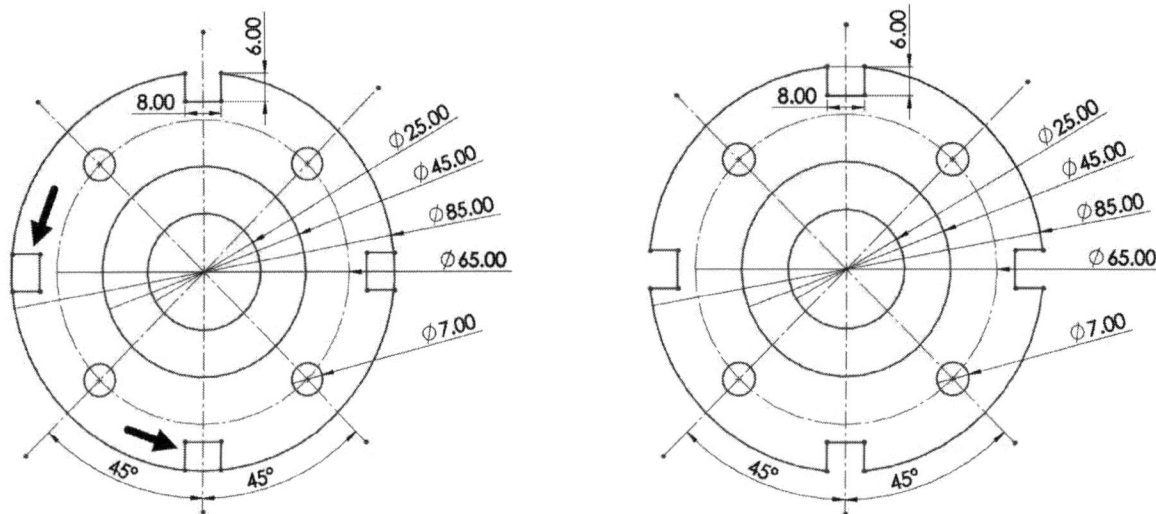

- Select both the centerlines and construction circle and press the **Delete** key from the keyboard to display the final sketch.

Note that **Sketcher Confirm Delete** message box will get displayed and click on the **Yes to All** button to continue. The dimensions associated with deleted entities also get deleted, as shown.

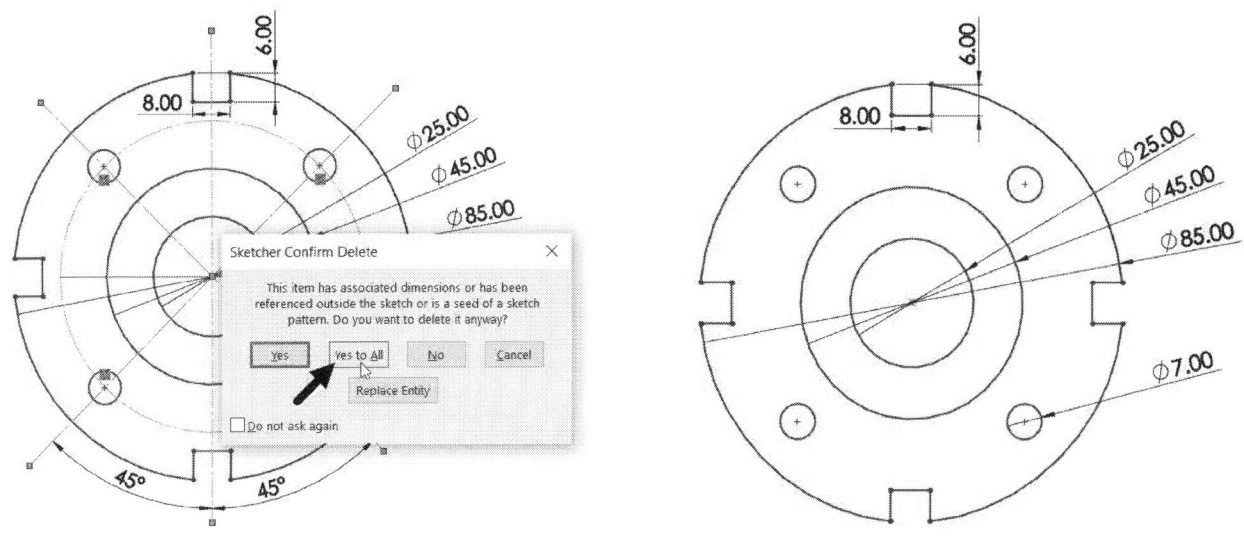

➢ The sketch is complete, click on the **Exit Sketch** button from the **Sketch CommandManager** to exit from the sketch environment and display the sketch created.

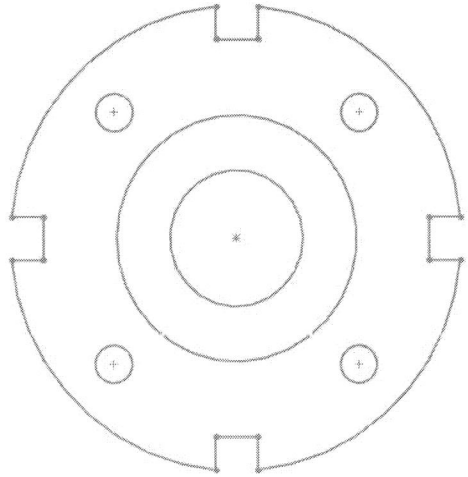

➢ Click on the **Save (Ctrl+S)** button from the Menu Bar to display the **Save As** dialog box.
➢ Next browse to the folder of chapter **2** and enter name **Ch02-exam03** in the **File name** edit box.
➢ Click on the **Save** button from the dialog box to save the file.
➢ Now enter the **Close** button from the upper right corner to close it.

Questions:

1. Which tool is selected to start a new file in SolidWorks and from where it is selected?
2. Which tool is used to apply dimensions in a sketch?
3. How can we create a tangent arc?
4. How can you change display visibility in SolidWorks?
5. How can you apply diametric dimension to a circle or arc?
6. List the tools in Rectangle flyout?
7. Which tool is selected to create a circle by defining three points?
8. Which tool is used to create a straight slot?
9. How can you toggle between Line and Arc tool?
10. How can you edit any spline created?

Exercises:

Exercise 1

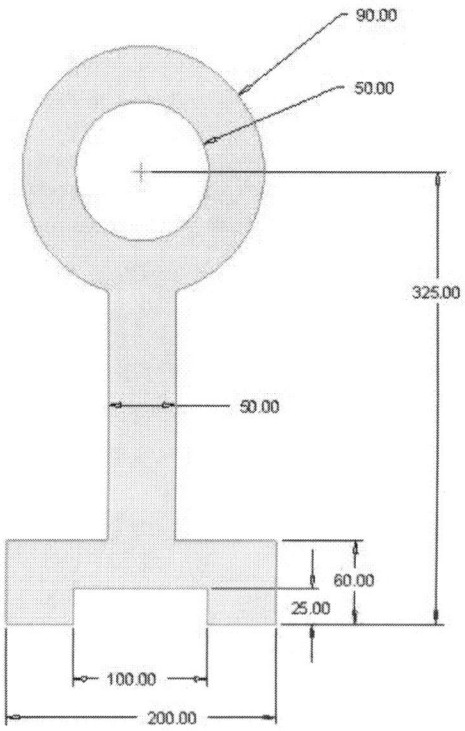

Exercise 2

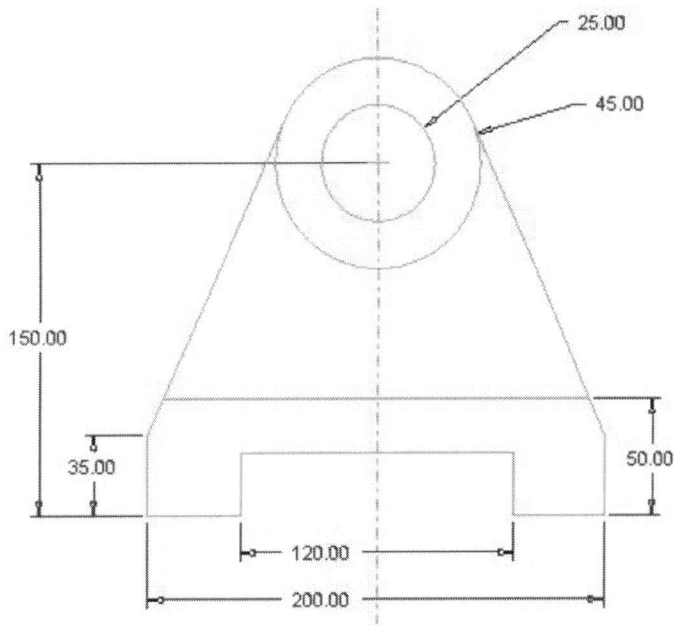

Exercise 3

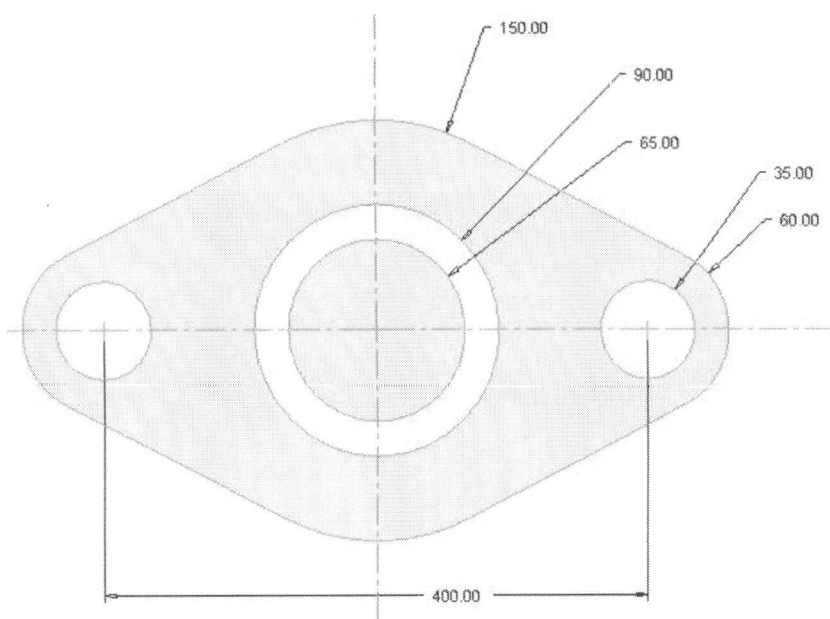

Chapter 03: Advance Sketching & Editing Tools

This chapter covers the advanced sketching tools and methods & commands to edit sketches used in the part environment. The commands and methods are discussed in context to the part environment. In SolidWorks, you can edit sketches by using different editing tools available in the SolidWorks environment. You will learn about editing sketches in this chapter.

The topics covered in this chapter are:

- ❖ Fillet
- ❖ Chamfer
- ❖ Trim
- ❖ Convert Entities
- ❖ Offset
- ❖ Text
- ❖ Mirror
- ❖ Patterns
- ❖ Learn use of tools that help you in editing sketch entities

The Fillet Tool

This tool is used to create a fillet or round a sharp corner created by intersection of two lines, arcs, circles, and rectangle or polygon vertices.

Sketch Fillet Tool

This tool is used to create a tangent arc at the intersection of two sketched entities by extending and trimming the entities.

> Click on the **Sketch Fillet** tool from the **Sketch CommandManager** to activate it and display the **Sketch Fillet PropertyManager**, as shown.
> Click on the entities (two lines, two arcs, or a line and an arcs) to create fillet between them, as shown.

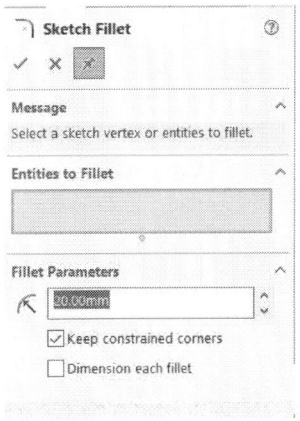
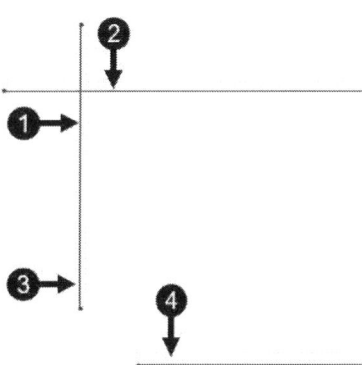

- The preview of fillets tangent to selected entities get visible with default radius value in the **Sketch Fillet PropertyManager**, as shown.
- Next, you can enter or adjust the required radius value in the **Fillet Radius** spinner of the PropertyManager if required.

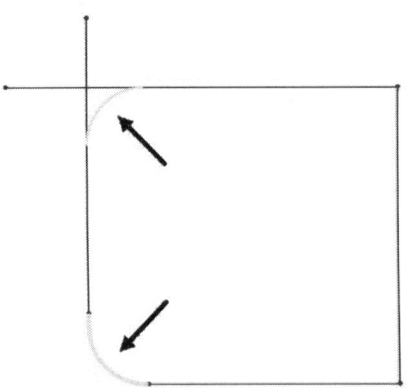
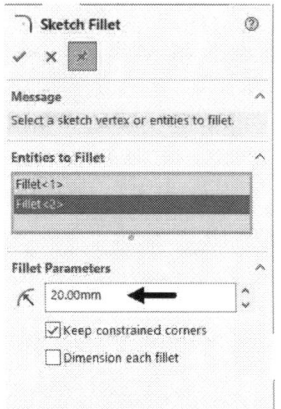

- Click on the **OK** button from the **Sketch Fillet PropertyManager** to display the fillets created, as shown.

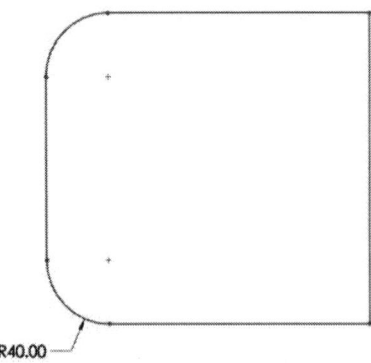

Note: The dimension of the radius will be only visible if the **View Sketch Dimensions** option is selected from the **View (Heads-up)** Toolbar, as shown below.

To display dimensions with each fillet, select the **Dimension each fillet** check box from the **Sketch Fillet PropertyManager**

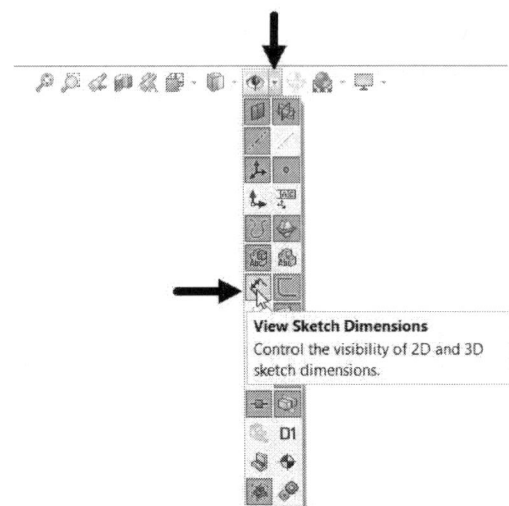

- The entities are automatically trimmed or extended to meet the end of the new fillet radius.
- The tool is still active and you can again enter required radius values and select other entities to create fillets, as shown.

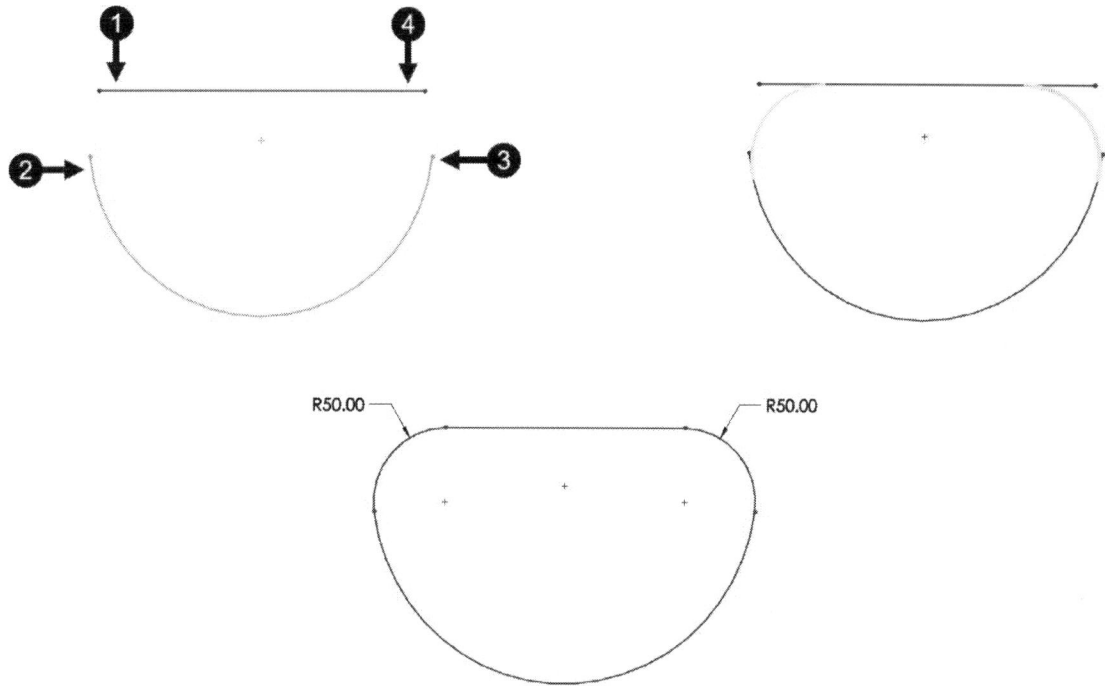

- Now, click on the **OK** button from the **Sketch Fillet PropertyManager** again to exit from this tool.

    Alternatively, press the **RMB** (Right mouse button) to display the shortcut menu and select the **OK** option to exit from this tool.

Sketch Chamfer Tool

This tool is used to create a chamfer between two selected entities by applying - two distance values, same distance value or distance and angle values. There are two radio buttons available in the **Sketch Chamfer PropertyManager**, used to create these three types of chamfers, disused next.

Angle-distance

This radio button is selected to create chamfer between two selected entities by using distance and angle values.

❖ Select **Sketch Fillet > Sketch Chamfer** option from the **Sketch CommandManager** to activate it and display the **Sketch Chamfer PropertyManager**, as shown.

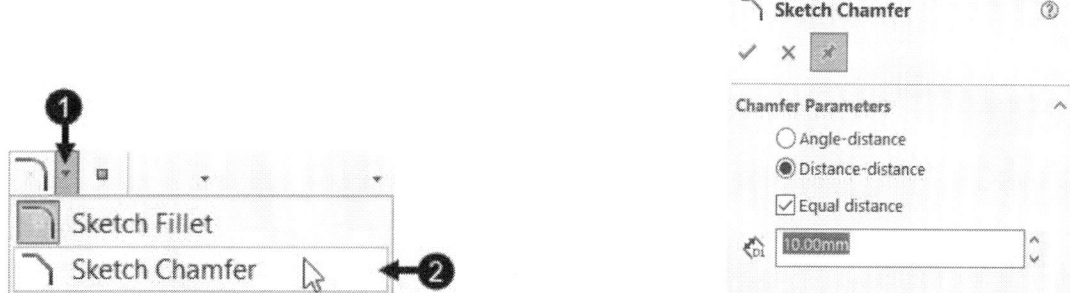

Advance Sketching & Editing Tools

- Select the **Angle-distance** radio button from the **Sketch Chamfer PropertyManager**, as shown.
- Enter or set the required distance and angle values in the **Distance 1** and **Direction 1 Angle** spinners, as shown.

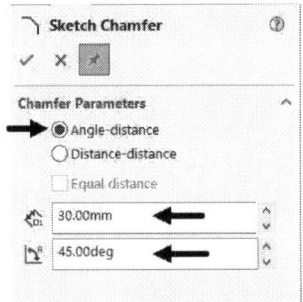

- Now, select the entities one by one to create chamfers between them, as shown.

    Note that the angle will be measured with respect to the first selected entity and distance with respect to the second selected entity.

- The entities are automatically trimmed or extended to meet the end of the new chamfer, as shown.

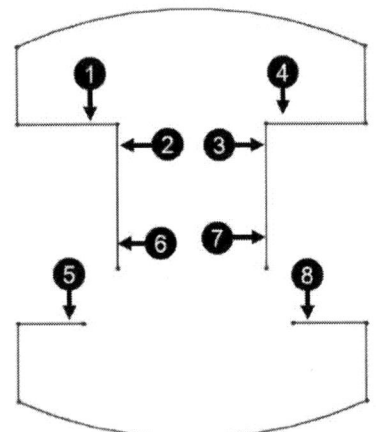 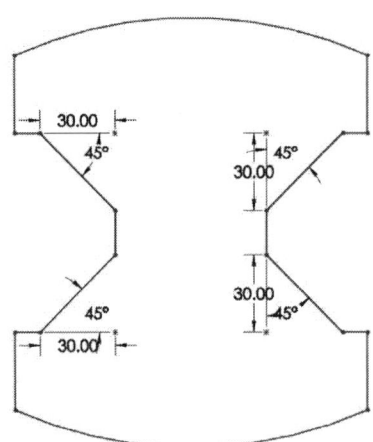

- Now, click on the **OK** ✓ button from the **Sketch Chamfer PropertyManager** to exit from this tool.

Distance-distance

This radio button is used to create chamfer between two selected entities by using same distance value or different distance values.

- Select the **Sketch Chamfer** option to activate it and display the **Sketch Chamfer PropertyManager**, as discussed above.
- Now select the **Distance-distance** radio button, if it is not selected by default, as shown.
- Next enter the required distance value in the **Distance 1** spinner of the PropertyManager, as shown.

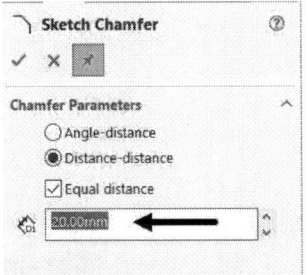

❖ Select the entities to create chamfer between them, as shown.

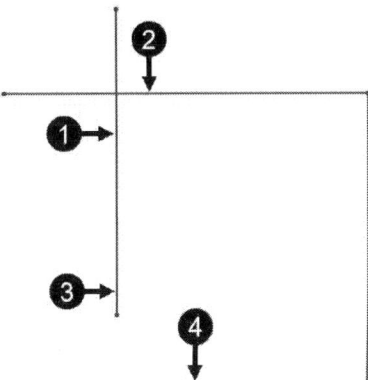

❖ The chamfer between selected entities with equal distance in both directions get visible, as shown.
❖ The entities are automatically trimmed or extended to meet the end of the new chamfer, as shown.

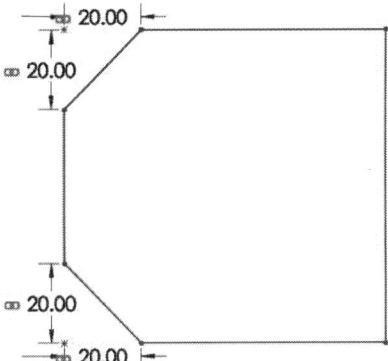

The tool is still active and to create chamfer with two different distances, follow the following steps.

❖ Deselect the **Equal distance** check box of the **Sketch Chamfer PropertyManager** to display the **Distance 2** spinner, as shown.
❖ Next, enter the required distance values in **Distance 1** and **Distance 2** spinners, as shown.

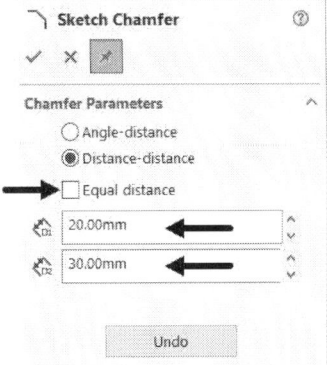

❖ Select the entities to create chamfer between them, as shown.
❖ The chamfer between selected entities with different distances in both directions get visible, as shown.

Note that the **Distance 1** value will be measured with respect to the first selected entity and **Distance 2** value with respect to the second selected entity.

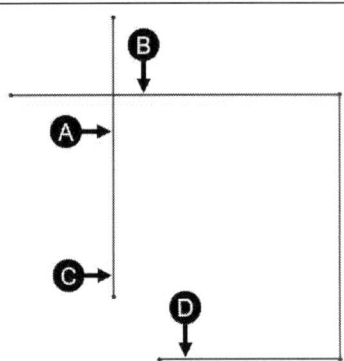 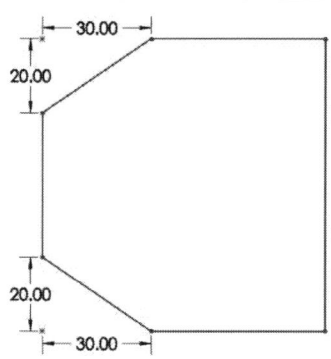

❖ Now, click on the OK ✓ button from the **Sketch Chamfer PropertyManager** to exit from this tool and display the chamfers created, as shown.

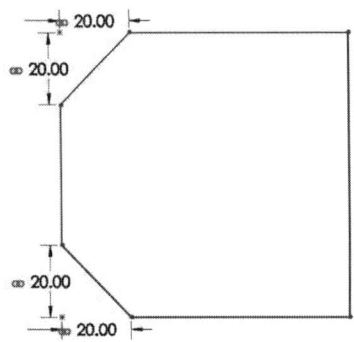 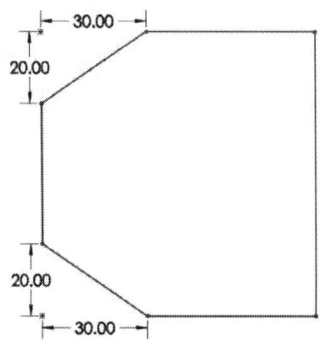

 Trim Entities Tool

This tool is used to trim/remove the unwanted portion of entities, intersecting other entities like line, circle, arc, ellipse, circle etc. The options/buttons available in the **Options** rollout of the **Trim PropertyManager** are discussed below.

Power Trim

This button is selected to trim/remove the unwanted portion of entities by dragging cursor over it.

➢ Select the **Trim Entities** tool from the **Sketch CommandManager** to activate it and display the **Trim PropertyManager**, as shown.

➢ Select the **Power trim** button if it is not selected by default, as shown.

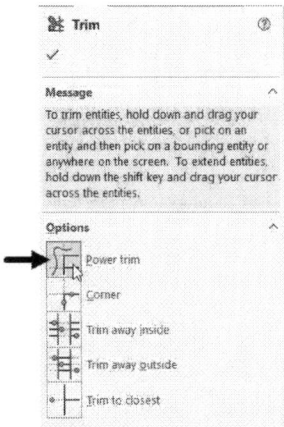

Advance Sketching & Editing Tools

- Click in the drawing area and drag the cursor over the entities to be removed, by press and holding the **LMB** (Left Mouse Button).
- Release the finger over **LMB** to display the sketch with removed entities.

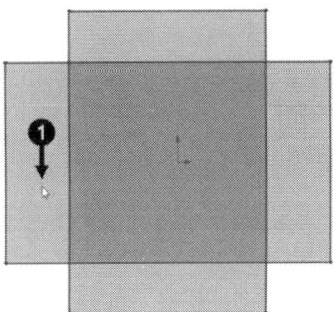 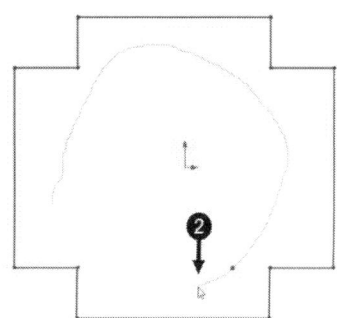

- Now, click on the **Close Dialog** button from the **Trim PropertyManager** to exit from the tool.

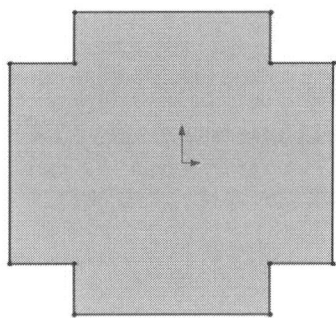

Corner

This button is selected to trim or extend the entities to form a corner.

- Activate the **Trim Entities** tool and select the Corner button from **Trim PropertyManager**.
- Select the line entities one by one to trim their unwanted portion and form a corner, as shown.

- Similarly, to extend the entities to form a corner, select the line entities one by one, as shown.

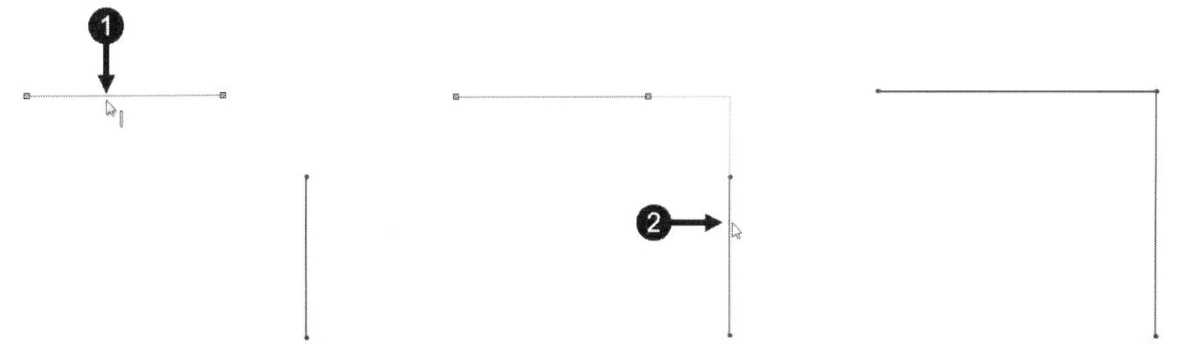

Advance Sketching & Editing Tools

Trim Away Inside

This button is selected to trim the portion of entities inside the boundaries.

- Activate the **Trim Entities** tool and select the **Trim Away Inside** button from **Trim PropertyManager**.
- Select the line entities as boundary entities, as shown.

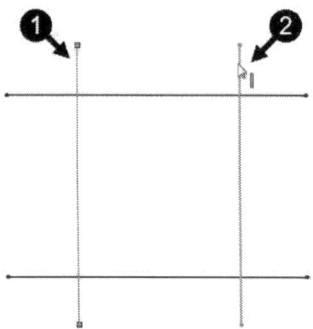

- Now select the entities to trim, as shown.
- Now, click on the **Close Dialog** button from the **Trim PropertyManager** to exit from the tool.

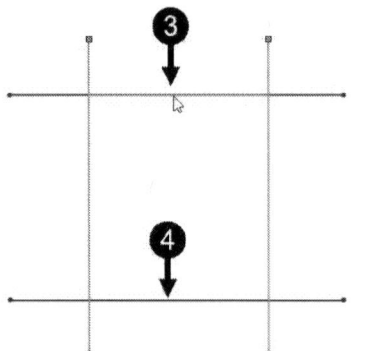
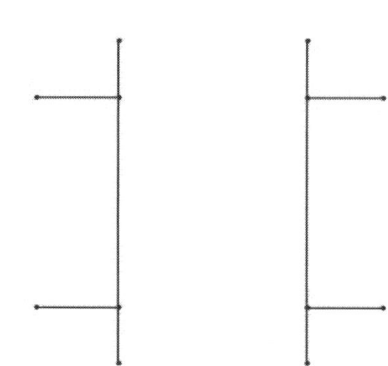

Trim Away Outside

This button is selected to trim the portion of entities outside the boundaries.

- Select the **Trim Away Outside** button from **Trim PropertyManager**, as shown.
- Select the line entities as boundary entities, as shown.

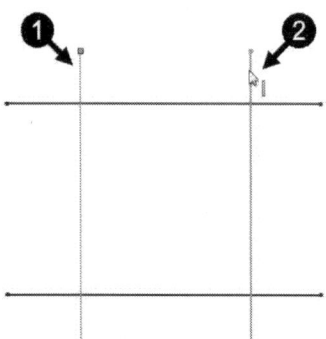

- Now select the entities to trim, as shown.
- Click on the **Close Dialog** button from the **Trim PropertyManager** to exit from the tool.

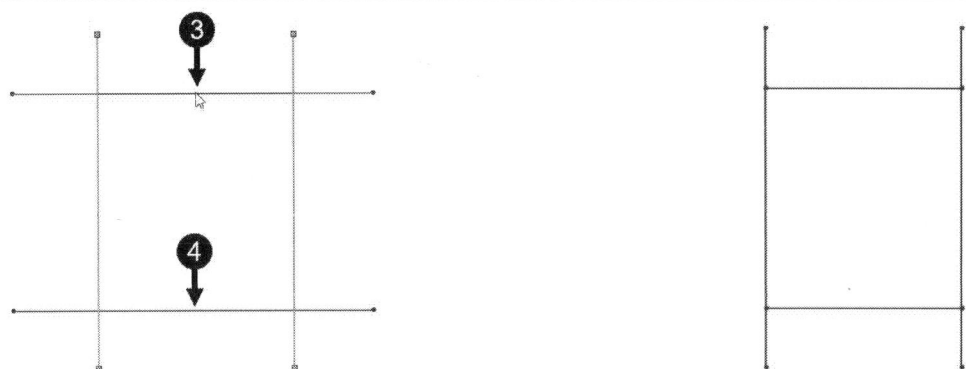

 **Trim to closest**

This button is selected to select an entity to trim to the nearest intersecting entity or to drag to an entity.

- Select the **Trim to closest** button from **Trim PropertyManager**.
- Select the line entities to trim, as shown.
- Click on the **Close Dialog** button from the **Trim PropertyManager** to exit from the tool.

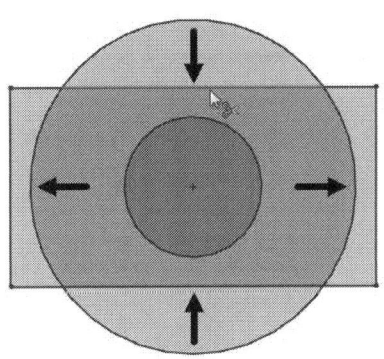 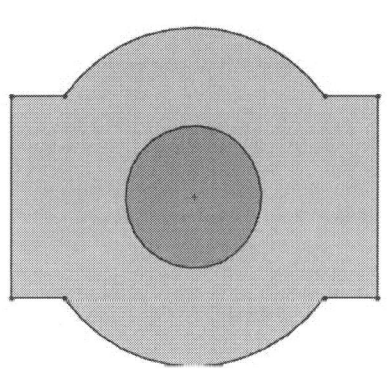

Extend Entities Tool

This tool is used to extend a sketch entity up to the next sketch entity.

- Select **Trim Entities > Extend Entities** tool from the **Sketch CommandManager** to activate it, as shown.

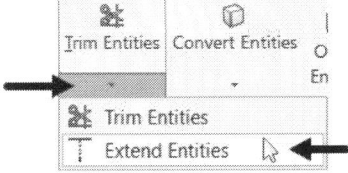

- Select the sketch entities to extend, as shown.
- The selected entities get extended to the next entities, as shown.

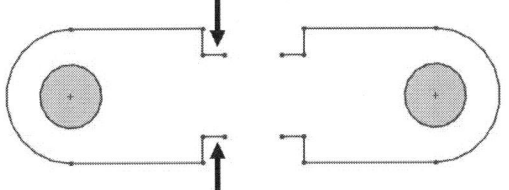 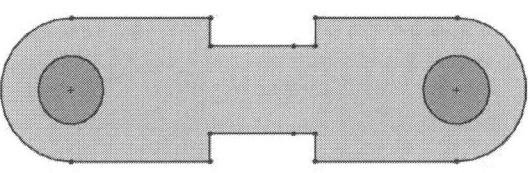

 ## Convert Entities Tool

The **Convert Entities** tool is used to create sketch entities by projecting edges of a model on the selected sketching plane.

> Create a reference plane parallel to the surface with entities to project.

The procedure to create a reference plane is discussed further in this book.

> Activate the **Sketch** tool from the **Sketch CommandManager** and select the Reference plane on which you want to project the sketching entities, as shown.
> Click on the **Convert Entities** button from the **Sketch CommandManager** to activate it and display the **Convert Entities PropertyManager**, as shown.

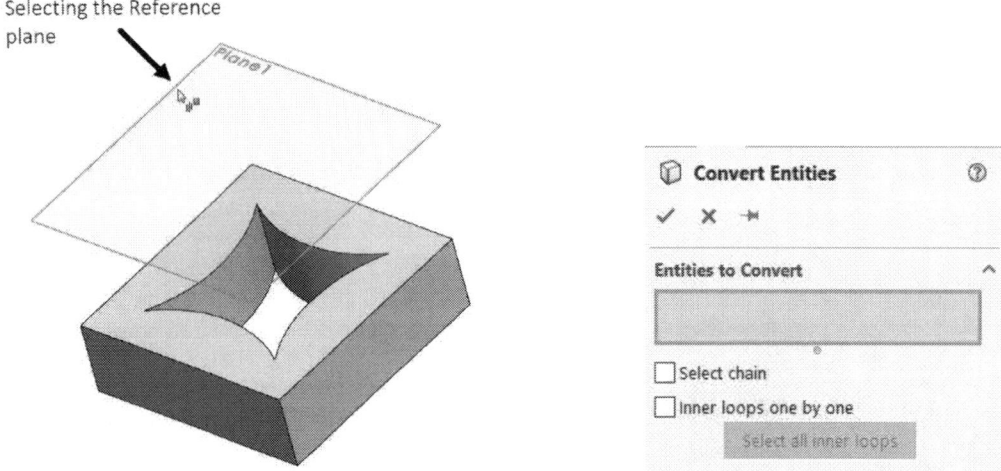

> Select the **Inner loops one by one** check box and select the upper surface of the model, as shown.
> Next, click on the **Select all inner loops** button of the **Convert Entities PropertyManager**, as shown.

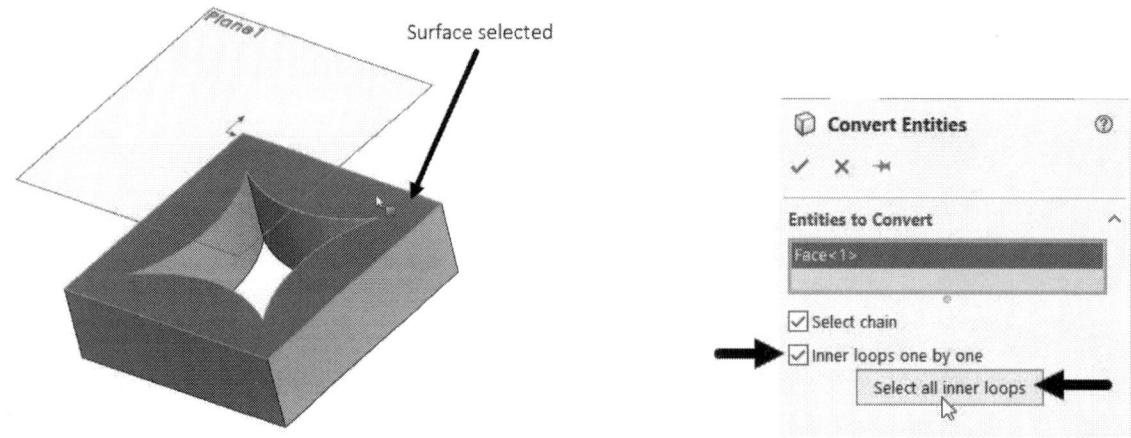

> Click on the **OK** button of the PropertyManager to exit from the tool and display the entities projected, as shown.

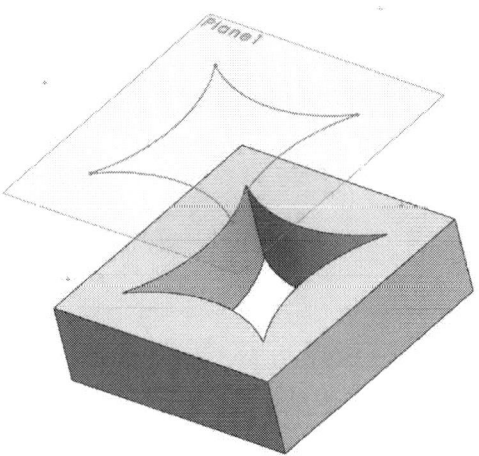

Text Tool

This tool is used to write text in the sketch environment and on the surface of a part. The text can be inserted on edges, curves, sketches, etc. The text sketched over surface of the part can be extruded and cut surfaces.

> Click on the **A** **Text** tool from the **Sketch CommandManager** to activate it and display the **Sketch Text PropertyManager**, as shown.
> Select the line entity to insert text along it, as shown.

Selecting line entitty

> Now write the text in the **Text** edit box of the Property Manager, as shown.
> The text entered get visible along the selected entity, as shown.

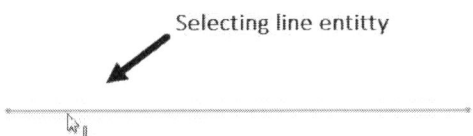

Similarly, you can write text along curve or round surfaces, as shown.

Advance Sketching & Editing Tools

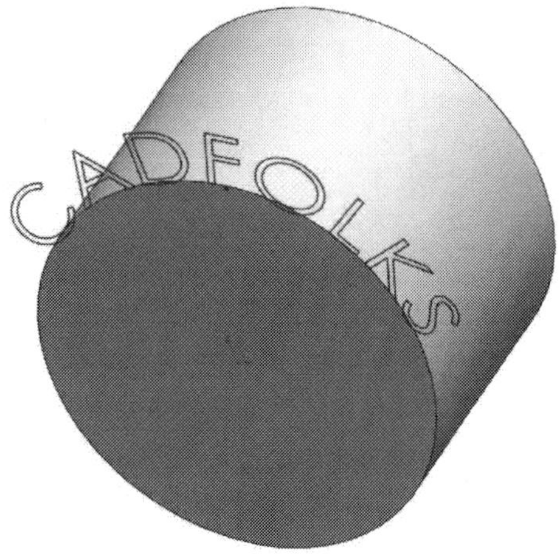

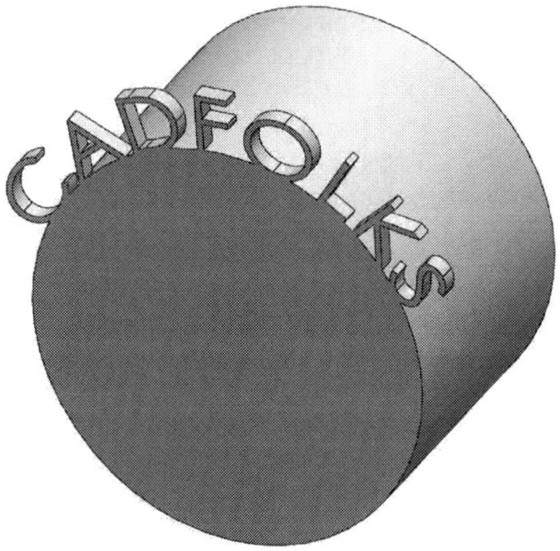

The options available in the **Sketch Text PropertyManager** can be used to edit the text entered, as shown

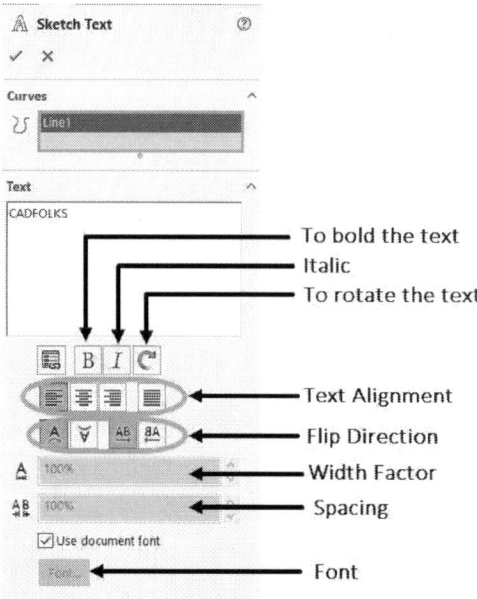

Note that the **Font** button, **Width Factor** and **Spacing** boxes get active only after deselecting the **Use document font** checkbox. To enter the required fonts, select the **Font** button to display the **Choose Font** dialog box, as shown.

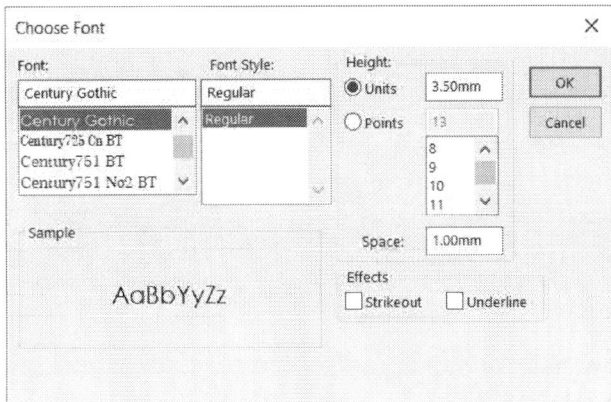

You can now select the required font and enter the required value for the size/height of text in their respective edit boxes.

Offset Entities Tool

The **Offset Entities** tool is used to create a duplicate geometry at a required offset distance from the selected geometry. You can offset sketch entities like lines, arcs, circles, set of model edges, loops etc. If you change the original entity then the offset entity changes accordingly.

Click on the **Offset Entities** tool from the **Sketch CommandManager** to activate it and display the **Offset Entities** PropertyManager, as shown. The use of options in the **Parameters** rollout of the PropertyManager are discussed below.

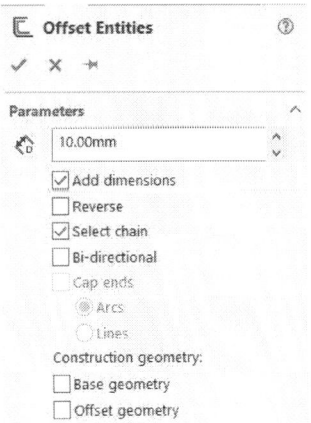

Offset Distance

The **Offset Distance** edit box is used to enter the required offset distance value at which you want to offset any entity. You can use its spinner to adjust the distance value, as shown. Alternatively, you can press and hold the **LMB** (left mouse mutton) and drag the cursor to see the dynamic preview, as shown.

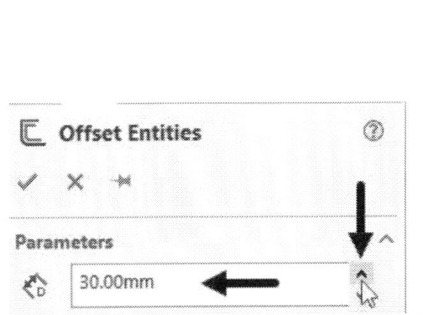
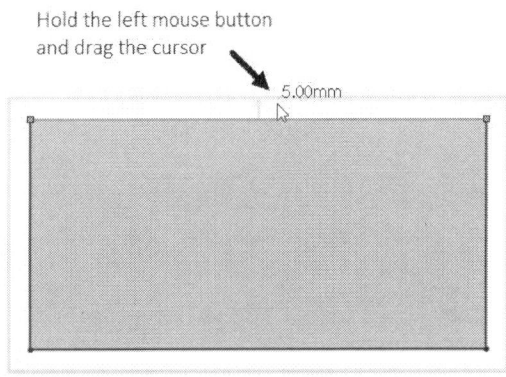

Advance Sketching & Editing Tools

Add dimensions

The **Add dimensions** check box is selected to display the offset distance in sketch after offsetting any sketch entity/entities.

Reverse

The **Offset Distance** check box is selected to change direction of offset.

Select chain

This check box is selected by default and is used to select chain of entities and entities connected with the selected entity, as shown.

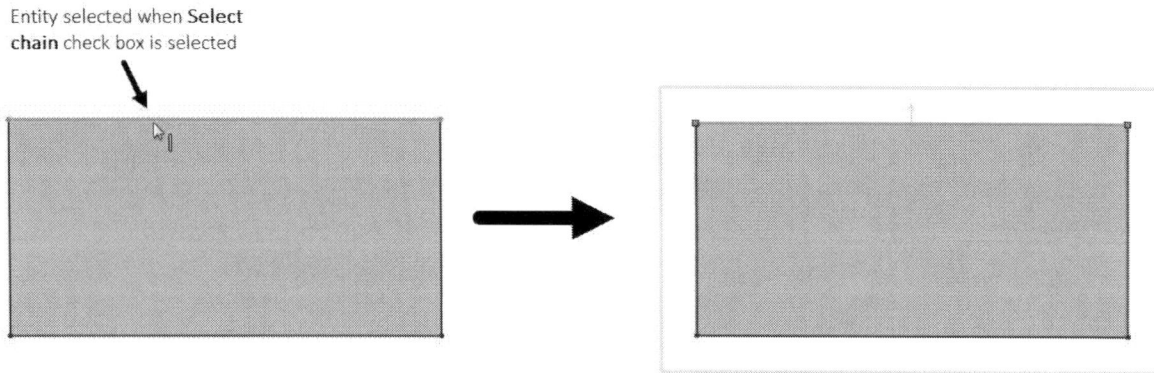

To offset a single entity, deselect the **Select chain** check box and then select the entity to offset, as shown.

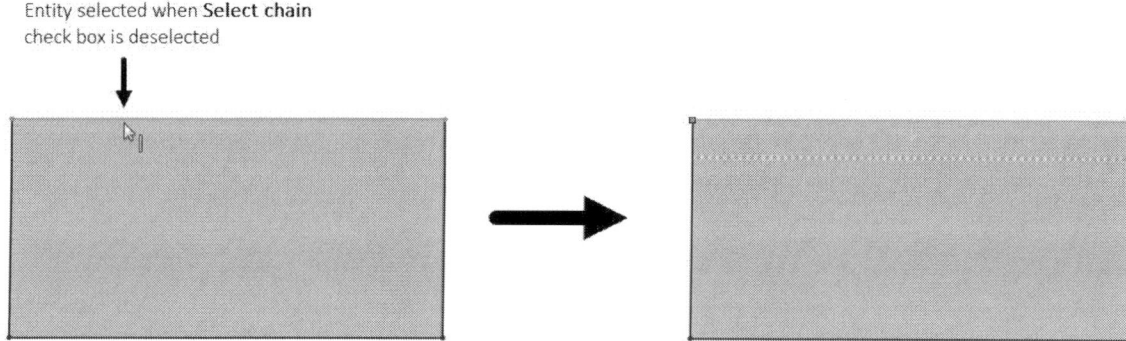

Bi-directional

The check box is selected to offset entities in two directions, as shown.

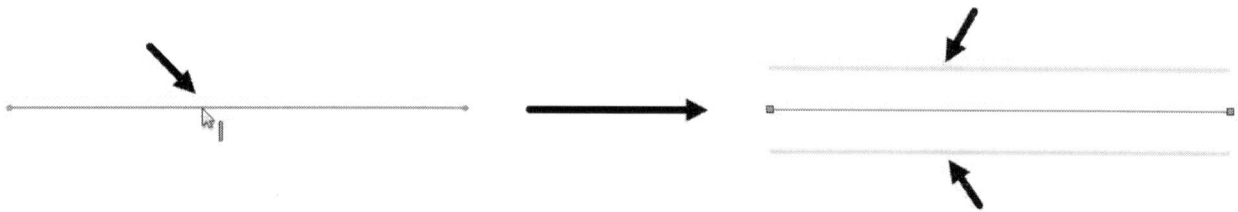

Cap ends

The check box is selected to offset entities with caps at their both ends, as shown.

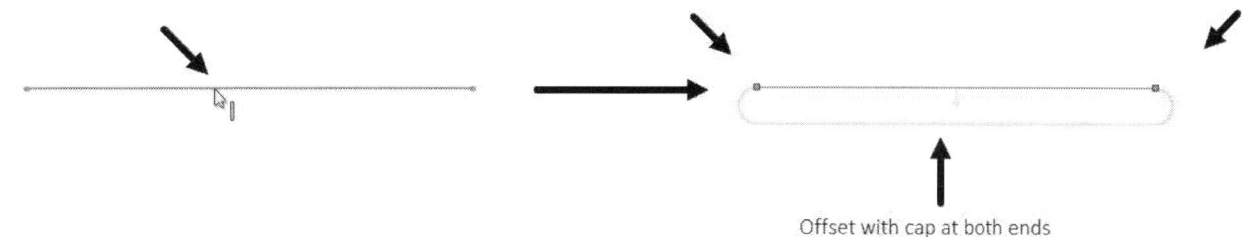

You can offset an entity in two direction with caps at both ends by selecting the **Bi-directional** check box also, as shown.

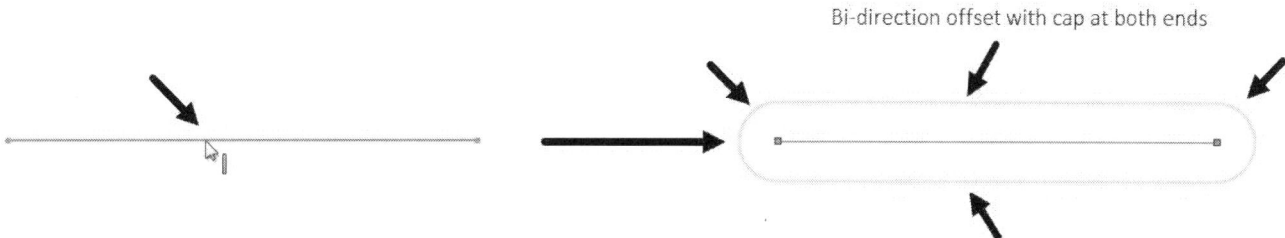

Note that you can also select the **Lines** radio button as cap ends at both ends.

Construction geometry

The radio button under **Construction geometry** are used to convert the selected sketch entity to a construction line and offset the entity or vice-versa. These radio buttons are discussed below.

Base geometry

This radio button is selected to convert the selected sketched entity to construction entity and create offset entity at a distance, as shown.

Offset geometry

This radio button is selected to offset construction entity at a distance, as shown.

Similarly, you use these options with other entities, as shown.

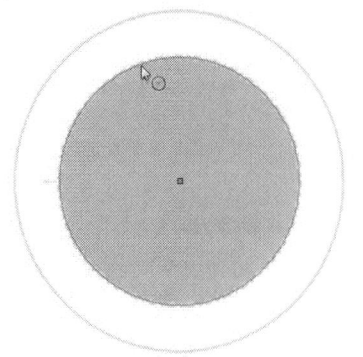 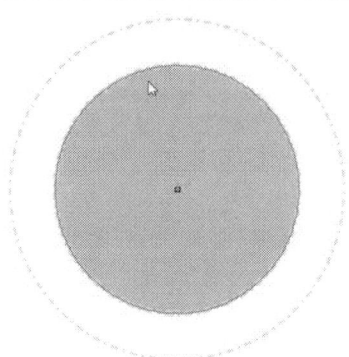

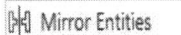 **Mirror Entities Tool**

The **Mirror Entities** tool is used to create a mirror copy of selected sketch entity about a centerlines, lines, model edges and linear edges on drawing. This is very useful for creating symmetrical sketches.

> Click on the **Mirror Entities** tool from the **Sketch CommandManager** to activate it and display the **Mirror PropertyManager**, as shown.

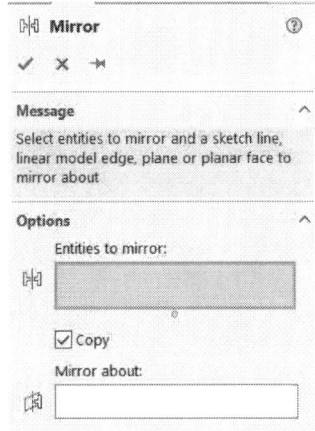

> Select the sketch entities to mirror, as shown.

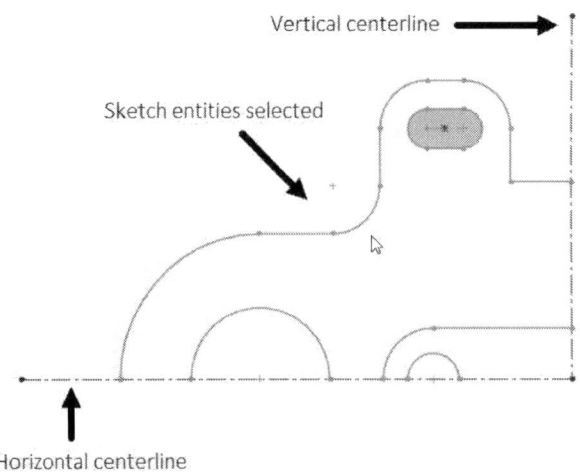

> Now click on the **Mirror about** in the PropertyManager.
> Select the horizontal centerline to display the mirrored entities along it, as shown.

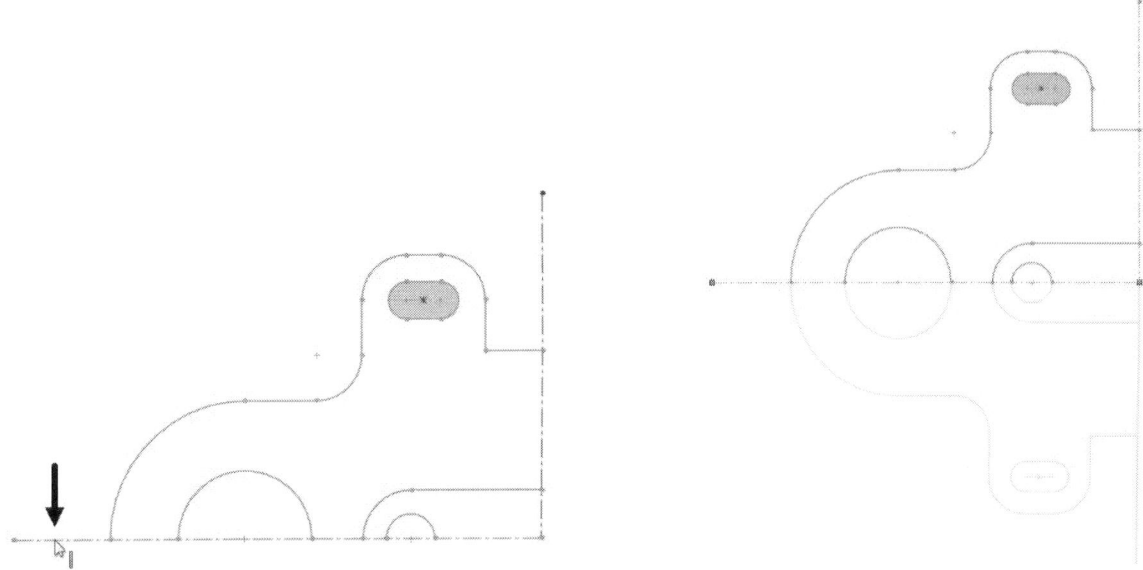

➤ Click on the **OK** ✓ button from the PropertyManager to exit the tool and display the mirrored entities, as shown.

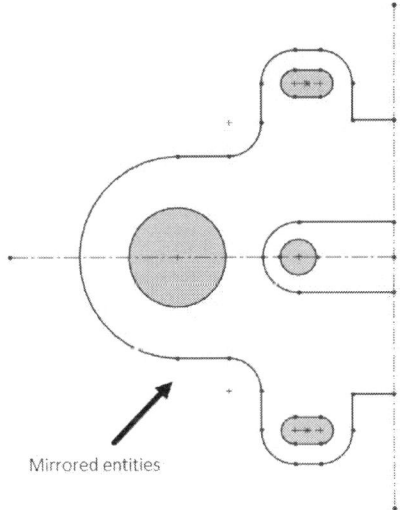

Mirrored entities

➤ Similarly select the entities and then select the vertical centerline to mirror entities along it, as shown.

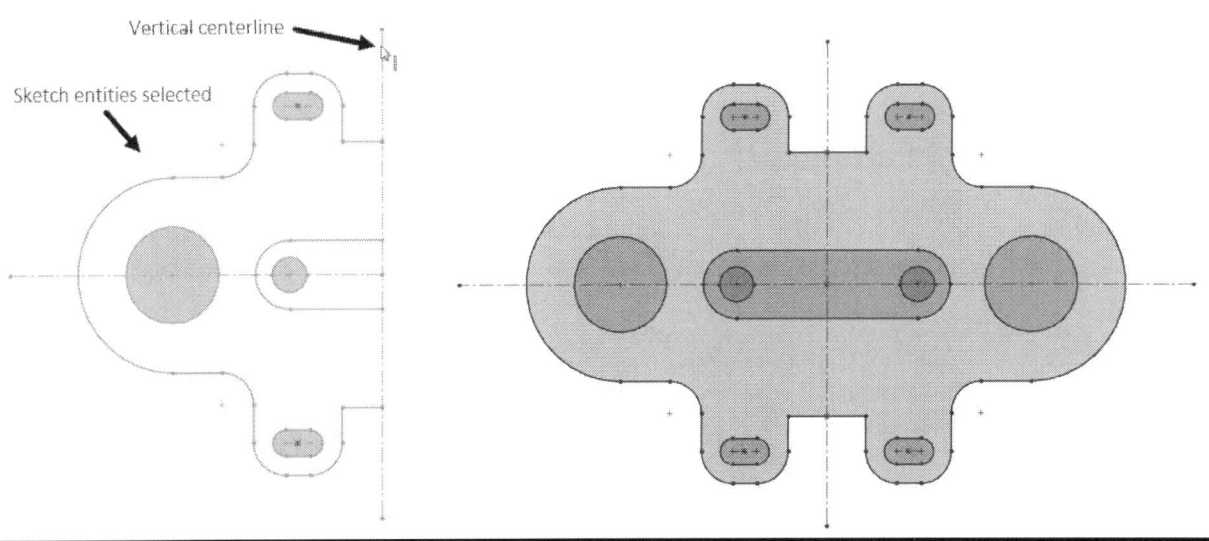

Creating Patterns

The Pattern tools are used to create replica of sketch entities in a particular sequence like along linear edges or around circular edges. You can save much time using this tool as you can create multiple copies of an entities. Also, if you make changes to original entity, the pattern/child features will be updated automatically. There are two option in the drop-down to create patterns, discussed below.

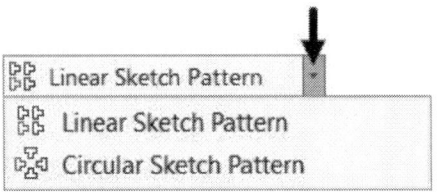

 **Linear Sketch Pattern**

This option is selected to create the pattern feature by defining directions. The directions can be defined by selecting Plane, edge, or axis.

➢ Click on the **Linear Sketch Pattern** button to activate it and display the **Linear Pattern** PropertyManager, as shown.
➢ As the X & Y axis are selected by default, select the entity to be patterned, as shown.

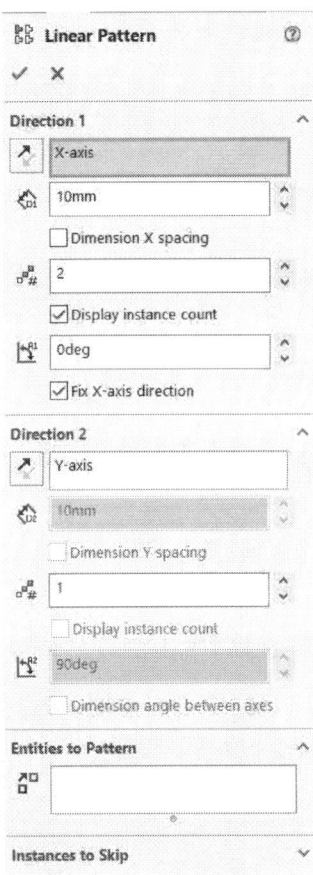
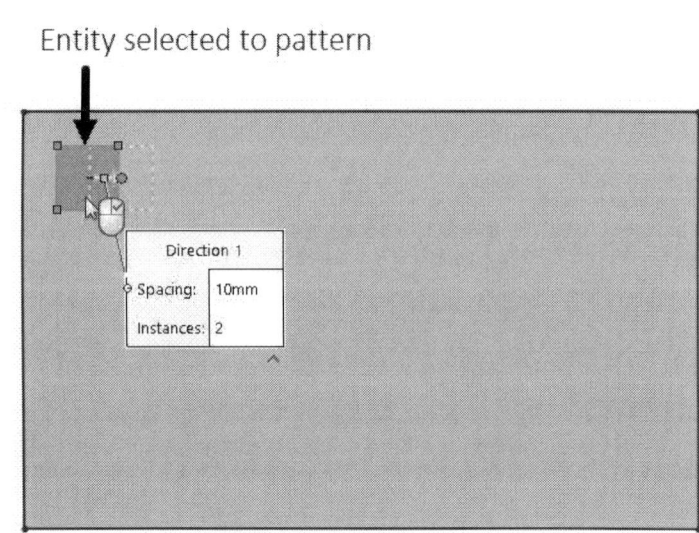

Next, you need to enter the required values in the PropertyManager to create patterns. The use of these options is shown below.

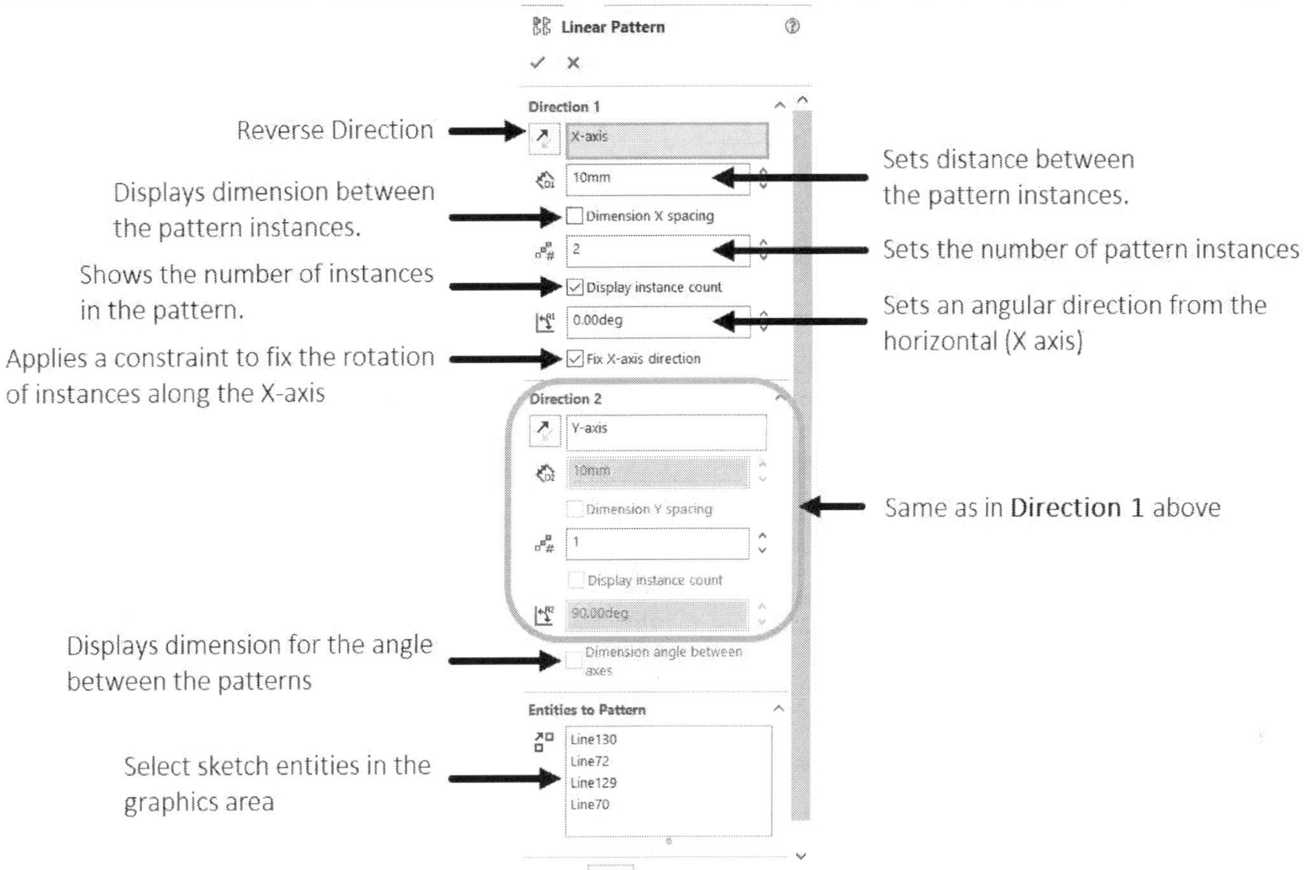

Linear Pattern

- **Reverse Direction** → X-axis
- **Sets distance between the pattern instances.** → 10mm
- **Displays dimension between the pattern instances.** → Dimension X spacing
- **Sets the number of pattern instances** → 2
- **Shows the number of instances in the pattern.** → Display instance count
- **Sets an angular direction from the horizontal (X axis)** → 0.00deg
- **Applies a constraint to fix the rotation of instances along the X-axis** → Fix X-axis direction

Direction 2 — Same as in **Direction 1** above

- **Displays dimension for the angle between the patterns** → Dimension angle between axes
- **Select sketch entities in the graphics area** → Entities to Pattern (Line130, Line72, Line129, Line70)

➤ Enter the required values and click on the  ✓ **OK** button of the PropertyManager to exit the tool and display the patterned entities, as shown.

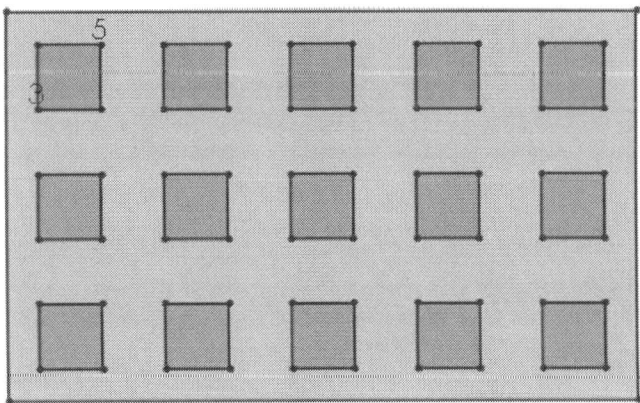

Circular Sketch Pattern

This option is selected to create the pattern feature by defining a center point for the pattern. The patterns then get created around the defined center point.

➤ Click on the **Circular Sketch Pattern** option from the **Linear Sketch Pattern** flyout of the Sketch CommandManager to activate it and display the **Circular Pattern** PropertyManager, as shown.

➤ Click over [ ] box of the PropertyManager and click on the center point of the circle to create patterns around it, as shown.

Advance Sketching & Editing Tools

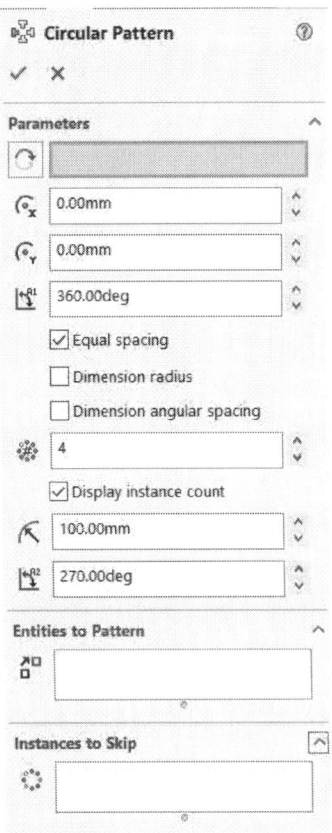
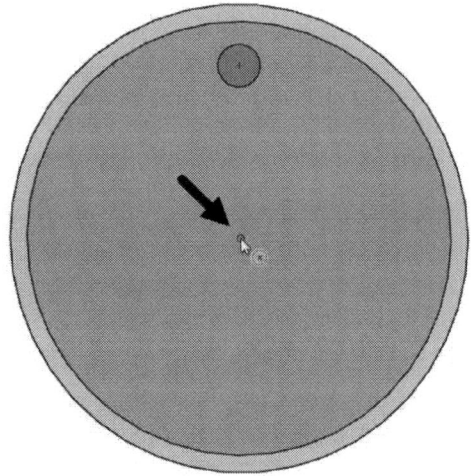

Next, select the entities to pattern and you need to enter the required values in the PropertyManager to create patterns. The use of these options is shown below.

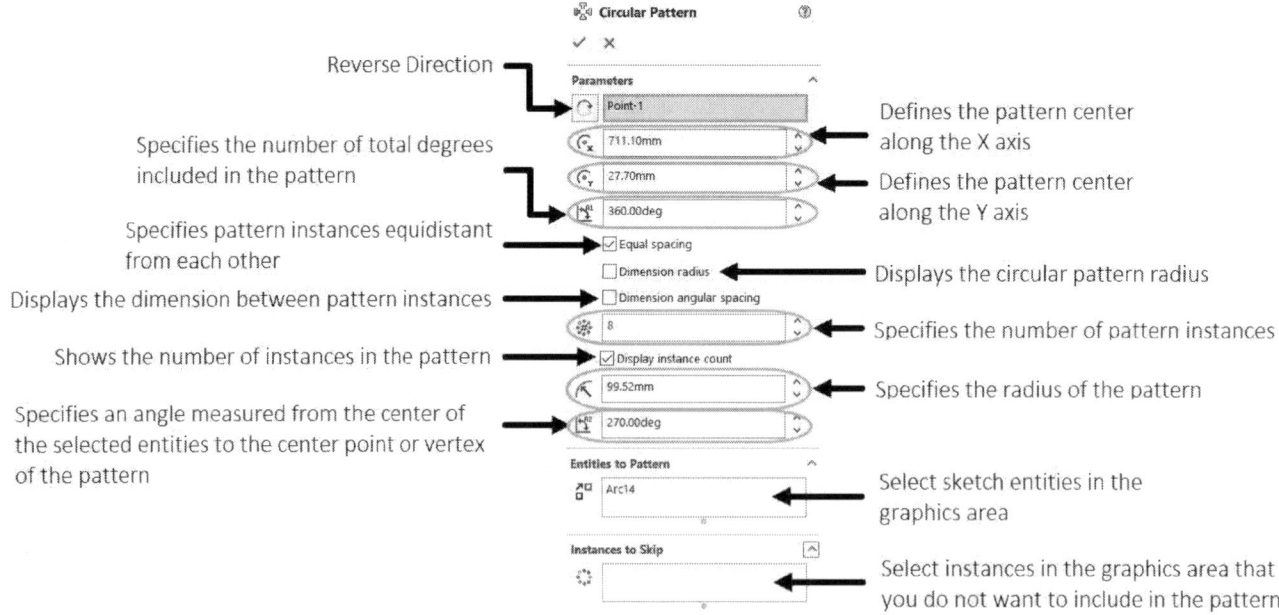

> Enter the required values and click on the ✓ OK button of the PropertyManager to exit the tool and display the patterned entities, as shown.

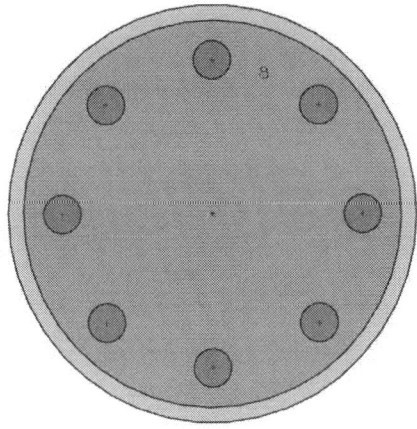

Editing Patterns
After creating the patterns, you can edit them ap per your requirements.

Editing Linear Pattern
To edit the linear patterns:

- Right click over any of the pattern instances to display the shortcut menu.
- Next, select the **Edit Linear Pattern** option from the shortcut menu, as shown.
- Now you can edit or make the required changes in the **Linear Pattern** PropertyManager displayed, as shown.

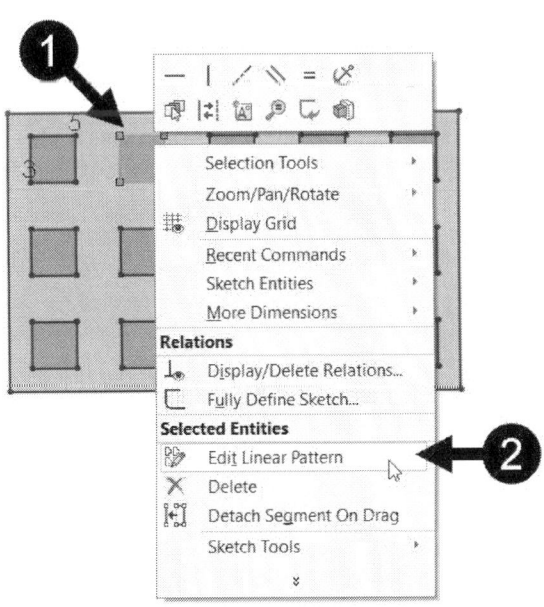
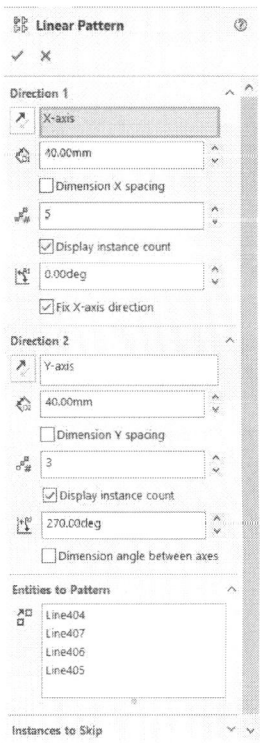

Editing Circular Pattern
To edit the circular patterns:

1. Right click over any of the pattern instances to display the shortcut menu.
2. Next, select the **Edit Circular Pattern** option from the shortcut menu, as shown.
3. Now you can edit or make the required changes in the **Circular Pattern** PropertyManager displayed, as shown.

Advance Sketching & Editing Tools

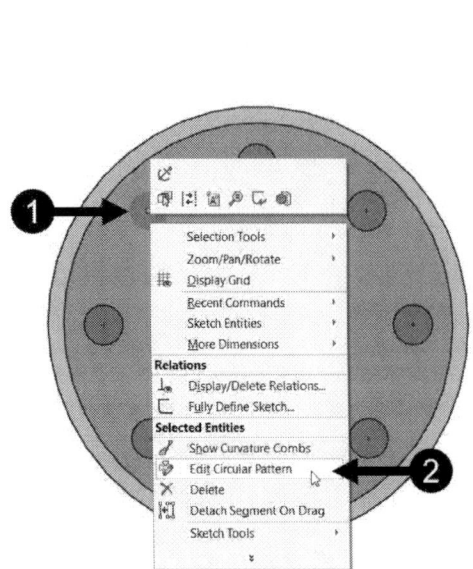 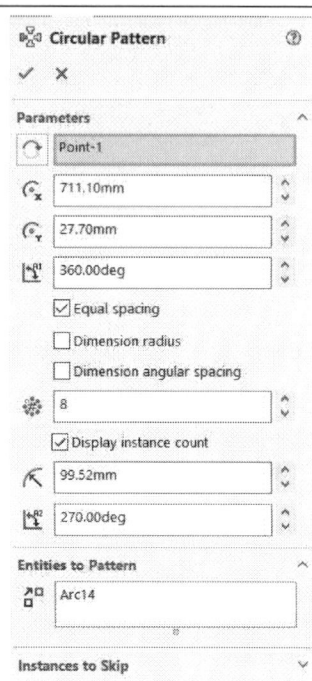

Editing Tools

In previous chapters, you have learned to create some simple drawings using the basic drawing tools. However, to create complex drawings, you may need to perform various editing operations. The tools to perform the editing operations are available in the **Move Entities** flyout in the **Sketch CommandManager**. You can click the down arrow to find more editing tools. Using these editing tools, you can modify existing objects or use existing objects to create new or similar objects. These tools are discussed below.

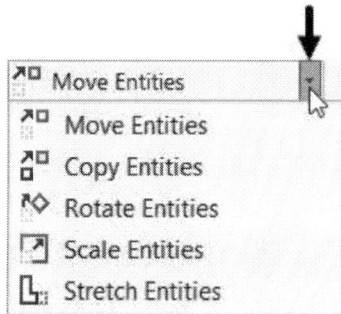

These editing tools are explained next, one-by-one.

The Move Entities tool

The **Move**  tool is used to move a selected object(s) from one location to a new location without changing its orientation. To move objects, you need to select this tool and select the objects **Move Entities** from the drawing area. After selecting objects, you need to specify the 'base point' and the 'destination point'.

➤ Create the drawing as shown below.

- Click on the **Move Entities** button from the **Sketch CommandManager** to activate it and display the **Move PropertyManager**, as shown below.
- Select the circle entity to move and click on the **Start point** box of the PropertyManager.

    Alternatively, you can press the RMB (Right Mouse Button) after selecting the entity to move.
- Next, click on the center of the circle to select it as the base point, as shown.
- Move the cursor up to some distance toward right, as shown.

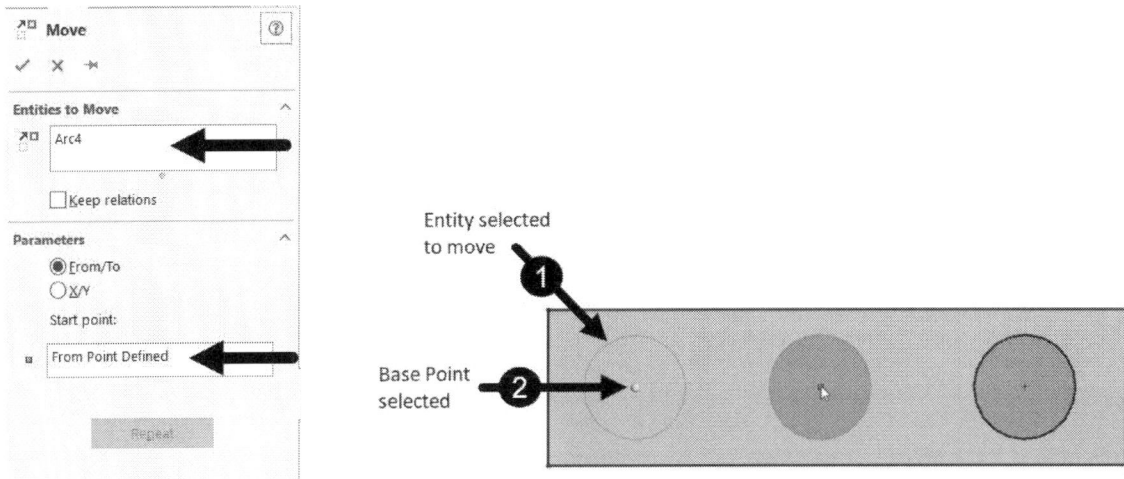

- Next click to place the moved circle entity, as shown.

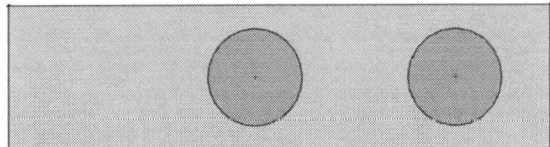

Note: You can also move any object to a required distance in X & Y direction by selecting the **X/Y** radio button of the **Move PropertyManager** and entering the required value in their respective edit boxes, as shown below.

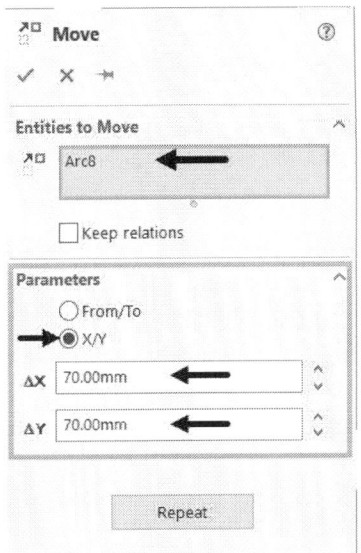
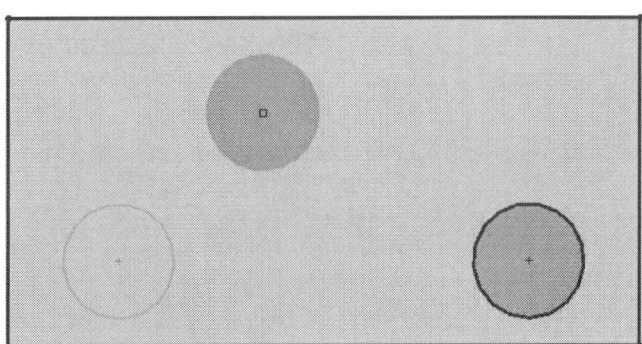

Advance Sketching & Editing Tools

The Copy Entities tool

The **Copy Entities**  tool is used to copy objects and place them at a required location. This tool is similar to the **Move** tool, except that object will remain at its original position and a copy of it will be placed at the new location.

➢ Draw a rectangle and two concentric circles inside it, as shown.

➢ Select **Move Entities > Copy Entities** from the **Sketch CommandManager** to activate it and display the **Copy PropertyManager**, as shown below.

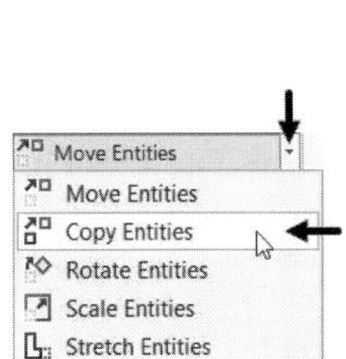
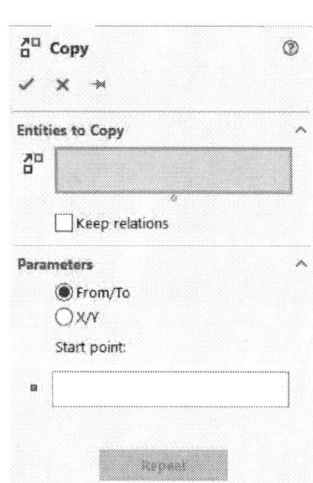

➢ Select the circle entities, and then right-click to accept the selection, as shown.
➢ Click on the center of the circles to select it as the base point.
➢ Move the cursor up to some distance towards right to place the copied entities.
➢ Next click to place the copied entities at the required location.

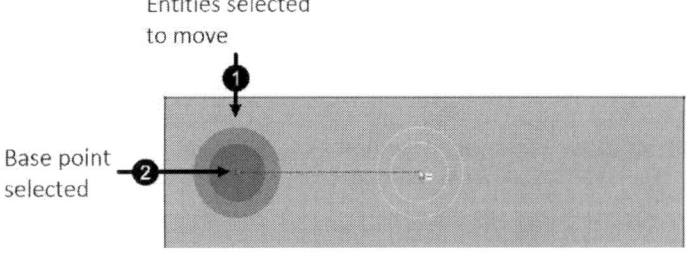

The Rotate Entities tool

The **Rotate Entities** tool is used to rotate an object or a group of objects about a base point. To rotate objects, you need to activate this tool and select the objects from the drawing window. After selecting objects, you need to specify the 'base point' and the angle of rotation. The object(s) will be rotated about the base point.

➢ Select **Move Entities > Rotate Entities** from the **Sketch CommandManager** to activate it and display the **Rotate PropertyManager**, as shown below.

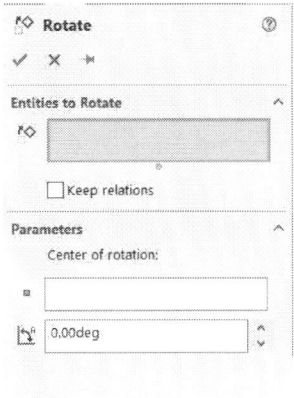

- Select all sketch entities and then right-click to accept the selection, as shown below.
- Click on the endpoint of the bottom line on left to select it as the base point, as shown.

- Next, using the spinner specify the required angle of rotation.

  Alternatively, enter the required angle value in the edit box of the PropertyManager, as shown.

- Click on the ✓ OK button of the PropertyManager to exit the tool and display the entities rotated, as shown.

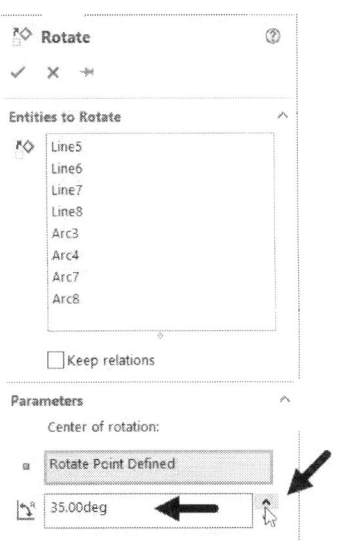

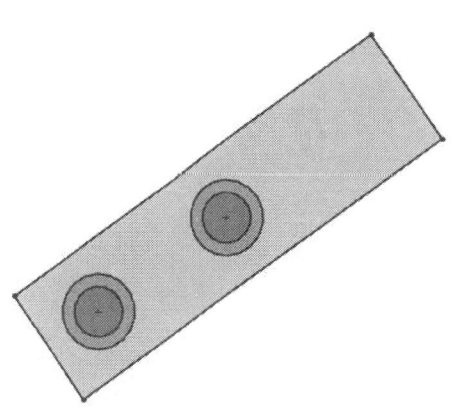

The Scale Entities tool

The **Scale Entities** tool is used to change the size of objects. You can reduce or enlarge the size without changing the shape of an object. To scale objects, you need to activate this tool and select the objects from the drawing window. After selecting objects, you need to specify the 'base point' and the scale factor. The scale factor is the ratio between the original size of the object and the size to be achieved. For example, if you specify the Scale Factor as **2**, the size of the object will be doubled.

➢ Select **Move Entities > Scale Entities** from the **Sketch CommandManager** to activate it and display the **Scale PropertyManager**, as shown below.

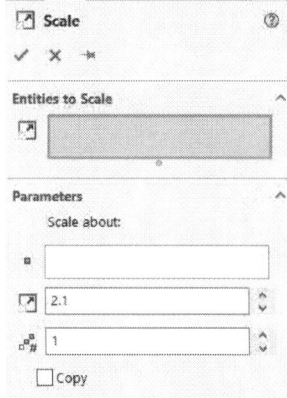

➢ Select all sketch entities and then right-click to accept the selection, as shown below.
➢ Click on the endpoint of the bottom line on left to select it as the base point, as shown.
➢ Next, using the spinner specify the required Scale Factor, as shown.

Alternatively, enter the required Scale Factor value in the edit box of the PropertyManager, as shown.

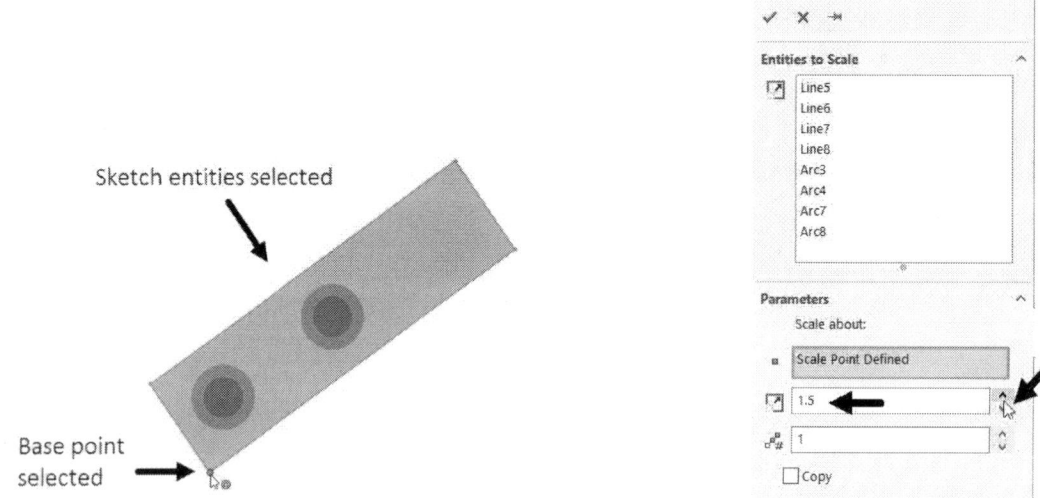

As you change the Scale Factor value, the size of object changes accordingly, as shown.

➢ Next, click on the ✓ **OK** button of the PropertyManager to exit the tool and display the entities rotated, as shown.

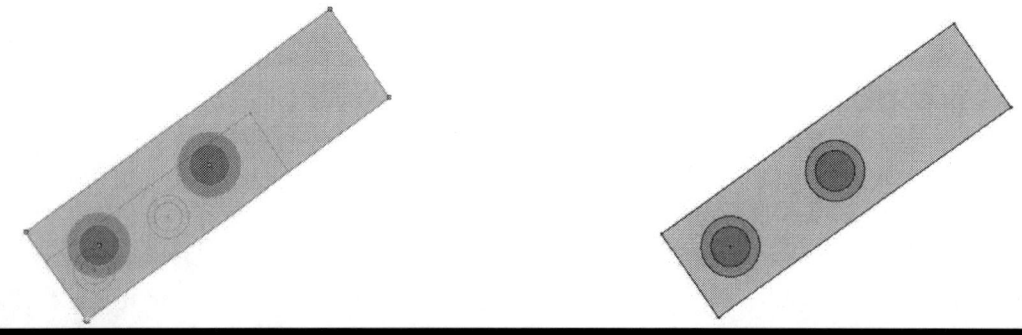

Note that the **Copy** check box in the **Scale PropertyManager** is selected to create copy of scaled entities, as shown.

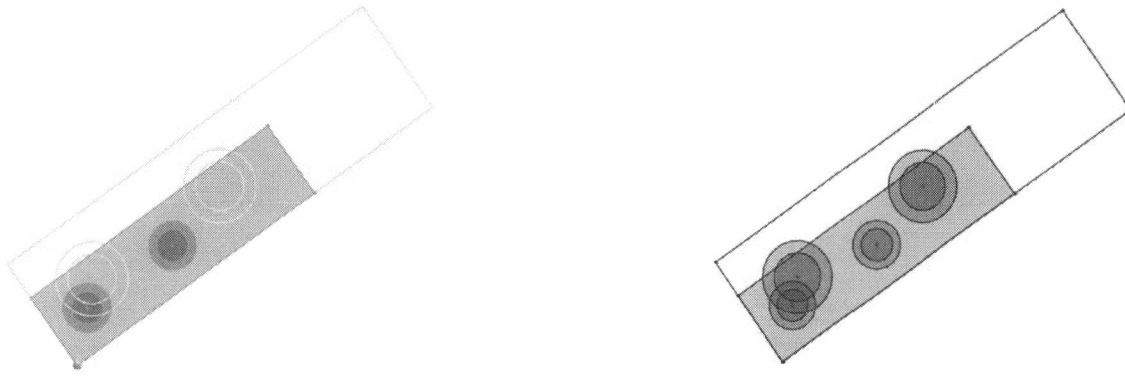

The Stretch Entities tool

The **Stretch** tool is used to lengthen or shorten drawings or parts of drawings. Note that you cannot stretch circles using this tool. Also, you need to select the portion of the drawing to be stretched by dragging a window.

> Select **Move Entities > Stretch Entities** from the **Sketch CommandManager** to activate it and display the **Stretch PropertyManager**, as shown below.

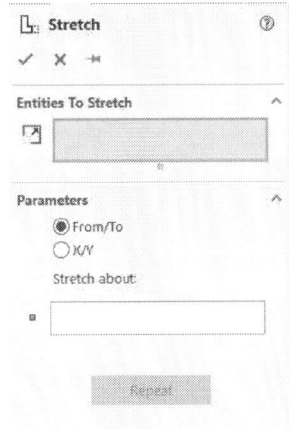

> Select the 3-line entities and then right-click to accept the selection, as shown below.
> Click on the bottom endpoint of the line entity to select it as the base point, as shown.
> Next, more the cursor up to some distance to stretch the line entities or object, as shown.
> Click at the required location to display the stretched entities/object, as shown.

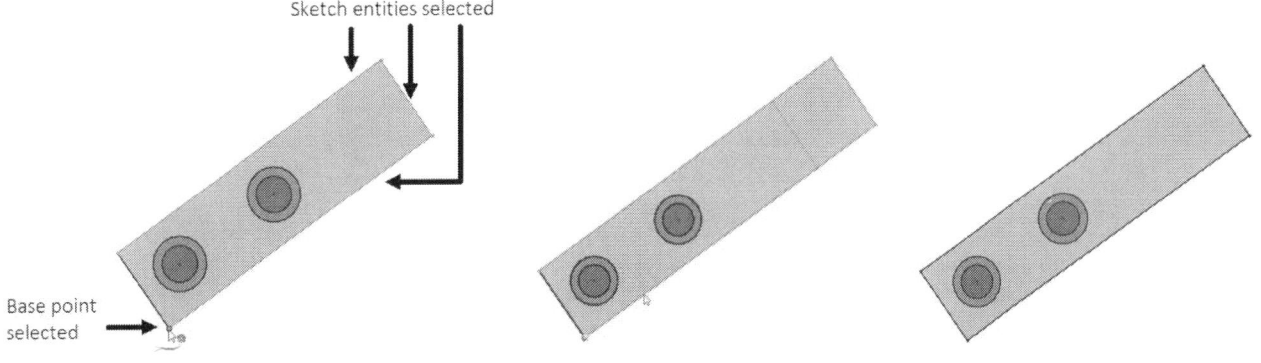

Advance Sketching & Editing Tools

Questions:

1. What is the use of **Scale Entities** tool and how it can be used?
2. How you can create mirror copy of selected sketch entity using the **Mirror Entities** tools?
3. How is **Sketch Chamfer** option used and where is it available?
4. Which tool is used to create a duplicate geometry at a required offset distance?
5. What is the use of **View Sketch Dimensions** option?
6. Which button is selected to trim or extend the entities to form a corner?
7. Which tool is used to create sketch entities by projecting edges of a model?
8. What is the use of **Power trim** button?
9. Which tool is selected to create pattern along the selected edge or direction axis?
10. Where is **Circular Sketch Pattern** option available and how can we use it?

Exercises:

Exercise 1

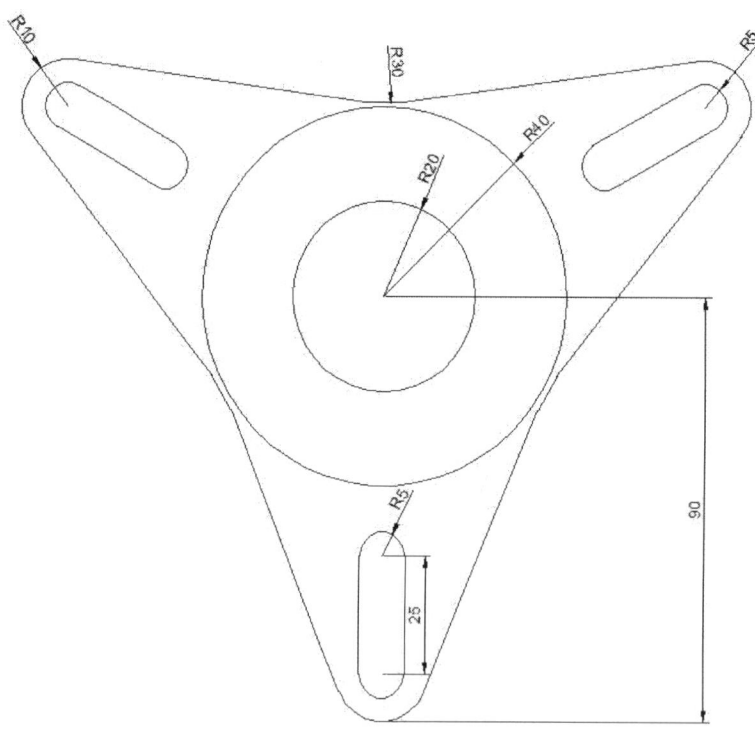

Exercise 2

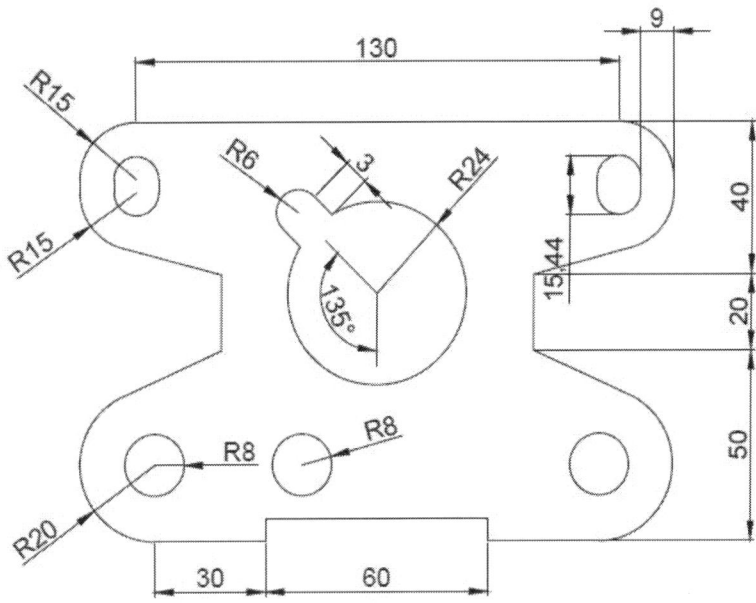

Exercise 3

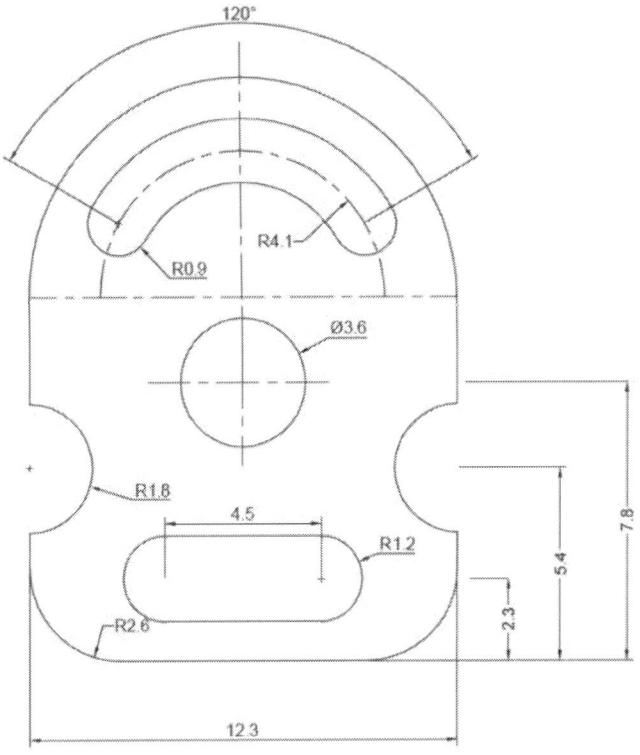

Chapter 04: Applying Dimensions & Geometric Relations

In SolidWorks, you first create a rough sketch, and then apply dimensions and constrains to it, that define its shape and size. The dimensions define the size, length, and angle of a sketch element, whereas constrains define the relations between sketch entities. In this chapter, you will learn how to apply dimensions and geometric relations to the sketches created in the sketching environment

The topics covered in this chapter are:

- ❖ Applying Geometric Relations to the sketch
- ❖ Modifying the dimensions
- ❖ Applying geometric relations
- ❖ Display & deleting geometric relations

Dimensioning

In SolidWorks there are different types of tools/options that are used for applying dimensions to the sketch. These options are available in the **Smart Dimension** flyout, as shown. These tools are discussed one by one.

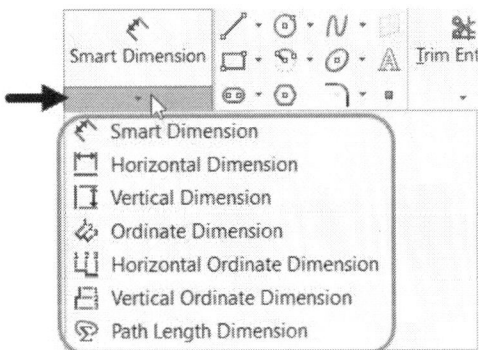

 **Smart Dimension**

The **Smart Dimension** tool is used to generate the dimensions with respect to the entity selected like horizontal dimensions, vertical dimensions for line entities and radius, dimeter for circle/arc entities etc.

- ➤ Click on the **Smart Dimension** button from the **Sketch CommandManager** to activate it.
- ➤ Click on the required entity to generate/display its dimension, as shown.
- ➤ Move the cursor up to some distance and press the **LMB** (Left Mouse Button) to place the dimension, as shown.

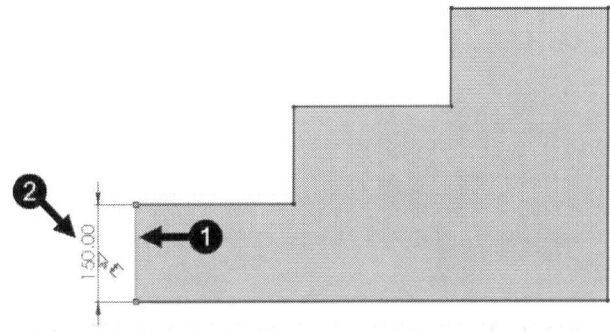

- The dimension of the selected entities gets displayed in the **Modify** dialog box. You can enter the required dimension value in it, as shown.
- Click on the ✓ button to display the dimension generated and exit the **Modify** dialog box, as shown.

  You can also edit the dimensions at any time by using the **Modify** tool, discussed further in this book.

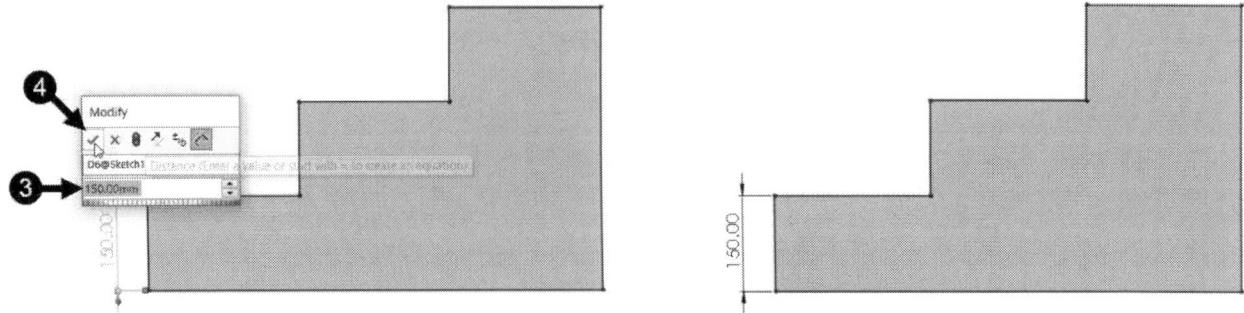

- Press the **ESC** button to deactivate the **Smart Dimension** button.

 Horizontal Dimension

This option is selected to generate horizontal dimensions if the sketch

- Select the **Horizontal Dimension** option (**Sketch > Smart Dimension > Horizontal Dimension**) to activate it, as shown above.
- Select the horizontal line entity or points of line entities one by one horizontally to generate its horizontal dimension, as shown.
- Move the cursor up to some distance and click to place the dimension generated, as shown.

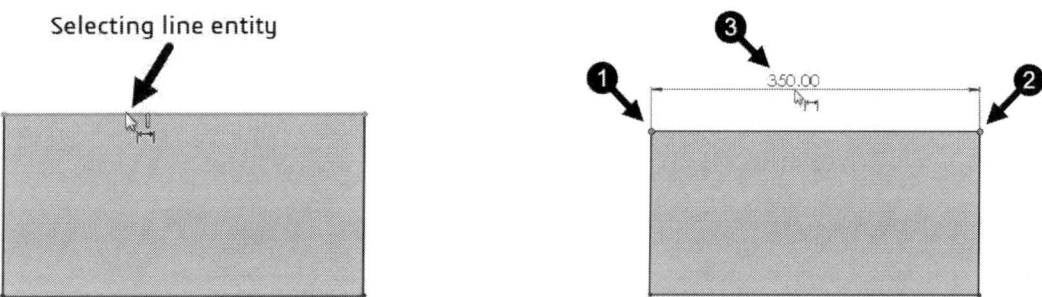

- The dimension of the selected entities gets visible in the **Modify** dialog box, as shown.
- Enter the required dimension value in it, if required, as shown.
- Next, click on the ✓ button of **Modify** dialog box to exit it and display the dimension generated, as shown.

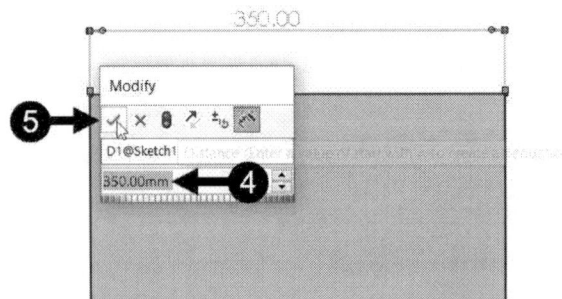

Applying Dimensions and Geometric Relations

Vertical Dimension

This option is selected to generate horizontal dimensions if the sketch

- Select the **Vertical Dimension** option (**Sketch > Smart Dimension > Vertical Dimension**) to activate it, as shown above.
- Select the vertical line entity or points of line entities vertically to generate its vertical dimension, as shown.
- Move the cursor up to some distance and click to place the dimension, as shown.

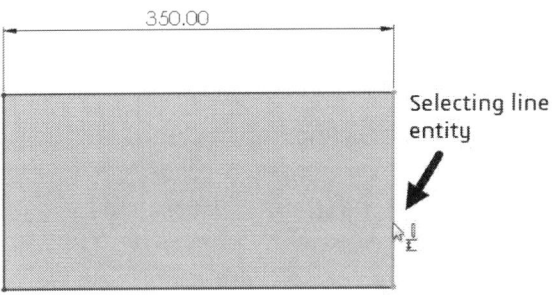
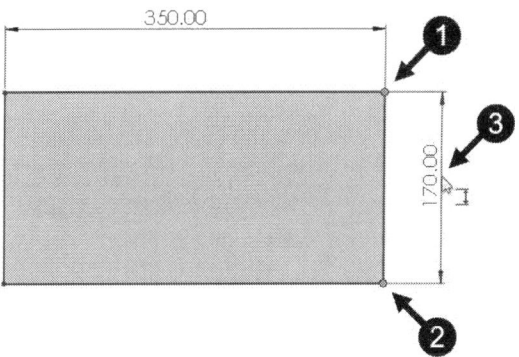

- The dimension of the selected entities gets visible in the **Modify** dialog box.
- Enter the required dimension value in it, as shown.
- Next, click on the ✓ button of **Modify** dialog box to exit it and display the dimension generated, as shown.

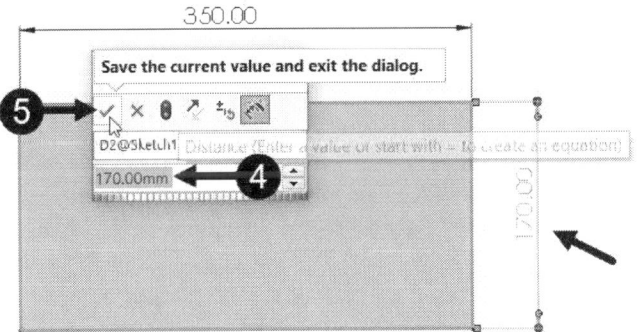

Note: You can also generate horizontal or vertical dimension by activating any of the **Horizontal Dimension** or **Vertical Dimension** tool and by selecting respective entities.

To generate vertical dimension by selecting **Horizontal Dimension** tool, you need to select two horizontal entities and vice versa, as shown.

The symbol of the selected dimension option gets visible with the cursor, while selecting the respective option, as shown.

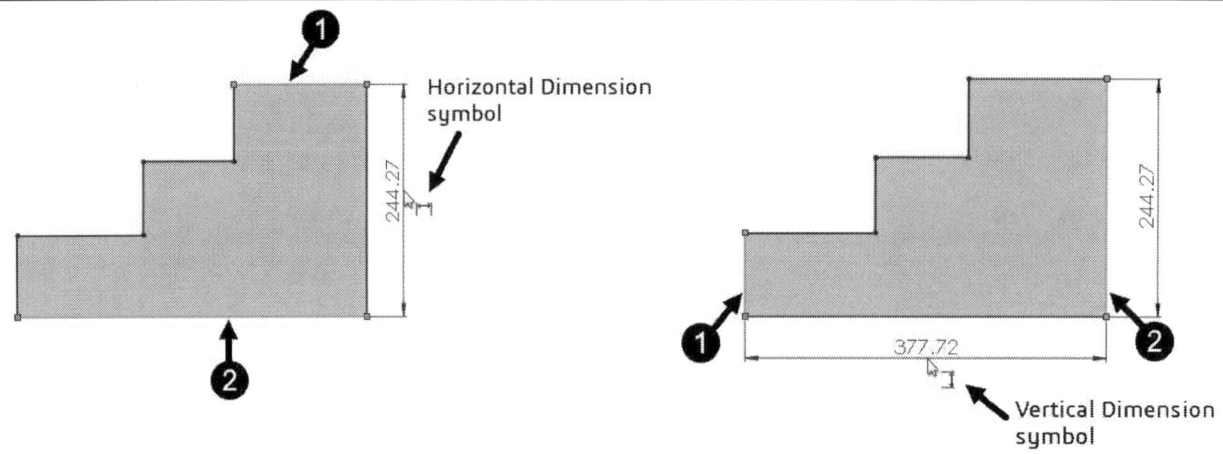

Ordinate Dimension

This tool is used to generate ordinate dimensions from a zero ordinate in the sketch. The ordinate dimensions are measured with respect to the initially selected entity/axis. All dimensions are aligned with each other automatically. While moving/dragging any single dimension; other aligned dimension moves relatively. To disconnect this alignment, right-click to display the shortcut menu and select the **Break Alignment** option from it.

There are two methods to measure ordinate dimensions - horizontal and vertical, defined by the orientation of the selected point, as shown. Both are discussed one by one below.

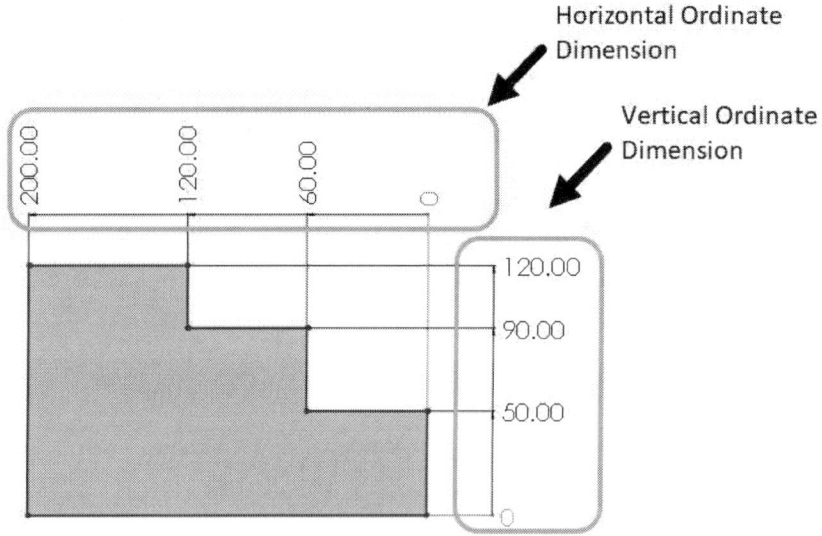

Horizontal Ordinate Dimension

This option is selected to measure ordinate dimensions horizontally.

- Select the **Horizontal Ordinate Dimension** option (**Sketch > Smart Dimension > Horizontal Ordinate Dimension**) to activate it, as shown above.
- Click on the vertical line entity, as shown earlier.
- Move the cursor up to some distance in upwards direction and click to define the "0" (Zero) ordinate, as shown.
- Next click other vertical line entities to display other dimensions automatically, as shown.

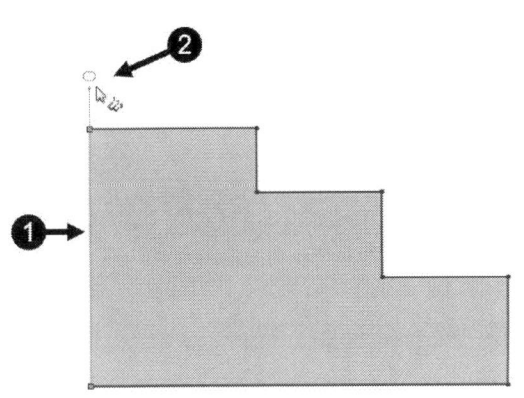 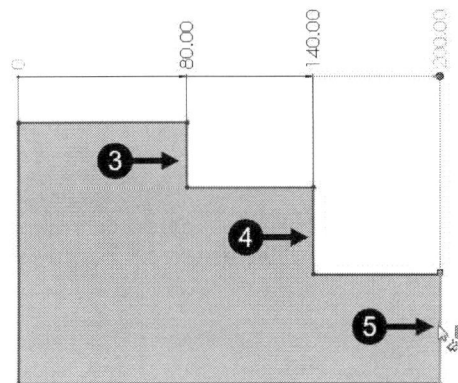

Vertical Ordinate Dimension

This option is selected to measure ordinate dimensions vertically.

- Select the **Vertical Ordinate Dimension** option (**Sketch > Smart Dimension > Vertical Ordinate Dimension**) to activate it, as shown above.
- Click on the vertical line entity, as shown earlier.
- Move the cursor up to some distance in upwards direction and click to define the "0" (Zero) ordinate, as shown.
- Next click other vertical line entities to display other dimensions automatically, as shown.

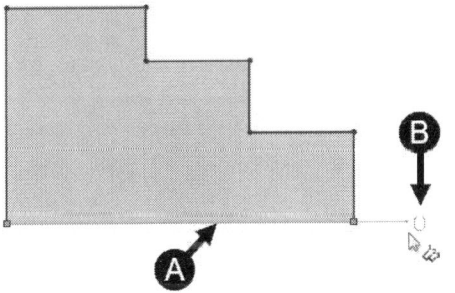 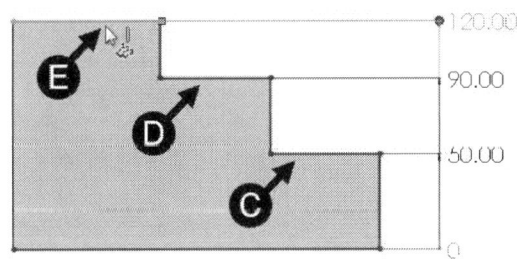

Path Length Dimension

This option is selected to generate dimension of combination of sketch entities.

- Select the **Path Length Dimension** option (**Sketch > Smart Dimension > Path Length Dimension**) to activate it and display the **Path Length PropertyManager**, as shown.
- Select the sketch entities one by one, as shown.
- Click on the OK ✓ button of the PropertyManager to exit it and display the Path Length generated, as shown.

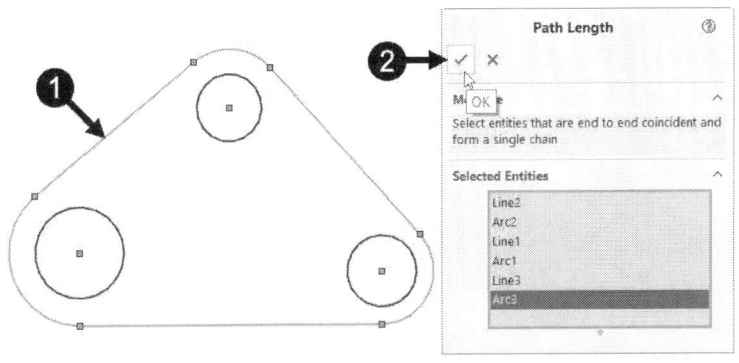 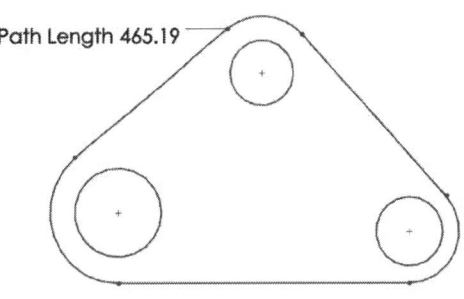

Applying Dimensions and Geometric Relations

Geometric Relations / Constraints

The geometric relations/constraints are logical operations that are used to control the position and shape/size of the drawing, by applying relationships between sketch elements. Before moving to create a feature, it is considered a good practice to ensure that the sketch is fully constrained. The term, 'fully-constrained' means that the sketch has a definite shape and size. You can make a sketch fully-constrained by using dimensions and applying constraints. These relations/constrains can be applied after activating **Add Relation** option and displaying the **Add Relations** dialog box, as shown.

> Select the **Add Relation** option from the **Display/Delete Relations** flyout to display the **Add Relations PropertyManager**, as shown.
> Next, after clicking on any entity or entities, the respective geometric relations get visible in the PropertyManager, as shown.
> Next you can apply the required relation by selecting it from the dialog box.

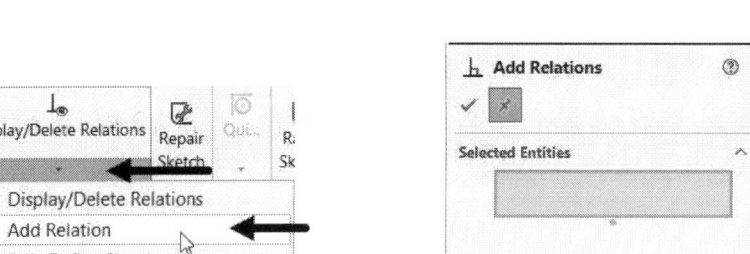
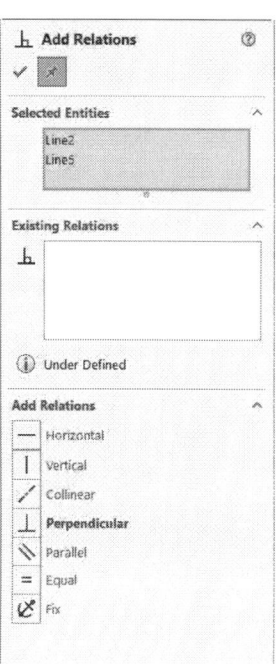

These geometric relations are discussed one by one below:

Horizontal

This relation is used to make entities horizontal or apply horizontal relation among selected entities.

1. Select the **Add Relation** option (**Sketch > Display/Delete Relations > Add Relation**) to activate it and display the **Add Relations PropertyManager**, as shown above.
2. Select the line entity/entities, as shown.
3. Next click on the **Horizontal** button from the PropertyManager to apply and display entities with Horizontal relation, as shown.
4. Click on the **OK** button of the PropertyManager to exit it and click to display entities with horizontal relations, as shown.

   You can also select an external entity such as an edge, plane, axis, or sketch curve on an external sketch that will act as a line to apply this relation.

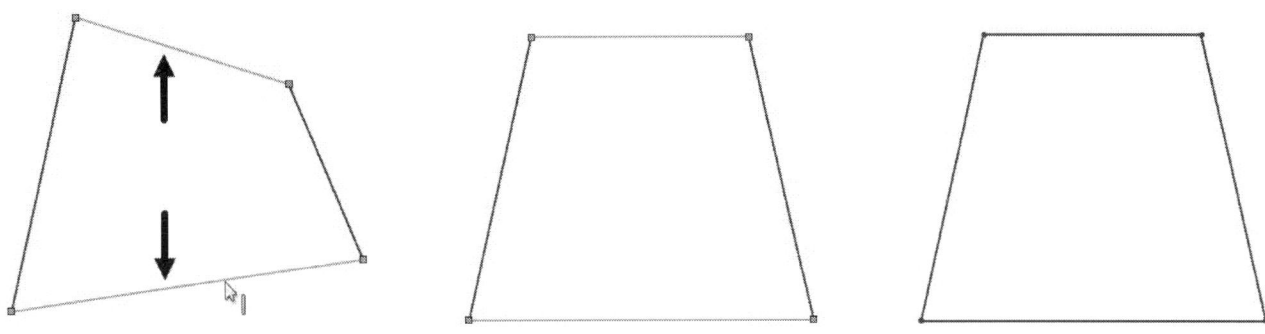

┼ Vertical

This relation is used to make entities vertical or apply vertical relation among selected entities.

> Select the **Add Relation** option to activate it and display the **Add Relations PropertyManager**, as shown above.
> Select the line entity/entities, as shown.
> Next click on the **Vertical** button from the PropertyManager to apply and display entities with vertical relation, as shown.
> Click on the **OK** button of the PropertyManager to exit it and click to display entities with vertical relations, as shown.

Note that the applied relations will be visible after selecting the **View Sketch Relations** button from the **Hide/Show Items** flyout in the **View (Head-Up)** toolbar, as shown.

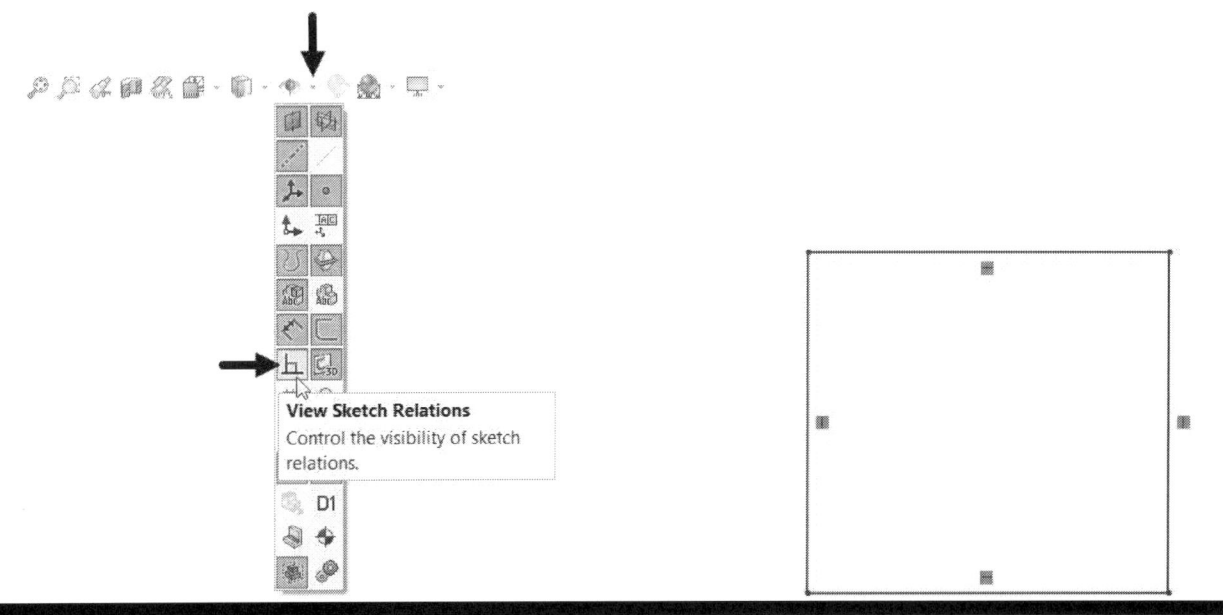

Applying Dimensions and Geometric Relations

Collinear

This relation is used to make the selected line to lie on the same straight/infinite line.

- Select the **Add Relation** option to activate it and display the **Add Relations PropertyManager**.
- Select the entities one by one, as shown.
- Next click on the **Collinear** button from the PropertyManager to apply collinear relation.
- Click on the **OK** button of the PropertyManager to exit it and display entities with collinear relation and ▨ symbol, as shown.

Perpendicular

This relation is used to make two lines perpendicular to each other.

- Select the **Add Relation** option to activate it and display the **Add Relations PropertyManager**, as shown above.
- Click on line 1 & 2 one by one to apply Perpendicular Constraint among them, as shown.
- Next click on the **Perpendicular** ⊥ button from the PropertyManager to apply perpendicular relation and display entities with symbol ▨, as shown.
- Similarly, you can apply perpendicular relation between other line by clicking them in the sequence 3 & 4, 5 & 6, and 7 & 8 as shown.
- Click on the **OK** button of the PropertyManager to exit it and display all entities with perpendicular relation and ▨ symbol, as shown.

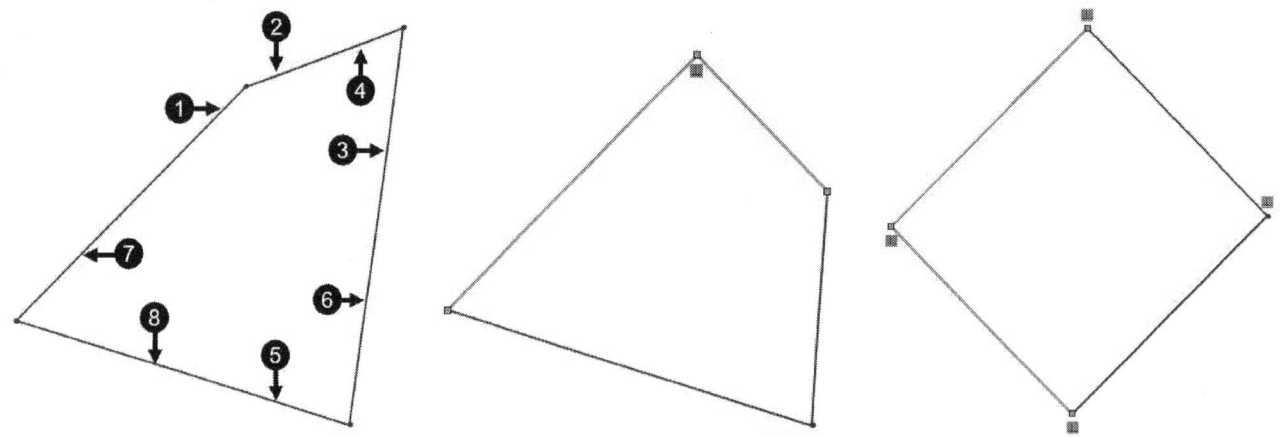

Parallel

This relation is used to make two lines parallel to each other.

- Select the **Add Relation** option to activate it and display the **Add Relations PropertyManager**.
- Select the entities one by one, as shown.
- Next click on the **Parallel** button from the PropertyManager to apply parallel relation.
- Next, click on the **OK** button of the PropertyManager to exit it and display entities with parallel relation and ▨ symbol, as shown.

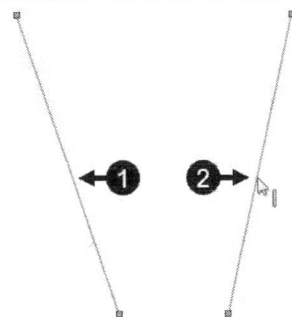 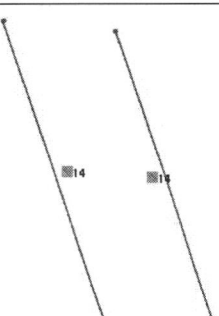

Equal

This relation is used to make the dimensions of selected similar entities equal to each other like equal length for line entities and equal radii for selected arcs & circles.

- Select the **Add Relation** option to activate it and display the **Add Relations PropertyManager**.
- Select the entities one by one, as shown.
- Next click on the **Equal** button from the PropertyManager to apply equal relation.
- Next, click on the **OK** button of the PropertyManager to exit it and display entities with equal relation and ▄ symbol, as shown.

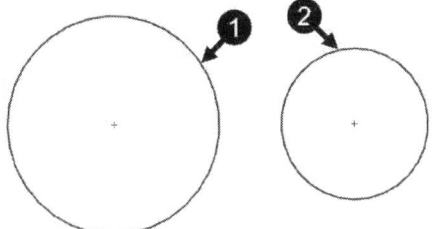 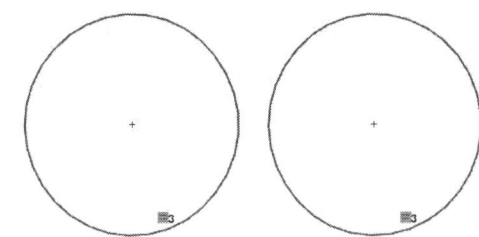

- Similarly, you can apply equal relation to line entities to make their length equal, as shown.

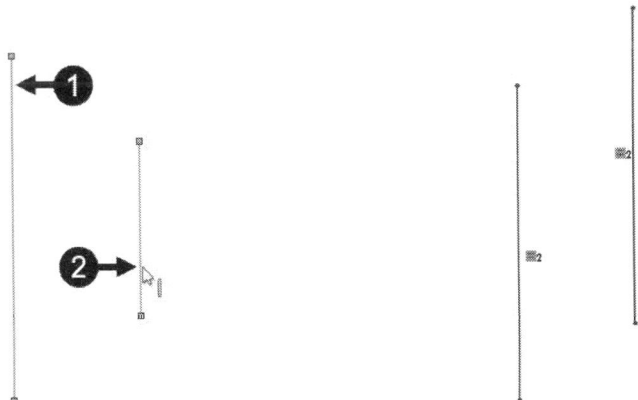

Note: You need to apply dimension to one of the entities with respect to which you want to apply **Equal** constraint. Unless system will assume their mean dimensions and apply it to both entities.

⌀ Tangent

This relation is used to make an arc, circle, or line entity tangent to each other.

- Select the **Add Relation** option to activate it and display the **Add Relations PropertyManager**.
- Select the entities one by one, as shown.
- Next click on the **Tangent** ⌀ button from the PropertyManager to apply tangent relation.

Applying Dimensions and Geometric Relations

- Click on the **OK** button of the PropertyManager to exit it and display entities with tangent relation and ◆ symbol, as shown.

- Similarly, apply tangent relation among other entities, as shown.

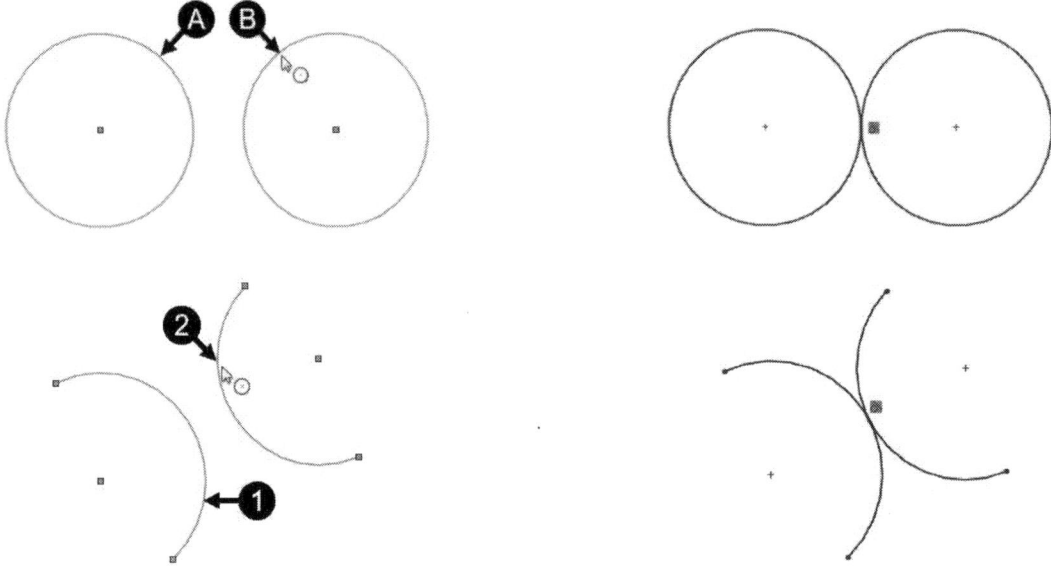

⚘ Coincident

This relation is used to make a line entity coincident to selected point entity.

- Select the **Add Relation** option to activate it and display the **Add Relations PropertyManager**.
- Select the end point of the line entity and then select another line entity, as shown.
- Next click on the **Coincident** button from the PropertyManager to apply coincident relation.
- Click on the **OK** button of the PropertyManager to exit it and display entities with coincident relation and ▨ symbol, as shown.

  Similarly, you can apply coincident relation between arc, circle, and ellipse with the selected point, as shown.

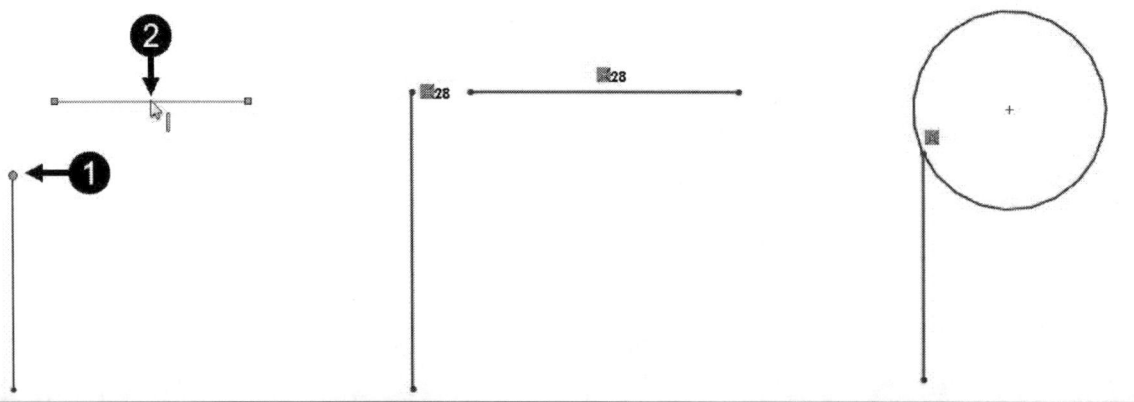

Applying Dimensions and Geometric Relations 4-10

Midpoint

This relation is used to force a point to get aligned with the midpoint of a line entity.

> Select the **Add Relation** option to activate it and display the **Add Relations PropertyManager**.
> Click on the center point of the circle entity and then click on the line entity, as shown.
> Next click on the **Midpoint** button from the PropertyManager to apply midpoint relation.
> Click on the **OK** button of the PropertyManager to exit it and display entities with midpoint relation and ▨ symbol, as shown.

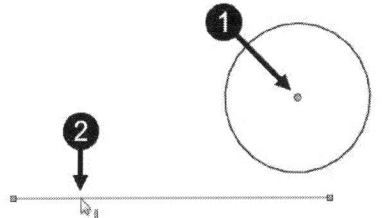 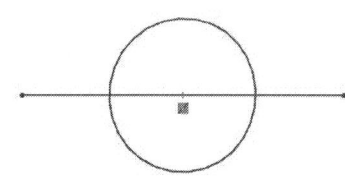

 Concentric

This constraint is used to make the center points of arcs, circles or ellipses coincident.

> Select the **Add Relation** option to activate it and display the **Add Relations PropertyManager**.
> Click on the two circles one by one, as shown.
> Next click on the **Concentric** button from the PropertyManager to apply concentric relation.
> Click on the **OK** button of the PropertyManager to exit it and display entities with concentric relation and ◉ symbol, as shown.

Similarly, you can apply coincident relation between arcs and ellipse, as shown.

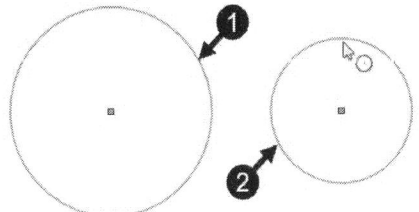 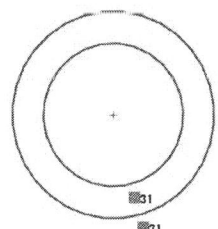 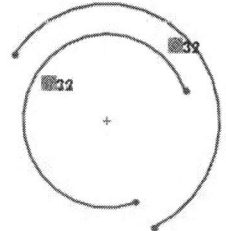 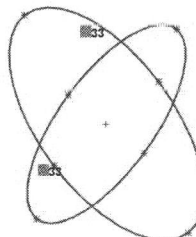

Intersection

This relation is used to move a selected point at the intersection of two selected lines.

> Select the **Add Relation** option to activate it and display the **Add Relations PropertyManager**.
> Click on line entities and point entity one by one, as shown.
> Next click on the **Intersection** button from the PropertyManager to apply intersection relation.
> Click on the **OK** button of the PropertyManager to exit it and display entities with intersection relation and ▨ symbol, as shown.

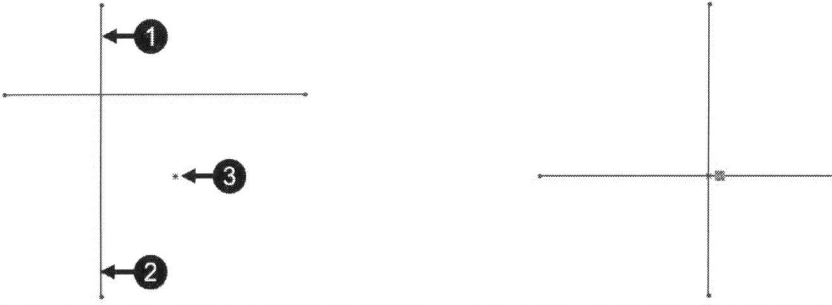

Applying Dimensions and Geometric Relations

Cordial

This relation is used to move a selected circle or arc to share the same center point and the same radius with another circle or arc.

➢ Select the **Add Relation** option to activate it and display the **Add Relations PropertyManager**.
➢ Click on two arc entities one by one, as shown.
➢ Next click on the **Coradial** button from the PropertyManager to apply coradial relation.
➢ Click on the **OK** button of the PropertyManager to exit it and display entities with coradial relation and ■ symbol, as shown.

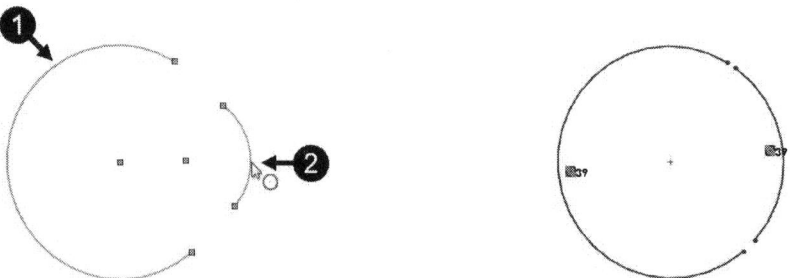

Symmetric

This relation is used to make two entities symmetric about a centerline. The entities will have same size, position and orientation about a line.

➢ Select the **Add Relation** option to activate it and display the **Add Relations PropertyManager**.
➢ Click on the centreline and then click on two circle entities one by one, as shown.
➢ Next click on the **Symmetric** button from the PropertyManager to apply symmetric relation.
➢ Click on the **OK** button of the PropertyManager to exit it and display entities with symmetric relation and ■ symbol, as shown.

 Fix

This relation is used to fix the position of the selected entity.

➢ Select the **Add Relation** option to activate it and display the **Add Relations PropertyManager**.
➢ Click on the line entity, as shown.
➢ Next click on the **Fix** button from the PropertyManager to apply fix relation.
➢ Click on the **OK** button of the PropertyManager to exit it and display entities with fix relation and ■ symbol, as shown.

If you apply fix relation to line or arc entities, you can change their sizes by dragging their endpoints, as shown.

✓ Merge

This relation is used merge two selected sketch points or endpoints in a single point.

> - Select the **Add Relation** option to activate it and display the **Add Relations PropertyManager**.
> - Click on the endpoints of two line entities, as shown.
> - Next click on the **Merge** button from the PropertyManager to apply merge relation.
> - Click on the **OK** button of the PropertyManager to exit it and display entities with merge relation, as shown.

Turn ON/OFF Dimensions and Constraints

After applying dimensions and constraints, if you want to turn on/off their visibility, in the graphics area. Follow the steps.

> - Click on the **Hide/Show Items** flyout of the **View (Heads-Up) Toolbar**, as shown.

> - Next you can control the visibility of dimension and relations in the drawing area by clicking on the **View Sketch Relations** and **View Sketch Dimensions** buttons displayed, as shown.

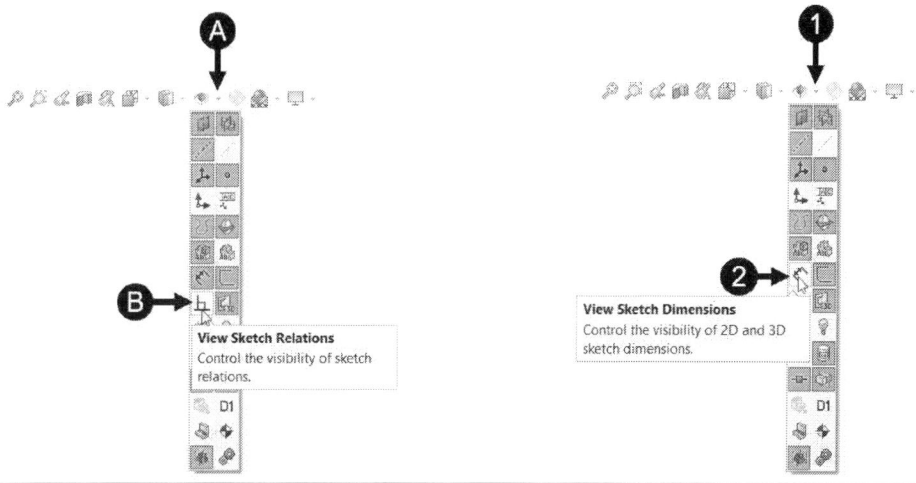

Applying Dimensions and Geometric Relations   4-13

Examples:

Example 1

In this example, you will create the sketch shown below.

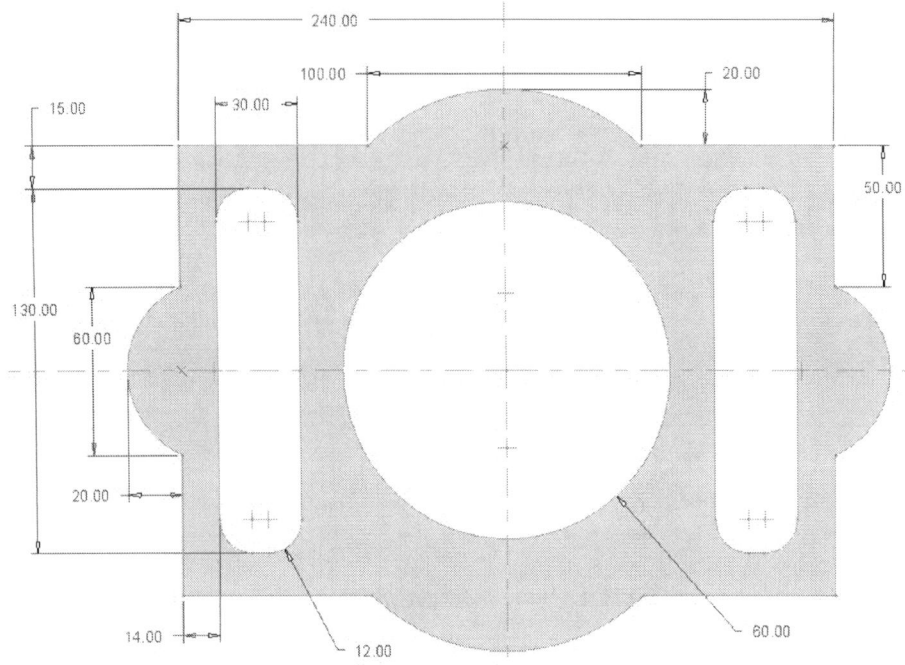

- Start SolidWorks 2021 by clicking **SOLIDWORKS 2021** icon on your desktop.
- Click on the **New** (📄) button from the **Menu Bar** to display the **New SOLIDWORKS Document** dialog box, as shown.

   Alternatively, press **Ctrl + N** key from the keyboard to display the **New SOLIDWORKS Document** dialog box.

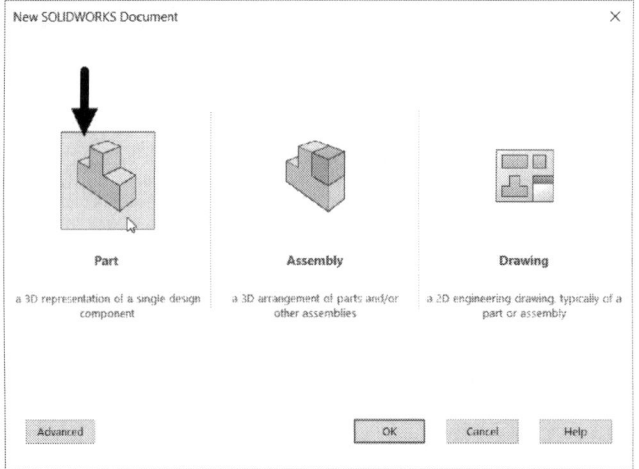

- Click on the **Part** button from the dialog box, if it is not selected by default and then click on **OK** button from dialog box to enter in the Sketching Environment.

   Alternatively, you can double click on the **Part** button to enter in the Sketching Environment.
- Next for the better visibility of display, change the background colour to white, as discussed in previous chapter.

➢ Click on the **Sketch** tab to display tools used in creating sketch, as shown.

➢ Click on the **Sketch** button from the **Sketch CommandManager** and then click on the **Front** plane to make it parallel to the screen, as shown.

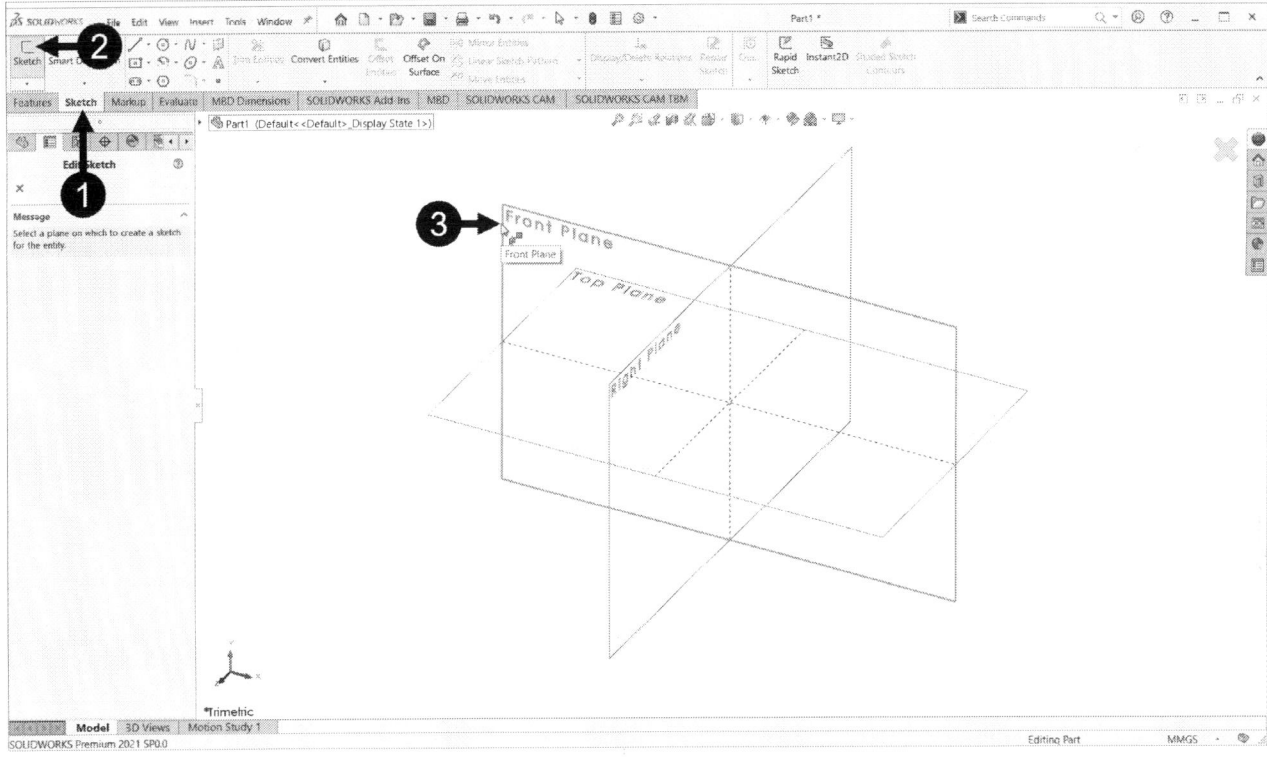

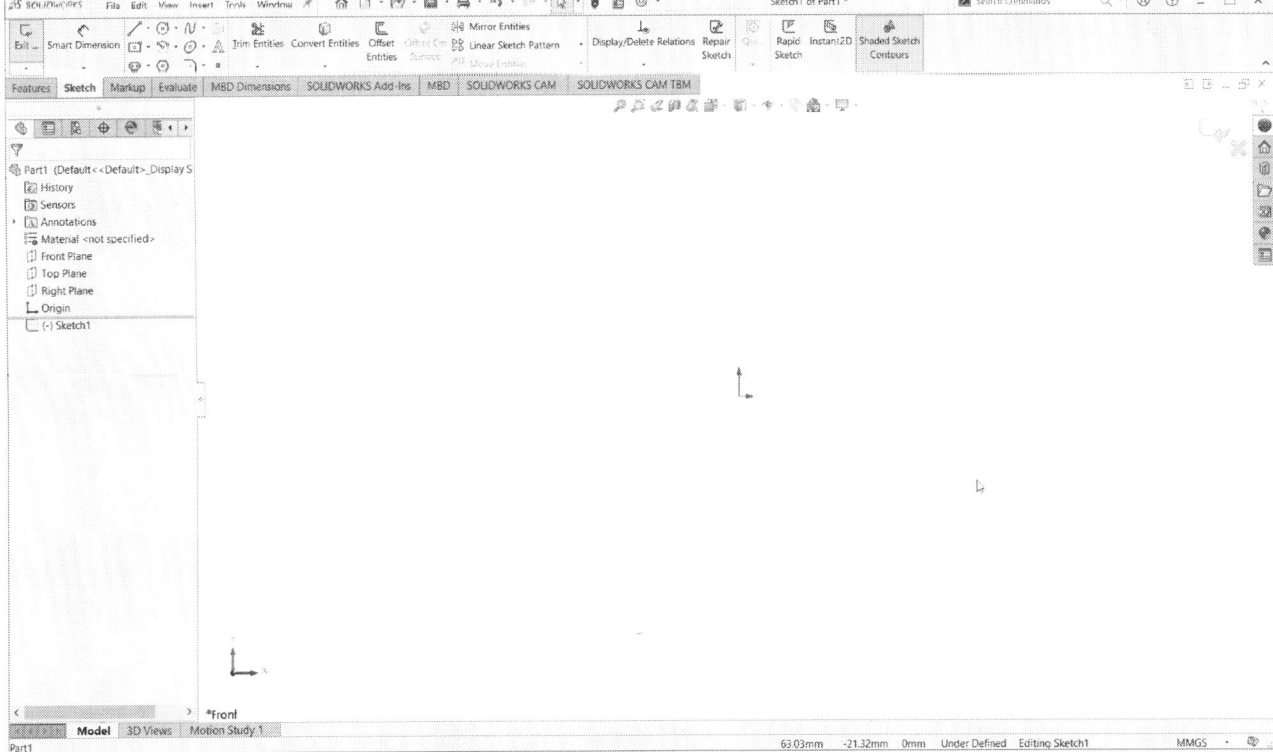

➢ Select the **Corner Rectangle** tool (**Sketch > Rectangle > Corner Rectangle**) to activate it.

Applying Dimensions and Geometric Relations 4-15

- Next to draw a rectangle (240X160) click anywhere in the drawing area and drag the cursor up to some distance, as shown.
- Next enter **160** as width of rectangle, as shown.

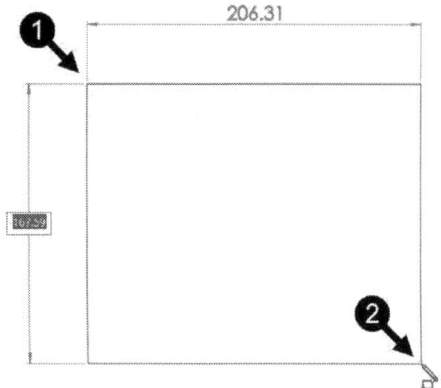 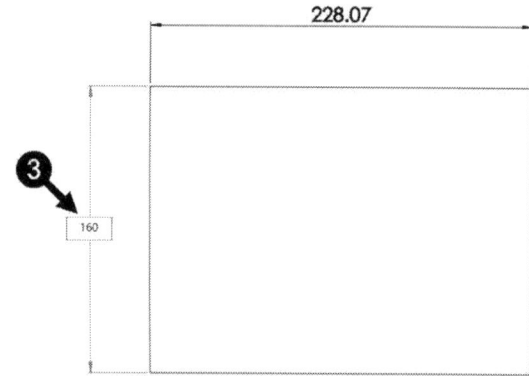

- Press the **Tab** key to move cursor to length edit box and enter **240** as length of rectangle, as shown.
- Next press the **Enter** key to display the rectangle (240 X 160), as shown.

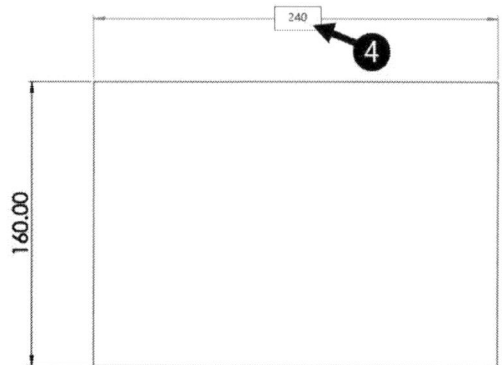 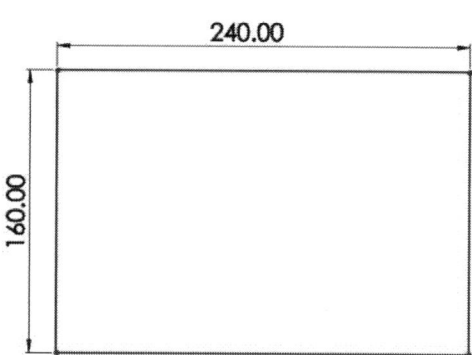

- Click on the **Centerline** tool (**Sketch** > **Line** > **Centerline**) to activate it.
- Move the cursor over upper horizontal line until its midpoint get visible, as shown.
- Move the cursor slightly upwards and click to define start point of centreline, as shown.
- Move the cursor vertically downwards and click to define endpoint of centreline, as shown.
- Next press the **Esc** key to exit **Centerline** tool and display the centreline created, as shown.

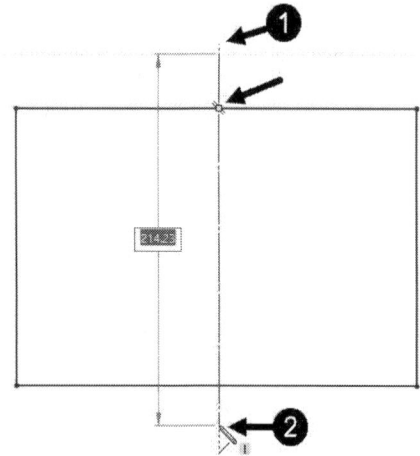 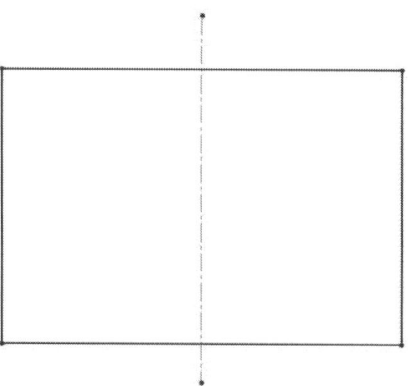

- Similarly create the horizontal centreline, as shown.

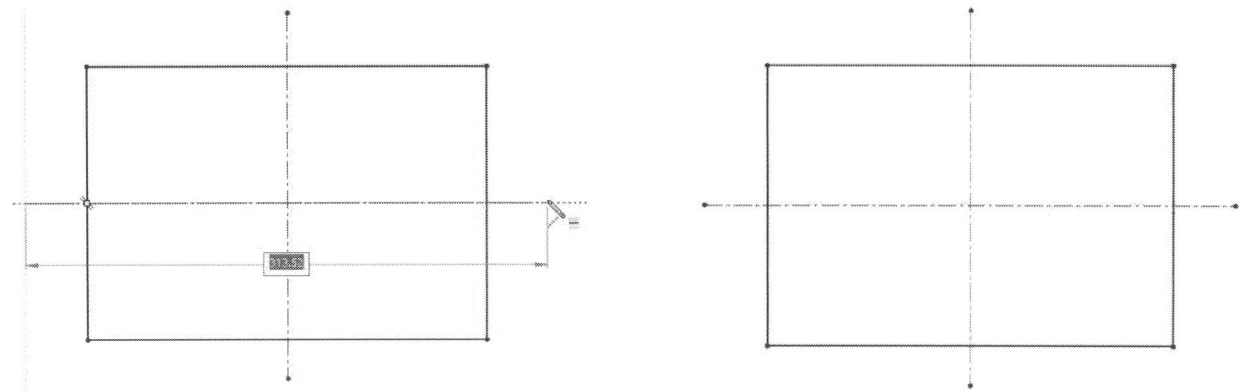

- Activate the **Circle** tool and draw a circle with diameter 120 at the center of rectangle, as shown.

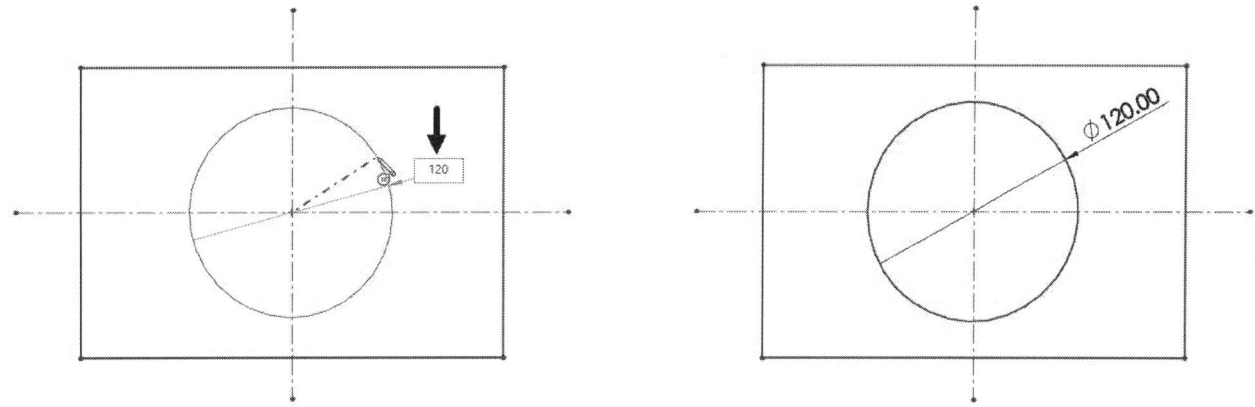

- Activate the **3 Point Arc** tool (**Sketch > Arc > 3 Point Arc**) and draw an arc with given dimensions, as shown.

  Also, use the **Symmetric** relation to make it symmetric with respect to the vertical centreline, if required, as shown.

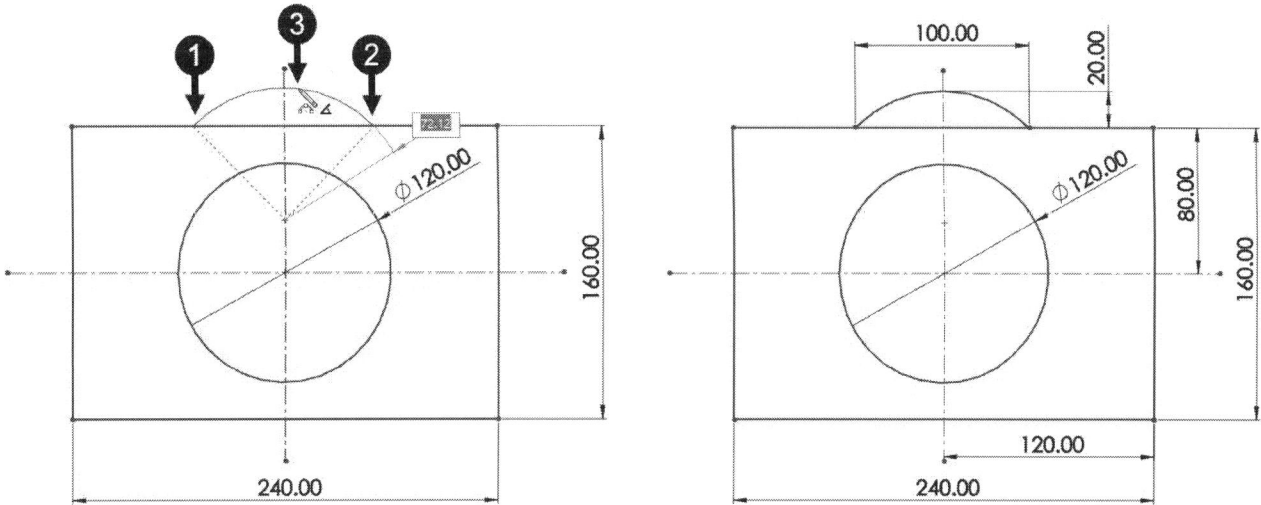

- Similarly draw another arc on the left of the rectangle, as shown.

Applying Dimensions and Geometric Relations

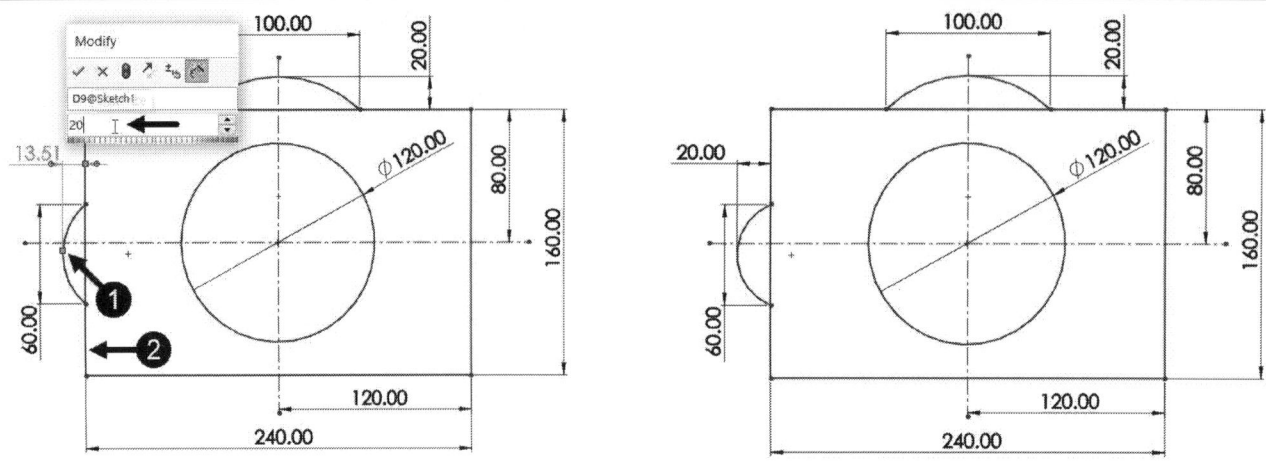

The arc is not symmetric, so you need to apply symmetric relations for it.

➢ Select the **Add Relation** option to activate it and display the **Add Relations PropertyManager**.
➢ Click on the horizontal centreline and then click on point entities one by one, as shown.
➢ Next click on the **Symmetric** button from the PropertyManager to apply symmetric relation, as shown.

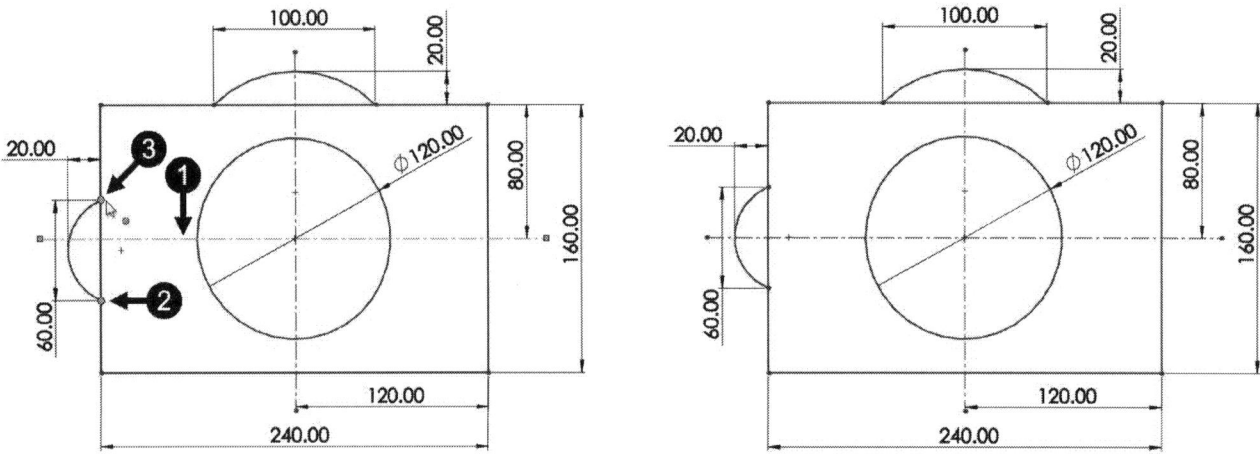

➢ Select the upper arc and then select the **Mirror Entities** tool to display **Mirror PropertyManager**.
➢ Next click in the **Mirror about** box of the PropertyManager and select the horizontal centerline to display preview of mirror entity on opposite direction, as shown.
➢ Now click on the **OK** button of the PropertyManager to exit and display the mirror entity, as shown.

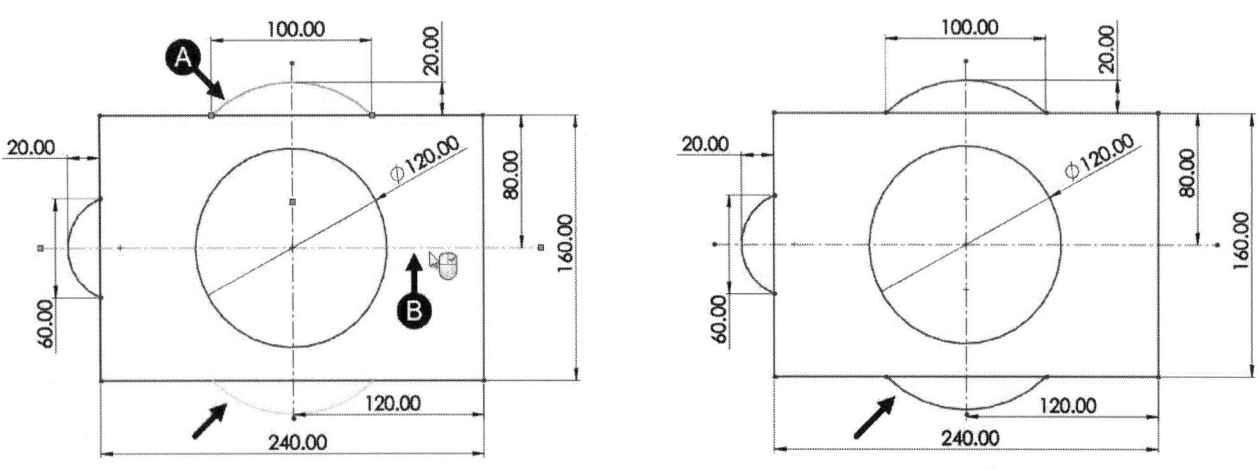

Applying Dimensions and Geometric Relations   4-18

> Similarly mirror the left side arc with respect to the vertical centreline, as shown.

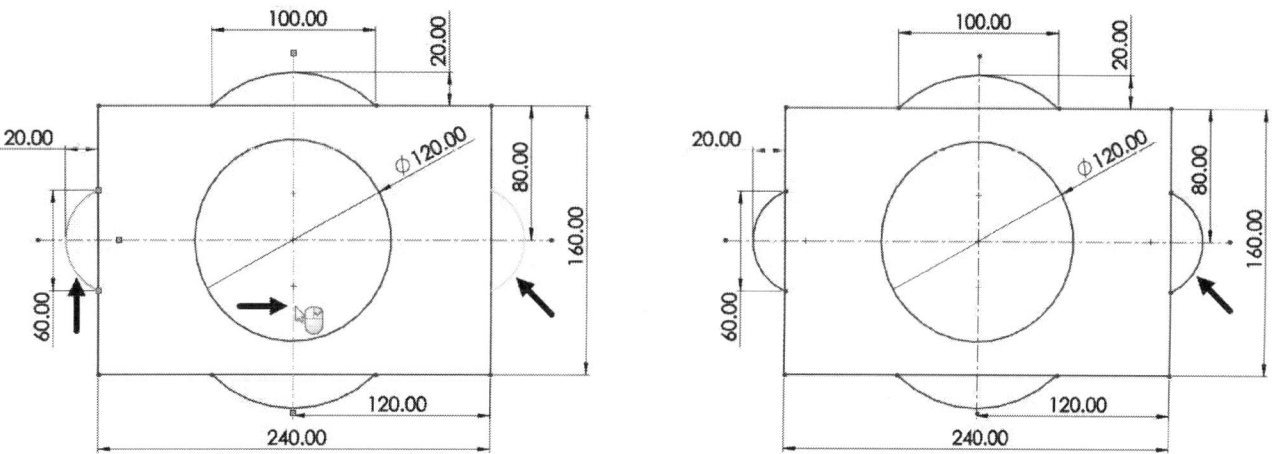

> Next draw a rectangle with given dimensions and symmetric with respect to horizontal centreline, as shown.

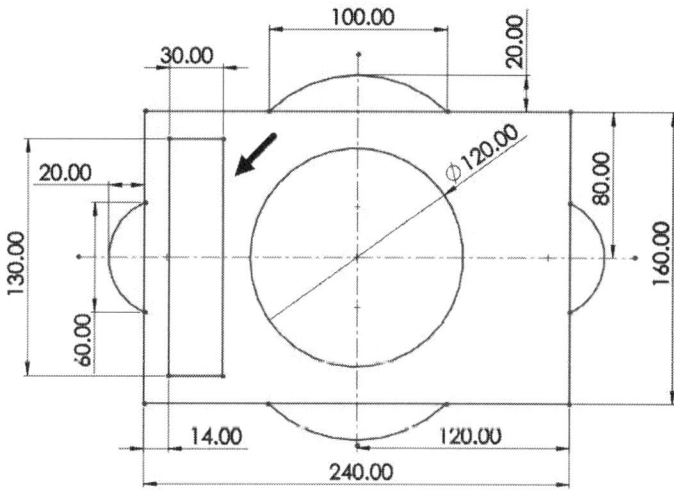

> Now select the **Sketch Fillet** tool from **Sketch CommandManager** to display **Sketch Fillet PropertyManager**. For applying round edges to the recently drawn rectangle.
> Select the two line entities of the rectangle one by one to display preview of round corner, as shown.
> Next enter **12** as fillet radius in the PropertyManager.
> Click on the **OK** button of the PropertyManager to exit it and display the fillet feature, as shown.

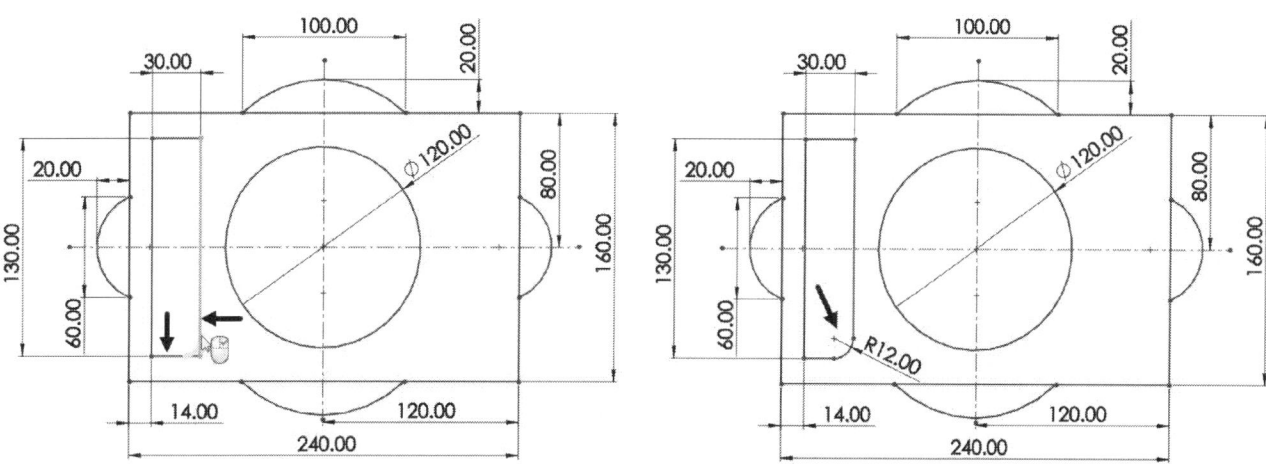

Applying Dimensions and Geometric Relations

➢ Similarly, apply the fillet with same fillet radius to other corners of rectangle, as shown.

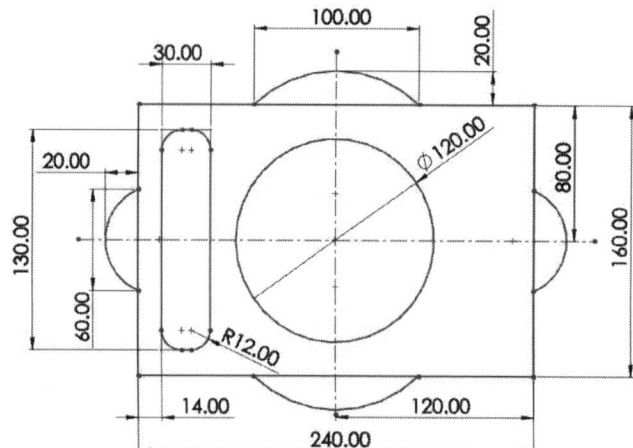

➢ Now drag the cursor over the rectangle with filleted corners to select it, as shown.
➢ Next select the **Mirror Entities** ▯ Mirror Entities tool to display **Mirror PropertyManager**.
➢ Click in the **Mirror about** box of the PropertyManager and select the vertical centerline to display preview of mirror entity with respect to it, as shown.
➢ Now click on the **OK** button of the PropertyManager to exit and display the mirror entity, as shown.

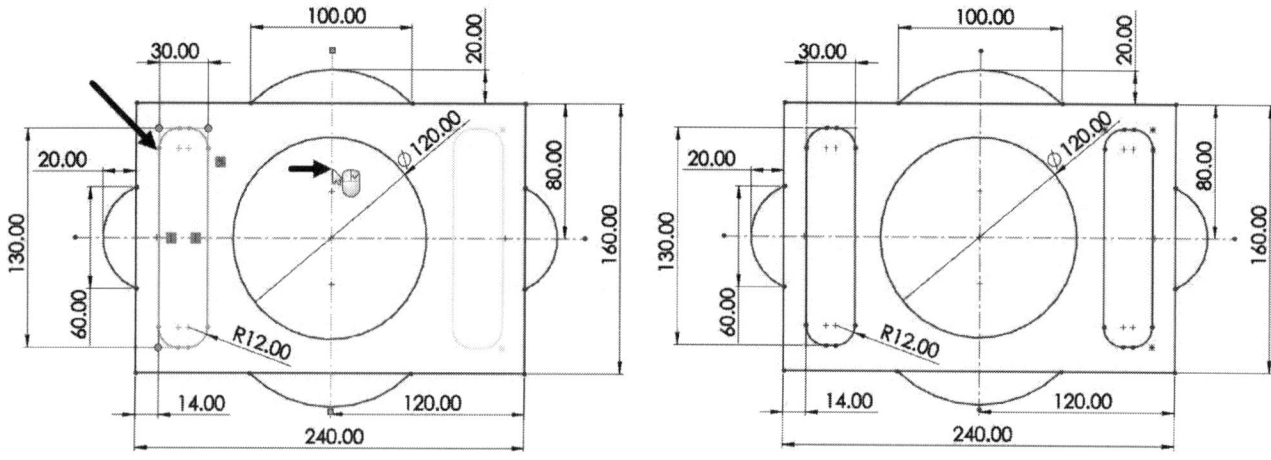

➢ Now activate the **Trim Entities** tool from the **Sketch CommandManager** and move the cursor over entities to trim, as shown.
➢ Now click on the **OK** button of the PropertyManager to exit it and display the entities, as shown.

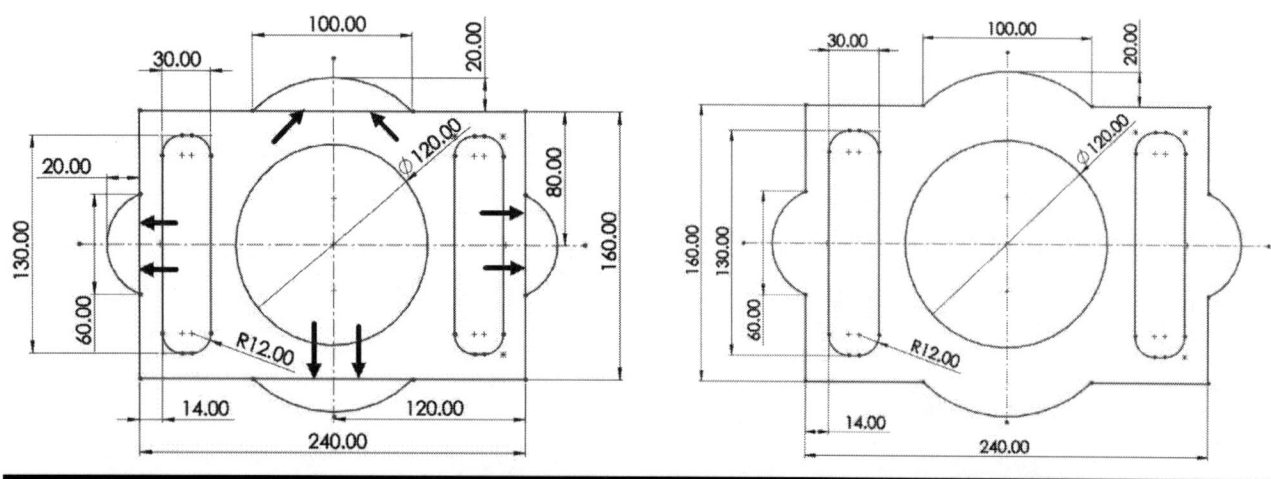

Applying Dimensions and Geometric Relations

➢ Next modify the dimensions, as shown.

➢ The sketch is complete, click on the **Exit Sketch** button from the **Sketch CommandManager** to exit from the sketch environment and display model.

Alternatively, you can click on the button from the top right corner of the drawing area to exit from sketch environment.

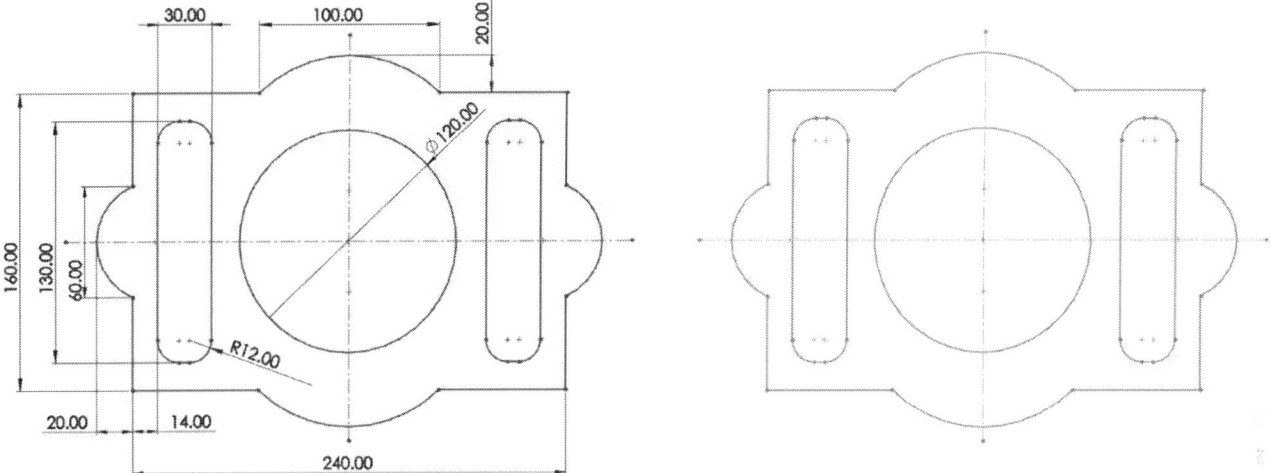

➢ Click on the **Save (Ctrl + S)** button from the **Menu Bar** to display the **Save As** dialog box.
➢ Next browse to the folder of **chapter 4** and enter name **Ch04-exam01** in the **File name** edit box.
➢ Click on the **Save** button from the dialog box to save the file.
➢ Now enter the **Close** button from the upper right corner to close it.

Example 2

In this example, you will create the sketch shown below.

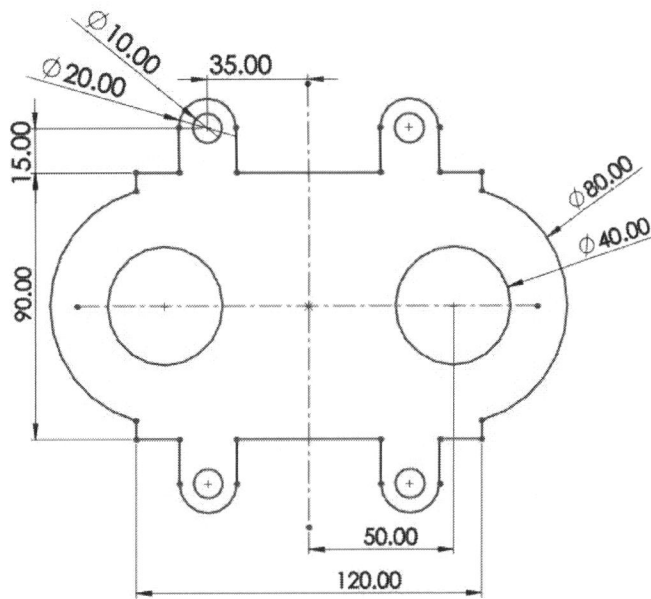

➢ Start SolidWorks 2021 by clicking **SOLIDWORKS 2021** icon on your desktop.

- Click on the **New** (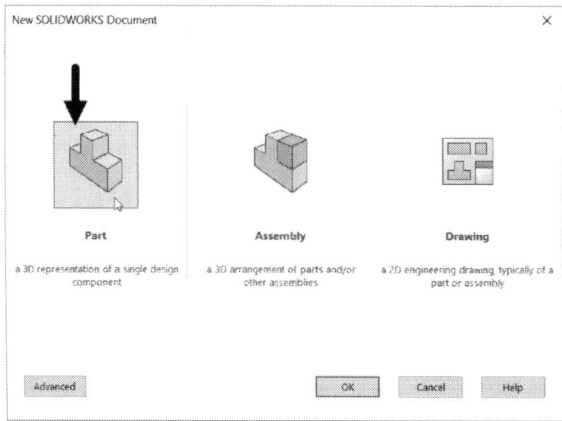) button from the **Menu Bar** to display the **New SOLIDWORKS Document** dialog box, as shown.

  Alternatively, press **Ctrl + N** key from the keyboard to display the **New SOLIDWORKS Document** dialog box.

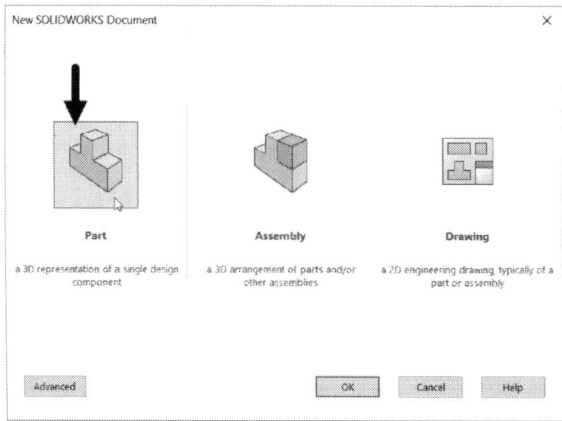

- Double click on the **Part** button to enter in the Sketching Environment.
- Next for the better visibility of display, change the background colour to white, as discussed in previous chapter.
- Click on the **Sketch** tab to display tools used in creating sketch.
- Click on the **Sketch** button from the **Sketch CommandManager** and then click on the **Front** plane to make it parallel to the screen, as shown in previous example.
- Select the **Centerline** tool from the **Line** drop-down of the **Sketch CommandManager**, as shown.
- Draw two centerlines, as shown.

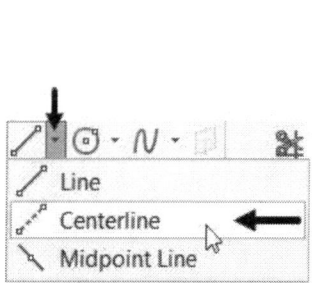 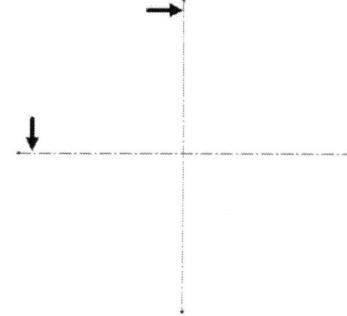

- Select the **Center Rectangle** tool (**Sketch > Rectangle > Center Rectangle**) to activate it, as shown.
- Next, click at the intersecting point of two centerlines to define its start point, as shown.
- Move the cursor up to some distance and click to define second point of the rectangle that also defines its width and length, as shown.

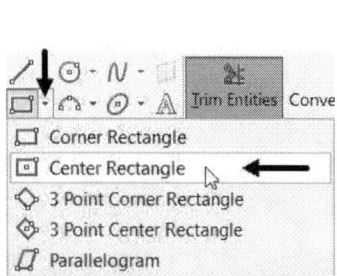 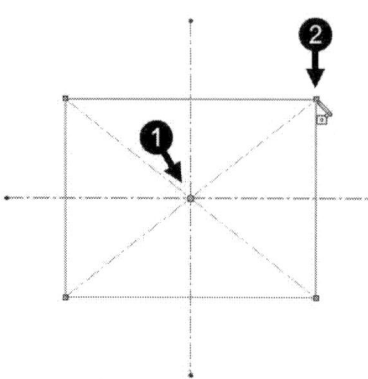

Applying Dimensions and Geometric Relations

- Select the **Smart Dimension** tool from the **Sketch CommandManager** and apply dimensions, as shown.
- Activate the **Circle** tool and draw two circles as shown, as shown.

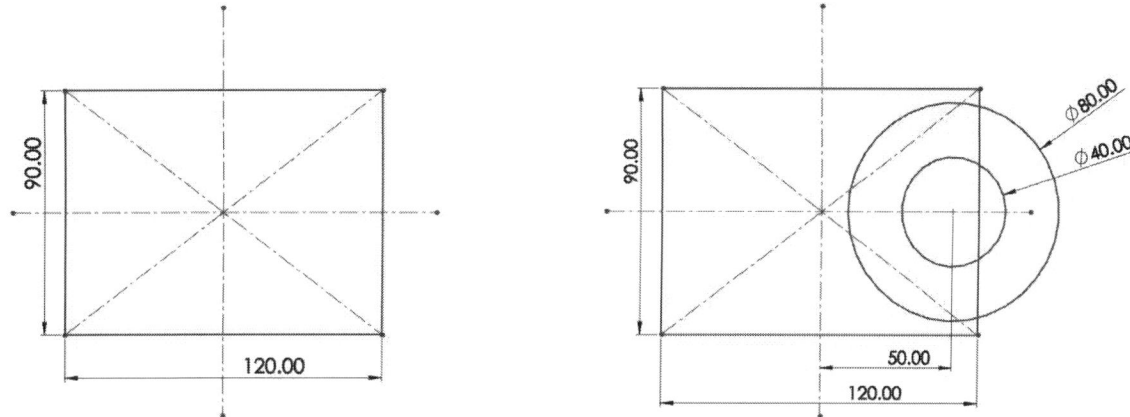

- Select the **Mirror Entities** tool to activate it and select both circles one by one to mirror, as shown.
- Next click in the **Mirror about** selection box of the PropertyManager and select the vertical center line to display preview of mirrored feature, as shown.
- Click on the **OK** button of the PropertyManager to exit it and display the mirrored feature, as shown

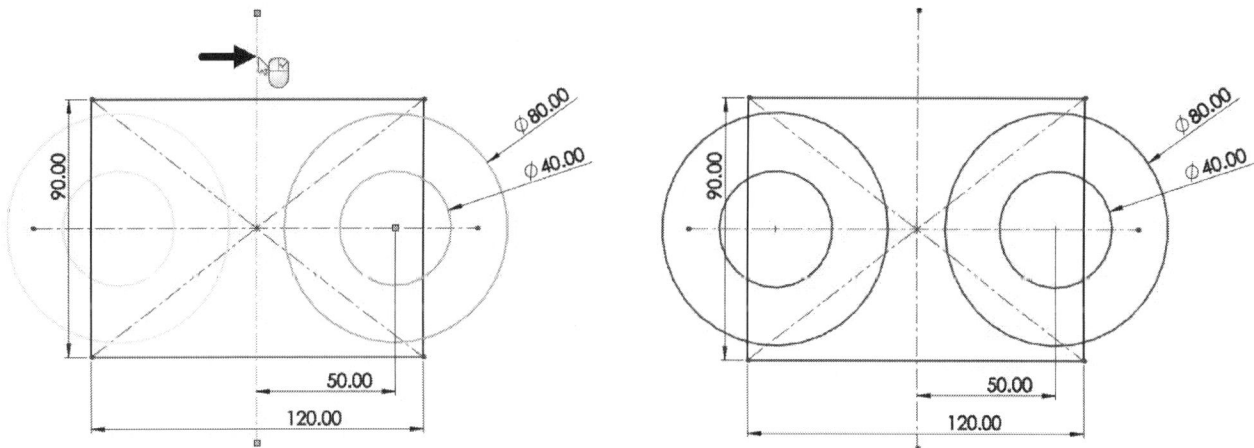

- Select the **Trim Entities** tool from the **Sketch CommandManager** to activate it.
- Move the cursor over unwanted entities, as shown. Similarly, remove other entities, as shown.
- Press and hold the **LMB** and drag the cursor over the entities to trim, as shown. Also remove the entities under inner circles.

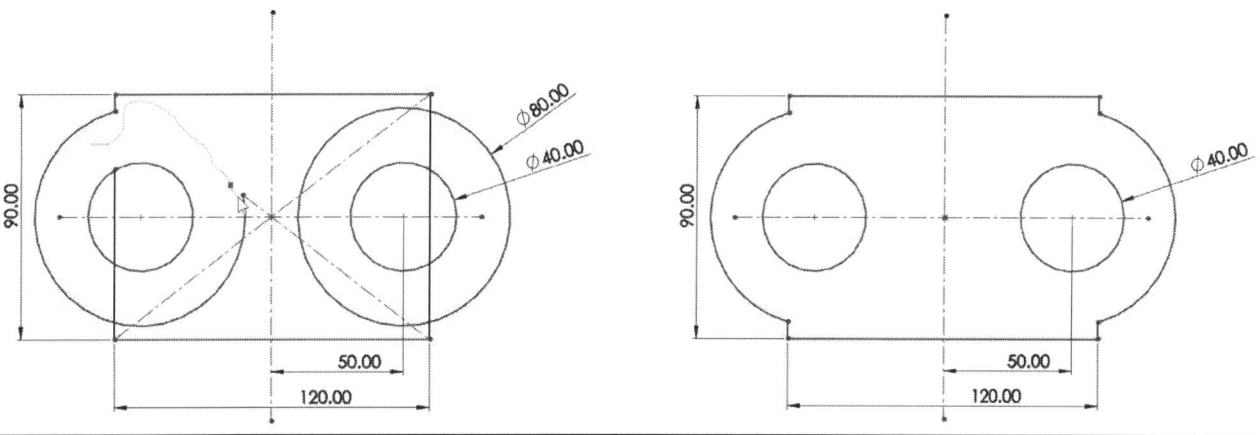

Applying Dimensions and Geometric Relations

➢ Again, activate the **Circle** tool and draw two concentric circles, as shown.

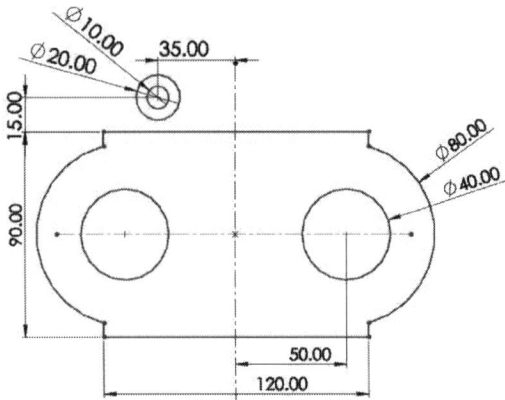

➢ Activate the **Line** tool and move the cursor over recently drawn outer circle and click where the cursor sticks on its left, as shown.
➢ More the cursor downwards and draw the line entity, as shown.
➢ Press **Esc** key to deactivate the Line tool.
➢ Create line entity on other side also. You can also do the same by creating a centerline and using the **Mirror** tool, as discussed earlier.

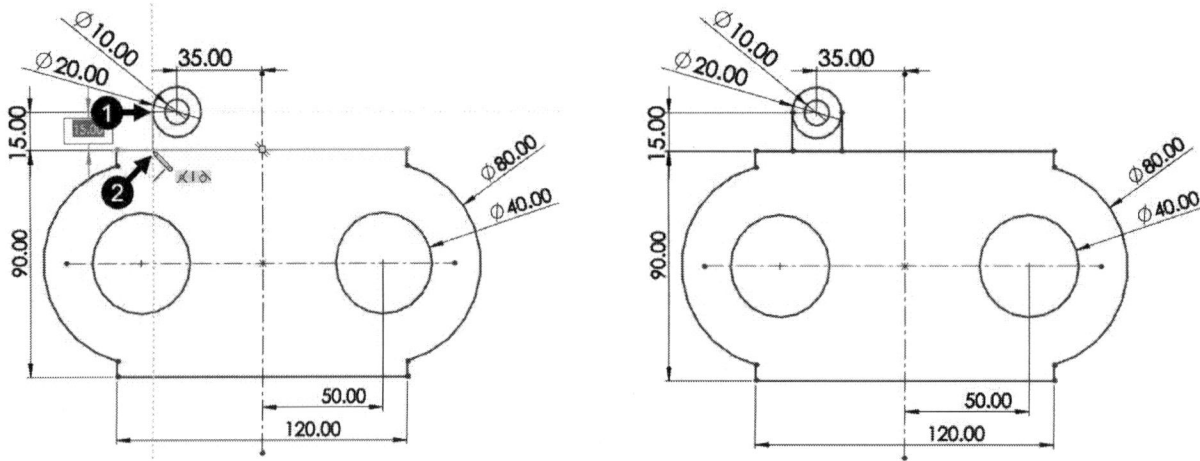

➢ Now activate the **Mirror Entities** tool and select the recently drawn sketch, as shown.
➢ Next click in the **Mirror about** selection box of the PropertyManager and select the vertical center line to display preview of mirrored entities, as shown.
➢ Click on the **OK** button of the PropertyManager to exit it and display the mirrored entities, as shown.

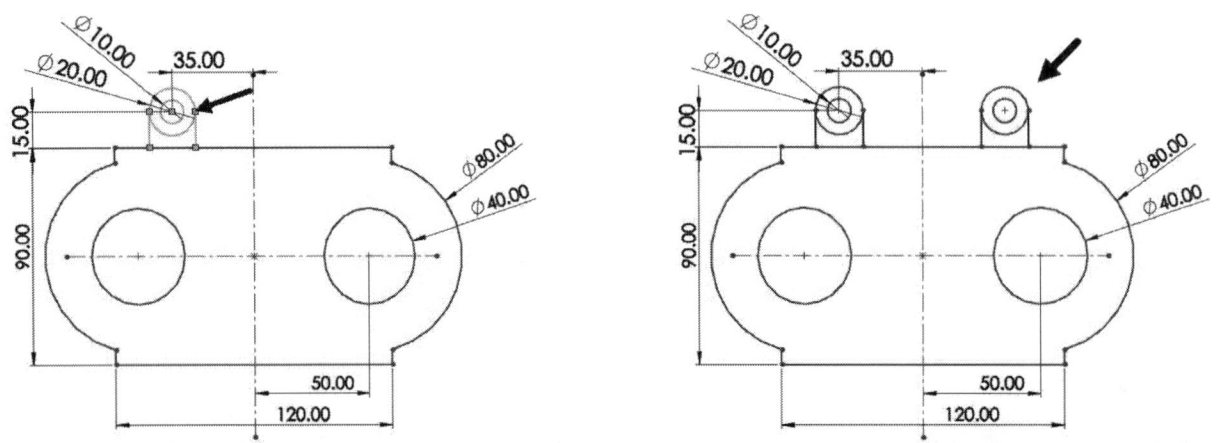

Applying Dimensions and Geometric Relations

➤ Similarly, select both of the top entities and using the horizontal centreline create mirror entities, as shown.

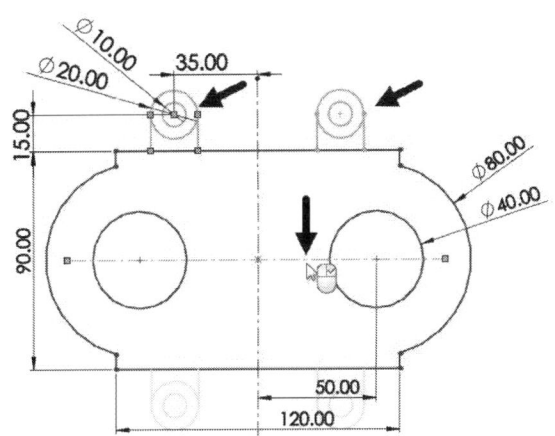 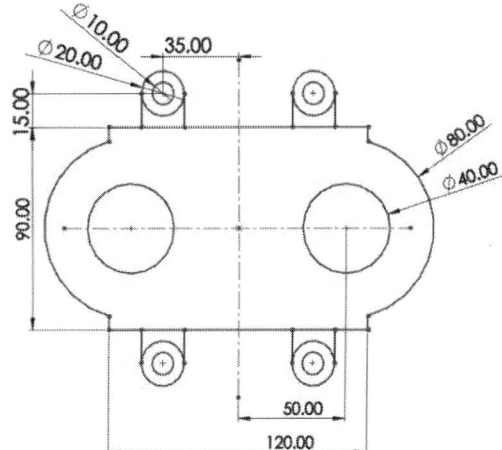

➤ Using the **Trim Entities tool,** trim the unwanted entities (as discussed above), as shown.

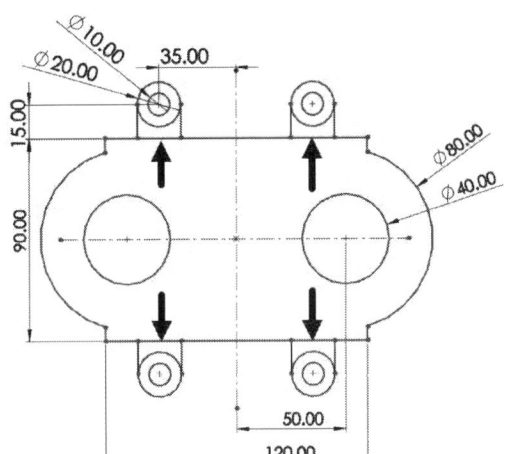 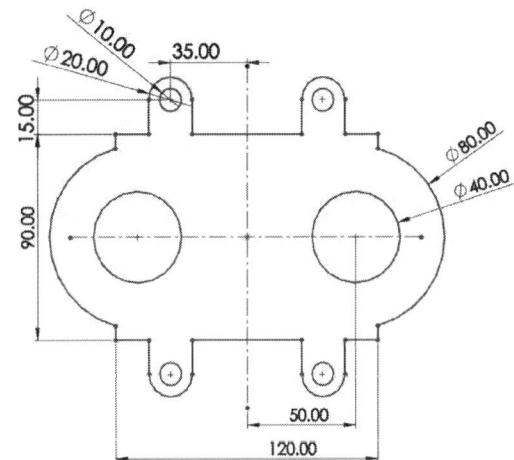

➤ The sketch is complete, click on the **Exit Sketch** button from the **Sketch CommandManager** to exit from the sketch environment and display model.

Alternatively, you can click on the button from the top right corner of the drawing area to exit from sketch environment.

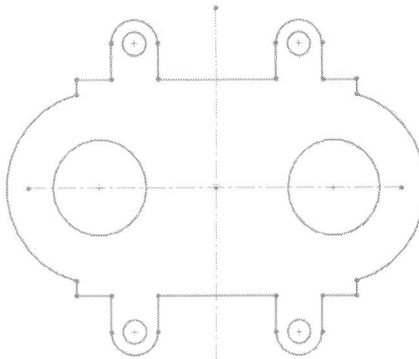

➤ Click on the **Save (Ctrl + S)** button from the **Menu Bar** to display the **Save As** dialog box.
➤ Next browse to the folder of **chapter 4** and enter name **Ch04-exam02** in the **File name** edit box.
➤ Click on the **Save** button from the dialog box to save the file.
➤ Now enter the **Close** button from the upper right corner to close it.

Applying Dimensions and Geometric Relations 4-25

Example 3

In this example, you will create the sketch shown below.

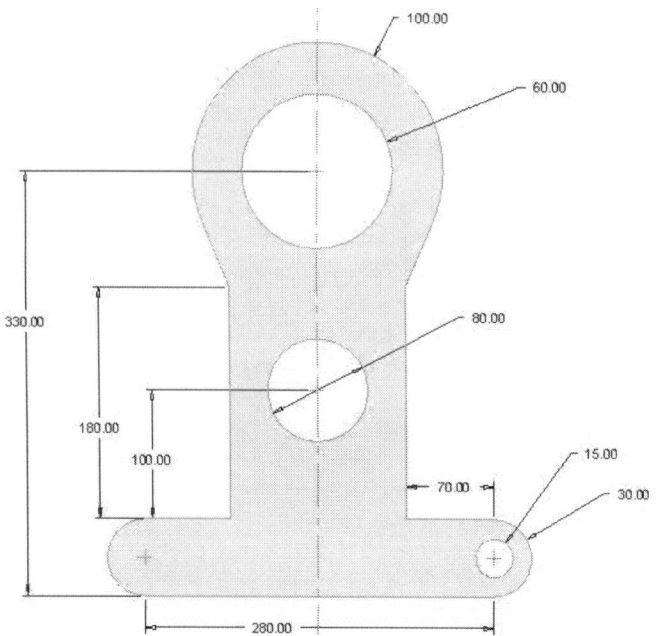

- Start SolidWorks 2021 by clicking **SOLIDWORKS 2021** icon on your desktop.
- Click on the **New** (📄) button from the **Menu Bar** to display the **New SOLIDWORKS Document** dialog box, as shown.

  Alternatively, press **Ctrl + N** key from the keyboard to display the **New SOLIDWORKS Document** dialog box.

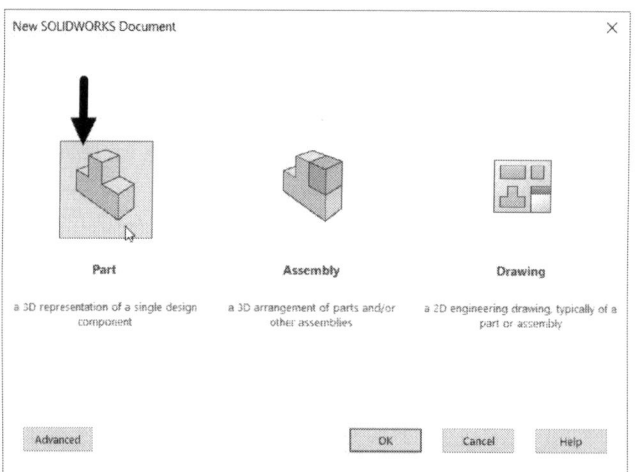

- Double click on the **Part** button to enter in the Sketching Environment.
- Next for the better visibility of display, change the background colour to white, as discussed in previous chapter.
- Click on the **Sketch** tab to display tools used in creating sketch.
- Click on the **Sketch** button from the **Sketch CommandManager** and then click on the **Front** plane to make it parallel to the screen, as shown in previous example.

- Select the **Corner Rectangle** tool (**Sketch > Rectangle > Corner Rectangle**) to activate it and draw the sketch, as shown.

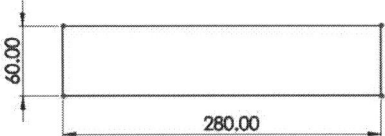

- Create the vertical centerline at the middle of the rectangle, as shown.

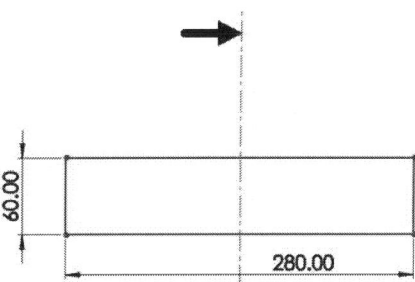

- Select the **Add Relation** option from the **Display/Delete Relations** drop down to display the Add Relations PropertyManager, as shown.

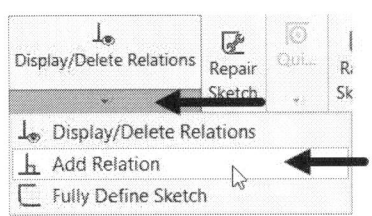 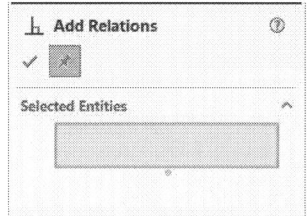

- Select the two vertical lines of rectangle and then select the vertical centreline, as shown.
- Next select the **Symmetric** button from the PropertyManager to apply Symmetric relation.

  Note that as the relations are not visible, select the **View Sketch Relations** button from the **Hide/Show Items** flyout in the **View (Head-Up)** toolbar to make all relations visible, as shown. Note that, you can toggle between visibility of relations in the drawing area by using the same button.

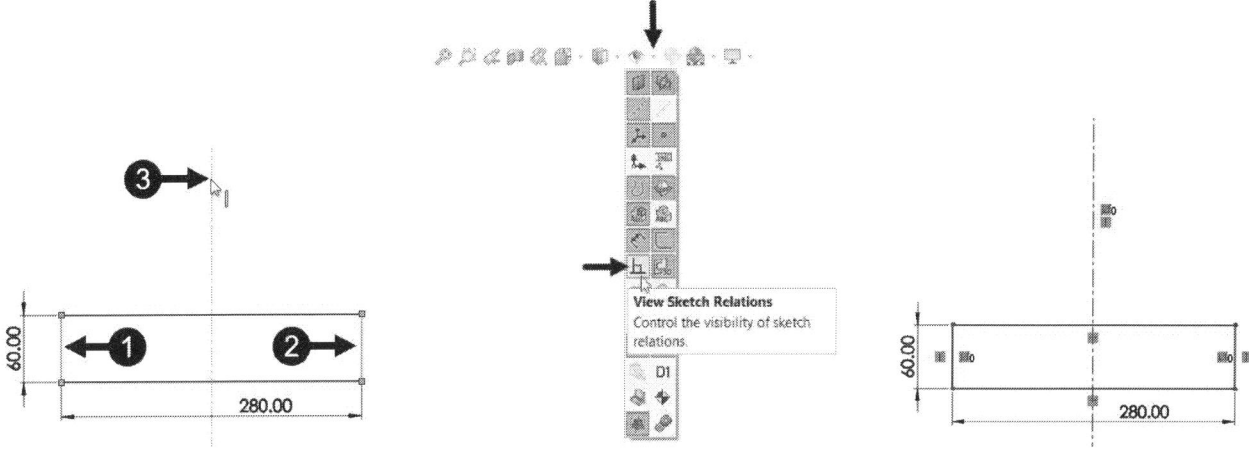

- Activate the **Line** tool and draw the line entity on the left side of the centerline and apply the dimensions, as shown.

Applying Dimensions and Geometric Relations 4-27

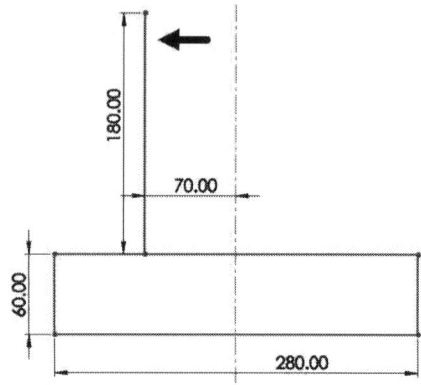

- Now activate the **Mirror Entities** tool and select the line entity, as shown.
- Next click in the **Mirror about** selection box of the PropertyManager and select the vertical center line to display preview of mirrored entities, as shown.
- Click on the **OK** button of the PropertyManager to exit it and display the mirrored entities, as shown.

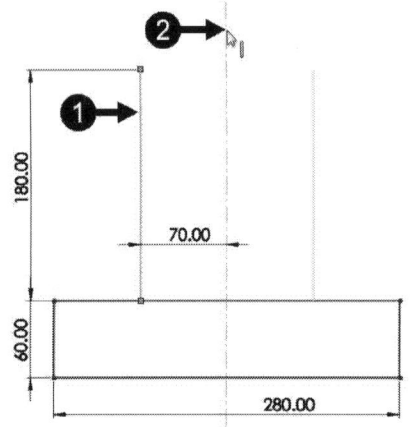
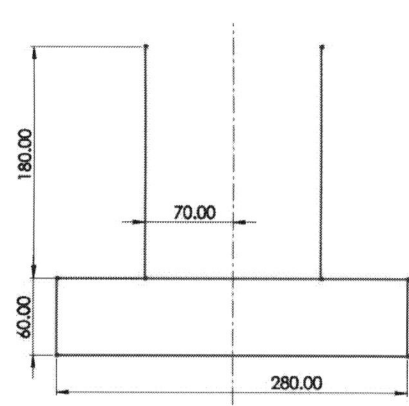

- Now select the **3 Point Arc** tool from the **Arc** drop-down.
- Click at the upper two points of the line entities one-by-one, as shown.
- Move the cursor in upward direction and enter **100** in the dimension edit box displayed, as shown.
- Press the **Enter** key and then the **Esc** key to display arc entity created, as shown.
- Using the **Smart Dimension** tool, apply dimension to recently created arc entity, as shown.

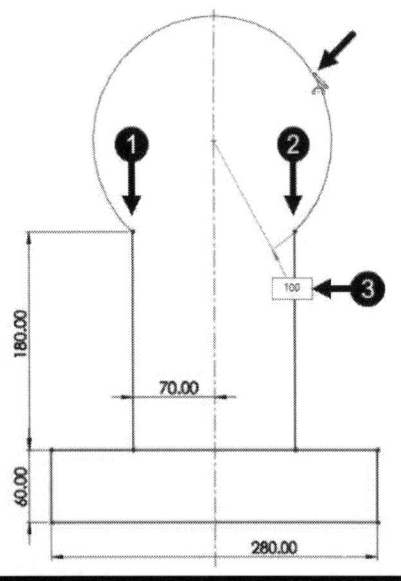
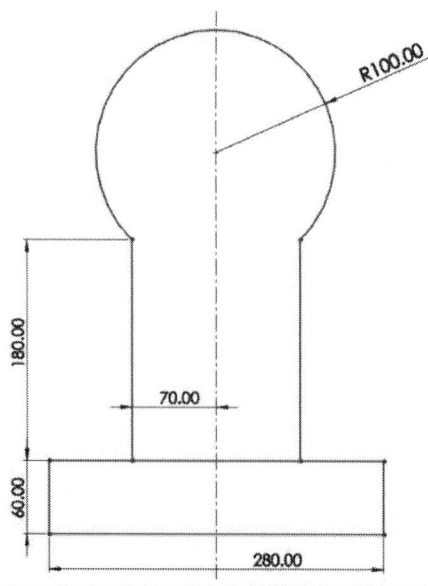

- Now activate the **Center** tool from the **Circle** drop-down.
- Click at the center of the recently drawn arc.
- Move the cursor upto some distance and enter **120** in the dimension edit box displayed, as shown.
- Activate the **Smart Dimensions** tool and apply the dimension to the recently drawn circle, as shown.

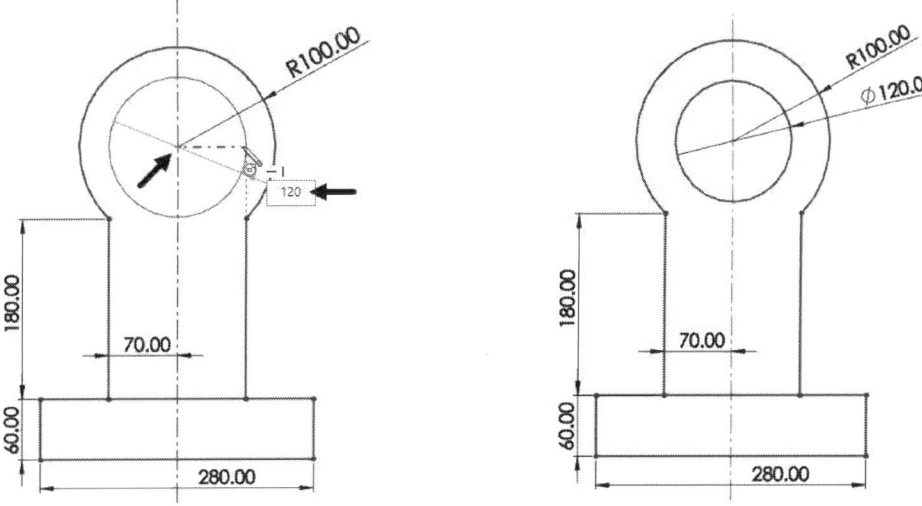

- Create another circle and apply dimensions, as shown.

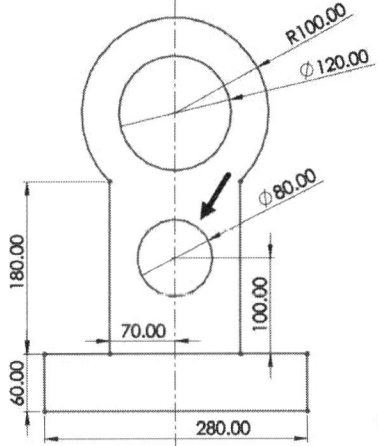

- Activate the **Centerpoint Arc** tool from the **Arc** drop-down.
- Click at the midpoint of the bottom right vertical line, as shown.
- Then click at the two endpoint of the line entity one-by-one to display arc, as shown.

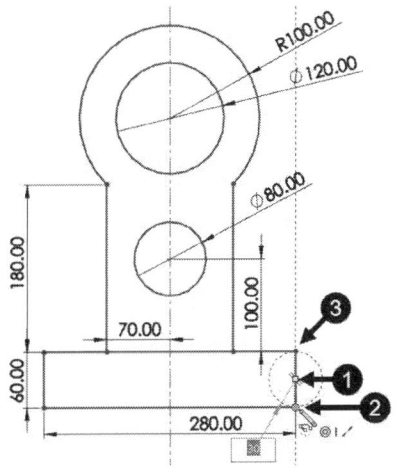 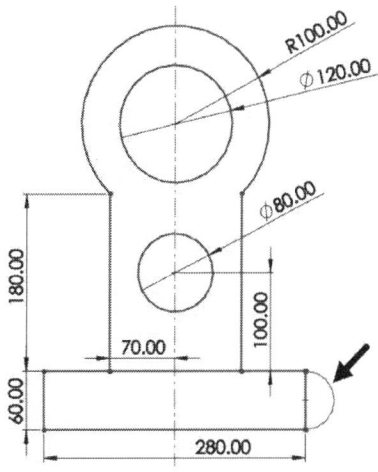

Applying Dimensions and Geometric Relations

➢ Activate the **Mirror** Entities tool and mirror the recently created arc entity, as shown.

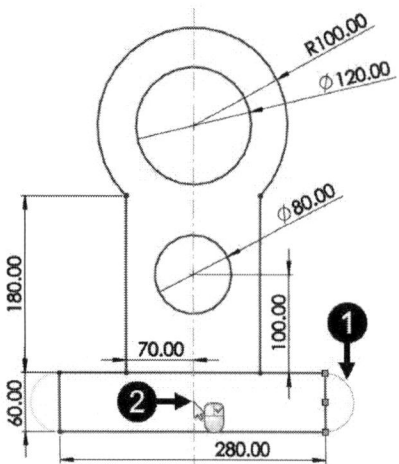 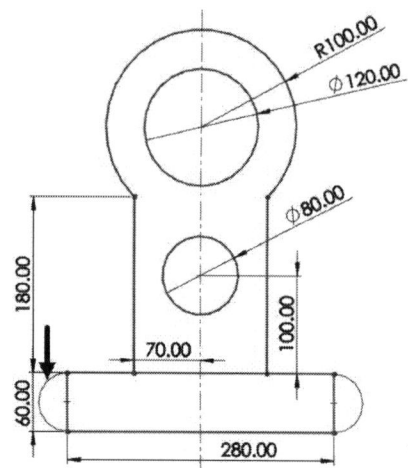

➢ Using the centerpoint of both arcs draw the circles, as shown.

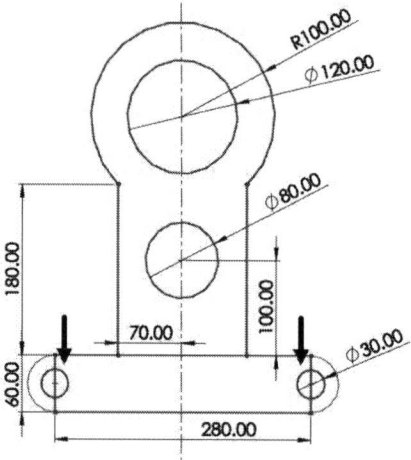

➢ Activate the **Trim Entities** tool and trim the unwanted entities, as shown.

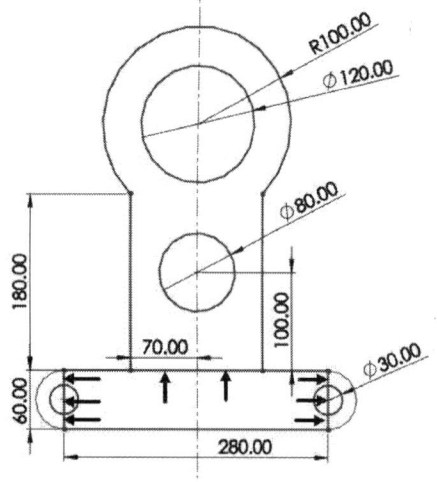 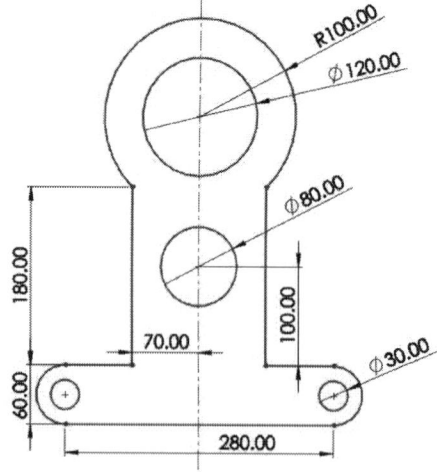

➢ Activate the **Sketch Fillet** tool from the **Sketch CommandManager** to display the **Sketch Fillet PropertyManager**.
➢ Enter **20** in the **Fillet Radius** box of the PropertyManager and select the edges to round their corners, as shown.
➢ Click on the OK button of the PropertyManager to display the filleted features, as shown.

Applying Dimensions and Geometric Relations

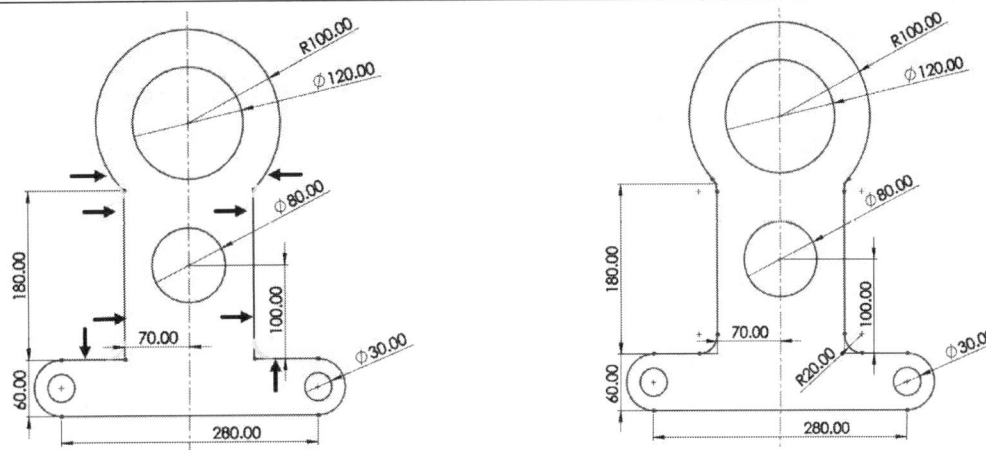

As discussed earlier, you can toggle the visibility of all relations by selecting the **View Sketch Relations** button from the **Hide/Show Items** flyout in the **View (Head-Up)** toolbar, as shown.

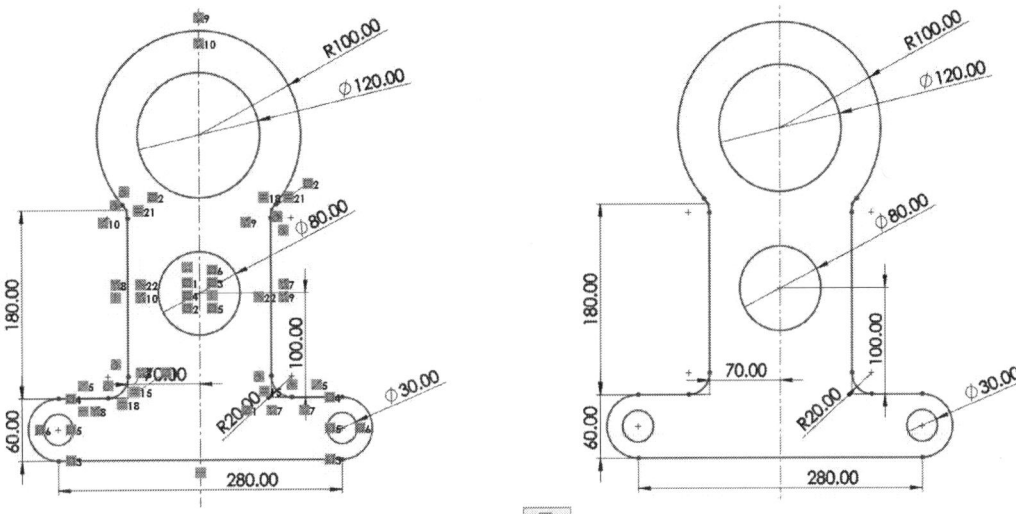

> The sketch is complete, click on the **Exit Sketch** button from the **Sketch CommandManager** to exit from the sketch environment and display model.

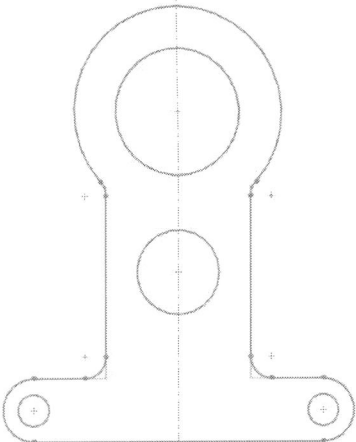

> Click on the **Save (Ctrl + S)** button from the **Menu Bar** to display the **Save As** dialog box.
> Next browse to the folder of **chapter 4** and enter name **Ch04-exam03** in the **File name** edit box.
> Click on the **Save** button from the dialog box to save the file.
> Now enter the **Close** button from the upper right corner to close it.

Questions:

1. What is the use of **Smart Dimension** tool?
2. What is the use of **Ordinate Dimension** tool?
3. How can we apply **Collinear** and **Coincident** relation between selected entities?
4. How can we use **Path Length Dimension** option and where is it available?
5. What is the use of **Merge** relation?
6. How can you measure vertical dimensions vertically?

Chapter 05: Solid Modeling Tools

Sketch-Based features are used to create basic and simple parts. Most of the times, they form the base for complex parts as well. These features are easy to create and require a single sketch. Now, you will learn the commands to create these features.

The topics covered in this chapter are:

- ❖ Extruded Boss/Base Tool
- ❖ Extruded Cut Tool
- ❖ Revolved Boss/Base Tool
- ❖ Revolve the Sketch as Surface
- ❖ Revolved Cut Tool

 ## Extruded Boss/Base Tool

The Extrude is the process of creating a two-dimensional profile and converting it into three-dimensional, perpendicular to the sketching plane and by giving it the required depth value. In order to create a cylinder, draw a circle and after selecting the **Extrude Boss/Base** tool, select it. The **Extrude Boss/Base** tool allows you to create a solid or surface, and add material. After selecting this tool from the **Features CommandManager**; the **Boss-Extrude PropertyManager** will be displayed as shown.

Some of the important options used in the **Boss-Extrude PropertyManager** are discussed next.

From

The options in the **Start Condition** drop down under **From** rollout are used to set the starting condition for the extrude feature.

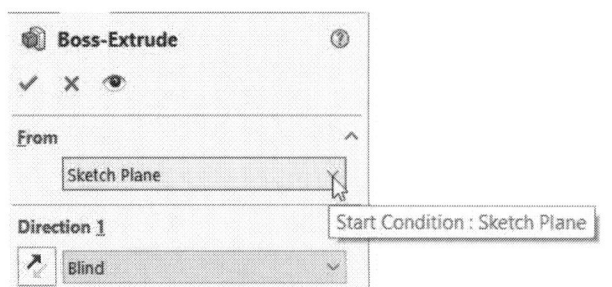 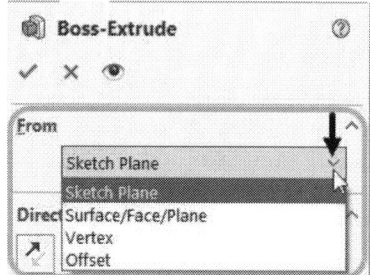

Sketch Plane

This option is selected to start the extrude from the plane on which the sketch is located, as shown. It is selected by default.

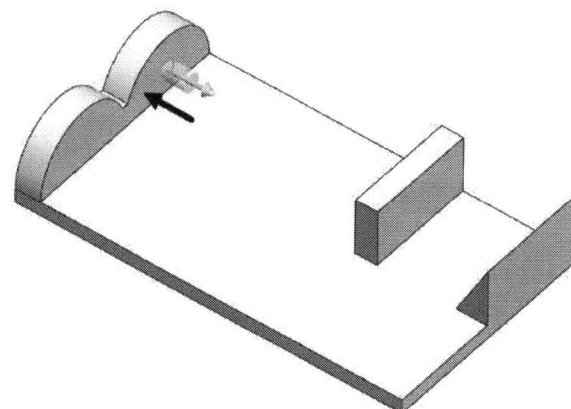

Surface/Face/Plane

This option is selected to start the extrude from the selected face/surface/plane, as shown.

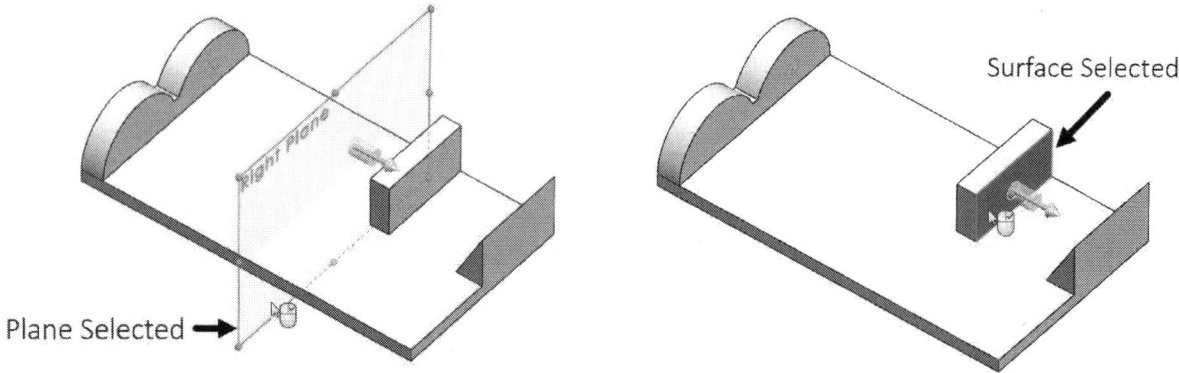

Vertex

This option is selected to start the extrude from the selected vertex, as shown.

Solid Modeling Tools

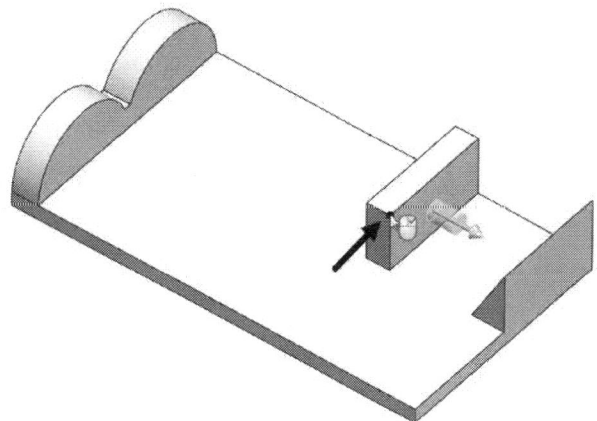

Offset

This option is selected to start the extrude at offset distance from the current sketching plane, as shown. By entering the required offset distance value in the **Enter Offset Value** spinner, as shown.

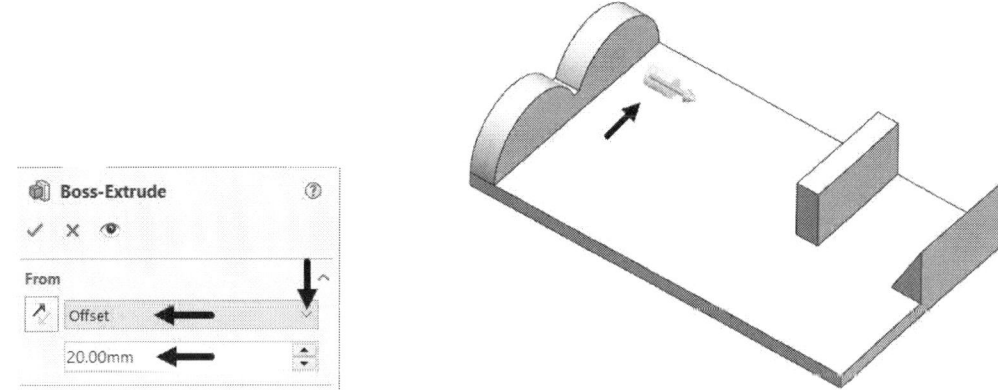

Direction 1

The options in this rollout are used to set the end condition for extruding the sketch in one direction from the sketching plane. The options in this rollout are discussed next.

End Condition

This options in this drop-down list are used to specify depth or depth values while using the **Extrude** tool to extrude the sketch. These options are discussed next.

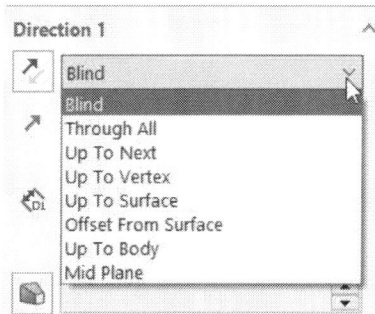

You can click on the ↗ **Reverse Direction** button to extrude the sketch in opposite direction.

> **Note:** Some of the options in the **End Condition** drop-down will not be available while creating the first feature.

Blind

This option is selected by default and is used to extrude a sketch from the sketching plane by the specified depth value, entered in the **Depth** spinner, as shown.

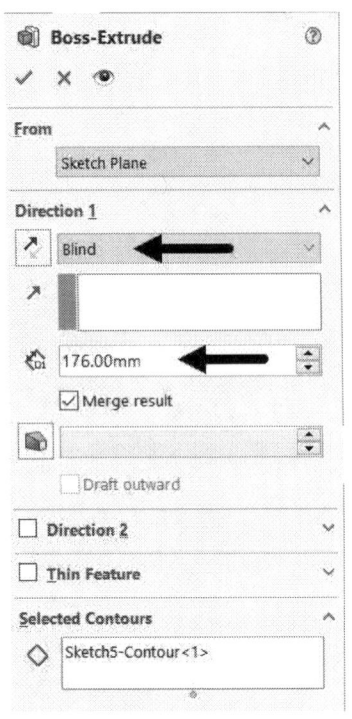

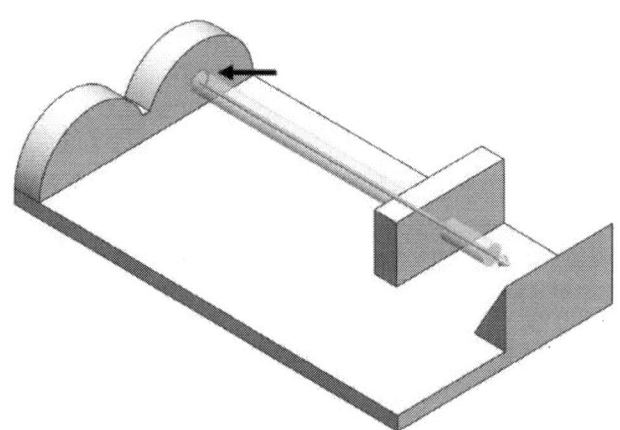

Through All

This option is selected to extrude the sketch through all surfaces, as shown.

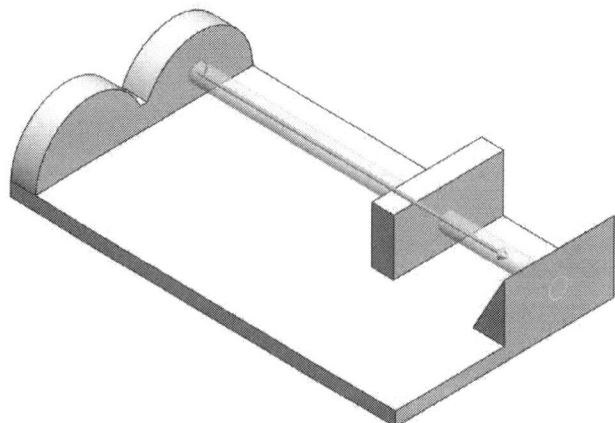

Up To Next

This option is selected to extrude a section up to the next surface, as shown. You cannot use a datum plane as a terminating surface.

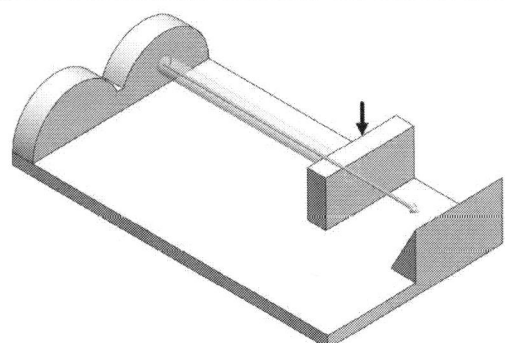

Up To Vertex
This option is selected to extrude a sketch up to the surface of the selected vertex, as shown.

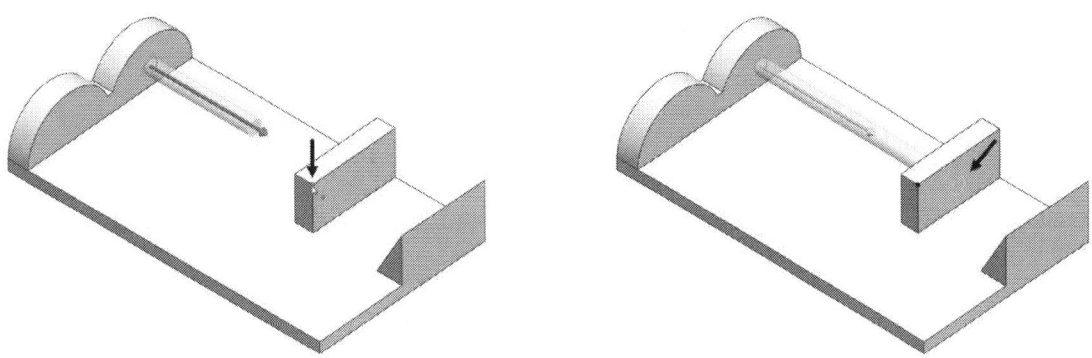

Up To Surface
This option is selected to extrude a section to the selected surface or plane, as shown.

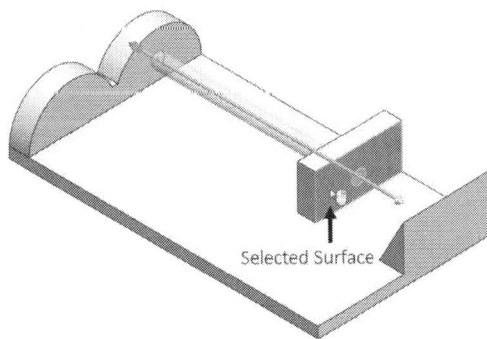

Offset From Surface
This option is selected to extrude a section up to the specified offset distance from the selected surface or plane, as shown.

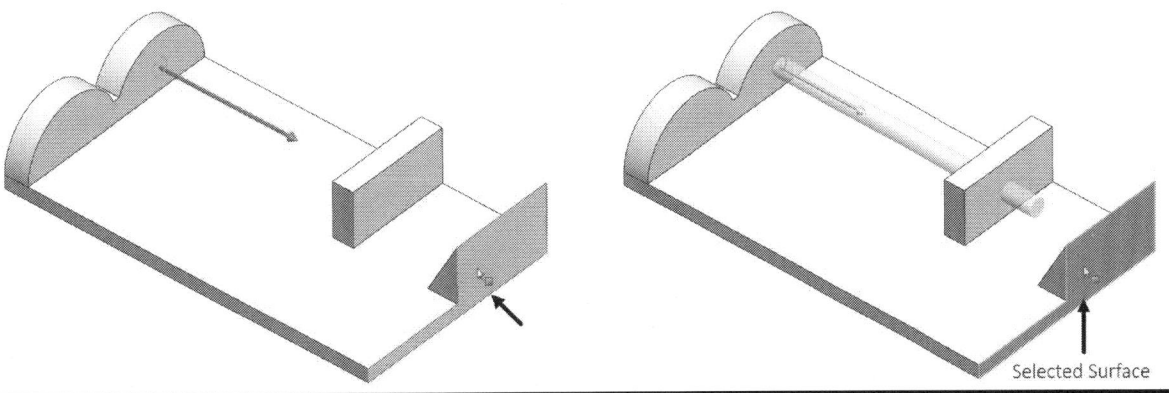

Up To Body

This option is selected to extrude a section up to the selected body, as shown.

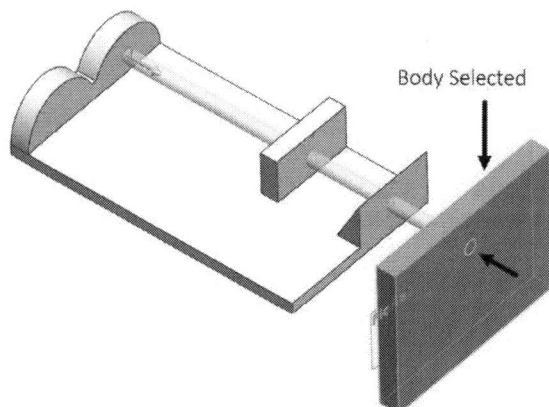

Mid Plane

The **Mid Plane** option is selected to extrude the sketch symmetrically in both the directions of the plane or selected surface on which the sketch is drawn, as shown.

You can also select and drag the handle to adjust the extruded sketch, as shown.

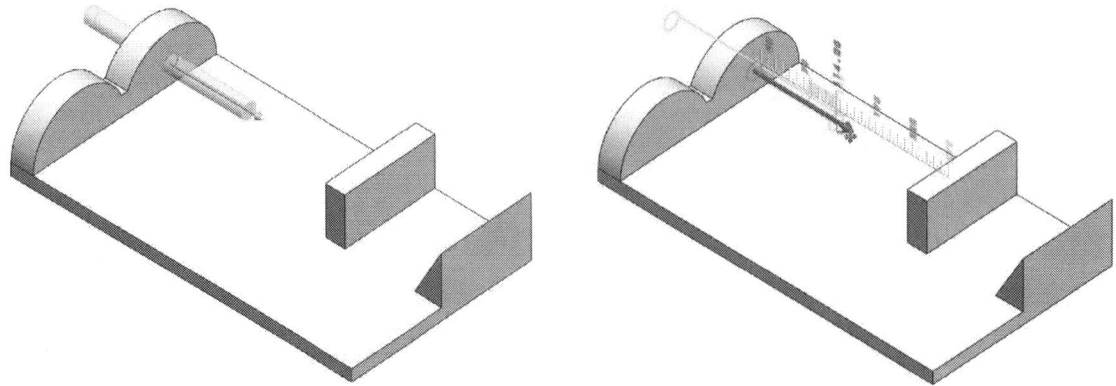

Direction of Extrusion

This is used to extrude a section along the direction vector like linear edges, vertices, reference points, sketch points and so on. Below is the figure in which the section is extruded along the line entity, selected as a direction vector.

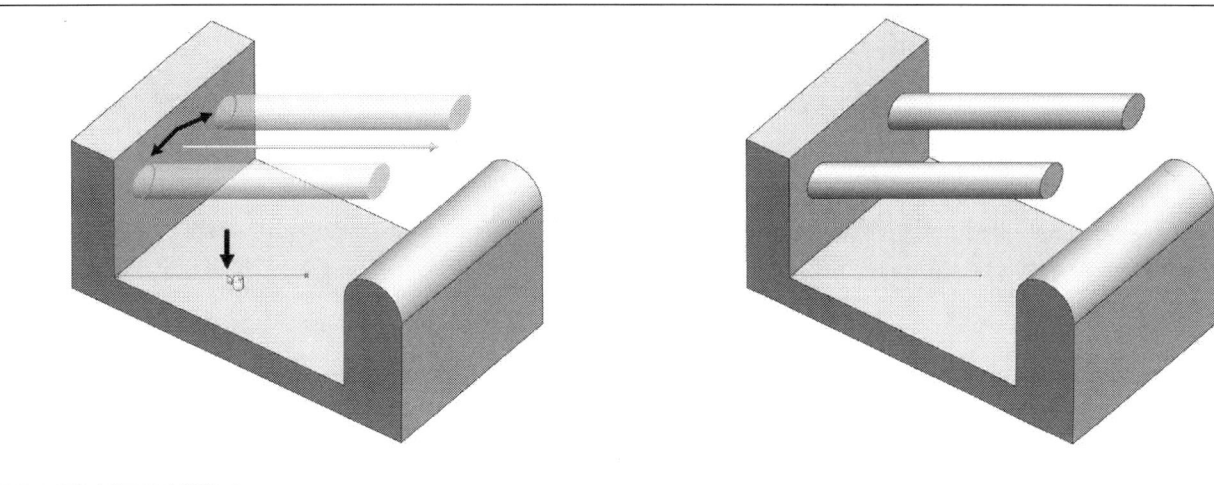

 Depth Spinner

This spinner is used to set the required depth value for the extruding feature. You can also enter required depth value in it.

Merge result

This checkbox is selected to merge the resultant body with the existing body if possible. Unless the feature creates an individual sold body.

Draft On/Off

This button is selected to specify the draft angle to taper the resultant feature while extruding the sketch. This button is not selected by default.

> Select the **Draft On/Off** button to activate **Draft Angle** spinner, as shown.

 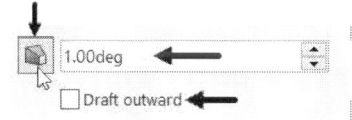

> Enter the required draft angle value in the **Draft Angle** spinner to display preview of the extrude feature with taper inwards, as shown.
> Select the **Draft outward** checkbox to taper the feature outwards, as shown.

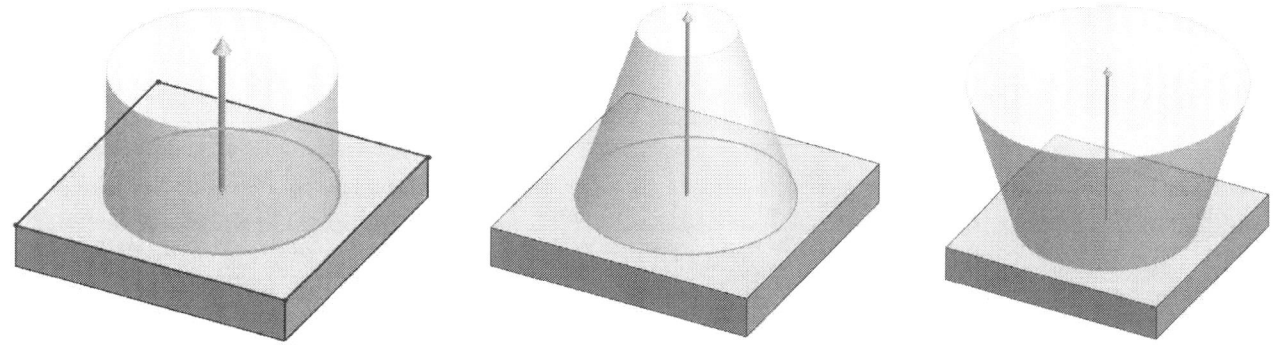

☐ Direction 2   Direction 2

This checkbox is selected to extrude the sketch in both directions or with different depth values from the sketching plane. Note that, this checkbox will not be available, if you select **Mid Plane** from the **End Condition** drop-down list of the **Boss-Extrude PropertyManager**, as discussed earlier.

The **Direction 2** rollout and its option get activated only after selecting **Direction 2** checkbox. The use of options in this rollout is same as of options in the **Direction 1** rollout, as discussed above.

☐ Thin Feature   Thin Feature

This checkbox is selected to activate the options used for creating thin features with required thickness like sheet metal components. The use of options in this rollout will be discussed further in this book.

◇   Selected Contours

This is used to select partial region/sketch to create extrude features along it.

> ➢ Activate the **Extruded Boss/Base** tool to display the **Boss-Extrude PropertyManager**.
> ➢ Now click on the partial region of sketch to extrude it and display the preview of extruded feature, as shown.

   Also, the selected sketch gets visible in the **Selected Contours** box of the PropertyManager, as shown.

> ➢ Next, you can enter the required depth value in the **Depth** spinner or select and drag the extruded handle, as shown.

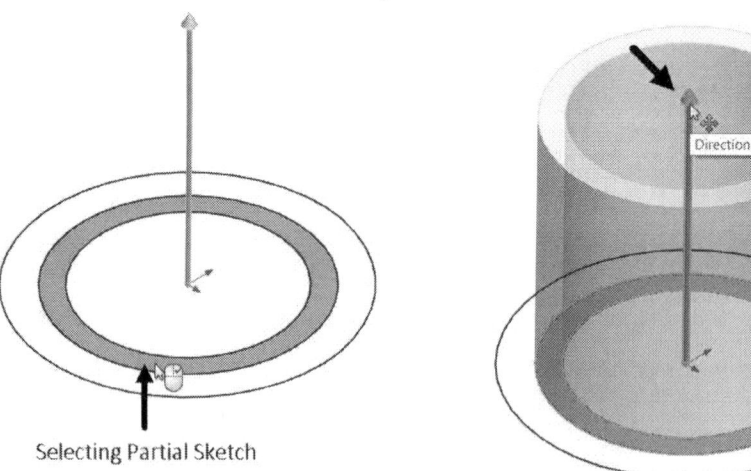
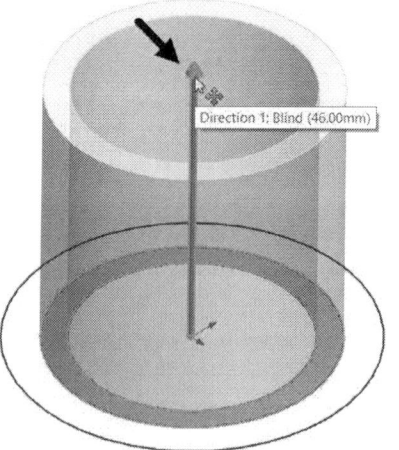

Selecting Partial Sketch

Note: To extrude other portions of sketch later, you need to make the sketch entities visible. To toggle between visibility of sketch entities, right click over the **Sketch** from the **FeatureManager Design Tree** and select the **Show** 👁 or **Hide** 🚫 button from the shortcut menu displayed, as shown.

Solid Modeling Tools

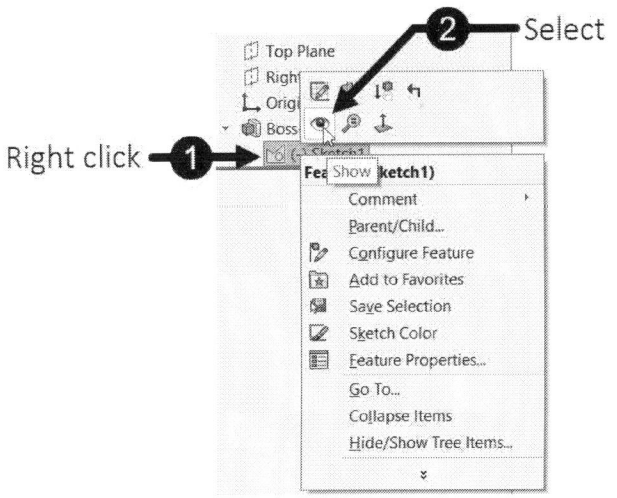
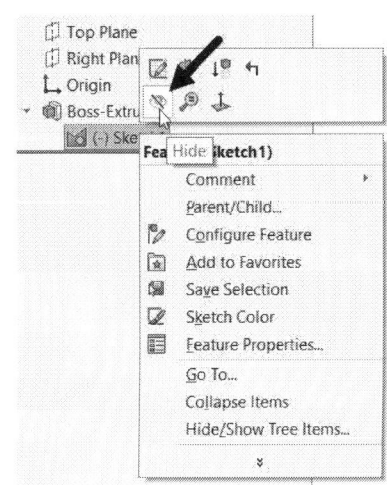

> Now select the other portion of sketch to extrude it, as shown.

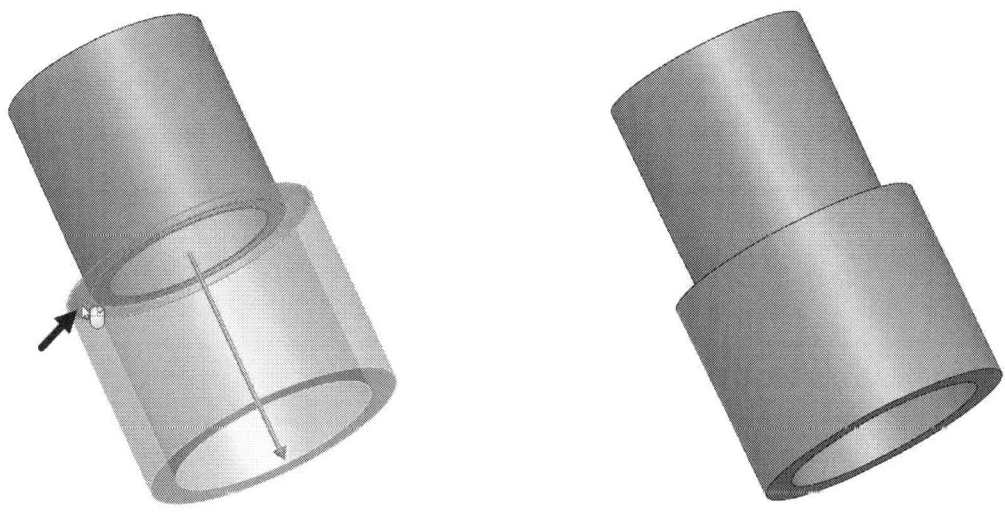

To deselect any unwanted contours:

> Right-click over the sketch to be removed from the **Selected Contours** box to display the shortcut menu, as shown.
> Next, select the **Delete** option to deselect it, as shown.

> To clear all selected regions/sketches, again right click in the **Selected Contours** box and select the **Clear Selections** from the shortcut menu, as shown.

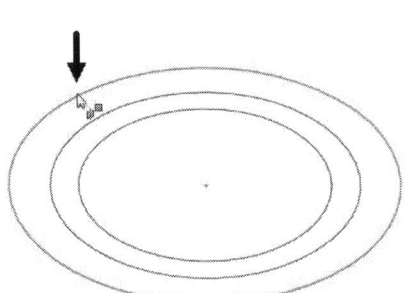
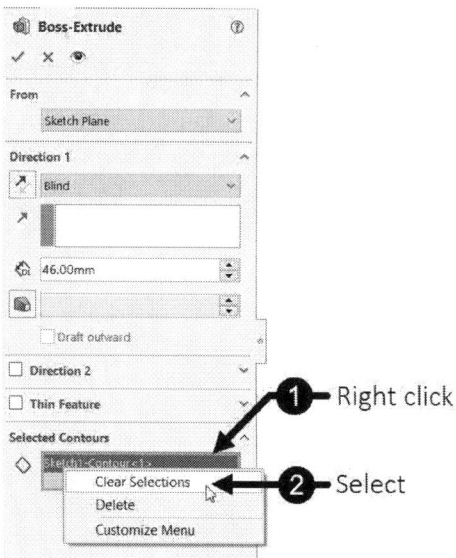

Extruded Cut Tool

The Extruded cut is the process of removing the material from the previously created features. By creating a two-dimensional profile and then extruded perpendicular to the sketching plane to remove material from the previously created features by selecting the required options. After selecting **Extruded Cut** tool from the **Features CommandManager**; the **Cut-Extrude PropertyManager** will get displayed as shown.

The use of options in **Cut-Extrude PropertyManager** is same as discussed earlier in **Boss-Extrude PropertyManager**. The only difference is these options are used to remove material. Some of the important options used in the **Cut-Extrude PropertyManager** are discussed next.

From

The options in the **Start Condition** drop down under **From** rollout are used to set the starting condition for the extrude cut feature.

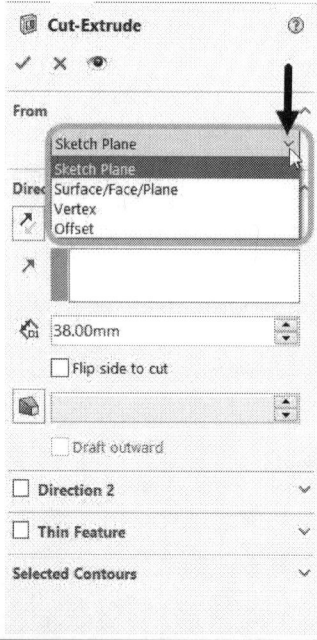

Sketch Plane

This option is selected to start the extruded cut from the plane on which the sketch is located.

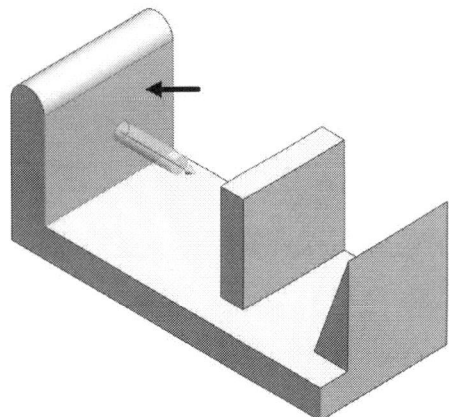

Surface/Face/Plane

This option is selected to start the extruded cut from the selected face/surface/plane, as shown.

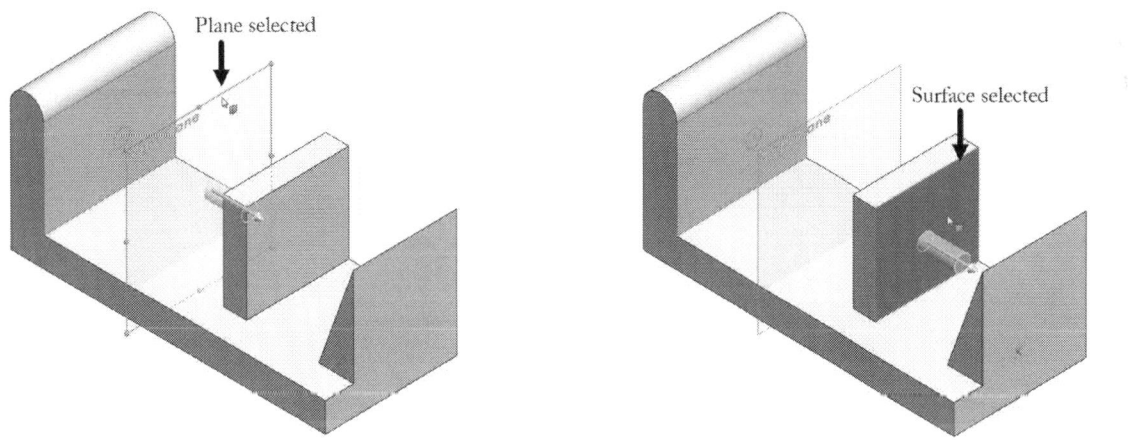

Vertex

This option is selected to start the extruded cut from the selected vertex, as shown.

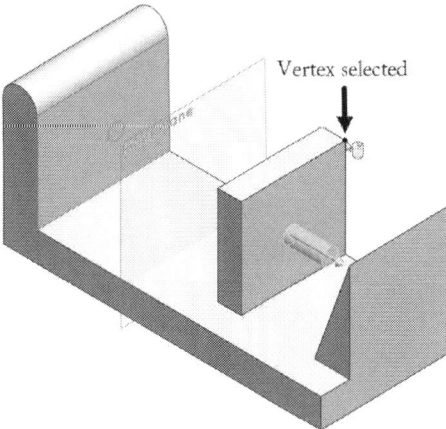

Offset

This option is selected to start the extruded cut at offset distance from the current sketching plane, as shown. By entering the required offset distance value in the **Enter Offset Value** spinner, as shown.

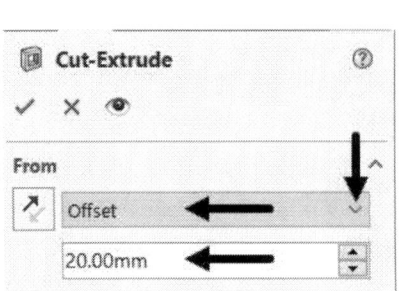
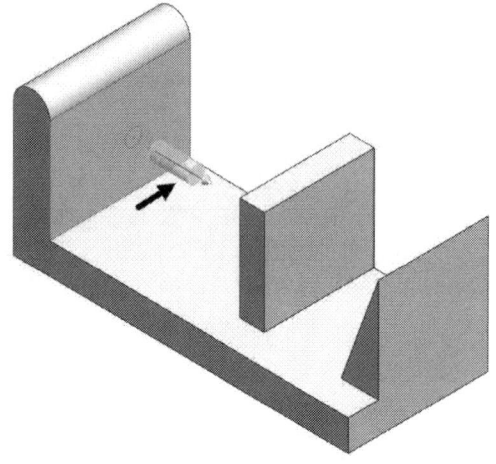

Direction 1

The options in this rollout are used to set the end condition or target for extruding the sketch in one direction from the sketching plane. The options in this rollout are discussed next.

End Condition

This options in this drop-down are used to specify depth or depth values while using the **Extruded Cut** tool to extrude the sketch. These options are discussed next.

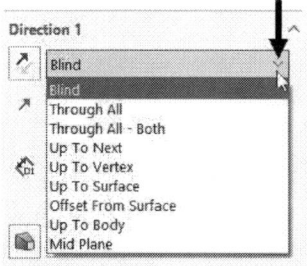

Blind

This option is selected by default and is used to extrude the sketch to the specified depth value, entered in the **Depth** spinner to cut the solid feature, as shown.

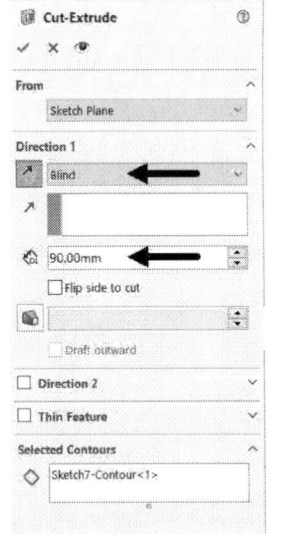
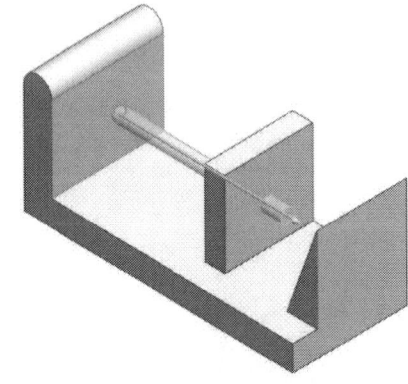
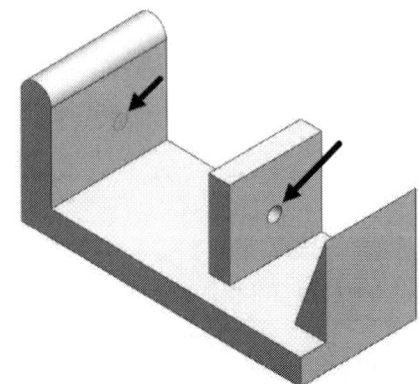

Through All

This option is selected to extrude the sketch through all surfaces to cut the solid feature, as shown.

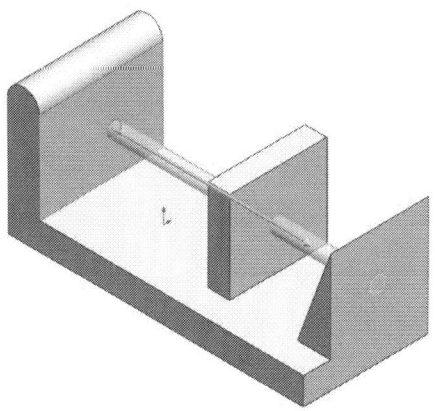 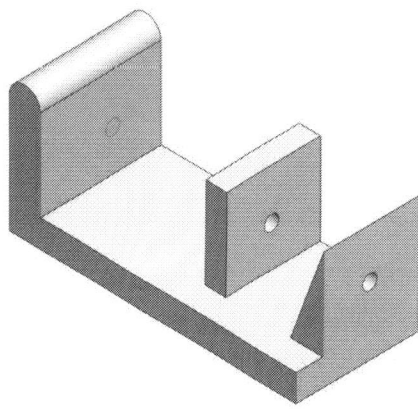

Through All - Both

This option is selected to extrude the sketch through all surfaces in both directions to cut the solid feature, as shown.

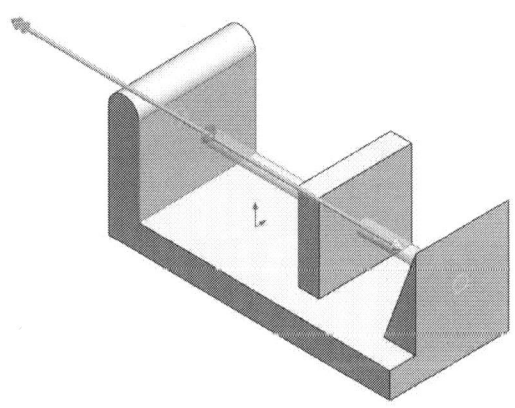 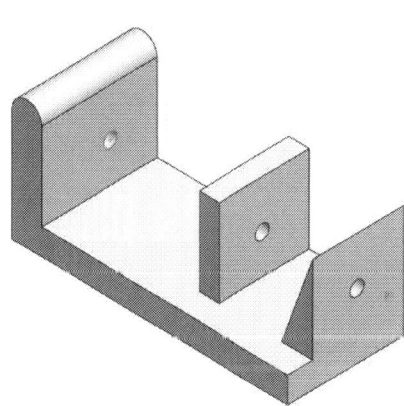

Up To Next

This option is selected to extrude the section up to the next surface to cut the solid feature, as shown.

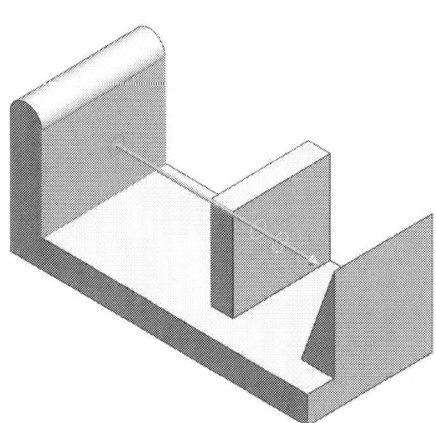 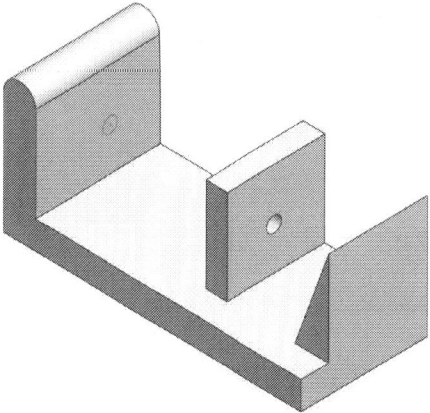

Up To Vertex

This option is selected to extrude the section up to the surface of the selected vertex to cut the solid feature, as shown.

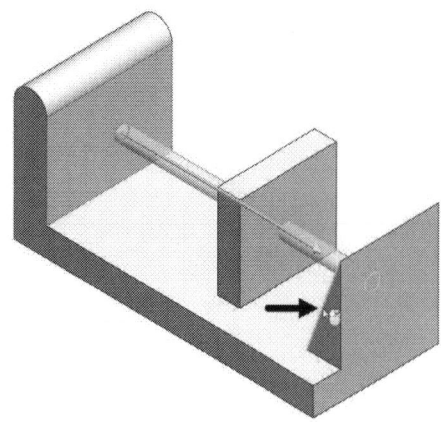 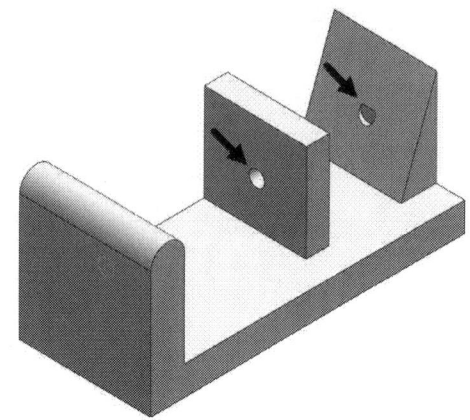

Up To Surface

This option is selected to extrude the section up to the selected surface or plane to cut the solid feature, as shown.

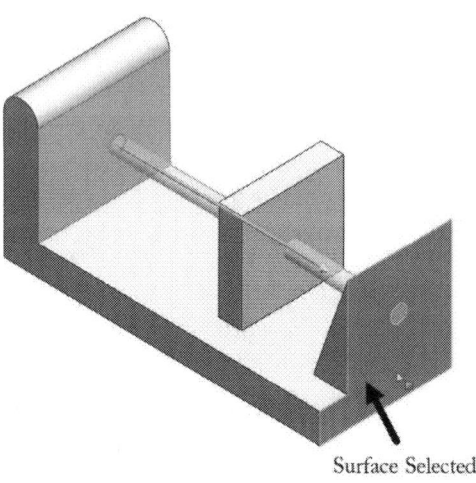 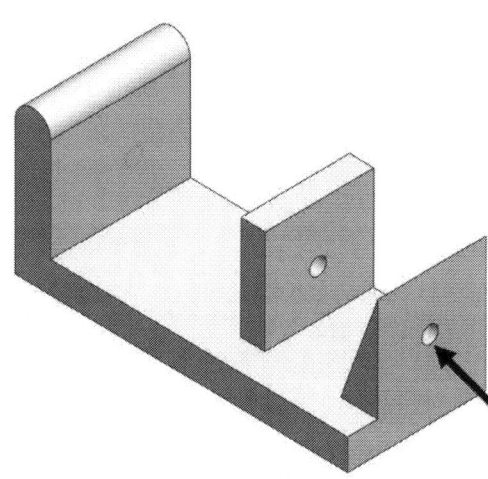

Surface Selected

Offset From Surface

This option is selected to extrude the section with specified offset distance from the selected surface or plane to cut the solid feature, as shown.

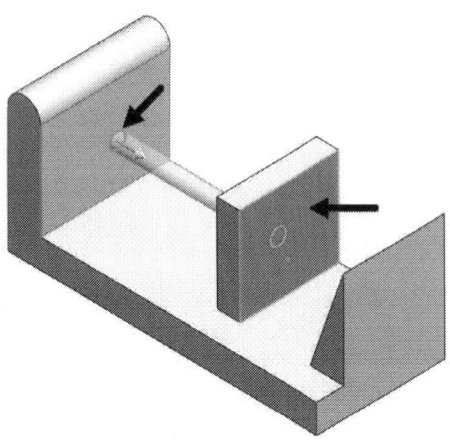 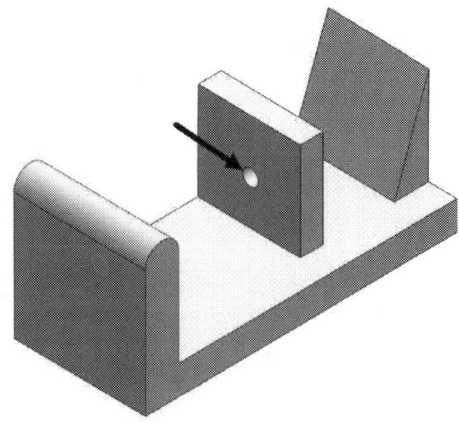

Up To Body

This option is selected to extrude the section up to the selected body to cut the solid feature, as shown.

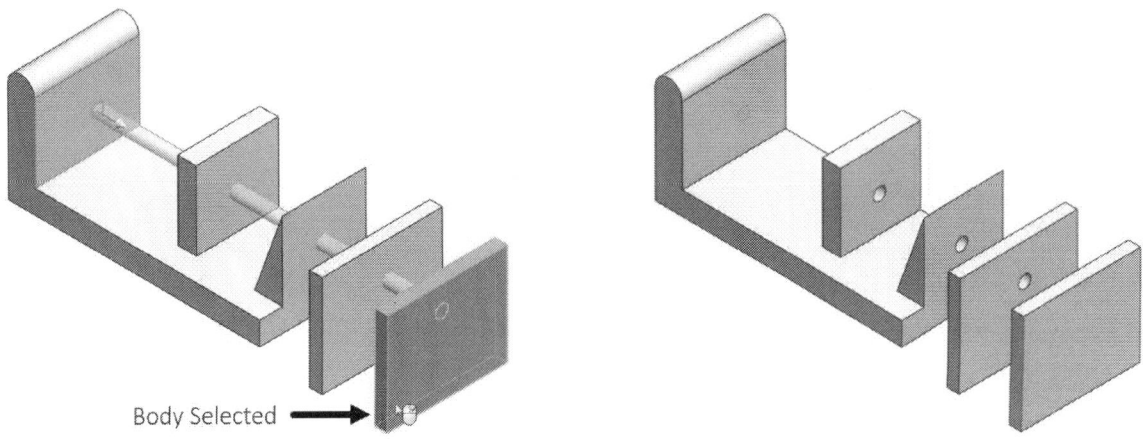

Body Selected

Mid Plane

The **Mid Plane** option is selected to extrude the sketch symmetrically in both the directions of the plane or selected surface on which the sketch is drawn to cut the solid feature, as shown.

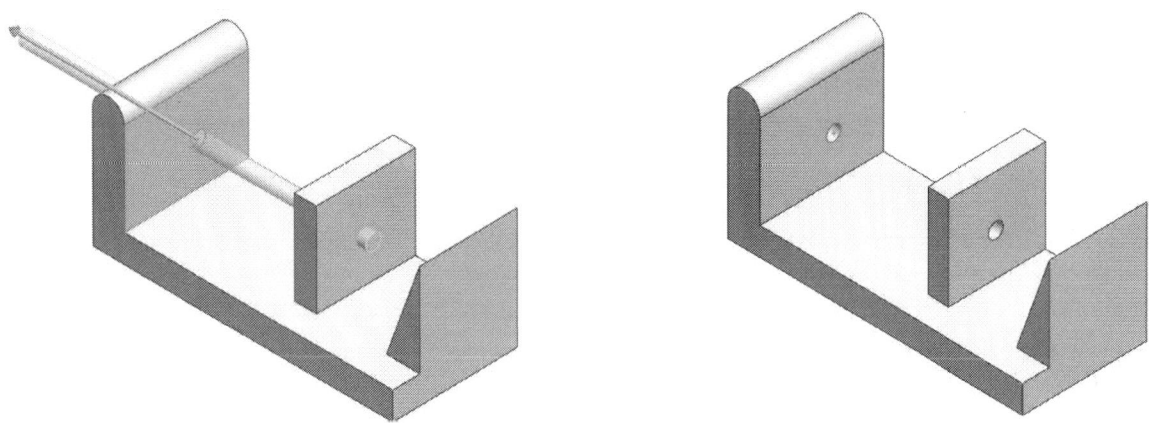

You can also select and drag the handle to adjust the extruded sketch, as shown.

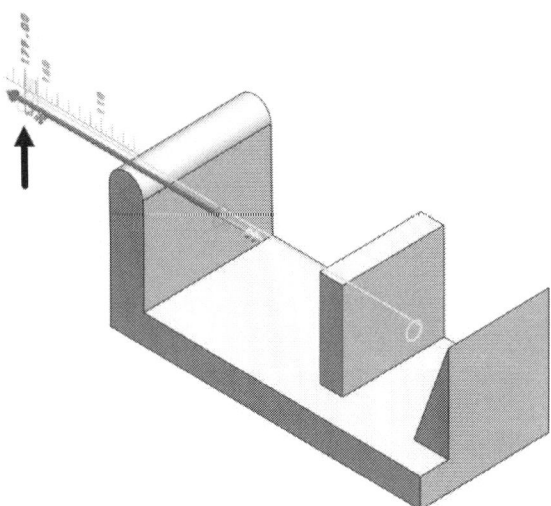

Direction of Extrusion

This is used to extrude a section along the direction vector like linear edges, vertices, reference points, sketch points and so on. Below is the figure in which the section is extruded along the line entity, selected as a direction vector.

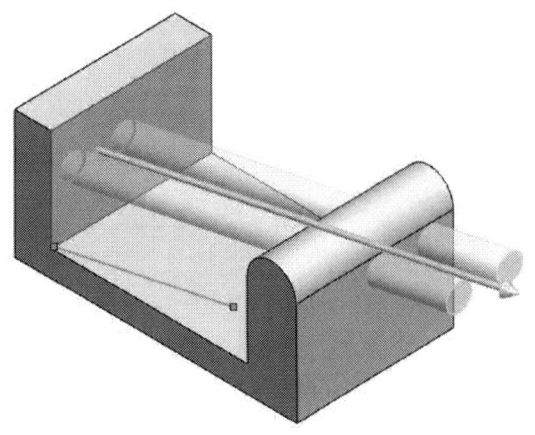 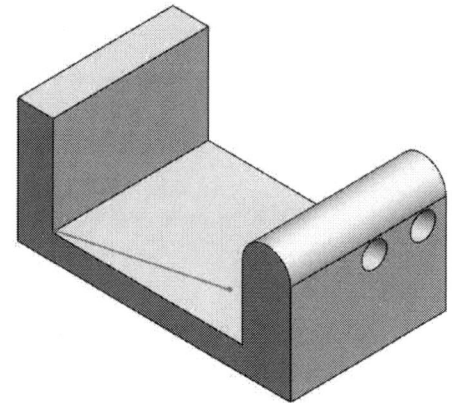

Depth Spinner
This spinner is used to enter the depth value for the extruding feature to cut the solid feature.

Draft On/Off
This button is selected to specify the draft angle to taper the resultant feature while extruding the sketch. By default, this button is not selected.

> Select the **Draft On/Off** button to activate **Draft Angle** spinner and **Draft outward** checkbox, as shown.

 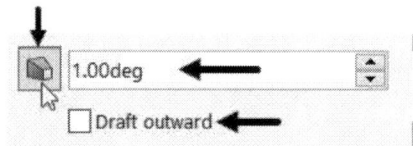

> Enter the required draft angle value in the **Draft Angle** spinner to create cut feature with taper inwards, as shown.

> Similarly, you can create cut feature with taper outwards, by selecting the **Draft outward** check box, as shown.

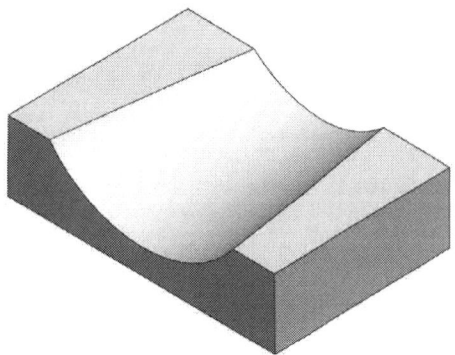 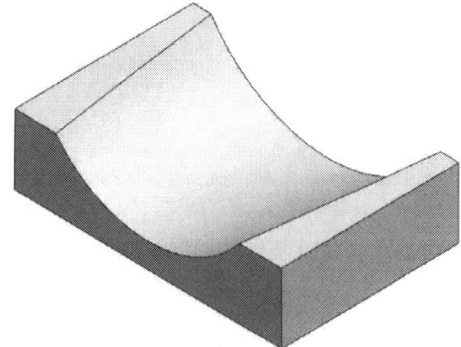

Cut feature without selecting **Draft outward** check box - **Taper Inwards**

Cut feature without selecting **Draft outward** check box - **Taper Outwards**

Direction 2
This checkbox is selected to extrude the sketch in both directions from the sketching plane. The use of options in this rollout is same like options in the **Direction 1** rollout, as discussed above. Note that, this checkbox will not be available, if you select **Mid Plane** from the **End Condition** drop-down list of the **Cut-Extrude PropertyManager**, as discussed earlier.

Below you can see Cut feature with specified **Draft Angle** values extruded in both directions after selecting **Direction 2** check box.

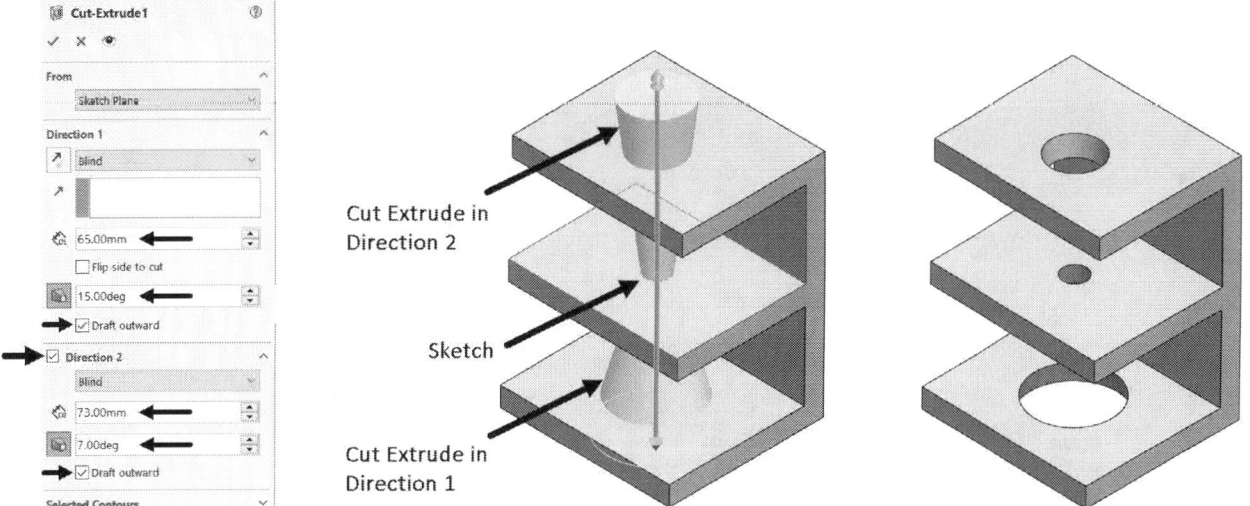

Revolved Boss/Base Tool

This revolve feature is the process of revolving a 2D sketch about a centerline at a specified angle by using the **Revolved Boss/Base** tool. It can be used to add the material.

Revolve the sketch as Solid

➢ Draw the sketch with a centerline, as shown.
➢ Click on the **Revolved Boss/Base** tool from the **Feature CommandManager** and select the axis to display **Revolve PropertyManager**, as shown.

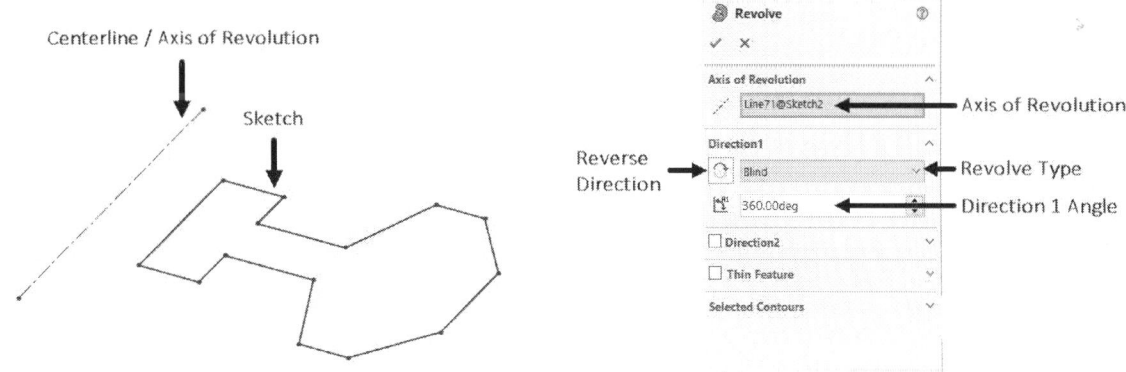

➢ Also, the sketch will be revolved with 360 degrees angle and the preview of the revolve feature get visible, as shown.

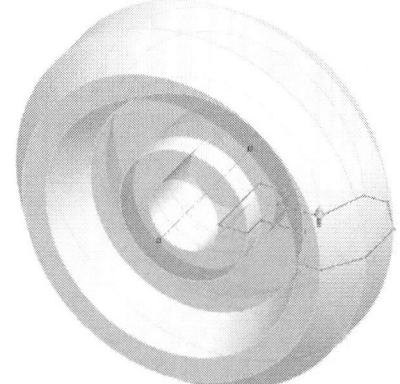

The **Axis of Revolution** option in the **Revolve PropertyManager** is used to specify the axis, about which the sketch revolves. The **Angle** spinner is used to specify the angle of rotation. By default, the sketch will be revolved with 360 degrees. You can enter the required angle value in it. The use of other options in this PropertyManager is same as that of the options in the **Boss-Extrude** PropertyManager, previously discussed.

➢ Now, click on the **OK** button to exit the tool and display the revolve model, as shown.
➢ Similarly, you can create revolve model with 270 degrees, as shown.

Also, to reverse the direction of revolution, you can use the **Reverse Direction** button under **Direction 1** rollout of the PropertyManager, if required.

Model revolved with 360 degrees

Model revolved with 270 degrees

➢ Next, you can use the **MMB** (middle mouse button) to rotate the model to change the orientation of the model, if required.

Revolve the sketch as Surface

The **Thin Feature** checkbox in the **Revolve PropertyManager** is used to create an revolve feature of thin surface or an open loop.

➢ Draw the open sketch with centerline, as shown.

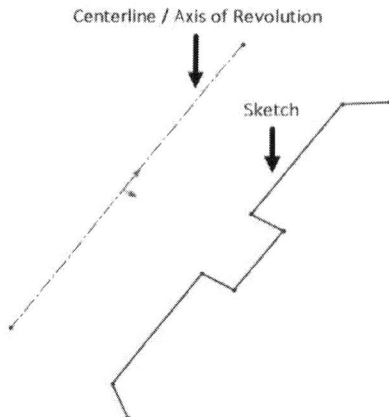

➢ Next activate the **Revolved Boss/Base** tool from the **Feature CommandManager** to display **Revolve PropertyManager**, as shown.
➢ Select the centerline as axis of revolution and click on the **No** button of the SOLIDWORKS message box displayed, to display the preview of revolve feature, as shown.

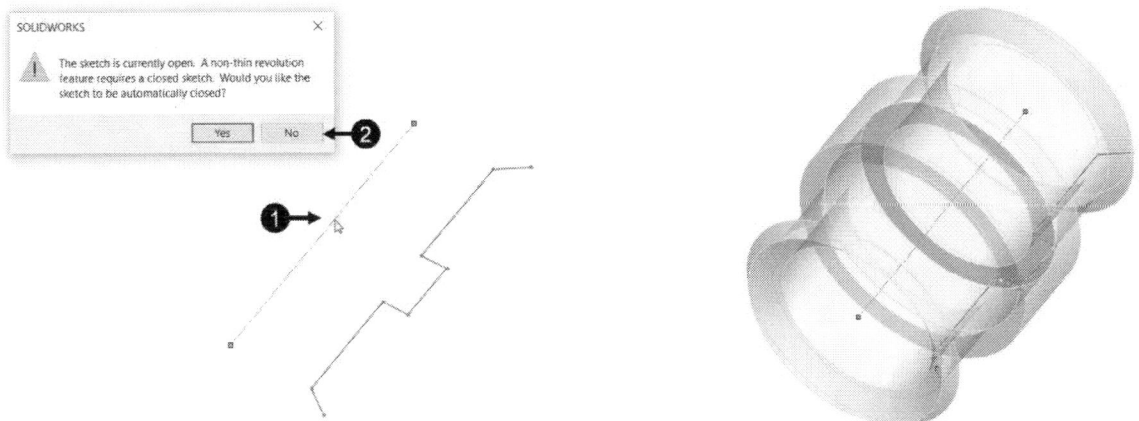

You can also specify the side for the material addition by selecting the **Reverse Direction** button and the required option from the **Type** drop-down list of the PropertyManager, as shown.

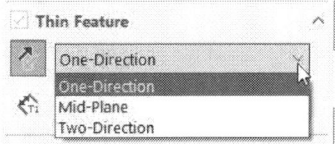

> Enter the required angle and thickness in their corresponding edit boxes of the PropertyManager, as discussed above.
> Also, click on the **Reverse Direction** button under **Direction 1** rollout of the PropertyManager, to reverse the direction of revolution, if required.
> Now, click on the **OK** button from the PropertyManager to exit the tool and display the revolve feature with thin surface, as shown.

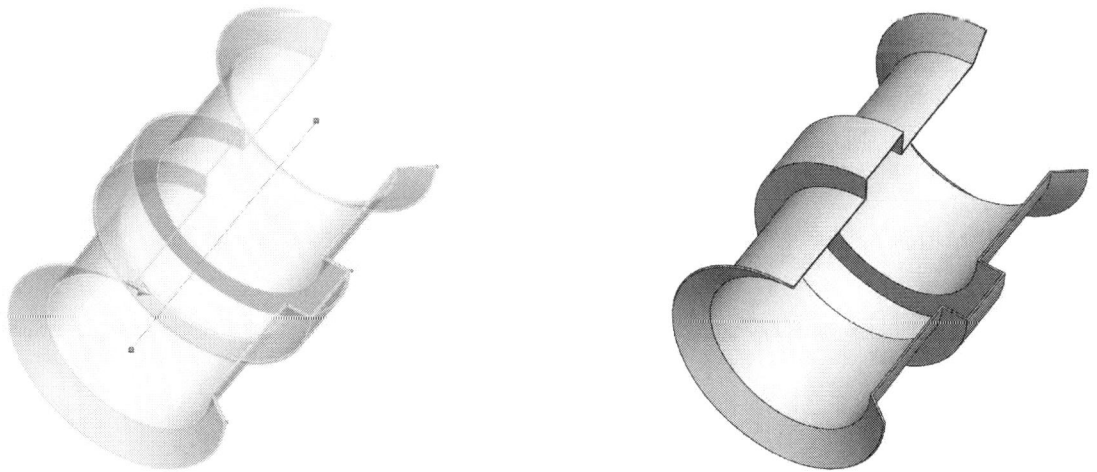

Note that if you select the **Yes** button from the **SOLIDWORKS** message box displayed earlier then the system will automatically convert it into close sketch. And then will create close revolve feature, as shown.

Solid Modeling Tools

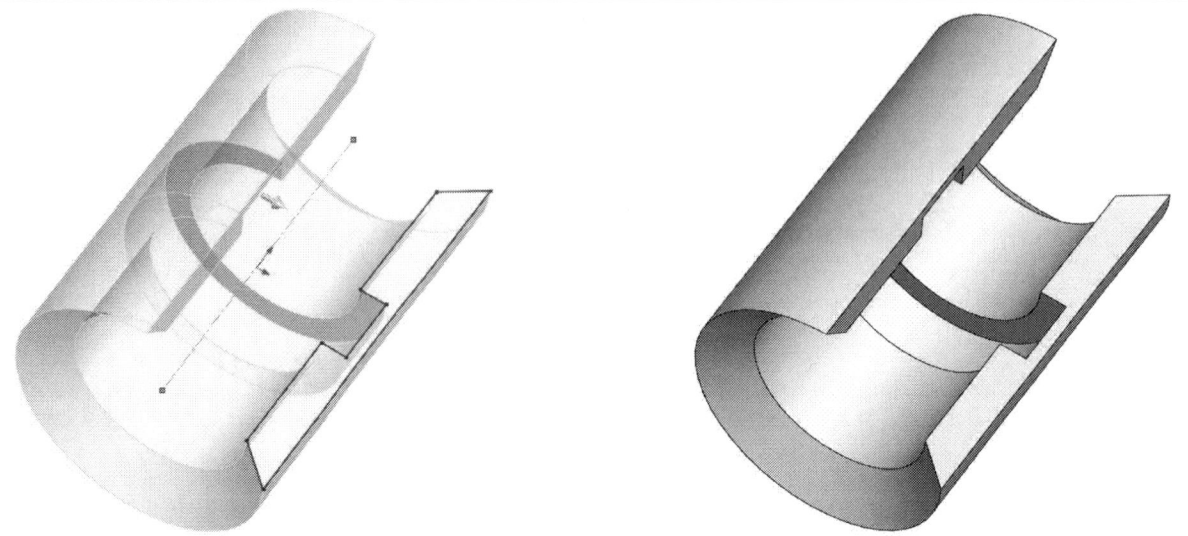

Revolved Cut Tool

This tool is used to remove the material from the existing feature, by revolving a sketch around an axis, as discussed earlier in Revolved boss/base tool.

Removing Material by Using Revolved Cut Tool

To use the **Revolved Cut** tool in removing material from existing feature, follow the steps:

➢ Draw the sketch on an existing feature created along with the centerline, as shown.

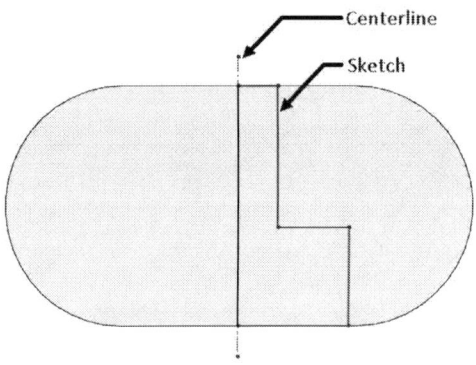

➢ Click on the **Revolved Cut** tool from the **Feature CommandManager** and select the axis to display preview of revolved feature along with **Revolve PropertyManager**, as shown.

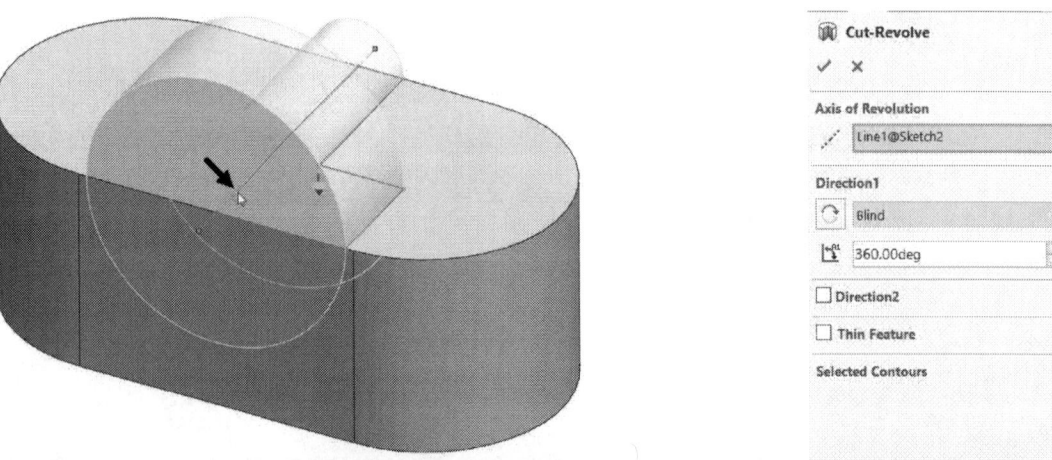

- You can enter **180** in the **Direction 1 Angle** spinner to remove material with revolving sketch at 180 degrees, as shown.
- Click on the **Reverse Direction** button to reverse direction of revolve feature, if required.
- Now, click on the **OK** button from the PropertyManager to exit the tool and display the 3D model with revolve cut feature, as shown.

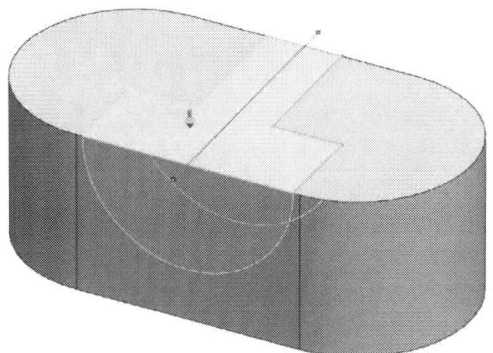
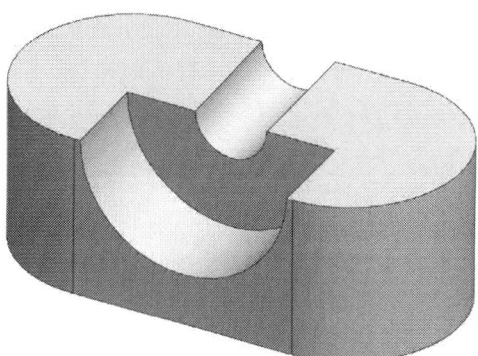

Examples:

Example 1

In this example, you will create the model shown below.

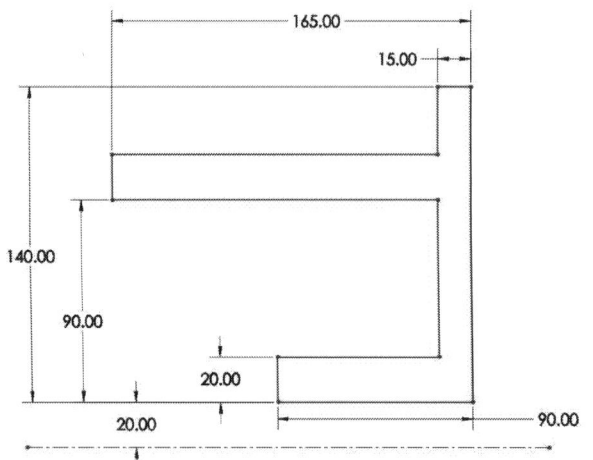
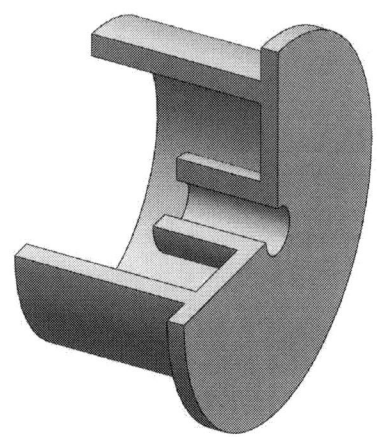

- Start SolidWorks 2021 by clicking **SOLIDWORKS 2021** icon on your desktop.
- Click on the **New** (□) button from the Menu Bar to display the **New SOLIDWORKS Document** dialog box, as shown.

    Alternatively, you can press **Ctrl + N** key from the keyboard to display the dialog box.

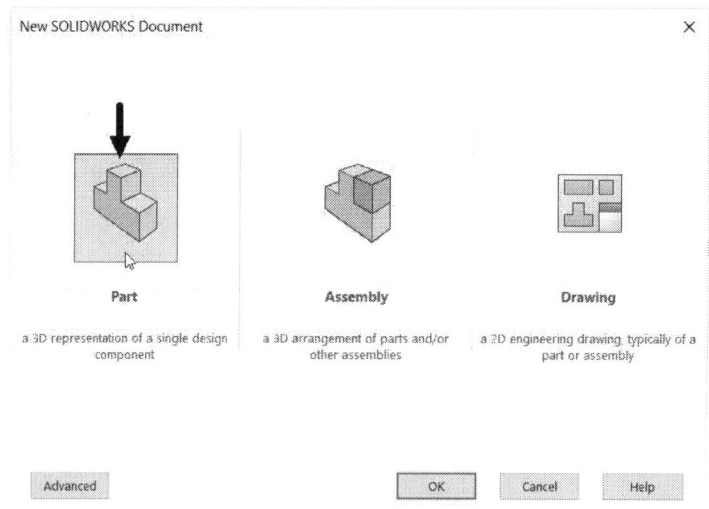

- Click on the **Part** button from the dialog box, if it is not selected by default and then click on **OK** button to enter in the Sketching Environment.

    Alternatively, you can double click on the **Part** button to enter in the Sketching Environment.
- Click on the Sketch tab to display **Sketch CommandManager** and tools used in creating sketch.
- Click on the **Sketch** button from the **Sketch CommandManager** and then click on the **Front** plane or vice-versa.
- Select the **Line** tool and draw the sketch over it, as shown.
- Now draw a centerline by using the **Centerline** tool, as shown.

> Activate the **Smart Dimension** tool and apply dimensions to the recently created sketch, as shown.

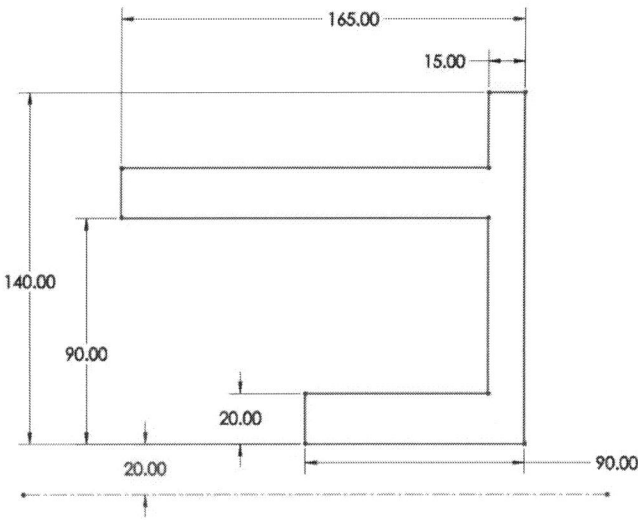

> Now click on the **Exit Sketch** button from the **Sketch CommandManager** to exit from the sketch environment.

Alternatively, you can click on the icon on the top right corner of the display.

> Select the **Revolved Boss/Base** tool from the **Features CommandManager** and select the centerline to display PropertyManager & preview of the revolve feature, as shown.

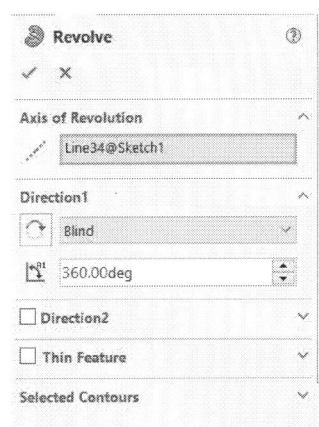 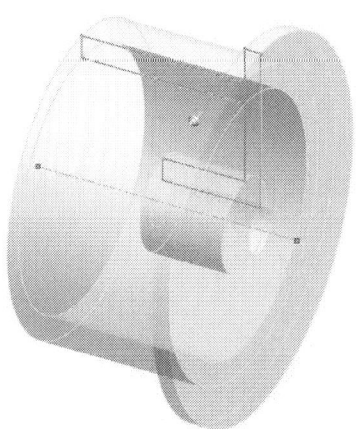

> Replace revolve angle **360** with **270** and click on the **Reverse Direction** button to change angle direction, from the **Revolve PropertyManager**.

Solid Modeling Tools

➢ Now click on the OK ☑ button to apply changes and display the revolved feature, as shown.

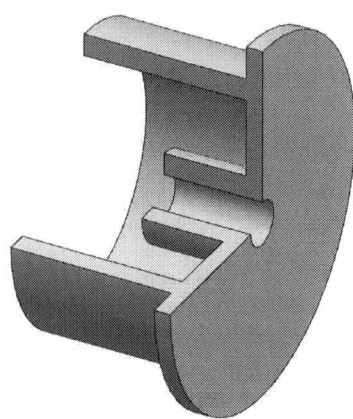

➢ Click on the **Save (Ctrl+S)** button from the Menu Bar to display the **Save As** dialog box.
➢ Next browse to the folder of chapter 5 and enter name **Ch05-exam01** in the **File name** edit box.
➢ Click on the **Save** button from the dialog box to save the file.
➢ Now enter the **Close** ☒ button from the upper right corner to close it.

Example 2 (Millimeter)

In this example, you will create the model shown below.

➢ Start SolidWorks 2021 by clicking **SOLIDWORKS 2021** icon on your desktop.
➢ Click on the **New** (🗋) button from the Menu Bar to display the **New SOLIDWORKS Document** dialog box.

  Alternatively, you can press **Ctrl + N** key from the keyboard to display the dialog box.

➢ Click on the **Part** button from the dialog box, if it is not selected by default and then click on **OK** button to enter in the Sketching Environment.

  Alternatively, you can double click on the **Part** button to enter in the Sketching Environment.

Note: After opening the SolidWorks, by default the **New SOLIDWORKS Document** dialog box with **Part** button selected get displayed. You can simply click on the **OK** button to enter in the Sketching Environment.

➢ Click on the Sketch tab to display tools used in creating sketch.
➢ Click on the **Sketch** button and then click on the **Front** plane or vice-versa.
➢ Select the **Line** tool and draw the sketch with centerline, as shown.

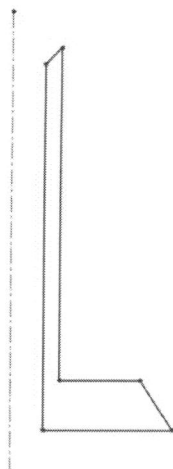

➢ Activate the **Smart Dimension** tool, apply the diametric dimensions, as shown.

Note that you need to apply the **Coincident** constraint between the top of the sketch and the Top plane and origin, as shown. The sketch will become Fully Defined.

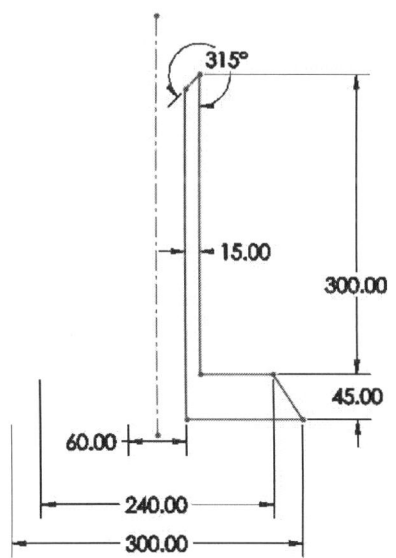 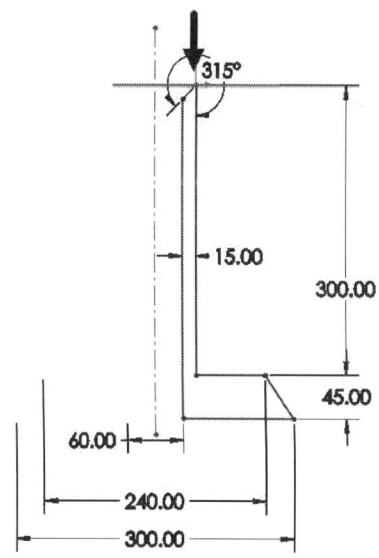

➢ Now click on the **Exit Sketch** button from the **Sketch CommandManager** to exit from the Sketch Environment.

Alternatively, you can click on the icon on the top right corner of the display.

➢ Select the **Revolved Boss/Base** tool from the **Features CommandManager** and select the centerline to display PropertyManager & preview of the revolve feature, as shown.
➢ Create the revolve feature at **360** degrees angle, as shown.

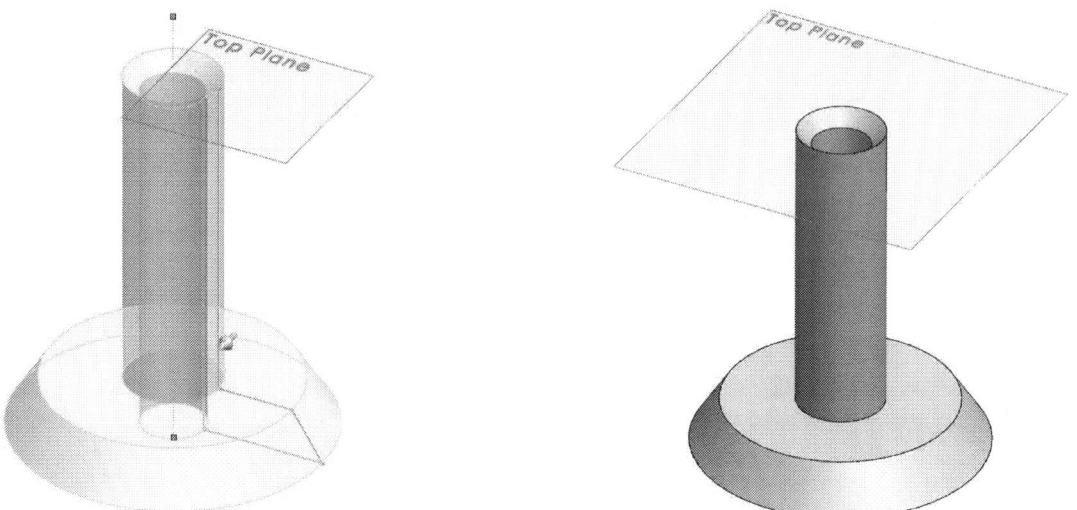

- Again, activate the **Sketch** tool and select the **Top** plane to draw sketch over it.
- Using the **Circle** tool draw a circle of **90** dia.
- Again, draw another construction circle of **216** dia., as shown.
- Similarly draw the centerlines across these circles.
- Using the **Smart Dimension** tool, generate the diametric dimensions of both circles, as shown.

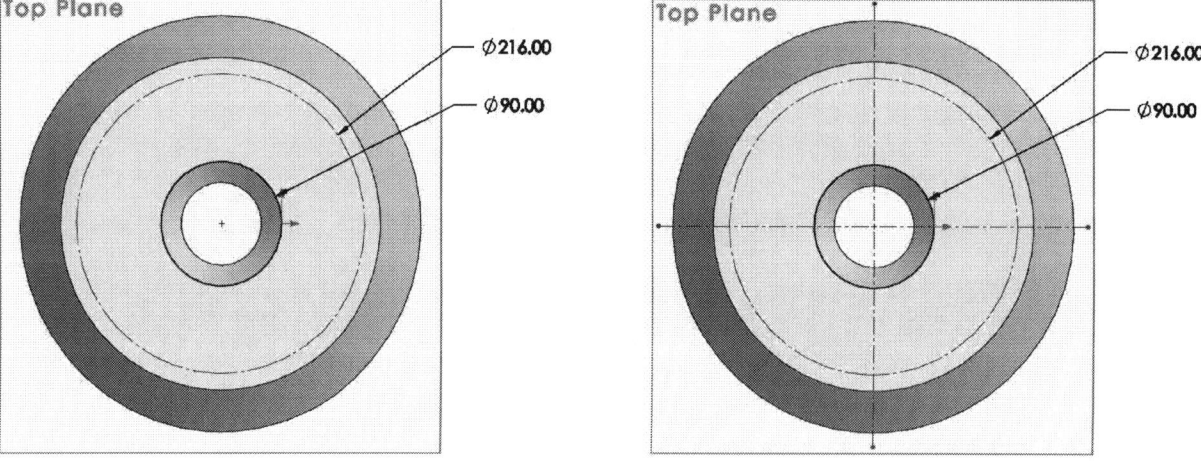

- Again, activate the **Circle** tool and create the circle entities at the intersection of centerline/construction line and the construction circle, as shown.

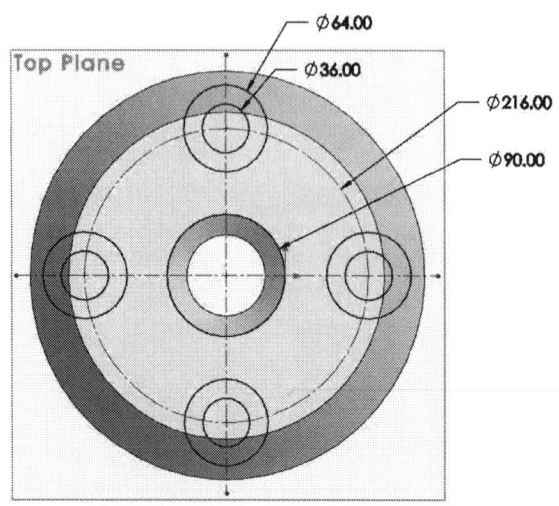

➤ Activate the **Trim Entities** tool from the **Sketch CommandManager** to trim unwanted entities, as shown.

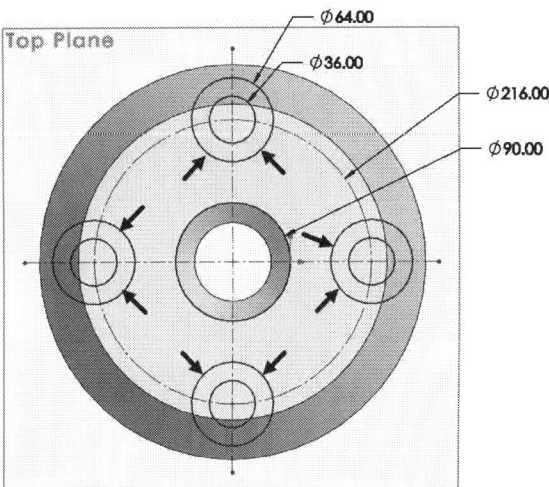 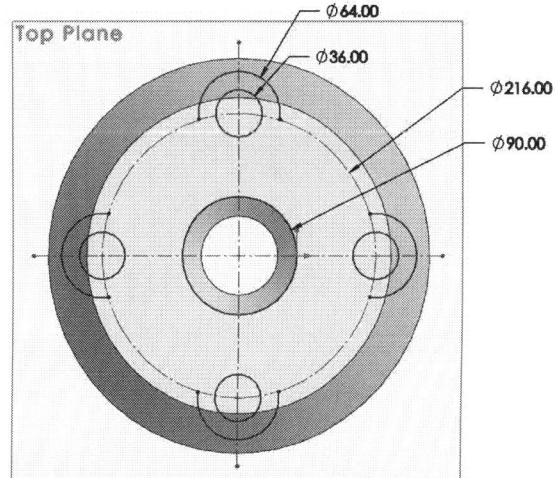

➤ Now, activate the **Tangent Arc** tool from the **Arc** drop-down and draw tangent arcs arc, as shown.

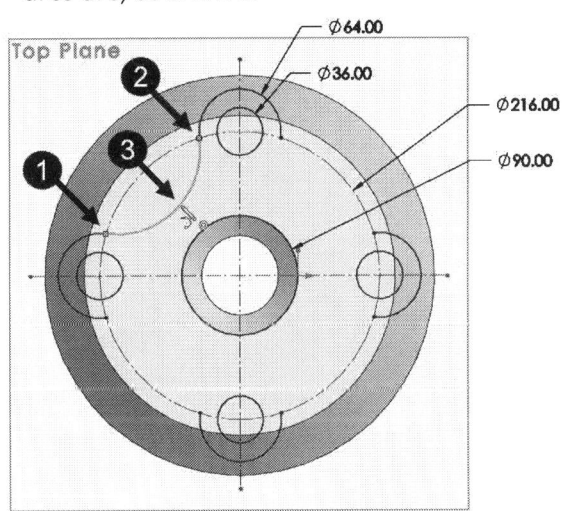 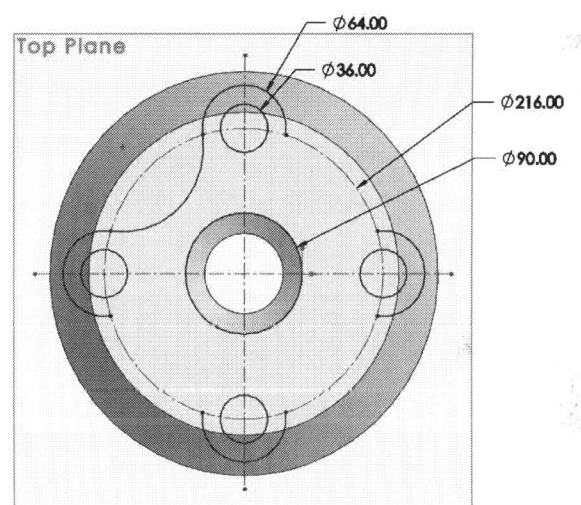

➤ Activate the **Mirror Entities** tool from the **Sketch CommandManager** to display the **Mirror PropertyManager**, as shown.
➤ Now select the arc to be mirrored, as shown.
➤ Click in the **Mirror about** selection box of the PropertyManager and select the centerline, as shown.

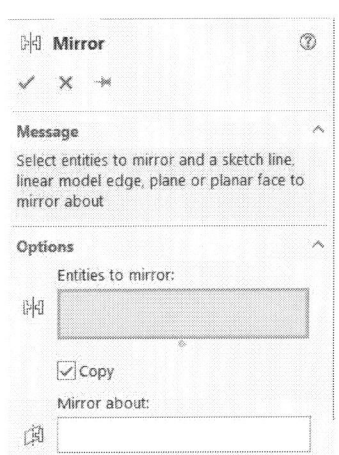 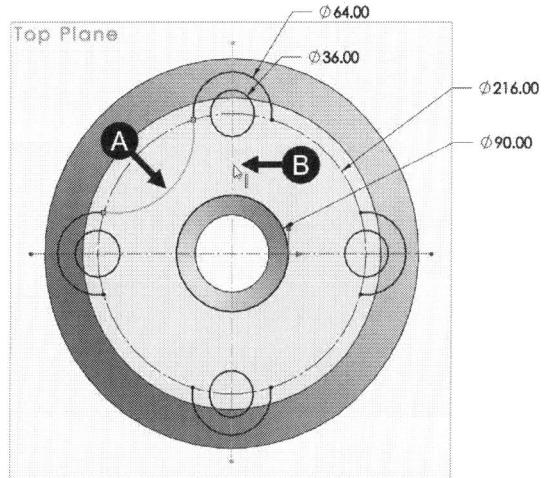

➤ The preview of the mirror feature gets visible and click on the **OK** button of the PropertyManager to display the mirrored feature, as shown.

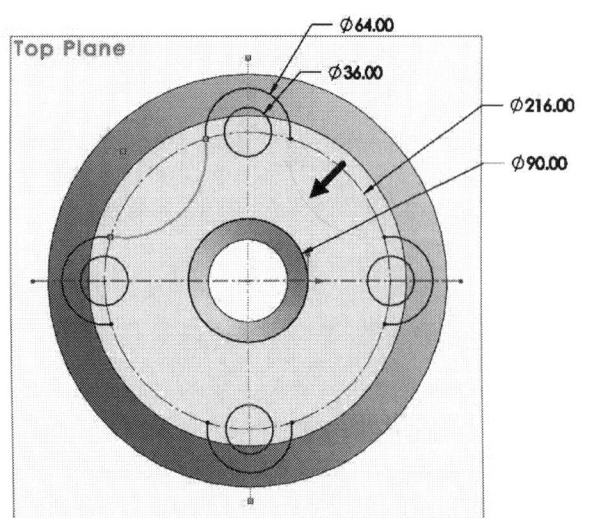
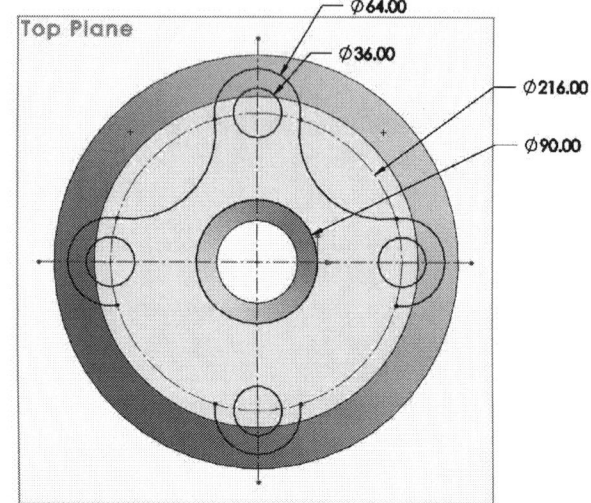

➤ Similarly, create mirror of another 2 arcs, as shown.

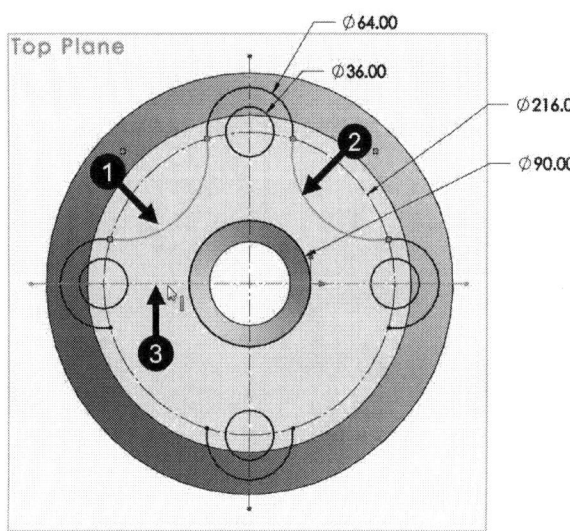
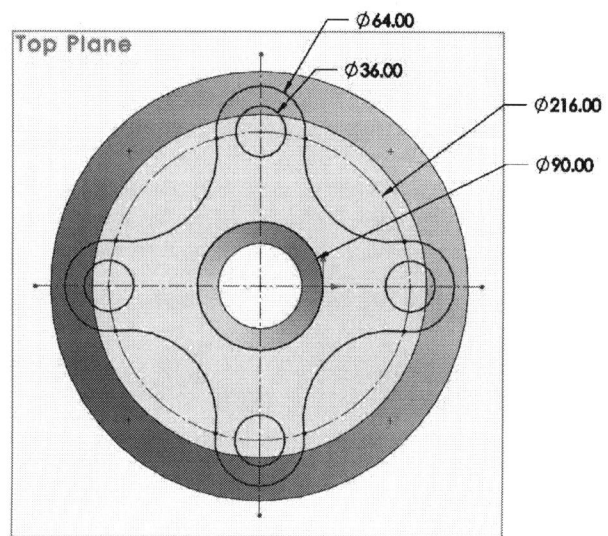

➤ Also select the construction circle and press the **Delete** key from the keyboard to remove it. The **Sketcher Confirm Delete** message box get visible, as shown. Click on **Yes** to continue.

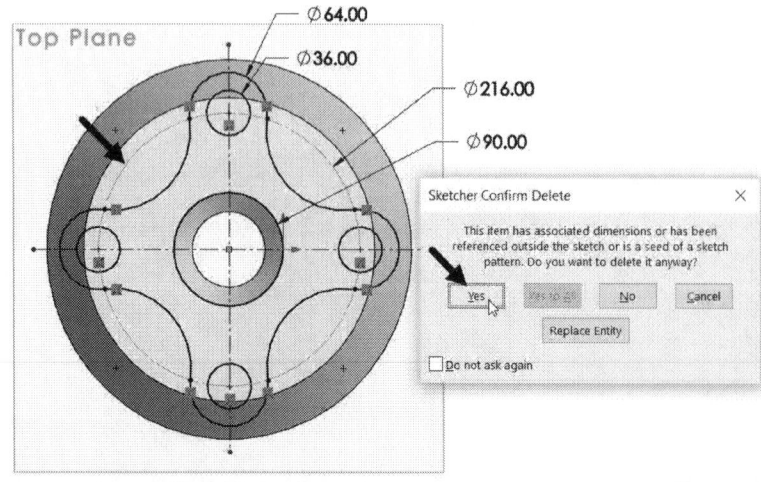

For the better visibility, right click over the **Top Plane** from the **FeatureManager Design Tree** and select the **Hide** button from the shortcut menu displayed to hide it, as shown.

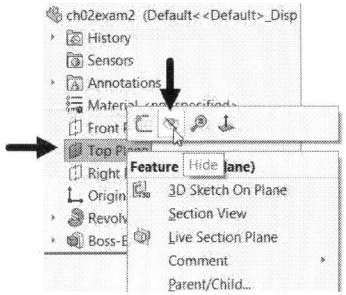

> Now click on the **Exit Sketch** button from the **Sketch CommandManager** to exit from the sketch environment.
> Activate the **Extrude Boss/Base** tool and select the sketch to extrude it, as shown.

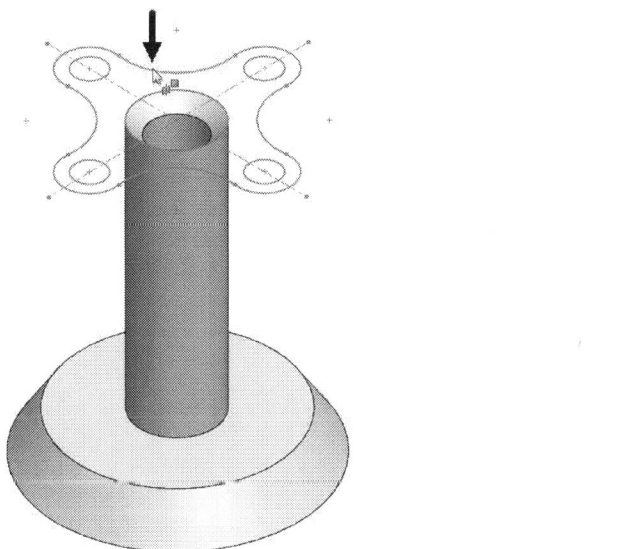
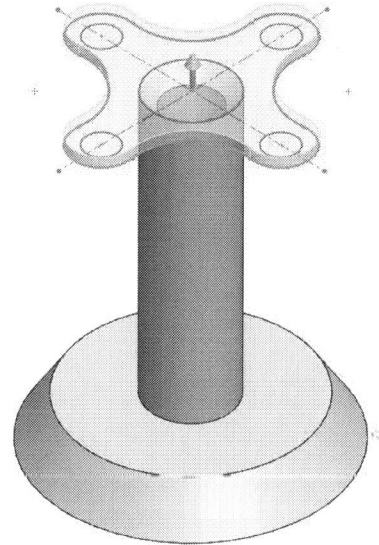

Here you need to delete the selected sketch from the **Selected Contours** rollout of the Boss-Extrude PropertyManager, as shown. Select the required entities and the system will automatically display preview of extruded feature of self-selected entities, as shown.

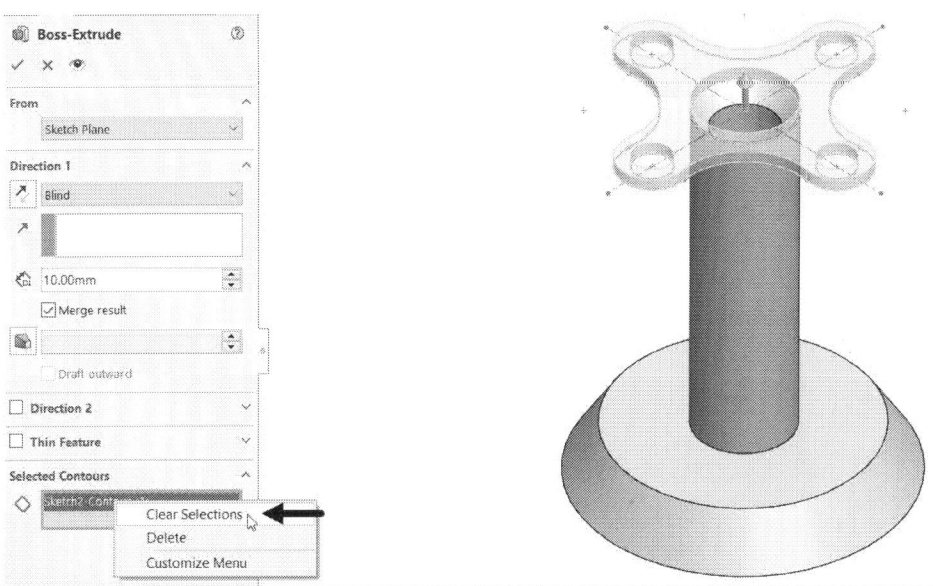

Solid Modeling Tools

➤ Enter **40** in the **Depth** spinner and click on the **Reverse Direction** button to extrude it upto 40 distance in downwards direction, as shown.

➤ Now click on the **OK** button from the PropertyManager to exit it and display the extruded feature, as shown.

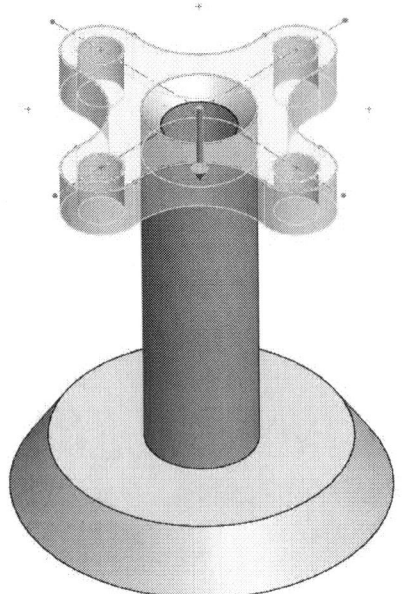
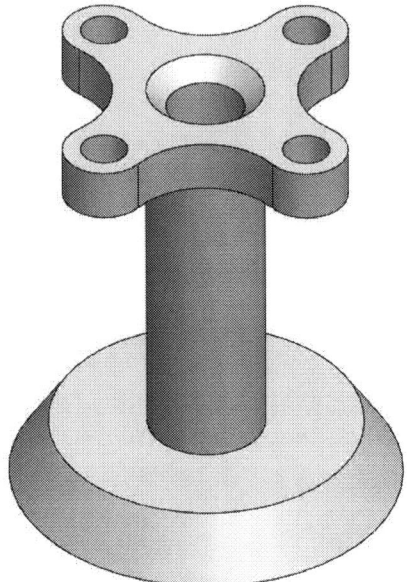

➤ Click on the **Save (Ctrl+S)** button from the Menu Bar to display the **Save As** dialog box.
➤ Next browse to the folder of chapter 5 and enter name **ch05-exam02** in the **File name** edit box.
➤ Click on the **Save** button from the dialog box to save the file.
➤ Now enter the **Close** button from the upper right corner to close it.

Questions:

1. Which tool is used to create a revolve feature?
2. How can you remove material from a solid model using the **Extrude** tool?
3. What is the use of the **Depth Value** drop-down in **Extrude** PropertyManager?
4. What is the procedure to create a surface feature using **Revolve** tool?
5. How can you extrude a sketch in both direction?
6. Which tools are activated for creating a construction circle?
7. Which checkbox is selected to activate the options used for creating thin features?
8. What is used to select partial region/sketch to create extrude features?

Exercises:

Exercise 1

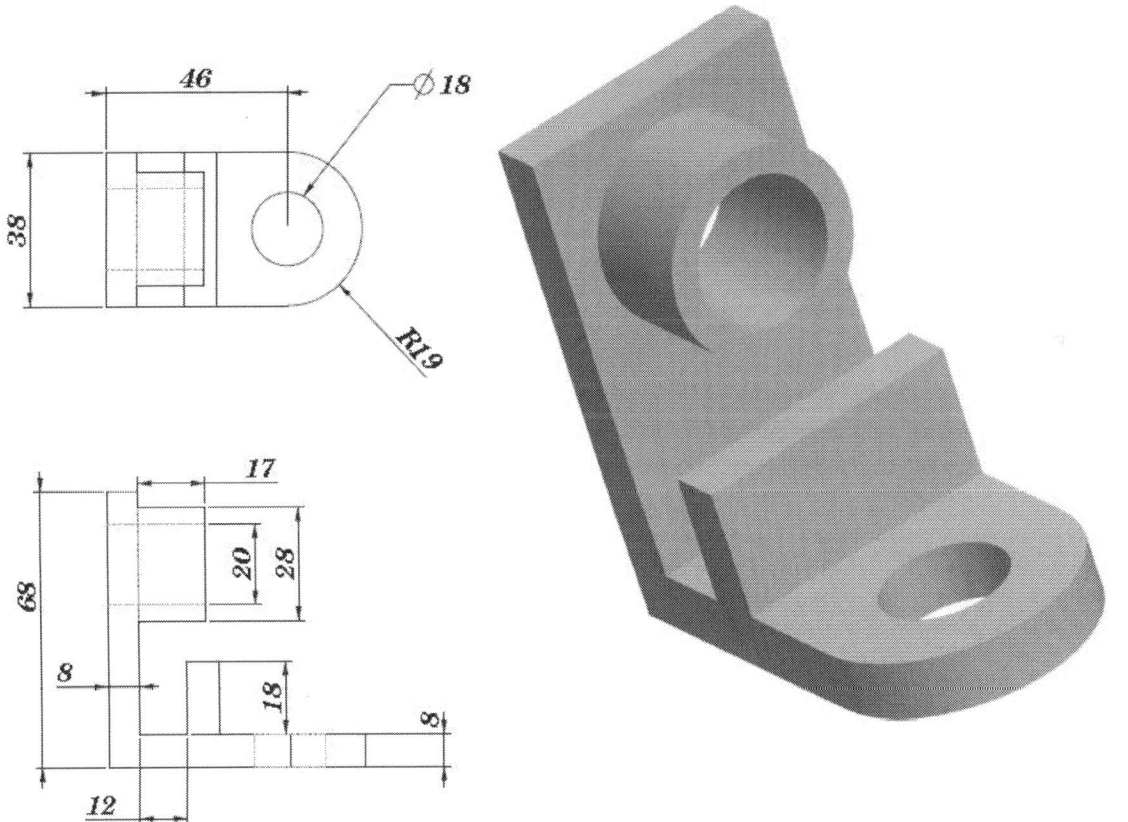

Exercise 2

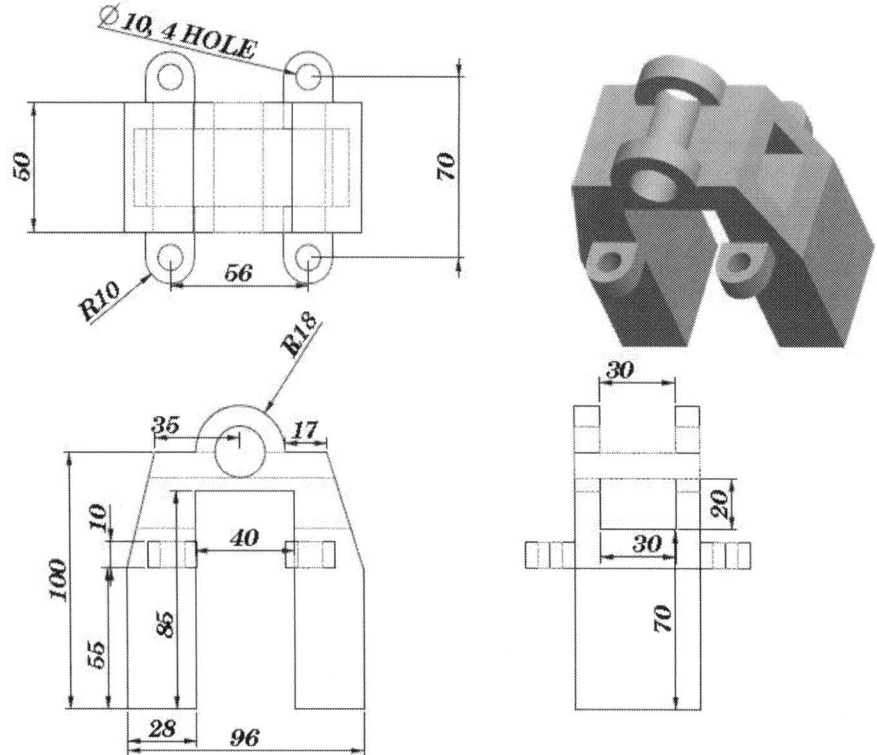

Exercise 3

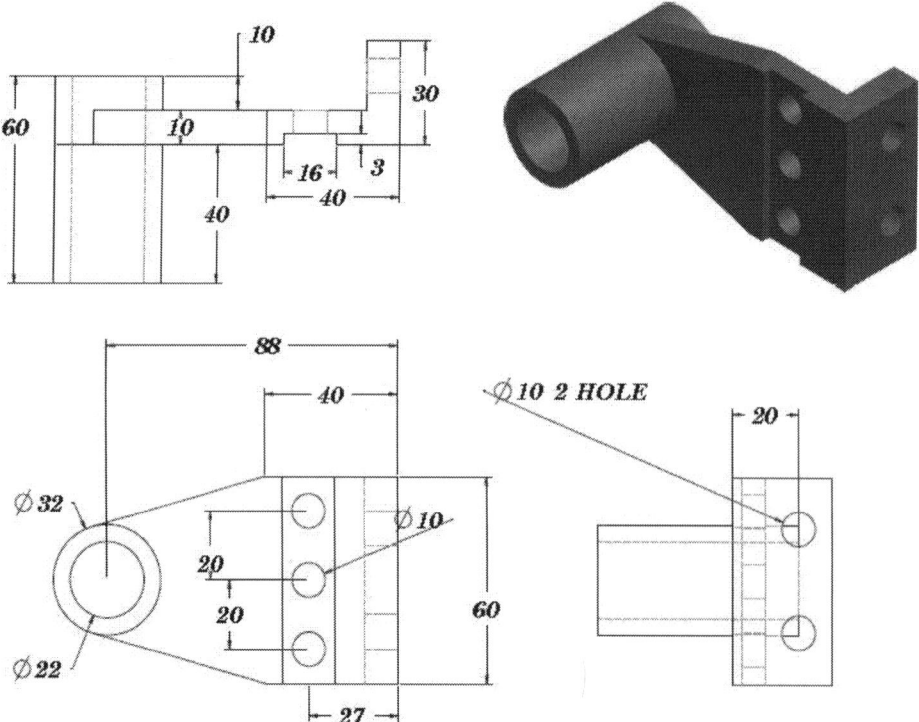

Chapter 06: Reference Geometry and Curves

Reference features are considered as non-solid features, used during the construction of other features. The most common reference features include reference planes, reference axes, reference coordinate systems, and reference point. The references are very useful, when you are working over very complex models in SolidWorks. Now, you will learn the tools to create these features.

The topics covered in this chapter are:

- ❖ Reference plane
- ❖ Reference axes
- ❖ Reference point
- ❖ Reference Coordinate system
- ❖ Center of Mass
- ❖ Mass Properties

Reference Features

Reference features are considered as non-solid features, used during the construction of other features. The datum features do not add or remove material from the model, so it will not affect the mass properties of the model. The various reference features are planes, axes, points and coordinate systems. The reference features are very useful, when you are working over very complex models in SolidWorks. Now, you will learn the tools to create these features.

The visibility of the reference features (reference planes, reference axes, reference lines etc) can be toggled on/off using the buttons available in the ⦿ **Hide/Show Items** drop-down, in the **Graphics** toolbar located at the top of the user interface, as shown.

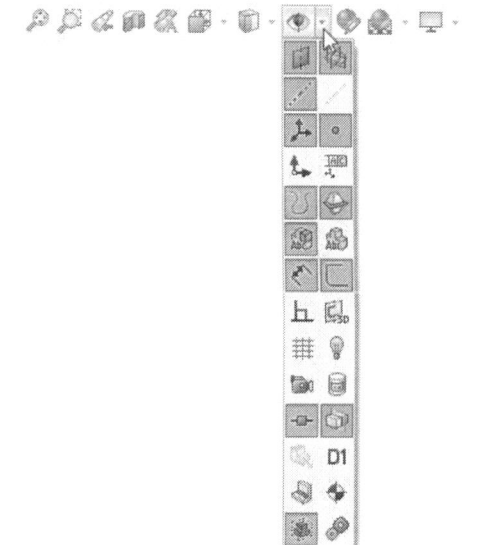

Default Plane

Each time when you start a new part file and enter Sketching environment, SolidWorks automatically displays default planes - **Front Plane**, **Top Plane**, and **Right Plane**, as shown below. Planes and coordinate system make up a specific type of features in SolidWorks, known as default features. These features act as support to your 3D geometry. In addition to the default features, you can create your own additional planes and coordinate systems too. Until now, you have known to create sketches on any of the default planes. If you want to create sketches and geometry at locations other than default planes, you can create new reference planes manually. You can do so by using the **Reference Geometry** tool, as shown.

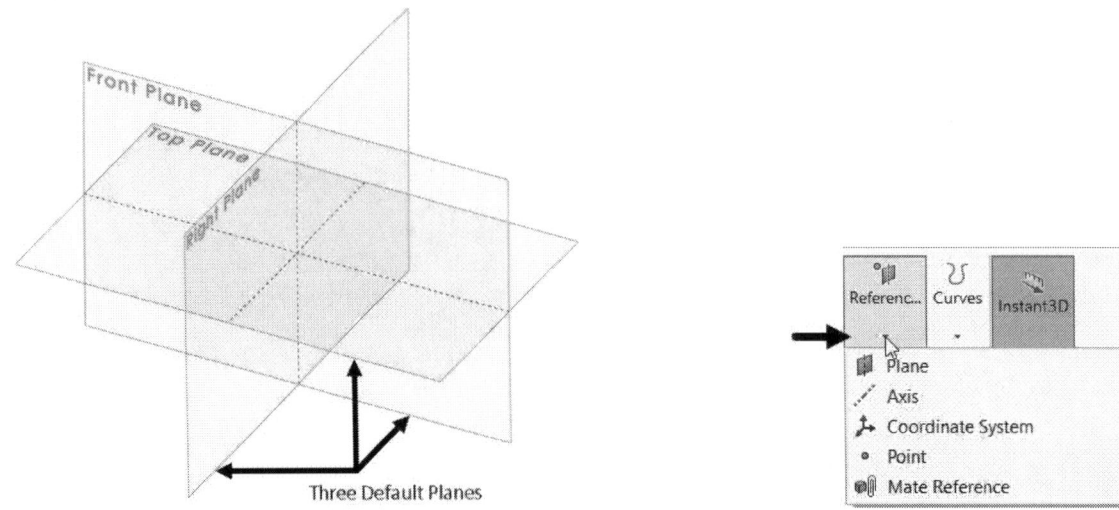

Three Default Planes

Below are combinations given according to which, you can create reference planes:

- Reference plane, offset from any existing/default plane or flat surface.
- Reference plane, through an axis, curve, or edge.
- Reference plane, normal to an existing plane or flat surface.
- Reference plane, parallel to an existing plane or flat surface.
- Reference plane, at a specified angle to an existing plane or flat surface.
- Reference plane, tangent to any selected cylindrical surface.

Uses of Reference Plane

Some of the important uses of Reference Plane are:

- Used in creating sketching planes and reference planes.
- Used as dimensioning and alignment references in the sketch.
- Used for creating cross sections.
- Used as reference plane for the **Mirror** tool.

Creating Reference Plane

There are different procedures to create reference planes, as discussed one-by-one below:

Creating An Offset Plane

The reference plane created using this method, will be parallel to a face or another plane (default plane or any previously created reference plane).

- Select the **Plane** tool (**Features > Reference Geometry > Plane**) to display **Plane PropertyManager**, as shown.

Reference Geometry and Curves

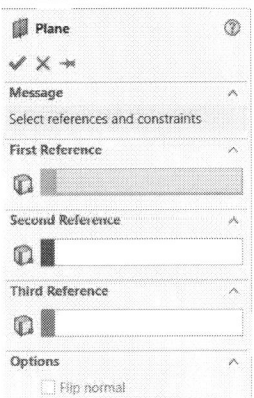

- Select the flat surface, to display preview of reference plane at default distance, as shown

  The selected face gets displayed in the PropertyManager, as shown.

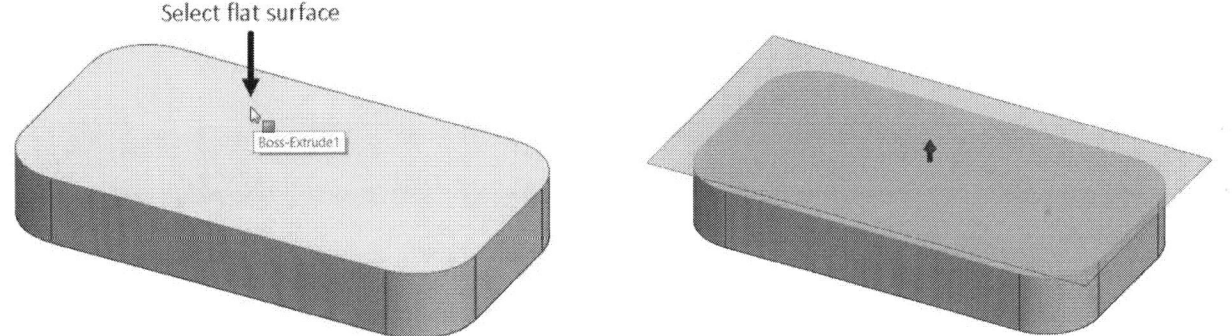

- Enter the required distance value in the **Offset distance** spinner of the **Plane PropertyManager** for the reference plane, as shown.

  To create multiple reference planes at uniform distance from each other you can enter the required no of planes in the **Number of planes to create** spinner, as shown. And **Flip offset** checkbox is selected to flip its direction.

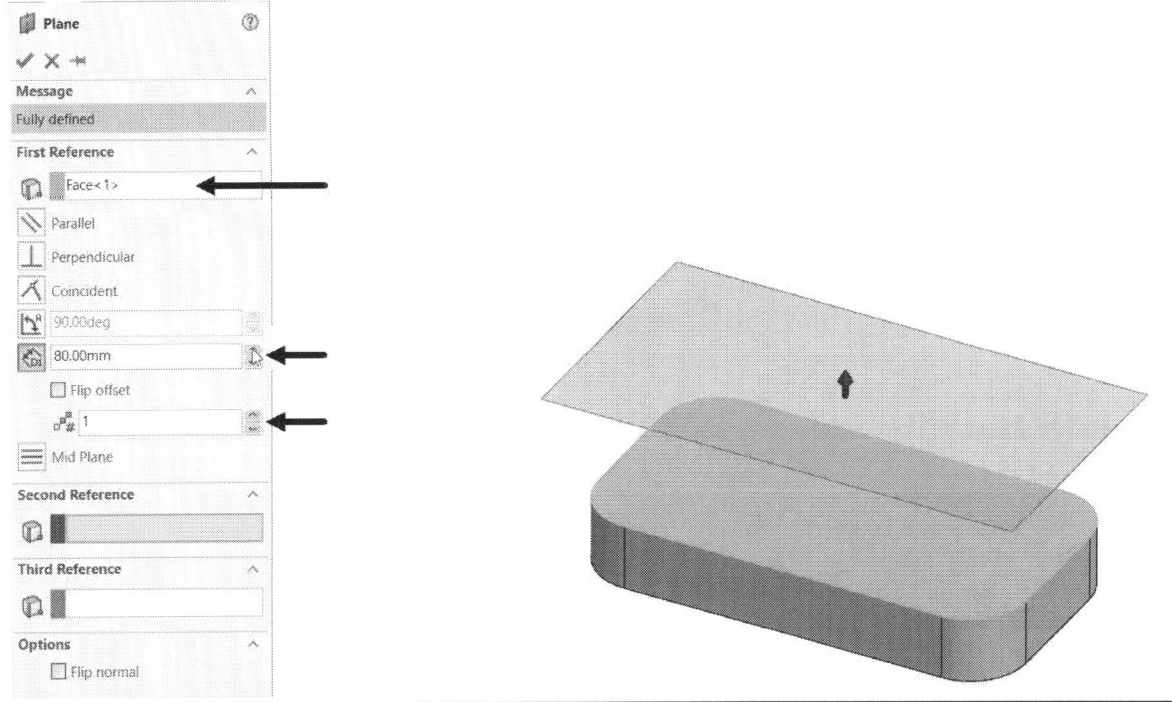

➢ Click on the **OK** button of the **Plane PropertyManager** to display the plane created, as shown.

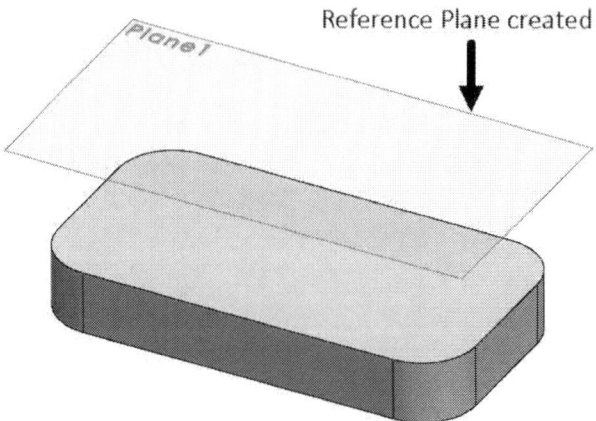

Similarly, you can create the offset plane from any default reference plane at an offset distance, after selecting it, as shown.

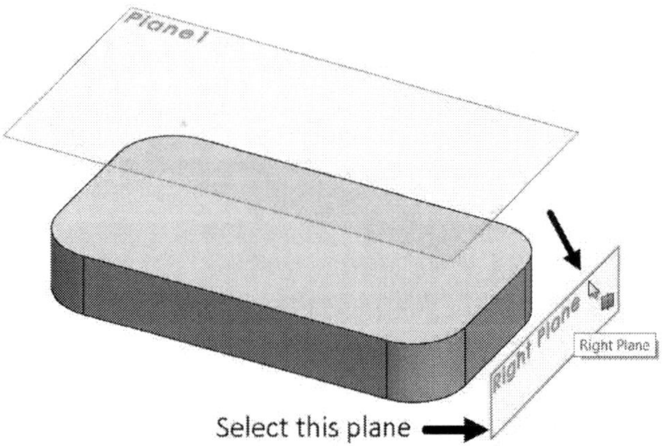

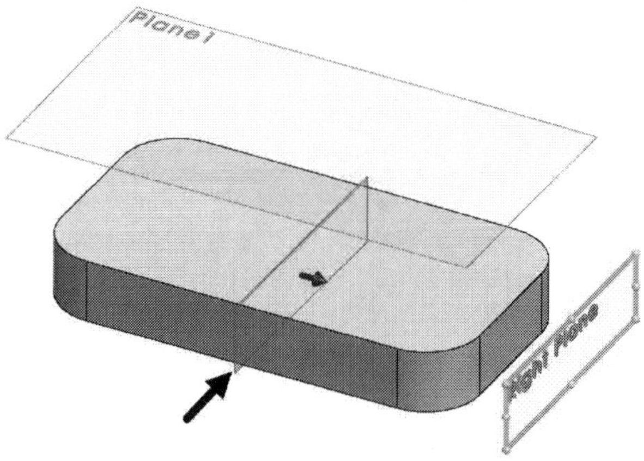

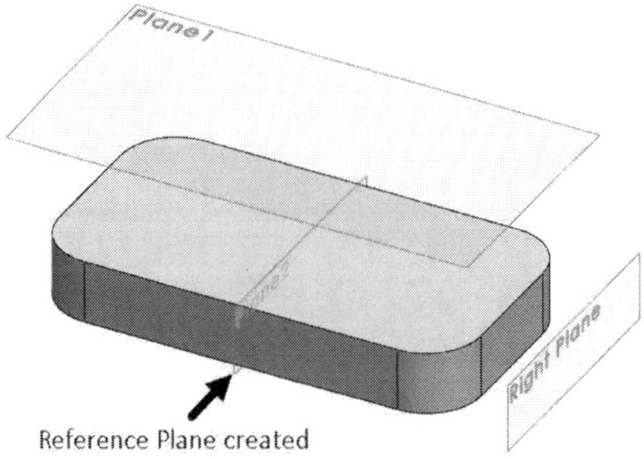

You can also, drag the reference plane by dragging it, as discussed below:

➢ Click on the reference plane that you want to drag, as shown.
➢ Press and hold the **LMB** (left mouse button) on the end point with the dimension, as shown.
➢ Next, you can drag it up to the required distance, as shown.

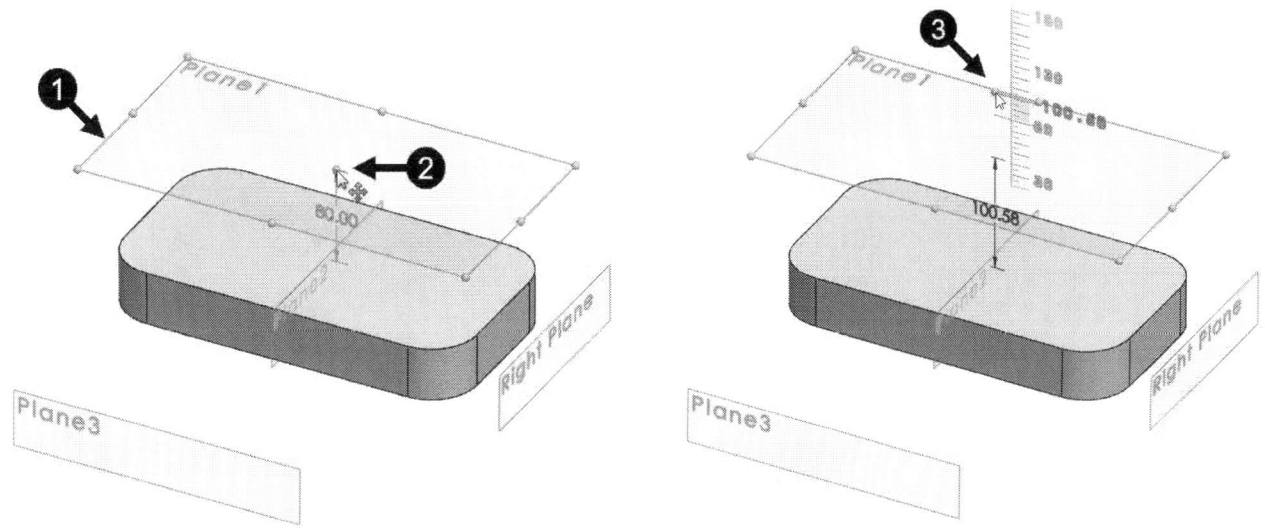

Creating Plane Through Selected Points

This method is used to create the reference plane, passing through three selected points.

> Select the **Plane** [Plane] tool (select **Features > Reference Geometry > Plane**) to activate it.
> Select or define the first, and second points of the model, one-by-one to display preview of reference plane, as shown.
> Now select the third point to display reference plane created through selected points, as shown.

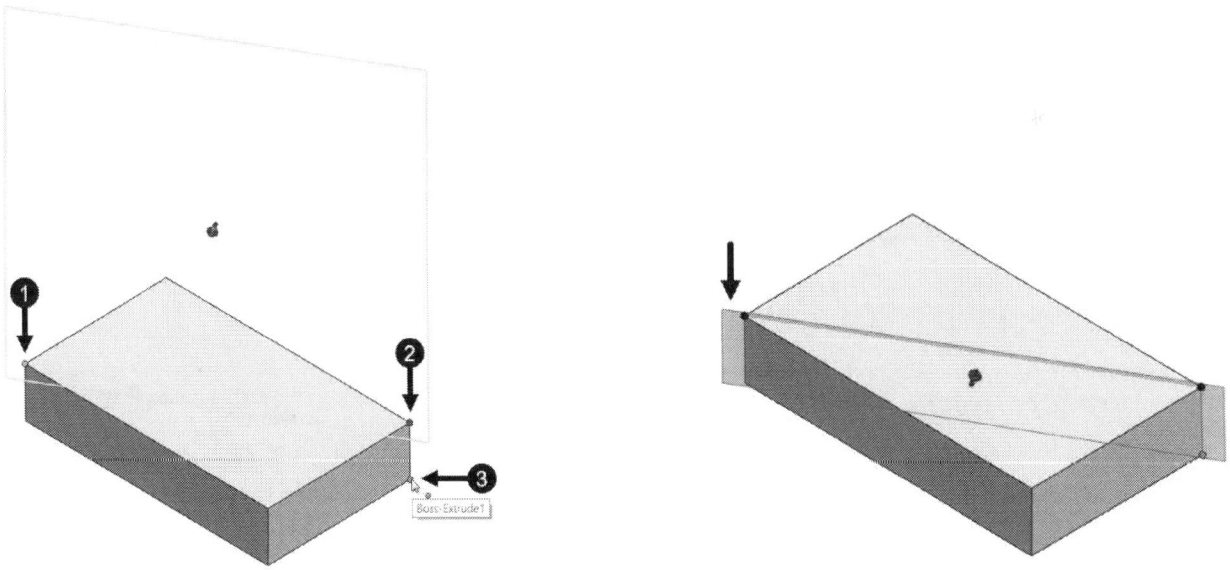

Similarly, you can create reference plane through selected line entity and point, as shown.

Reference Geometry and Curves

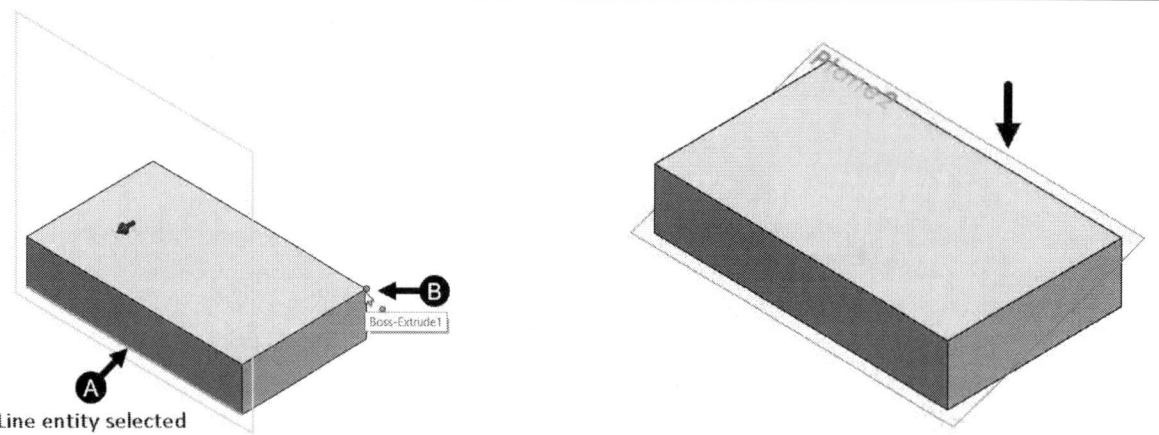

Creating Plane At An Angle

This method is used to create the reference plane at an angle from the selected flat surface.

➤ Select the **Plane** [Plane] tool (select **Features > Reference Geometry > Plane**) to display **Plane PropertyManager**, as shown earlier in this chapter.
➤ Select the flat surface to display datum plane parallel to it, as shown.

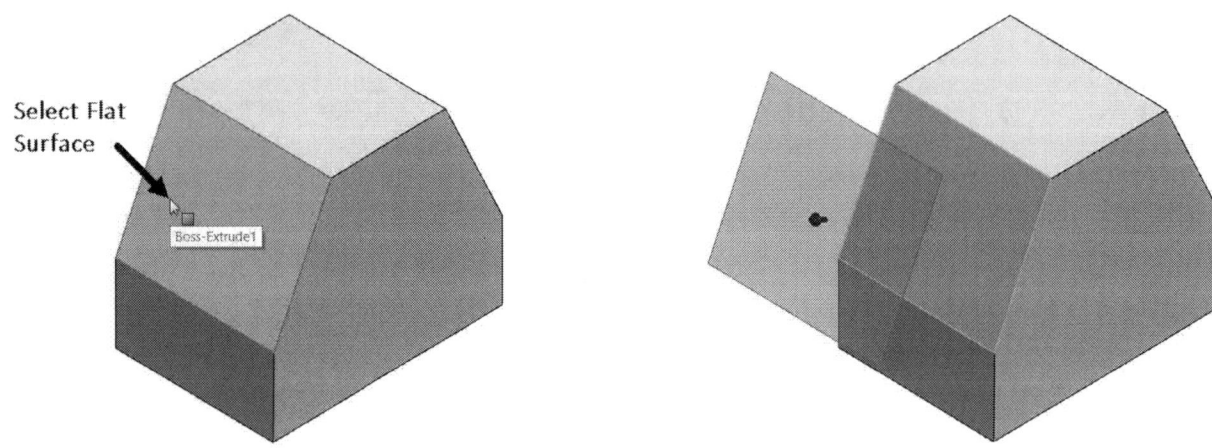

➤ Select the edge to display reference plane at an angle, as shown.

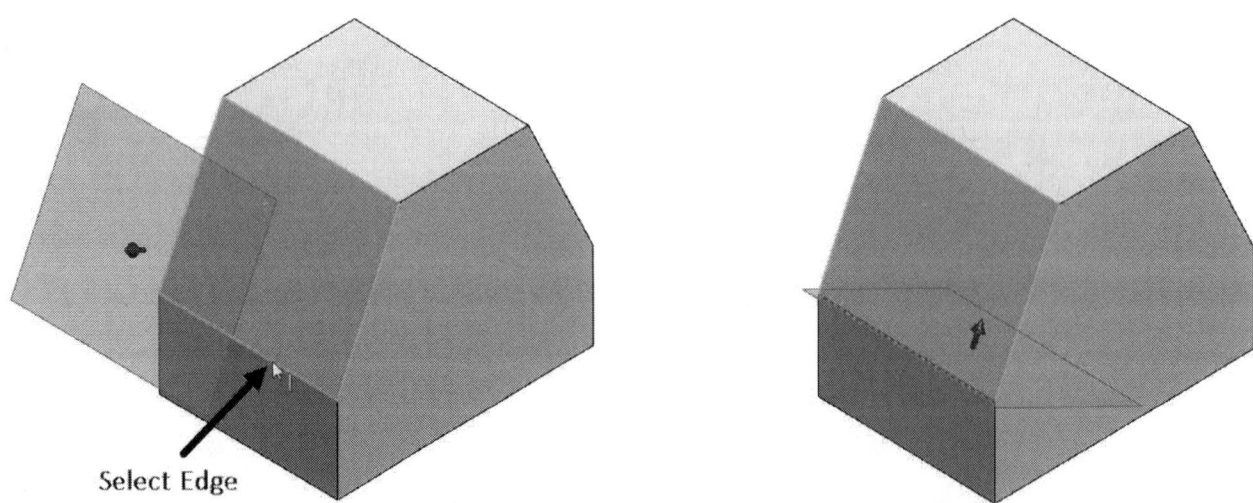

➤ Select the **At angle** button from the **Plane PropertyManager** to activate **Angle** spinner, as shown.
➤ Next, enter or adjust the required angle value in the **Angle** spinner, as shown.

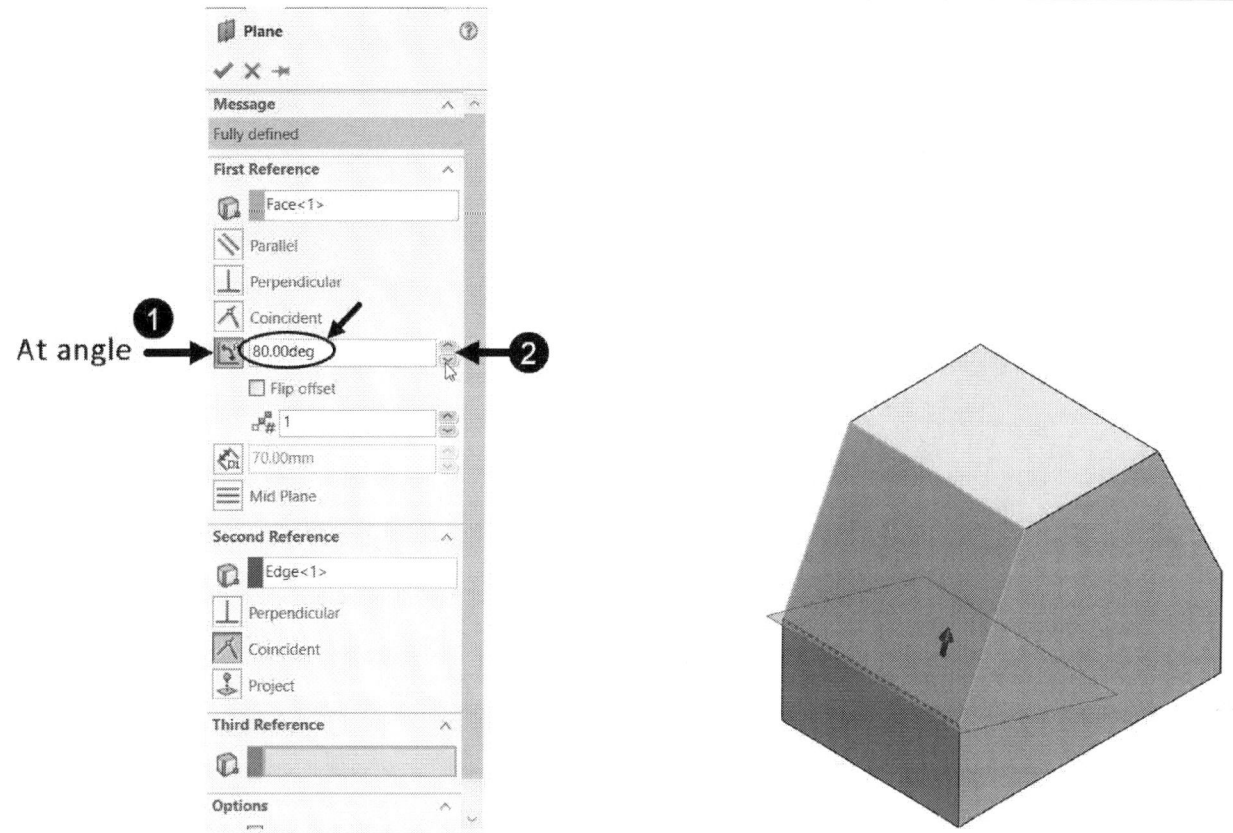

- Now, click on the OK ✓ button from the PropertyManager to exit it and display the reference plane created at the angle value entered, as shown.

For the better visibility of plane, the display style of model is changed to the **Wireframe** mode from the **Display Style** flyout of the **View (Heads-Up)** toolbar, as shown.

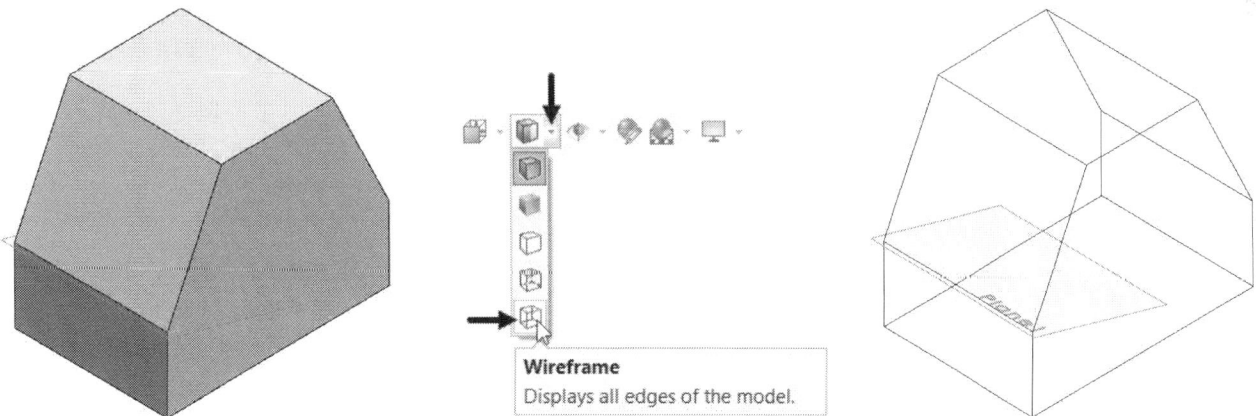

Creating Tangent Plane

This method is used to create a reference tangent plane across the selected round surface.

- Select the **Plane** tool (select **Features > Reference Geometry > Plane**) to activate it.
- Select the round surface, to display the preview of the reference tangent plane, as shown.

Reference Geometry and Curves

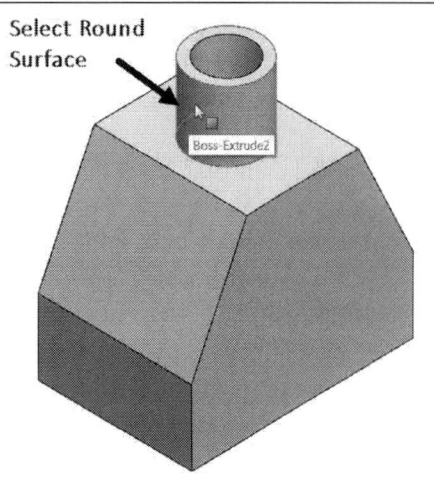 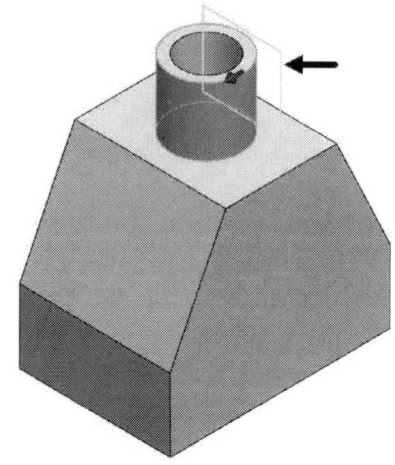

- Select the point for second reference, as shown.
- Select the OK ✓ button from the PropertyManager to display the tangent reference plane, as shown.

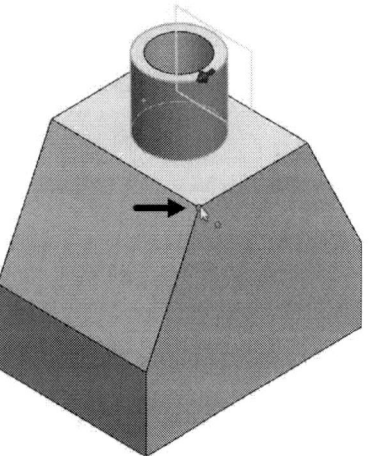 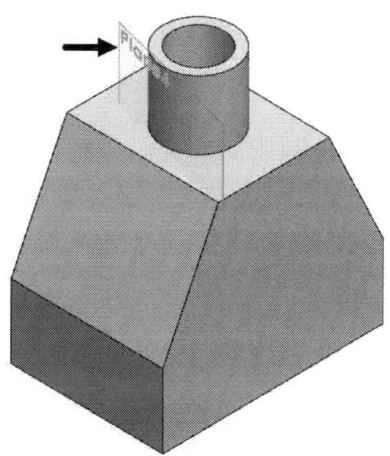

Creating Parallel Plane

This method is used to create a reference plane parallel to the selected plane or flat surface.

- Select the **Plane** [Plane] tool (select **Features > Reference Geometry > Plane**) to activate it and display the **Plane PropertyManager**, as shown.
- Click on the flat surface to display the preview of reference plane, offset to it, as shown.

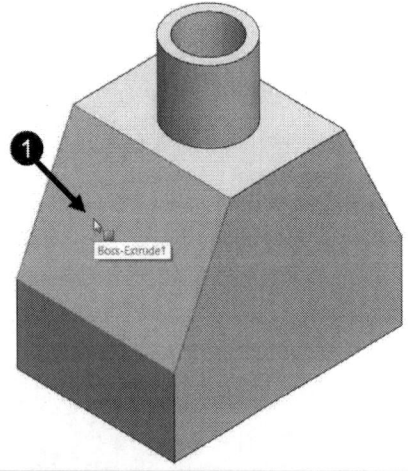 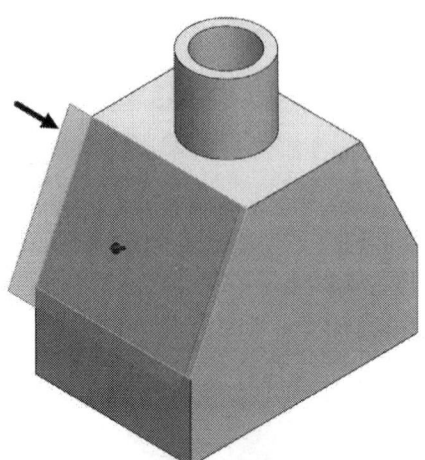

- Now click on the **Parallel** button from the PropertyManager, as shown.
- Next select any midpoint or end point of any edge, or any sketched point for the second reference, as shown.

The reference plane parallel to the selected flat surface get visible, passing through the selected point, as shown.

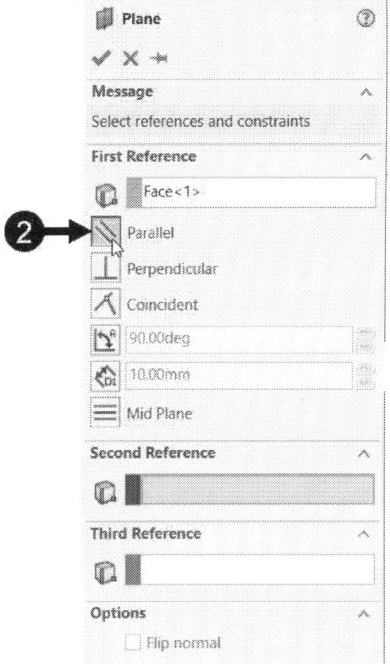
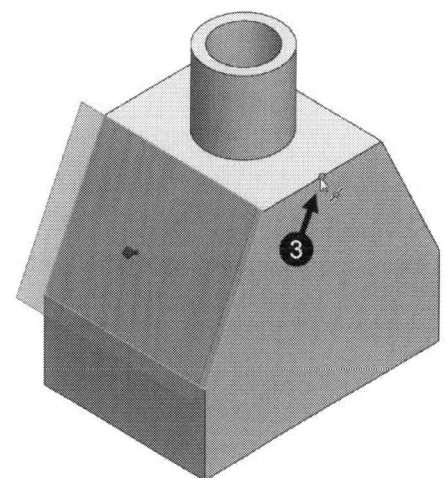

- Now click on the **OK** button from the PropertyManager to display the parallel plane, as shown.

For the better visibility of plane, the **Display Style** is changed to the **Wireframe** mode, as shown earlier.

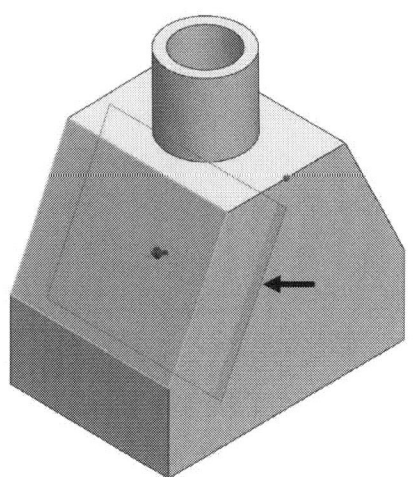
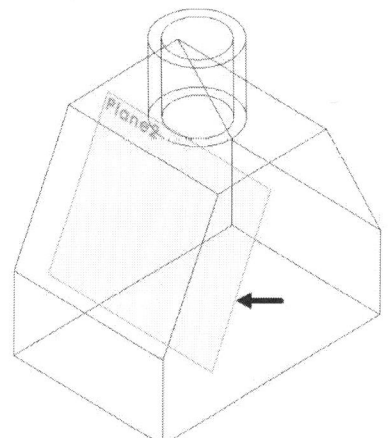

Similarly, you can create a parallel reference plane, parallel to the selected plane, as shown.

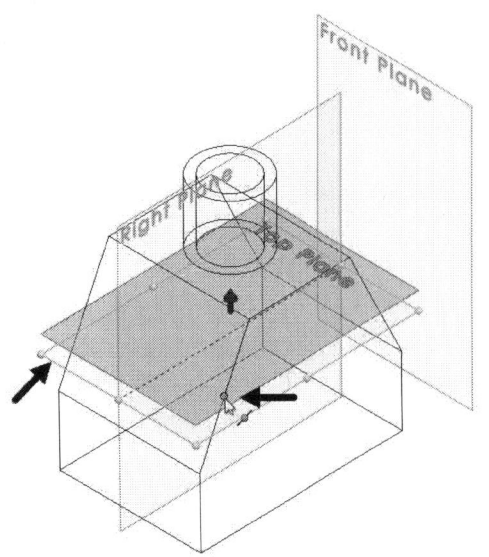 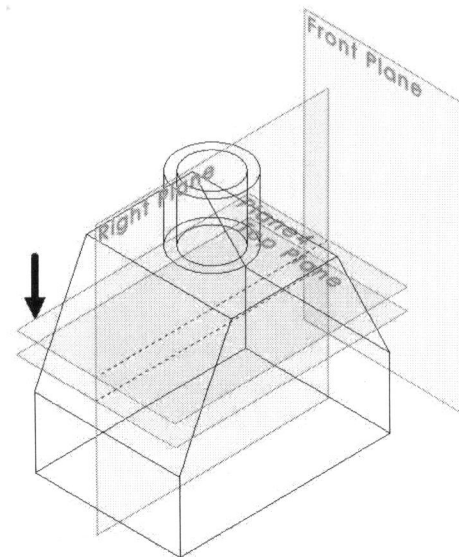

Reference Axis

The axis is another very important reference feature. The reference axis can be created by activating the **Axis** tool (**Features > Reference Geometry > Axis**). This tool is very useful while creating rotational features.

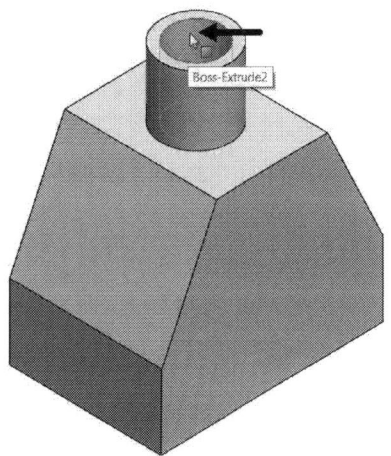 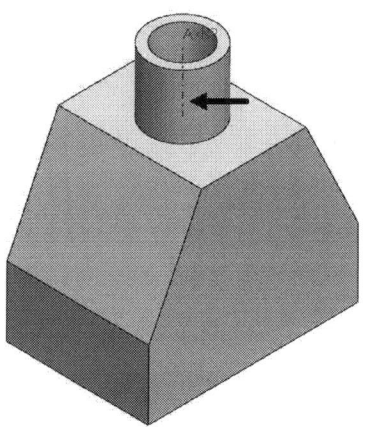

Below are combinations according to which, reference axis can be created:

- Reference axis, normal to a plane or flat surface
- Reference axis, through a point
- Reference axis, through a linear edge
- Reference plane, through the center of a cylindrical surface
- Reference plane, at an intersection of two planes or flat surfaces

Uses of Axis

Some of the important uses of axis are:

- Used in creating centerlines in drawings
- Used in creating coaxial holes
- Used to indicate symmetry in drawings

Creating Reference Axis

The **Axis** ✎ Axis tool is used to create reference axis. There are different methods to create reference axis, as discussed one-by-one below:

One Line/Edge/Axis

This button is selected to create a reference axis, passing through selected line/edge/axis.

- Select the **Axis** ✎ Axis tool (**Features > Reference Geometry > Axis**) to activate it and display the **Axis PropertyManager**, as shown.
- Click on the One Line/Edge/Axis **One Line/Edge/Axis** option of the PropertyManager and select the edge to display preview of reference axis through/across it, as shown.

Tip: You can also directly click on line/edge/axis, the system will then select respective button from the PropertyManager automatically.

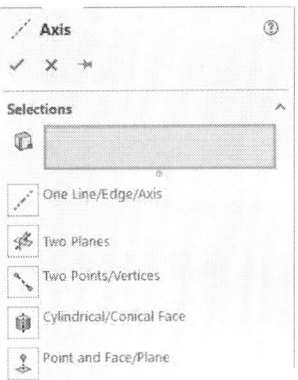 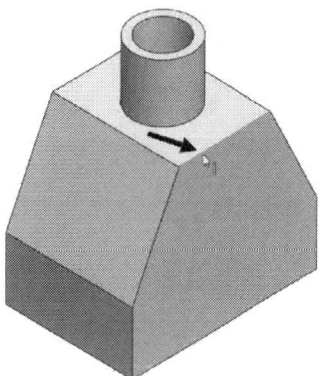

- Now click on the **OK** button of the PropertyManager to display the reference axis along the selected edge, as shown.

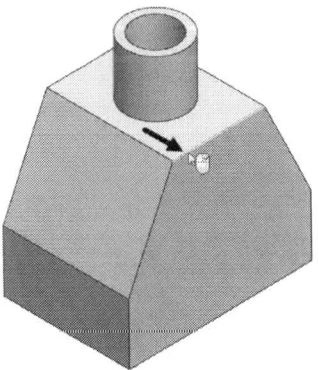 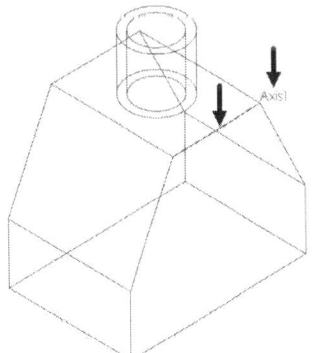

- Similarly, you can select any construction line to create reference axis across it, as shown.

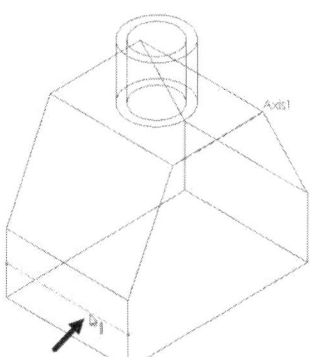 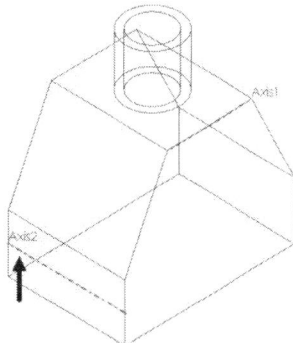

Reference Geometry and Curves

Two Planes

This button is selected to create a reference axis where the two planes intersect each other.

- Select the **Axis** ⟋ Axis tool to activate it and display the **Axis PropertyManager**, as shown above.
- Click on the **Two Planes** option of the PropertyManager, as shown above.
- Select the two planes one by one to display preview of reference axis, as shown.
- Next click on the **OK** button of the PropertyManager to display the reference axis along the selected planes, as shown.

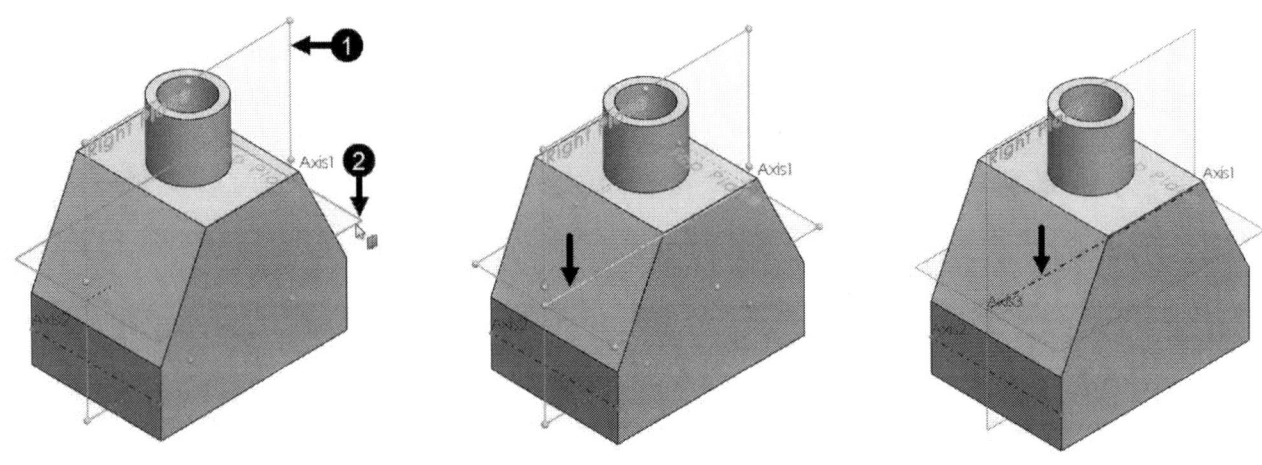

Two Points/Vertices

This button is selected to create a reference axis that passes through two points or two vertices.

- Select the **Axis** ⟋ Axis tool to activate it and display the **Axis PropertyManager**, as shown above.
- Click on the **Two Points/Vertices** option of the PropertyManager.
- Select the two points one by one to display preview of reference axis, as shown.
- Next click on the **OK** button of the PropertyManager to display the reference axis along the selected points, as shown.

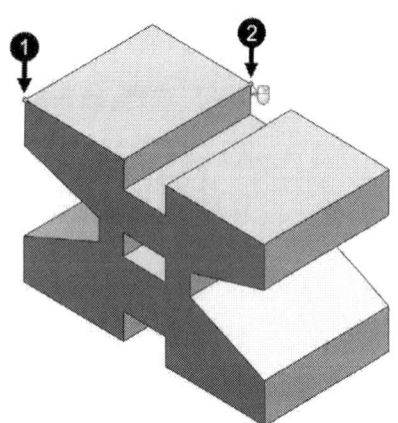 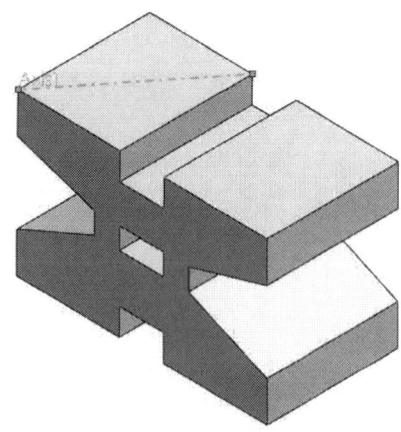

Cylindrical/Conical Face

This button is selected to create a reference axis along cylindrical or conical surfaces after selecting them.

- Select the **Axis** ⟋ Axis tool to activate it and display the **Axis PropertyManager**, as shown above.
- Click on the **Cylindrical/Conical Face** option of the PropertyManager.

Reference Geometry and Curves

- Click on the cylindrical surface to display the preview of reference axis along it, as shown.
- Next click on the **OK** button of the PropertyManager to display the reference axis along the cylindrical surface, as shown.

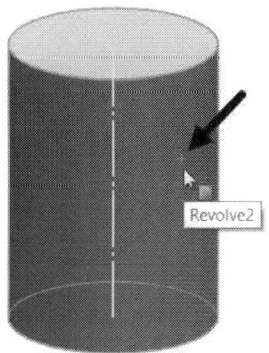 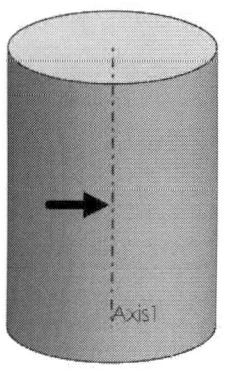

Similarly, you can create reference axis along conical surface, as shown.

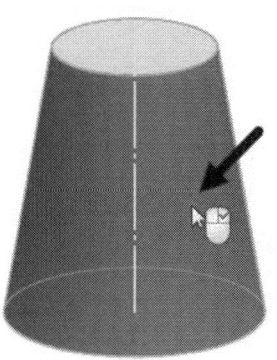 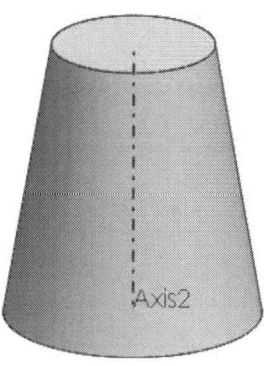

Point and Face/Plane

This button is selected to create a reference axis passing through the selected point and normal to the selected face/plane.

- Select the **Axis** tool to activate it and display the **Axis PropertyManager**, as shown above.
- Click on the **Point and Face/Plane** option of the PropertyManager.
- Select the point and then click on the face to display the preview of reference axis passing through the selected point, normal to the face selected, as shown.
- Next click on the **OK** button of the PropertyManager to display the reference axis, as shown.

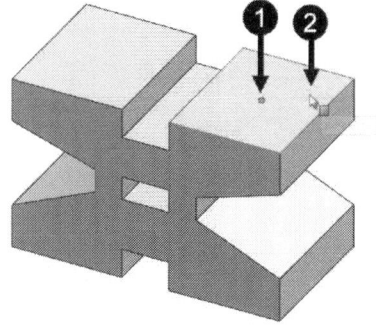 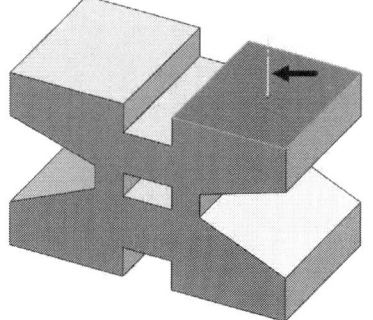 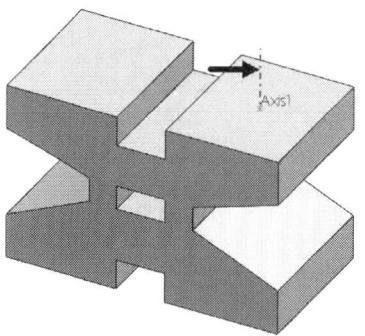

Similarly, create one more axis, as shown.

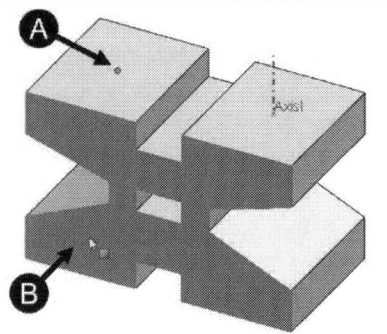 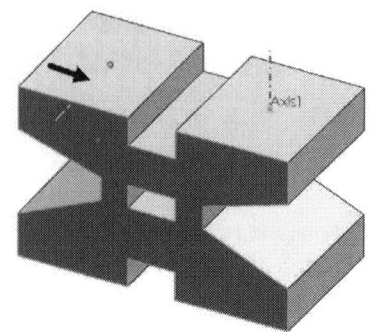 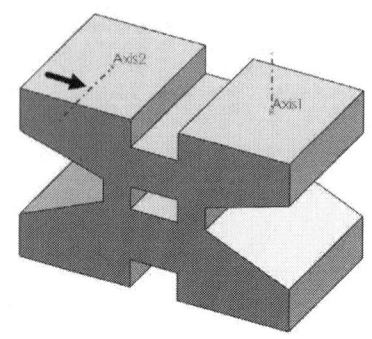

Reference Coordinate System

This tool is used to create a user defined reference coordinate system other than the default coordinate system.

> Click on the **Coordinate System** tool to activate it and display the **Coordinate System PropertyManager**, as shown.
> Click to definite the point for the origin of coordinate system and display temporary coordinate system, as shown.

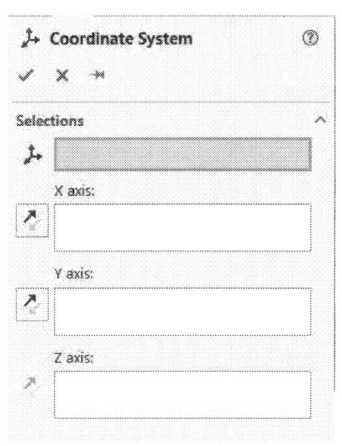 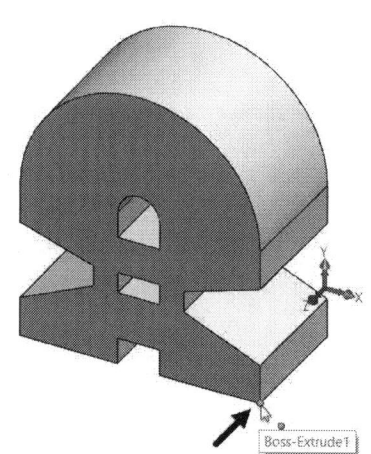 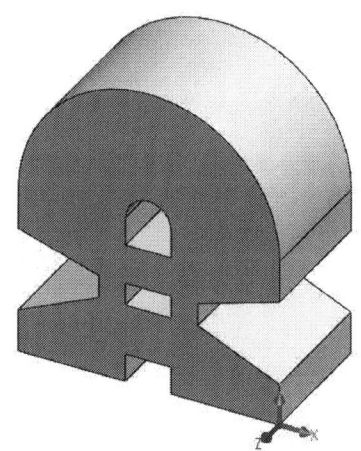

> Next select the line entity to align the X axis, as shown. You can also select point of the line entity.

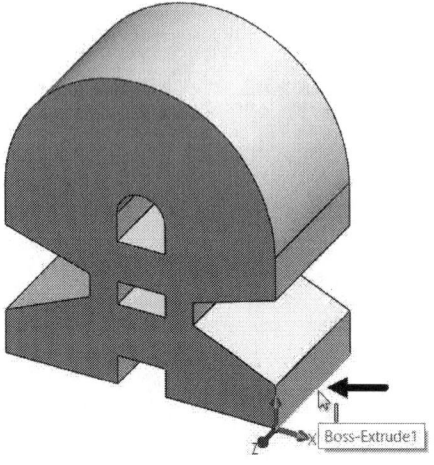 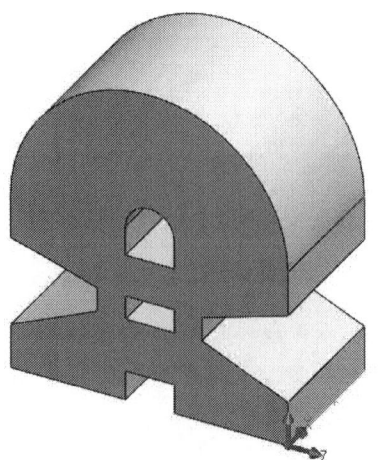

> Also select another line entity to align the Y axis, as shown.

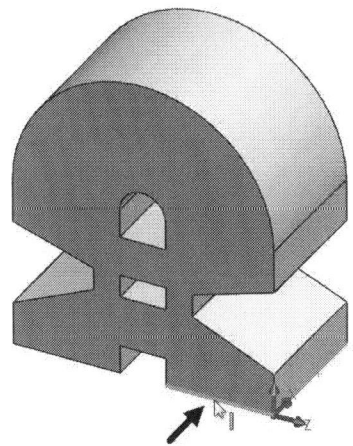 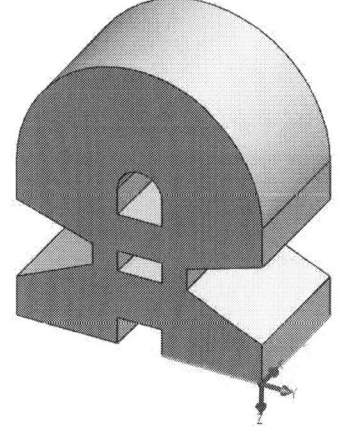

Note that you can click on the [↗] buttons of the PropertyManager to reverse the direction of the respective axis, if required.

➤ Now, click on the [✓] OK button of the PropertyManager to display the reference coordinate system, as shown.

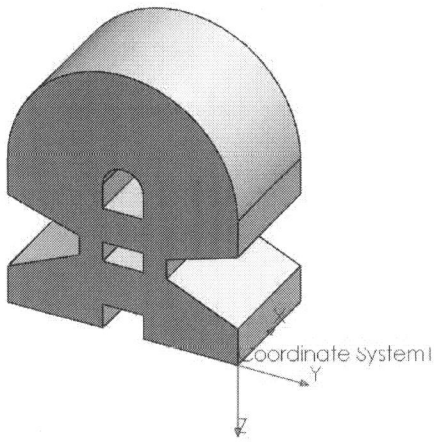

Creating Reference Point

The **Point** ● Point tool is used to create reference point. There are different methods to create reference point, as discussed one-by-one below:

Arc Center

This option is selected to create a reference point at the center of the selected arc or circle.

➤ Select the **Point** ● Point tool (**Features > Reference Geometry > Point**) to activate it and display the **Point PropertyManager**, as shown.

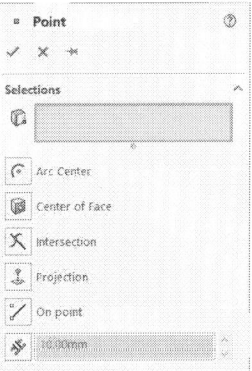

Reference Geometry and Curves   6-15

- Click on the circular edge to display the preview of reference point at its center, as shown.

  Note that system will select the **Arc Center** option of the PropertyManager automatically.

- Next click on the **OK** button of the PropertyManager to display the reference point created, as shown.

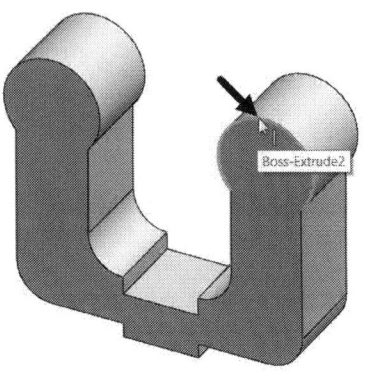 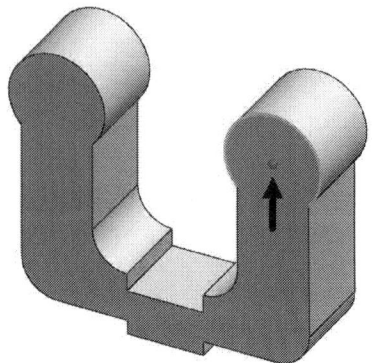 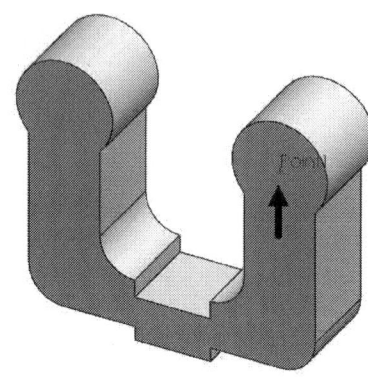

Center of Face

This button is used to create a reference point at the center of mass of the selected face.

- Select the **Point** • Point tool (**Features > Reference Geometry > Point**) to activate it and display the **Point PropertyManager**, as shown above.
- Click on the face to display the preview of reference point at its center of mass, as shown.

  Note that system will select the **Center of Face** option of the PropertyManager automatically.

- Next click on the **OK** button of the PropertyManager to display the reference point created, as shown.

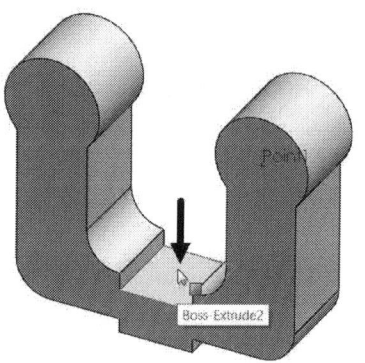 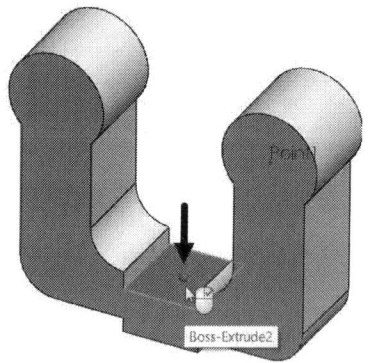 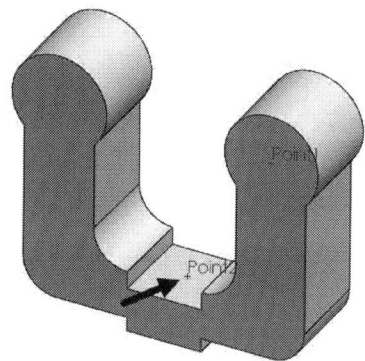

Similarly, you can create reference point of non-planer face also, as shown.

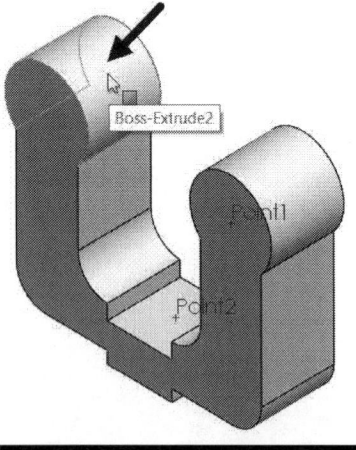 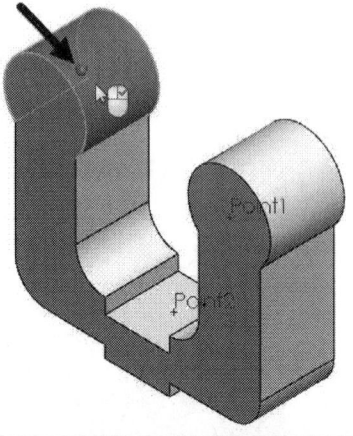 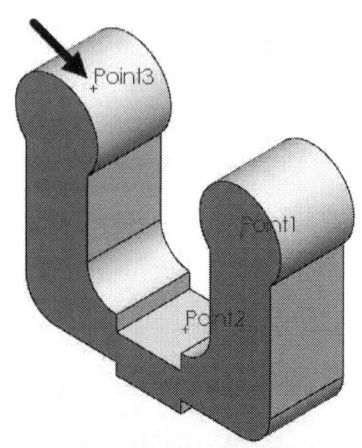

Intersection

This button is used to create a reference point at the intersection of the two selected entities like edges, curves, and sketch segments.

- Select the **Point** ● Point tool (**Features > Reference Geometry > Point**) to activate it and display the PropertyManager.
- Click on the **Intersection** ✕ Intersection option of the PropertyManager, as shown above.
- Next select two edges one by one to display the preview of reference point at the point where they intersect each other, as shown.
- Next click on the **OK** button of the PropertyManager to display the reference point created, as shown.

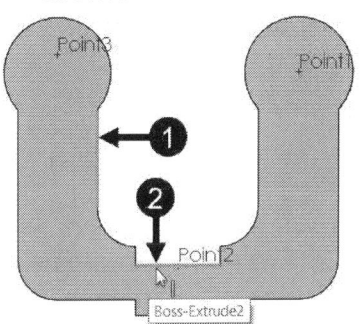 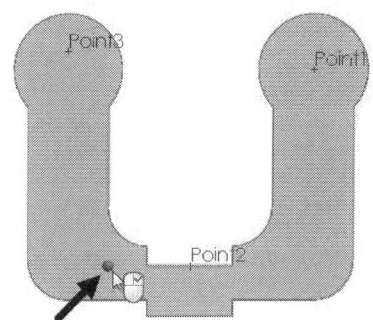 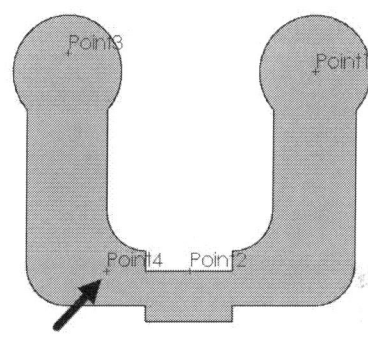

Projection

This option is used to create a reference point from one entity projected onto another. You can project points, endpoints of curves and sketch segments, and vertices of solids and surfaces onto planes and faces (planar or non-planar). The point is projected normal to the plane or face.

- Select the **Point** ● Point tool (**Features > Reference Geometry > Point**) to activate it and display the PropertyManager.
- Next, select the point to project and then click on the plane on which you want to project it to display the preview of the projected reference point, as shown.

    Note that system will select the **Projection** option of the PropertyManager automatically.

- Now click on the **OK** button of the PropertyManager to display the projected reference point, as shown.

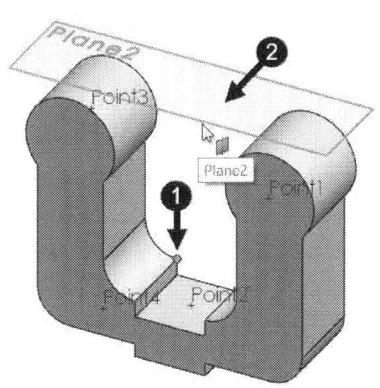 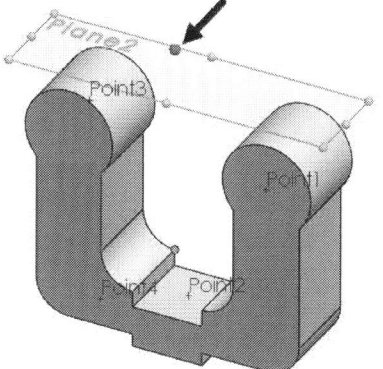 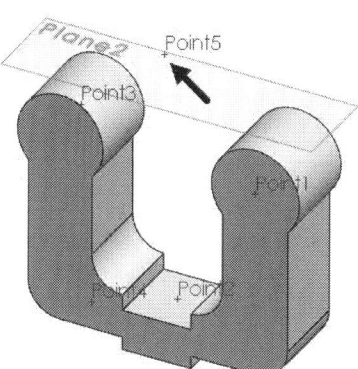

On point

Creates a reference point on a sketch point and on the end of a sketch section.

Along curve distance or multiple reference point

Creates a set of reference points along edges, curves, or sketch segments. Select the entity and create the reference points using these options:

Center of Mass

The **Center of Mass** tool is used to indicate the global center of mass of the entire model.

➤ Select the **Center of Mass** tool (**Features > Reference Geometry > Center of Mass**) to activate it.
➤ After selecting this tool, system will automatically locate the point on the model, as shown.
➤ Also, the **Center of Mass** node will be added to the **FeatureManager Design Tree** under the **Origin** node, as shown.

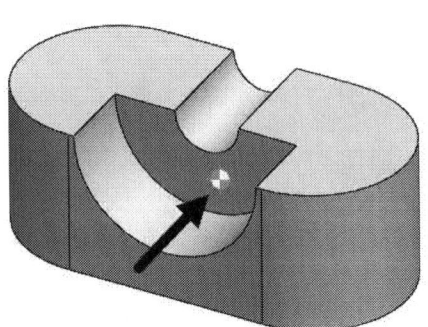
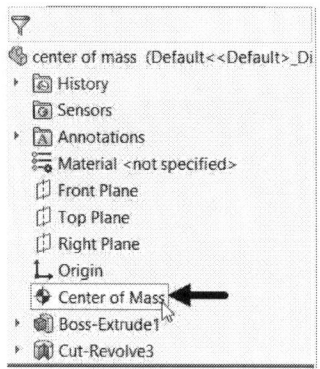

Mass Properties

The **Mass Properties** tool is used to get the mass properties of a solid model in part or assembly of the current session. Mass properties includes density, mass, volume, surface area, center of mass, principal axes of inertia, principal moments of inertia, and moments of inertia.

Select the **Mass Properties** tool (**Evaluate > Mass Properties**) to display the **Mass Properties** dialog box, as shown. Also, a 3D triad will be placed at the center of the model. You can now check the mass properties of the current model in the dialog box displayed.

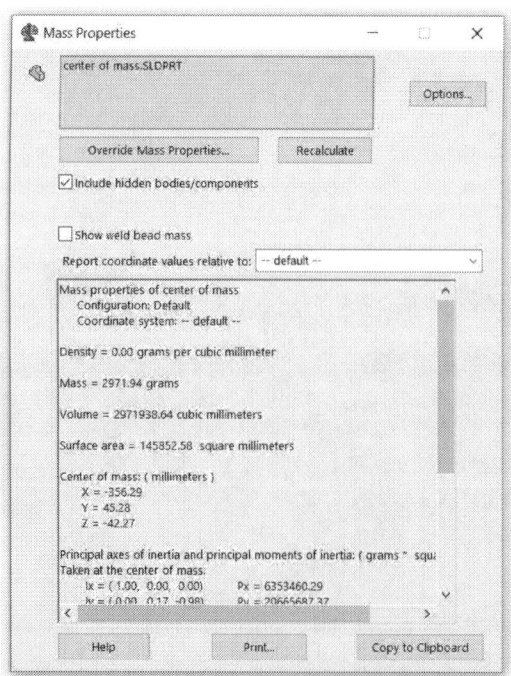

Reference Geometry and Curves

Questions:

1. How can you create an offset plane?
2. How can you create a reference plane passing through three points?
3. How can you create a plane at an angle?
4. Which tool is used to create a reference axis?
5. Which button is used to create a reference point at its center of mass?
6. Which option is used to create a reference point from one entity projected onto another?
7. Which option is selected to create a reference point at the center of the selected arc or circle?
8. Which button is selected to create a reference axis along cylindrical or conical surfaces?

Chapter 07: Hole Features and Pattern Geometry

So far, all of the features that were covered in previous chapter were based on two-dimensional sketches. However, there are certain features in SolidWorks that do not require a sketch at all. Features that do not require a sketch are called Dress-Up or Placed features. You can simply place them on the models. However, you must have some existing geometry to add these features. Unlike a sketch-based feature, you cannot use a Dress-Up feature for a first feature of a model. For example, to create a Mirror feature, you must have an already existing feature to be mirrored or to create a Pattern feature, you must have an already existing feature to be patterned. In this chapter, you will learn how to add Holes and Dress-Up features to your design.

The topics covered in this chapter are:

- ❖ Hole features
- ❖ Creating Simple Hole
- ❖ Hole Wizard Tool
- ❖ Creating Counterbore Hole
- ❖ Creating Countersink Hole
- ❖ Creating Counterbore Slot
- ❖ Creating Mirror feature
- ❖ Creating Pattern features

Hole

As you know, it is possible to use the **Extrude** tool to create cuts and remove material. But, if you want to drill holes that are of standard sizes, the **Hole** tool is a better way to do this. The reason for this is it has many hole types already predefined for you. All you have to do is choose the correct hole type and size. The other benefit is when you are going to create a 2D drawing, SolidWorks can automatically place the correct hole annotation. The various types of holes are discussed next.

Create simple hole

The Simple tool is used to create simple hole.

➢ Activate the **Simple Hole** tool (**Insert > Features > Simple Hole**) from the Menu bar to display the **Hole PropertyManager**, as shown.

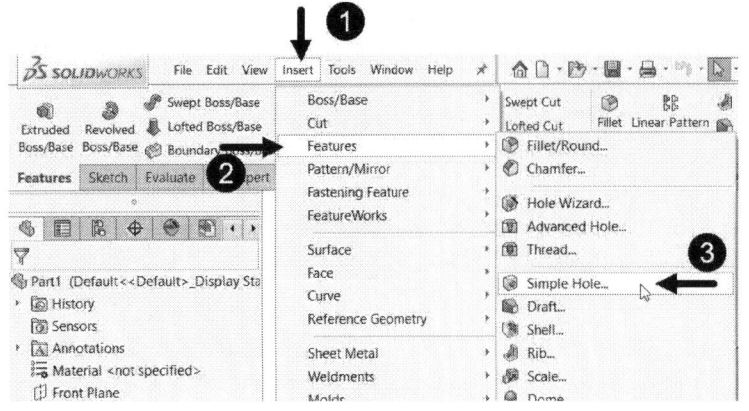
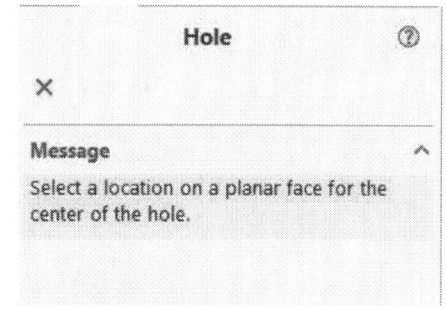

> Now click on the planer face to place the hole and display the preview of simple hole, as shown.

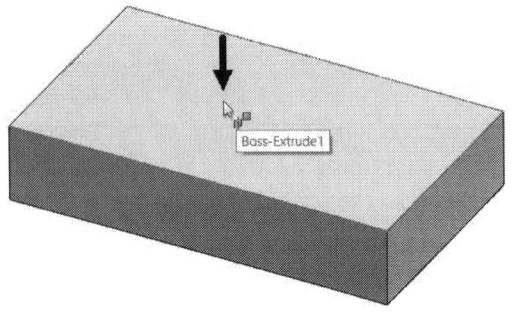
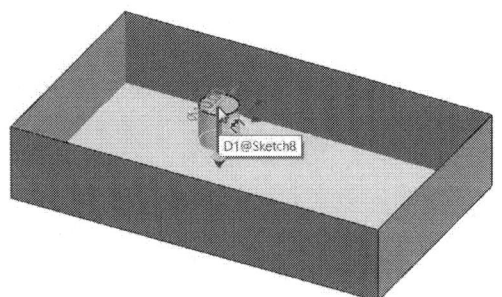

> The simple hole with the default dimension gets displayed and you can enter the required values in the PropertyManager, as shown.

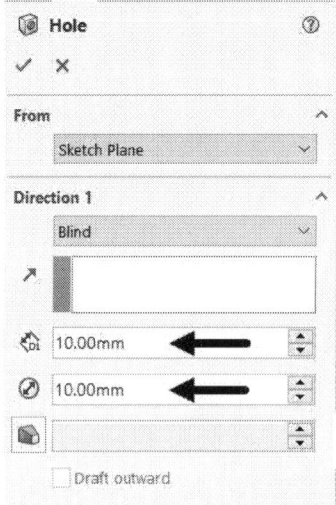

> Now click on the **OK** button of the PropertyManager to display the simple hole, as shown.

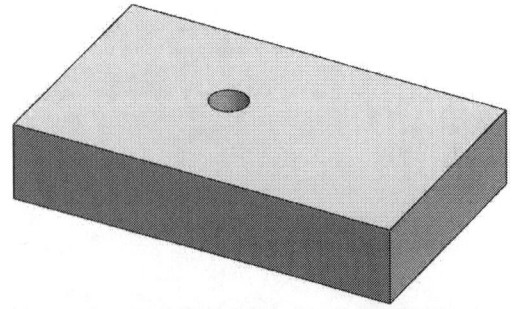
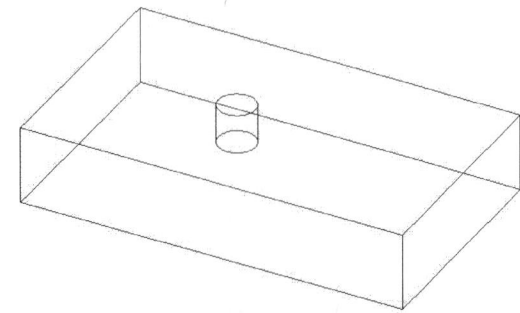

Hole Wizard

This tool is used to add standard holes like counterbore, countersink, tapped, drilled, and pipe tap holes. In SolidWorks there are various types of standard holes/slots grouped in the library. These options can be used for creating different types of holes. You can also create customized hole using this tool.

> Activate the **Hole Wizard** tool from the **Feature CommandManager** to display **Hole Specification PropertyManager**, as shown.

Some of the important options available in the **Hole Specification PropertyManager** and procedure of creating various types of hole features are discussed next.

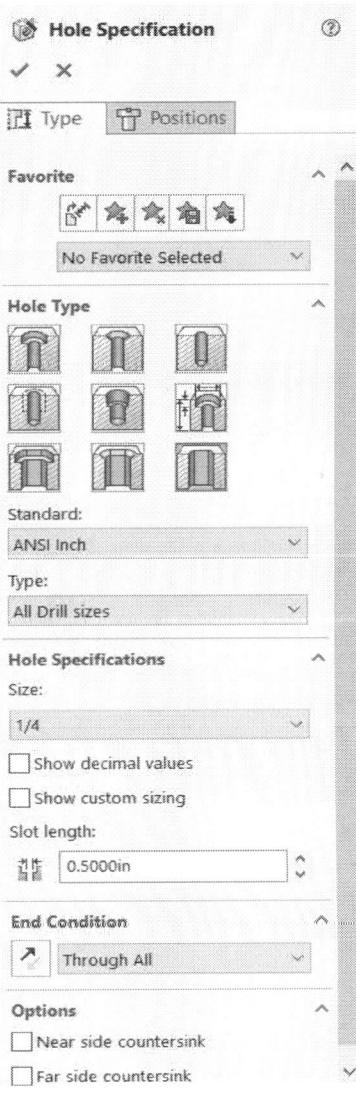

Favourite
The options in this rollout are used to add and manage a list of styles for Hole Wizard that you need to reuse in model.

Hole Type Rollout
The **Hole Type** rollout of the **Hole Specification PropertyManager** is used to define the type of the standard hole to be created.

Hole Features and Pattern Geometry   7-3

Creating Counterbore Hole
To create a Counterbore hole feature.

- Activate the **Hole** tool from the **Features CommandManager** to activate it and display the **Hole Specification PropertyManager**, as shown.
- Select the **Counterbore** button under **Hole Type** rollout if it is not selected by default, as shown.
- Next, select the required options from their respective drop-down lists available in the PropertyManager one by one, as shown.

  The use of options available in the drop-downs of **Hole Specification PropertyManager** are discussed further in this chapter.

- Also enter or adjust the required values for the hole feature in their respective spinners of the PropertyManager, as shown.

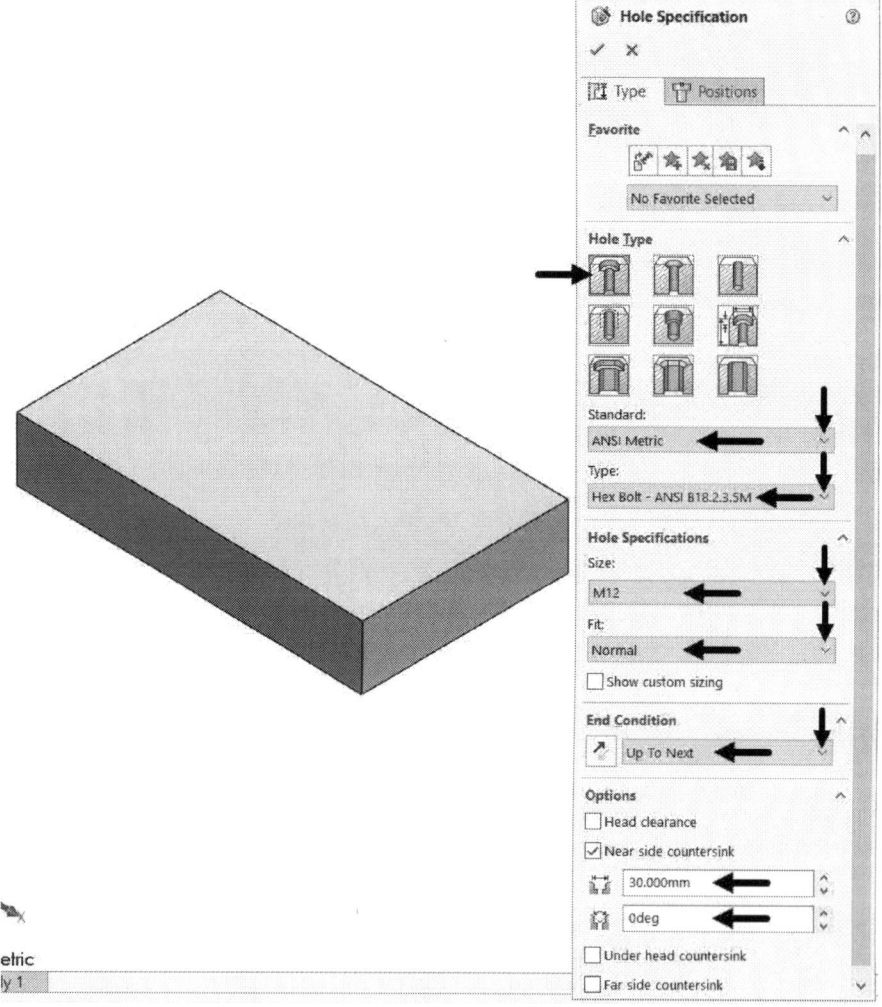

- Now, click on the **Position** tab of the PropertyManager and click over the flat surface of the model to place the hole over it and display the preview of hole feature, as shown.
- Click again on the selected surface to define position/location for hole feature and display preview of placed counterbore hole, as shown.

Hole Features and Pattern Geometry

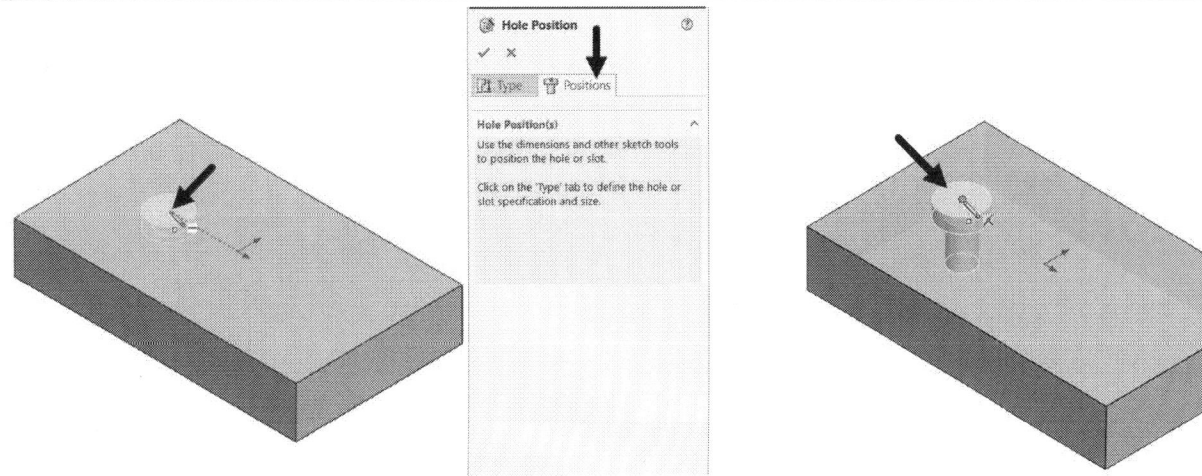

- Select the **Smart Dimension** tool from the **Sketch CommandManager** to activate it.
- Select the top edge and center point of the hole to display the dimension, as shown.
- Click to place the dimension created and enter the required distance value in the **Modify** edit box displayed, as shown

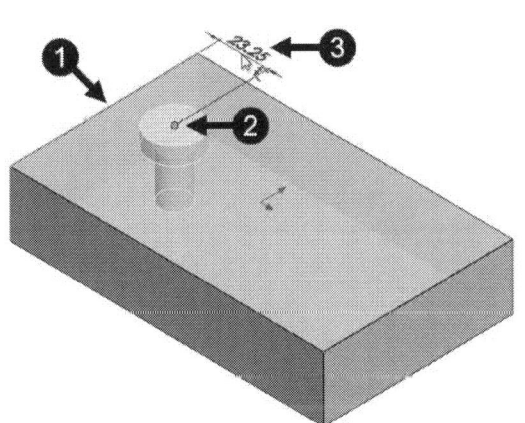 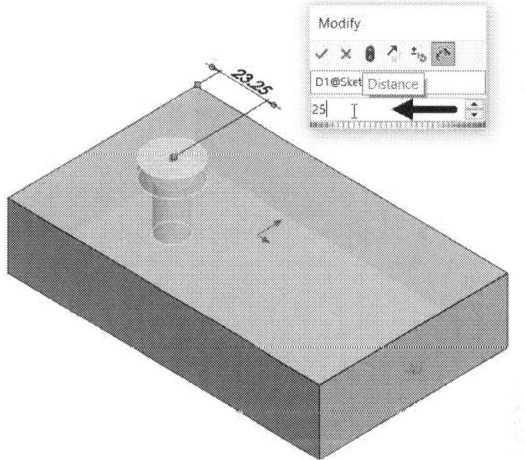

- Similarly enter the required distance value in other direction, as shown.

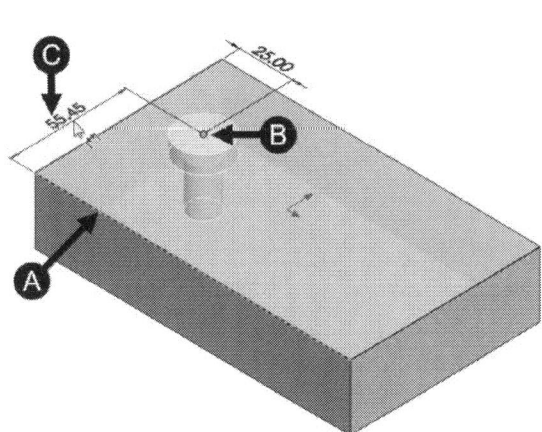 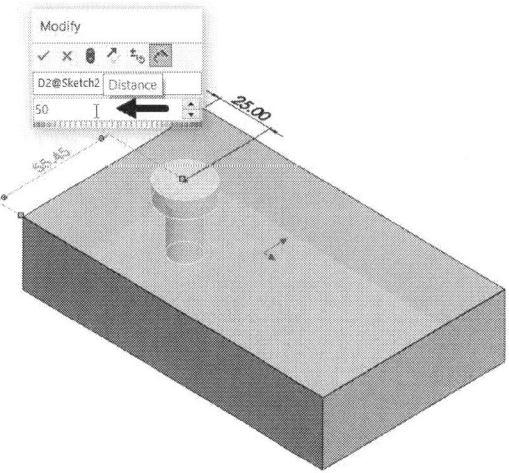

- Now click on the **OK** button of the PropertyManager to display model with Counterbore hole, as shown.

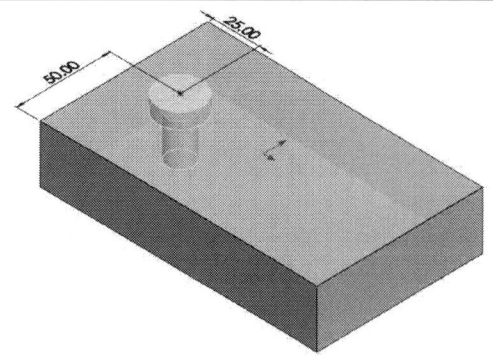 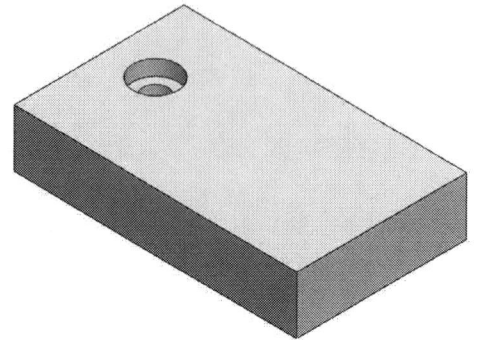

For the better visibility of hole feature, the display style of model is changed to the **Wireframe** mode and **Hidden Lines Visible** mode from the **Display Style** flyout of the **View (Heads-Up)** toolbar, as shown.

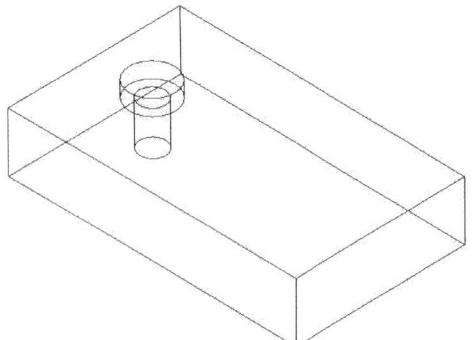 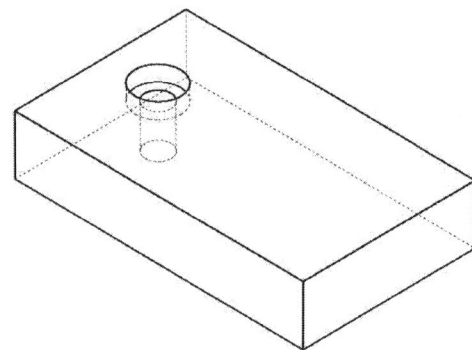

> Now click on the **OK** button of the PropertyManager to display model with Counterbore hole, as shown.

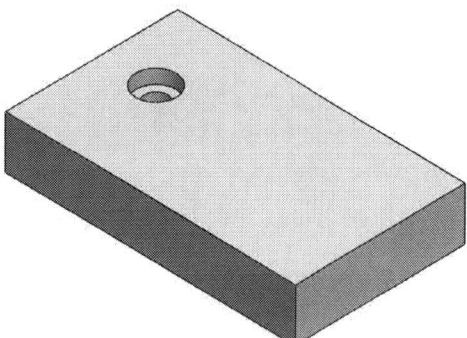 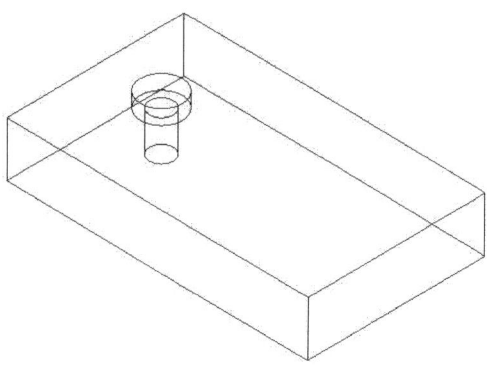

The other options available in **Hole Specification PropertyManager** are discussed next and these options vary depending on the Hole type:

Standard

The **Standard** drop-down list under **Hole Type** rollout has options that are used to define the hole standards, as shown.

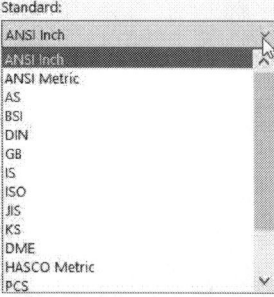

Type

The options available in this drop-down list defines the drill sizes, tap drills, dowel holes, or screw clearance, as shown.

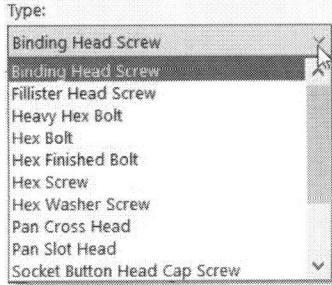

Hole Specifications Rollout

The **Hole Specifications** rollout, in the **Type** tab of the **Hole Specification PropertyManager** is used to define the size and fit of the standard hole to be created, as shown and discussed below.

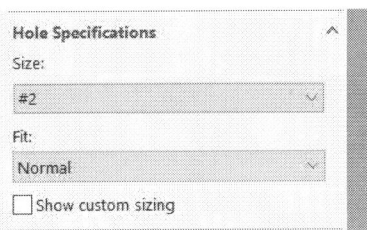

Size

The options available in this drop-down list are used to defines size of fastener to be inserted in the hole, as shown above.

Fit

The options available in this drop-down list are used to define the fastener fit - Close, Normal, or Loose, as shown. Note that this drop-down list will be available for Counterbore and Countersink only.

Show custom sizing

The options available in this drop-down list under Hole Specifications drop-down defines fastener size, as shown.

End Condition Rollout

The options in the **End Condition** rollout in **Hole Specification PropertyManager** are used to define the hole depth by selecting the required option. The use of these options is same as discussed in previous chapters. The **Reverse Direction** button is used to flip direction of hole, as shown.

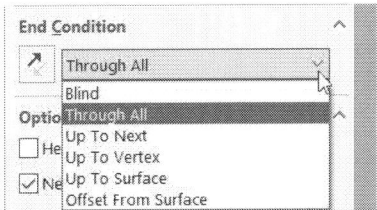

Note that, additional options will get displayed for defining the depth for threads, if you create tapered hole or a tapped hole.

Options Rollout

The use of options in this rollout are explained one by one below.

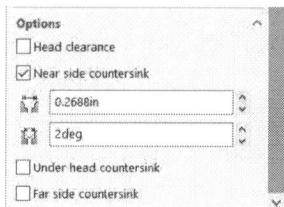

Head clearance

This check box is selected to define the clearance distance between the head of the fastener and the placement plane of the hole feature. When you select this check box, the **Head Clearance** spinner will get displayed and you can set the clearance value in this spinner.

Near side countersink

This check box is selected to define the diameter and the angle for the countersink on the upper face, which is the placement plane of the hole feature. After selecting this check box, the **Near Side Countersink Diameter** and **Near Side Countersink Angle** spinners will be displayed. You can set the values of the diameter and angle using their respective spinners, as shown above.

Under head countersink

This check box is selected to define the diameter and the angle for the countersink to be applied at the end of the counterbore head. When you select this check box, the **Under Head, Countersink Diameter** and **Under Head Countersink Angle** spinners will be displayed. You can set the values of the diameter and the angle using the corresponding spinners.

Far side countersink

This check box is selected to define the diameter and the angle for the countersink on the bottom face of the hole feature. When you select this check box, the **Far Side Countersink Diameter** and **Far Side Countersink Angle** spinners will be displayed. You can set the values of the diameter and the angle using their respective spinners.

Tip: To edit any Hole feature, right click on it from the **FeatureManager design tree** to display the shortcut menu, as shown. Click on the **Edit Feature** button to display the **Hole Specification PropertyManager**. Next, you can select the required option and enter the required values in it.

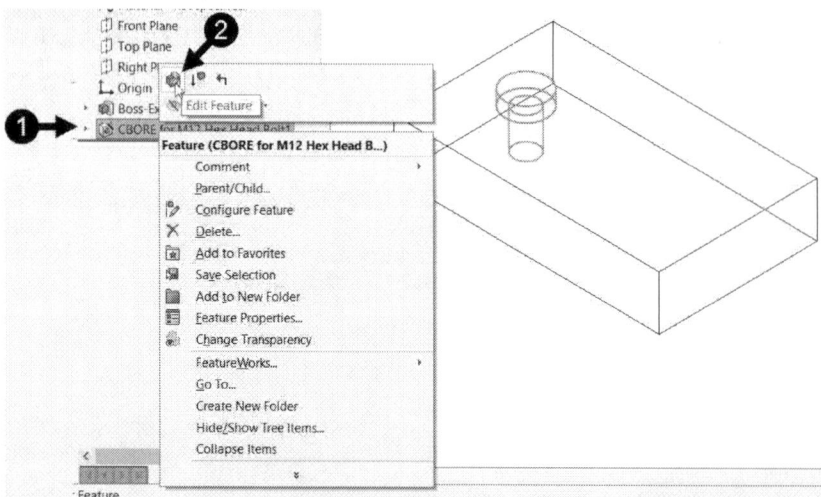

Hole Features and Pattern Geometry

Creating Countersink Hole

To create a Countersink hole feature, select the **Countersink** button under the **Hole Type** rollout, as shown. Next follow the step similarly as discussed above while creating a Counterbore hole, as shown.

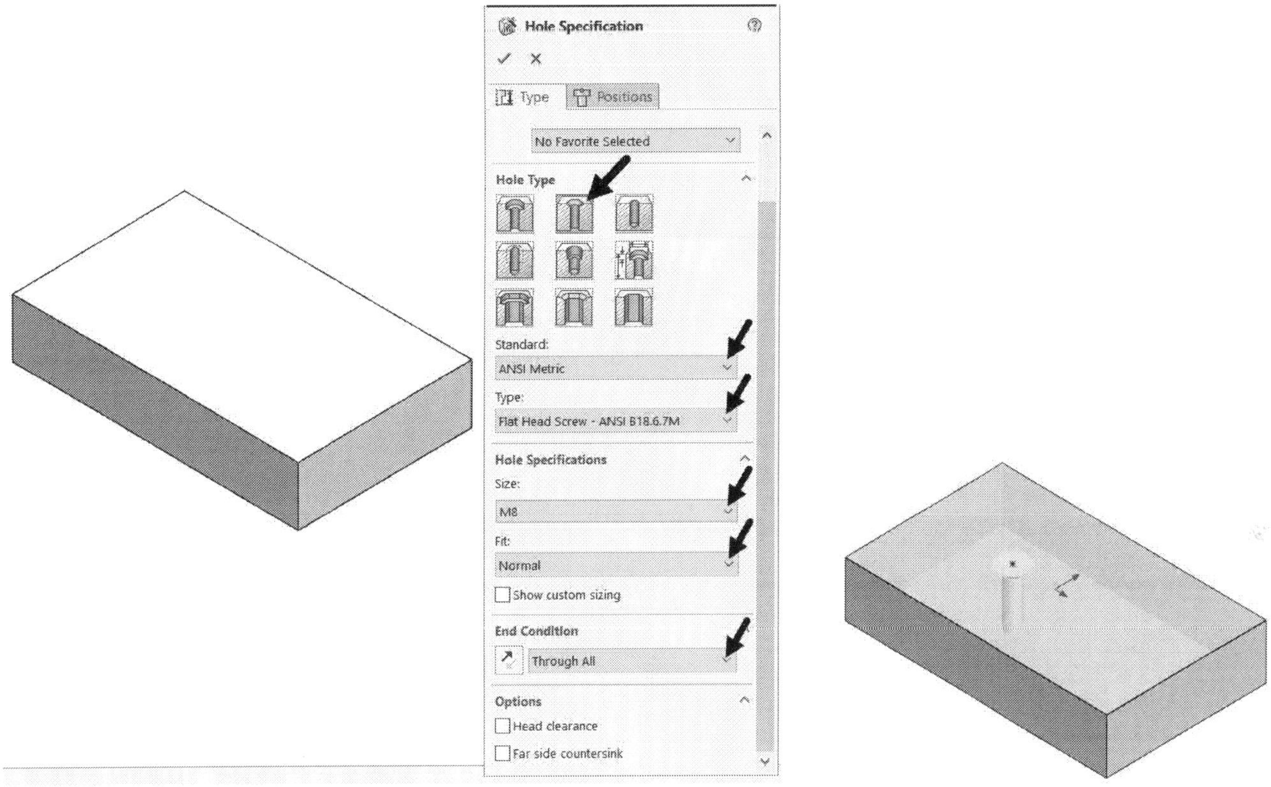

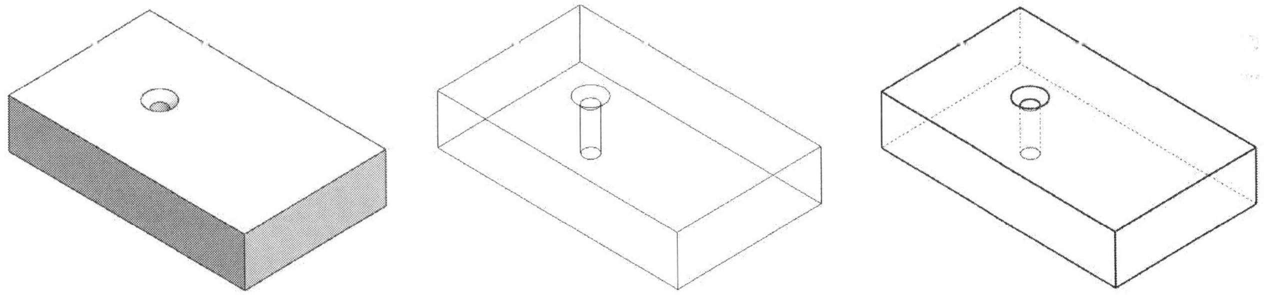

Creating Hole

To create a hole feature.

- Select the **Hole** button from the **Hole Type** drop-down, as shown.
- Select the required options from the drop-downs of the PropertyManager and enter required values in their respective edit boxes, as shown.
- Next click on the **Position** tab of the PropertyManager and double click on the
- Now, click on the **Position** tab of the PropertyManager and click over the flat surface of the model to place the hole over it and display the preview of hole feature.
- Click again on the selected surface to define position/location for hole feature and display preview of hole placed.
- Click on the **OK** button of the PropertyManager to display the model with Hole feature, as shown.

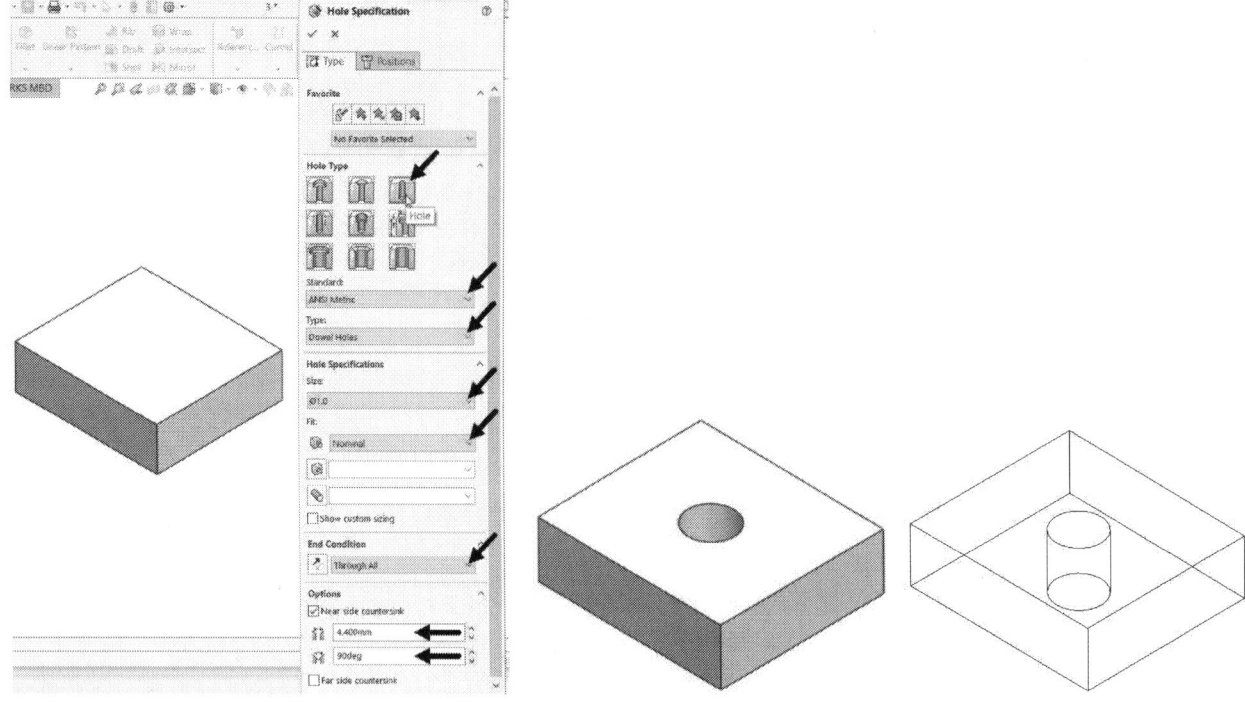

Similarly, you can create Straight Tap hole, Tapered Tap hole and Legacy hole by following the same step as discussed earlier in this chapter while creating the Counterbore hole.

Creating Counterbore Slot
To create a Counterbore slot feature.

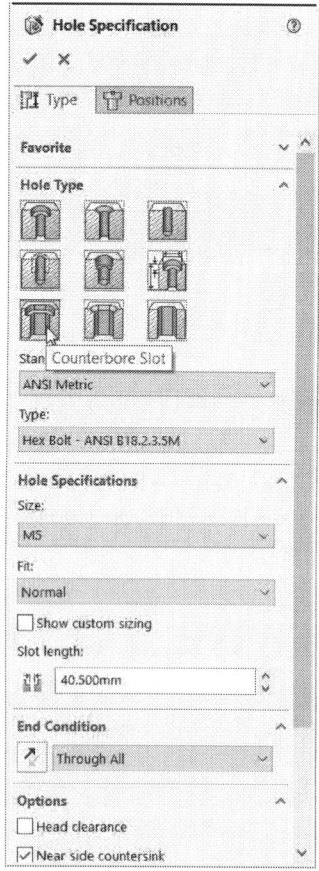

- Click on the **Hole Wizard** tool from the **Features CommandManager** to activate it and display the **Hole Specification PropertyManager**, as shown above.
- Select the **Counterbore Slot** button under **Hole Type** drop-down, as shown.
- Next, select the required options from the different drop-downs of the PropertyManager one by one, as shown.

  The use of options available in the drop-downs is same as discussed above in this chapter.

- Also enter the required values in the respective selection boxes of the PropertyManager, as shown.
- Now, click on the **Position** tab of the PropertyManager and click over the flat surface of the model to place the slot over it and display the preview of counterbore slot feature, as shown.
- Click again on the selected surface to define position/location for hole feature and display preview of placed counterbore slot, as shown.

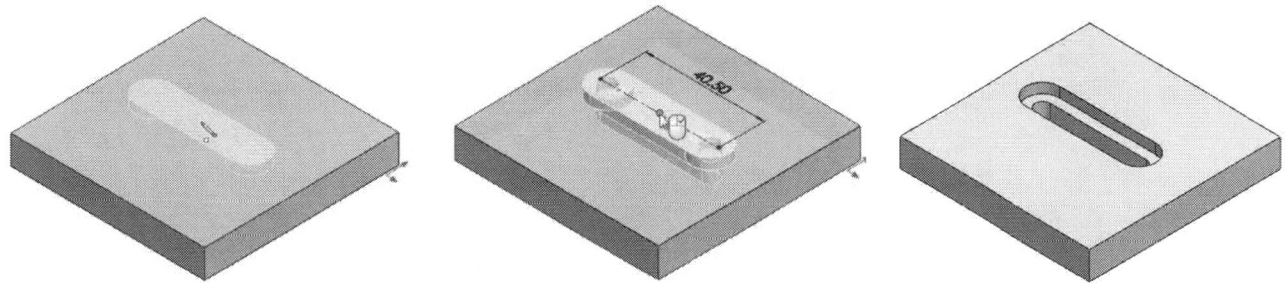

> Using the **Smart Dimension** tool from the **Sketch CommandManager** and by applying dimensions, you can set the location of slot at required location, as discussed earlier.

For the better visibility of slot feature, the display style of model is changed to the **Wireframe** mode and **Hidden Lines Visible** mode from the **Display Style** flyout of the **View (Heads-Up)** toolbar, as shown.

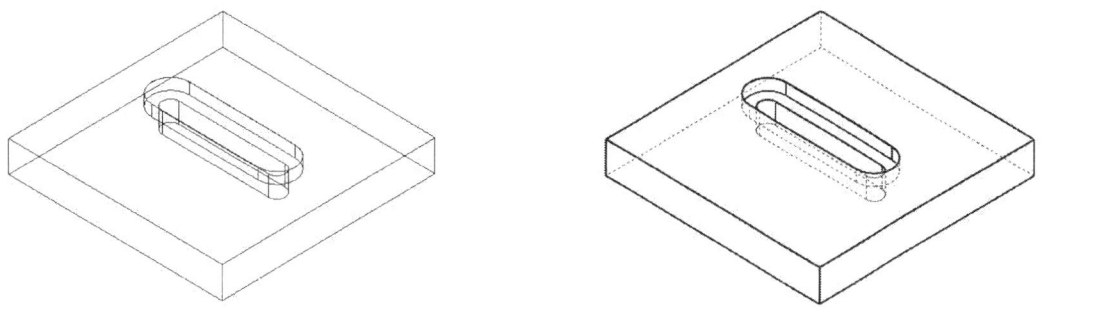

Similarly, you can create **Countersink** slot, and **Slot** by following the same step as discussed above.

Mirror

This tool is useful while designing a symmetric part by saving your time. By using this tool, you can copy individual features of the entire body. For creating a mirror feature in Part environment or 3D geometry, you need to have place or face to use it as the mirroring element. You can use default planes, model faces or sometime you need to create a datum/reference plane.

Mirror a Feature/Features of a Model

> Click on the **Mirror** tool from the **Features CommandManager** to activate it and display the **Mirror PropertyManager**, as shown.
> Select the Plane as the mirror plane, as shown.
> Select the features to mirror and display the preview of mirror features, as shown
> Click on the **OK** button of the PropertyManager to display the part will Mirror Feature, as shown.

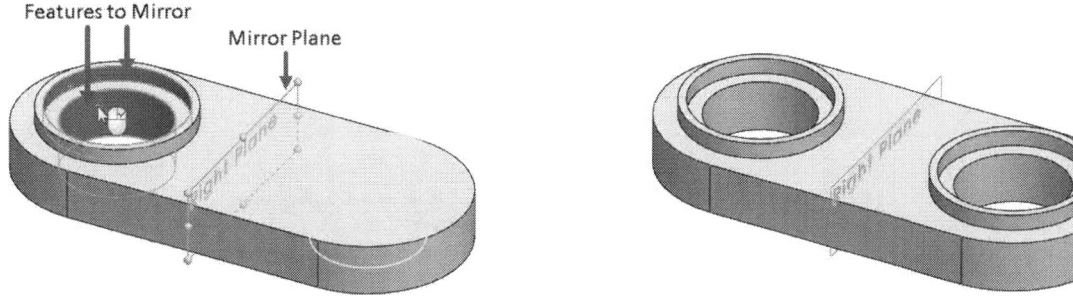

Now, if you make changes to original feature, the mirror feature will be updated automatically, as shown.

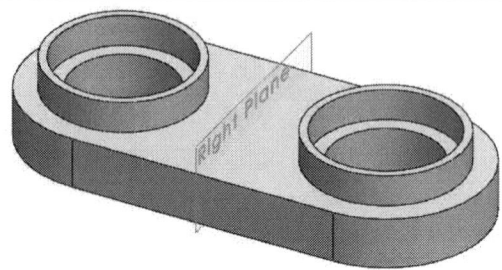

Mirror the Whole Model

If the part you are creating is completely symmetric, you can save more time by creating half of it and mirroring the entire geometry rather than individual features.

> Activate the **Mirror** tool.
> Click on the face of the model to select it as the mirror face, as shown.

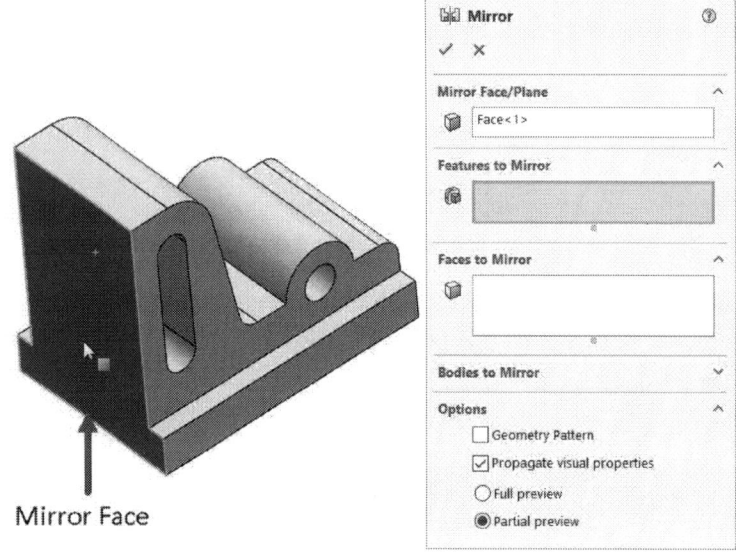

Mirror Face

> Click on all features from the **FeatureManager design tree** on the left side of the screen to display preview of mirror feature, as shown.
> Click on the **OK** button of the PropertyManager to display the Mirror Feature, as shown.

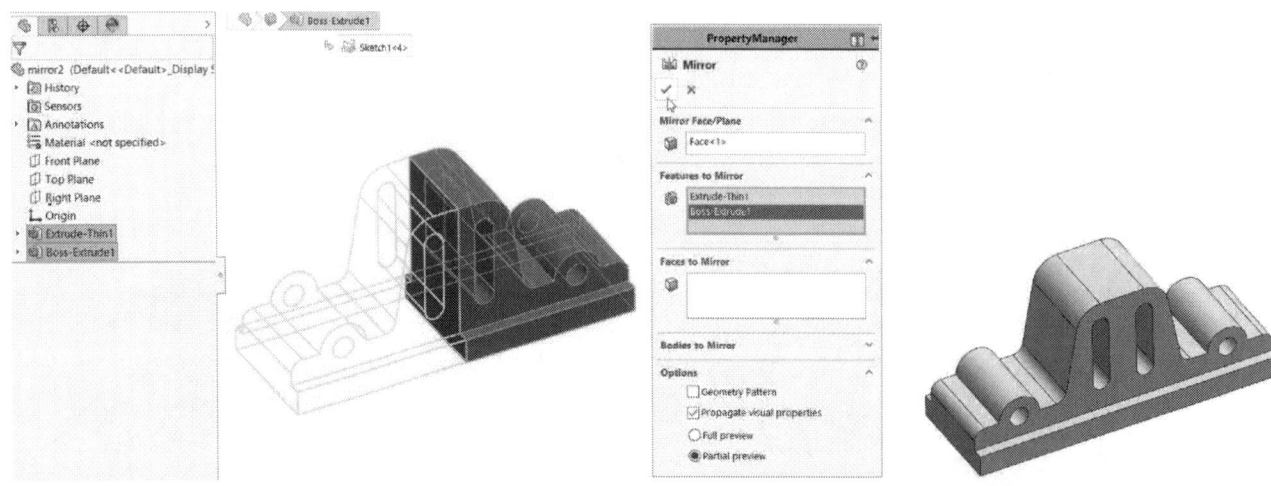

Hole Features and Pattern Geometry

Pattern Tools

In SolidWorks, there are various Pattern tools, used to create replica of a feature using different options - **Linear Pattern**, **Circular Pattern**, **Curve Driven Pattern**, **Sketch Driven Pattern**, **Table Driven Pattern**, **Fill Pattern** and **Variable Pattern**, available in the **Linear Pattern** flyout, as shown. You can save much time using this tool as you can create multiple copies of a feature. Also, if you make changes to original feature, the pattern/child features will be updated automatically.

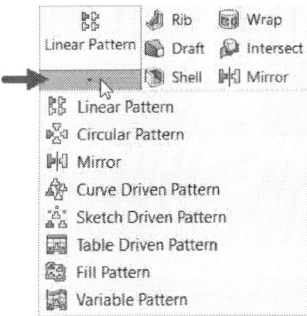

The Options available in the **Linear Pattern** flyout are discussed next.

 ## Linear Pattern

The **Linear Pattern** tool is used to create multiple instances of selected feature or features with uniform space along a single or two linear paths.

> Click on the **Linear Pattern** tool from the **Features CommandManager** to activate it and display the **Linear Pattern PropertyManager**, as shown.
> Click on the edges of the model to define both as Direction1 and Direction2 to pattern in both directions, as shown

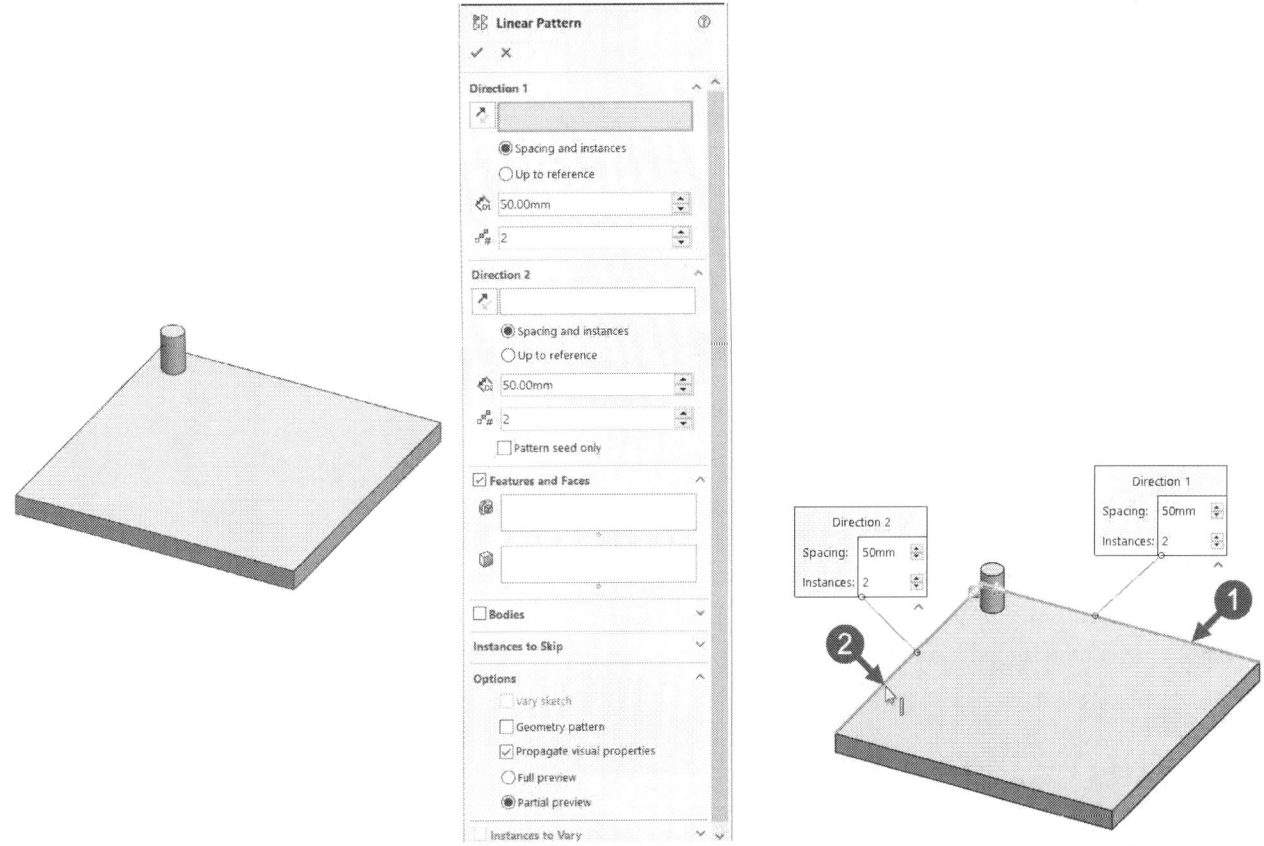

Hole Features and Pattern Geometry

➤ Click on the feature to be patterned and display preview of pattern feature, as shown.
➤ Now enter or adjust the required spacing value and number of instances in their respective spinners available in the **Direction1** and **Direction2** callout attached with selected edges, as shown.

Alternatively, you can enter these values in their respective edit boxes, available in the **Linear Pattern PropertyManager,** as shown above.

➤ Click on the **OK** button of the PropertyManager to display the Pattern Feature, as shown.

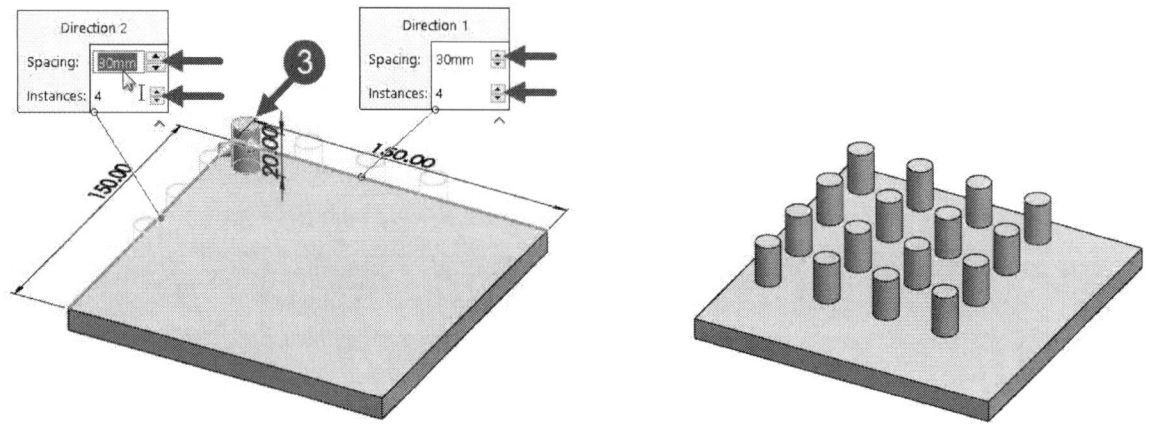

Editing the Linear Pattern

After creating the Pattern features, if any time you need to make changes in it, you can edit it.

➤ Right click on the **LPattern** Pattern Feature in the **FeatureManager** design tree and click on **Edit Feature** button from the shortcut menu displayed, as shown.

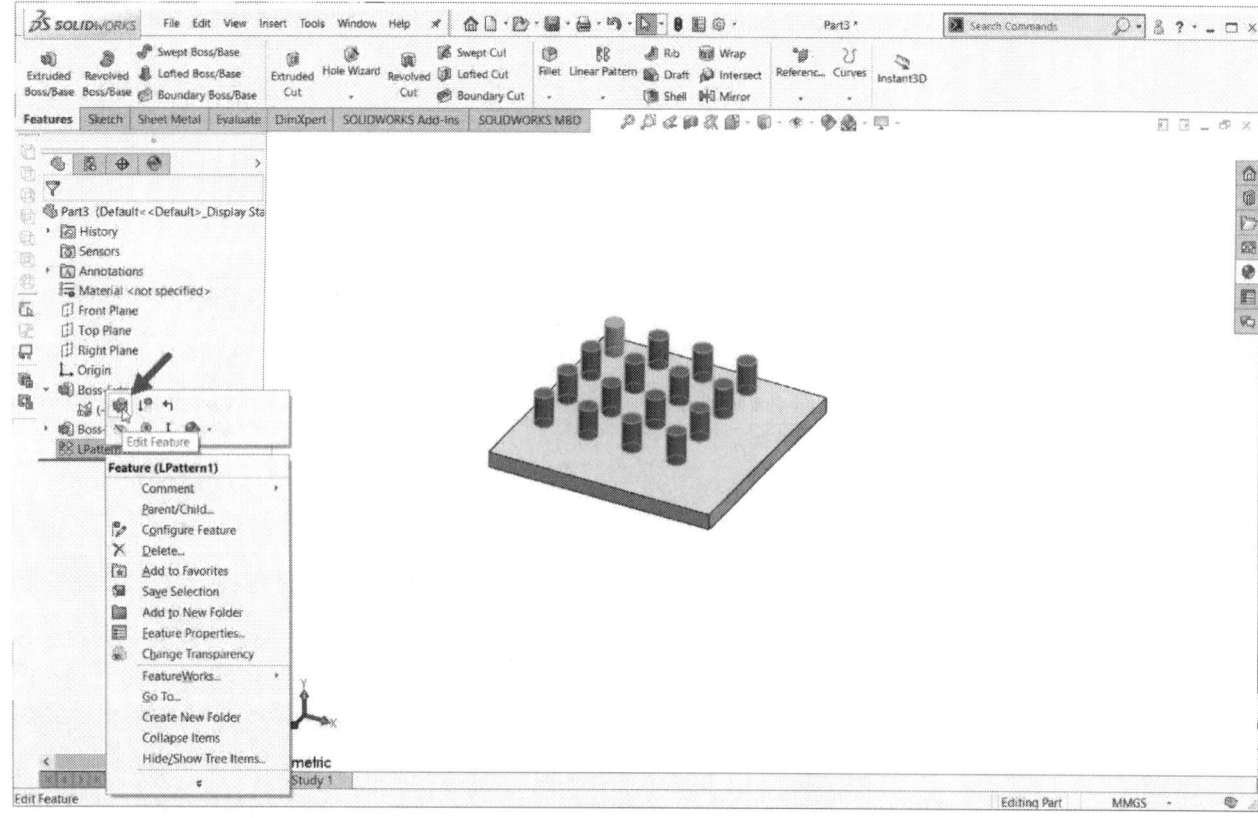

➤ The **Linear Pattern PropertyManager** will be displayed again and you can make the required changes in it by entering the required spacing and number of instance values, as shown.

Hole Features and Pattern Geometry

➢ Click on the OK button of the PropertyManager to display the part with edited Pattern Feature, as shown.

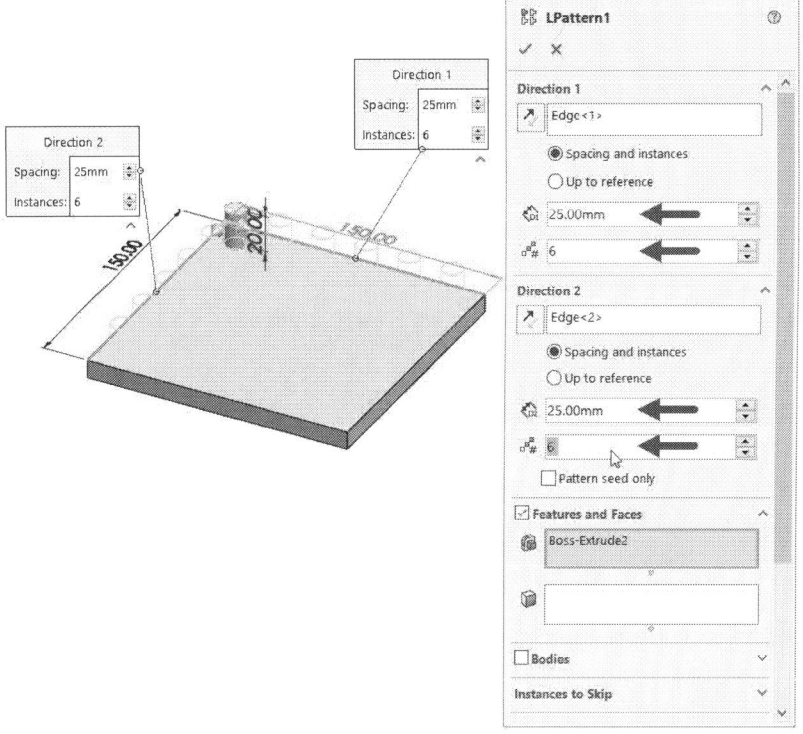

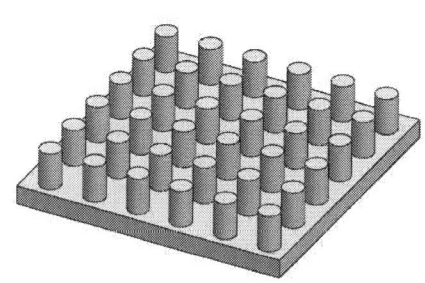 ## Circular Pattern

This tool is used to create multiple instances of selected feature or features with uniform space along an axis.

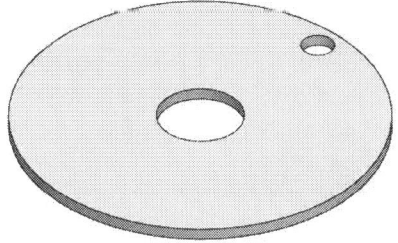 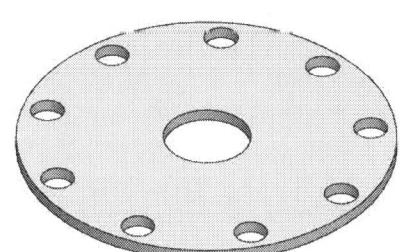

➢ Select the **Circular Pattern** option from the **Linear Pattern** flyout of the **Features CommandManager** to activate it and display the **CirPattern PropertyManager**, as shown.
➢ Click on the feature to be patterned, as shown.
➢ Click in the Pattern Axis box under **Direction 1** box of the PropertyManager, as shown
➢ Next, click on the circular face of the model to define it as Pattern Axis and display the preview of circular pattern feature along it, as shown
➢ Now enter or adjust the required angular spacing value and number of instances in their respective spinners available in the **Direction1** callout attached with selected face, as shown.

Alternatively, you can enter these values in their respective edit boxes, available in the **CirPattern PropertyManager,** as shown.

➢ Click on the OK button of the PropertyManager to display the Pattern Feature, as shown.

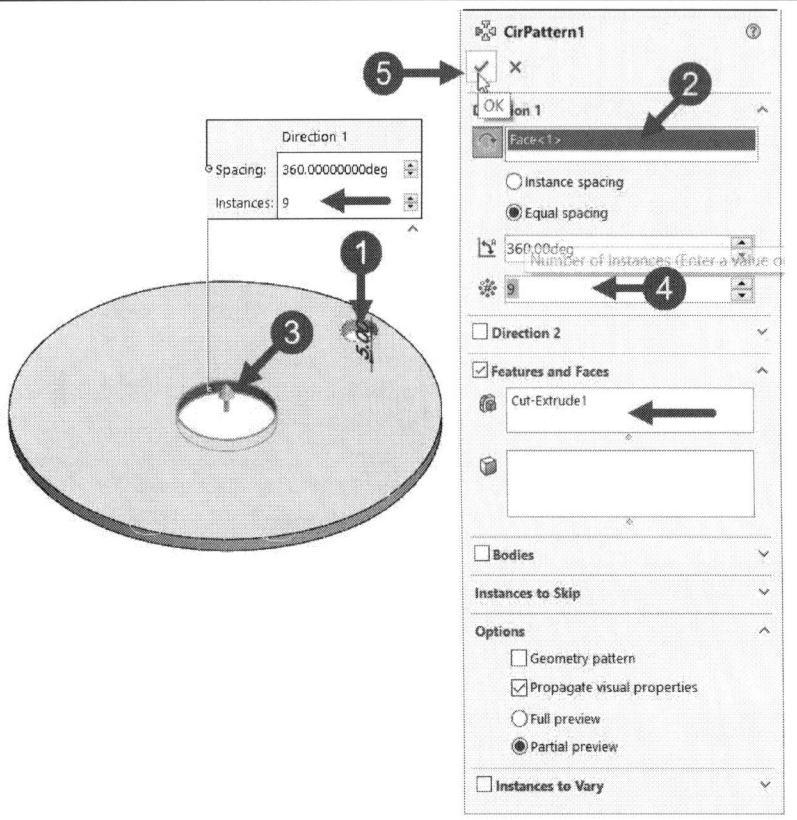

Curve Driven Pattern

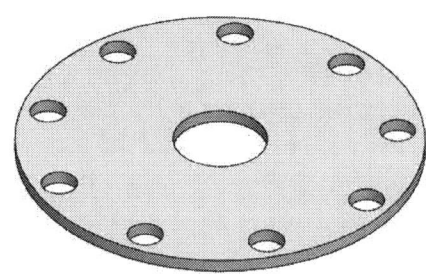

This tool is used to create multiple instances of selected feature or features with uniform space along a curve, as shown and as discussed.

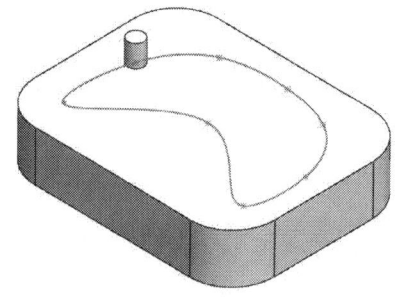 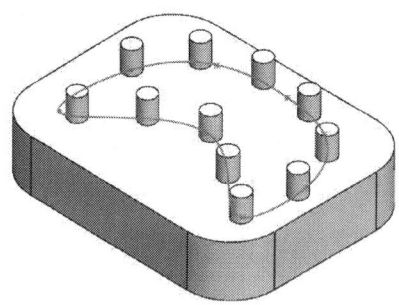 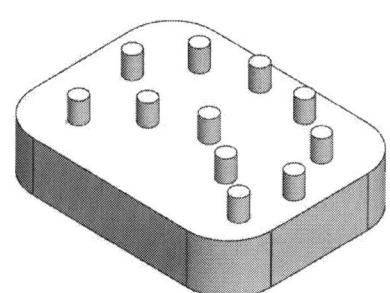

> Select the **Curve Driven Pattern** option from the **Linear Pattern** flyout of the **Features CommandManager** to activate it and display the **CrvPattern PropertyManager**, as shown.
> Select the curve and then select the feature to be patterned to display preview of patterned feature along the curve, as shown.
> Next, enter or adjust the required spacing value and number of instances in their respective spinners available under the **Direction1** rollout of the PropertyManager, as shown.

Alternatively, you can enter these values in their respective edit boxes, available in the **Direction1** callout attached with selected curve, as shown.

> Click on the **OK** button of the PropertyManager to display the Pattern Feature, as shown.

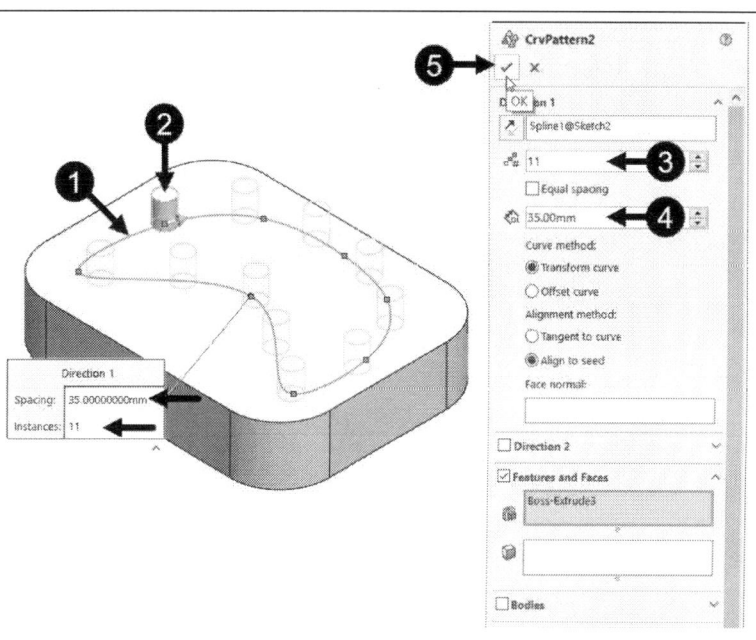
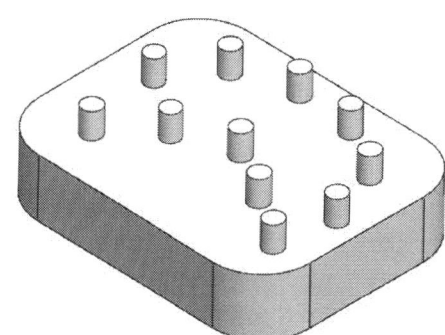

Sketch Driven Pattern

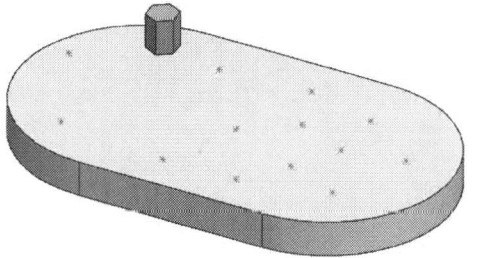 **Sketch Driven Pattern**

This tool is used to create multiple instances of selected feature or features along the point entities created in a single sketch, as shown and as discussed.

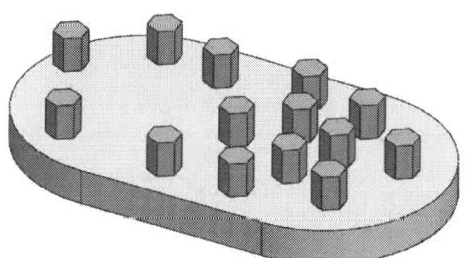

- Select the **Sketch Driven Pattern** option from the **Linear Pattern** flyout of the **Features CommandManager** to activate it and display the **Sketch Driven Pattern PropertyManager**, as shown.
- Click on any of the point entity created in the sketch and then click on the feature to be patterned to display preview of patterned feature along the point entities, as shown.
- Click on the **OK** button of the PropertyManager to display the Pattern Feature, as shown.

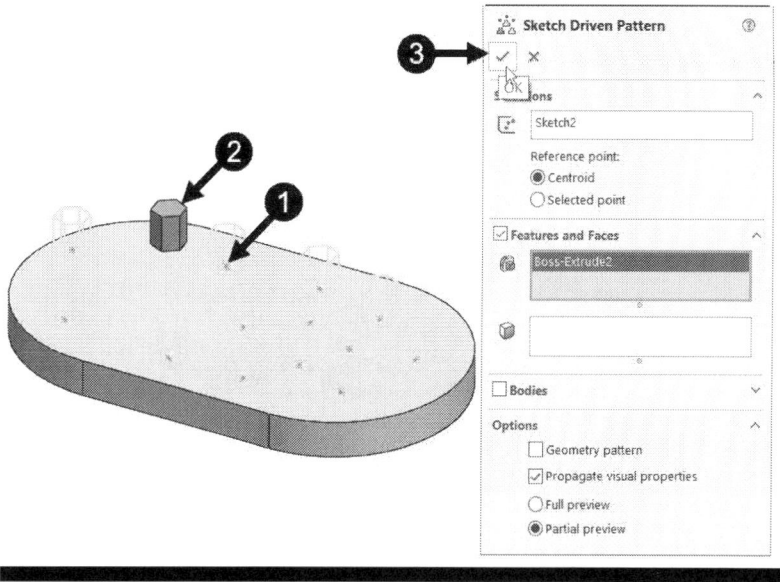
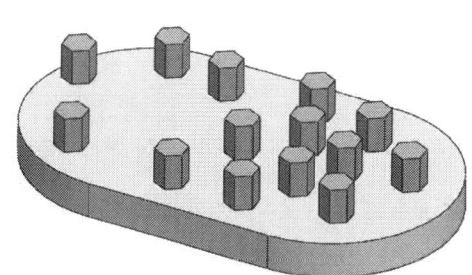

Exercises:

Exercise 1

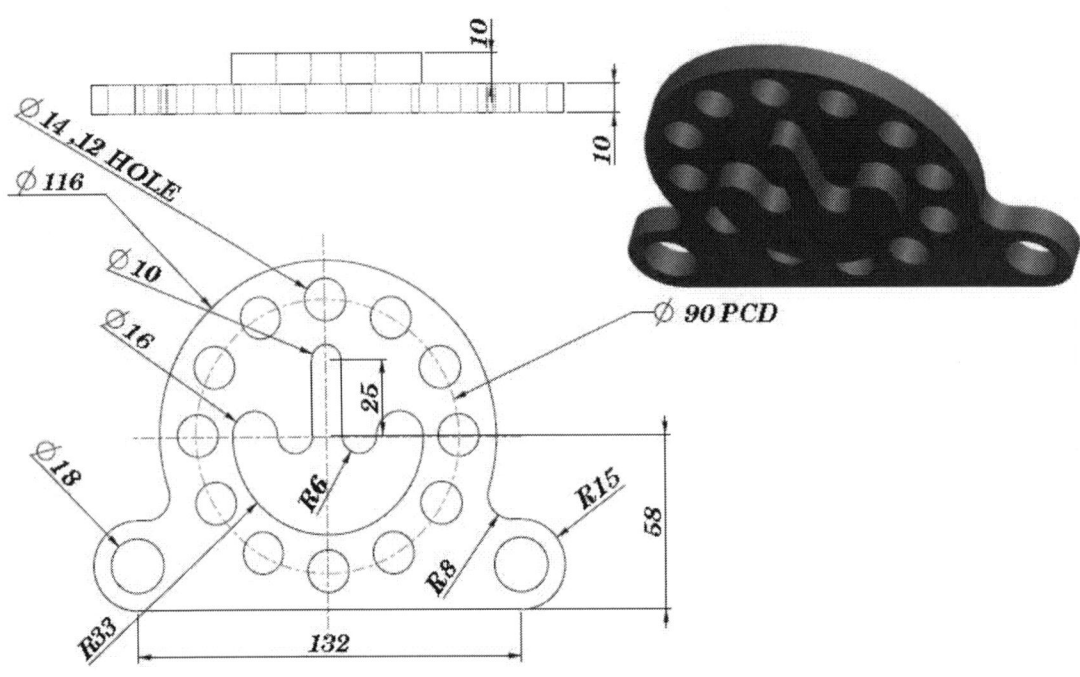

Exercise 2

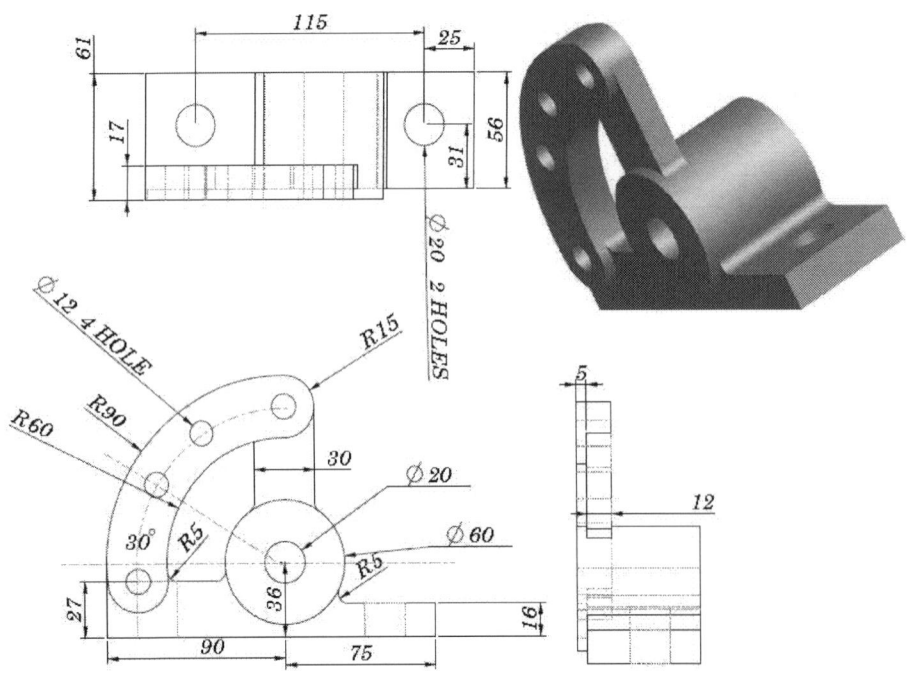

Questions:

1. How can we create a countersink hole?
2. How can we edit a hole feature?
3. In which PropertyManager, the **Near side countersink** checkbox is available?
4. Where is **Circular Pattern** tool available in the **CommandManager**?
5. How can we create pattern features using the **Circular pattern** tool?
6. How can we mirror multiple features in the Part Environment?
7. What is the use of **Curve Driven Pattern** option?
8. Which tool can be used to create multiple instances of selected feature or features along the point entities?

Chapter 08: Advanced Solid Modeling Tools

Sketch-Based features are used to create basic and simple parts. Most of the times, they form the base for complex parts as well. These features are easy to create and require a single sketch. Now, you will learn the tools to create these features in this chapter.

The topics covered in this chapter are:

- ❖ Swept Boss/Base tool
- ❖ Swept Cut tool
- ❖ Using the Swept Cut tool for Removing Material
- ❖ Loft Features
- ❖ Boundary Features

Swept Boss/Base Tool

The **Swept Boss/Base** tool is used to create a sweep based features by sweeping/extruding an open or close profile, along a path. This tool allows you to create a solid, & surface feature for the same.

➢ Draw the sketch on the **Top** plane, as shown.

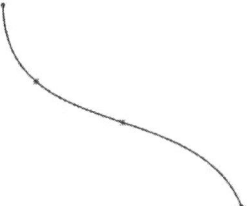

➢ Next create a plane, perpendicular at one end of the recently drawn sketch and draw another sketch over it, as shown.

Now you can use these two sketches as profile and path for creating the sweep feature, as shown.

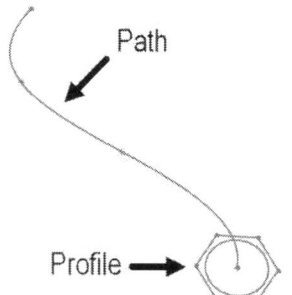

➢ Select the **Swept Boss/Base** tool from the **Features CommandManager** to display **Sweep PropertyManager**, as shown.

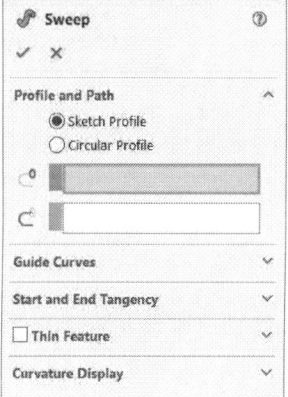

➢ Select the profile sketch first and then select the path sketch to display preview of sweep feature, as shown.

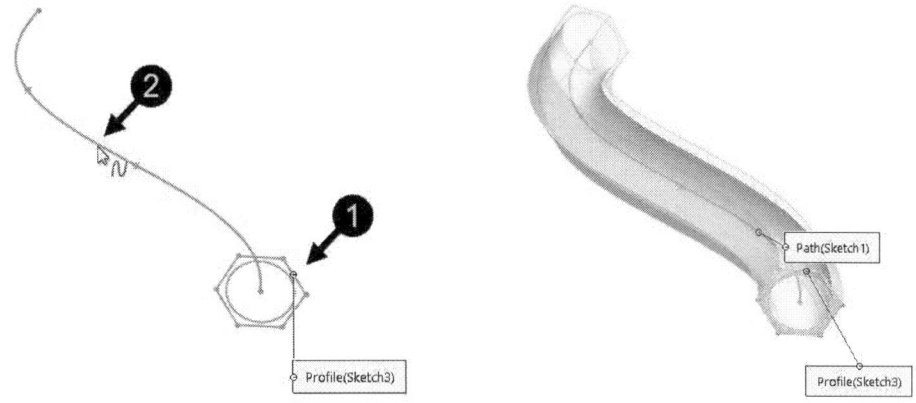

➢ Click on the **OK** button of the PropertyManager to display the sweep feature created, as shown.

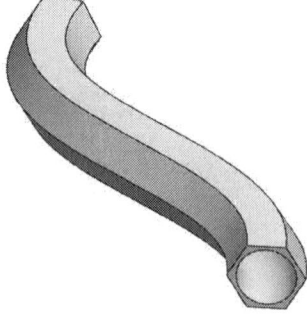

Similarly, you can create sweet feature of a close section/path, as shown.

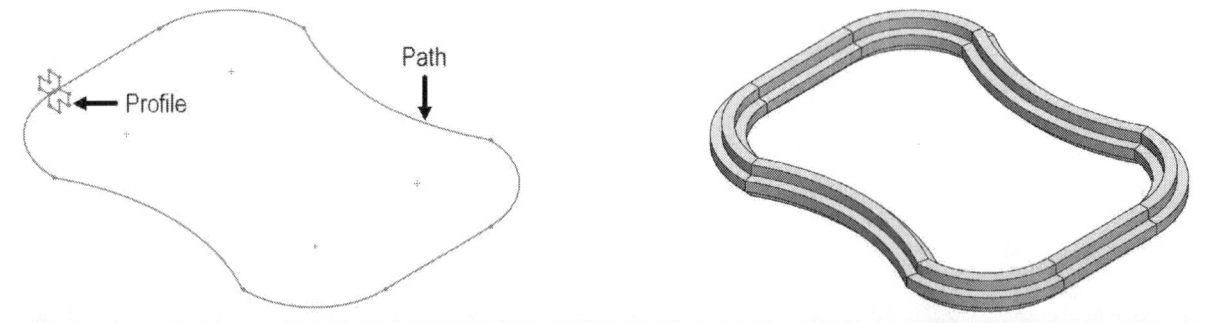

Note that you can also sweep a profile if it is not intersecting the path, as shown. The important thing is that the plane should be perpendicular at one end.

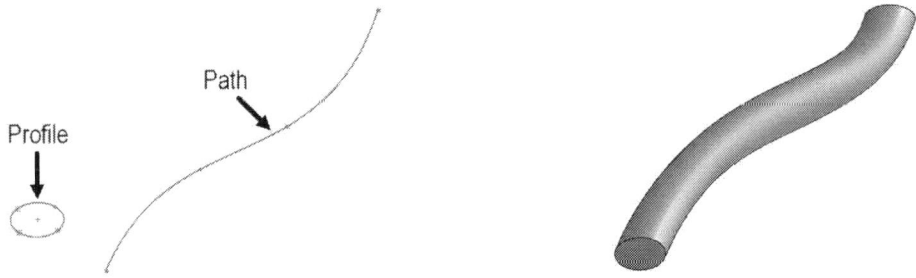

Sweep Feature with Guide Curve
You can sweet a profile sketch along the guide curve

➤ Draw the profile, path and guide curve sketches one by one, as shown.

Note that path sketch and guide curve sketch should be coincident with profile sketch and both sketches should be also created one by one.

➤ Activate the **Swept Boss/Base** tool and select the profile sketch and then select the path sketch, as shown.
➤ Next, click on the **Guide Curves** rollout of the PropertyManager and then click on the guide curve to display preview of sweep along guide curve, as shown.

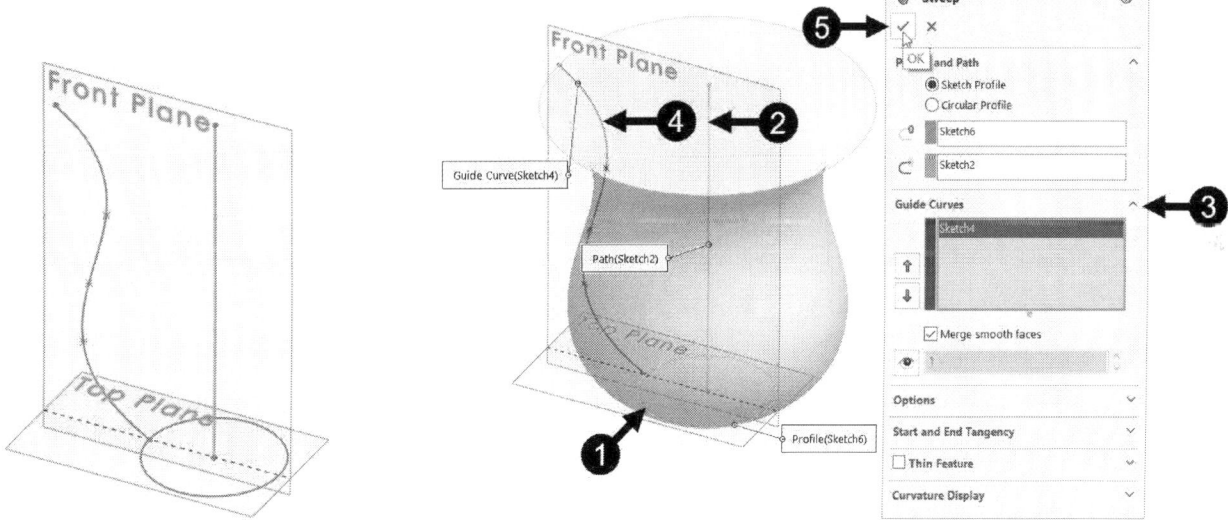

➤ Click on the OK ✓ button of the PropertyManager to display the sweep feature created, as shown.

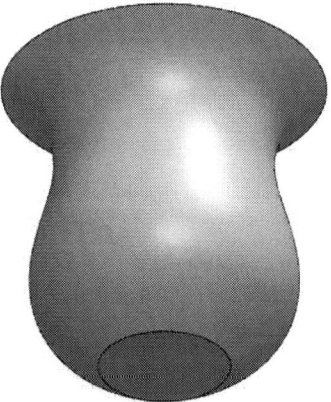

Advanced Solid Modelling Tools

Sweep Feature with Twist

You can sweep a profile sketch along the guide curve and then twist it, as shown.

- ➤ Draw the profile and path sketch, as shown.
- ➤ Activate the **Swept Boss/Base** tool and then select the profile and path sketch one by one.
- ➤ Click on the **Options** rollout of the PropertyManager and then select the **Specify Twist Value** option from the **Profile Twist** drop down list, as shown.
- ➤ Next enter or adjust the required twist angle in the **Twist Angle** spinner to display the preview of twisted sweep feature, as shown.

    Note that you can click on the **Reverse Twist Direction**  button to reverse its direction, if required.

- ➤ Click on the **OK** button of the PropertyManager to display the sweep feature created, as shown.

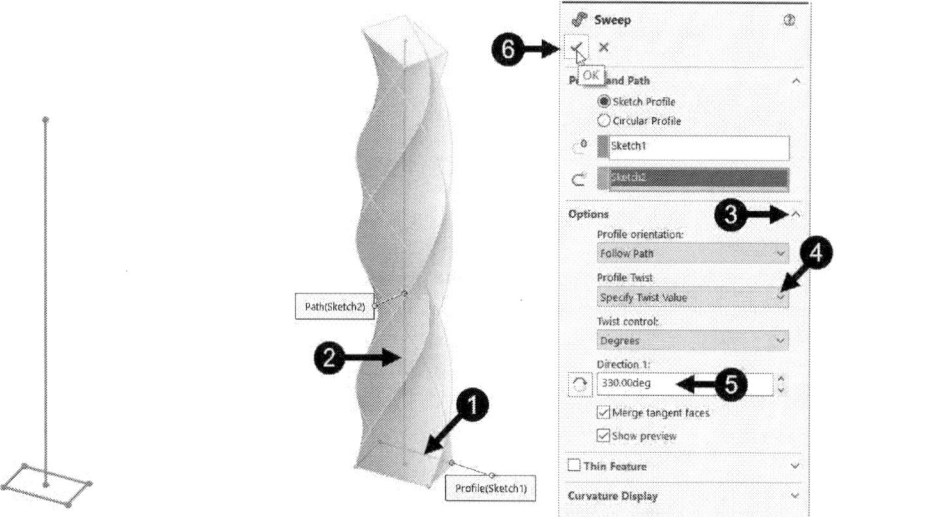

Using the Swept Cut tool for Removing Material

The **Swept Cut** tool can be used for removing material by sweeping/extruding a section/profile, along a path. The procedure of using this tool is same as that of **Swept Boss/Base** tool, as discussed previously. The only difference is that this tool cab be used only after creating a solid model.

- ➤ Draw two sketches on two different surfaces/planes of the model as profile and path, as shown.

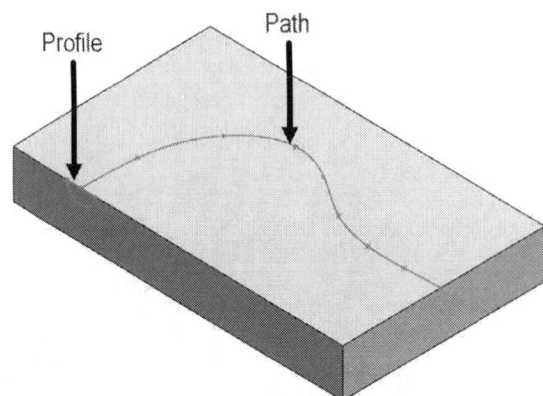

- ➤ Click on the **Swept Cut** button from the **Features CommandManager** to display **Cut-Sweep PropertyManager**, as shown.
- ➤ The **Sketch Profile** radio button in the PropertyManager is selected by default, as shown.

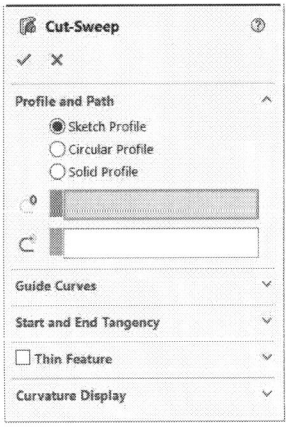

> Select the profile sketch first and then select the path sketch to display preview of sweep feature, as shown.

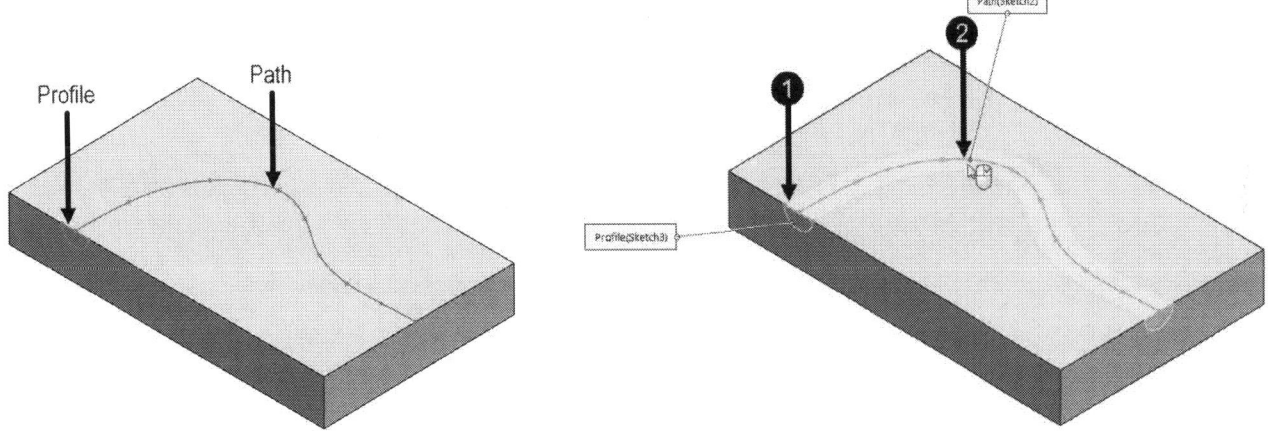

> Now click on the OK button from the PropertyManager to exit it and display the swept cut feature created, as shown.

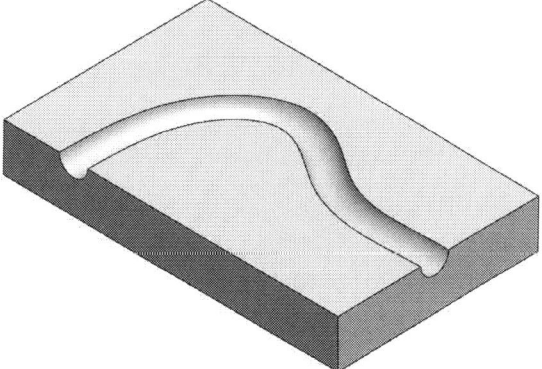

Swept Cut with Circular Profile radio button

The **Circular Profile** radio button is selected to sweep circular profile automatically along the path sketch created for removing material. There is no need to create a profile sketch.

> Create a sketch for path, as shown.
> Select the **Swept Cut** tool from the **Features CommandManager** to display **Cut-Sweep PropertyManager**, as shown.
> Next, select the **Circular Profile** radio button from the PropertyManager, as shown.

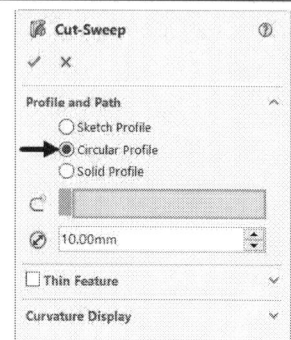

- Now click on the path sketch to display preview of swept cut feature, as shown.

  Note that, system automatically created a circular profile to sweep along the path created, as shown.

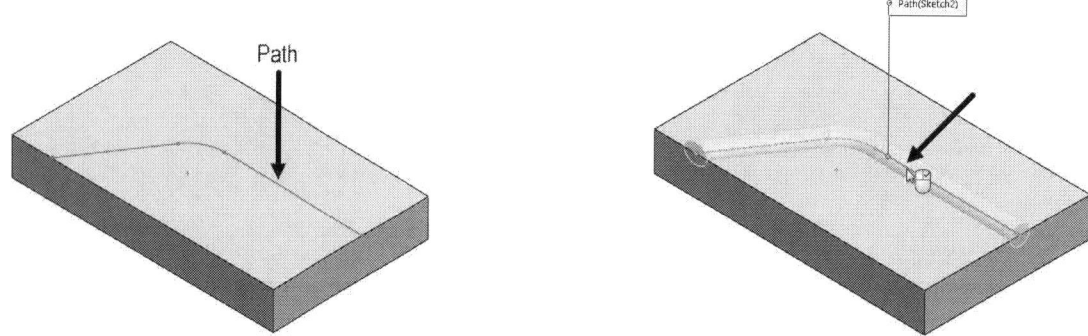

- Now click on the **OK** button from the PropertyManager to exit it and display the swept cut feature created, as shown.

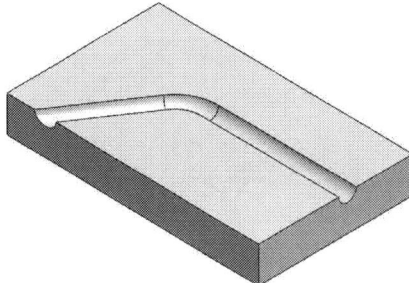

Swept Cut with Solid Profile radio button

The **Solid Profile** radio button is selected to sweep a solid profile along the path sketch created for removing material. The solid profile should be a revolved feature made of line and arcs or a cylindrical feature. And the path must be tangent continuous and begin at a point on or within the tool body profile. Note that the solid profile should not be merged with another solid model.

- Create a solid revolve feature as profile and another sketch as path for the swept cut feature, as shown.

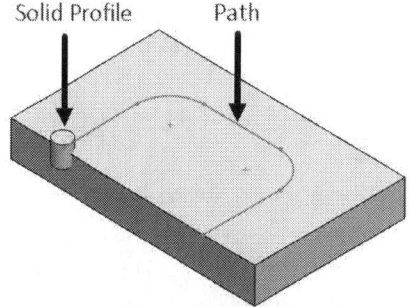

- Select the **Swept Cut** tool from the **Features CommandManager** to display **Cut-Sweep PropertyManager**, as shown.
- Next, select the **Solid Profile** radio button from the PropertyManager, as shown.
- Next select the solid profile and then select the path sketch, as shown.

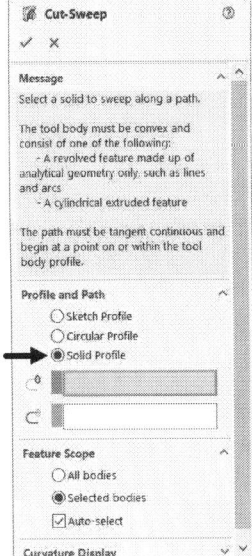
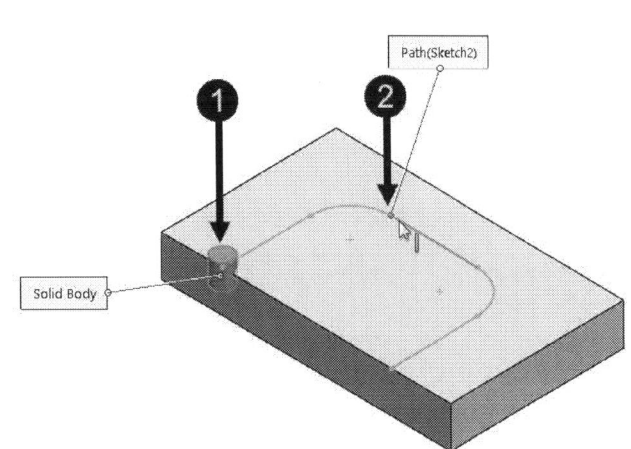

- Now click on the **OK** button from the PropertyManager to exit it and display the swept cut feature created, as shown.

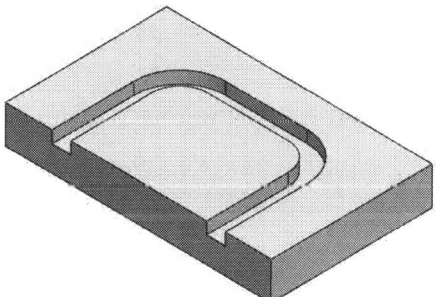

Lofted Bose/Base Tool

This tool is used to create a solid model by connecting two or more sketches created on different planes, as shown. The steps to create a lofted feature are explained below:

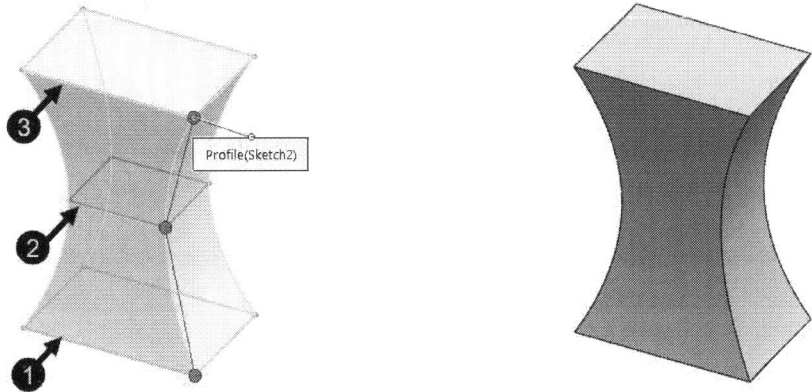

- Draw three different sketches on 3 different planes, as shown.
- Select the **Lofted Boss/Base** tool from the **Features CommandManager** to display **Loft PropertyManager**, as shown.

Advanced Solid Modelling Tools

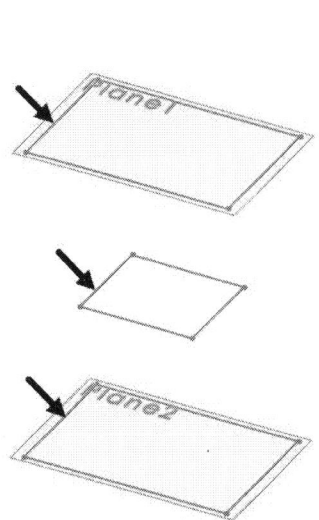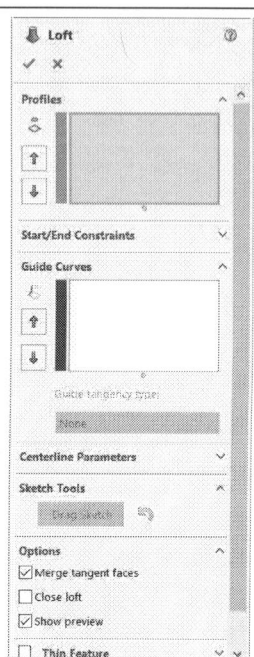

> Click on the sketch entities or constraints of all sketches one by one to display the lofted feature with green colored handles of the connector, as shown.

Note that the lofted feature will be created according to the order in which you select the sketch entities or constraints.

> You can change the shape of lofted feature by dragging the green colored handles of the connector attached with it, as shown.

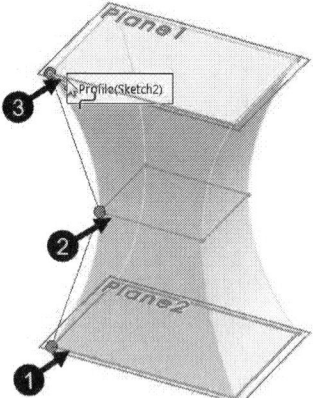

> Press and hold the LMB (left mouse button) on the green colored handle at left side of the middle sketch and drag it towards right, as shown.
> Release the LMB (left mouse button) to display the reshaped lofted feature, as shown.

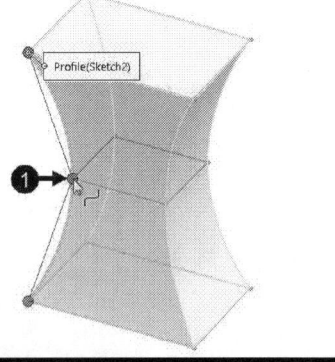 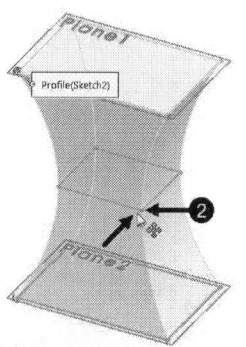 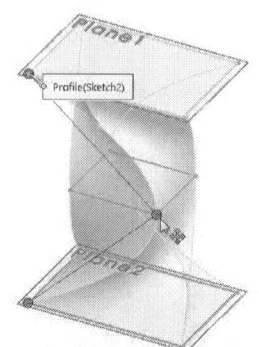

Similarly, you can drag the same handle back to its previous position, if required.

➤ Now click on the **OK** button from the PropertyManager to exit it and display the lofted feature created, as shown.

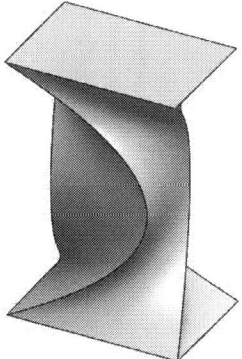

Lofted Feature by Defining Start and End Constraints

The options under the **Start/End Constraints** rollout of the **Loft PropertyManager** are used to define the constraints at the start and end sections of the loft feature. Click on the down arrow of the **Start/End Constraints** rollout to make **Start constraint** and **End constraint** drop-down list visible under it, as shown below. The use of these options is discussed next:

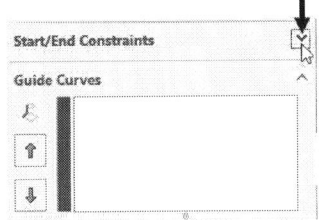 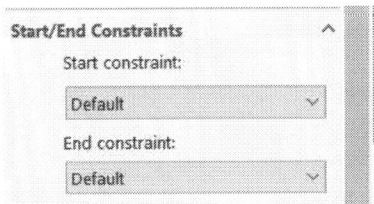 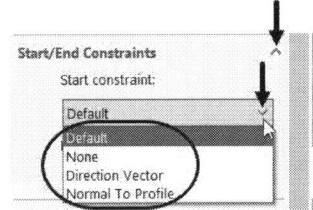

➤ Select the **Lofted Boss/Base** tool to display the **Loft PropertyManager**, as shown.
➤ Next, select the three sketches one by one to display preview of lofted feature, as shown.

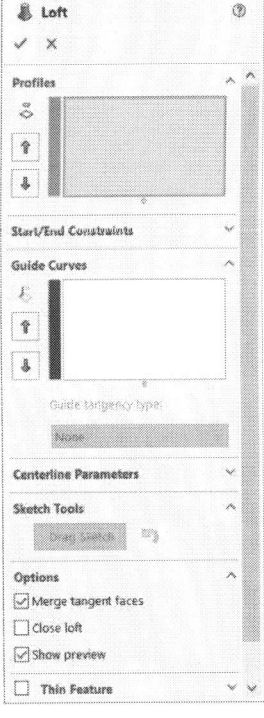 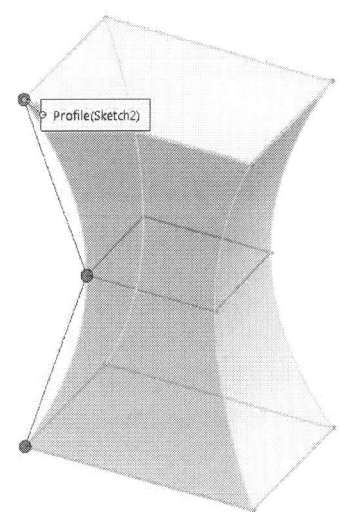

Advanced Solid Modelling Tools

- Click on the **Start/End Constraints** rollout to make **Start constraint** and **End constraint** drop-down list visible under it, as shown.
- Next, select the **Normal To Profile** option from the **Start constraint** drop-down list, as shown above.
- Next enter the required values in the edit boxes displayed under **Start constraint** drop-down list, as shown.
- Similarly enter the values in edit boxes under End constraint drop-down list also, as shown

    Note that while entering the values for Draft angles and Tangent Length for start and end sections, the preview of loft feature get changed accordingly, as shown.

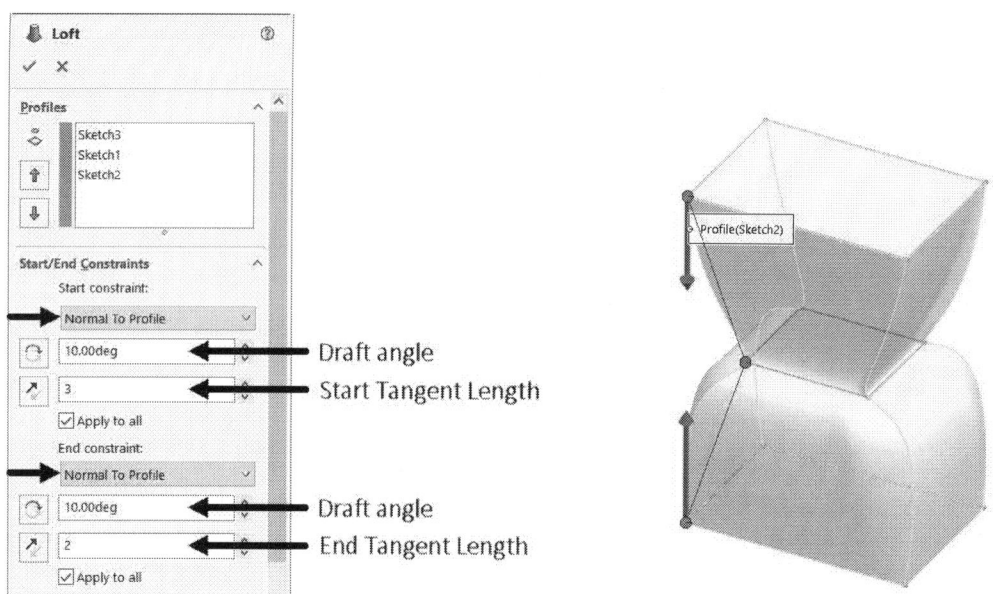

- Now click on the **OK** button from the PropertyManager to exit it and display the lofted feature created, as shown.

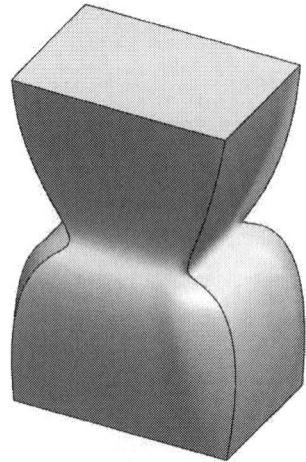

Lofted Feature with Guide Curve

To create a lofted feature with guide curves, follow the steps:

- Create three profile sketches on three different planes and two sketches for guide curves on single plane or different plane, as shown.
- Next, select the three profile sketches one by one and then click in the **Guide Curves** box of the **Loft PropertyManager**, as shown

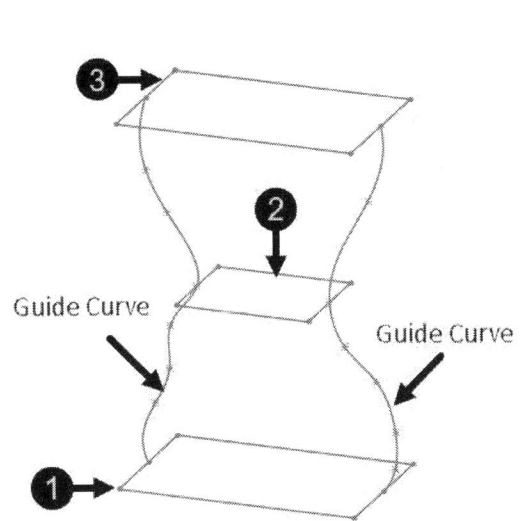
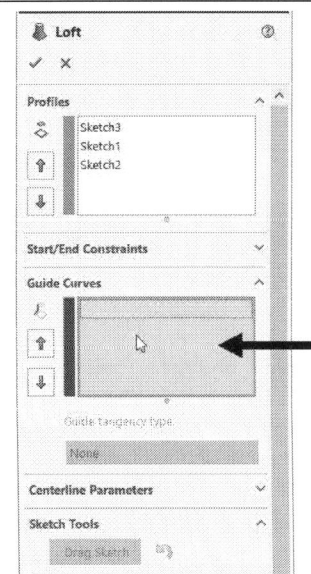

- Next select one of the guide curves and click on the **Select Open Loop** button, if required.
- Click on the **OK** button to display the preview of lofted feature with the selected guide curve, as shown.
- Similarly, select another guide curve.

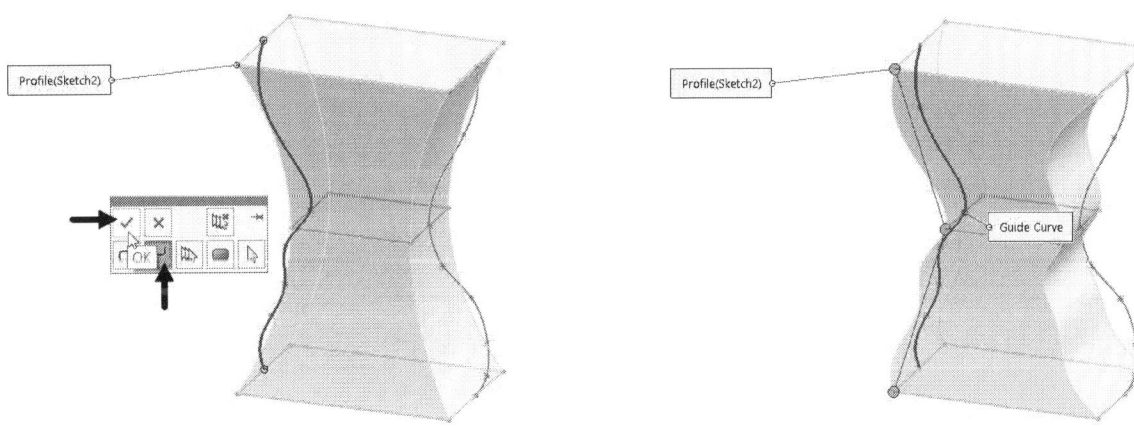

Note that you will not be asked to select the **Select Open loop** and then **OK** button for a single guide curve.

- Now click on the **OK** button from the PropertyManager to exit it and display the lofted feature with guide curves, as shown.

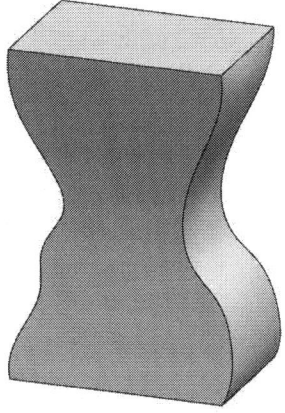

Advanced Solid Modelling Tools

Lofted Cut Tool

The use of **Lofted Cut** tool is almost same as that of the **Lofted Boss/Base** tool. The only difference is this tool is used to remove material from a solid model. The steps to create a lofted cut feature are:

- ➢ Create sketch on two planes or two faces of any solid model, as shown.
- ➢ Next click on the **Lofted Cut** tool to activate it and display the **Cut-Loft PropertyManager** and preview of lofted feature, as shown.

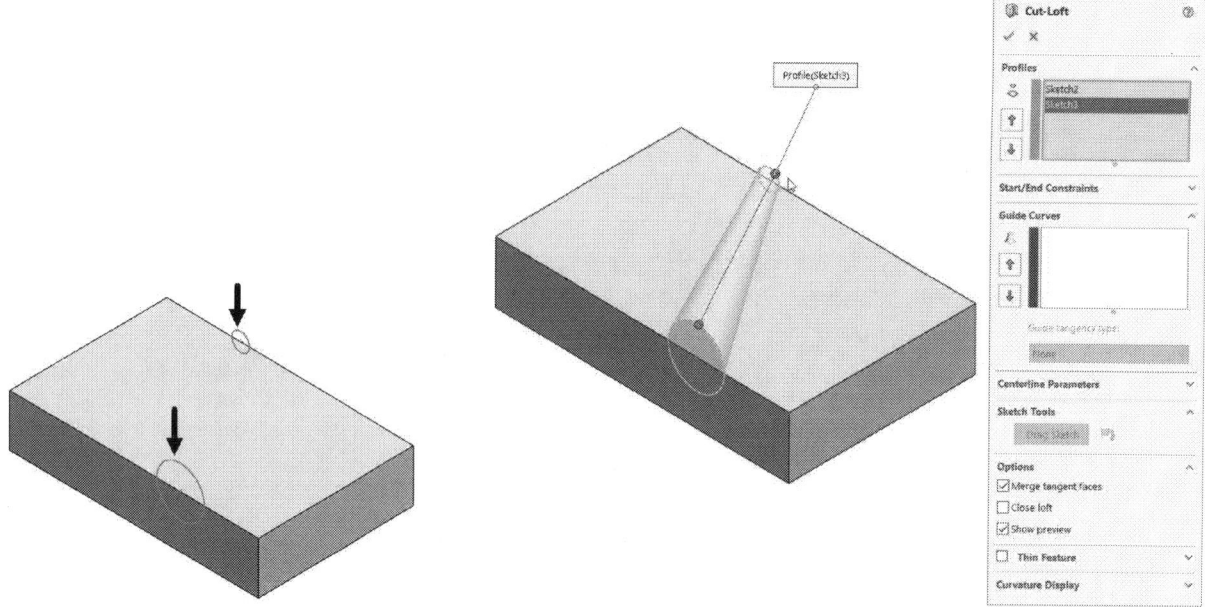

- ➢ Next click on the **OK** button of the PropertyManager to exit it and display the Lofted Cut feature, as shown.

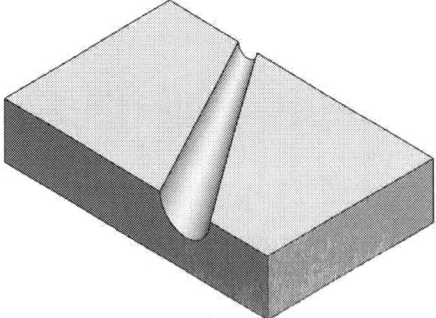

Boundary Bose/Base Tool

This tool is used to create feature by adding material in two directions. This tool is mostly used in creating complex or curved bodies. You need to create two profiles between which you can add material. You can specify sketch curves, faces, edges, or other sketch entities to control the shape of a boundary feature.

- ➢ Draw the sketch on **Top** Plane, as shown.

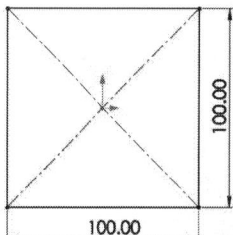

➢ Next create another sketch of two entities on **Front** Plane, as shown.

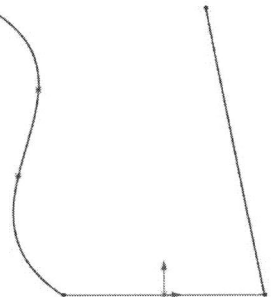

➢ Now select the **Boundary Boss/Base** tool from **Features CommandManager** to activate it and display the **Boundary PropertyManager**, as shown.
➢ Click on the profile sketch, as shown.

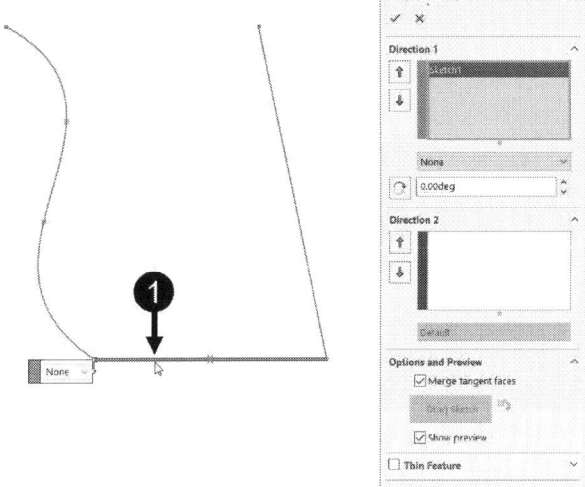

➢ Click in the **Curves** selection box and then click on the path sketch, as shown.
➢ Click on the **OK** button of the message box to select it and display preview of boundary boss/base feature, as shown.

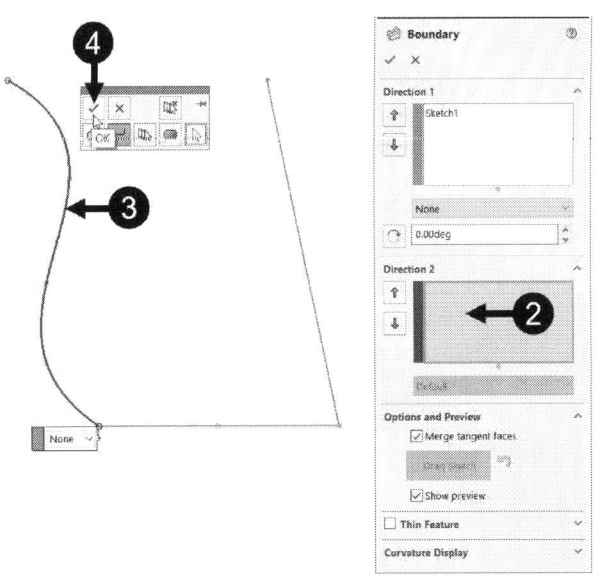
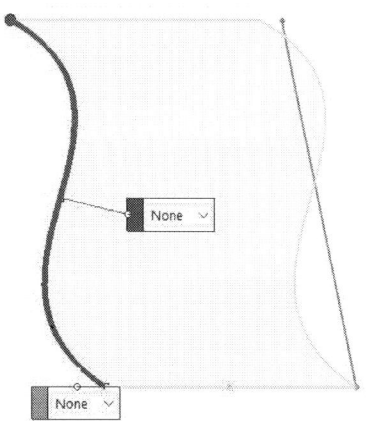

➢ Similarly select another sketch entity, as shown.

Advanced Solid Modelling Tools

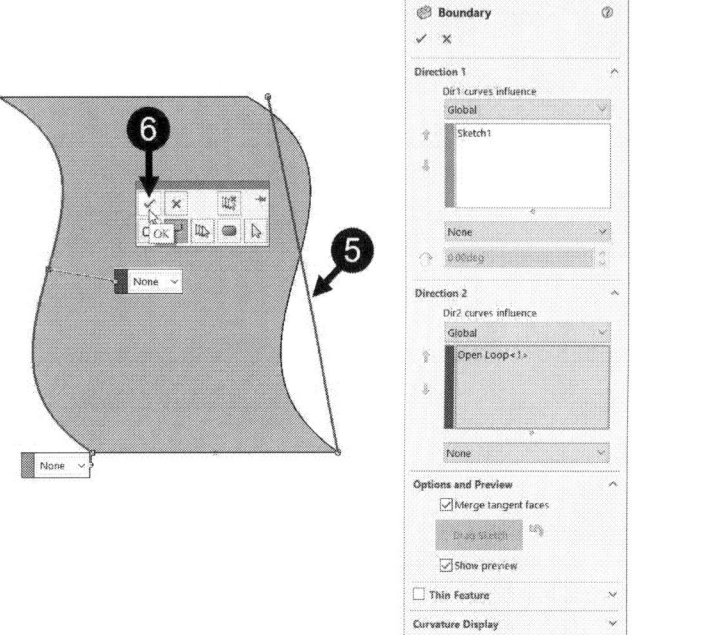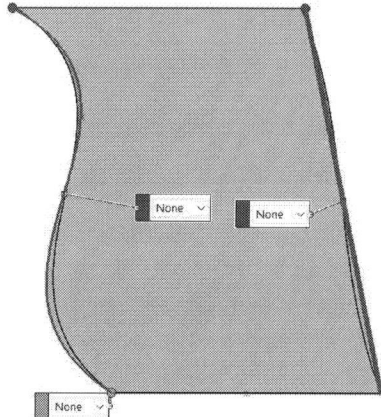

> Next, you can select the required option for all drop-down attached with control points, as shown.

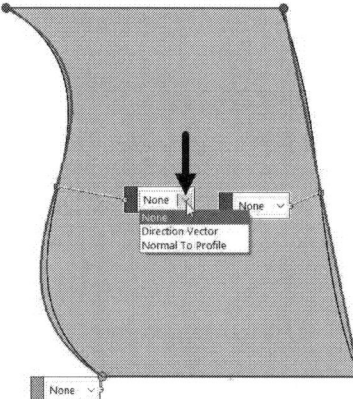

Note: The use of Loft and Boundary tools is almost same. But the only difference is the availability of drop-down attached with control points using this tool.

> Click on the **OK** button of the PropertyManager to exit it and display boundary boss/base feature, as shown.

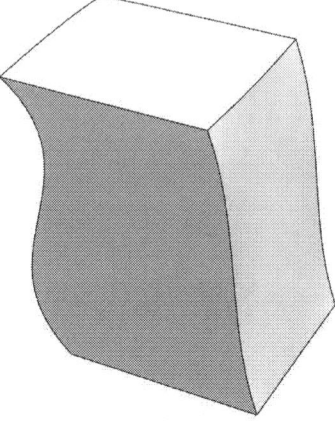

Note that you can also create boundary boss/base feature by creating single path sketch.

Boundary Cut Tool

This tool is used in removing material between two profiles in two directions. This tool is also mostly used in creating complex or curved bodies. You need to create two profiles between which you can remove material. You can specify sketch curves, faces, edges, or other sketch entities to control the shape of a boundary feature.

> Draw the sketch on different faces of model, as shown.

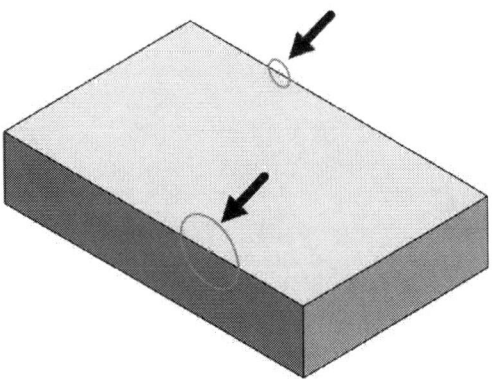

> Now select the **Boundary Cut** tool from **Features CommandManager** to activate it and display the **Boundary-Cut PropertyManager**, as shown.
> Select the two sketches one by one to display preview of Boundary Cut feature, as shown.

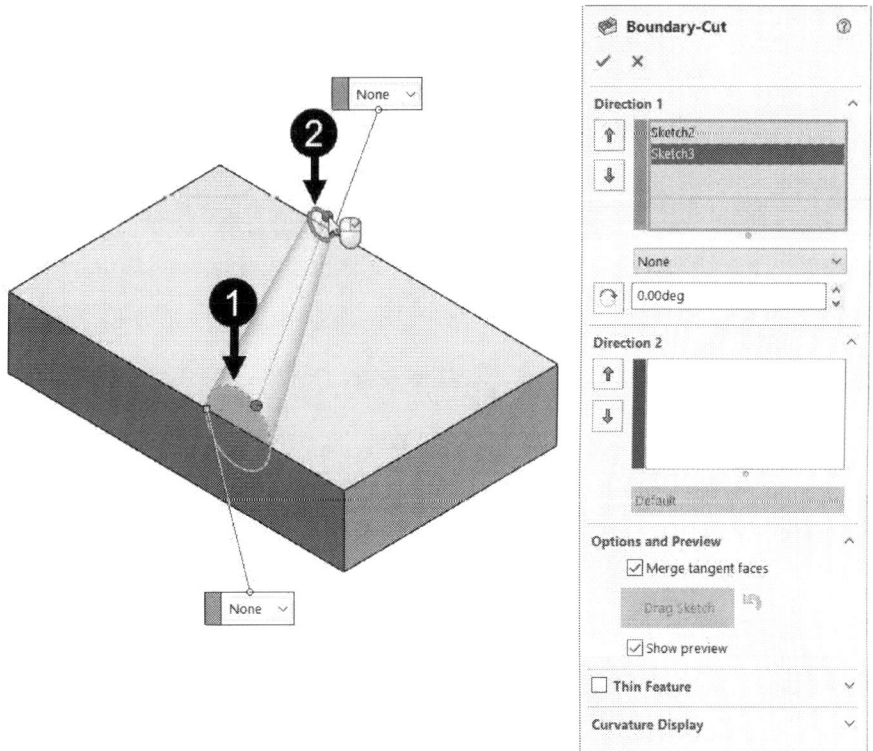

> Select the **Normal To Profile** option from the drop-downs attached with the control points to display boundary cut feature normal to the profile, as shown.

Similarly, you can use other options available in the drop-downs.

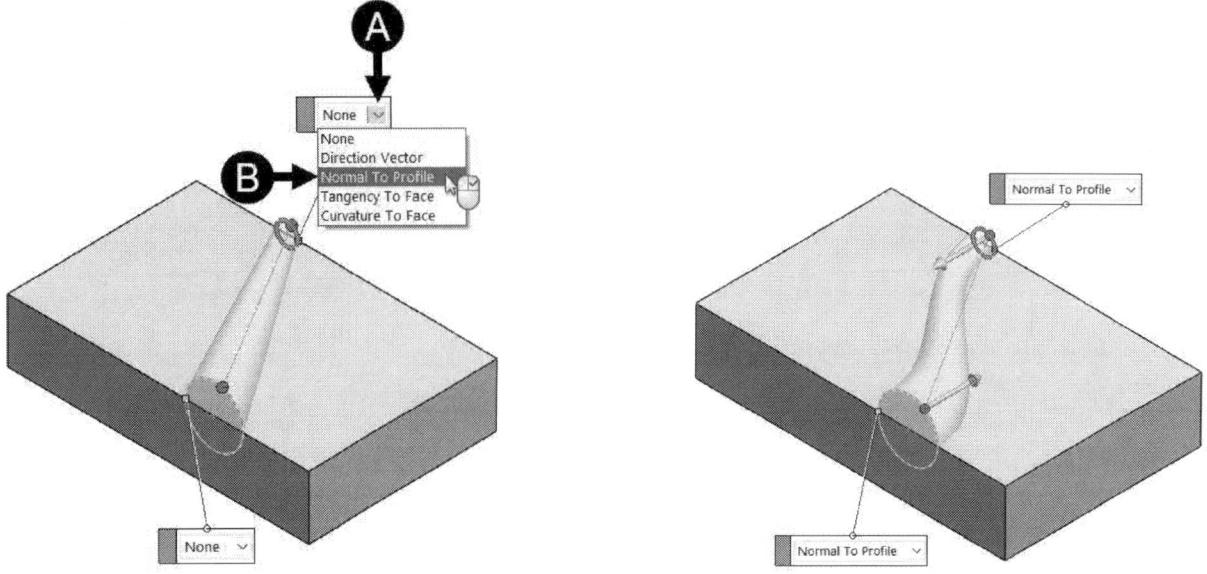

> Click on the **OK** button of the PropertyManager to exit it and display boundary cut feature, as shown.

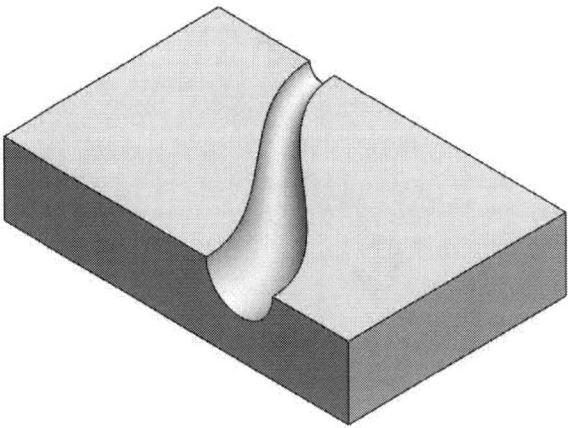

Examples:

Example 1 (Millimetres)

In this example, you will create the model shown below.

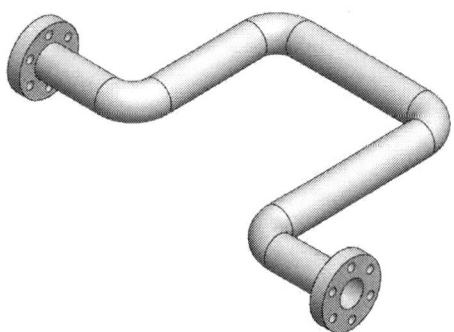

- Start SolidWorks 2021 by clicking **SOLIDWORKS 2021** icon on your desktop.
- Click on the **New** (📄) button from the **Menu Bar** to display the **New SOLIDWORKS Document** dialog box.
- Double click on the **Part** button of the dialog box to enter in the Sketching Environment.
- Click on the **Sketch** tab to display **Sketch CommandManager** and tools used in creating sketch.
- Click on the **Sketch** button from the **Sketch CommandManager** and then click on the **Top** plane.
- Using the **Line** and **Fillet** tool from the **Sketch CommandManager**, draw the sketch and apply dimensions, as shown.

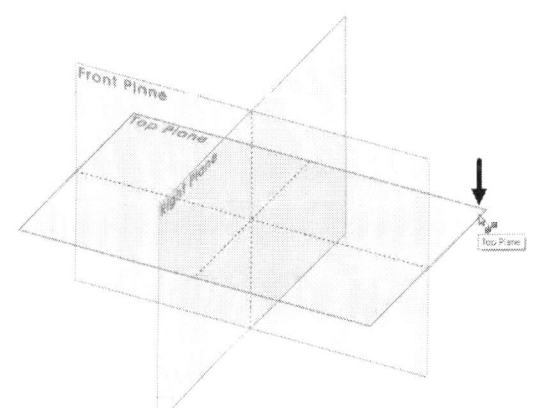
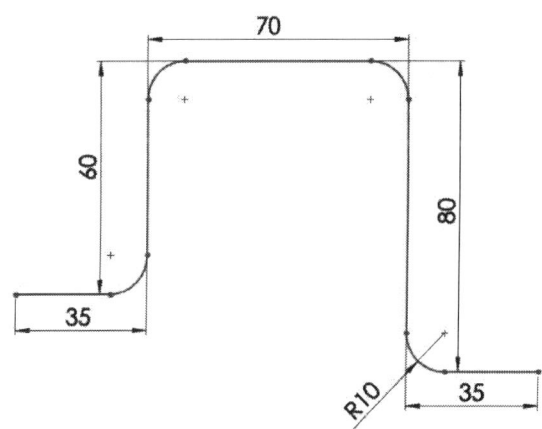

- Now click on the **Exit Sketch** button from the **Sketch CommandManager** to exit from the sketch environment.
- Next click on the **Plane** tool (**Features** > **Reference Geometry** > **Plane**) to activate it and display the **Plane PropertyManager**, as shown.
- Click on the left side line entity to define it as **First Reference**, as shown.
- Click on the left side point entity to define it as **Second Reference** and display preview of a Reference Plane normal to selected line entity, as shown.

Advanced Solid Modelling Tools

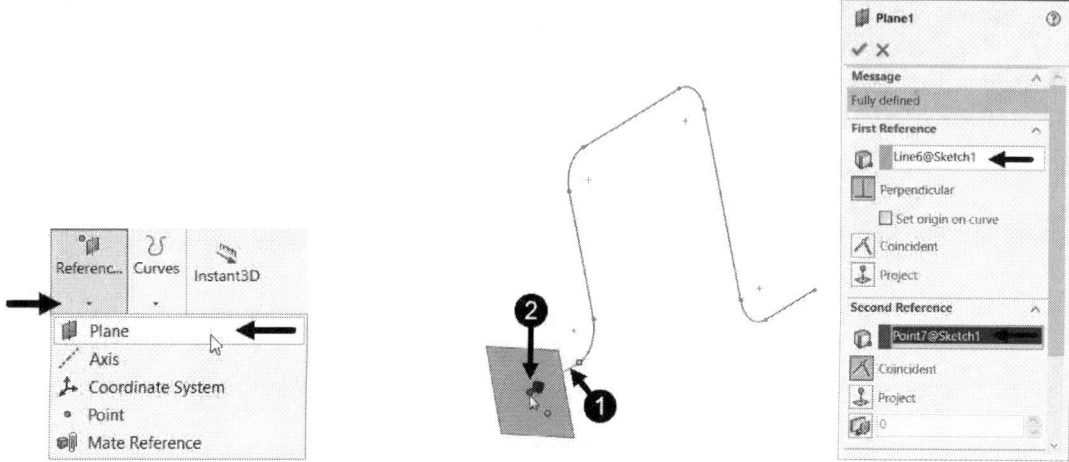

> Click on the **OK** button of the PropertyManager to exit it and display Reference Plane, as shown.

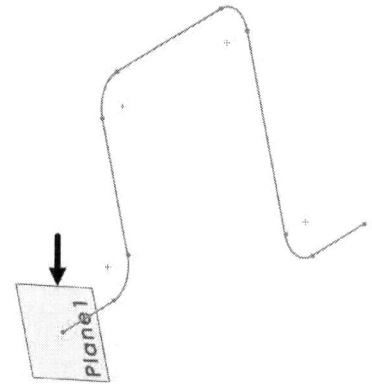

> Now draw the sketch of two circle entities on recently created reference plane, as shown.

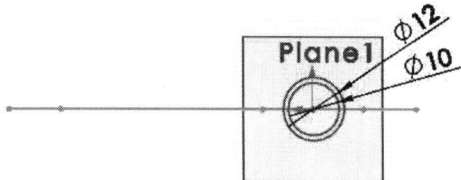

> Select the **Swept Boss/Base** tool from the **Features CommandManager** to activate it and display the **Sweep PropertyManager**, as shown.
> Next select the circles entities as profile and other sketch as path to display preview of Sweep feature, as shown.

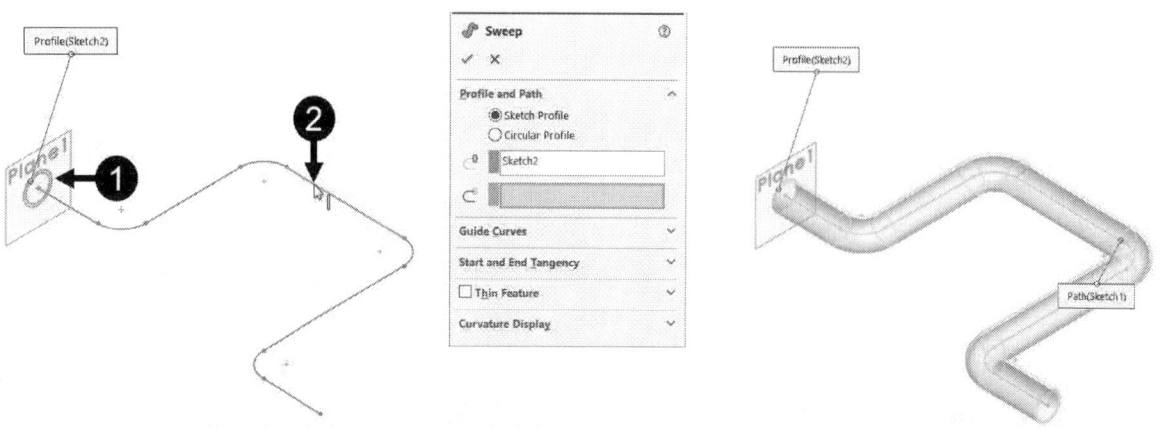

- Click on the **OK** button of the PropertyManager to exit it and display Sweep feature, as shown.

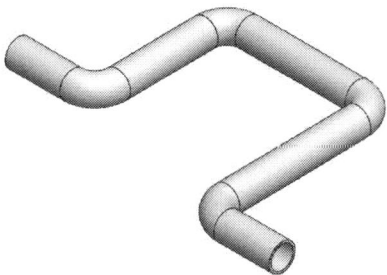

- Click on the **Sketch** button from the **Sketch CommandManager** to activate it.
- Select the flat surface of right end of the sweep feature to make it a sketching plane, as shown.
- Press the **Ctrl + 8** key to make the sketching plane parallel to the screen, as shown.

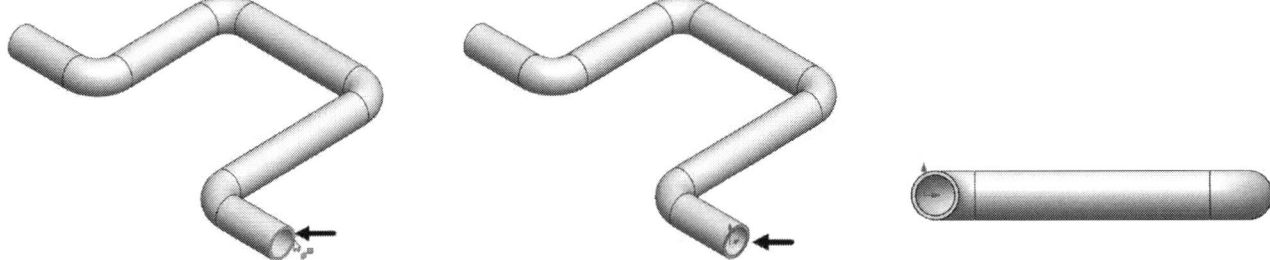

- Now draw the sketch of two circle entities and apply dimensions, as shown.

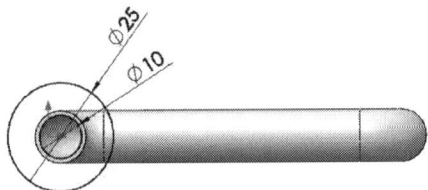

- Now using the **Extruded Boss/Base** tool, extrude the recently drawn sketch up to **5** as discussed in previous chapters.

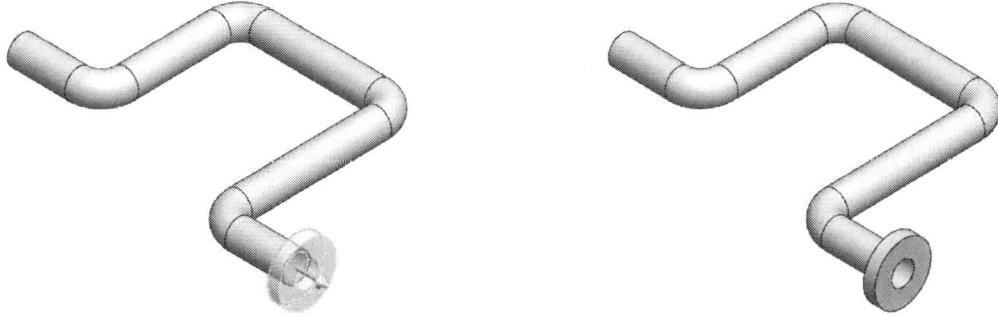

- Similarly create the same feature on the other end of the sweep feature, as shown.

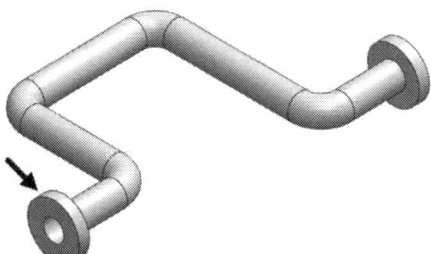

Advanced Solid Modelling Tools

- Again, select the **Sketch** button and select the left flat surface to make it a sketching plane, as shown.
- Draw the sketch of two circle entities, as shown.

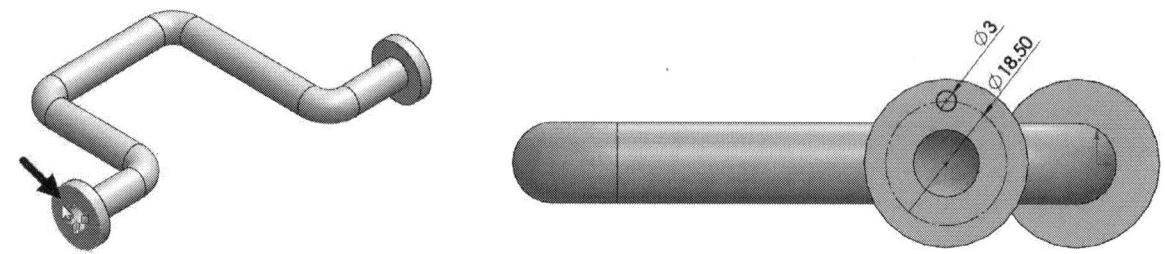

- Activate the **Extruded Cut** tool and select the recently drawn sketch to create Extruded Cut Feature, as shown.

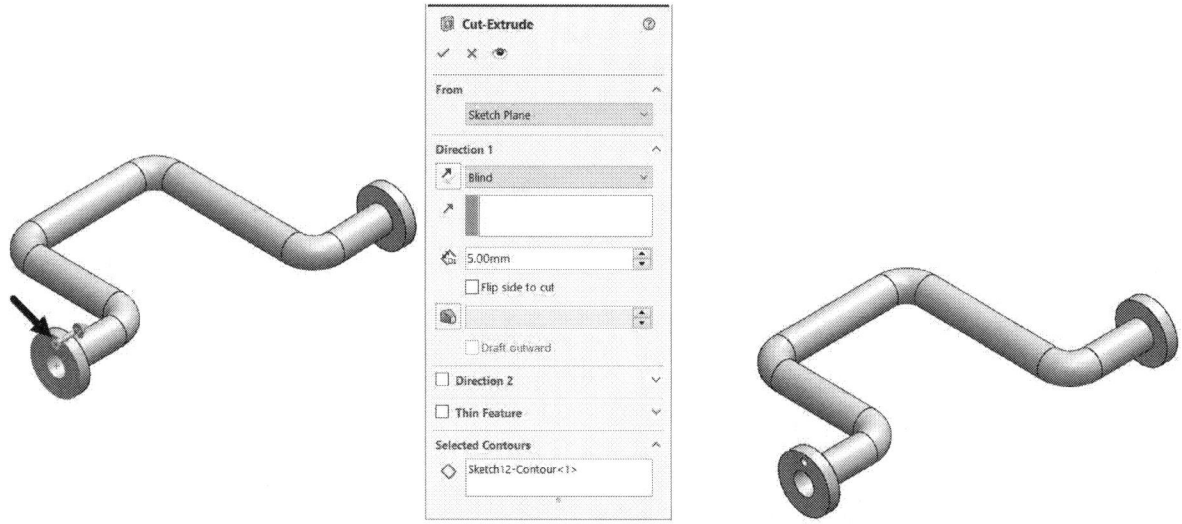

- Select the **Circular Pattern** option from the **Linear Pattern** drop-down to activate it and display the **CirPattern PropertyManager**, as shown.
- Select the previously created Extruded Cut feature, as shown.
- Click in the **Direction1** selection box of the PropertyManager, as shown.
- Select the circular edge of left Extruded feature to display preview of Circular Pattern Feature, as shown.

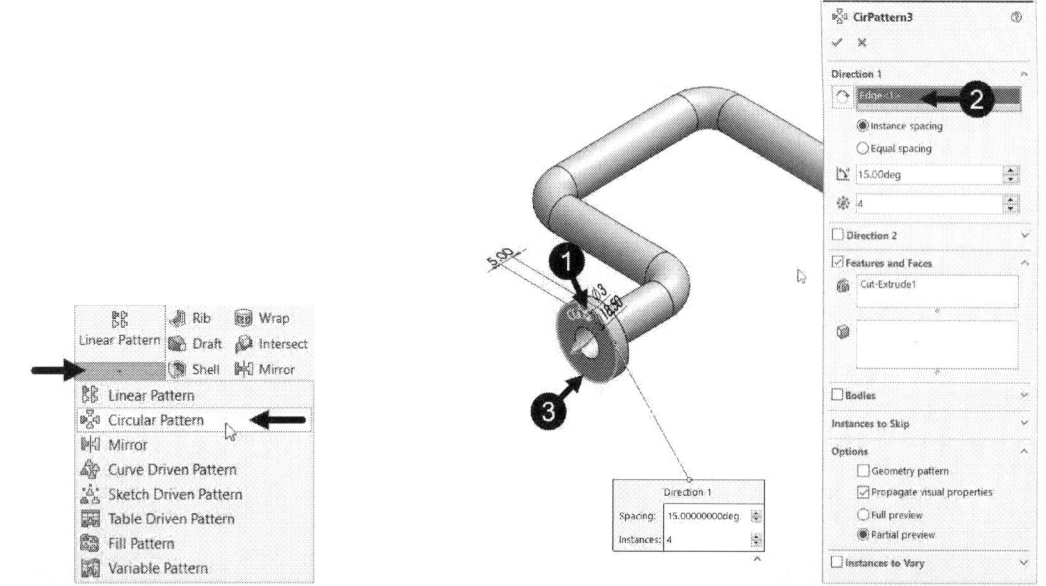

- Next set **6** in the **Number of Instances** edit box of the PropertyManager, as shown.
- Now select the **Equal spacing** radio button of the PropertyManager to display preview of Circular Pattern feature with equal angular spacing, as shown.
- Click on the **OK** button of the PropertyManager to exit it and display Circular Pattern feature created, as shown.

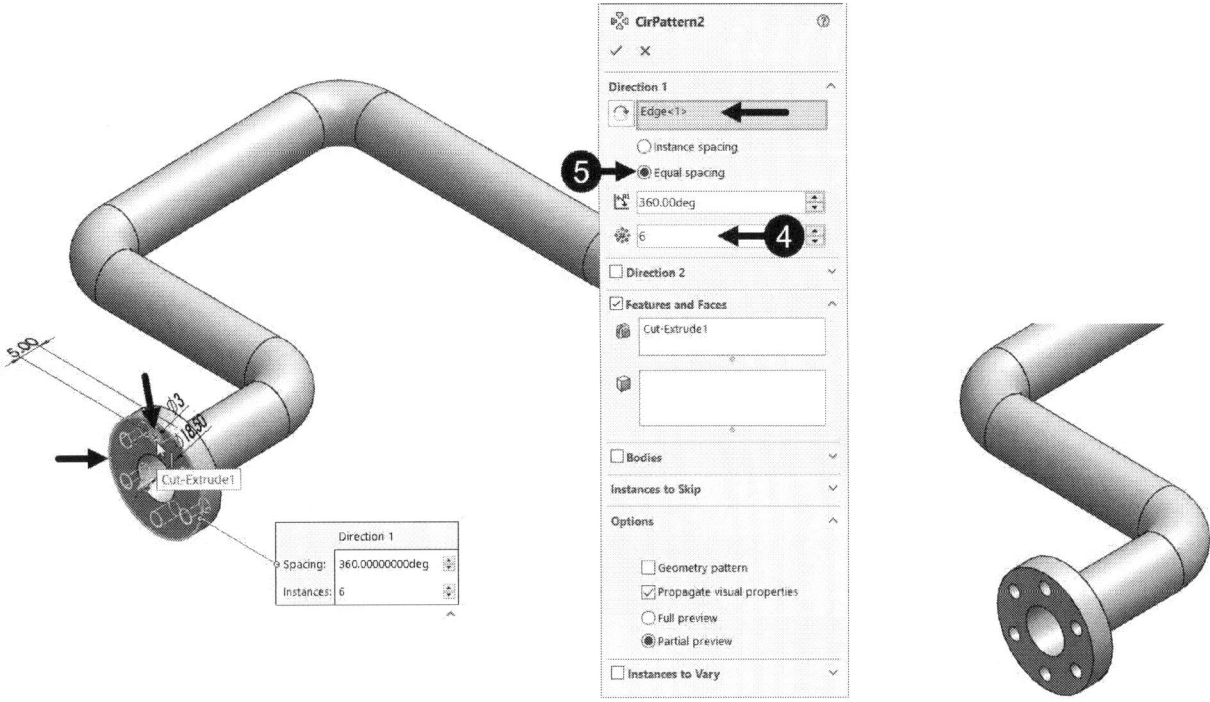

- Similarly create the Circular Pattern feature over another Extruded feature, as shown.

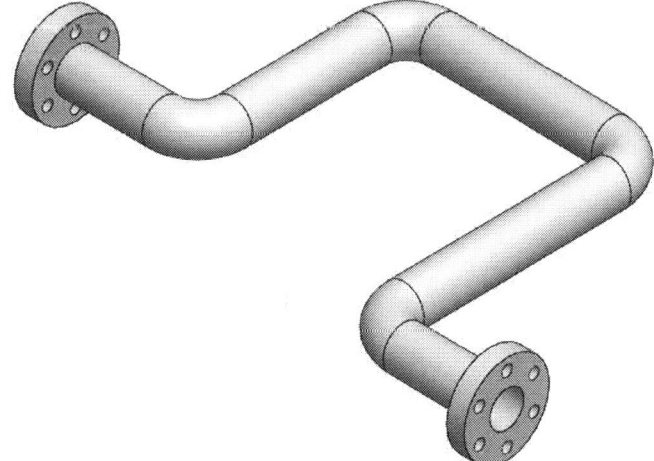

- Click on the **Save (Ctrl+S)** button from the **Menu Bar** to display the **Save As** dialog box.
- Next browse to the folder of chapter **8** and enter name **Ch08-exam01** in the **File name** edit box.
- Click on the **Save** button from the dialog box to save the file.
- Now enter the **Close** button from the upper right corner to close it.

Example 2 (Millimetres)   Using Swept Blend

In this example, you will create the model shown below.

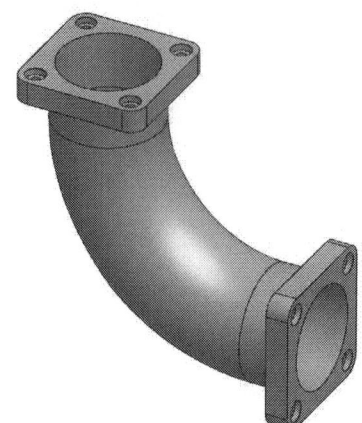

- Start SolidWorks 2021 by clicking **SOLIDWORKS 2021** icon on your desktop.
- Click on the **New** ( ) button from the **Menu Bar** to display the **New SOLIDWORKS Document** dialog box.
- Double click on the **Part** button of the dialog box to enter in the Sketching Environment.
- Click on the **Sketch** tab to display **Sketch CommandManager** and tools used in creating sketch.
- Click on the **Sketch** button from the **Sketch CommandManager** and then select the **Front** plane.
- Using the **Line** and **Fillet** tool from the **Sketch CommandManager**, draw the sketch and apply dimensions, as shown.

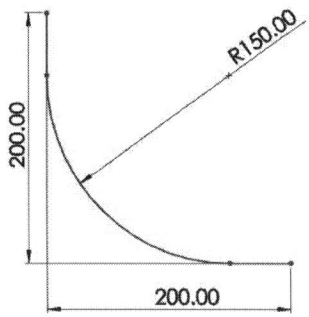

- Now click on the **Exit Sketch** button from the **Sketch CommandManager** to exit from the sketch environment.
- Click on the **Plane** tool (**Features > Reference Geometry > Plane**) to activate it.
- Next create a reference plane as discussed in previous example, as shown.

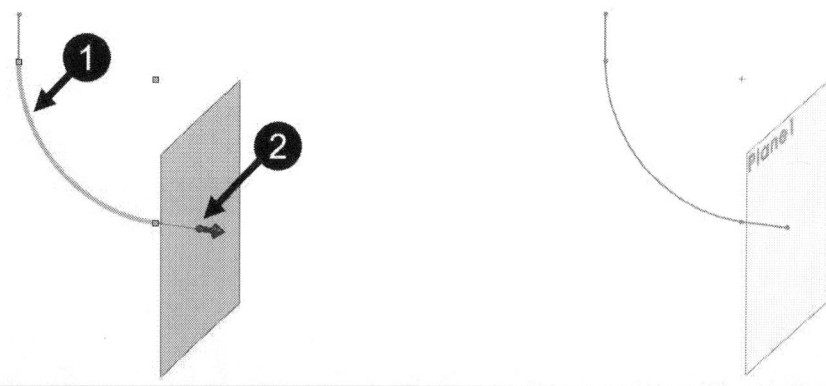

- Now draw the sketch of two circle entities on recently created reference plane, as shown.

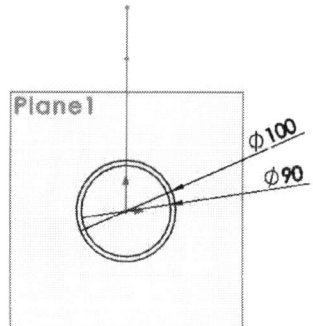

- Select the **Swept Boss/Base** tool from the **Features CommandManager** to activate it and display the **Sweep PropertyManager**, as shown.
- Next select the circles entities as profile and other sketch as path to display preview of Sweep feature, as shown.
- Click on the **OK** button of the PropertyManager to exit it and display Sweep feature, as shown.

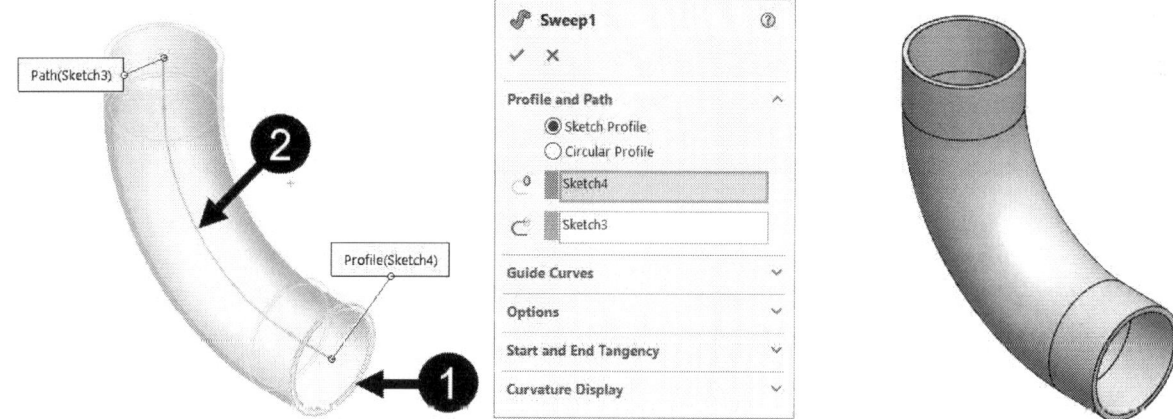

- Click on the **Sketch** button from the **Sketch CommandManager** to activate it.
- Select the flat surface of top end of the sweep feature to make it a sketching plane, as shown.
- Press the **Ctrl + 8** key to make the sketching plane parallel to the screen, as shown.
- Now draw the sketch of a circle and a rectangle entity and apply dimensions, as shown.

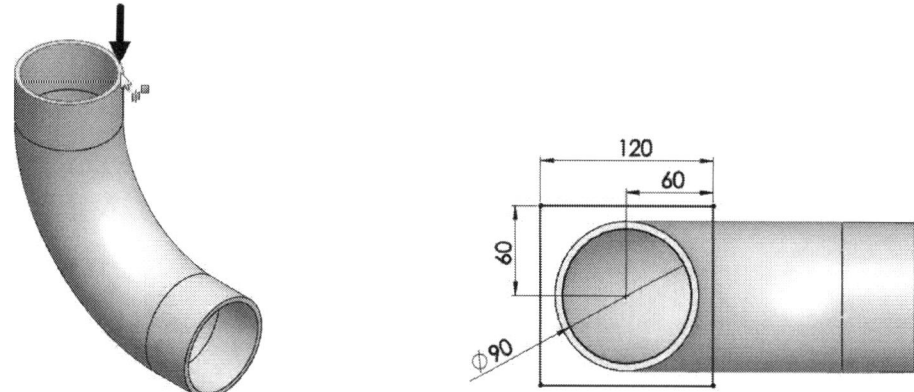

- Now using the **Extruded Boss/Base** tool and extrude the recently drawn sketch up to **20** as discussed, as shown.

Advanced Solid Modelling Tools

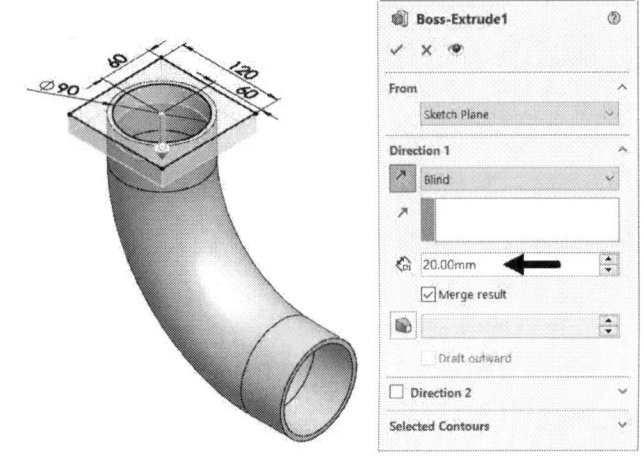
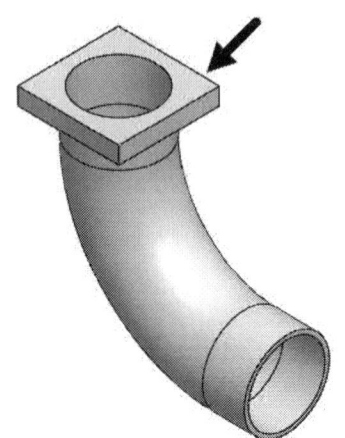

> Select the **Fillet** tool from the **Features CommandManager** to activate it and display the **Fillet PropertyManager**, as shown.

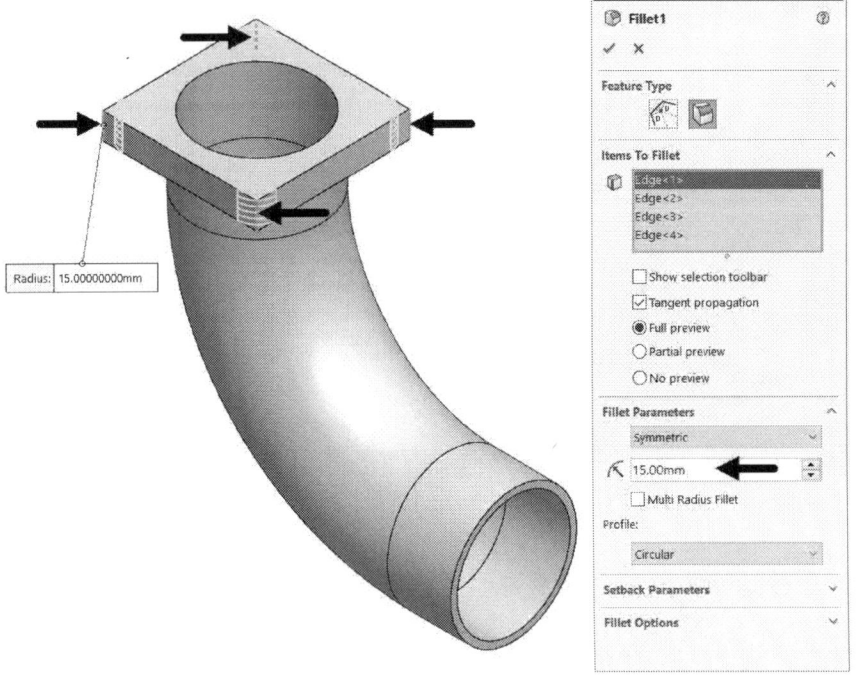
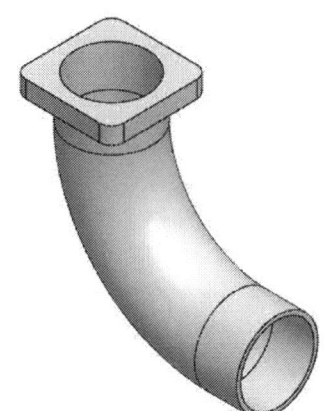

> Now, Select the **Hole Wizard** tool from the **Features CommandManager** to activate it and display the **Hole Specification PropertyManager**, as shown below.
> Click on the **Position** tab and click on the top planar face of the previously created Extruded Boss/Base feature of model, as shown.
> Move the cursor over right sided round corner to make its center point visible, as shown.
> Click on the displayed center point to define position for hole, as shown.

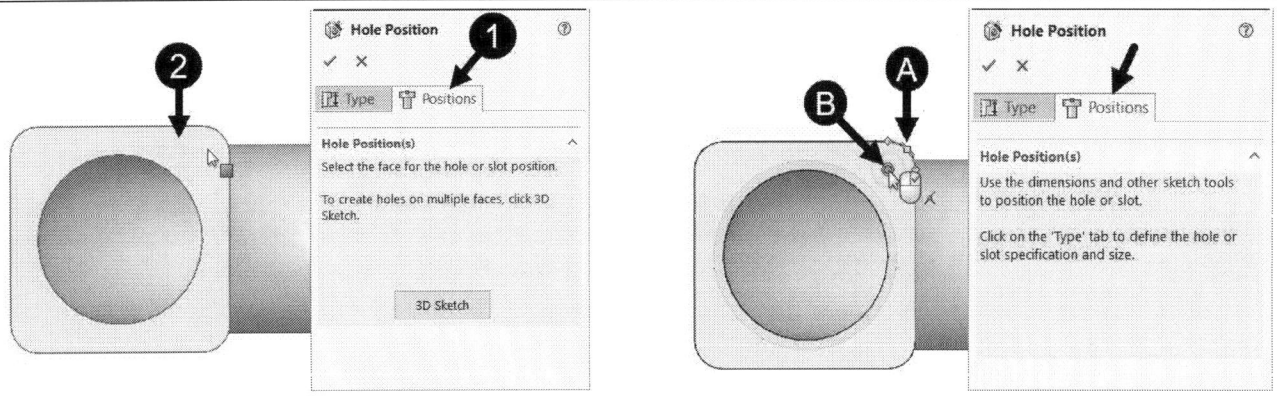

> Next, click on the **Type** tab of the PropertyManager and select required options for the hole feature, as shown.
> Click on the **OK** button of the PropertyManager to exit it and display the Hole feature created, as shown.

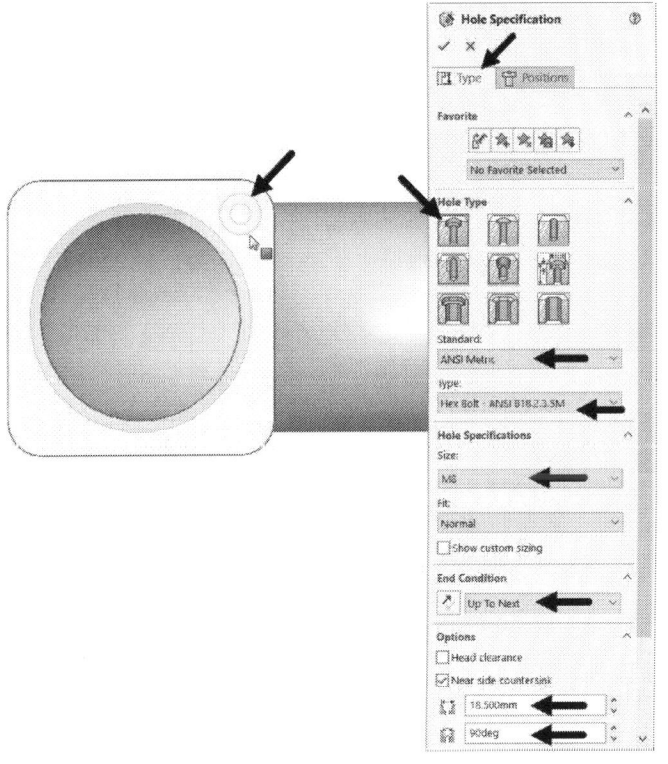

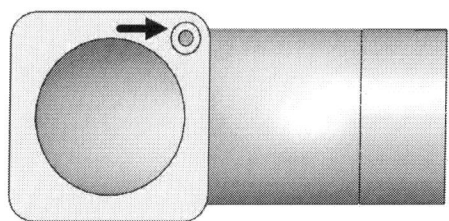

> Click on the **Linear Pattern** tool from **Features CommandManager** to activate it and display the **Linear Pattern PropertyManager**, as shown.
> Click on top horizontal line and then right vertical line to define both as Direction 1 & Direction 1, as shown.
> Next, select the previously created Hole feature and enter required details in the PropertyManager to display preview of Pattern feature, as shown.
> Click on the **OK** button of the PropertyManager to exit it and display the Pattern feature created, as shown.

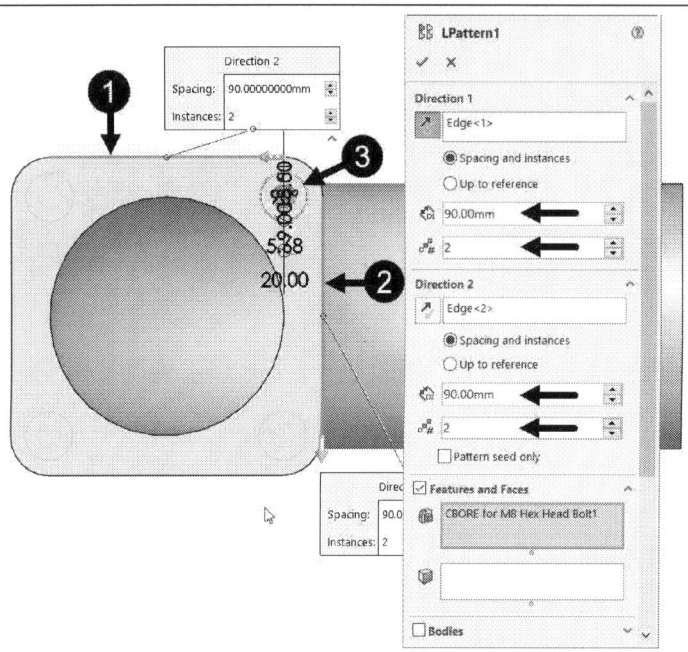
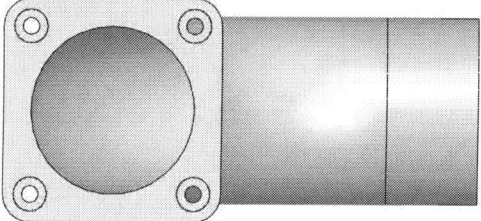

➤ Click on the **Plane** tool (**Features > Reference Geometry > Plane**) to activate it and display the Plane **PropertyManager**, as shown.
➤ Click on two planar face of the model to create or display preview of mid plane between both, as shown.
➤ Click on the **OK** button of the PropertyManager to exit it and display the Pattern feature created, as shown.

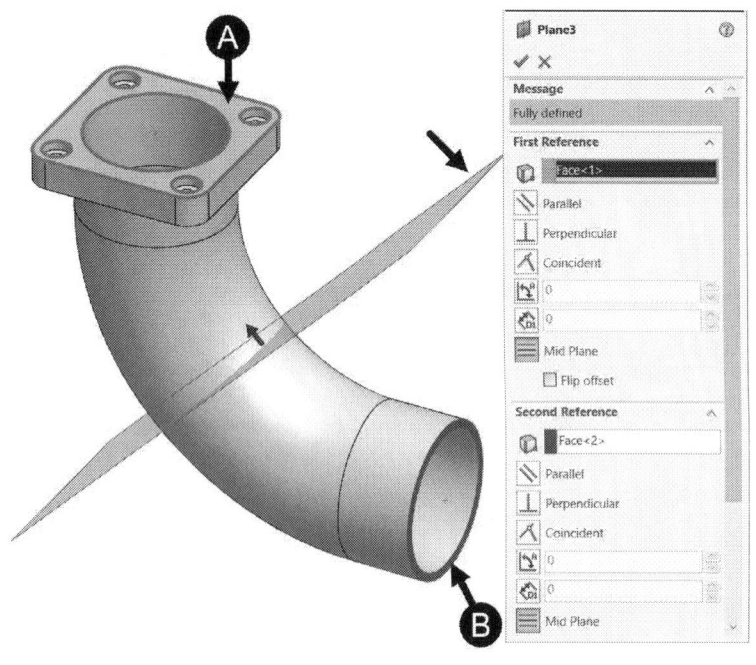
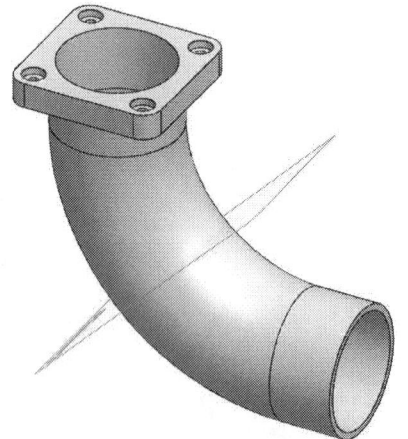

➤ Select the Mirror tool from **Features CommandManager** to activate it and display the **Mirror PropertyManager**, as shown.
➤ Click on the recently created plane and then select all features to mirror and display preview of all Mirrored features, as shown.
➤ Click on the **OK** button of the PropertyManager to exit it and display the Mirrored feature created, as shown.

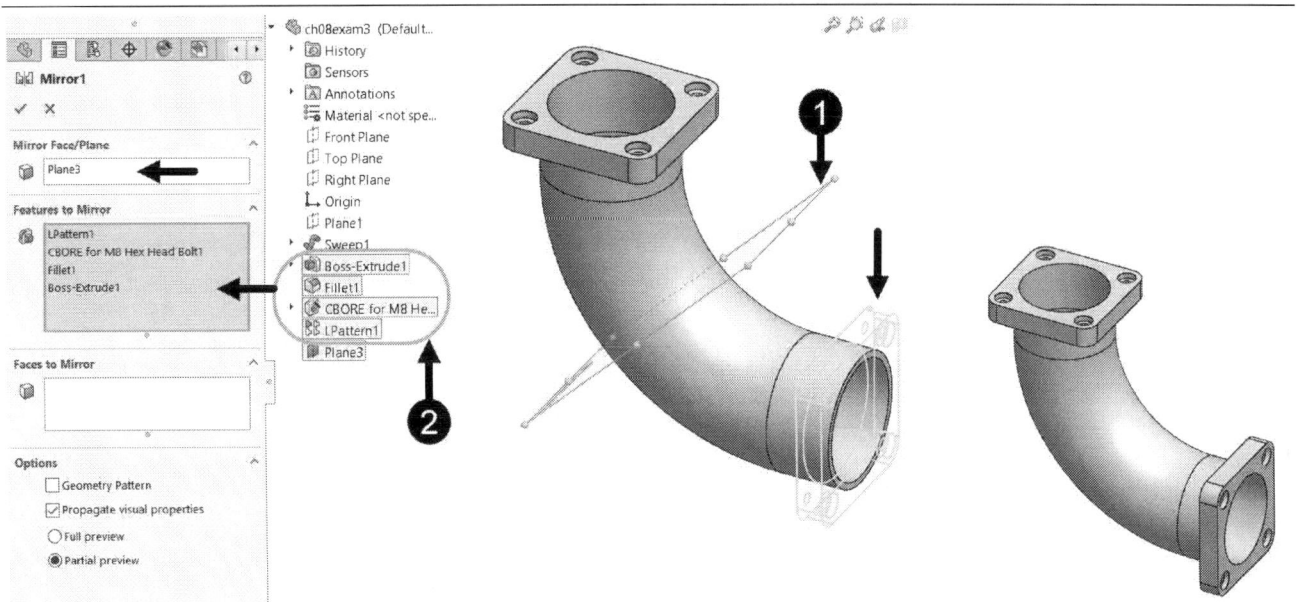

- Select the **Fillet** tool from **Features CommandManager** to activate it and display the **Fillet PropertyManager**, as shown.
- Click on two circular edges of the model and enter **5** as radius of fillet to display preview of Fillet feature, as shown.
- Click on the **OK** button of the PropertyManager to exit it and display the model with Fillet feature, as shown.

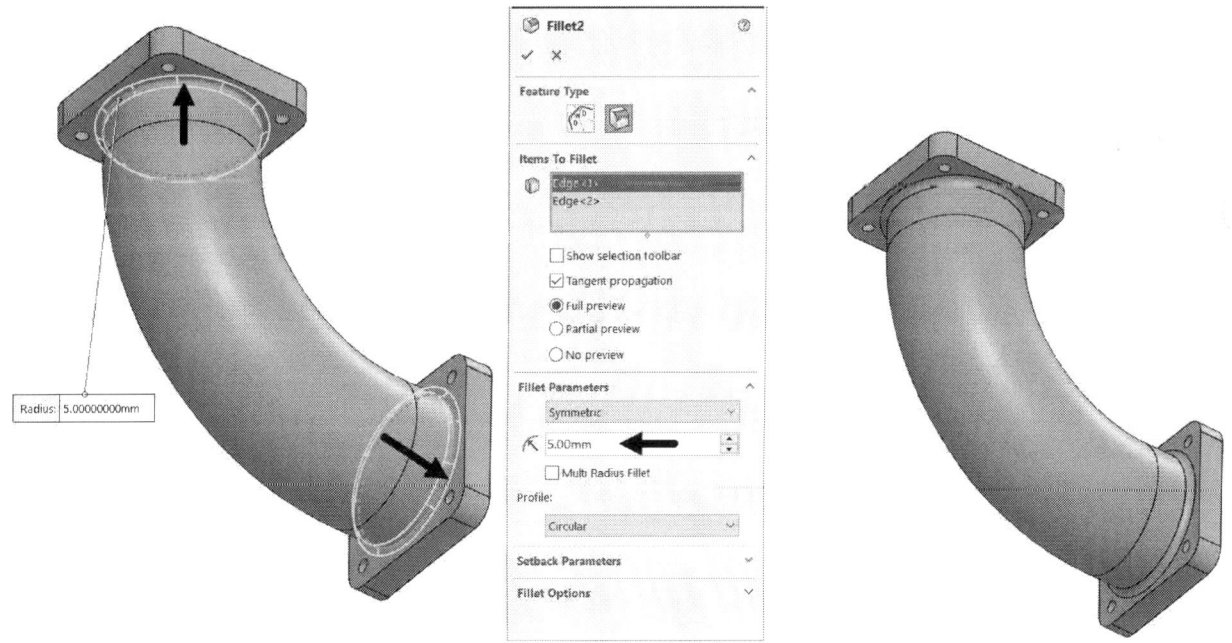

To change appearance of the model created, follow the steps:

- Click on the **Appearances, Scenes, and Decals** button on the right of the display screen, as shown.
- Next click on the required folder and then required option displayed under it to display model with new appearances, as shown.

Advanced Solid Modelling Tools

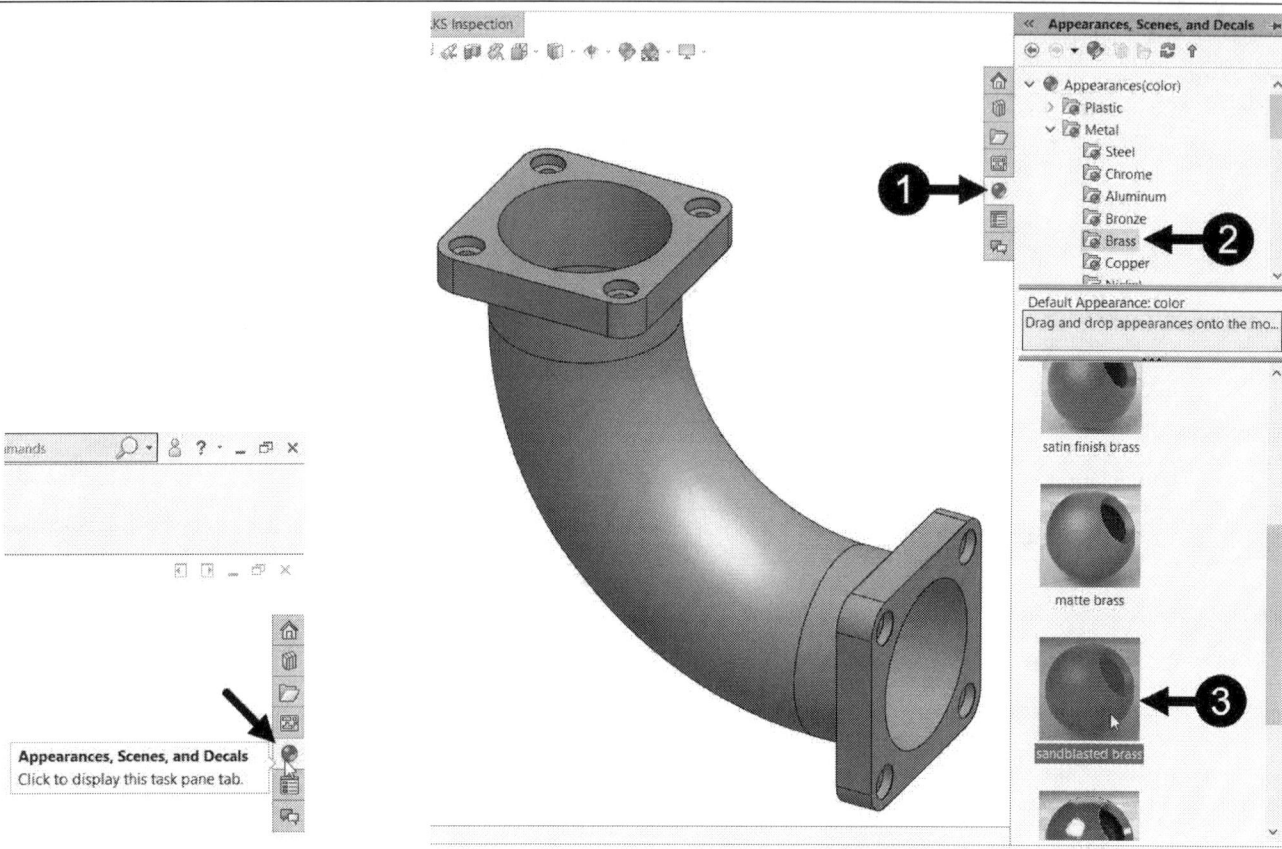

- Click on the **Save (Ctrl+S)** button from the **Menu Bar** to display the **Save As** dialog box.
- Next browse to the folder of chapter **8** and enter name **Ch08-exam02** in the **File name** edit box.
- Click on the **Save** button from the dialog box to save the file.
- Now enter the **Close** ⊠ button from the upper right corner to close it.

Questions:

1. What is the use of **Swept Boss/Base** tool?
2. How can you sweep a profile feature along a guide curve?
3. Which tool is used to remove material by sweeping the profile sketch?
4. Why **Solid Profile** radio button is selected?
5. How can we use **Lofted Cut** tool?
6. What is the main difference between Loft and Boundary tool?

Exercises:

Exercise 1

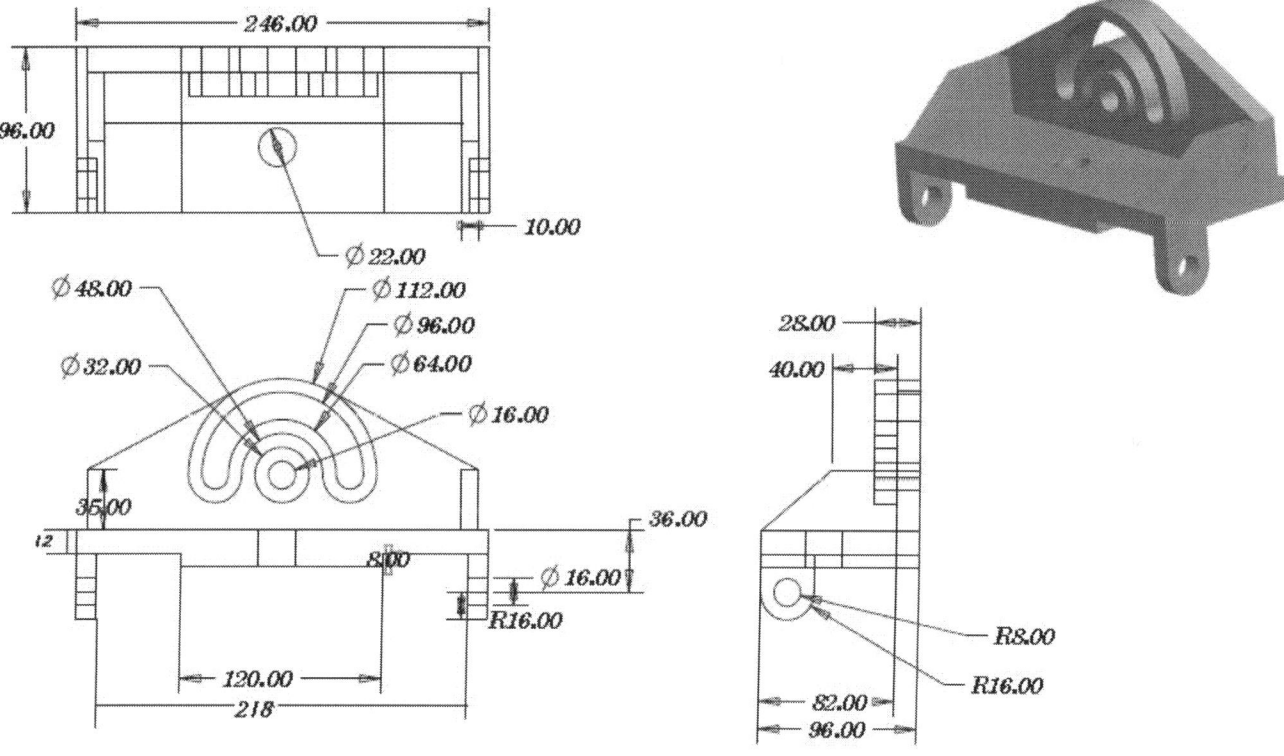

Exercise 2

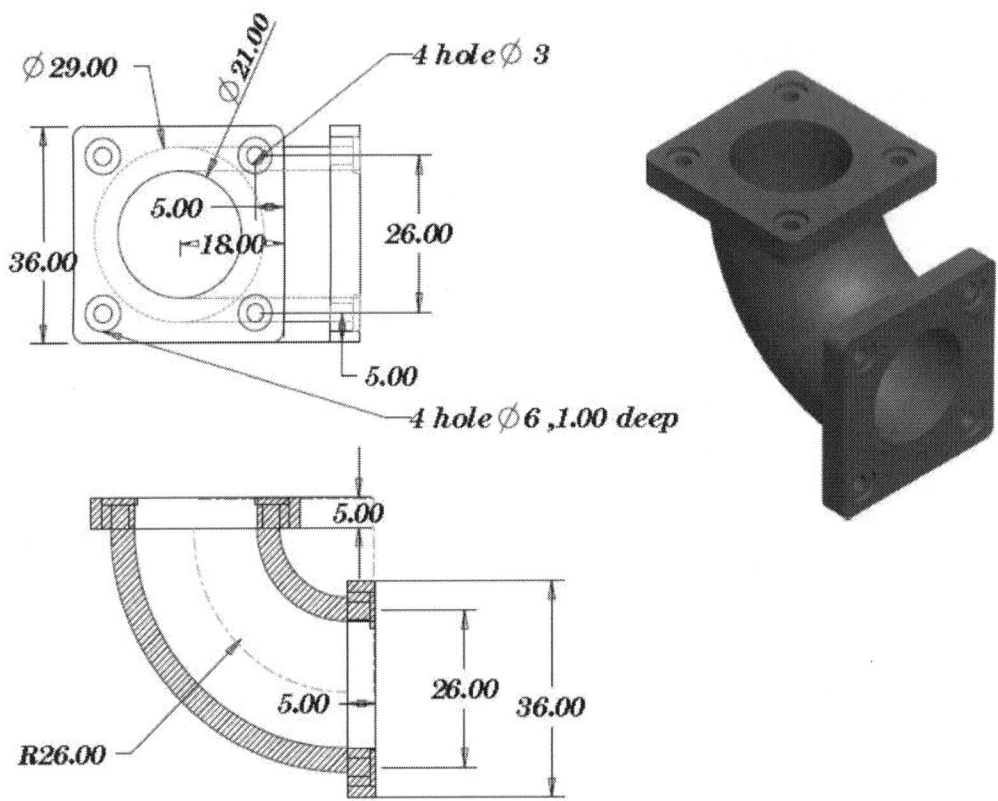

Chapter No 9: Advanced Solid Modeling Tools - II

The topics covered in this chapter are:

- ❖ Rib Feature
- ❖ Draft Feature
- ❖ Shell Feature
- ❖ Wrap Feature
- ❖ Mirror Feature
- ❖ Fillet Feature
- ❖ Chamfer Feature

Rib Feature

Ribs are the features that are used to strengthen the solid parts. This feature is almost similar to the extruded feature, the only difference is that it requires an open sketch. After selecting the open sketch and applying the required thickness, it automatically creates the rib feature. It also adds the material on both sides with symmetric thickness.

Create a Rib Feature

The steps to create rib feature are:

> Select the **Rib** tool from the **Features CommandManager** to display **Rib PropertyManager**, as shown.
> Select the required plane on which you want to create rib feature and enter in the sketching environment, as shown.

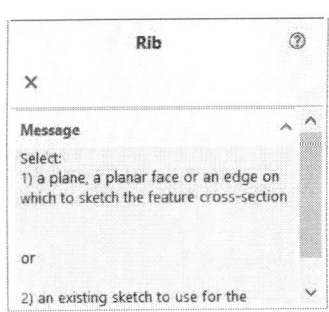 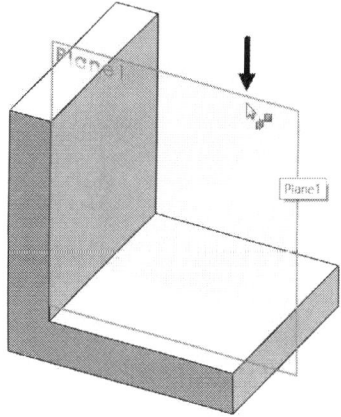

> Press the **CTRL + 8** key to adjust the sketching plane, parallel to the screen and draw the sketch, as shown.
> Click on the **Exit Sketch** button to exit the sketching environment and display the preview of rib feature along with **Rib1 PropertyManager**, as shown.

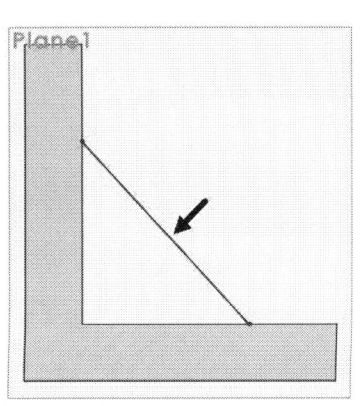 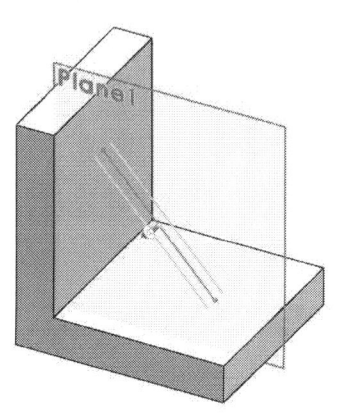 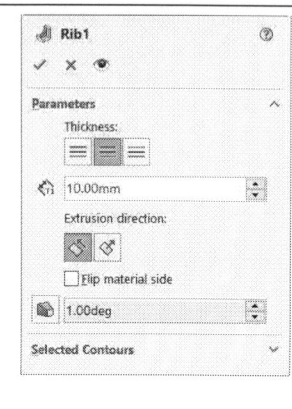

- Select the required **Thickness** button to define the side of the sketch to add material and thickness of the rib feature.
- Also, you can enter the required Rib Thickness and Draft Angel values in their respective spinners.

  The **Extrusion direction** buttons are selected to create the rib extrusion, parallel to the sketch or normal to the sketch.

- Next click on the **OK** button of the PropertyManager to display the Rib feature created, as shown.

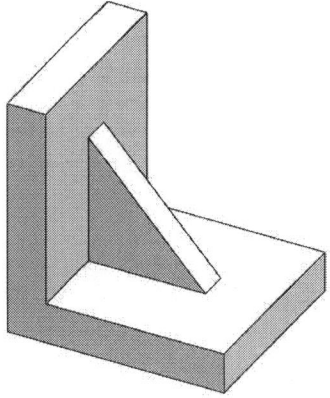

Create a Rib Feature by Selecting an Existing Sketch

To create a rib feature by selecting the previously created sketch, follow the steps:

- Draw a sketch on the required plane, as shown.
- Select the **Rib** tool from the **Features CommandManager** to display **Rib PropertyManager**, as shown.

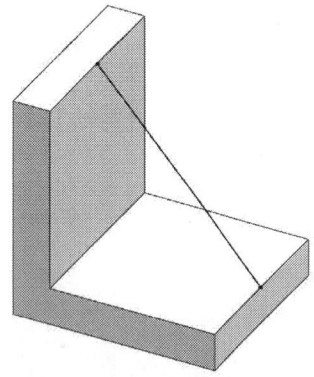 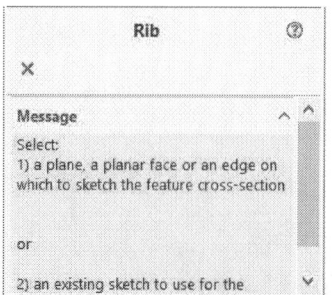

➢ Select the sketch to display preview of Rib feature and **Rib 1 PropertyManager** with all options, as shown.

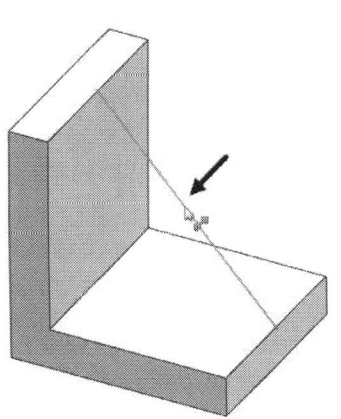 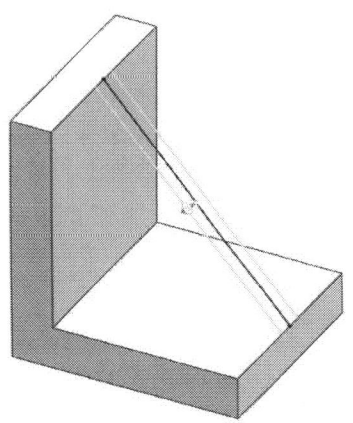 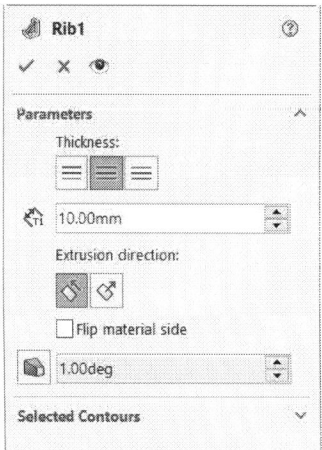

➢ You can select the required options and enter required values in the PropertyManager, as discussed earlier.
➢ Next click on the **OK** button of the PropertyManager to display the Rib feature created, as shown.

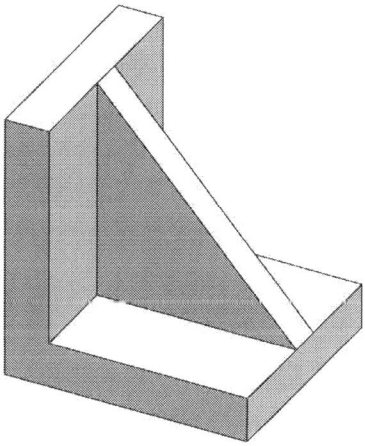

Draft Feature

The **Draft** tool is used to add taper to the selected faces of the model. This tool is mostly used to the model for molding and casting. After applying taper on faces, the model can be easily removed from the mold or die. To create a draft feature, follow the steps:

➢ Select the **Draft** tool from the **Features CommandManager** to display **DraftXpert PropertyManager**, as shown.
➢ Next click on the **Manual** button of the PropertyManager to display the **Draft PropertyManager**, as shown.

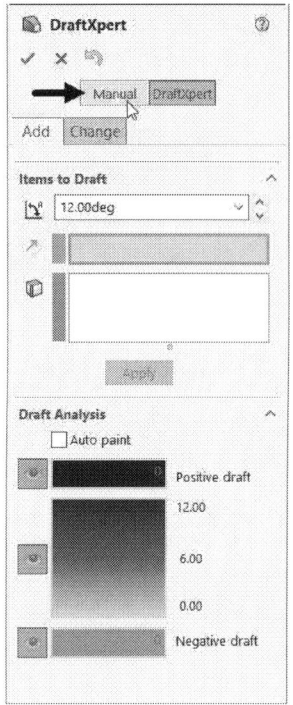 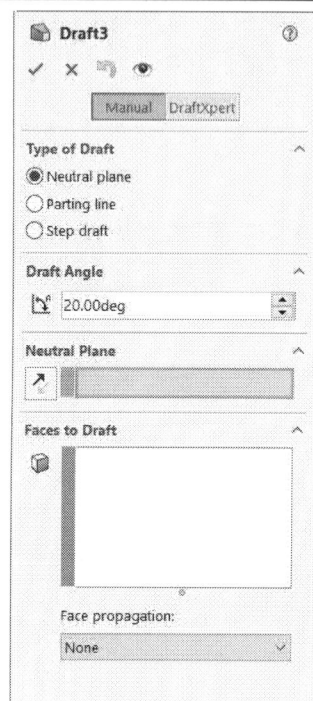

- ➢ Select the **Neutral** radio button under **Types of Draft** rollout of the PropertyManager, if it not selected by default.
- ➢ Now first select the face to define it as the Neutral plane with respect to which you can taper other faces, as shown.

The selected faces get visible in the respective boxes of the PropertyManager and you can edit and change them any time, as shown.

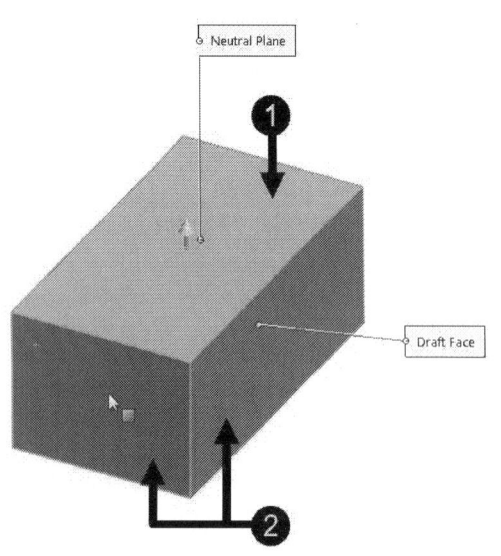 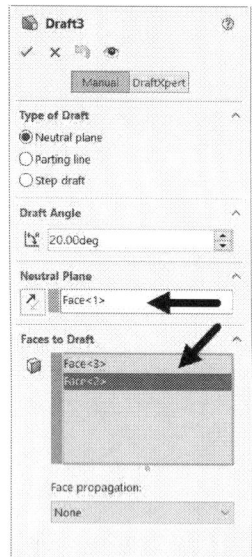

- ➢ Now enter the required draft angle value in the **Draft Angle** spinner of the PropertyManager. Also, you can select the **Reverse Direction** button to flip its direction.
- ➢ Now click on the **OK** button to exit the PropertyManager and display the draft feature, as shown.

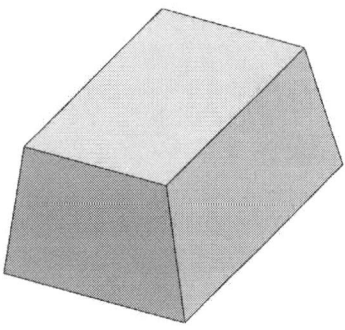

Shell Feature

The **Shell** tool is used to apply to solid model to make it hollow. Thus this is very time saving technique during creating thin walls solid models like tanks, containers, and bottles. To create a draft feature, follow the steps:

> Select the [Shell] **Shell** tool from the **Features CommandManager** to display **Shell PropertyManager**, as shown.

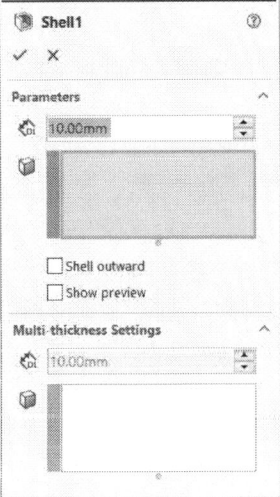

> Click on the face/faces to remove, as shown.
> Enter the required thickness in the **Thickness** spinner of the PropertyManager, as shown.
> Also, select the **Show preview** check box to display the preview of the model, as shown.

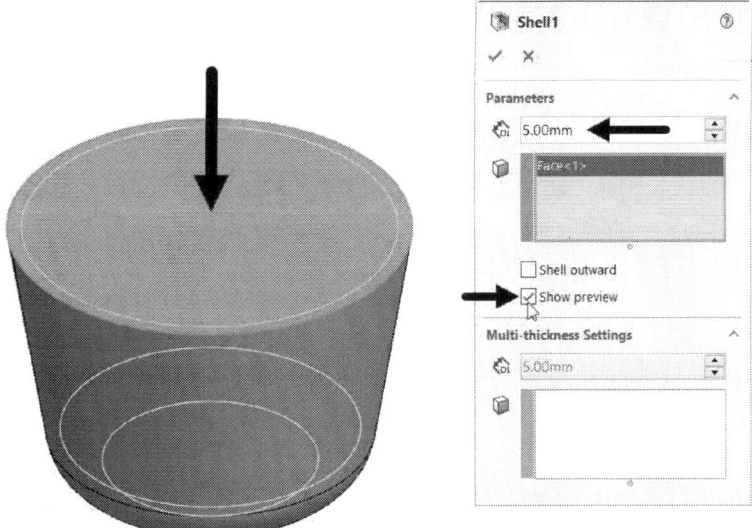

> Now click on the OK ☑ button to exit the PropertyManager and display the model with shell feature, as shown.

Note that model is rotated for the better visibility of inner surface of the model.

Shell with Multiple Thickness

You can also use Shell tool to create shell feature with multiple thicknesses by following the below given steps:

> Select the **Shell** tool to display the **Shell PropertyManager**, as shown.
> Enter the required thickness value in the **Thickness** spinner, as shown.
> Select the surface to remove, as shown.
> Select the **Show preview** check box to display preview of shell feature, as shown.
> Now click in the **Multi-thickness Faces** box to activate **Multi-thickness (es)** spinner above it, as shown.
> Select the two faces to create shell feature with different thickness value, as shown.
> Enter the required thickness value, as shown.

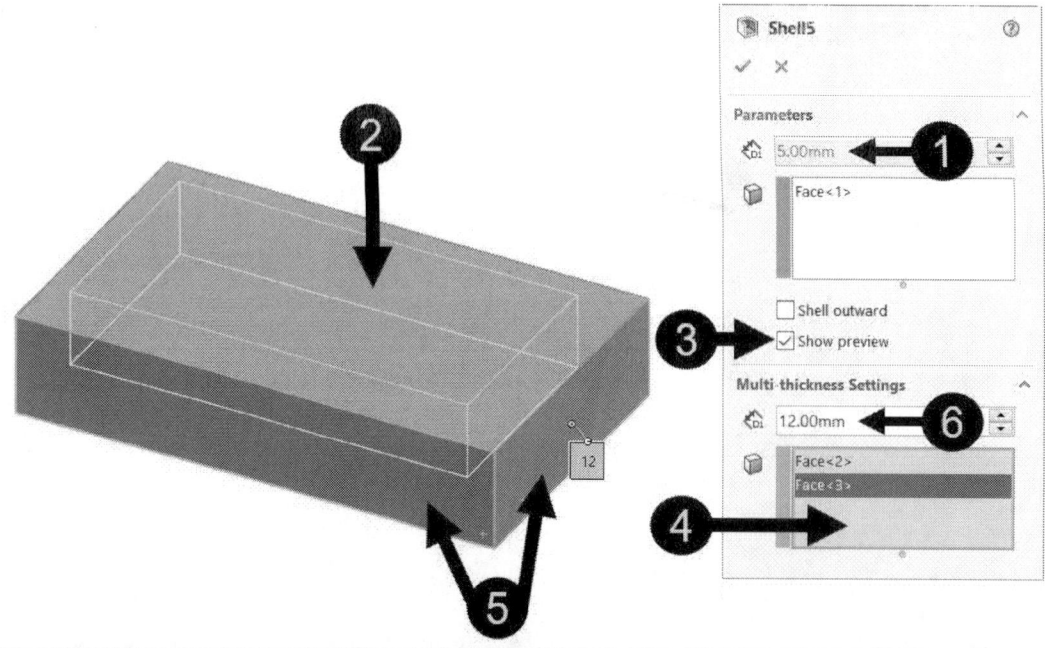

➤ Now click on the OK ☑ button to exit the PropertyManager and display the model with shell feature, as shown.

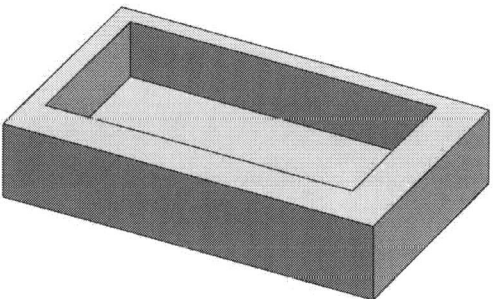

Wrap Tool

The **Wrap** tool is used to emboss, deboss or scribe a sketch or text on the selected planar or curved faces. The plane and selected faces should be parallel or tangent to each other, as shown. To create a draft feature, follow the steps:

➤ Draw the sketch on plane, parallel/tangent to the face to be selected, as shown.
➤ Select the sketch and then select the **Wrap** tool from the **Features CommandManager** to display **Wrap PropertyManager**, as shown.

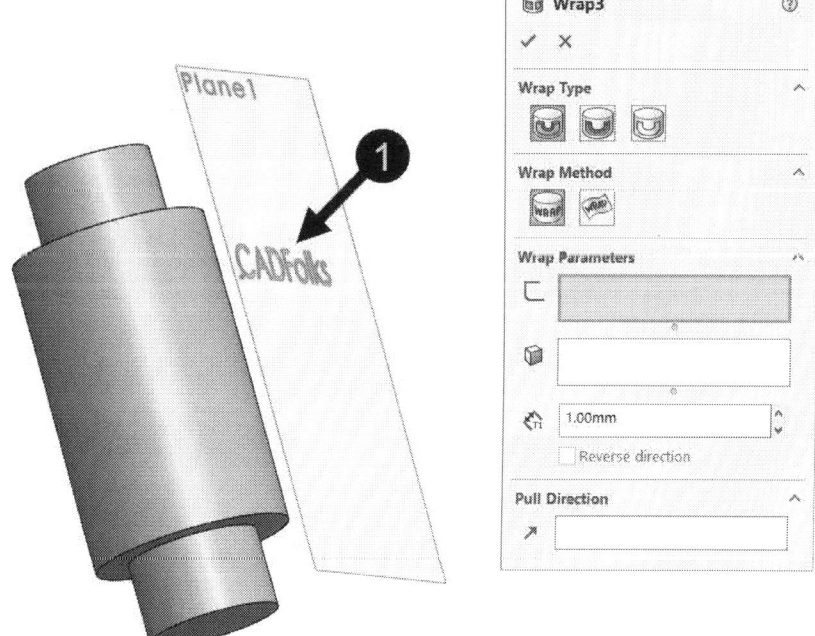

➤ Click on the required button from **Wrap Type** and **Wrap Method** rollout of the **Wrap PropertyManager**, as shown above.
➤ Click in the **Source Sketch** area under the **Wrap Parameters** rollout of the PropertyManager and select the sketch.
➤ Click in the **Face for Wrap Sketch** area and click on the face to display preview of wrap feature over it, as shown.
➤ Next, enter or adjust the required thickness value in the **Thickness** spinner, as shown.

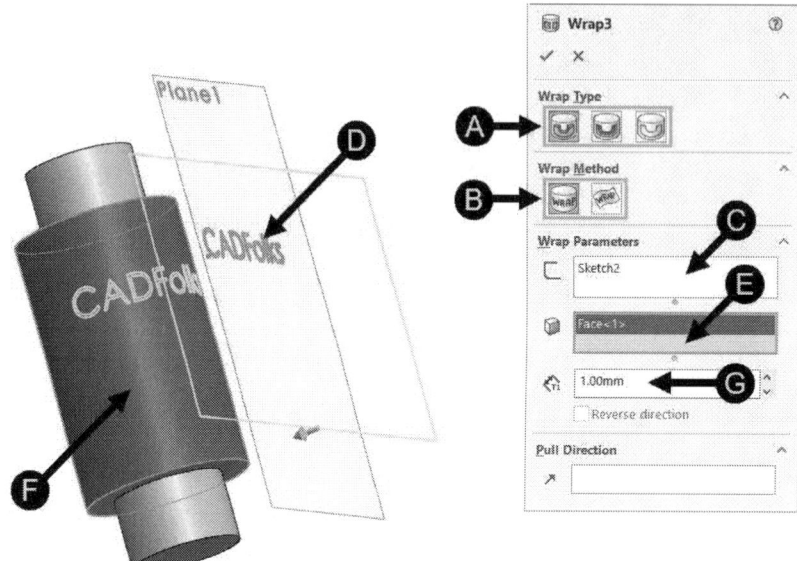

> Now click on the **OK** ✓ button to exit the PropertyManager and display the model with wrap feature, as shown.

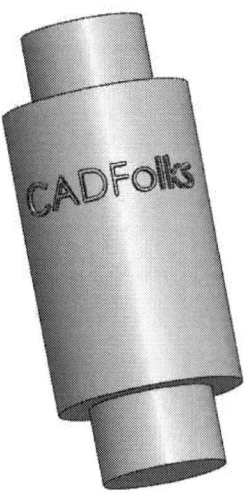

Similarly, you can deboss and scibe text or sketch over the selected circular face by selecting the **Deboss** and **Scibe** button under **Wrap Type** rollout of the **Wrap PropertyManager**, as shown.

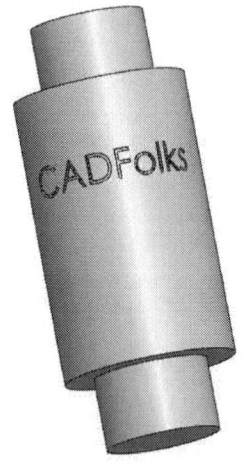 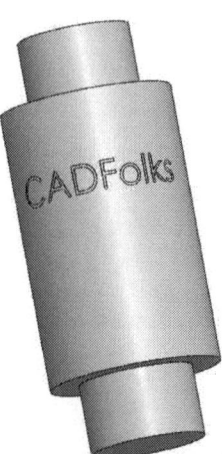

You can emboss, deboss and scibe on a planer face also, as shown.

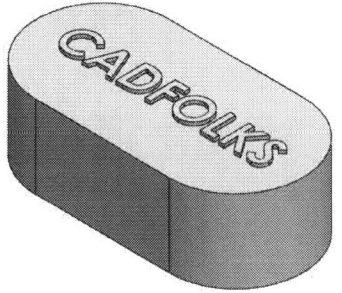
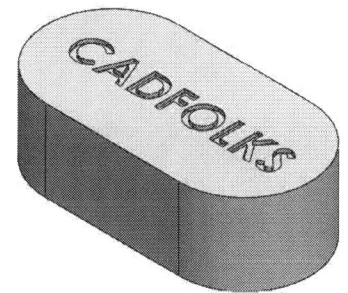
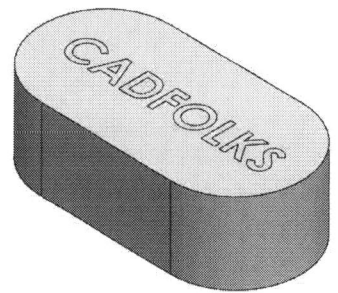

Mirror Tool

The **Mirror** tool is used to copy/mirror the selected feature and body about a selected mirror plane or planar face. This tool is useful while designing a symmetric part by saving your time. By using this tool, you can copy individual features of the entire body. For creating a mirror feature in 3D geometry, you need a place or planar face to use it as the mirroring element. You can use default planes, model faces or sometime you need to create a datum/reference plane.

Mirror a Feature/Features of a Model

➢ Create reference planes across the model to be used later as mirroring planes, as shown

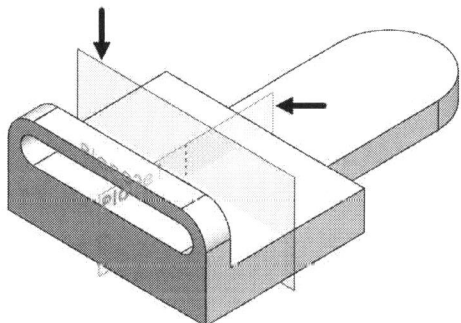

➢ Select the Mirror ![Mirror] tool from the **Features CommandManager** to display **Mirror PropertyManager**, as shown.
➢ Select the mirroring place with respect to which you want to create mirror feature, as shown.
➢ Next, select the feature to be mirrored and to display the preview of mirror feature, as shown.

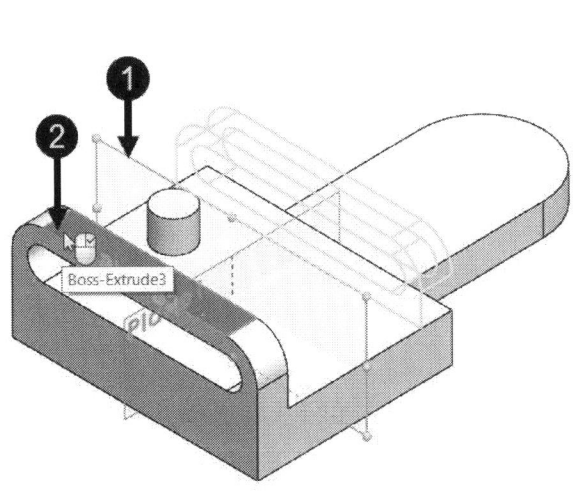
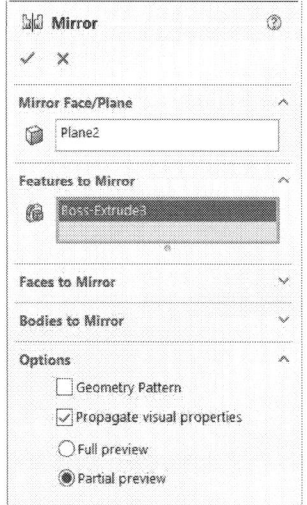

Advanced Solid Modelling Tools

➢ Now click on the OK ✓ button to exit the PropertyManager and display the model with mirror feature, as shown.

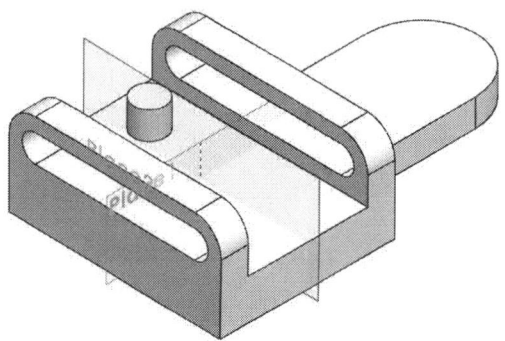

Similarly, you can mirror the features of the model by selecting faces.

➢ Again, activate the **Mirror** tool to display **Mirror PropertyManager**, as shown.
➢ Select the mirror plane and next click in the **Faces to Mirror** section box, as shown.
➢ Next, click on the faces of the cylindrical extruded feature to display preview of mirror feature, as shown.

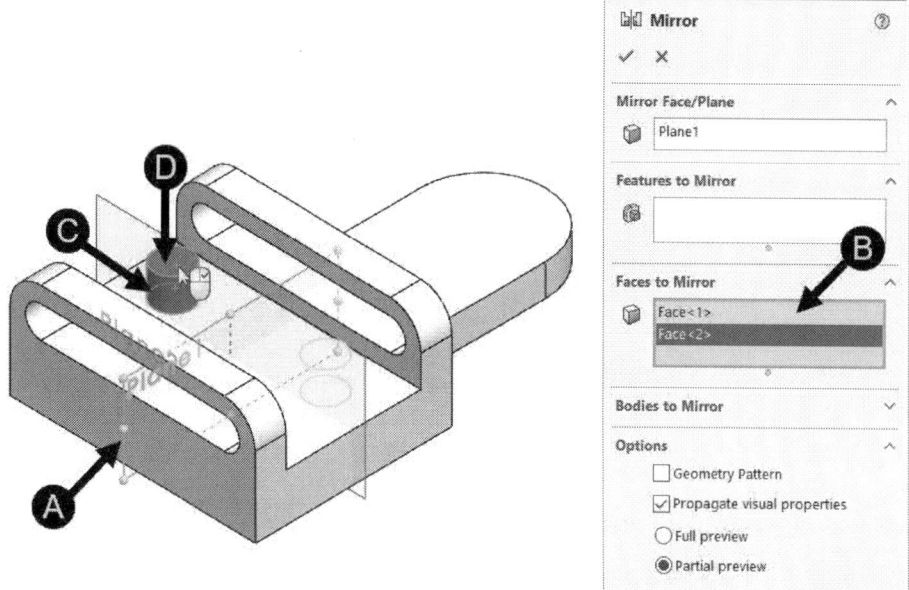

➢ Now click on the OK ✓ button to exit the PropertyManager and display the model with mirror feature, as shown.

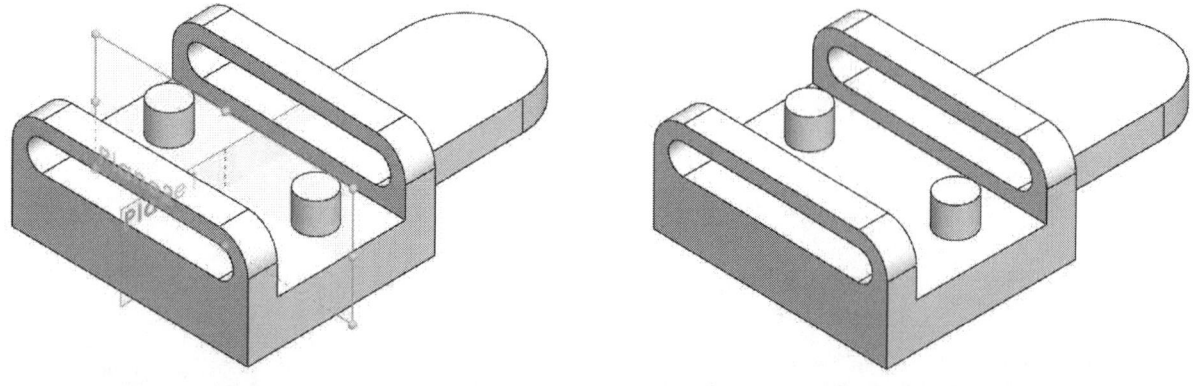

Mirror the Whole Model

If the part you are creating is completely symmetric, you can save more time by creating half of it and mirroring the entire geometry rather than individual features.

- ➢ Activate the **Mirror** tool.
- ➢ Select the planar face along which you want to mirror whole model, as shown.
- ➢ Next, select all the features of model or whole model to display preview of mirror feature, as shown.

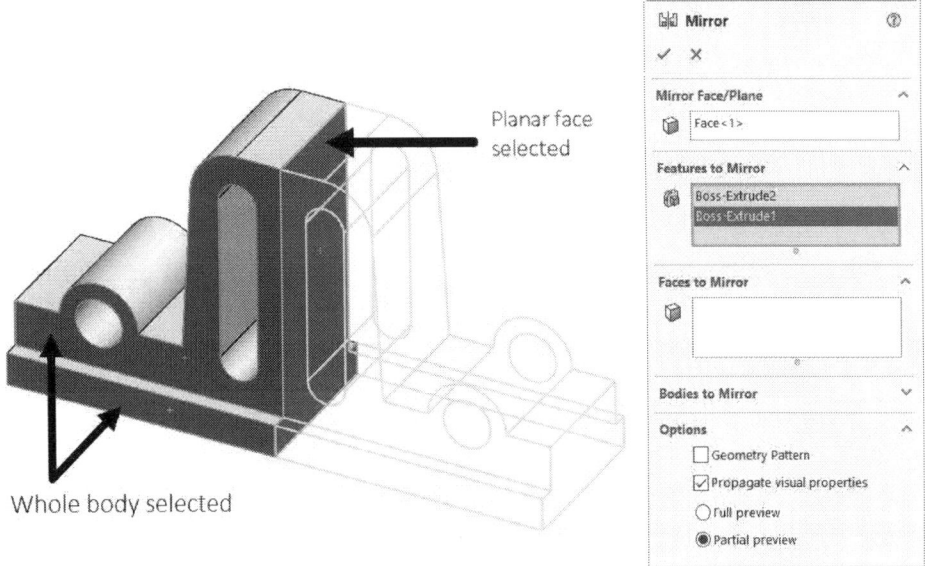

- ➢ Now click on the **OK** button to exit the PropertyManager and display the model with mirror feature, as shown.

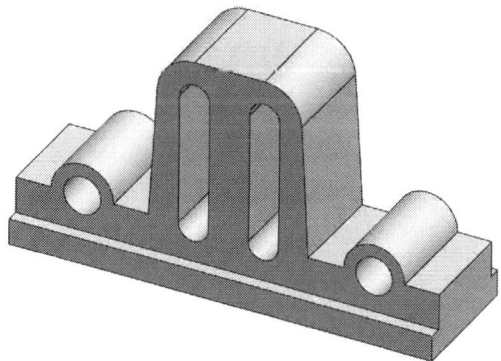

 ## Fillet Tool

The **Fillet** tool is used to remove edges or corners of the part model. The use of this tool is same like **Sketch Fillet** tool, discussed earlier in this book. There are four options available in the **Fillet PropertyManager**, used for creating fillet features, discussed below one-by-one:

 ### Constant Size Fillet

This option is used to create a fillet with constant radius along the selected entities. This option is selected by default.

- ➢ Select the **Fillet** tool (**Features > Fillet**) to display **Fillet PropertyManager**, as shown.

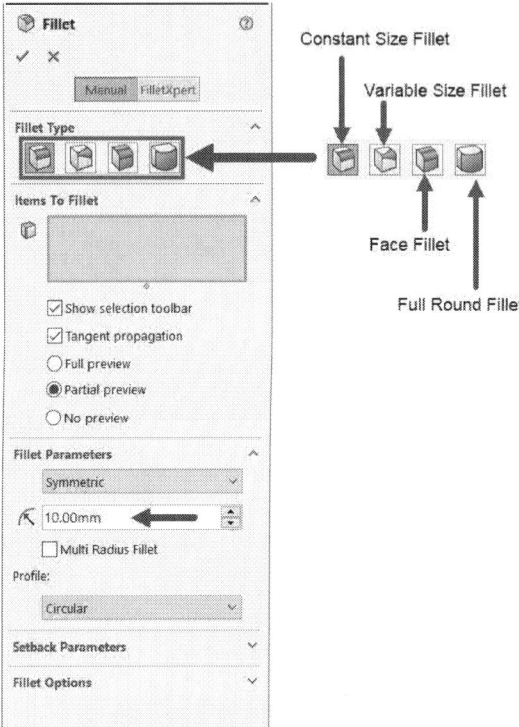

> Enter the required radius value for fillet in the PropertyManager, as shown.
> Select the edges to fillet to display the preview of fillet feature, as shown.

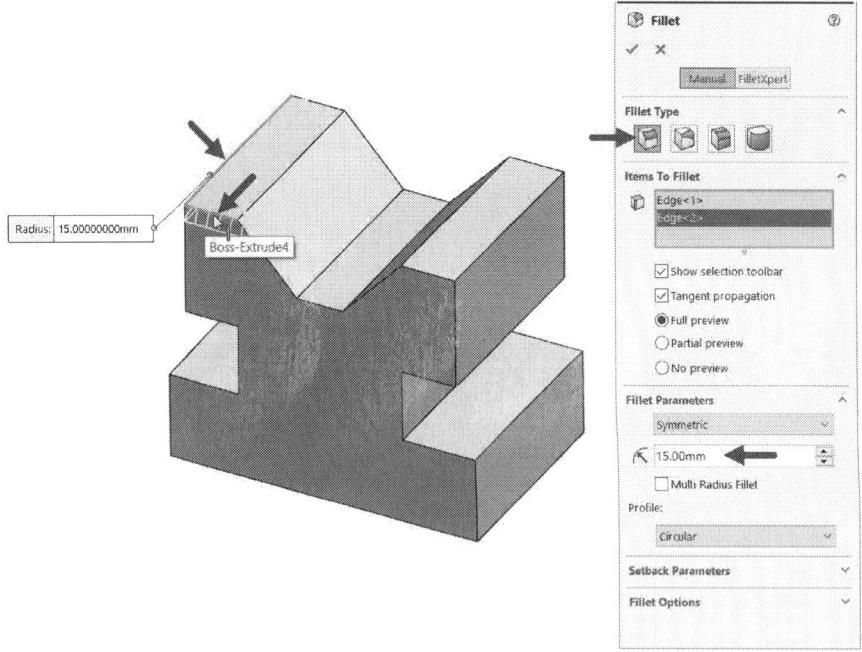

The names of the selected entities get displayed in the **Edges, Faces, Features and Loops** selection box. You can remove/deselect any single or all selected entities from it.

> Click on the **OK** button of the PropertyManager to display the fillet feature, as shown.

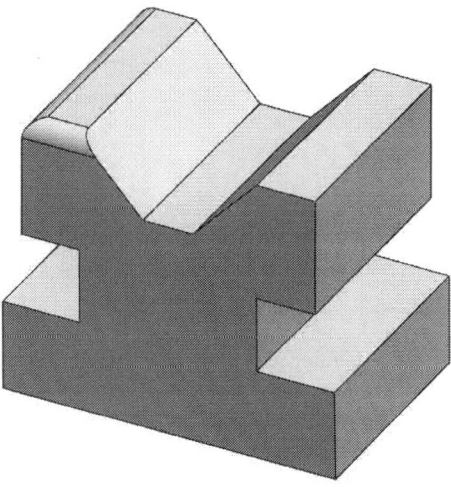

You can also select the face to create fillet to all edges of selected faces, as shown.

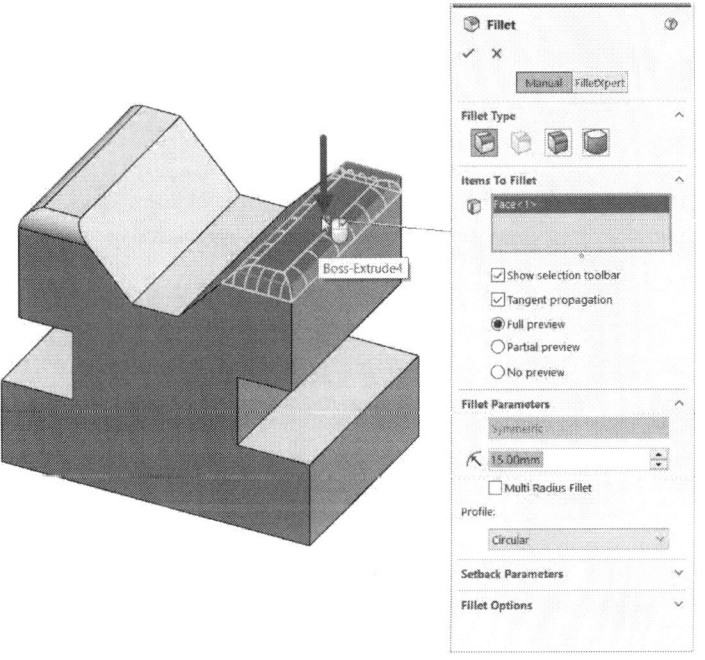
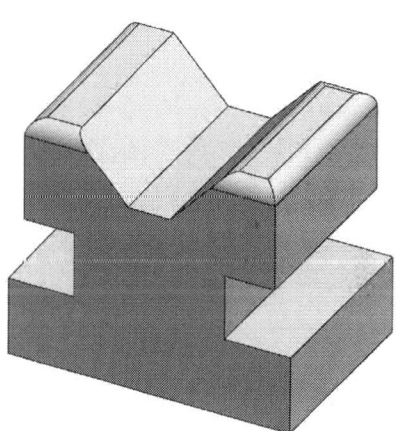

Variable Size Fillet

This option is selected to create a fillet with variable radii. You can use the variable points to define the fillet.

➢ Select the **Fillet** tool (**Features > Fillet**) to display **Fillet PropertyManager**, as shown above.
➢ Click on the **Variable Size Fillet** button of the PropertyManager, as shown.
➢ Next, select the entity to display variable points and instance points along it, as shown.

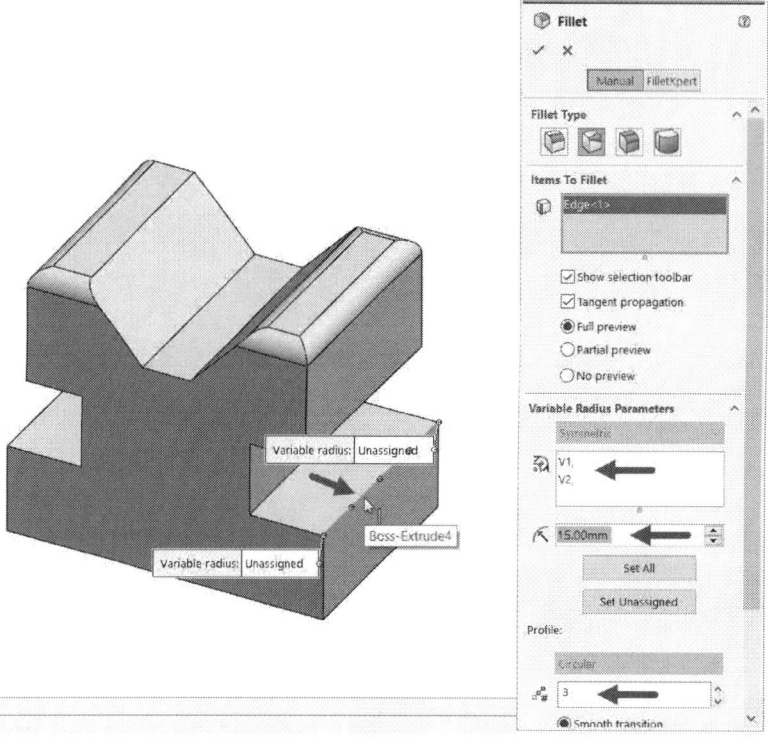

- Click on the variable points in the **Attach Radii** selection box of PropertyManager, as shown.
- Next, enter or adjust the radius values for both variables from the **Radius** spinner to display preview of variable size fillet, as shown.
- Enter or adjust the required no of instances from the **Number of Instances** selection box, as shown.
- Click on the **OK** button of the PropertyManager to display the fillet feature, as shown.

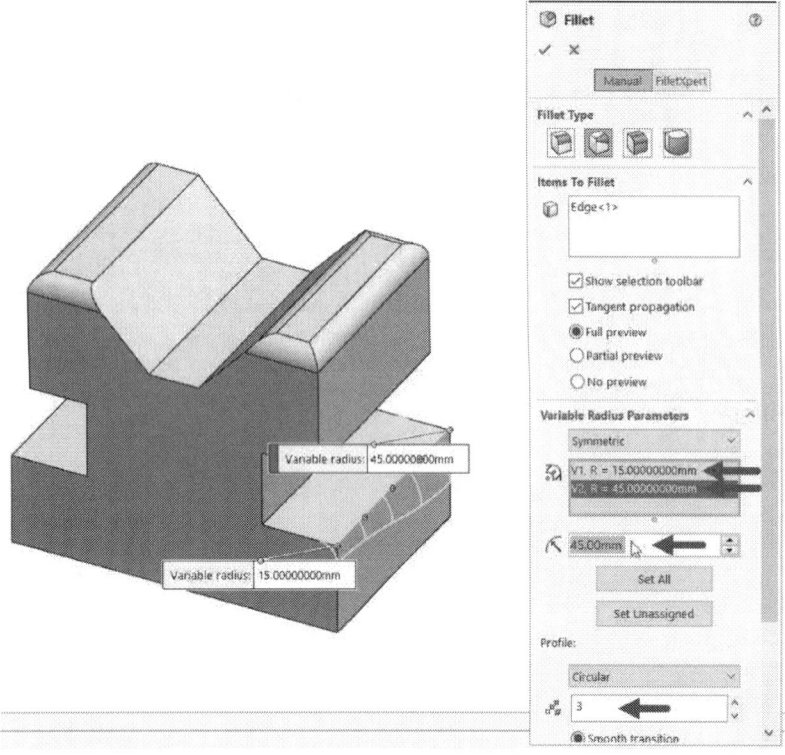
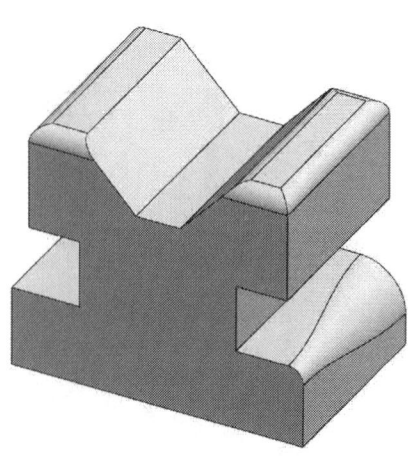

Face Fillet

This option is used to create fillet along non-adjacent & non-continuous faces by selected them one-by-one.

> - Select the **Fillet** tool (**Features > Fillet**) to display **Fillet PropertyManager**, as shown above.
> - Click on the **Face Fillet** button of the PropertyManager, as shown.
> - Next, click on one of the faces to display it in the **Face Set 1** selection box of the PropertyManager, as shown.
> - Next click in the **Face Set 2** selection box of PropertyManager and click on other face to display preview of fillet along selected faces, as shown.
> - Adjust the required radius value of fillet in the Radius selection box of the PropertyManager, as shown.
> - Click on the **OK** button of the PropertyManager to display the fillet feature, as shown.

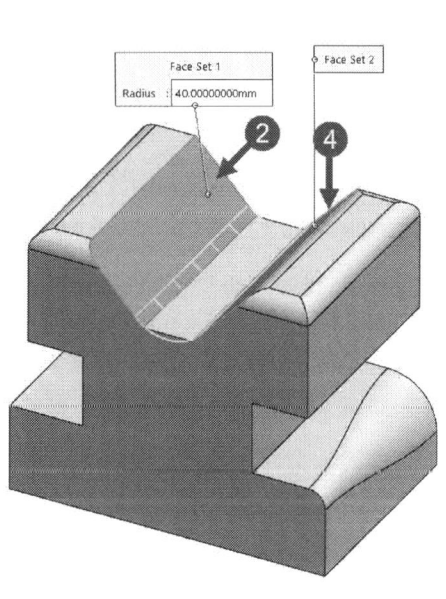 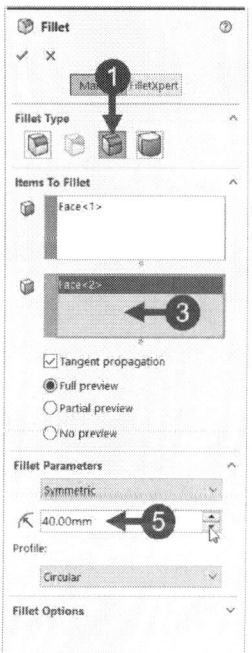 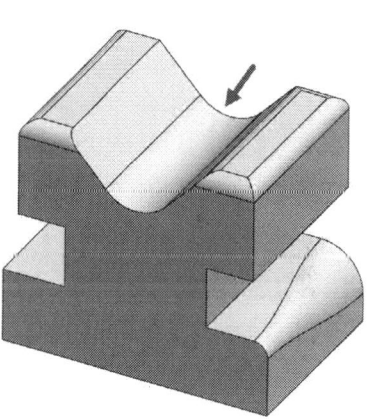

Full Round Fillet

This option is selected to create fillet, tangent to three adjacent faces.

> - Select the **Fillet** tool (**Features > Fillet**) to display **Fillet PropertyManager**, as shown above.
> - Click on the **Full Round Fillet** button of the PropertyManager, as shown.
> - Next, click on left side face of the model to display it in the **Side Face Set 1** selection box of the PropertyManager, as shown.
> - Next click in the **Center Face Set** selection box of the PropertyManager and click on the top face of the model, as shown.
> - Next click in the **Side Face Set 2** selection box of PropertyManager and click on right side face to display preview of fillet along selected faces, as shown.

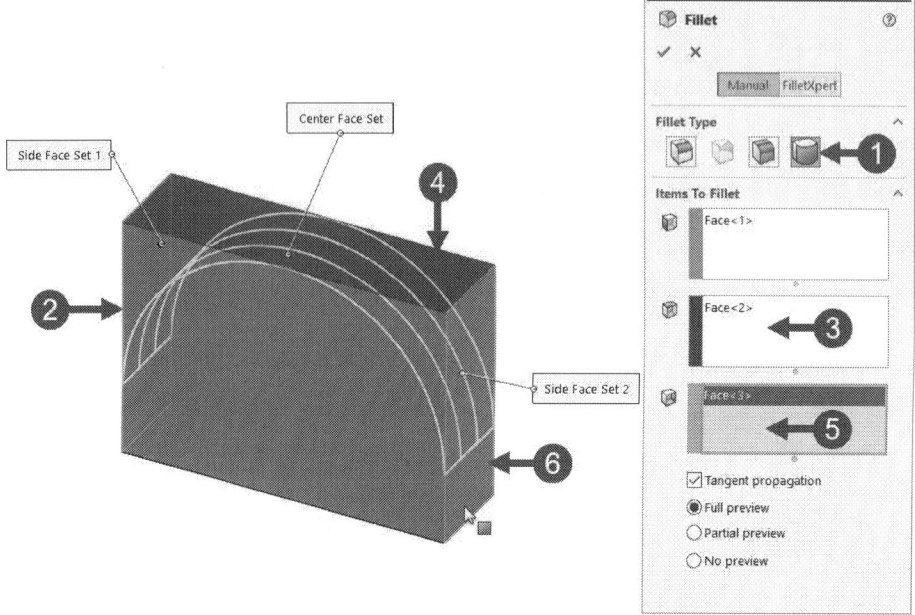

> Click on the OK ✓ button of the PropertyManager to display the fillet feature, as shown.

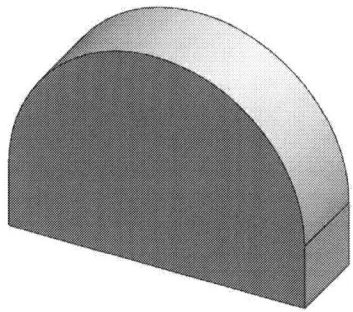

FilletXpert

This tool is selected to create single or multiple fillets together, once you activate/select it. It also helps in changing existing fillets and manage fillet corners.

> Select the **Fillet** tool (**Features > Fillet**) to display **Fillet PropertyManager**, as shown above.
> Click on the FilletXpert tab to display all options used in creating fillets using this tool, as shown.

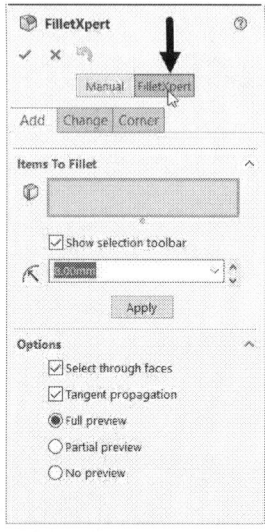

The tabs available in this PropertyManager are discussed below:

Add Tab

The options in this tab can be used for creating new constant radius and multiple radius fillets. This tab is selected by default.

- Select the entities to create fillets along them, as shown.
- Enter the required radius value for fillet in the respective edit box, as shown.

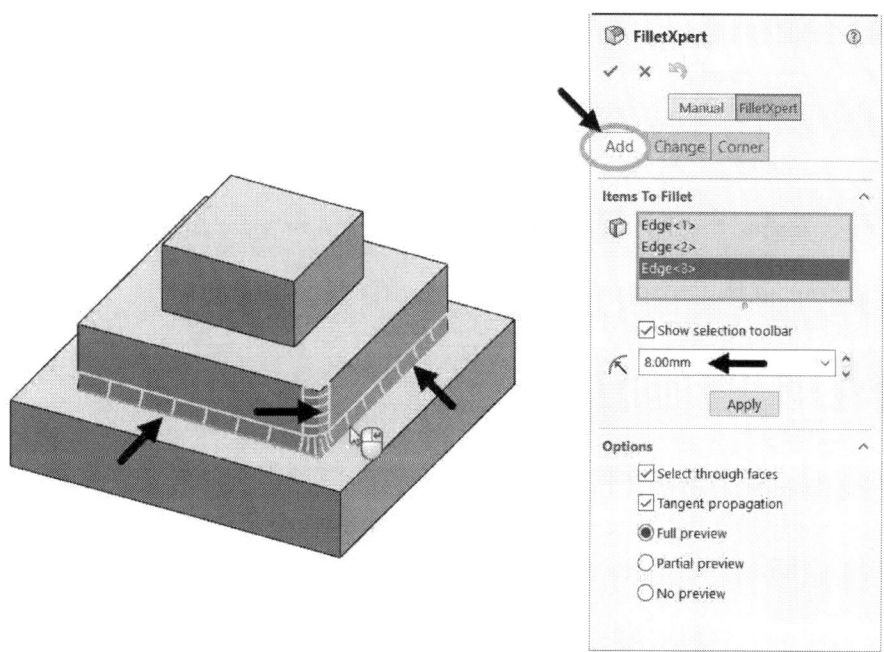

- Now click on the **OK** button of the PropertyManager to display the fillets created, as shown.

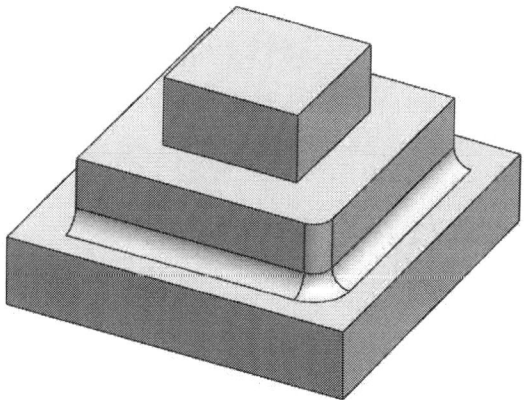

Note that, you can create fillets with multiple radius by clicking on the **Apply** button of the PropertyManager, after selecting any entity/edge and entering required radius.

- Select the entity and enter the required radius value for fillet, as shown.
- Next, click on the Apply button of the PropertyManager to display the fillet created, as shown.

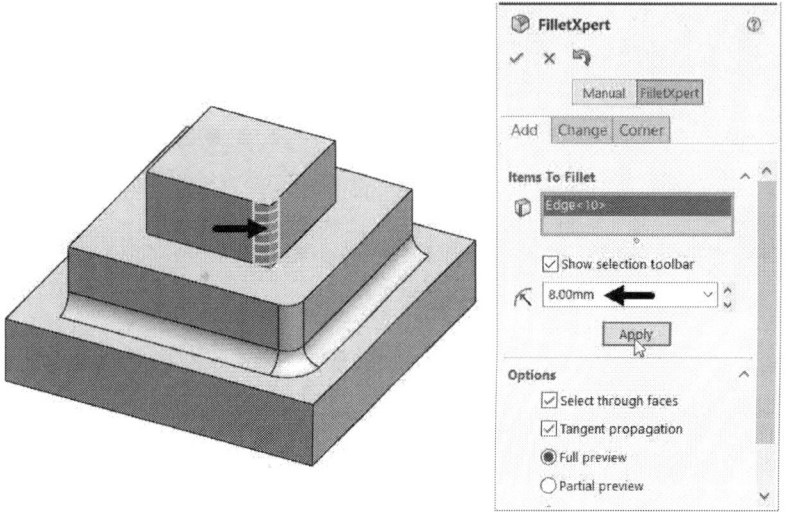
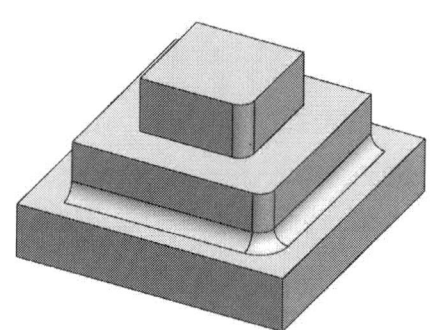

- The PropertyManager is still active, select new edges of model and enter required radius value for fillet, as shown.
- Again, click on the **Apply** button of the PropertyManager to display the fillet created, as shown.

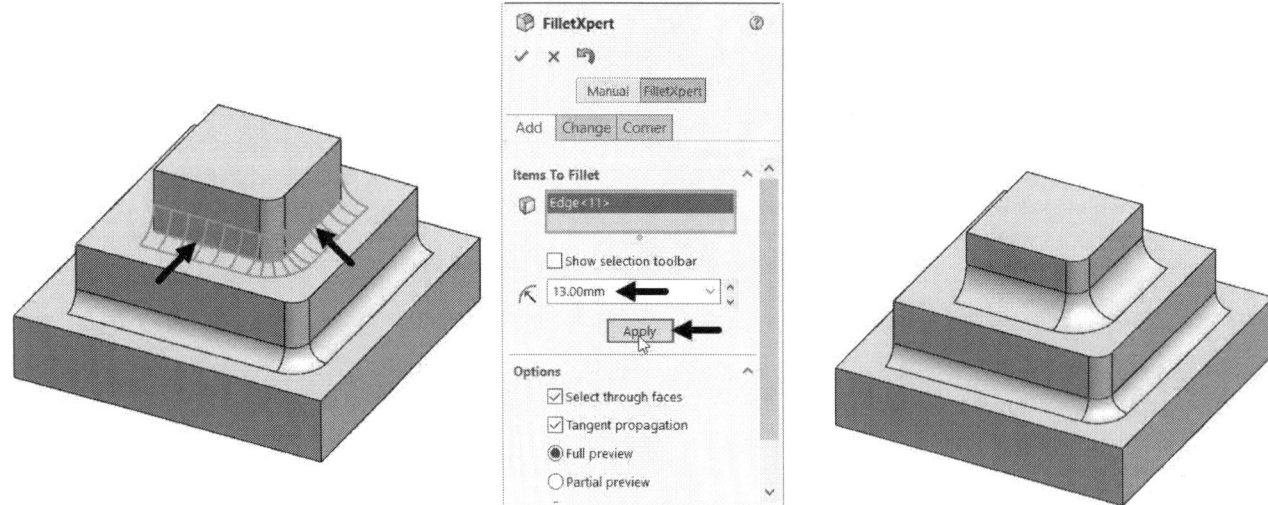

Change Tab

The options in this tab can be used to remove or resize previously created fillets with constant radius.

- Click on the **Change** tab of the PropertyManager, as shown.
- Next, click on the required fillet from the **Existing Fillets** rollout, as shown.

    Note that the respective selected fillet with constant radius gets highlighted automatically over the model, as shown.

- Enter the new radius value in the **Radius** edit box, as shown.
- Next, click on the **Resize** button to display the resized fillet, a shown.

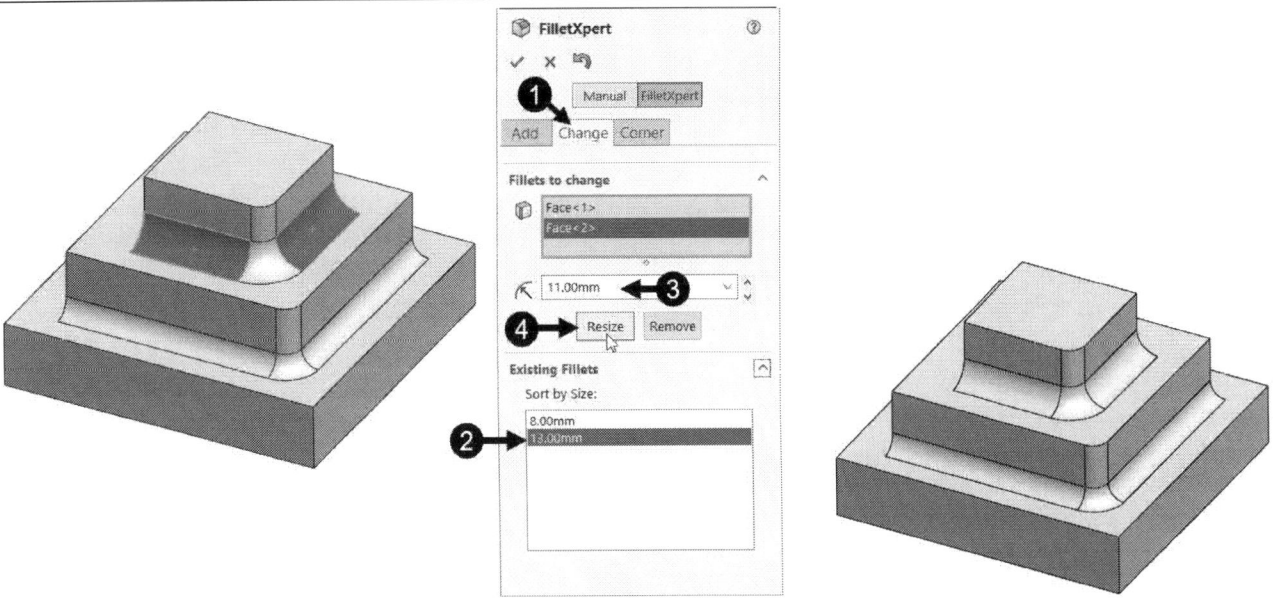

Note that to remove any fillet, you can simply click on Remove button of the PropertyManager after selecting it.

Corner Tab

The options in this tab can be used to create and manage fillet corner where three filleted edges meet at one vertex.

- Click on the **Corner** tab of the PropertyManager, as shown.
- Next, click on the fillet feature of the model, as shown.
- Next click over the **Show Alternatives** button of the PropertyManager to display the **Select Alternatives** display box, as shown.
- Next select the required button from the dialog box to apply change and display model with new corner, as shown.

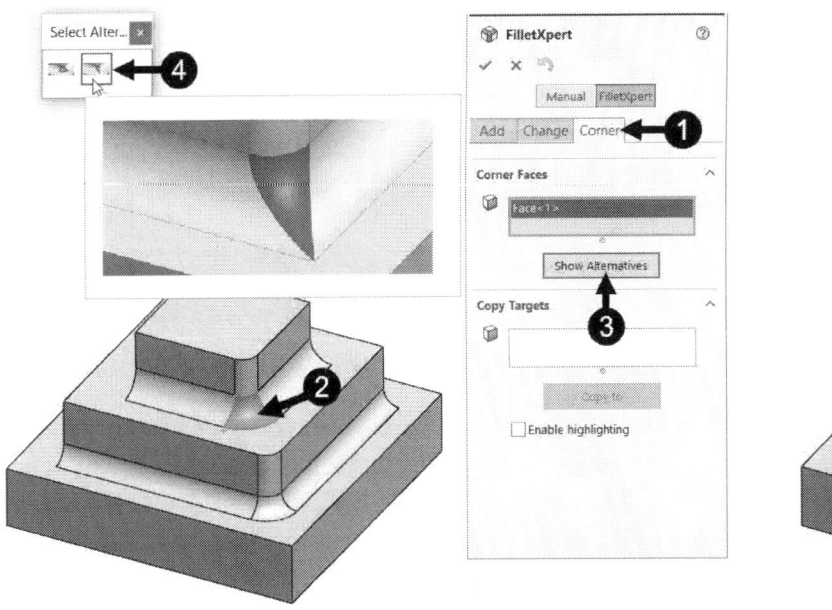
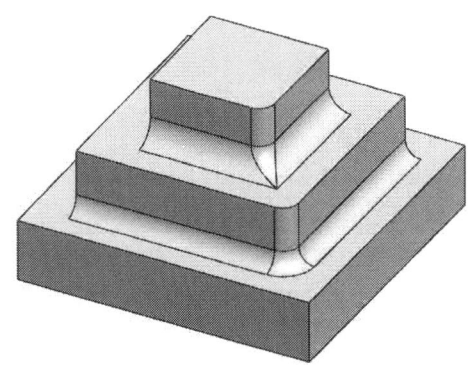

Chamfer Tool

The Chamfer tool available in the **Fillet** drop-down is used to replace the sharp corners with an inclined edge. The use of this tool is same like **Sketch Chamfer** tool, discussed earlier in this book. There are five options available in the **Chamfer PropertyManager** used for creating chamfer features, discussed below one-by-one:

Angle Distance

This option is used to create a chamfer by entering the required distance and angle values in their respective edit boxes in **Chamfer PropertyManager** or drawing area, as shown. This option is selected by default.

- Select the **Chamfer** tool (**Features > Fillet > Chamfer**) to display **Chamfer PropertyManager**, as shown.
- Select the edge to display preview of chamfer feature along it, as shown.

  The **Angle Distance** button in **Chamfer PropertyManager** is selected by default, as shown.

- Note that a manipulator arrow with direction towards the point in which the distance is measured also appears, as shown. You can flip the direction by selecting the arrow or by selecting the Flip direction check box of the PropertyManager.
- Enter the required Angle and Distance values in their respective edit boxes of the PropertyManager or drawing area, as shown.
- Next, click on the **OK** button of the PropertyManager to display chamfer feature created, as shown.

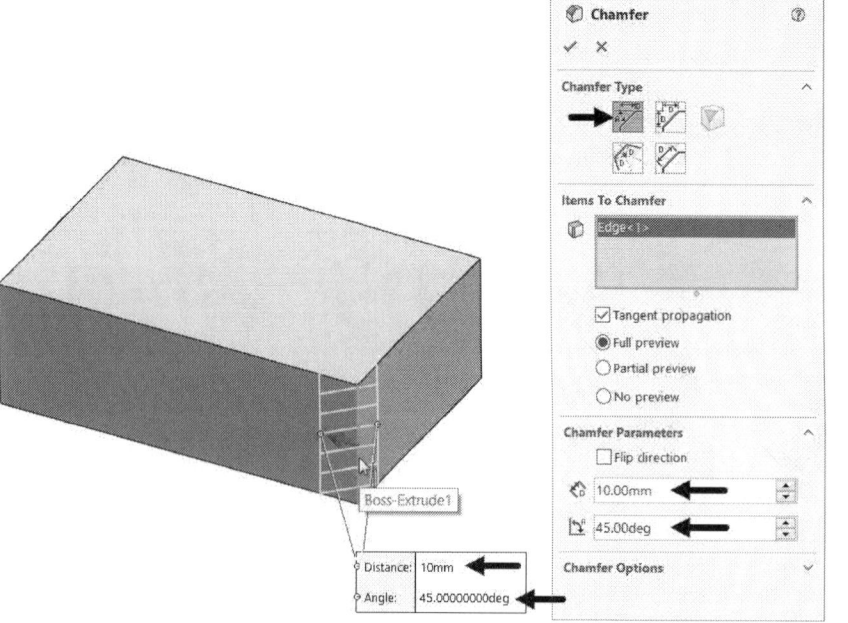

Distance Distance

This option is used to create a chamfer with uniform distance in both direction with distance value entered in the respective edit box in **Chamfer PropertyManager** or drawing area, as shown.

- Select the **Chamfer** tool (**Features > Fillet > Chamfer**) to display **Chamfer PropertyManager**, as shown.

- Click on the **Distance Distance** button of the PropertyManager and select the edge to display preview of chamfer feature along it, as shown.
- Enter the required distance value in their respective edit box of the PropertyManager or drawing area, as shown.
- Next, click on the **OK** button of the PropertyManager to display chamfer feature created, as shown.

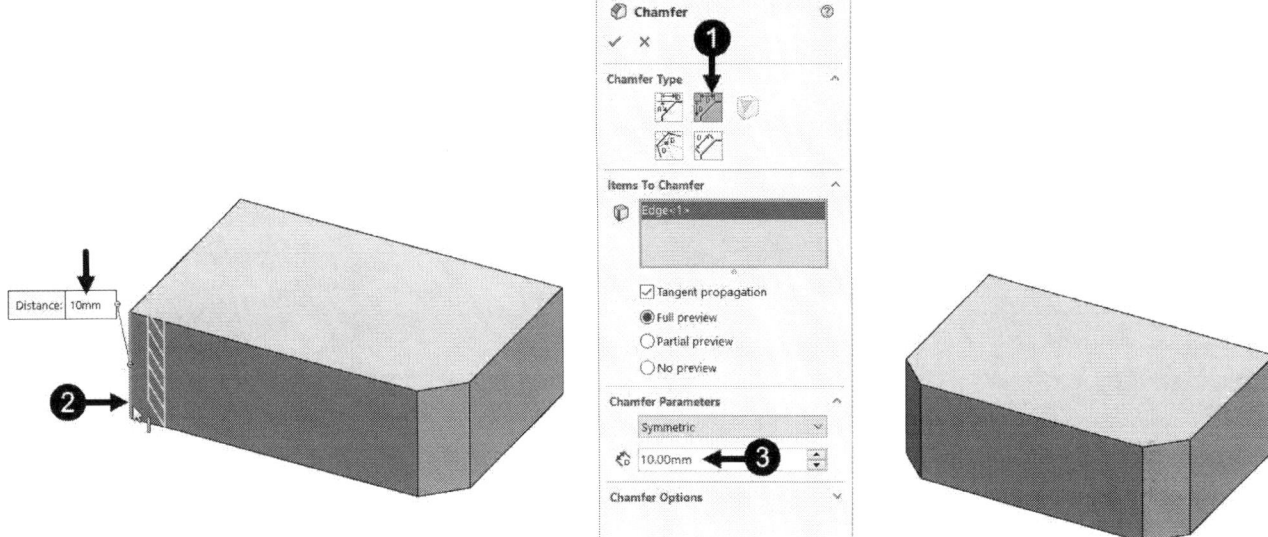

For the better visibility, press the **Space** button of keyboard and click to change its orientation, as shown. You can also use MMB (middle mouse button) in rotating it.

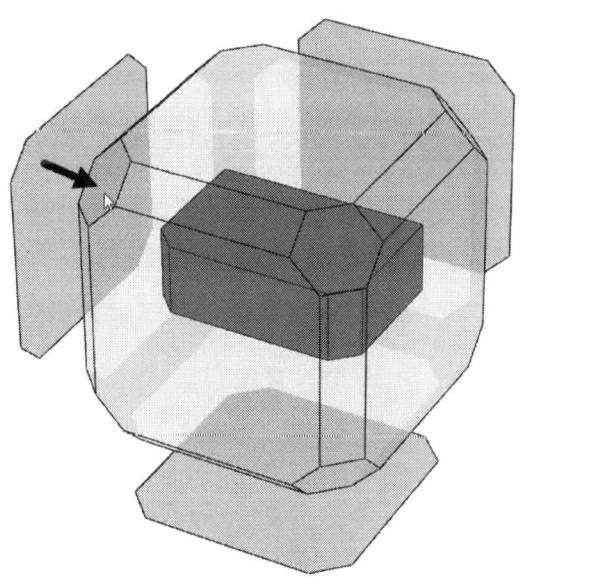

Vertex

This button is selected to create a chamfer along the selected vertex and entering required distance values for the three distances on each side of the selected vertex.

- Click on the **Vertex** button of the PropertyManager and select the vertex to display preview of chamfer feature along it, as shown.
- Enter the required distance value in their respective edit box of the PropertyManager or drawing area, as shown.

➤ Next, click on the **OK** button of the PropertyManager to display chamfer feature created, as shown.

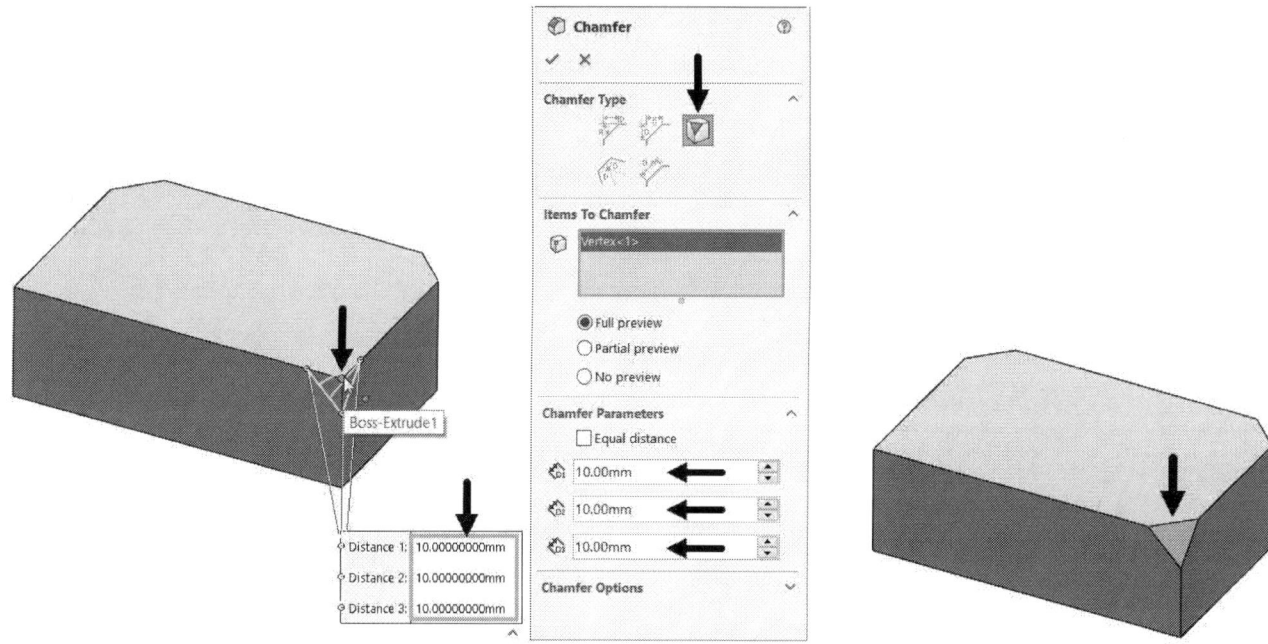

Note that if you select the **Equal distance** checkbox of the PropertyManager then you need to enter only one distance value for all sides, as shown.

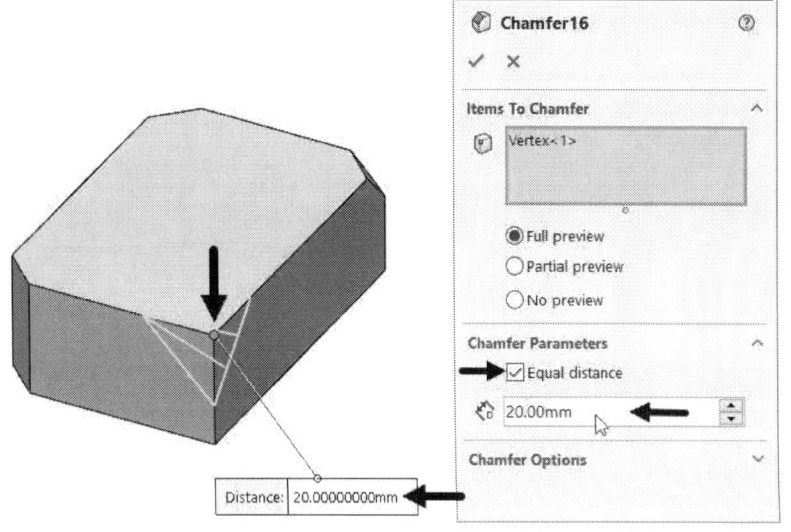

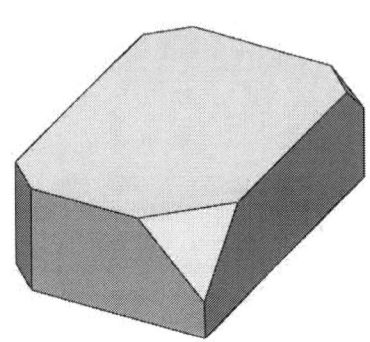 **Offset Face**

This button is selected to create a chamfer by offsetting the face adjacent to selected face or edge. The system calculates the intersection point of the offset faces, then calculates the normal from that point to each face to create the chamfer.

➤ Click on the **Offset Face** button of the PropertyManager and click on the face to display preview of chamfer feature at offset distance from it, as shown.
➤ Enter the required offset distance value in the respective edit box of the PropertyManager or drawing area, as shown.
➤ Next, click on the **OK** button of the PropertyManager to display chamfer feature created, as shown.

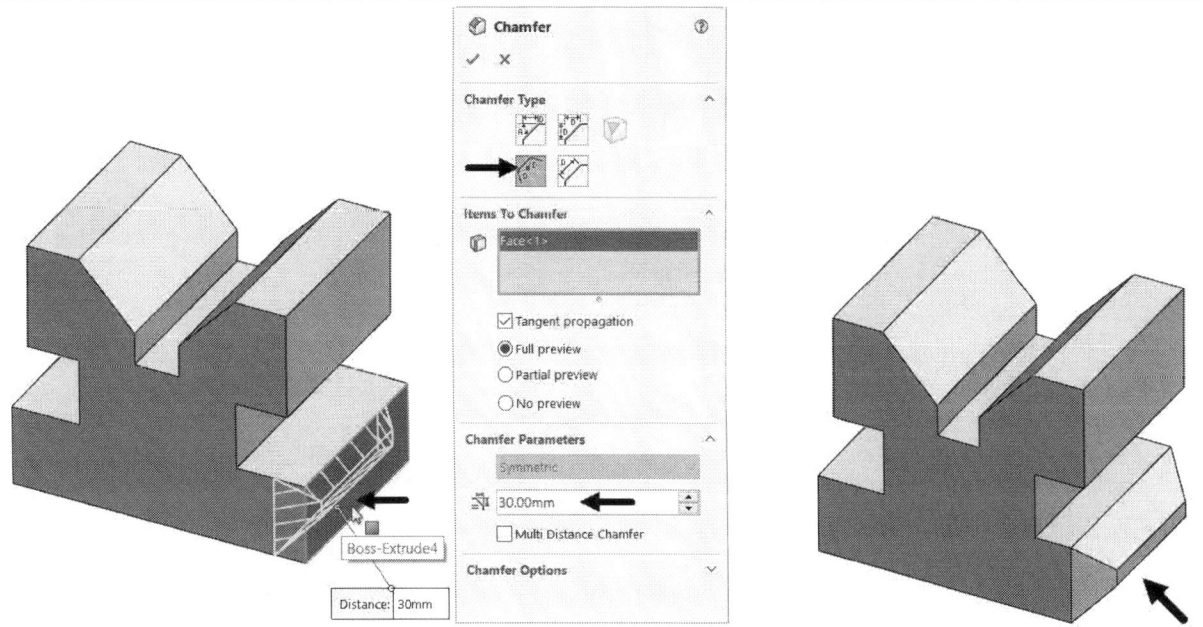

Face Face

This button is used to create chamfer along non adjacent & non continuous faces. It helps in creating symmetric, asymmetric, hold line, and chord width chamfers.

> Click on the **Face Face** button of the PropertyManager and click on one of the faces, as shown.
> Next click in the **Face Set 2** box of the PropertyManager and click on another face of the model to display preview of chamfer feature, as shown.
> Select the required chamfer method from the **Chamfer Method** drop-down of the **Chamfer Parameters** rollout of the PropertyManager, if required, as shown.
> Enter the required distance value in the respective edit box of the PropertyManager or drawing area, as shown.

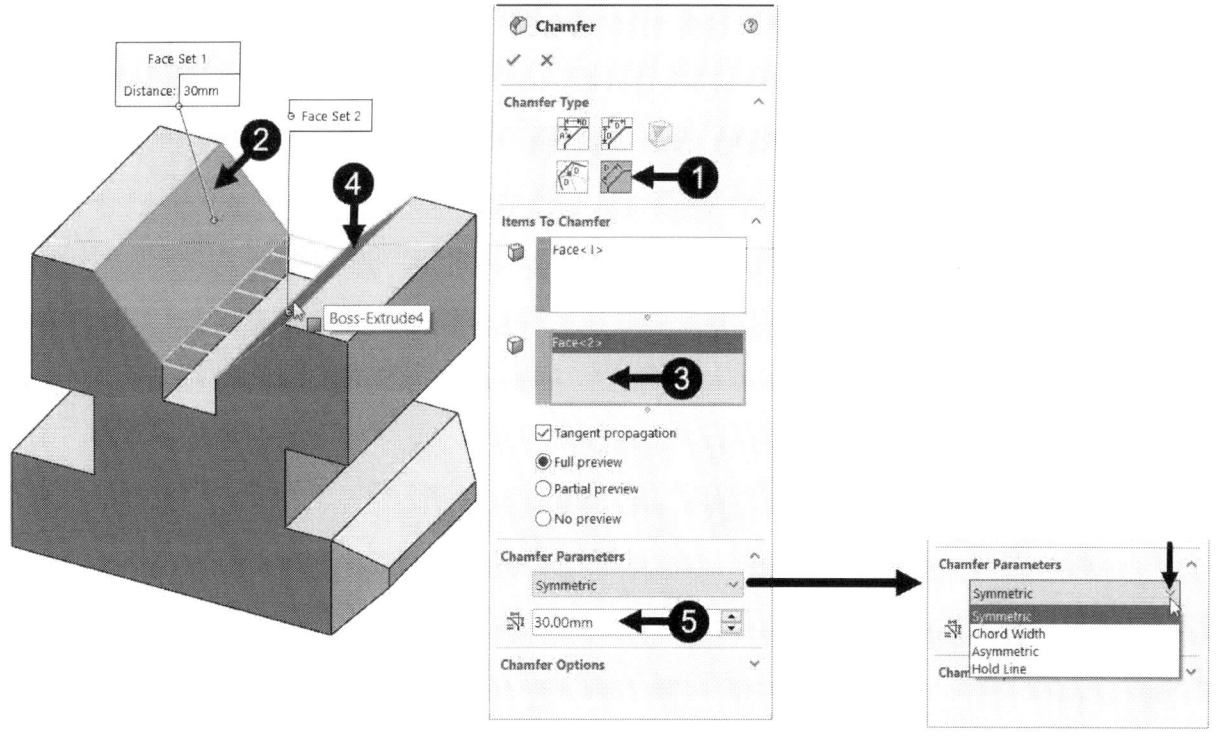

➢ Next, click on the **OK** button of the PropertyManager to display chamfer feature created, as shown.

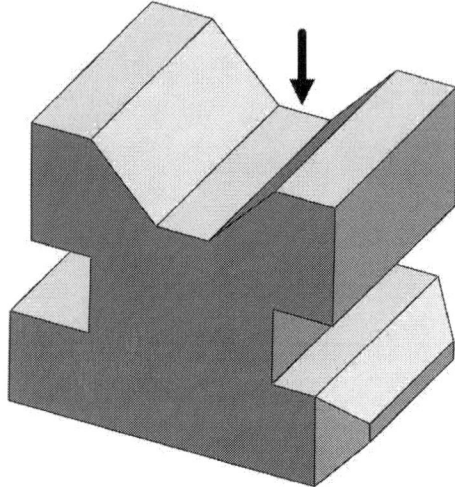

Questions:

1. Which tool is used to add taper to selected face of the model?
2. Which tool is used to make a solid model hollow?
3. Which tool is used to remove edges or corners of a model?
4. How can you use the **Shell** tool to make a shell feature with multiple thickness?
5. Which tool is used to emboss a sketch on planar face of model?
6. How can you mirror the whole model?
7. Which tool is used to replace the sharp corners with an inclined edge?
8. What is the use of **Rib** tool?

Exercises:

Exercise 1

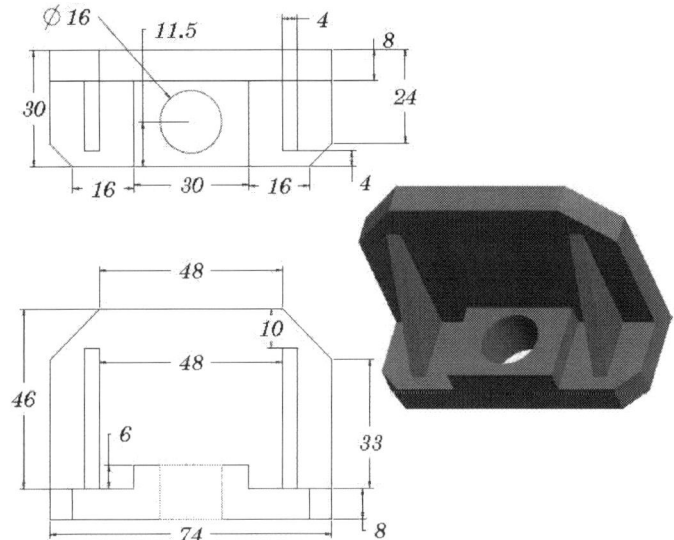

Exercise 2

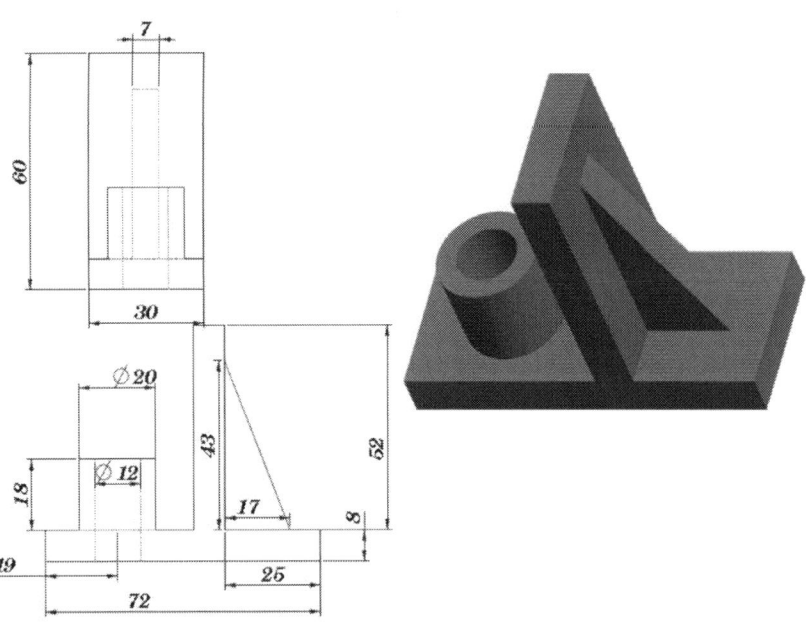

Advanced Solid Modelling Tools

Exercise 3

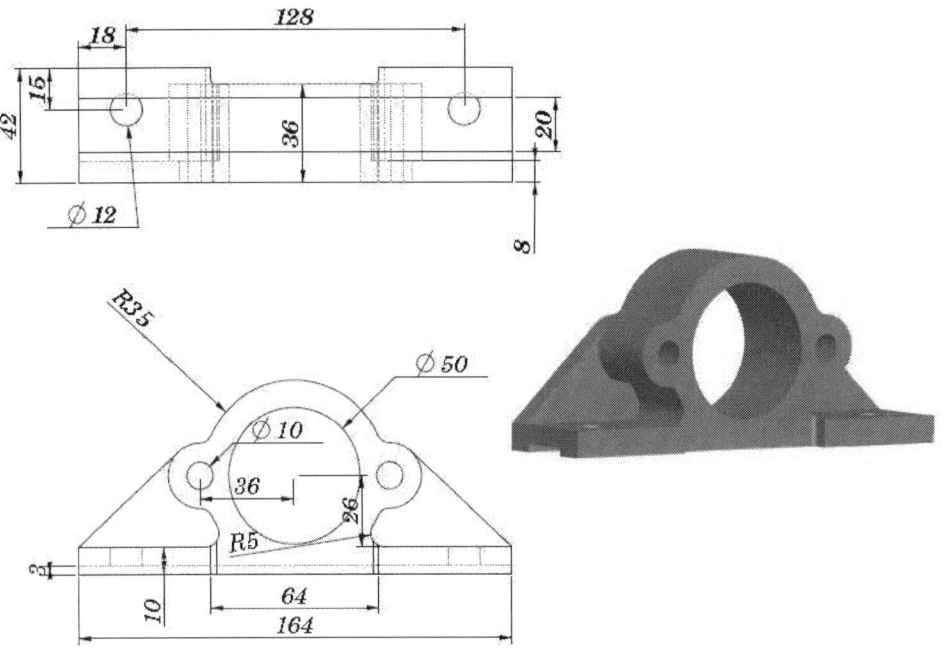

Exercise 4

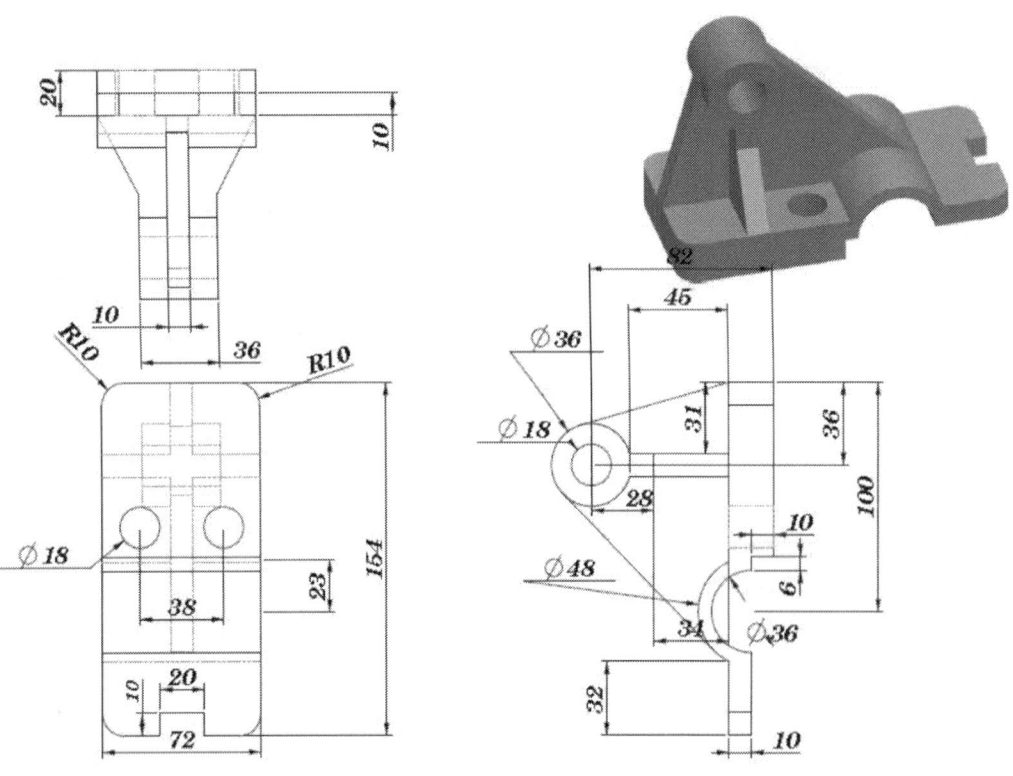

Chapter 10: Creating Assemblies

After creating individual components, you can bring them together into an assembly. By doing so, it is possible to identify incorrect design problems that may not have been noticeable at the part level. In this chapter, you will learn how to bring components into the Assembly environment and position them.

The topics covered in this chapter are:

- ❖ Starting an assembly
- ❖ Inserting Components
- ❖ Fixing the first component
- ❖ Inserting the second component
- ❖ Moving and rotating components
- ❖ Applying constraints
- ❖ Exploded view

Starting an Assembly

To begin an assembly file, click on the **New** button from the **Quick Access Toolbar** to display **New SOLIDWORKS Document** dialog box. From the dialog box, select the **Assembly** button and click on the **OK** button to entering in the assembly environment, as shown. The Assembly environment with **Assembly** tab opened and **Begin Assembly PropertyManager** get displayed, as shown below.

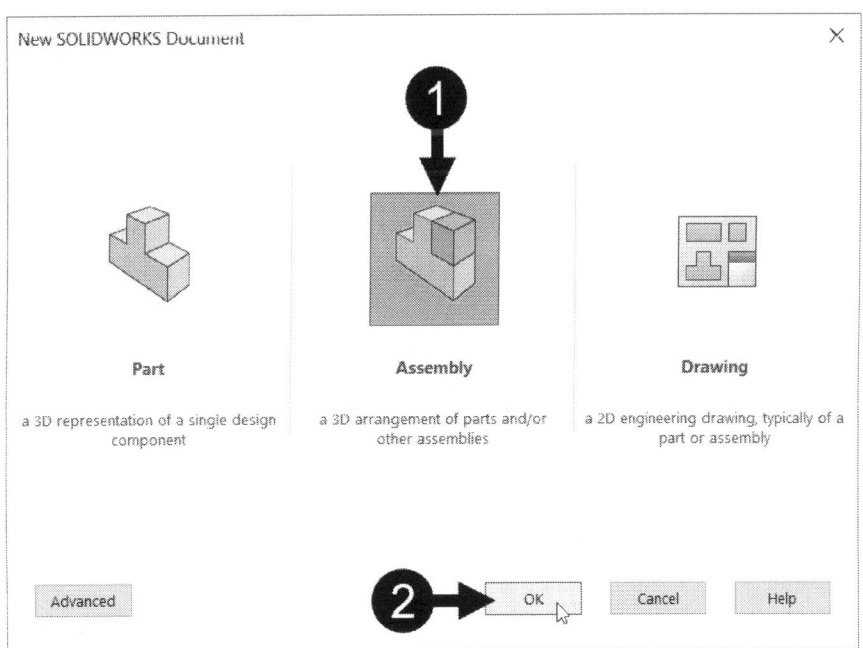

Assembly Environment

The Assembly environment has tools to combine individual parts in an assembly. There are two ways to create an assembly. The first way is to create individual parts in part environment and then assemble them in the Assembly environment, known as **Bottom-up assembly design**. The second way is to start an assembly file and create individual parts in it, known as **Top-down assembly design**.

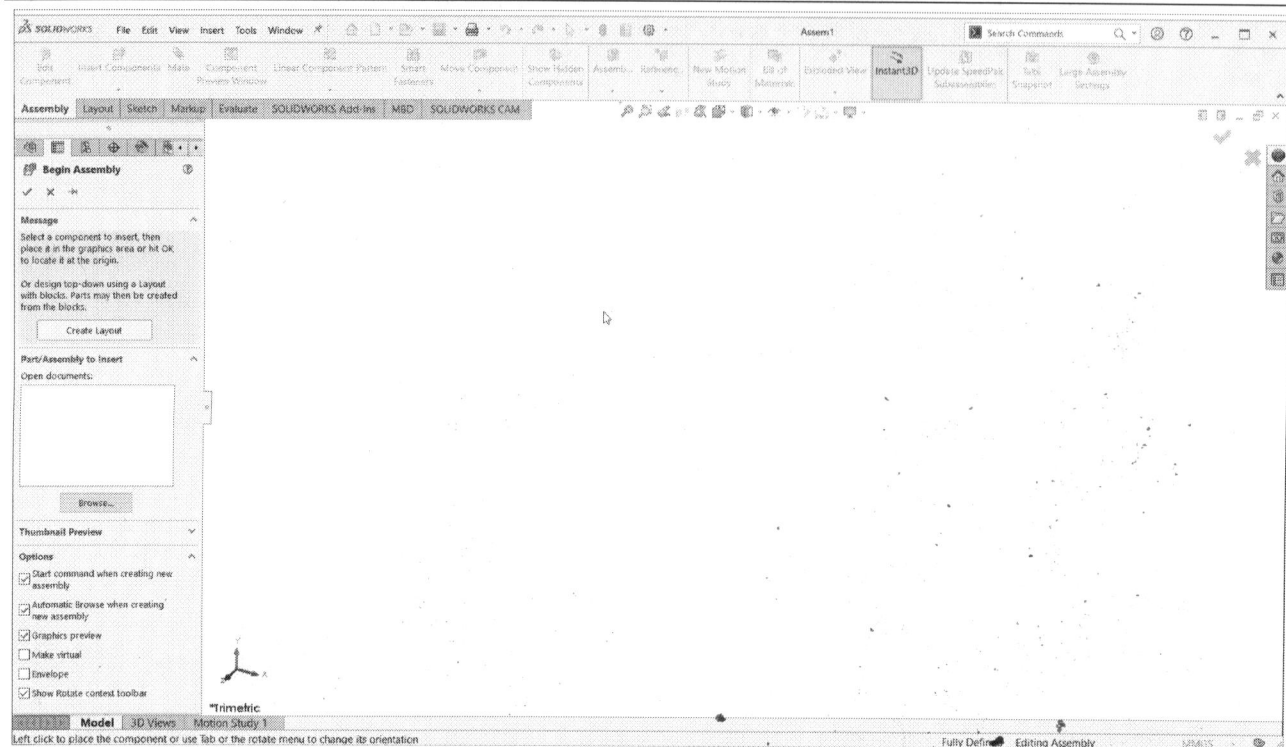

Note: Note that after entering in the assembly environment, by default the **Open** window get display automatically. You can then browse to the required folder and then select and import the required part file in the assembly environment, as shown.

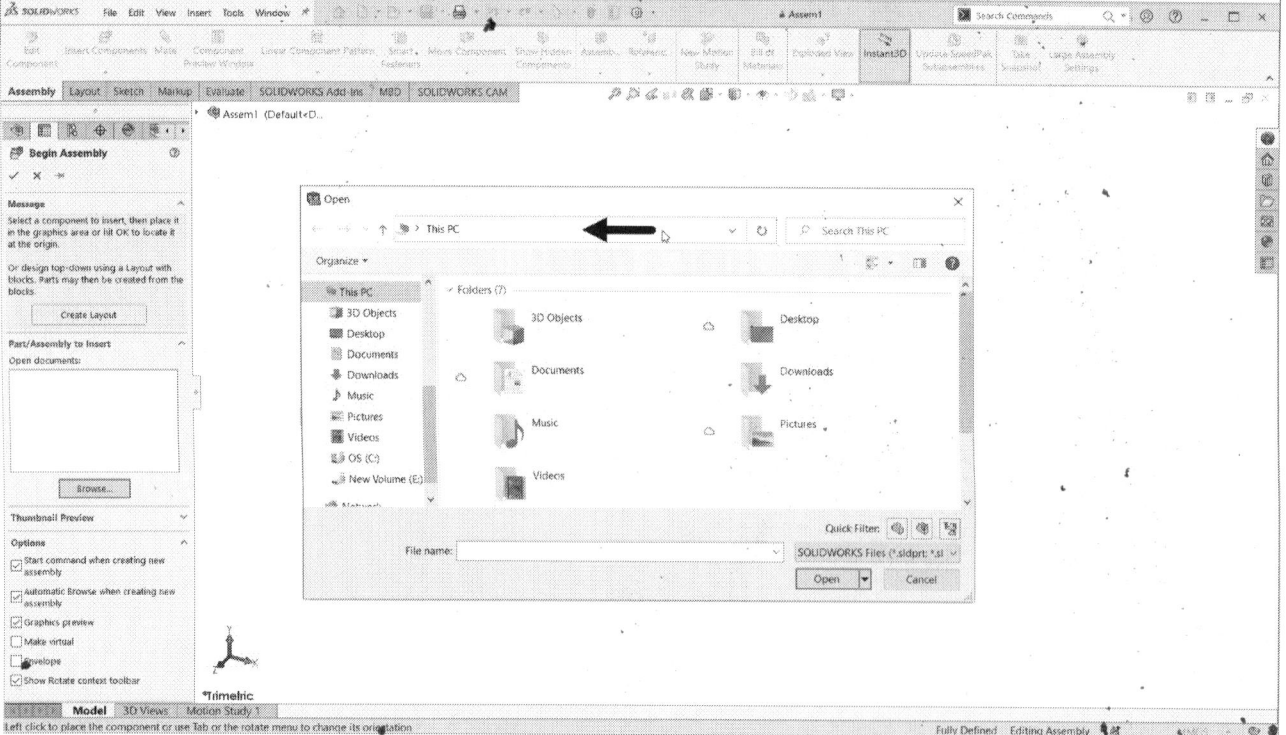

Inserting Components

There are two different methods to insert an existing part into an assembly. The first one is to insert using the **Insert Components** button. The second way is to drag it directly from Windows Explorer. In the second method, there is no need to open the components in **Open** window. You can simply drag-and-drop them into the assembly.

- Click on the **Insert Components** button from the **Assemble CommandManager** to display **Open** window, as shown.
- Browse to the required folder and select the required part file, as shown.
- Next click on the **Open** button to display it in the assembly environment, as shown.

    Alternatively, you can double click on the required file to import it.

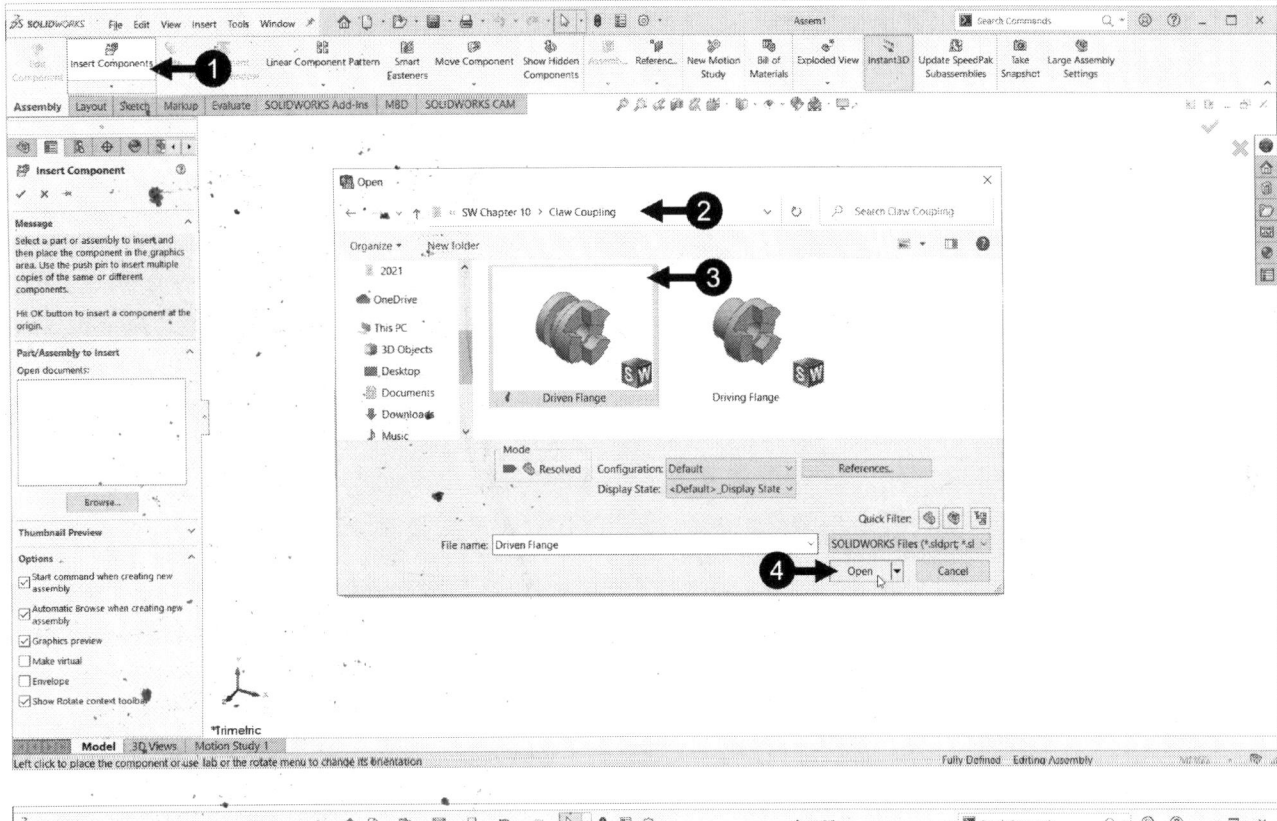

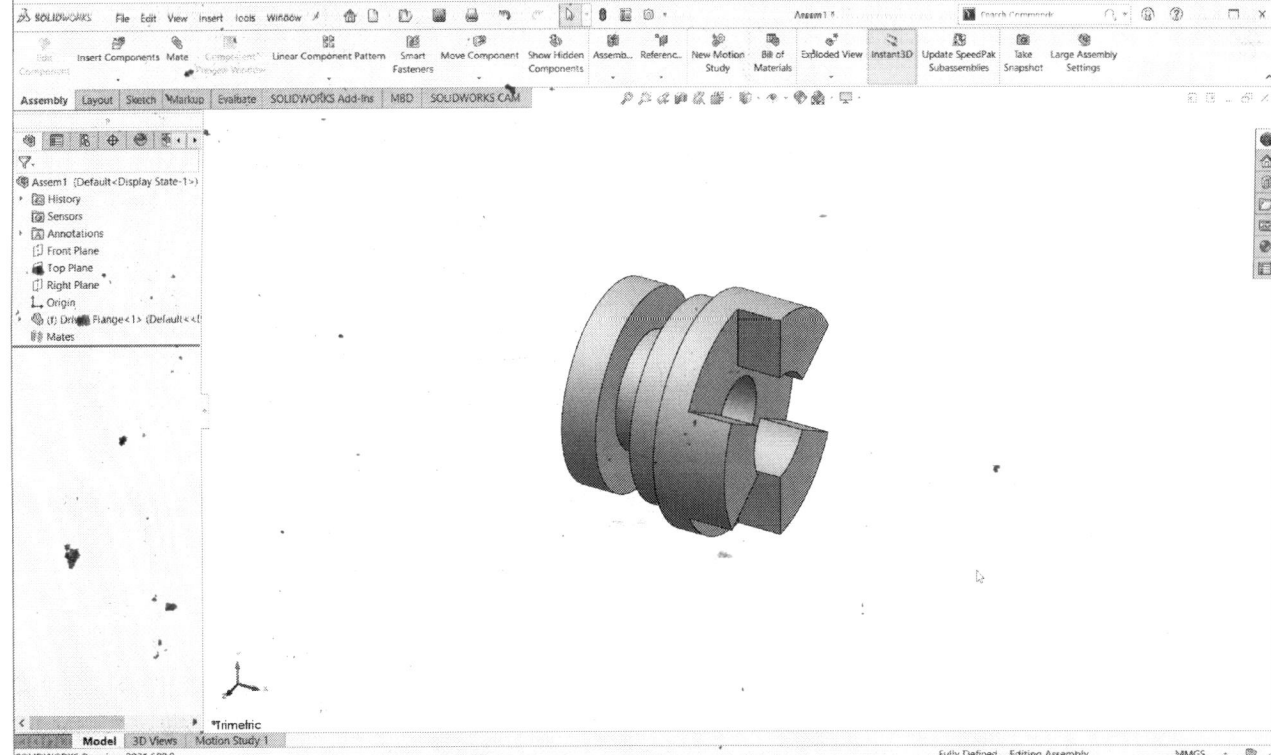

- After importing the first component, it gets fixed at the origin automatically.

Creating Assemblies 10-3

➤ Similarly, you can insert other components and you need to apply various mates to assemble them with respect to initially imported or fixed component. These mates/constraints are discussed further in this chapter.

Note: As the initially inserted component get fixed automatically with the origin. So, the component gets fully defined automatically. Thus, its degrees of freedom in the drawing area get removed.

➤ After inserting the first component, it gets fixed at the origin automatically, as shown. And then after inserting other components, you can assemble them with respect to it.
➤ Similarly, you can insert other components and you need to apply various mates to assemble them with respect to initially inserted or fixed component, as shown.

These mates/constraints are discussed further in this chapter.

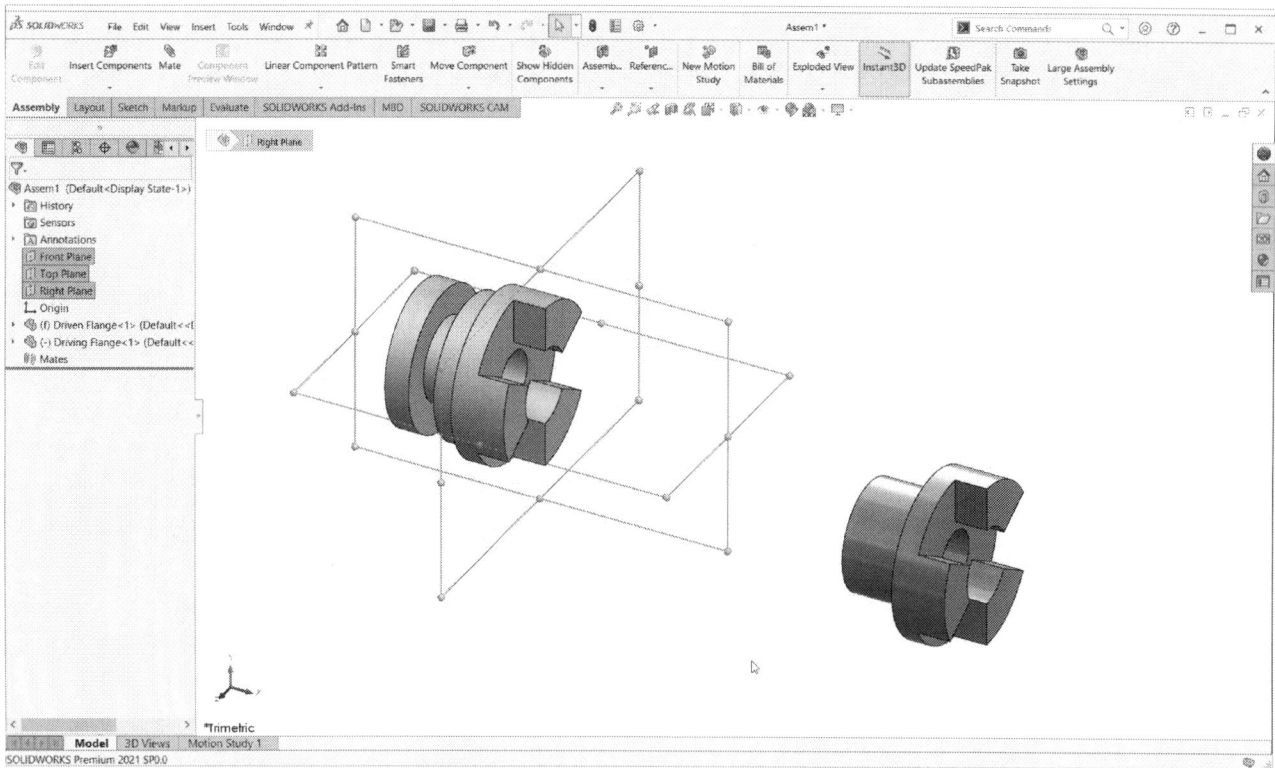

Applying Constraints

After inserting components into an assembly, you have to define relations/mates between them. By applying mates, you can make components to flush with each other or two cylindrical faces concentric with each other, and so on. As you add constraints between components, the degrees of freedom will be removed from them.

By default, there are six degrees of freedom for a part (three linear and three rotational). Eliminating degrees of freedom will make components attached and interact with each other as in real life. These constraints are available in the drop-down in the **Component Placement** dashboard. Now, you will learn to add constraints between components one by one.

Automatic Mate

After activating the **Mate** tool and selecting the entities, the system automatically applies the respective mate/constraint with respect to the selected entities. After selecting two flat surfaces; **Coincident** mate gets applied and after selecting two circles; **Concentric** mate get applied and so on.

- After inserting any component, select the **Mate** tool to activate it and display the **Mate PropertyManager**, as shown.
- Click on the two flat surface one-by-one to display preview of automatically applied **Coincident** mate between both, as shown.
- Next to apply any change or apply any other mate, you can click on the buttons available in the **Mate** pop-up toolbar displayed, as shown.

  The use of buttons in the **Mate** pop-up toolbar are displayed further in this chapter.

- Now click on the ✓ **Add/Finish Mate** button to apply mate and display components with applied mate, as shown.

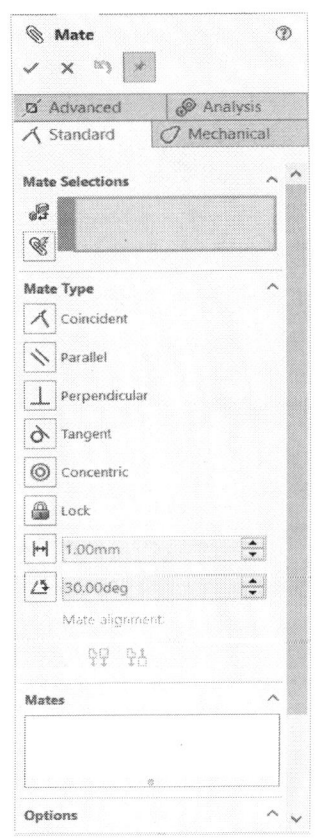
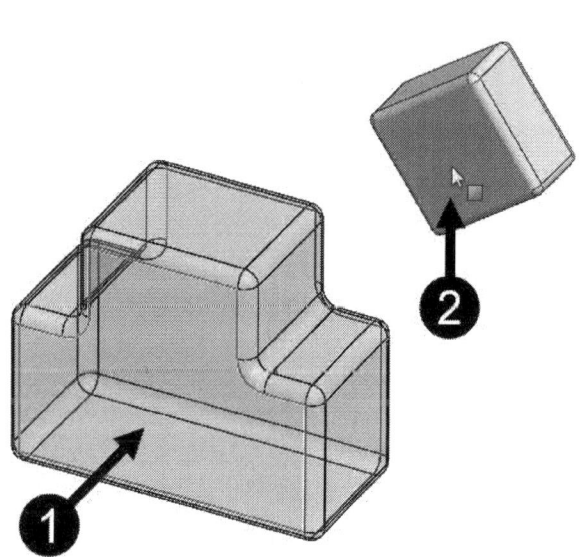
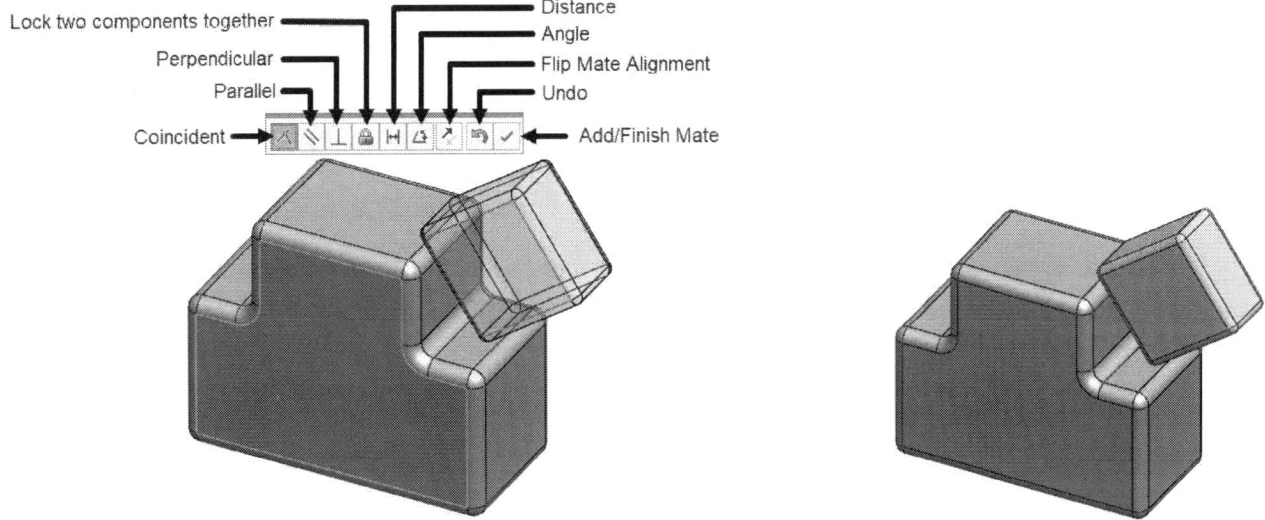

Creating Assemblies   10-5

➤ Click on the ✓ OK button of the **Mate PropertyManager** to exit it.

Similarly, after selecting circular surfaces of two components, **Concentric** constrains will be applied automatically, as shown.

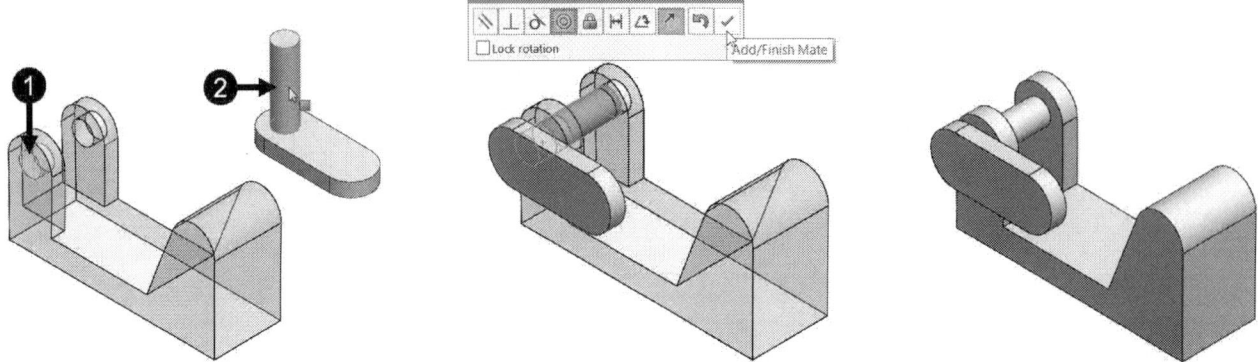

Note that, after activating the **Mate** tool and selecting two surfaces of two components, the **Mate** pop-up toolbar will also get display along with automatically applied respective mate, as shown above. And if required you can also select another mate from it. The use of other buttons in this pop-up toolbar are:

Flip Mate Alignment – This button is selected to flip the direction of applied mate.

Undo – This button is selected to go back after applying any mate.

Add/Finish Mate - After applying mates, this button is selected to exit pop-up toolbar and display components with applied mates.

Coincident Mate
The use of **Coincident** constraint is same as discussed above.

Parallel Mate
The **Parallel** mate makes an axis, face or edge of one part parallel to that of another part.

➤ Click on the **Parallel** button from the **Mate PropertyManager**, as shown above.
➤ Click on the two flat surfaces one by one to display preview of **Parallel** mate between them, as shown.
➤ Next click on the ✓ **Add/Finish Mate** button to apply mate and display components with applied mate, as shown.

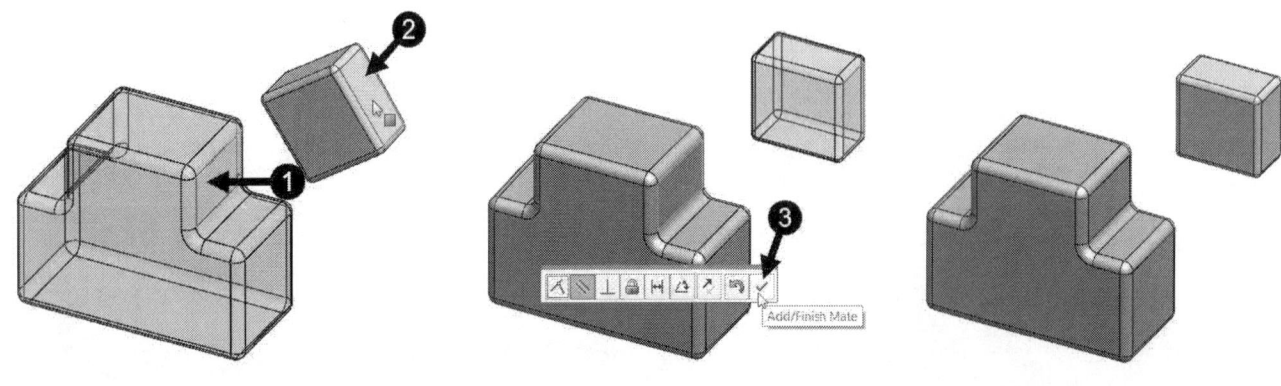

Creating Assemblies

Perpendicular Mate

The **Perpendicular** mate is used to make two selected surfaces or two axes perpendicular to each other.

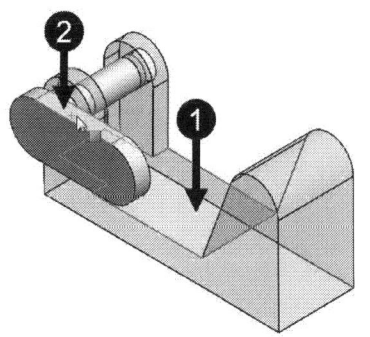 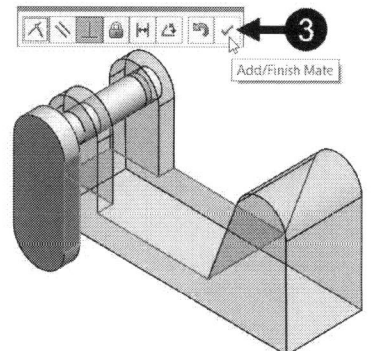 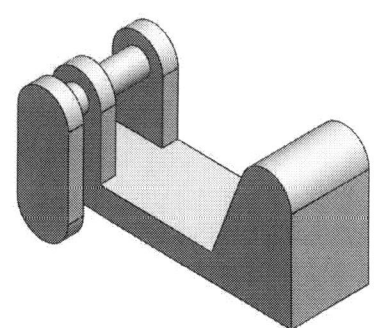

Tangent Mate

The **Tangent** mate is used to make the selected circular face tangent to the other selected face or plane.

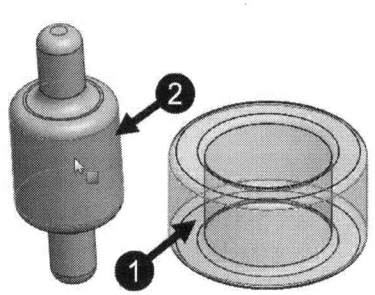 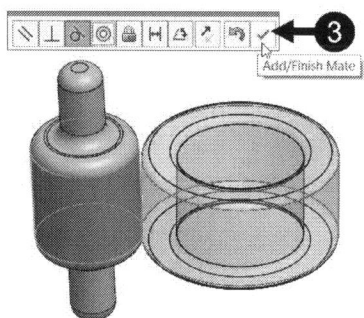 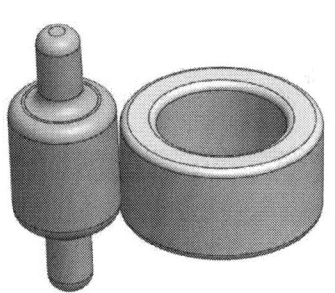

Concentric Mate

The **Concentric** mate is used to make the axes of two cylindrical faces coincide/concentric with each other.

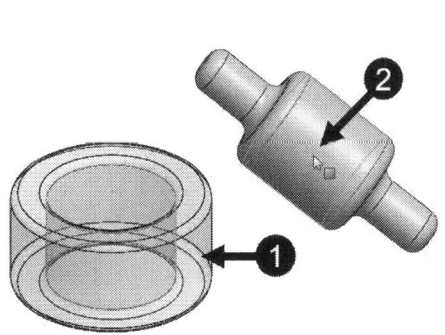 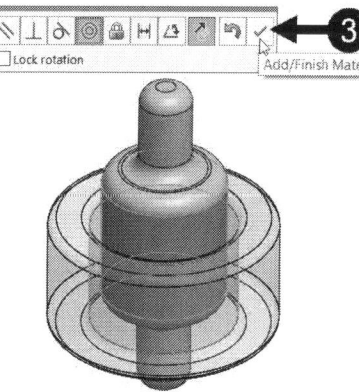 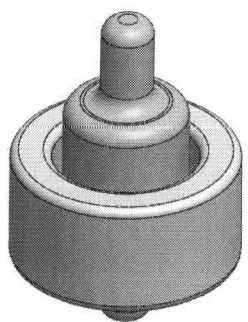

Lock two components together

The **Lock** mate is selected to lock two components together and thus maintains position and orientation with each other. Note that, after applying the **Lock** mate between components, if you move any component then other component/components also start moving with it.

Creating Assemblies   10-7

Distance Mate

The **Distance** mate is selected to place the selected faces at the specified distance between them.

- ➤ Click on the **Distance** button from the **Mate PropertyManager**, as shown above.
- ➤ Click on two surfaces to place distance between them.
- ➤ Next enter or adjust the required distance value in the **Distance** spinner of the **Mate** pop-up toolbar, as shown.
- ➤ Next click on the ✓ **Add/Finish Mate** button to place the selected items at the defined distance value, as shown.

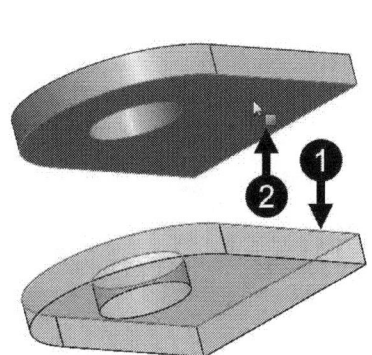
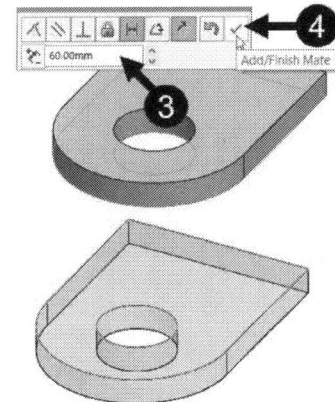
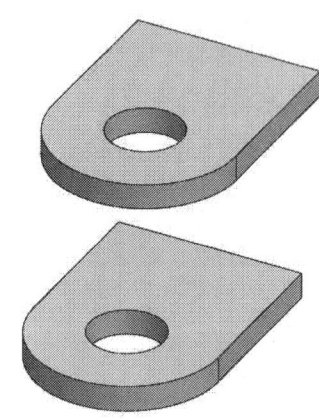

Angle Mate

The **Angle** button is used to position the selected faces at a specified angle.

- ➤ Click on the **Angle** button from the **Mate PropertyManager**, as shown above.
- ➤ Click on two flat surfaces to position them at an angle with each other, as shown.
- ➤ Next enter or adjust the required angle value in the **Angle** spinner of the **Mate** pop-up toolbar, as shown.
- ➤ Next click on the ✓ **Add/Finish Mate** button to place the selected items at the defined angle value, as shown.

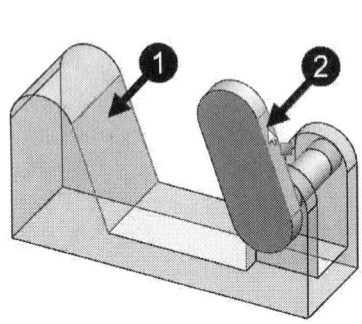
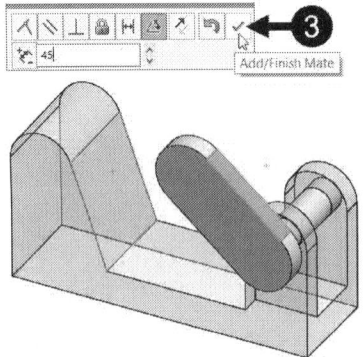
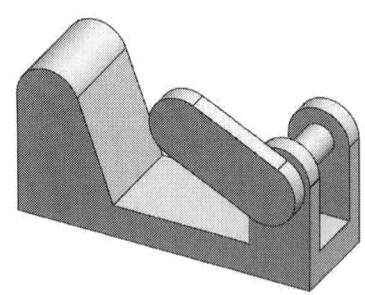

Fix

The **Fix** option from the shortcut menu is used to fix the component inserted in the assembly environment, as discussed earlier. After adding fixing the component, its degrees of freedom in the drawing area get removed and you cannot move or rotate it.

- ➤ Right click over the component to be fixed in the assembly environment area to display the shortcut menu, as shown.

- Next select the **Fix** option, the component gets fixed and you will not be able to move or rotate it.
- Also, if you need to move or rotate any fixed component then you need to remove **Fix** over it.
- Right click over the fixed component and select the **Float** option from the shortcut menu, as shown.
- Now you can again move and rotate the component.

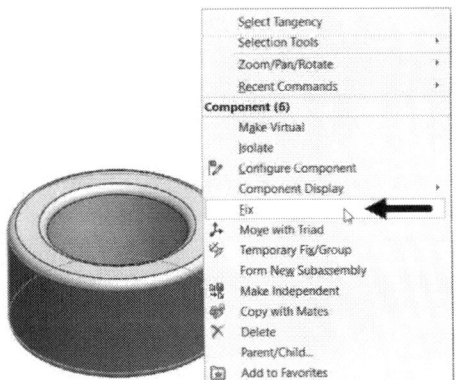 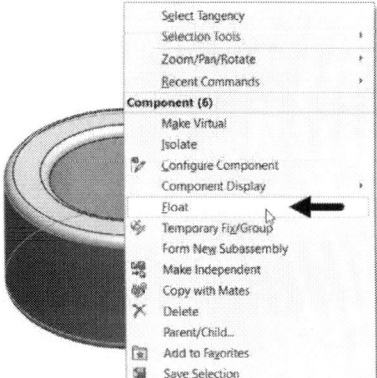

Advanced Mates

There are various buttons/options available under the **Advanced Mates** rollout of the Mate PropertyManager to be used during assembly. These are discussed below one by one.

Profile Center

This button is selected to center align rectangular and circular components to each other and makes the components fully defined.

- Activate the **Mate** tool to display **Mate PropertyManager**, as shown.
- Next click on the **Profile Center** button under the **Advanced Mates** rollout, as shown.
- Click on planar faces of cylindrical and rectangular components to display preview of components, center align with each other.
- Next click on the **OK** button of PropertyManager to display components center align with each other, as shown.

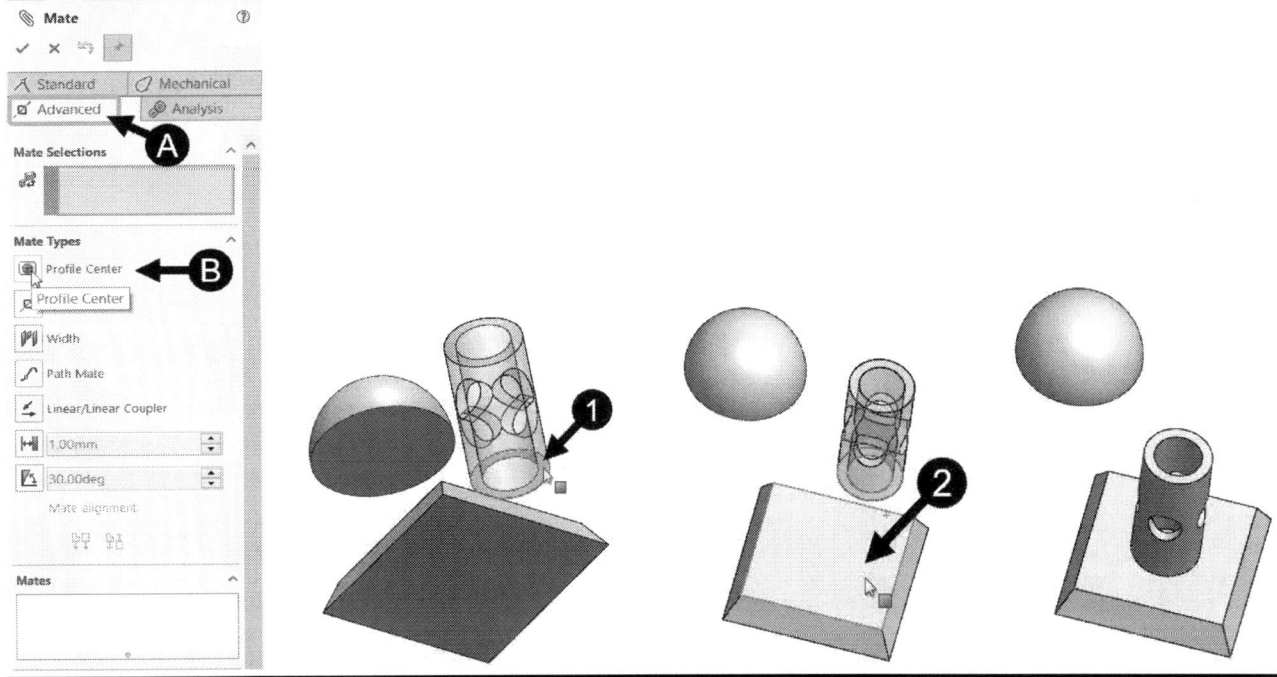

➢ Similarly, click on other two planar faces to center align them with each other, as shown.

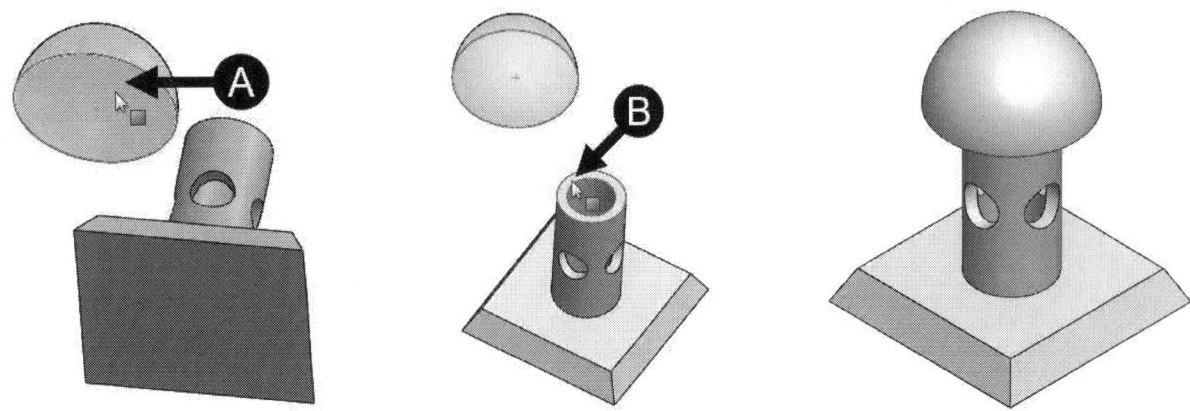

◲ Symmetric

This button is selected to force two similar components to be symmetric about a plane or a planar face.

➢ Activate the **Mate** tool to display **Mate PropertyManager**, as shown.
➢ Next click on the **Symmetric** button under the **Advanced Mates** rollout, as shown.
➢ Select the Plane and then click on opposite planar faces of two similar component to make them symmetric about the plane, as shown.
➢ Next click on the **OK** ✓ button of PropertyManager to display component symmetric along the selected plane, as shown.

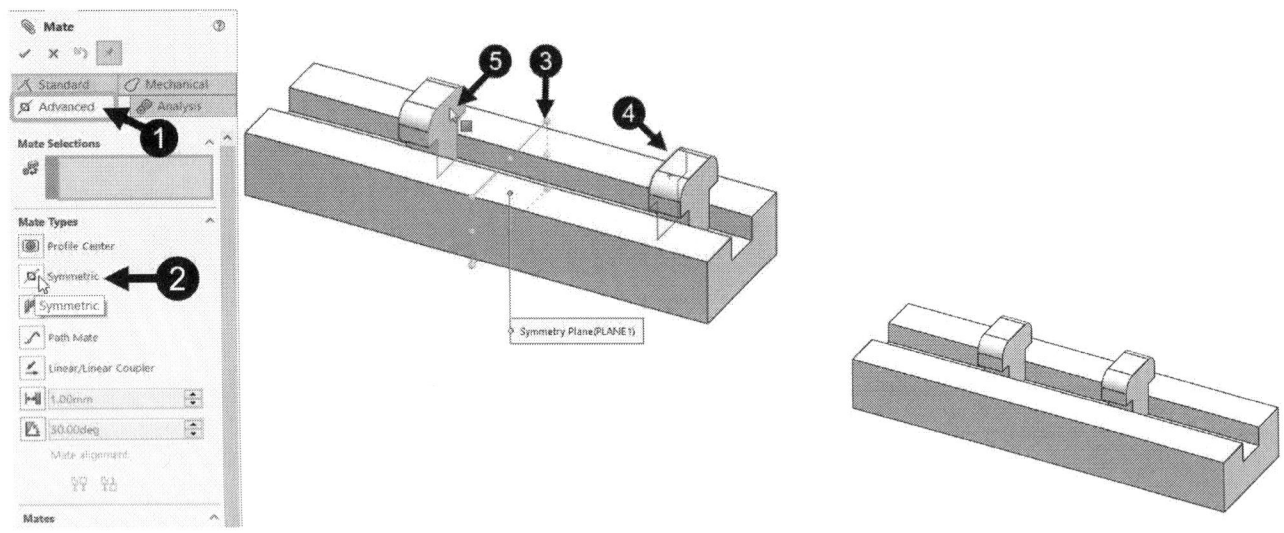

➢ To check its symmetry, select the right component and move it up to some distance towards right; another component will also move symmetrically, as shown.

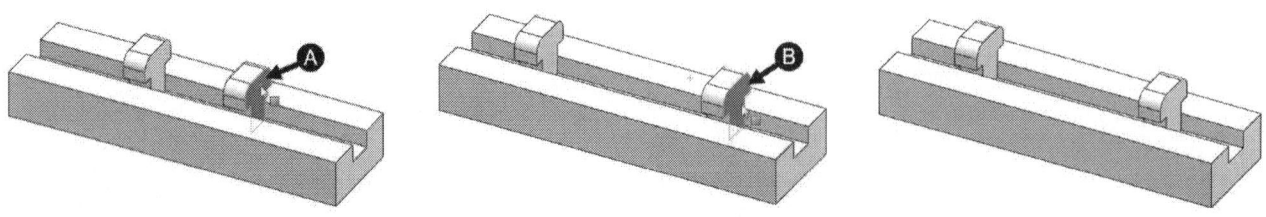

Width

This button is selected to constrain a component between two planar surfaces of another component.

➢ Activate the **Mate** tool to display **Mate PropertyManager**, as shown.

- Next click on the **Width** button under the **Advanced Mates** rollout, as shown above.
- Click on the two planar surfaces of the component to mate it with another component, as shown.

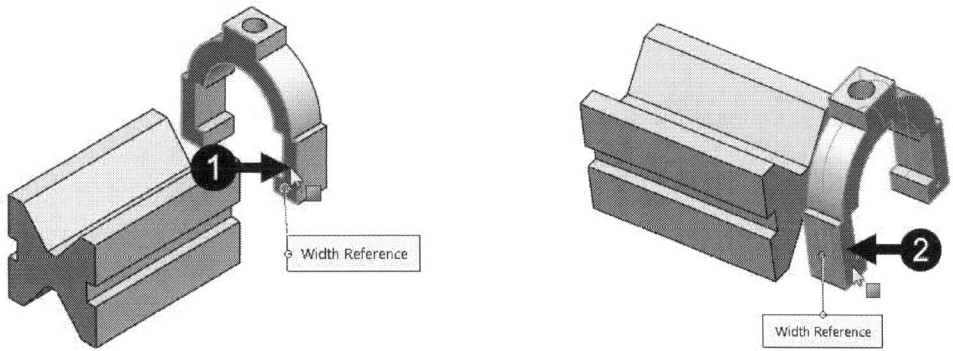

- Next click on two planar surfaces of another component to display preview of components with Width mate, as shown.

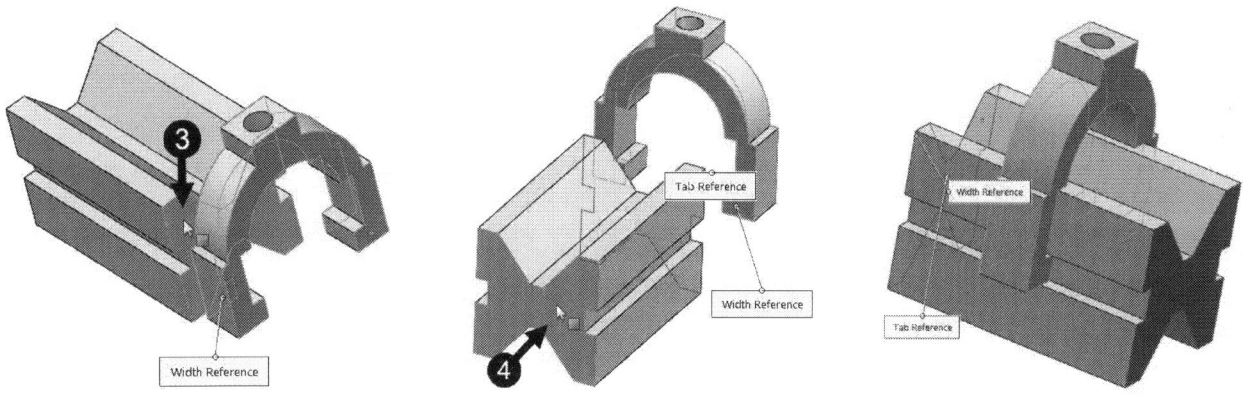

- Click on the **OK** button of the PropertyManager to display components with Width mate between each other, as shown.

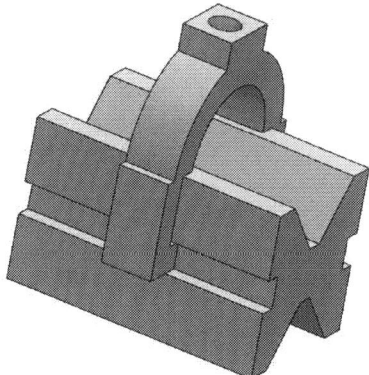

Path Mate

This button is selected to constrain a selected point of one component along a path on another component.

- Activate the **Mate** tool to display **Mate PropertyManager**, as shown above.
- Next click on the **Path Mate** button under the **Advanced Mates** rollout, as shown above.
- Click on the Point entity of component that you want to move along another component, as shown.
- Next click on the path along which you want to move the previously selected component entity and display preview of component sifted along it.

> Click on the OK ✓ button of the PropertyManager twice to display components with Path Mate and exit it, as shown.

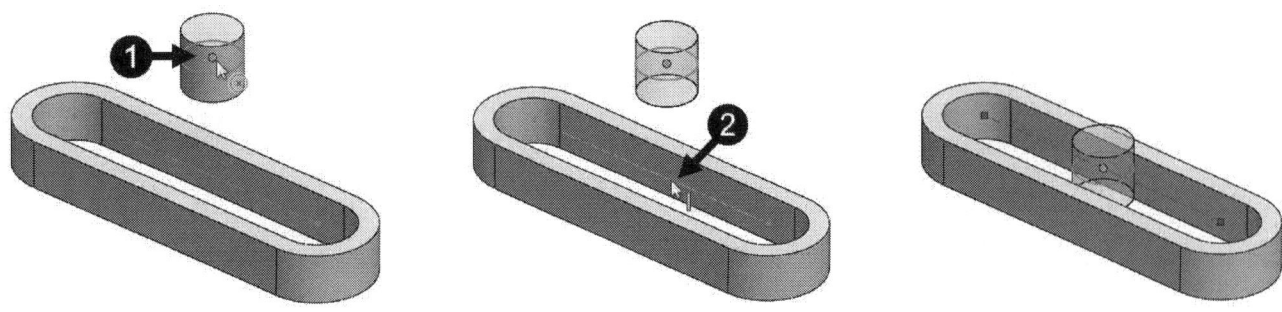

> Now you can move the component/point entity along the selected path, as shown.

> Note that you might not be able to move it smoothly until you apply any other mate also, as shown.

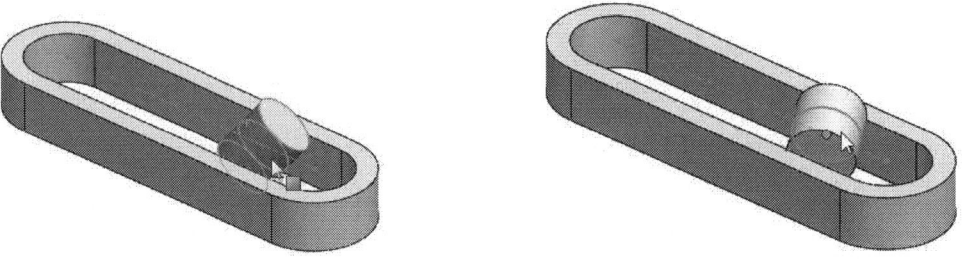

> Apply the **Parallel** Mate along the selected surface of components to move the component smoothly along the path, as shown.

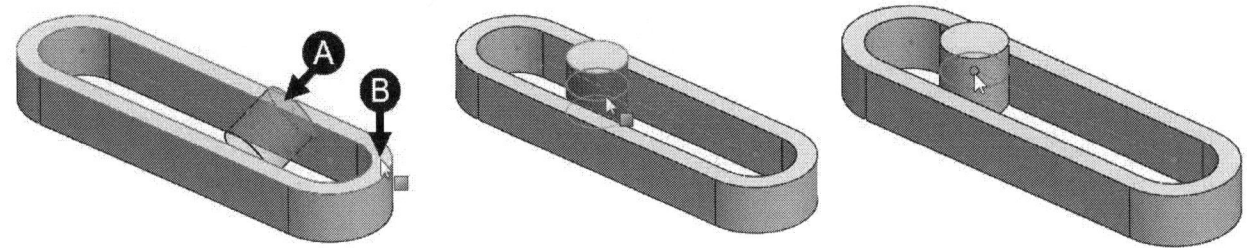

Linear/Linear Coupler

This button is selected to establish a relationship between the translation of one component with another component.

> Activate the **Mate** tool to display **Mates PropertyManager**, as shown above.
> Next click on the **Linear/Linear Coupler** button under the **Advanced Mates** rollout, as shown.
> Click on planar surfaces of two components one by one, as shown.
> Next enter required values in edit boxes under **Ratio** portion of PropertyManager, as shown.
> You can also select the **Reverse** check box, if required.
> Click on the OK ✓ button of the PropertyManager twice to display components with applied mate and exit it.
> Now if you move the component, another component with also move with respect to the other component and depending upon the values entered, as shown.

Creating Assemblies

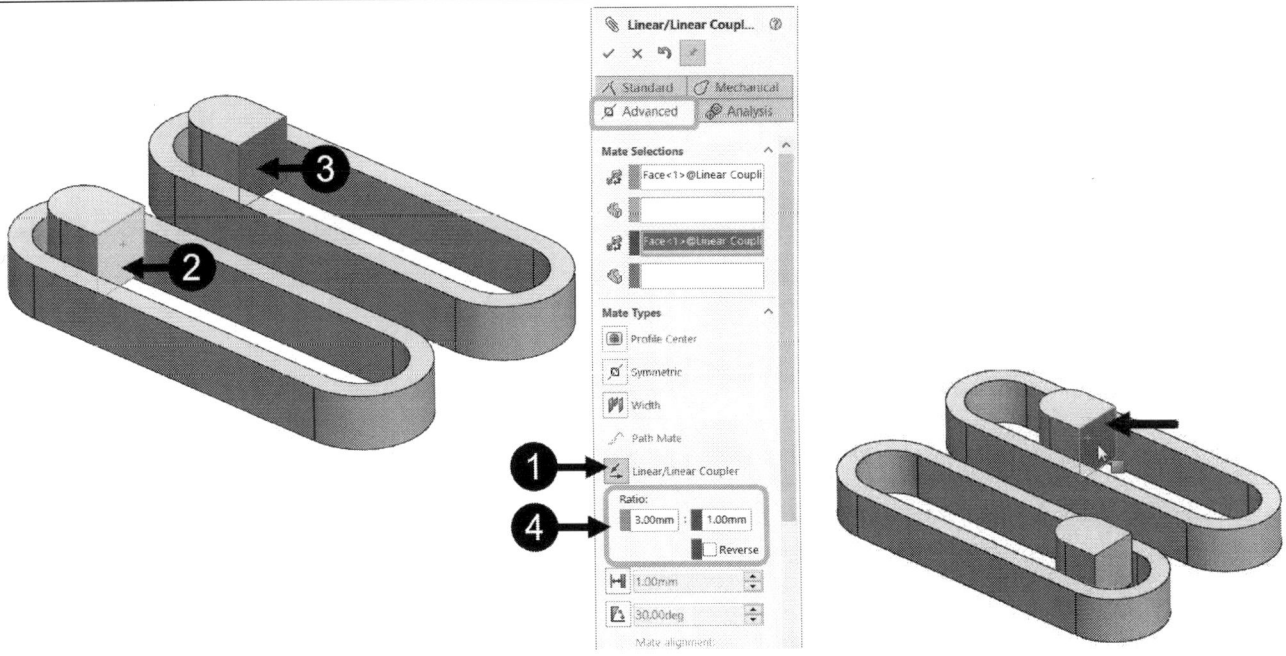

Distance

This button is selected to allows components to move within a range for distance mate by entering the required distance values in their respective edit boxes, as shown.

Angle

This button is selected to allows components to move within a range for angle mate by entering the required angular values in their respective edit boxes, as shown.

Mate Alignment

The buttons under **Mate Alignment** portion of the PropertyManager are used to toggle alignment of components after applying mates.

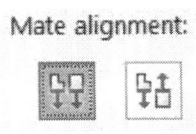

Aligned

Aligns the vectors normal to the selected faces in the same direction.

Anti-Aligned

Aligns the vectors normal to the selected faces in the opposite direction.

Exploded View

After assembling different components in an assembly, you can explode them.

➤ Click on the **Exploded View** button from the Assembly CommandManager to display the **Explode PropertyManager**, as shown.

➤ Select the component to display triad along it, as shown.

Using this triad, you can move & rotate the component up to the required distance and place it at the required location.

➤ Holing the triad handle, drag the component up to some distance, as shown.

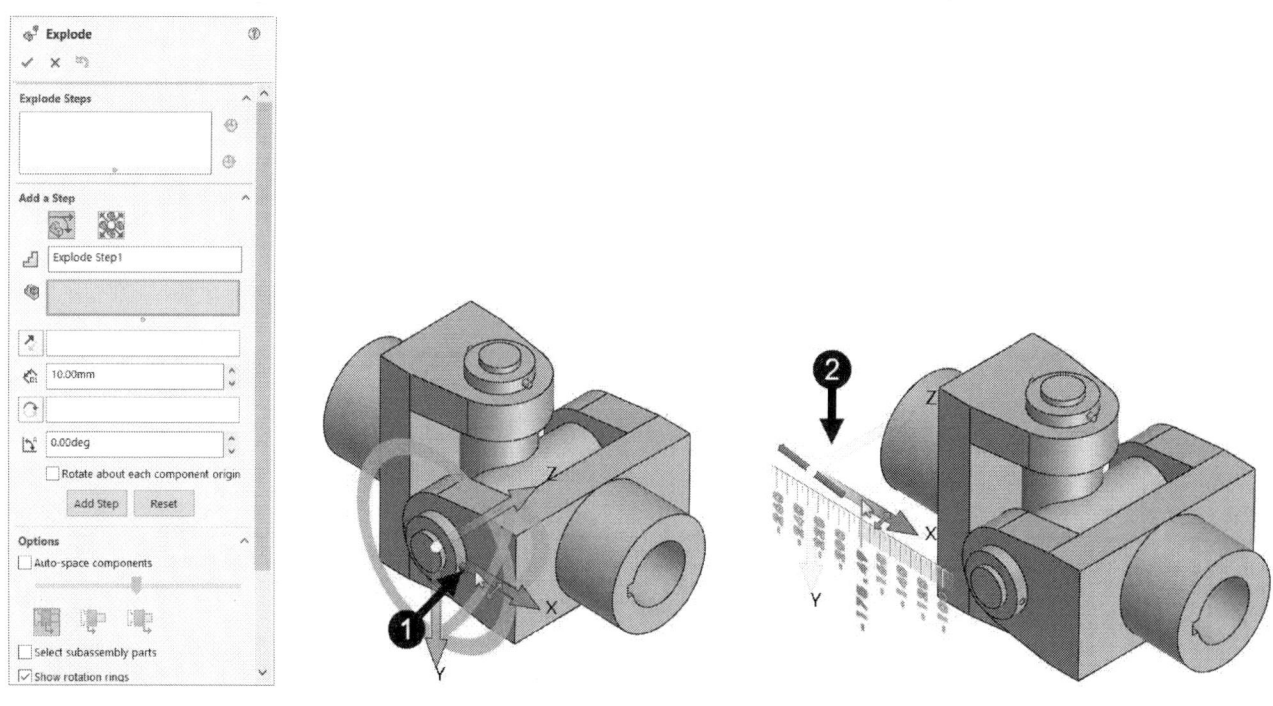

➤ Similarly, you can drag other components also, as shown.

Note that, you can move and rotate each component by entering the required distance and angular value in their respective edit boxes of the PropertyManager, as shown above.

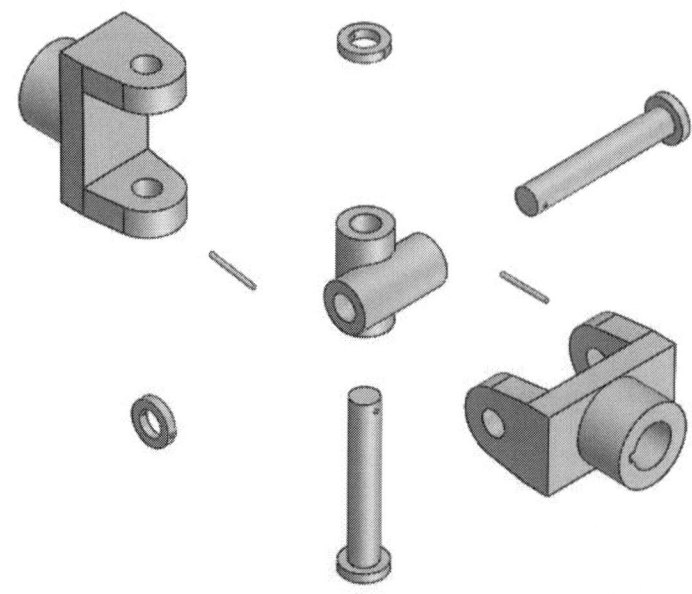

Creating Assemblies

- To rotate any component, first select the component and click and hold the cursor over torus handle of the triad displayed, as shown.
- Move the cursor up to some distance to display preview of rotated component, as shown.
- Release the finger over mouse button to display component rotated, as shown.

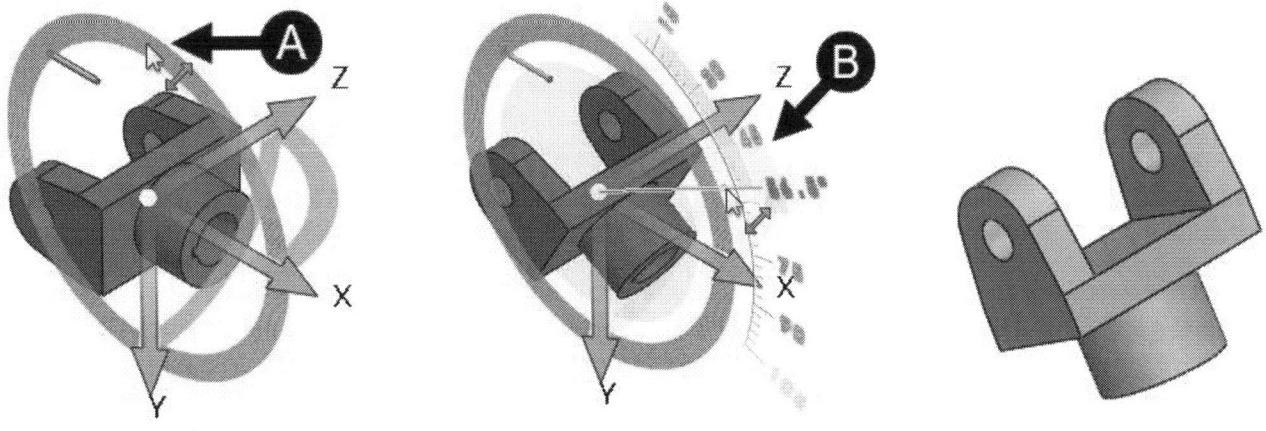

- Click on the 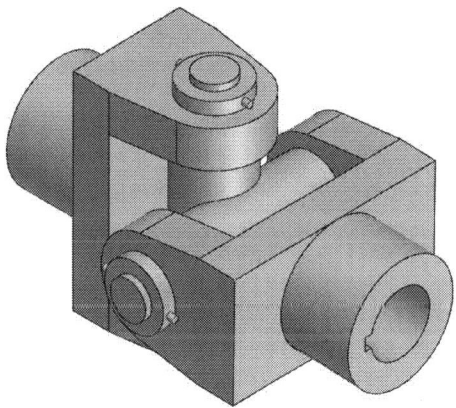 button to reassemble the exploded components, as shown.

Examples:

Example 1

In this example, you will first create the parts of Oldham's Coupling and then create the assembly shown next.

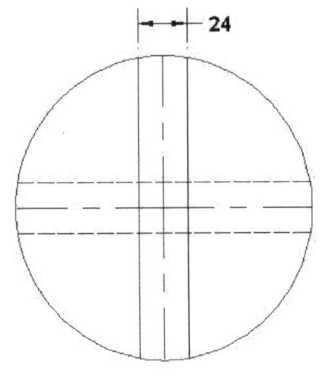

Centre Disc

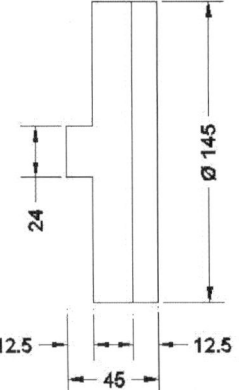

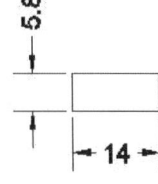

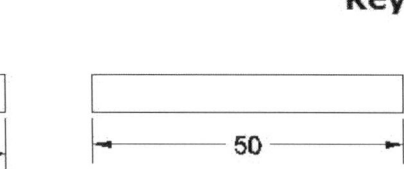

Key

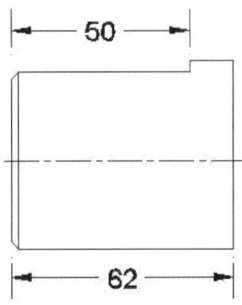

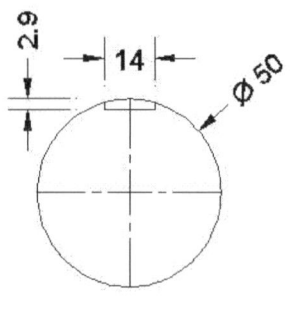

Shaft

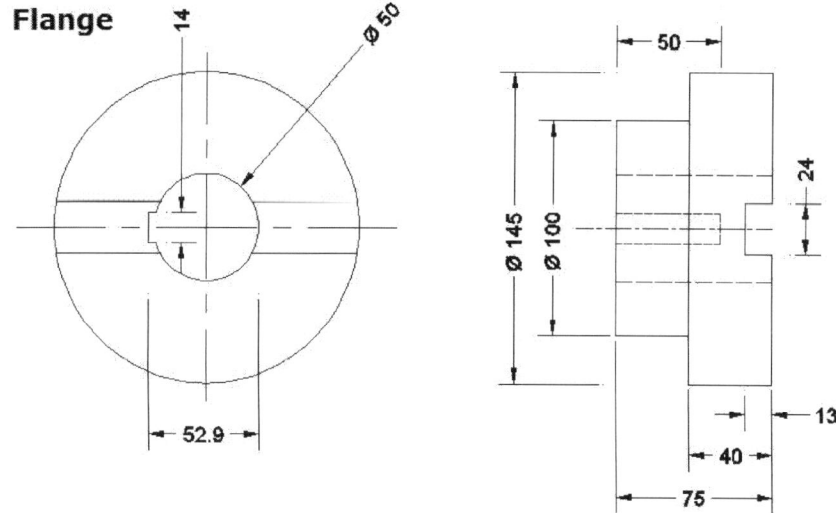

- Start SolidWorks 2021 by clicking **SOLIDWORKS 2021** icon on your desktop.

Note: After opening the SolidWorks, by default the **Welcome – SOLIDWORKS 2021** dialog box get displayed. You can simply double click on the **Assembly** button to enter in the Assembly Environment, as shown.

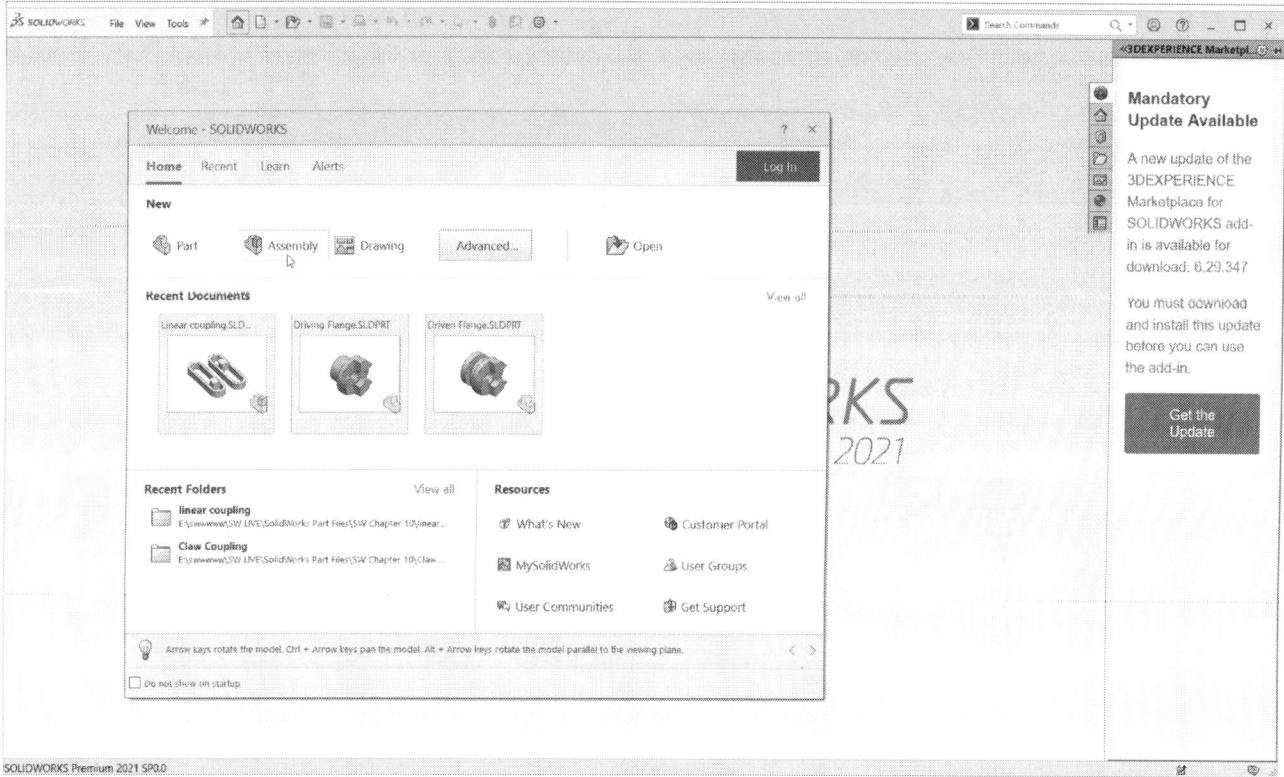

- The SolidWorks Assembly environment with **Open** window get displayed along with **Begin Assembly PropertyManager** on its left, as shown.
- From the **Open** window, browse to the respective folder and double click on **Centre Disc** component to insert it in Assembly environment, as shown.

Note: After entering the **Assembly** environment, for the first time by default the **Open** window will get displayed automatically, as shown.

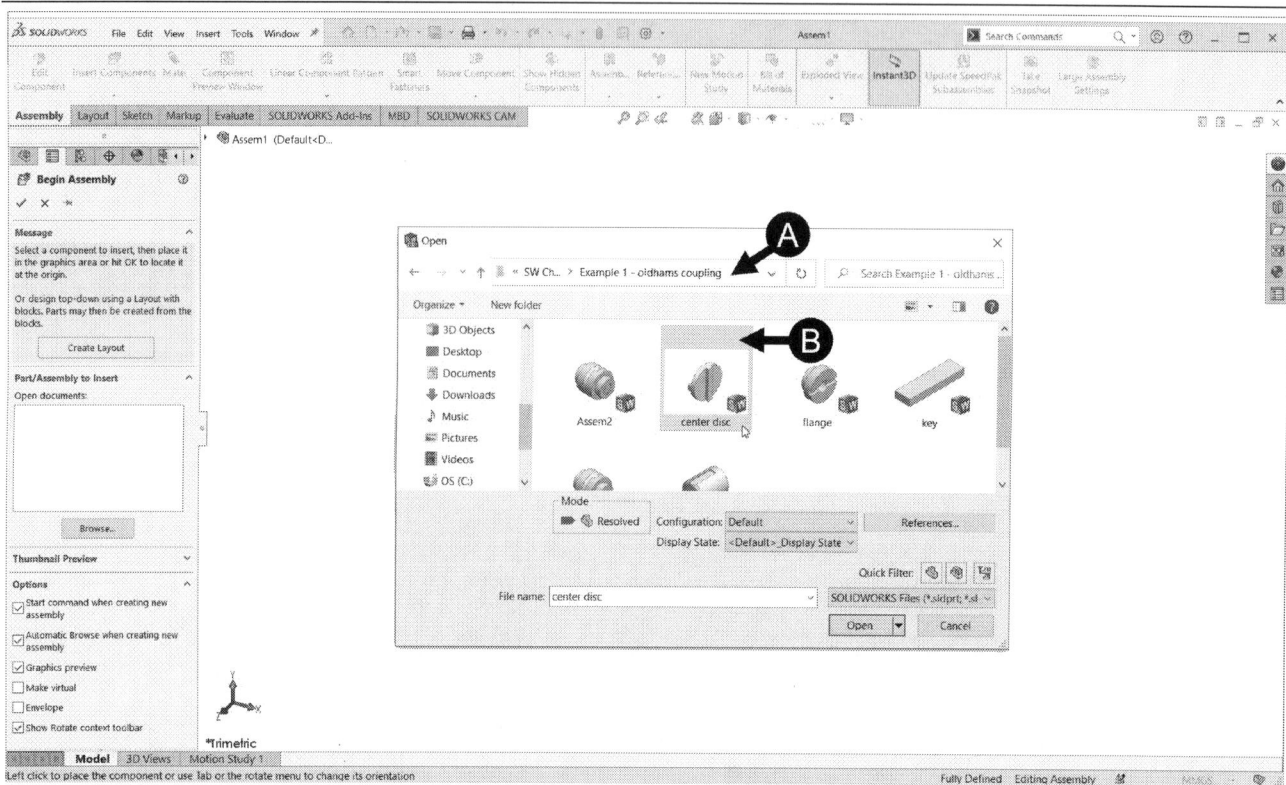

➤ Next, click anywhere in the drawing area to exit **Begin Assembly PropertyManager** and the component inserted get placed to origin automatically, as shown.

Note that as the first inserted component is placed to origin and become Fully Defined, as shown. So, while inserting other components, you can arrange/assemble them with respect to it.

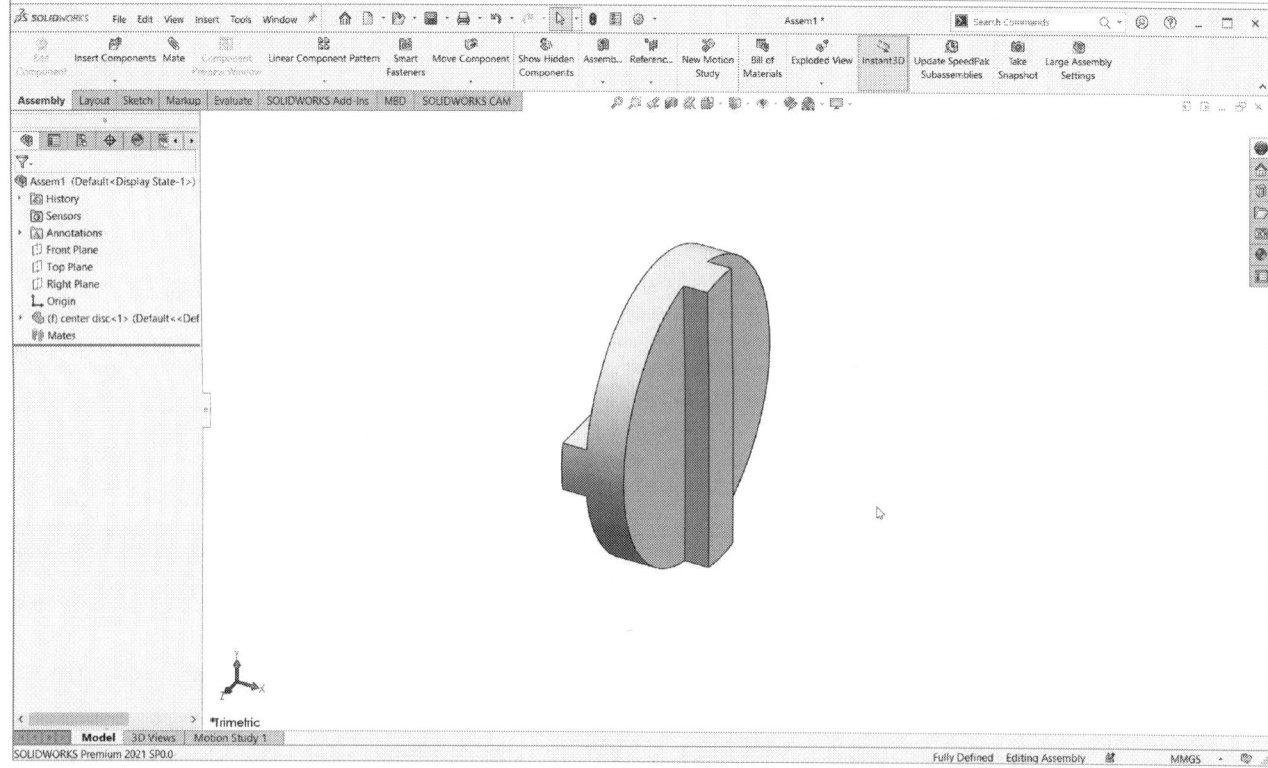

For better visibility of the component/part, the background colour is changed to **Plain White** from the **Apply Scene** button of the **View (Heads-Up)** toolbar, as discussed earlier in this book.

- Click on the **Insert Component** button to display **Open** dialog box along with **Import Component PropertyManager**, as shown.
- Double click on another component (**flange**) from the **Open** dialog box to import it, as shown.

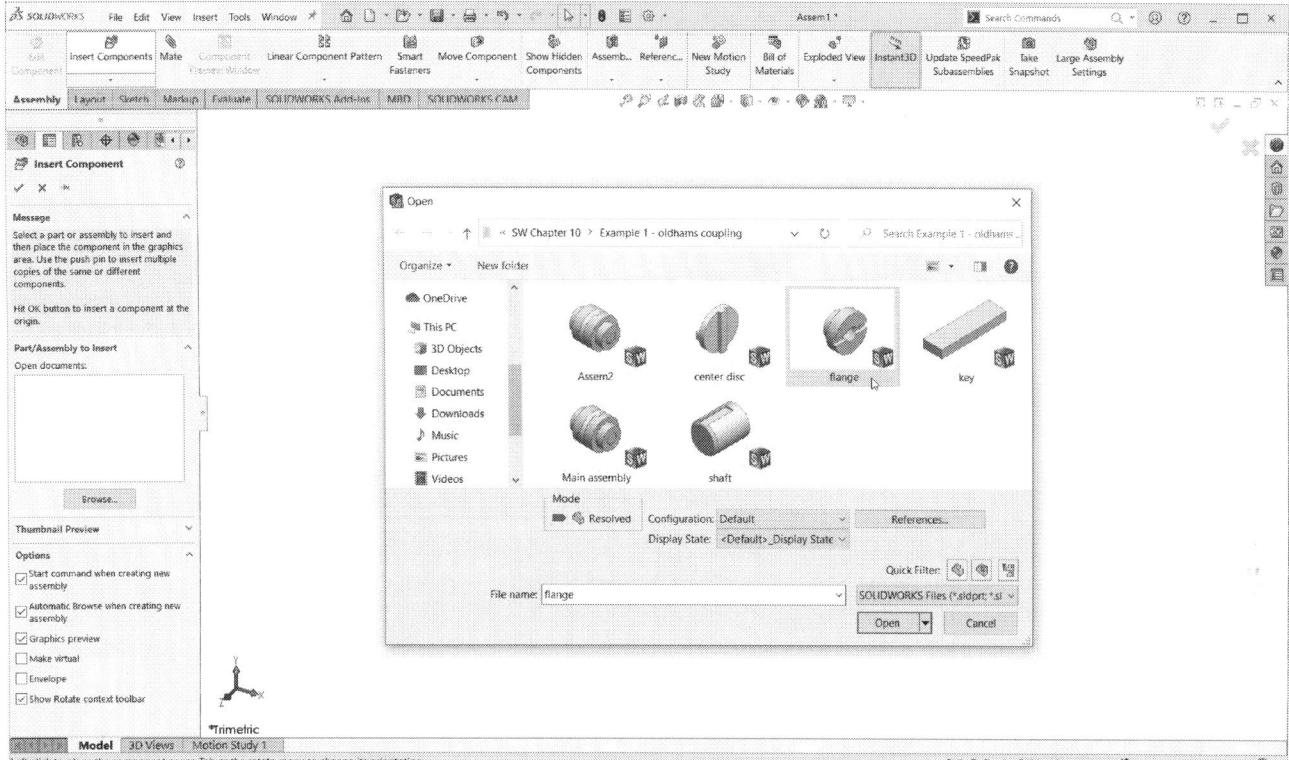

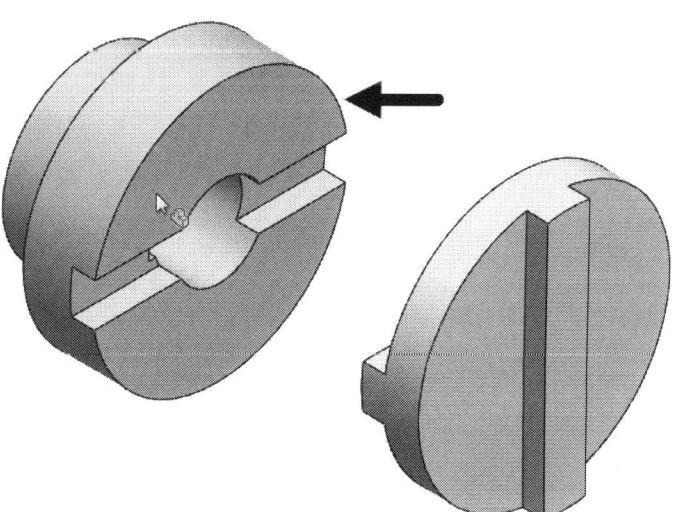

- Next, click on the **Mate** button to display **Mate PropertyManager**, as shown.

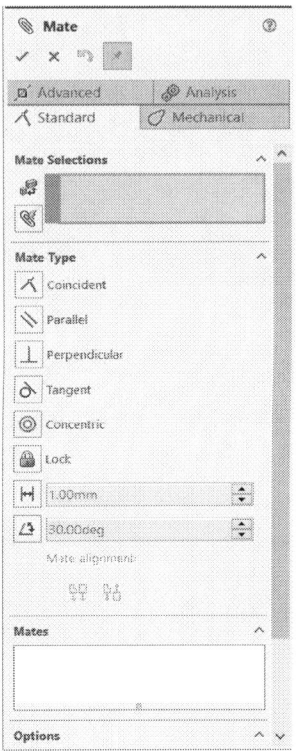

- Click on circular faces of two components one by one to apply and display preview of concentric relation/mate between both, as shown.
- Next click on **Add/Finish Mate** button to apply mate, as shown.

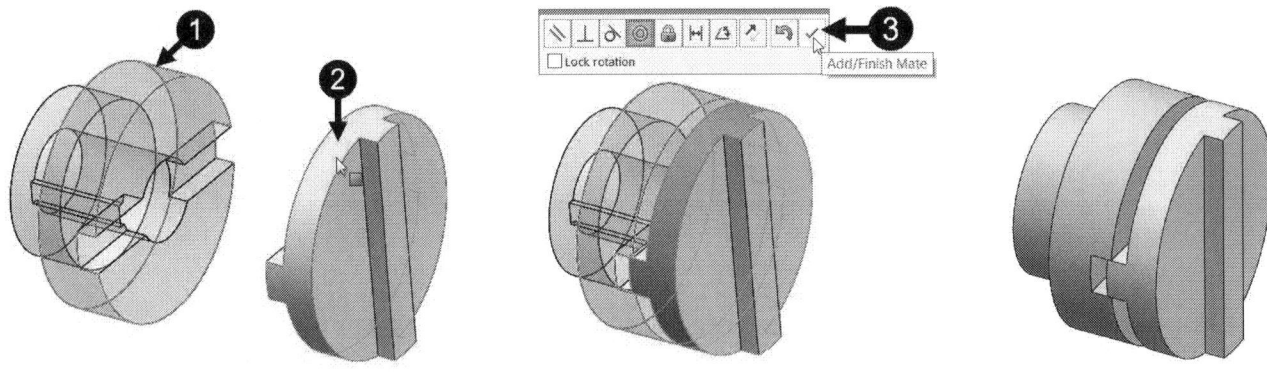

- Next, click on two planar faces one by one to apply **Coincident** relation between both, as shown.

    Note that, you can click on **Flip Mate Alignment** button to flip direction of applied mate, if required. You can also click on other buttons displayed as per your requirements, as shown.

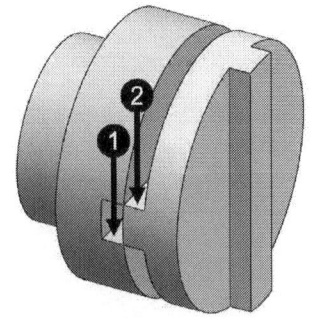 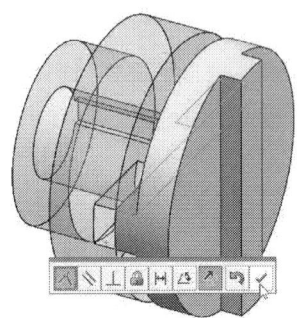 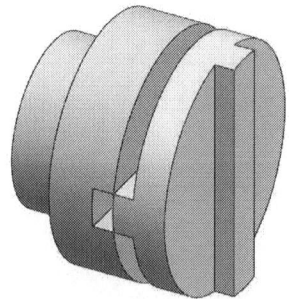

- Again select two planar faces to apply **Coincident** relation between both, as shown.

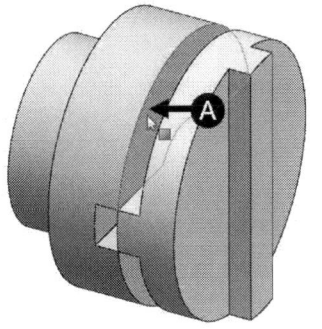 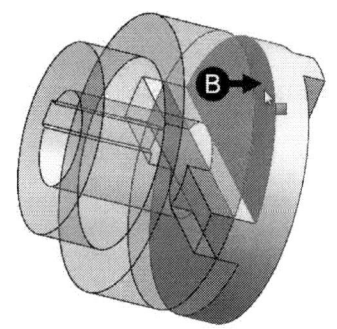 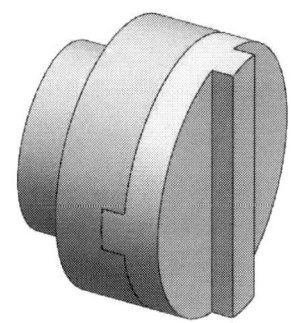

Similarly you need to assembly another **Flange** component on the other side of **Center Disc** (Fix component). You can either insert it similarly as discussed earlier or you can copy it from existing **Flange** component in the drawing area.

- Press and hold the **Ctrl** key and select the existing **Flange** component in the drawing area.
- Hold the **LMB** (left mouse button) also after selecting the **Flange** component.
- Move the cursor up to some distance and release the **LMB** to place copied **Flange** component, as shown.

Note that you can copy any component from **FeatureManager design tree** also, by following the same steps.

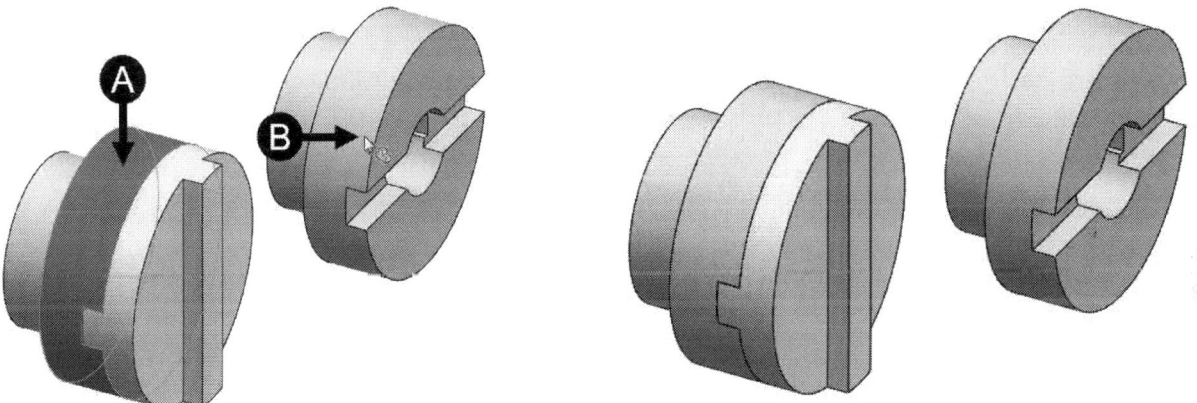

- Assemble the recently copied **Flange** component on the other side of **Center Disc**, as discussed earlier.

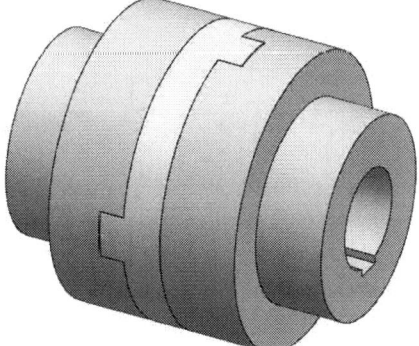

- Click on **OK** button of the **Mate PropertyManager** to exit it.
- Now insert another component which is **Shaft**, as shown.

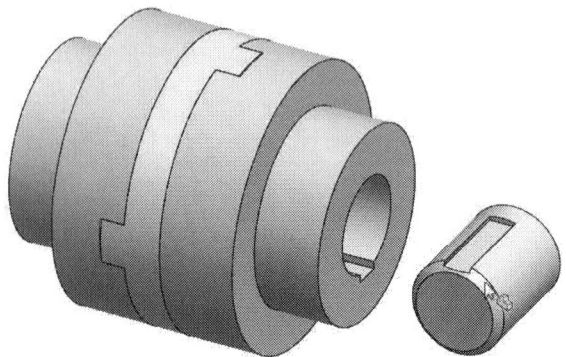

- Again, activate the **Mate PropertyManager** to apply mates.

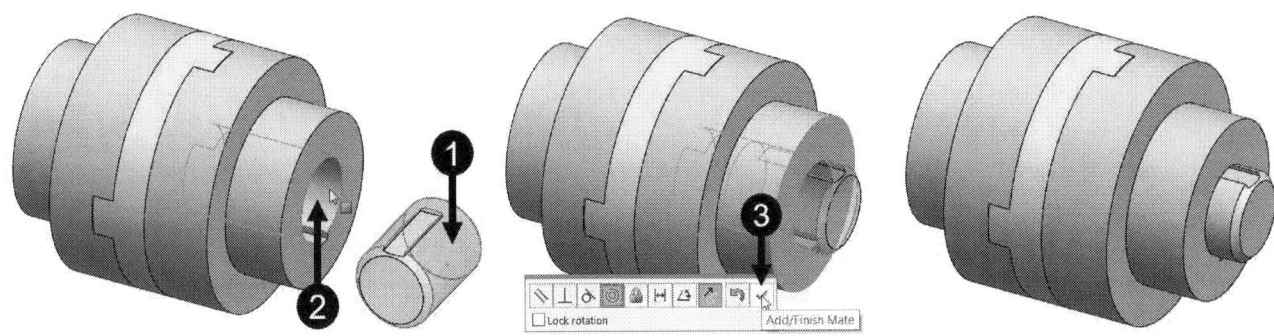

You can rotate the component using the **MMB** (Middle Mouse Button), as shown.

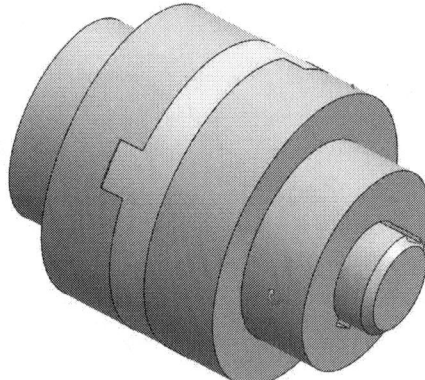

- Select the plane surface of the **Shaft** and then select the **Coincident** option from the dashboard.
- Select the plane surface of the **Flange** component.

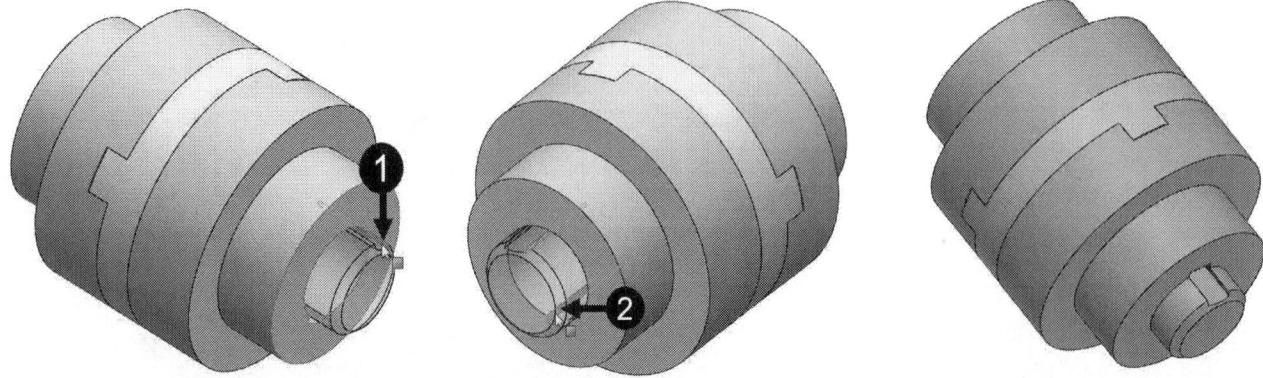

- Select another two flat surfaces to apply Coincident relations between them, as shown.

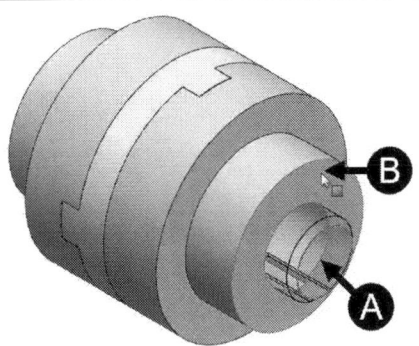 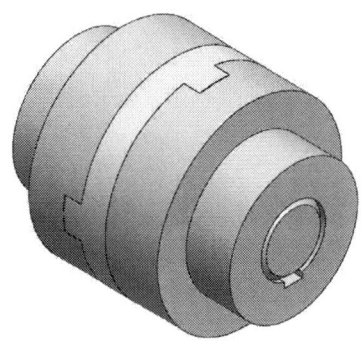

> Now insert another component (**Key**), as shown.
> Activate the **Rotate Components** option (**Features > Move Component > Rotate Component**), as shown.
> Using the **MMB** (middle mouse button) rotate the recently inserted component, as shown.

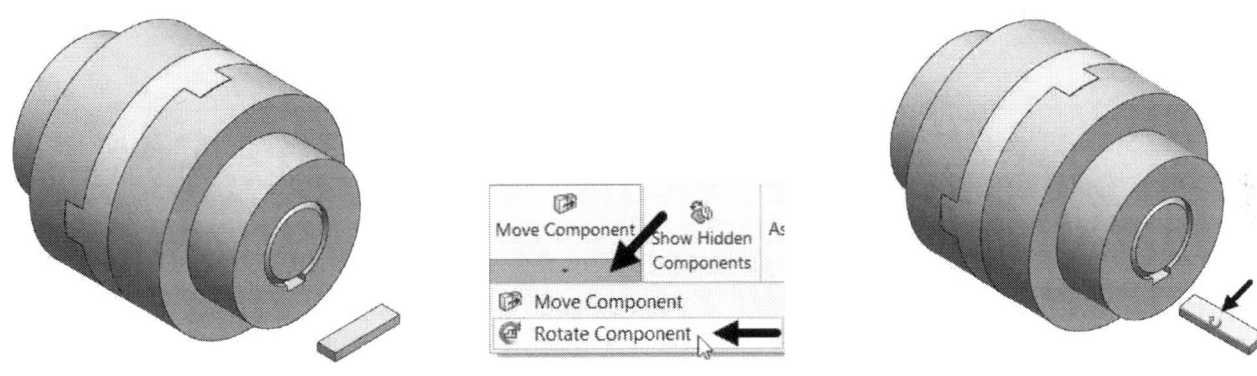

> Apply the **Coincident** mate between selected flat surfaces one by one, as shown.

Creating Assemblies

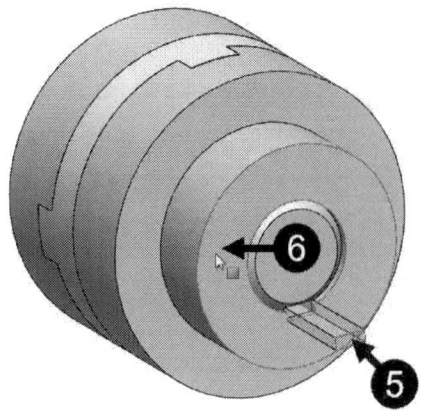 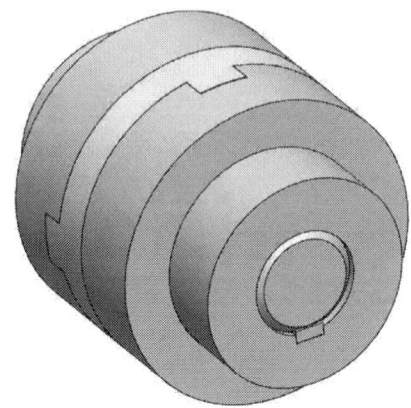

Similarly, assemble the **Key** and **Shaft** component on the other side after copying/inserting both, as discussed earlier in this example.

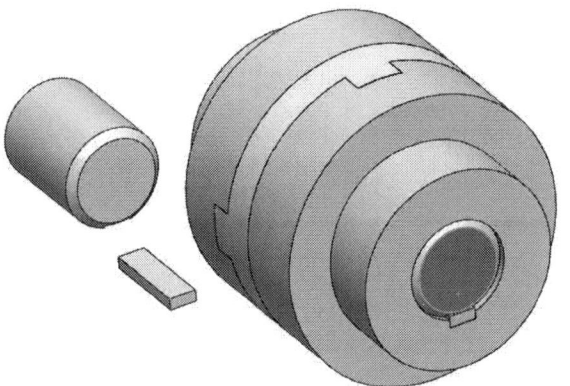 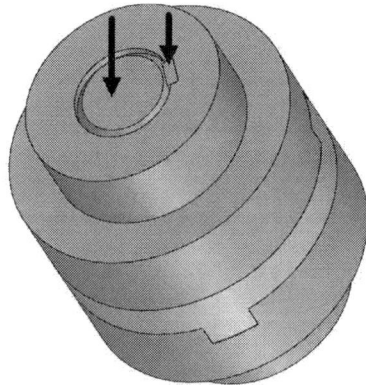

- Click on the **Save (Ctrl+S)** button from the Menu Bar to display the **Save As** dialog box.
- Next browse to the folder of chapter 10 and enter name **ch10-exam01** in the **File name** edit box.
- Click on the **Save** button from the dialog box to save the file.
- Now enter the **Close** ☒ button from the upper right corner to close it.

Example 2

In this example, you will first create the parts and then create the assembly shown next.

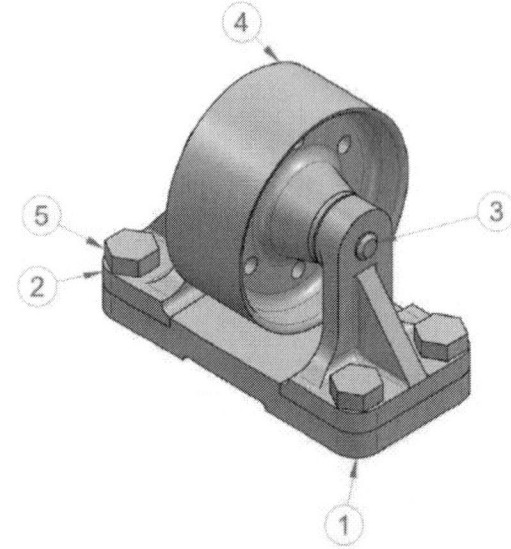

Item Number	File Name and extension	Quantity
1	Base	1
2	Bracket	2
3	Spindle	1
4	Roller-Bush assembly	1
5	Bolt	4

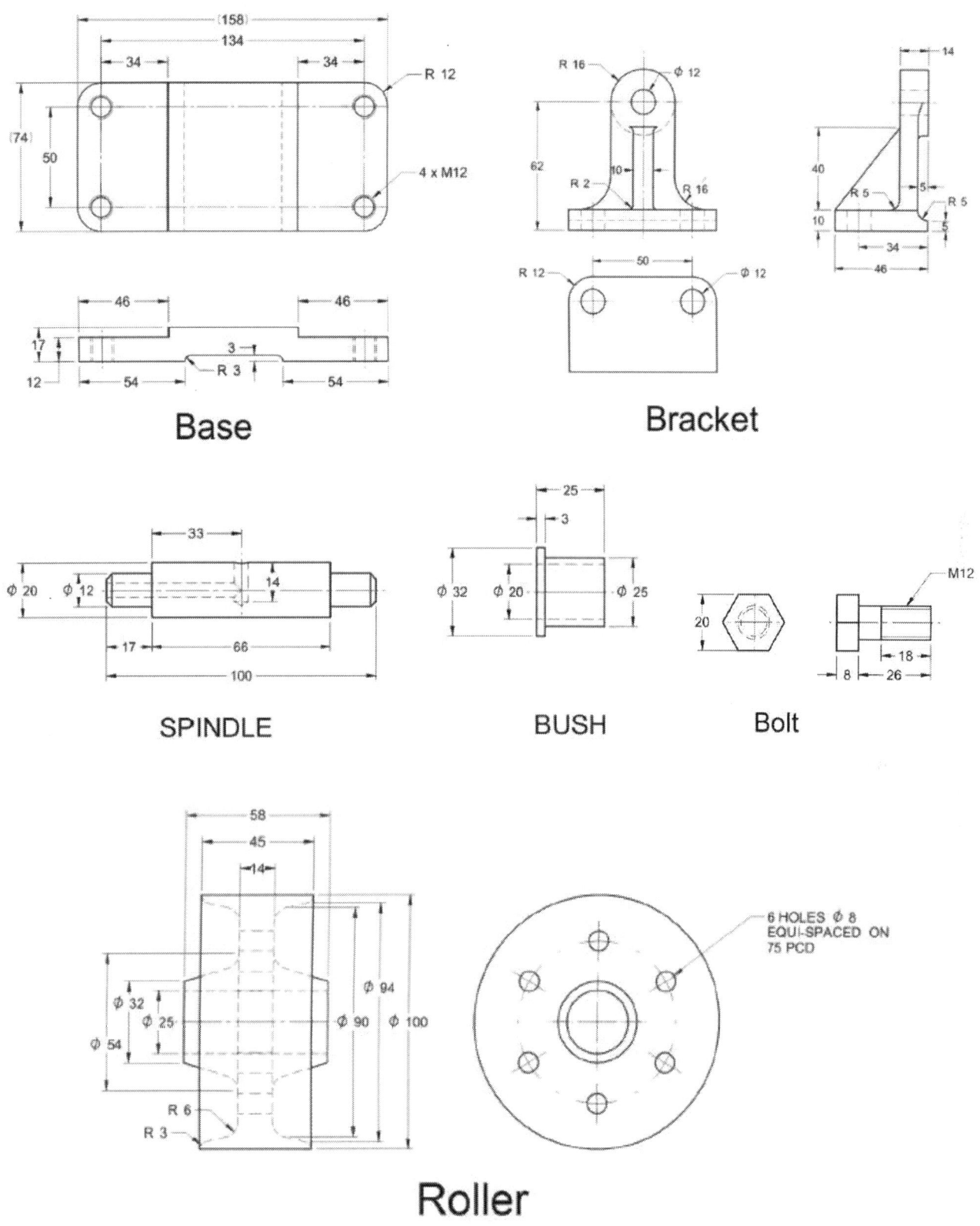

- Start SolidWorks 2021 by clicking **SOLIDWORKS 2021** icon on your desktop.
- Click on the **New** (📄) button from the **Menu Bar** to display the **New SOLIDWORKS Document** dialog box, as shown in previous chapters.

    Alternatively, you can press **Ctrl + N** key from the keyboard to display the dialog box.

➢ Double click on the **Assembly** button to enter in the Assembly Environment.

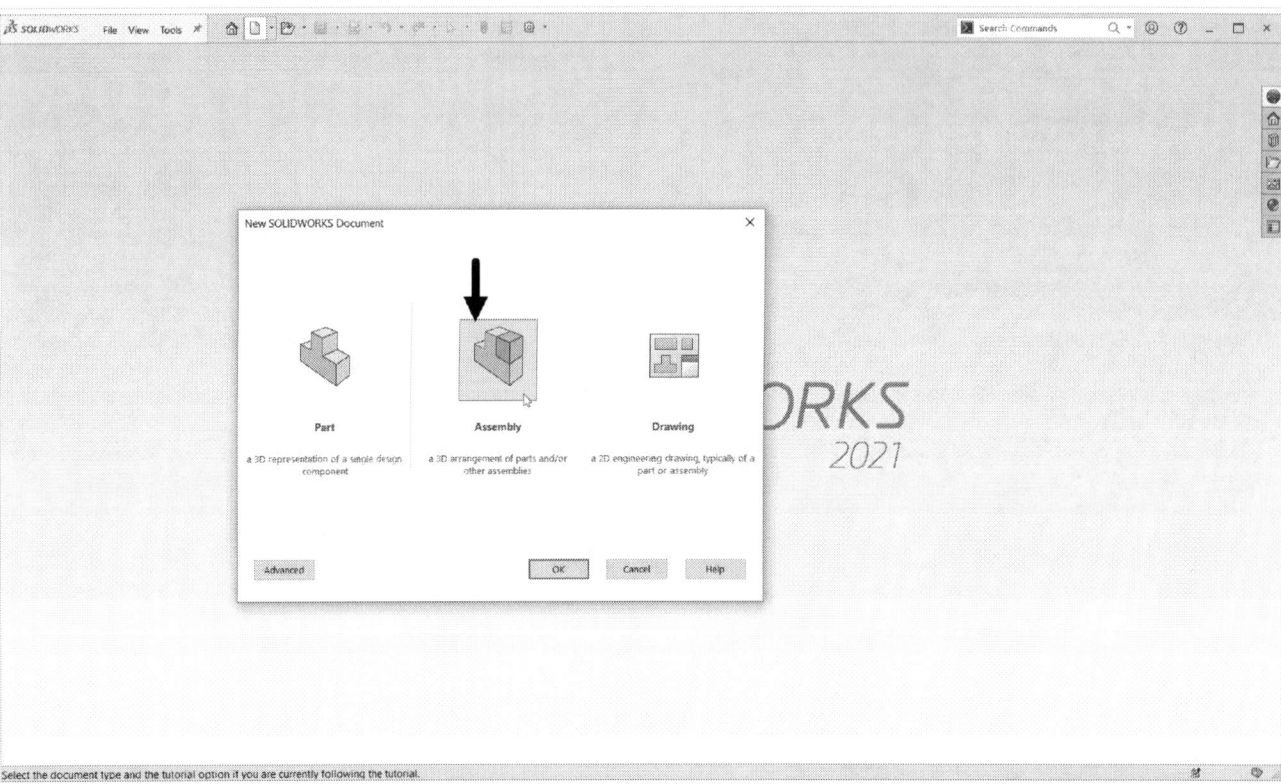

➢ The SolidWorks Assembly environment with **Open** window get displayed, as shown.
➢ From the **Open** window, browse to the respective folder and double click on **Base** component to insert it in Assembly environment, as shown.

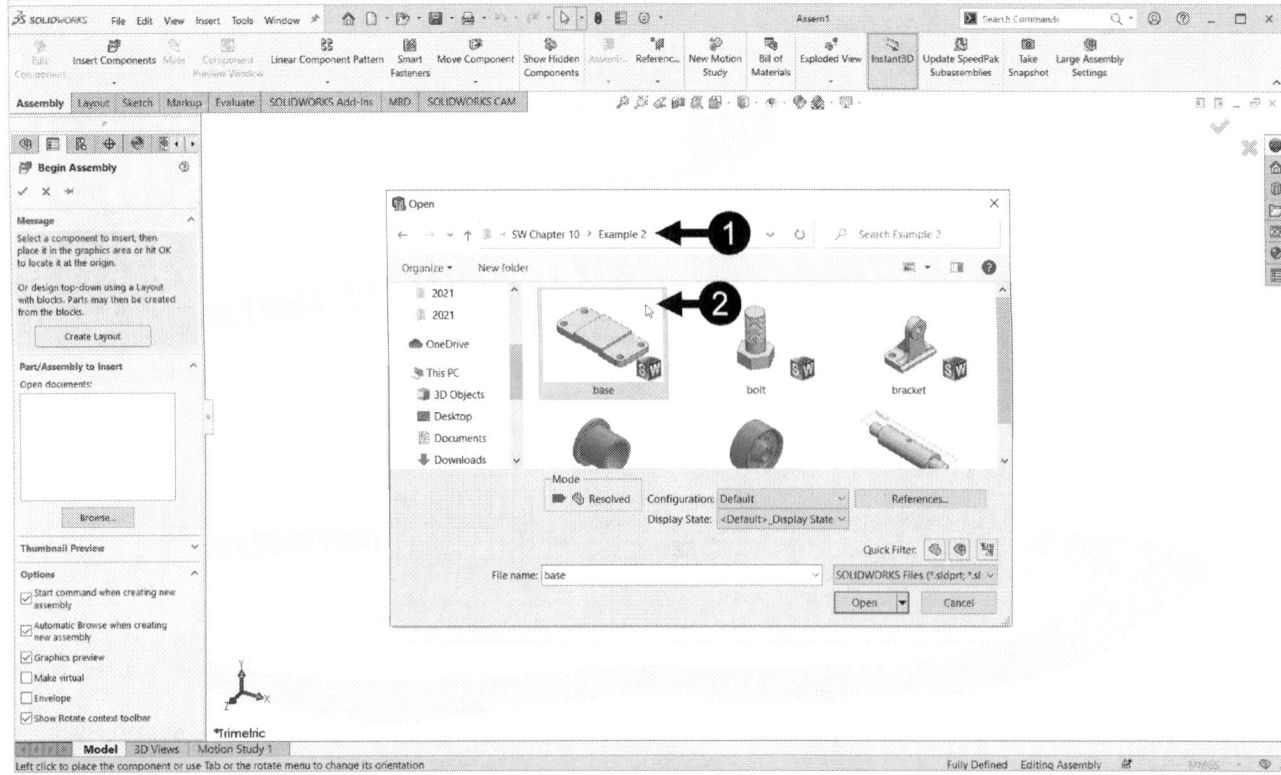

- Next, click anywhere in the drawing area to exit **Begin Assembly PropertyManager** and the component inserted get placed to origin automatically, as shown.

  As already discussed, the first inserted component is placed to origin and become Fully Defined, as shown. So, while inserting other components, you can arrange/assemble them with respect to it.

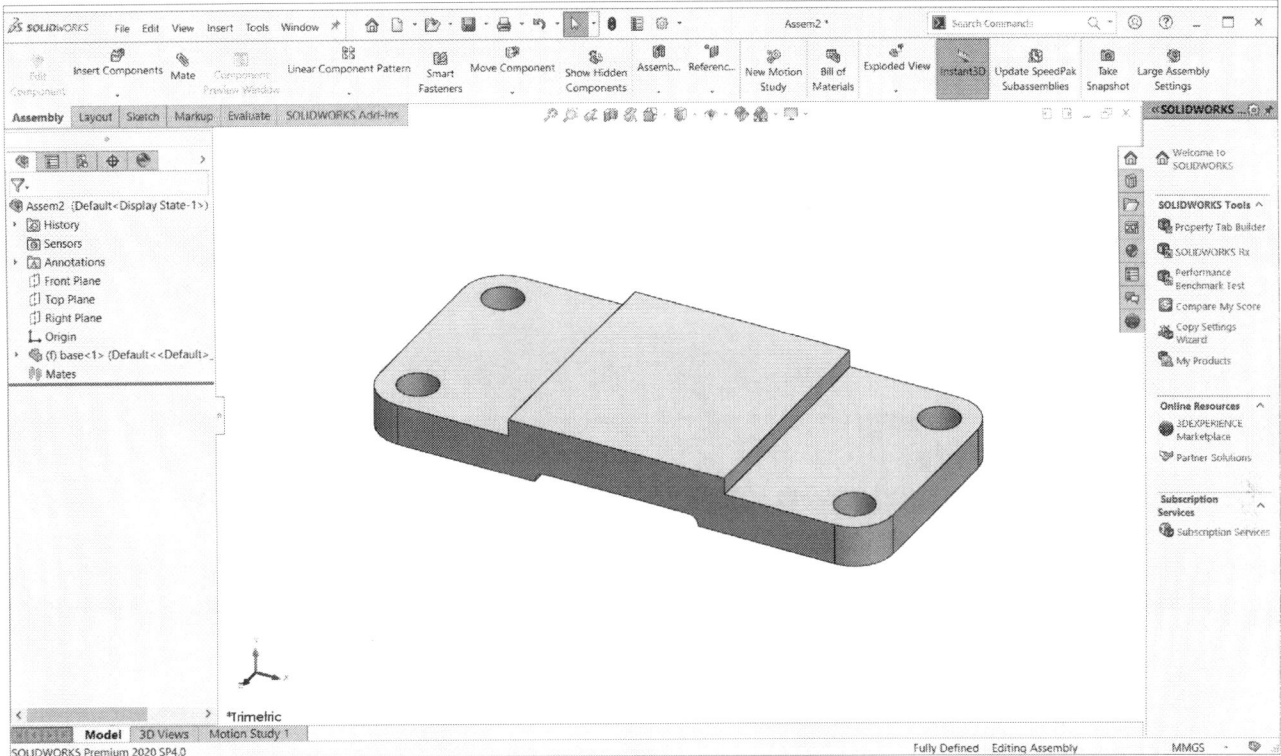

For better visibility of the component/part, the background colour is changed to **Plain White** from the **Apply Scene** button of the **View (Heads-Up)** toolbar, as discussed earlier in this book.

- Click on the **Insert Component** button to display **Open** dialog box along with **Import Component PropertyManager**, as shown.
- Double click on another component (**Bracket**) from the **Open** dialog box to import it, as shown.

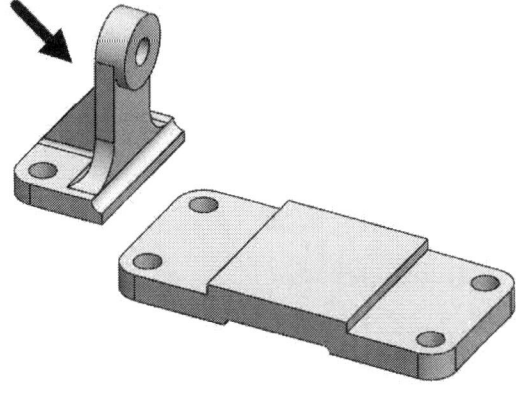

- Click on the **Mate** button of the **Assembly CommandManager** to display **Mate PropertyManager**, as shown.

Creating Assemblies

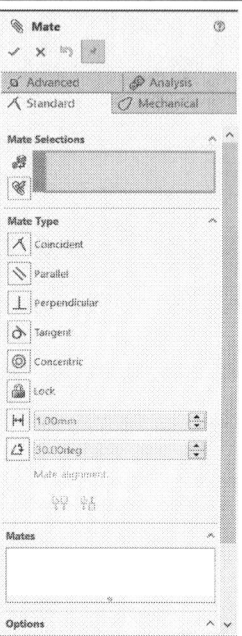

➢ Click on two circular faces of two components one by one to display preview of **Concentric** relation/mate between both, as shown.
➢ Next click on **Add/Finish Mate** button to apply mate, as shown.

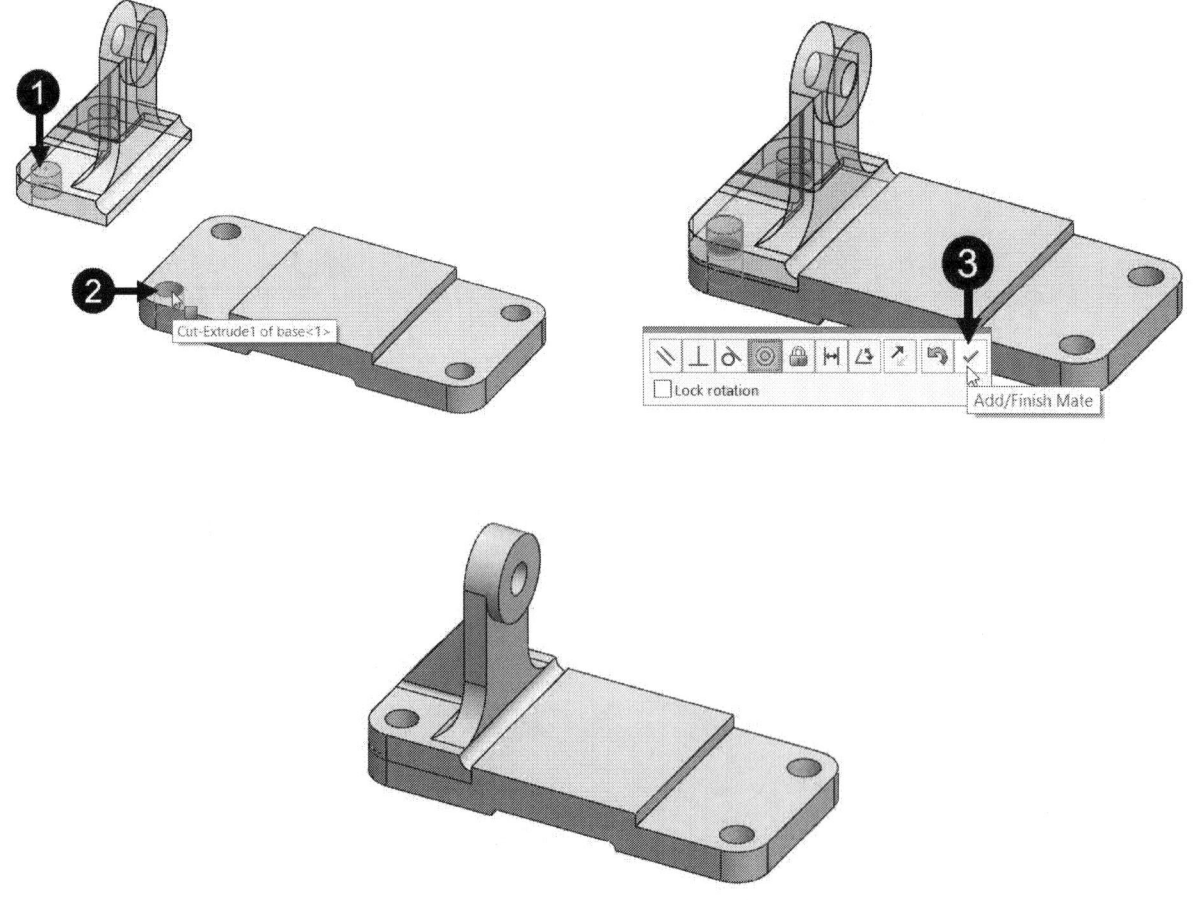

➢ Next, click on two flat surfaces of both components to display preview of **Coincident** mate between both, as shown.
➢ Next click on ✓ **Add/Finish Mate** button to apply mate, as shown.

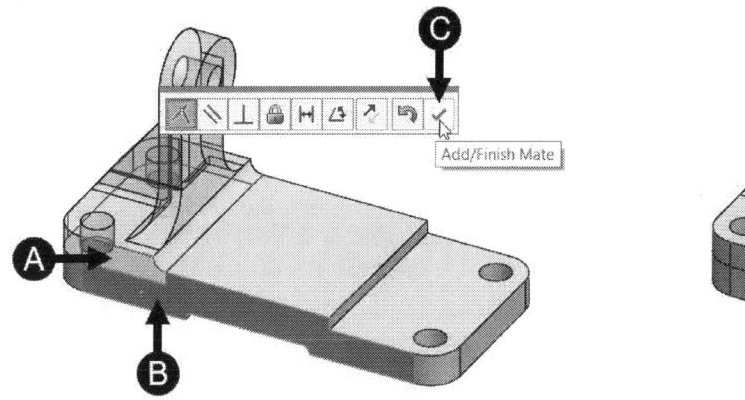
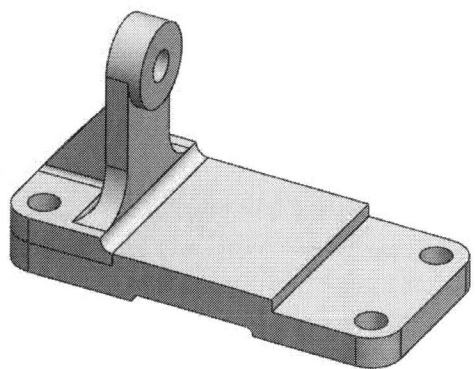

- Using **LMB** (Left Mouse Button) select and move the **Bracket** component up to some distance in upward direction and click to place it, as shown.
- Now click on the flat surface of Base component, as shown.
- Click on ✅ **OK** button of **Mate PropertyManager** to exit it.

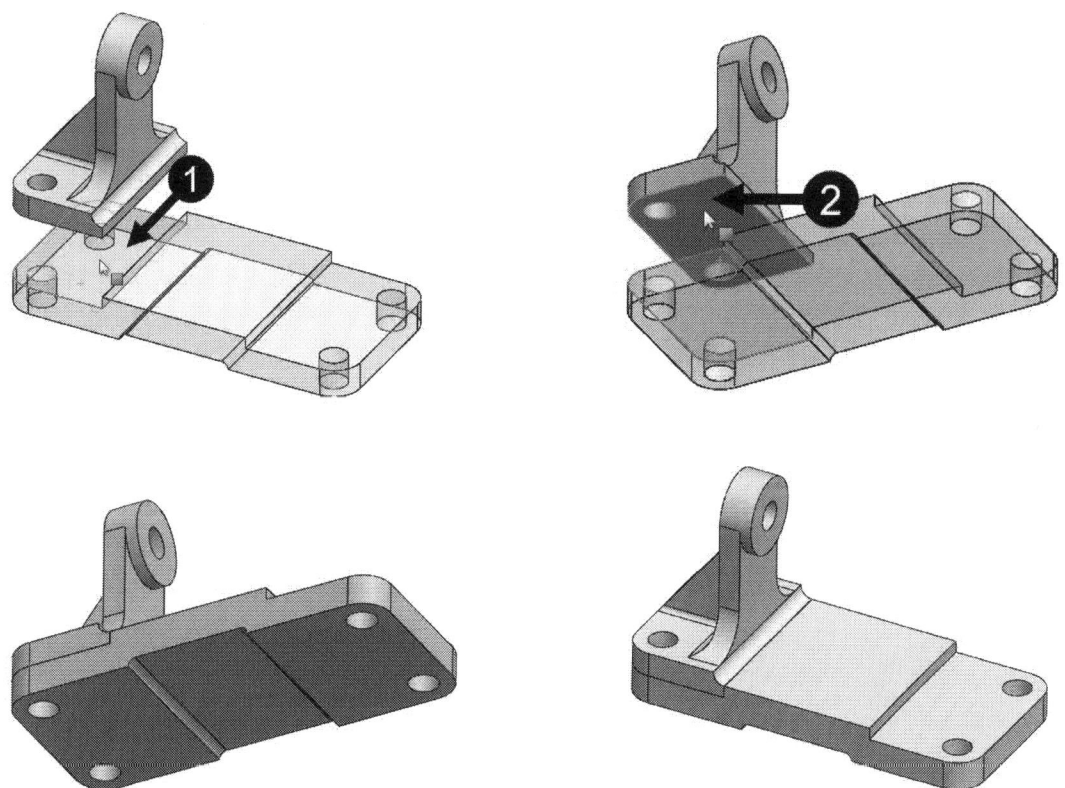

- Next, import one more component (**Bush**) as discussed earlier and as shown.
- Activate the **Mate** tool from **Assembly CommandManager**, as discussed earlier.

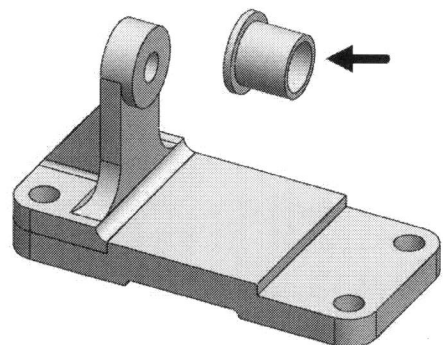

Creating Assemblies

- Now click on the flat surface of **Bush** component and **Bracket** component to display preview of **Coincident** mate/relation between both, as shown.
- Next click on ✅ **Add/Finish Mate** button to apply mate, as shown.

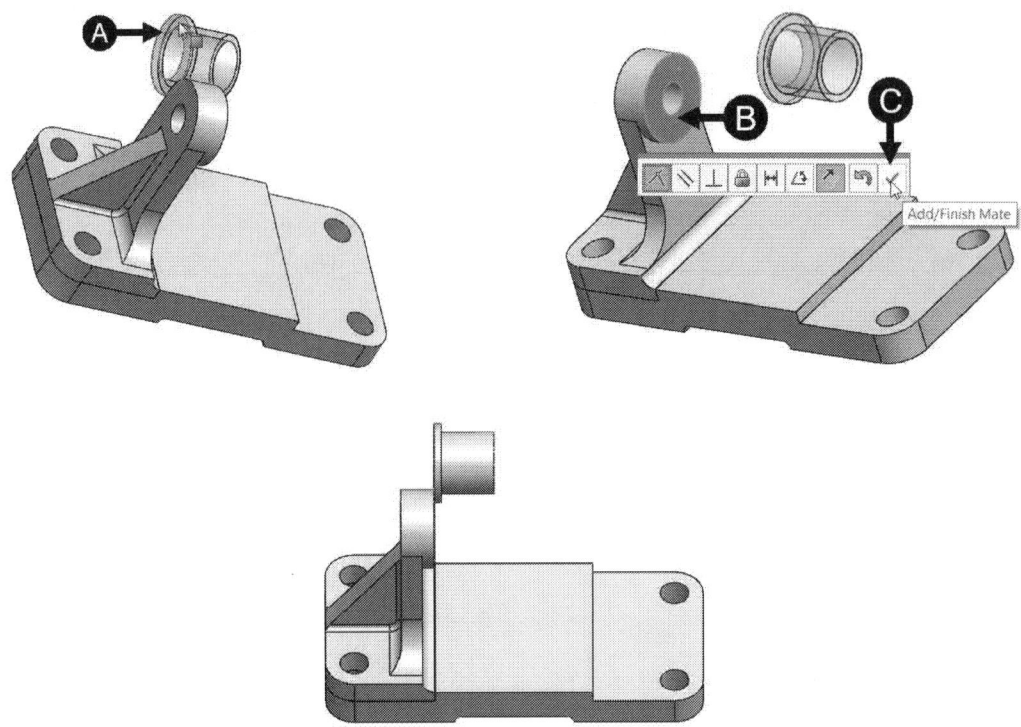

- Now click on the round surface of **Bush** component and **Bracket** component to display preview of **Concentric** mate/relation between both, as shown.
- Click on ✅ **Add/Finish Mate** button to apply mate & **OK** button of **Mate PropertyManager** to exit it.

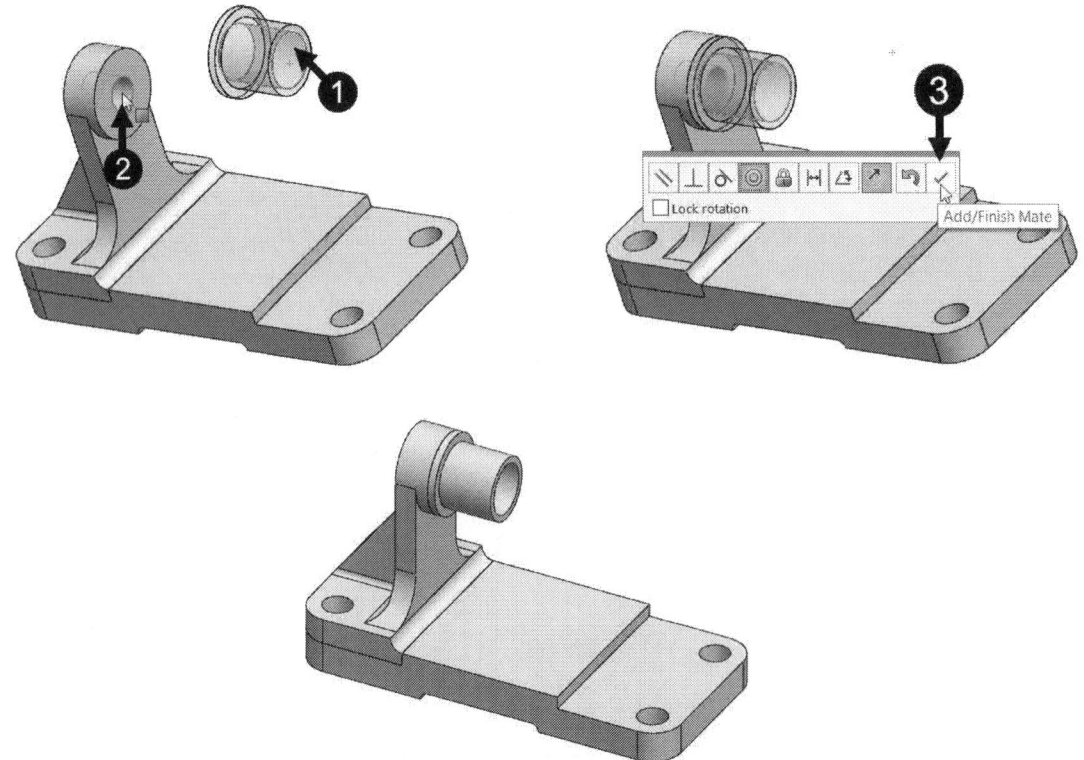

- Next, import **Spindle** component and activate the **Mate** tool, as shown.

- Now click on the round surface of **Spindle** component and **Bush** component to display preview of **Concentric** mate/relation between both, as shown.
- Click on ✅ **Add/Finish Mate** button to apply mate, as shown.

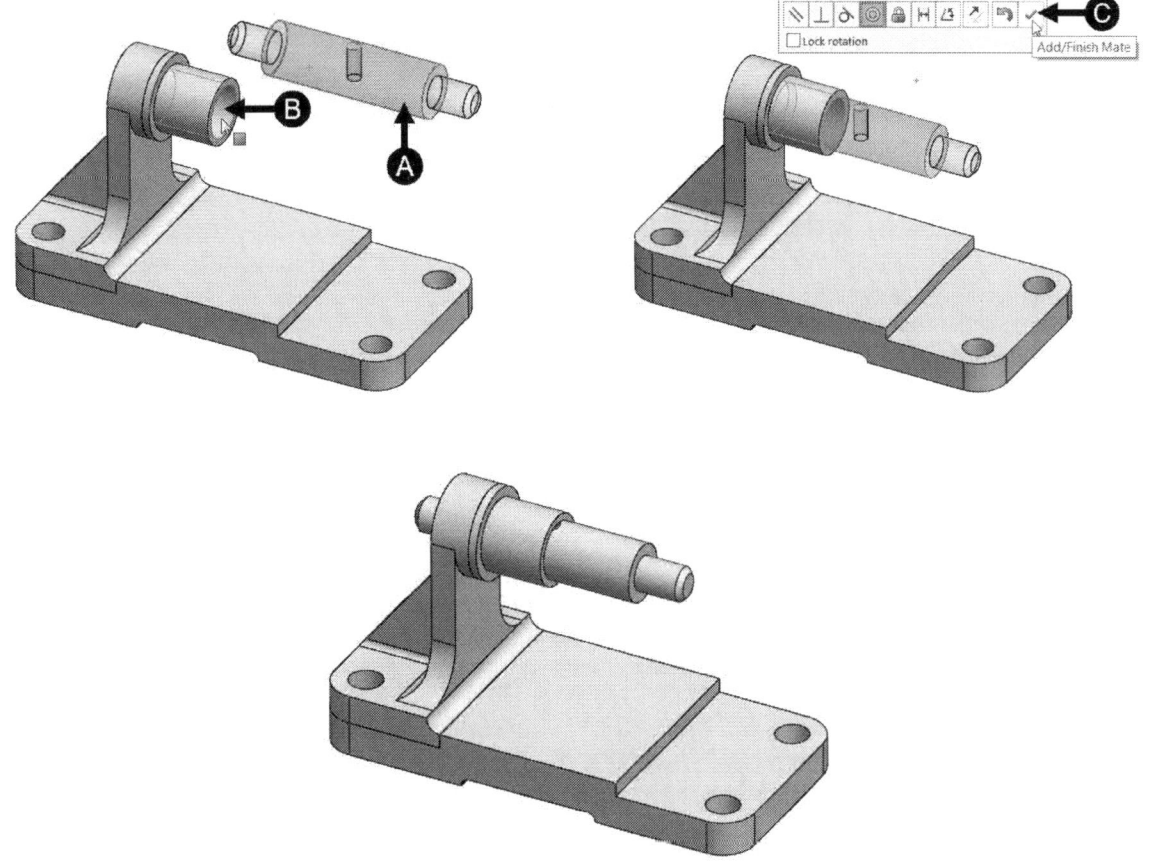

- Now click on the left flat surface of **Spindle** component and **Bracket** component to display preview of **Coincident** mate/relation between both, as shown.
- Next click on the **Distance** button and enter **3** in **Distance** edit box to apply distance between selected surfaces, as shown.
- Next click on ✅ **Add/Finish Mate** button to apply mate, as shown.

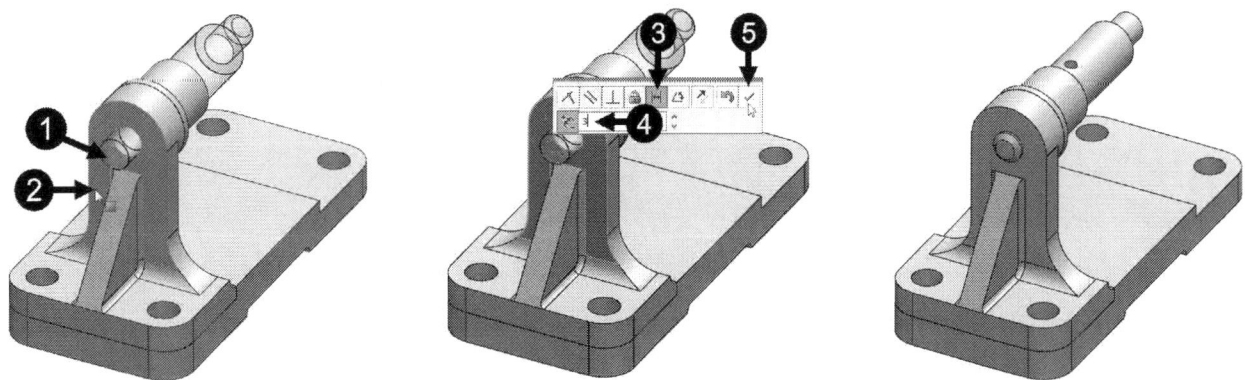

- Right click over the **Spindle** component to display the shortcut menu, as shown.
- Next, select the **Fix** option of shortcut menu to fix it, as shown.

Creating Assemblies

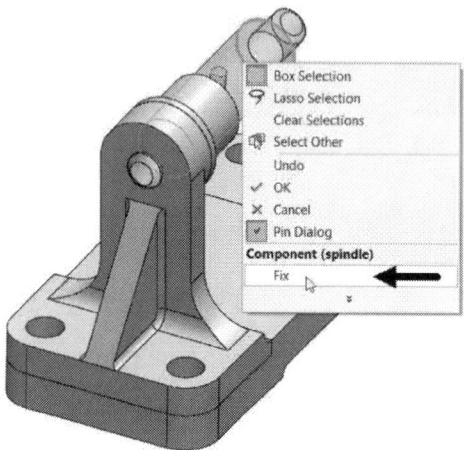

- Next, import **Roller** component and activate the **Mate** tool, as shown.
- Now click on the round surface of **Roller** component and **Spindle** component to display preview of **Concentric** mate/relation between both, as shown.
- Click on ☑ **Add/Finish Mate** button to apply mate, as shown.

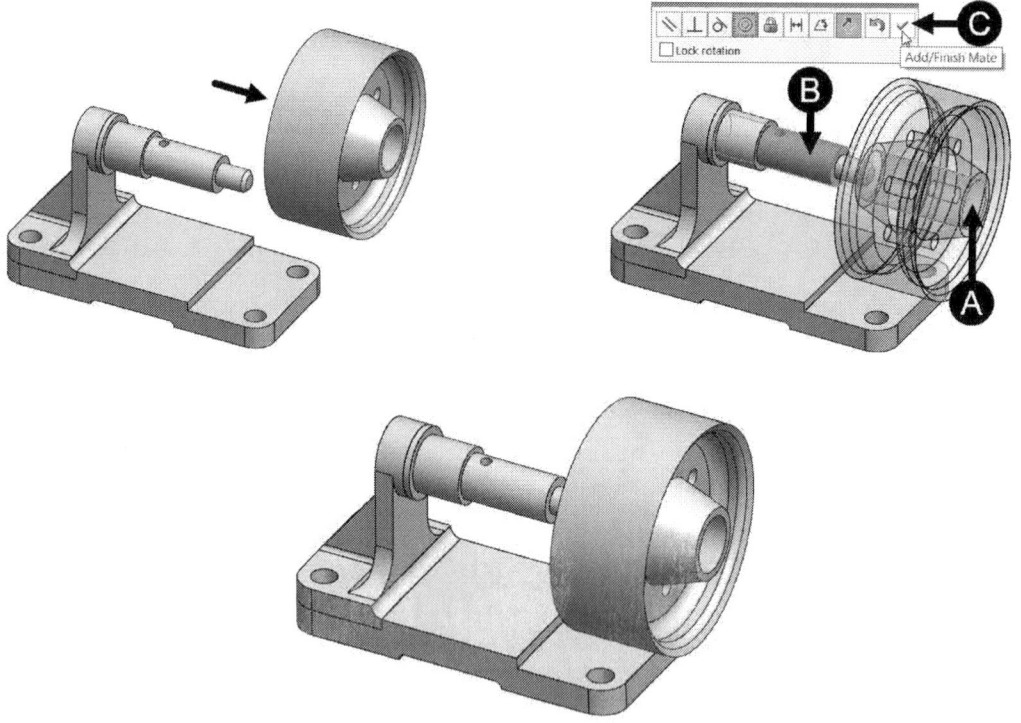

- Now click on the flat surface of **Roller** component and **Bush** component to display preview of **Coincident** mate/relation between both, as shown.

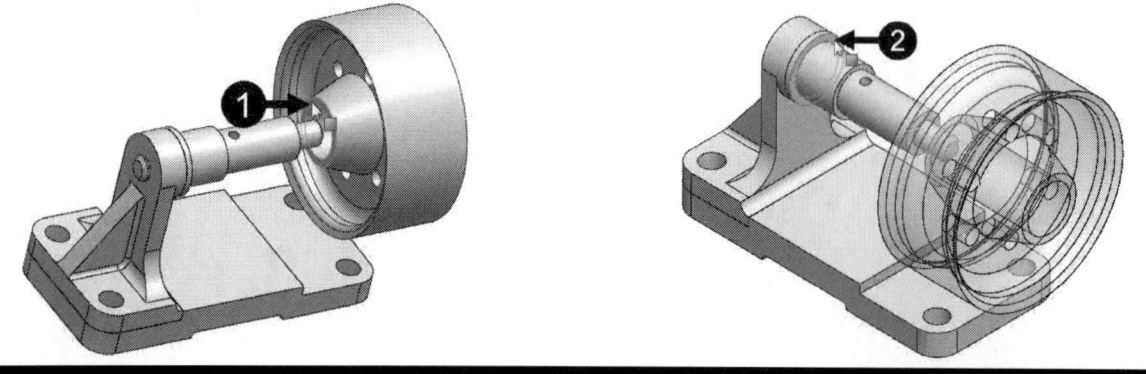

➤ Next click on the **Distance** button and enter **1** in **Distance** edit box to apply distance between selected surfaces, as shown.
➤ Next click on ✅ **Add/Finish Mate** button to apply mate, as shown.

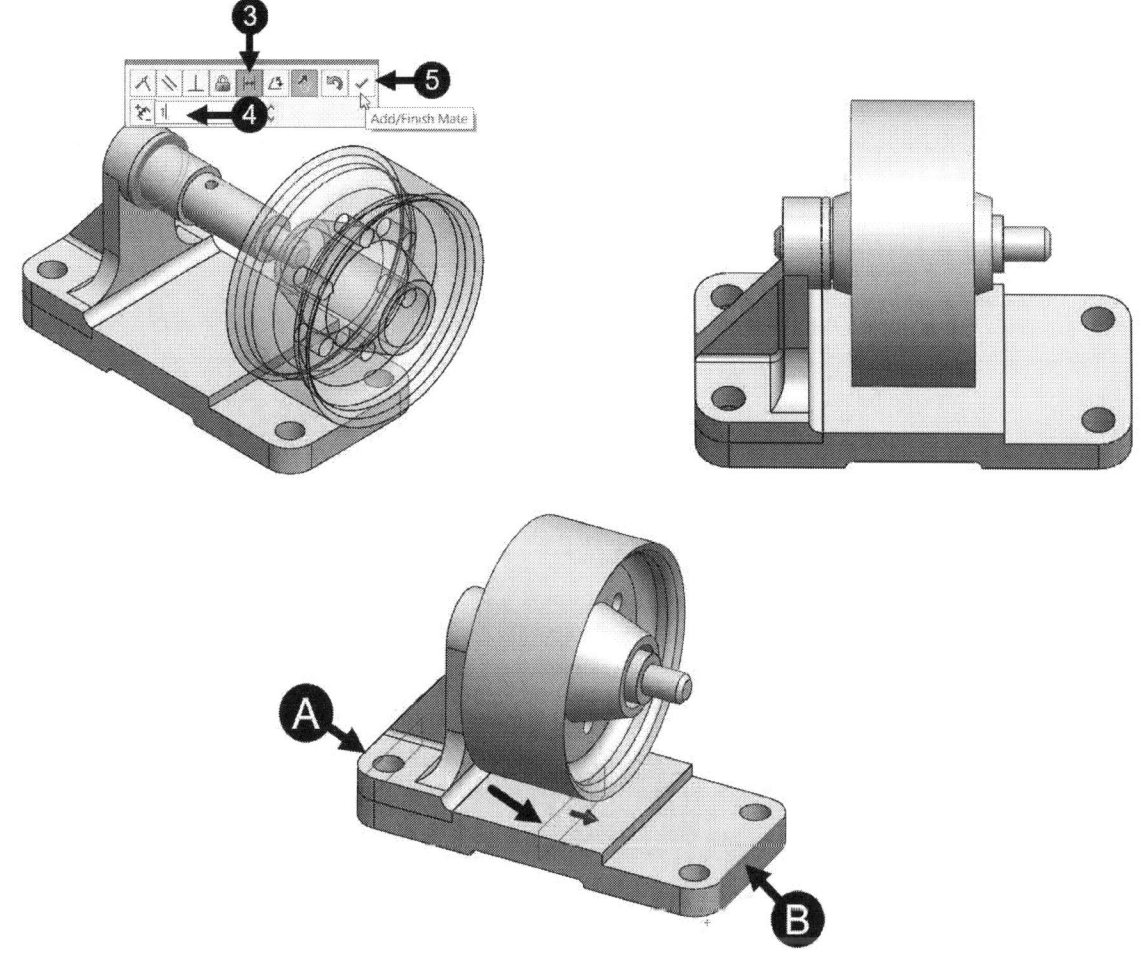

➤ Now click on the **Plane** tool (**Assembly > Reference Geometry > Plane**) to activate it.
➤ Click on planar surfaces on both sides of **Base** component to display preview of mid plane, as shown.
➤ Next click on ✅ **OK** button of **Plane PropertyManager** to exit it and display Reference Plane created, as shown.

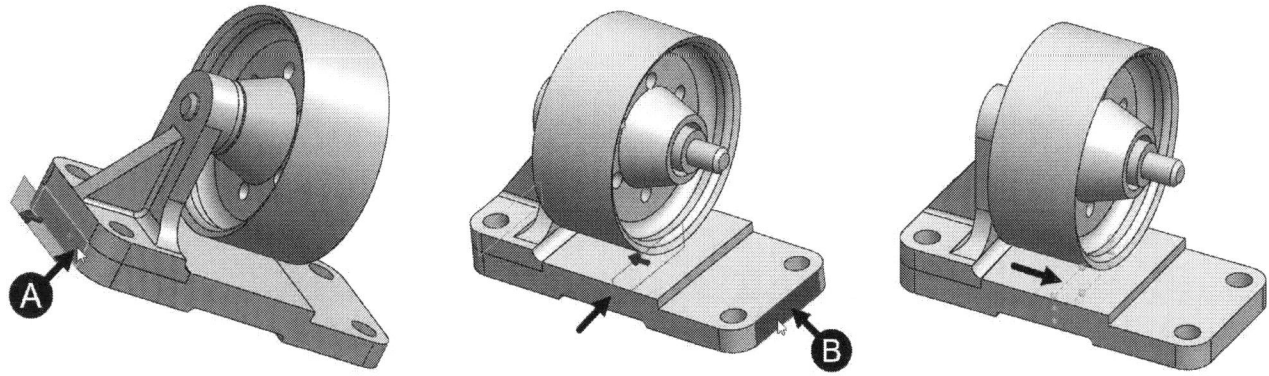

➤ Now select the **Mirror Components** option from the **Linear Component Pattern** flyout of the **Assembly CommandManager** to activate it and display the **Mirror Components PropertyManager**, as shown.

Creating Assemblies

> Click on the recently created **Plane** from the **FeatureManager Design Tree** displayed in the drawing area, as shown.

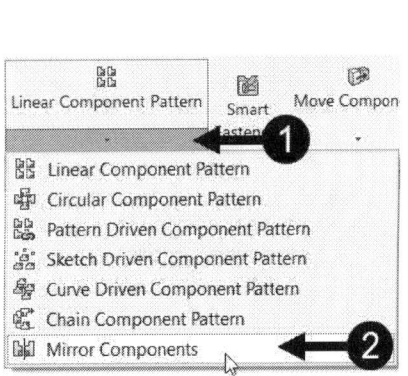 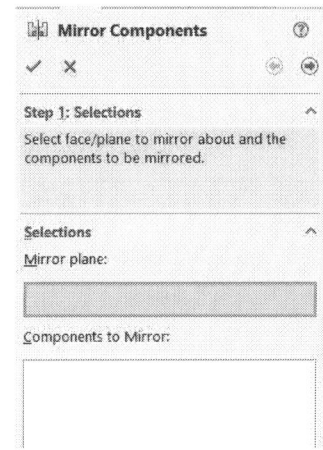 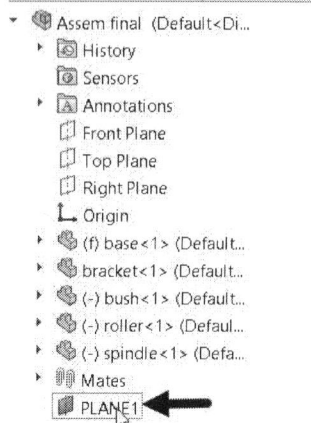

> Now select the components to mirror from the **FeatureManager Design Tree**, as shown.

Alternatively, you can select the required components by clicking on it from the drawing area. Also, the selected components get highlighted in the drawing area, as shown.

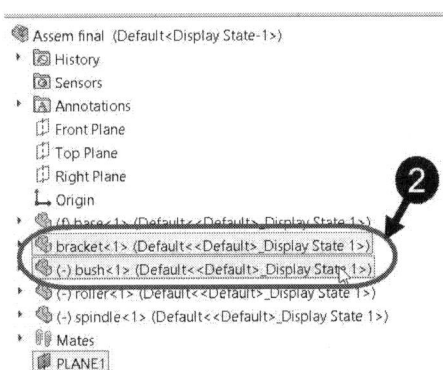 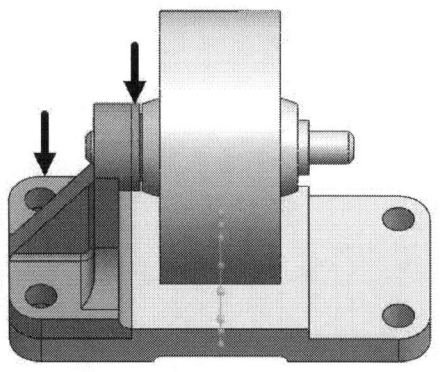

> Next click on ✓ **OK** button of **Mirror Components PropertyManager** to exit it and display mirrored components, as shown.

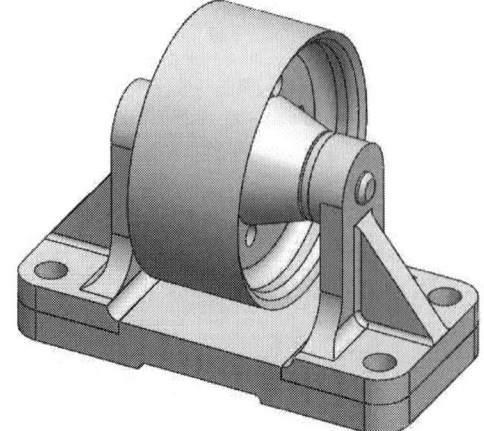

> Next, import **Bolt** component and activate the **Mate** tool, as shown.
> Now click on the round surface of **Bolt** component and **Bracket** component to display preview of **Concentric** mate/relation between both, as shown.
> Click on ✓ **Add/Finish Mate** button to apply mate, as shown.

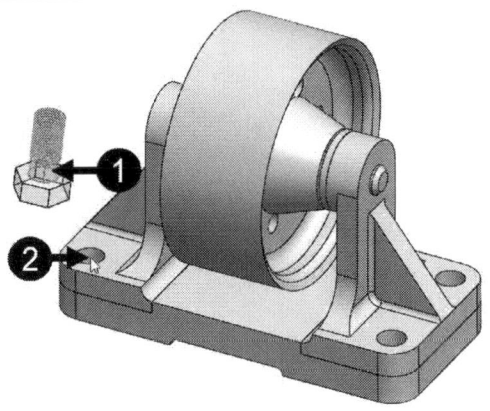 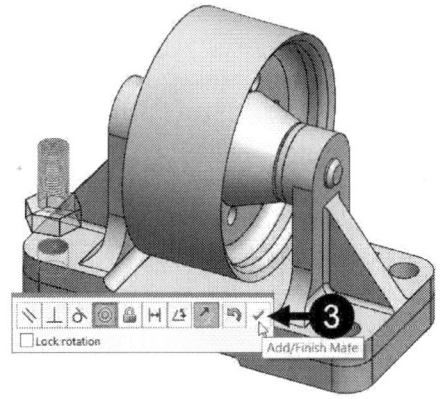

- Now click on the flat surface of **Bolt** and **Bracket** component to display preview of **Coincident** mate/relation between both, as shown.
- Next, if required click on the **Flip Mate Alignment** button to flip its direction, as shown.

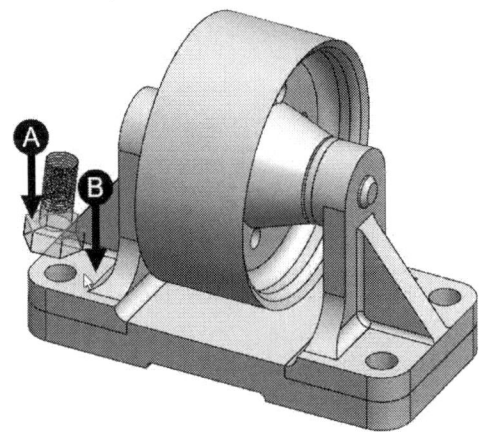 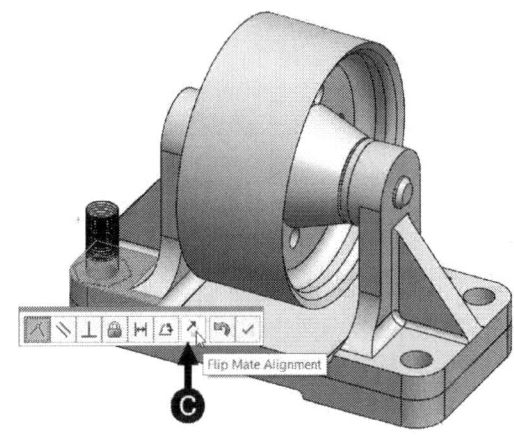

- Click on ✓ **Add/Finish Mate** button to apply mate, as shown.

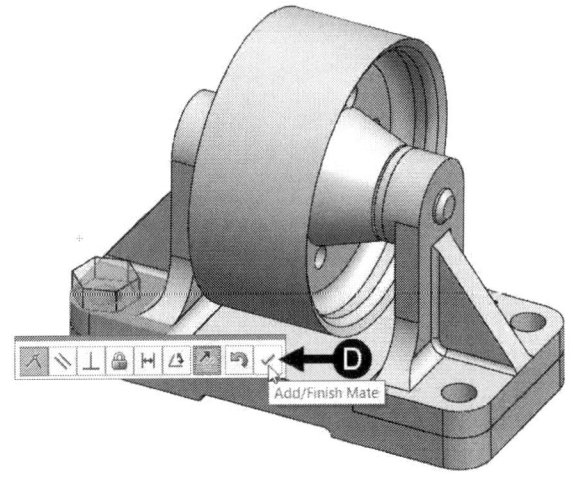 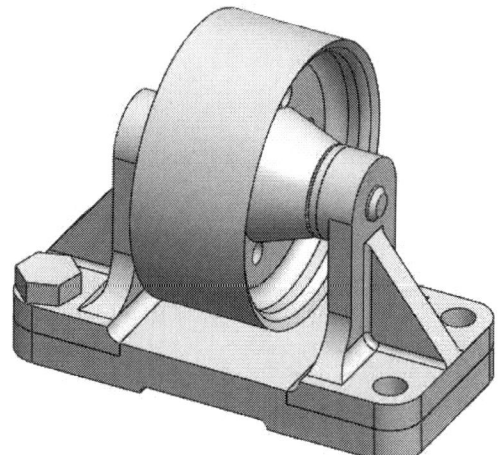

- Now click on the flat surface of **Bolt** and **Base** component to make both surfaces coincident with each other, as shown.
- Next click on ✓ **OK** button of **Mate PropertyManager** to exit it and display mirrored components, as shown.

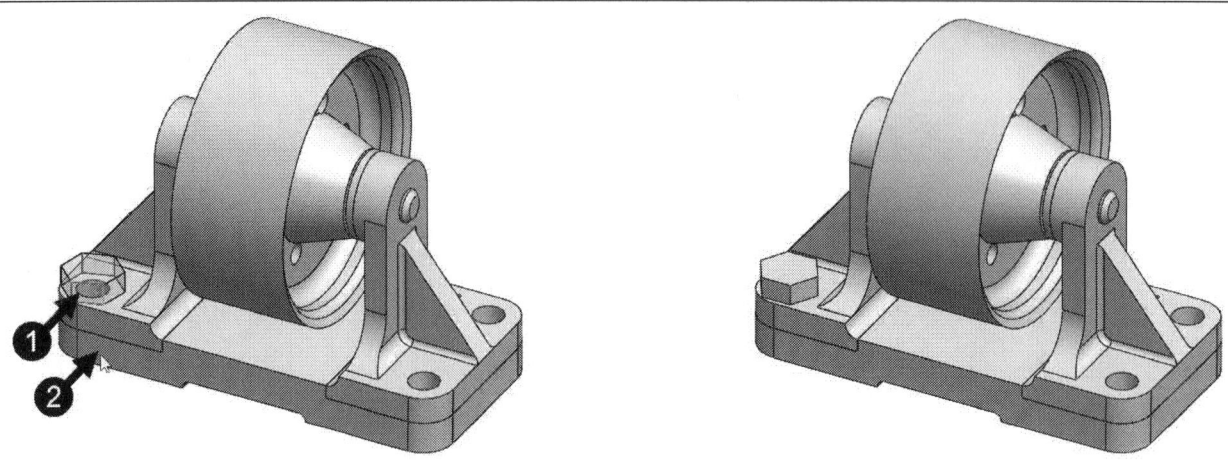

> Now click on the **Linear Component Pattern** tool from the **Assembly CommandManager** to activate it and display the **Linear Pattern PropertyManager**, as shown.
> Click on two edges to define as Direction 1 and Direction 2 and click on the **Bolt** component to Pattern, as shown.
> Next, enter the required entries in the Property Manager to display preview of Pattern feature, as shown.

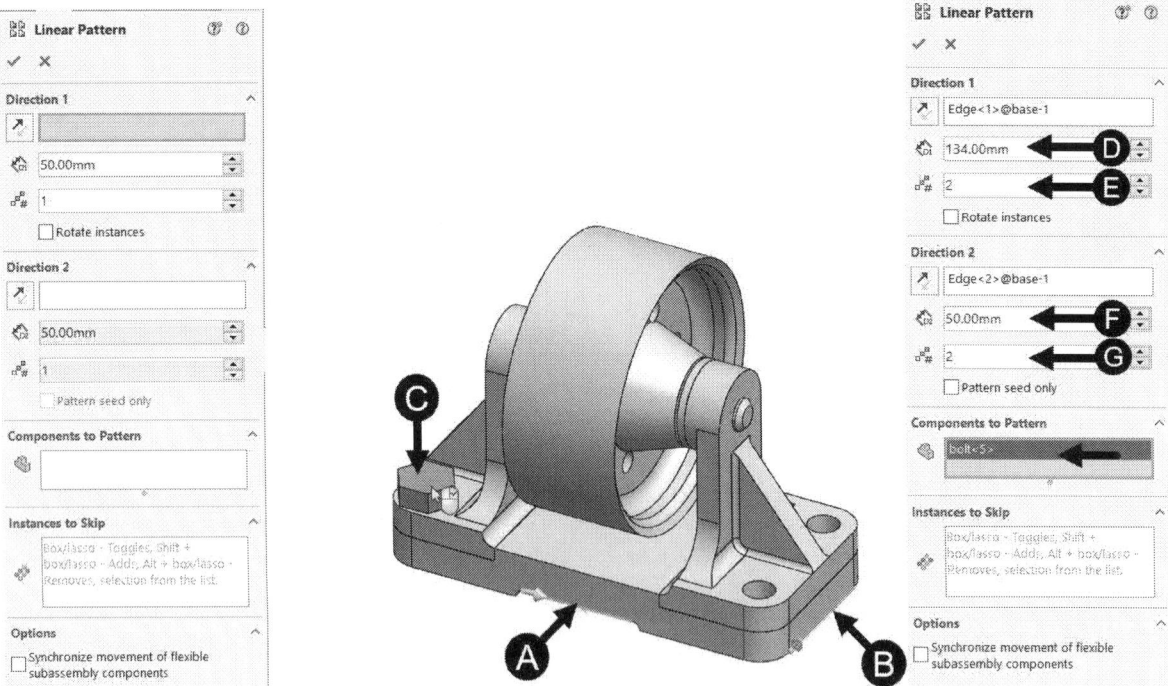

> Next click on ✓ **OK** button of **Linear Pattern PropertyManager** to exit it and display mirrored components, as shown.

Creating Assemblies

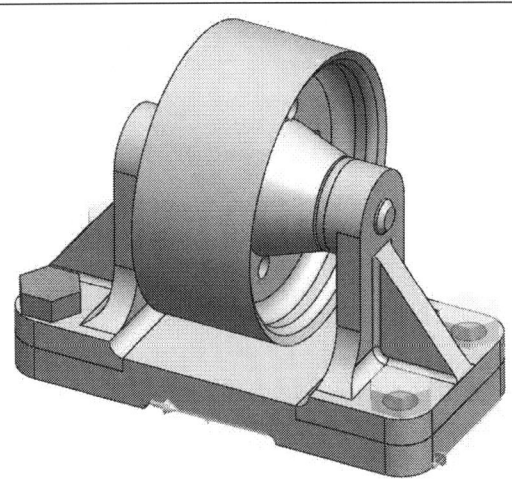 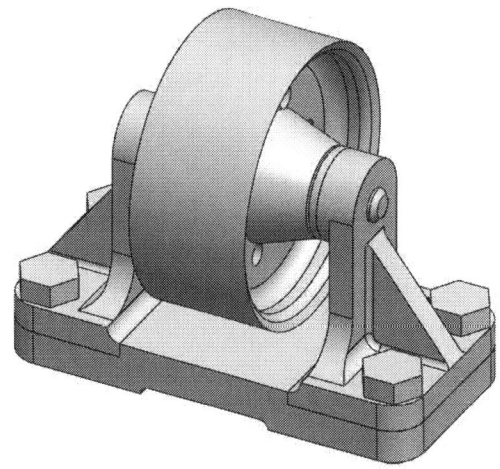

- Click on the **Save (Ctrl+S)** button from the Menu Bar to display the **Save As** dialog box.
- Next browse to the folder of chapter 10 and enter name **ch10-exam02** in the **File name** edit box.
- Click on the **Save** button from the dialog box to save the file.
- Now enter the **Close** ⌧ button from the upper right corner to close it.

Questions:

1. Which tool is used to import a component in the assembly environment?
2. What is the procedure of fixing a component in the assembly environment?
3. Which tool is used to apply concentric relation between two round surfaces?
4. Which tool is used to explode the assembly components?
5. What is the procedure to move components manually after exploding them?
6. What is the use of Symmetric mate and how can you use it?

Exercises:

Exercise 1

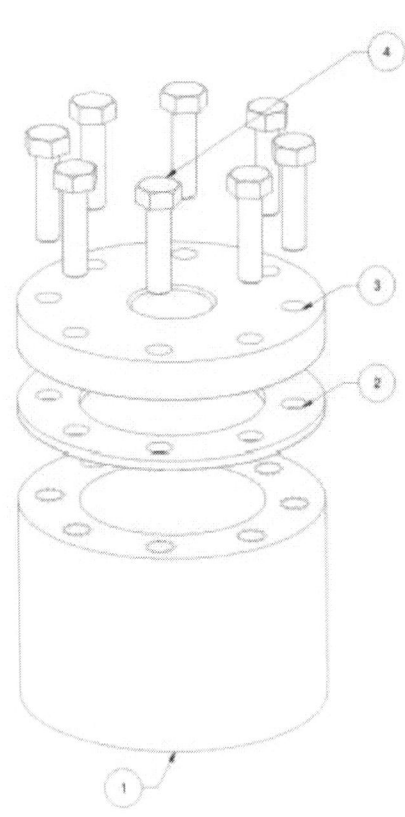

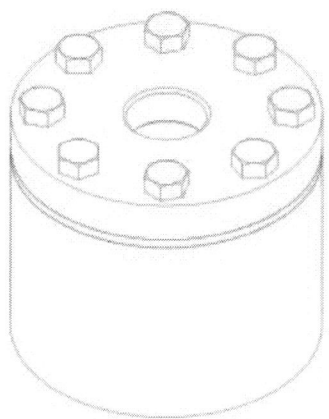

4	HEX BOLT ADJMBX1.25X30	8
3	COVER PLATE	1
2	GASKET	1
1	CYLINDER BASE	1
PC NO	PART NAME	QTY

Creating Assemblies

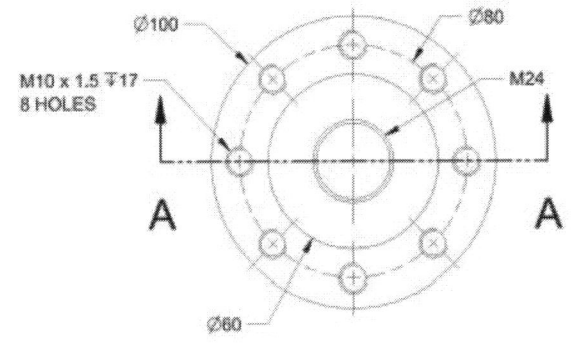
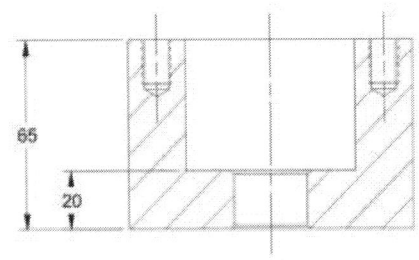

Cylinder Base

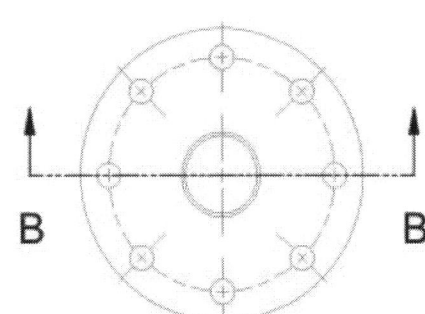
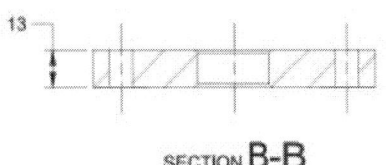

Cover Plate

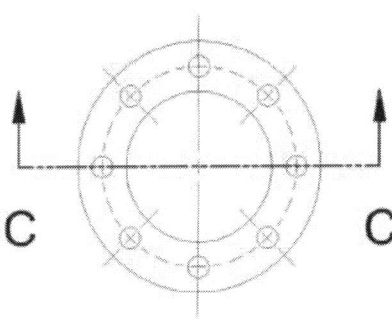

Gasket

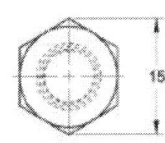
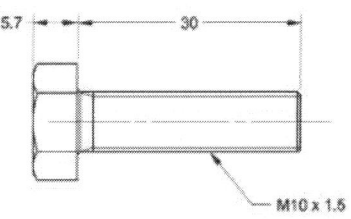

Screw

Chapter 11: Drawings and Views

Drawings are used to document your 3D models in the traditional 2D format including dimensions and other instructions useful for the manufacturing purpose. In SolidWorks, you first create 3D models and assemblies, and then use them to generate the drawing. There is a direct association between the 3D model and the drawing. When changes are made to the model, every view in the drawing will be updated. This relationship between the 3D model and the drawing makes the drawing process fast and accurate. Because of the mainstream adoption of 2D drawings of the mechanical industry, drawings are one of the three main file types you can create in SolidWorks.

The topics covered in this chapter are:

- Starting a Drawing
- Drawing Sheet Selection
- Edit Sheet Size
- Generating standard views
- Generating Model Views
- Projected view
- Auxiliary view
- Section View
- Detail View
- Broken Out Section view
- Break
- Generating the Drawing view of an Exploded Assembly
- Generating Bill of Material
- Adding Balloons
- Customize the Title Block
- Applying Dimensions to the Drawing View
- Generate Dimensions of the Drawing View

Starting a Drawing in SolidWorks 2021

To start a drawing in SolidWorks 2021:

- Click on the **New** button from the menu bar to display the **New SOLIDWORKS Document** dialog box, as shown.
- Next double click on the **Drawing** button of the dialog box to enter in the Drawing environment and display the **Sheet Format/Size** dialog box, as shown.

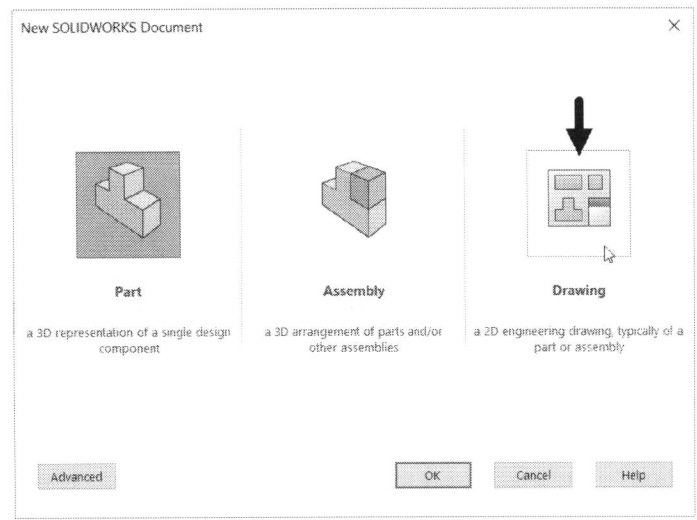

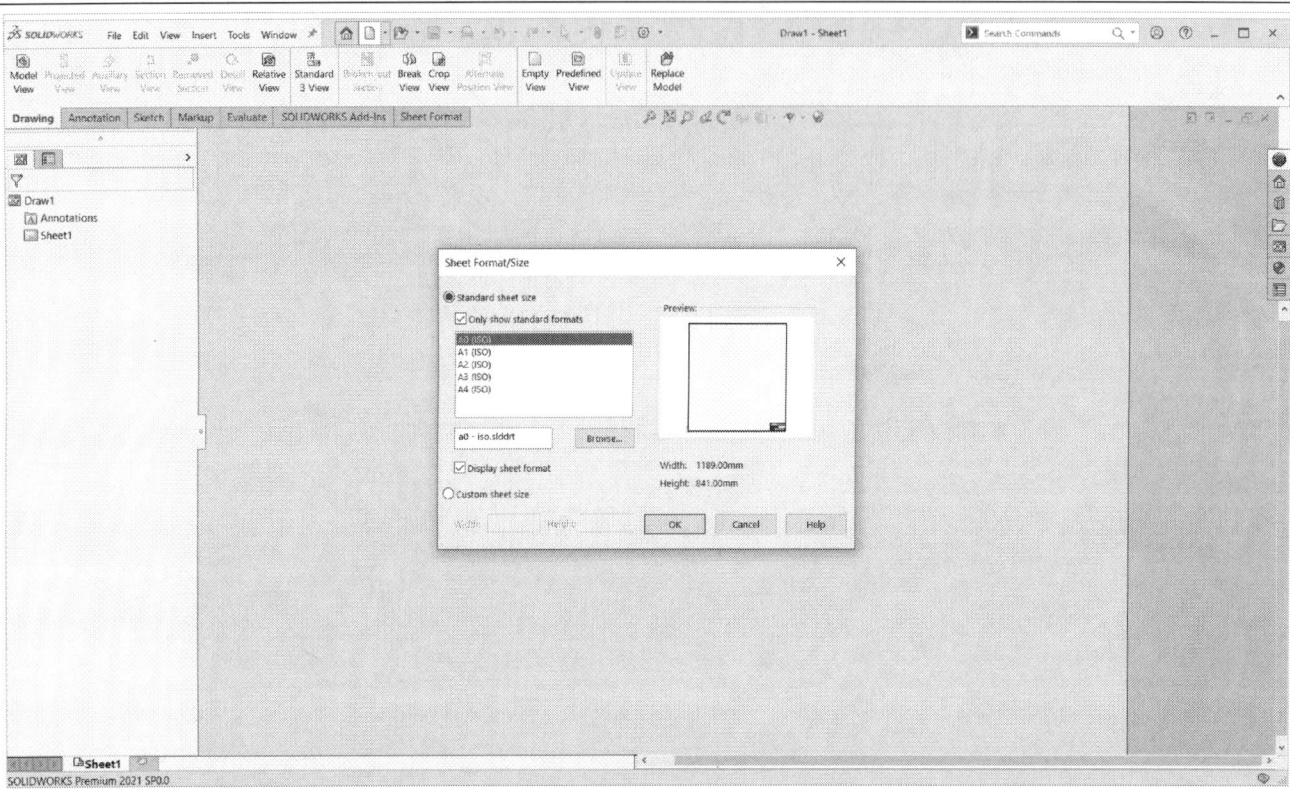

Note: If you have started SolidWorks recently then **Welcome – SolidWorks 2021** dialog box get displayed automatically, as shown. You can simply click on the **Drawing** button to enter in the Drawing Environment, as shown.

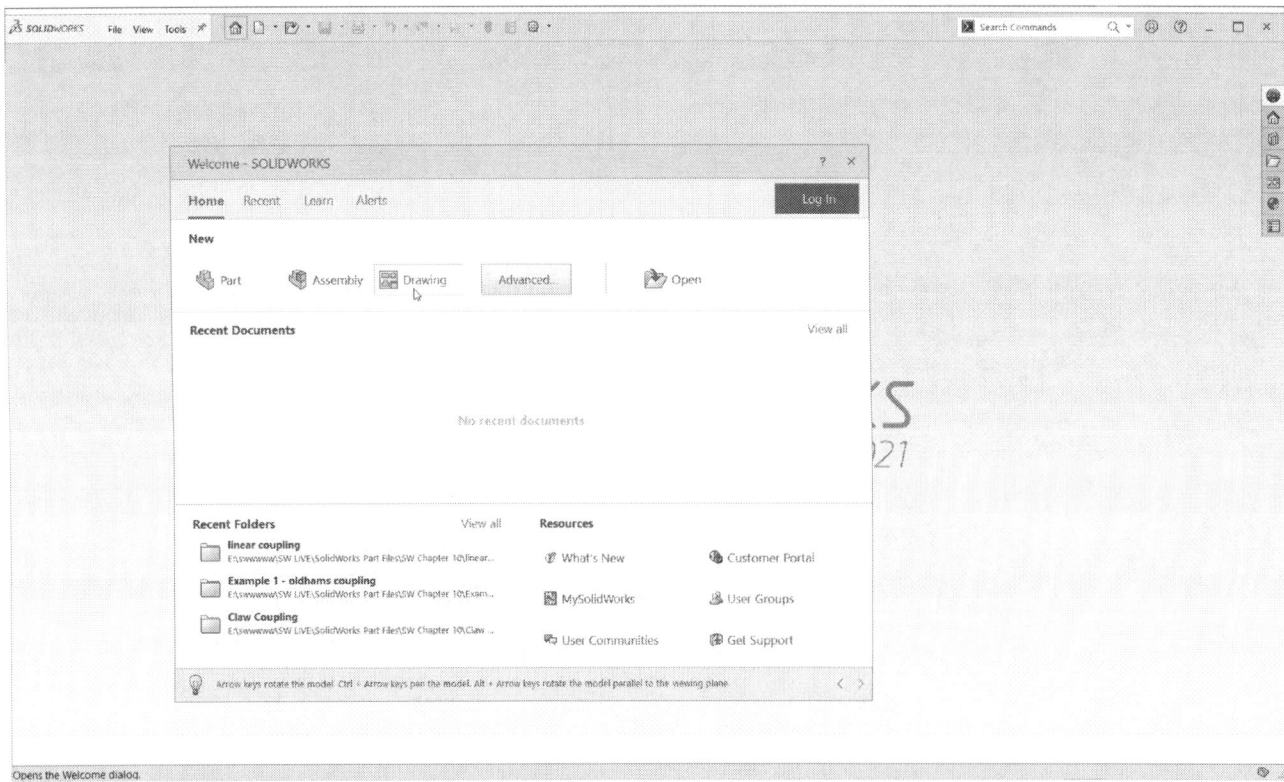

Tip: You can click on the Home button from the **Quick Access toolbar** to display the **Welcome – SolidWorks 2021** dialog box any time.

➢ Next, click on the **OK** button of the **Sheet Format/Size** dialog box to display the drawing sheet in Drawing Environment with **Model View** dialog box, as shown.

Note that you can insert and generate drawing views of a model by using **Model View** dialog box, displayed by default. And the procedure to use it is discussed further in this chapter.

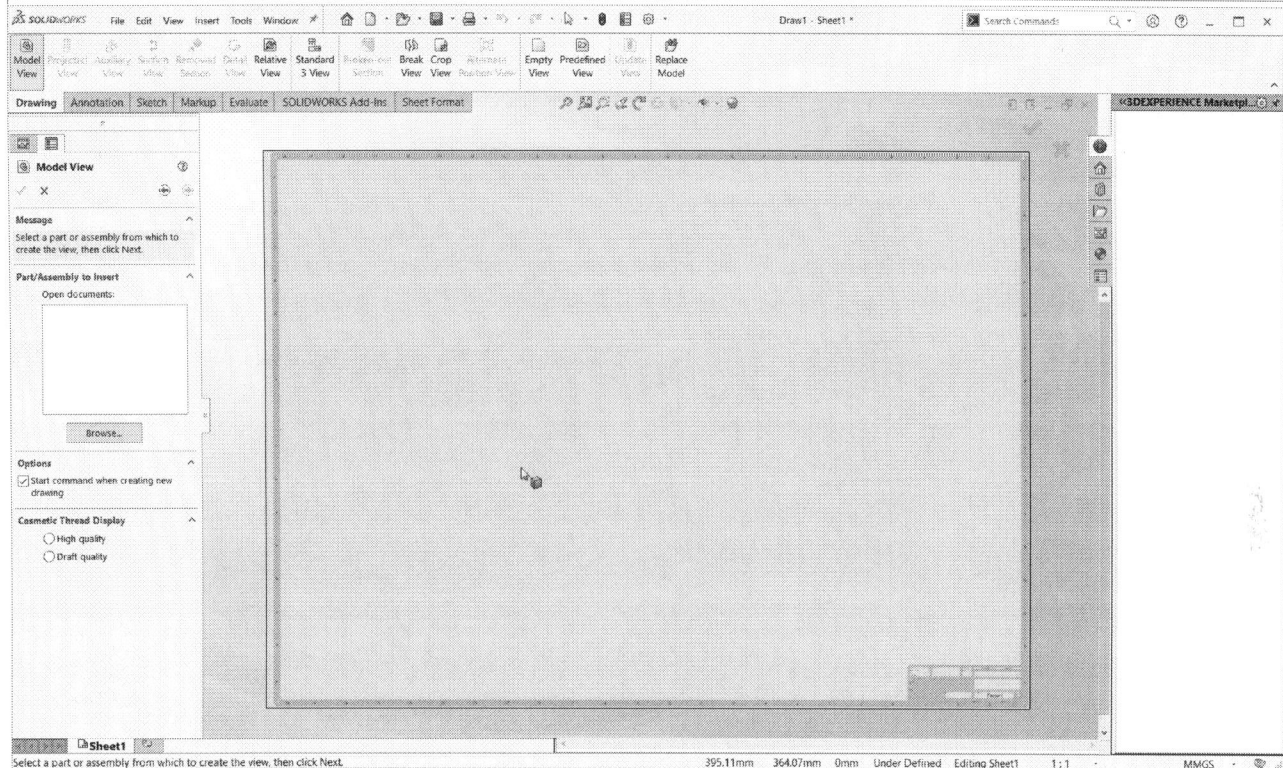

Drawing Sheet Selection

After entering the Drawing Environment, the **Sheet Format/Size** dialog box get displayed automatically, as shown above.

➢ Double click on the required drawing template file of the dialog box to start a new drawing file with **Model View PropertyManager** displayed, as shown.

Note that by default the **Sheet Format/Size** dialog box with standard sheet size formats only get displayed, as shown. You can deselect the **Only show standard formats** checkbox to display all sheet size formats, as shown.

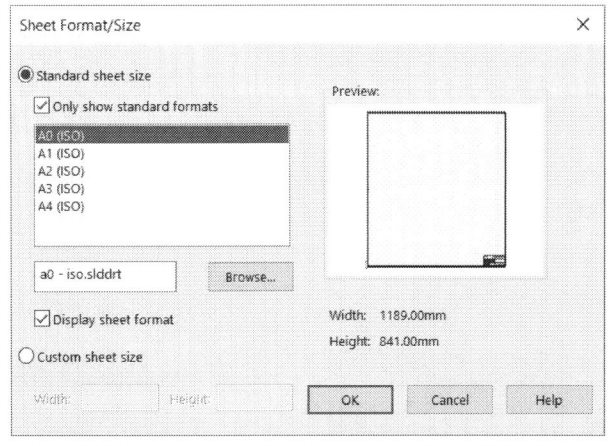
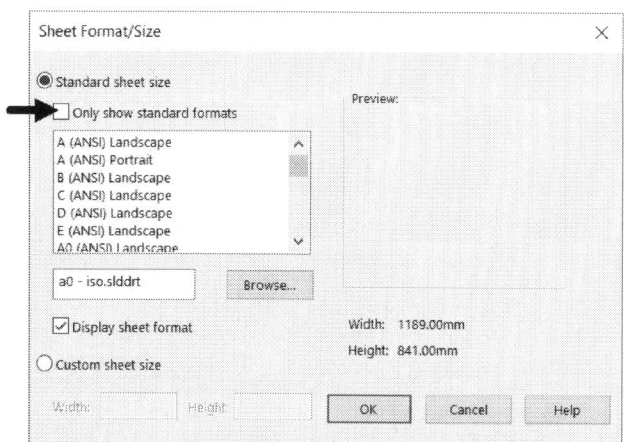

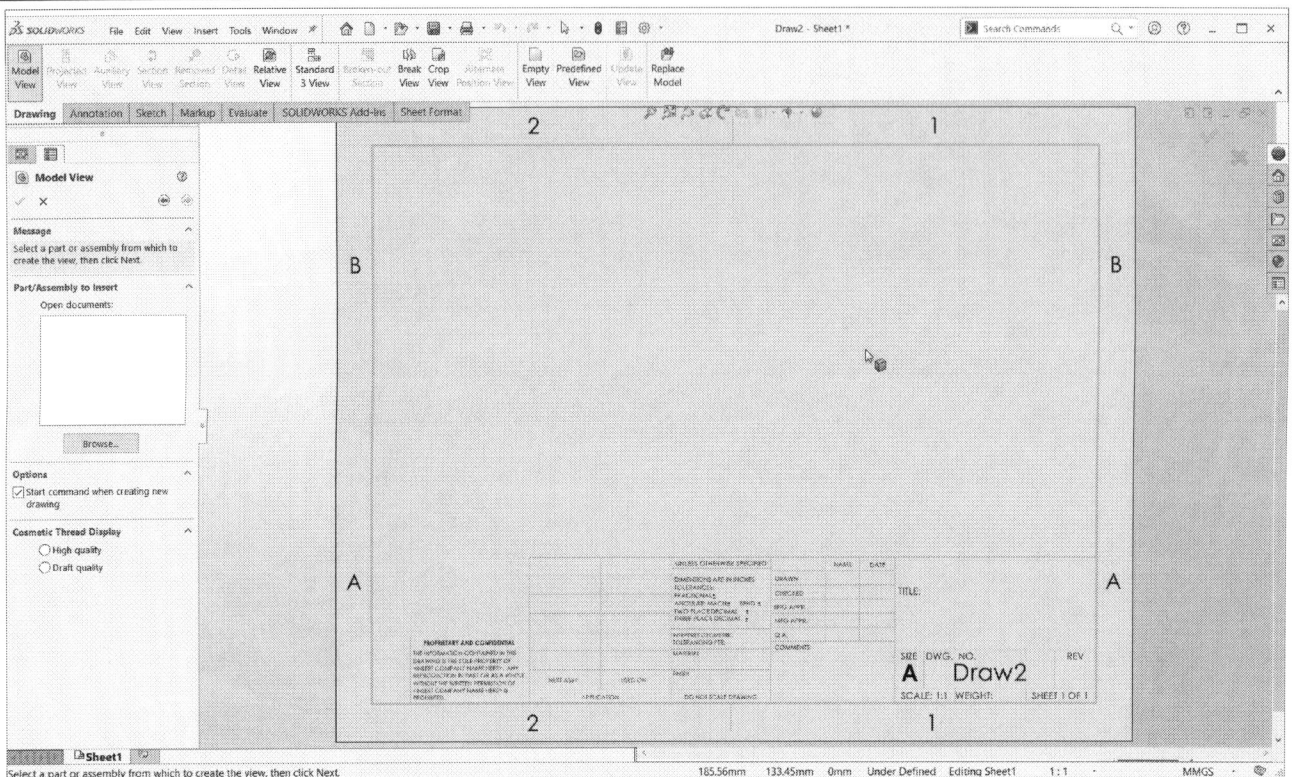

Edit Sheet Size

To edit the sheet size:

> ➤ Right click on the **Sheet** tab at the bottom of drawing area to display the shortcut menu, as shown.
> ➤ Select the **Properties** option to display the **Sheet Properties** dialog box, as shown.
> ➤ Next select the required sheet size and other required options from the dialog box, as shown.
> ➤ You can also customize the sheet size by selecting the **Custom sheet size** radio button of the dialog box and enter the required values in their respective edit boxes, as shown.
> ➤ Next, you can click on the **Apply Changes** button to exit the dialog box and apply changes, as shown.

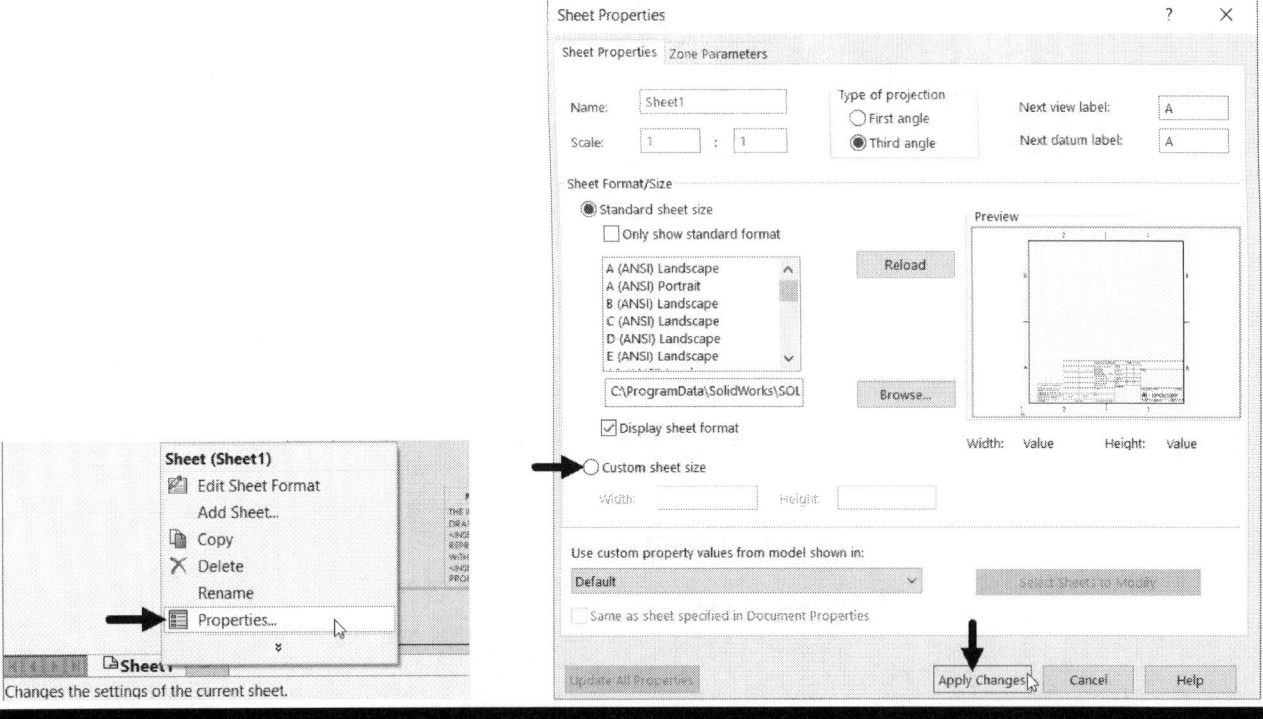

Creating a Drawing from any Opened Part or Assembly

You can start a new drawing file when the part file or the assembly file of which you want to generate the drawing views is already opened in another window.

> Click on the **New > New Drawing Part/Assembly** option from the **Quick Access toolbar** to display the Drawing Environment with **Sheet Format/Size** dialog box, as shown.

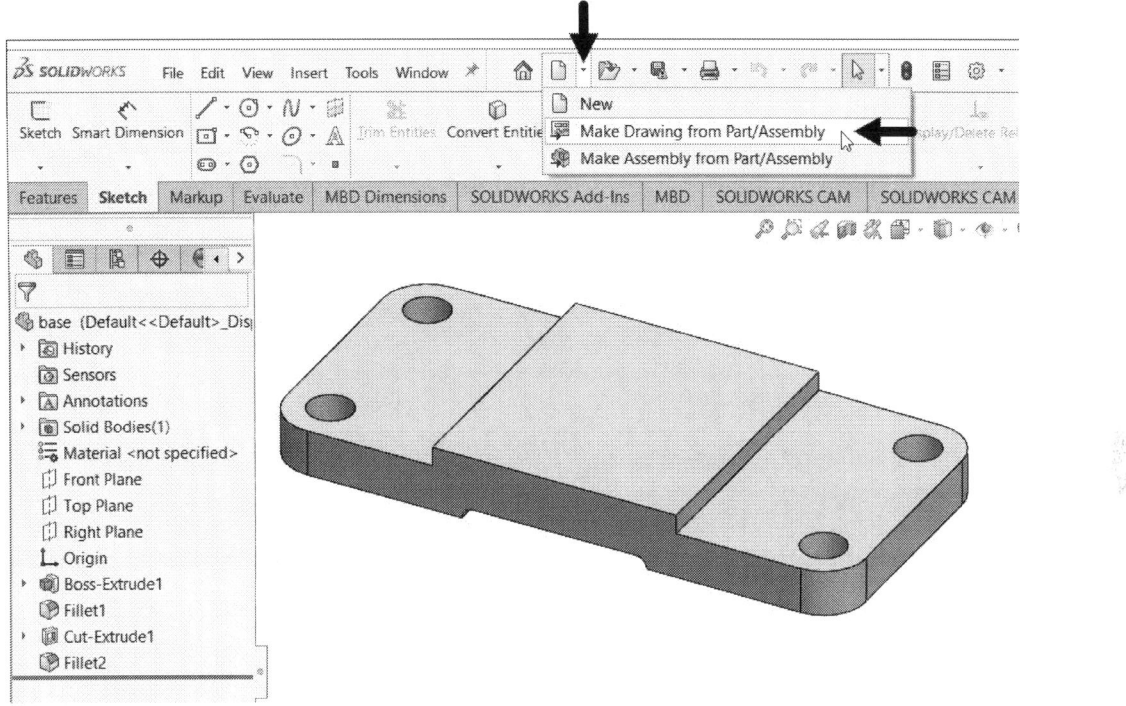

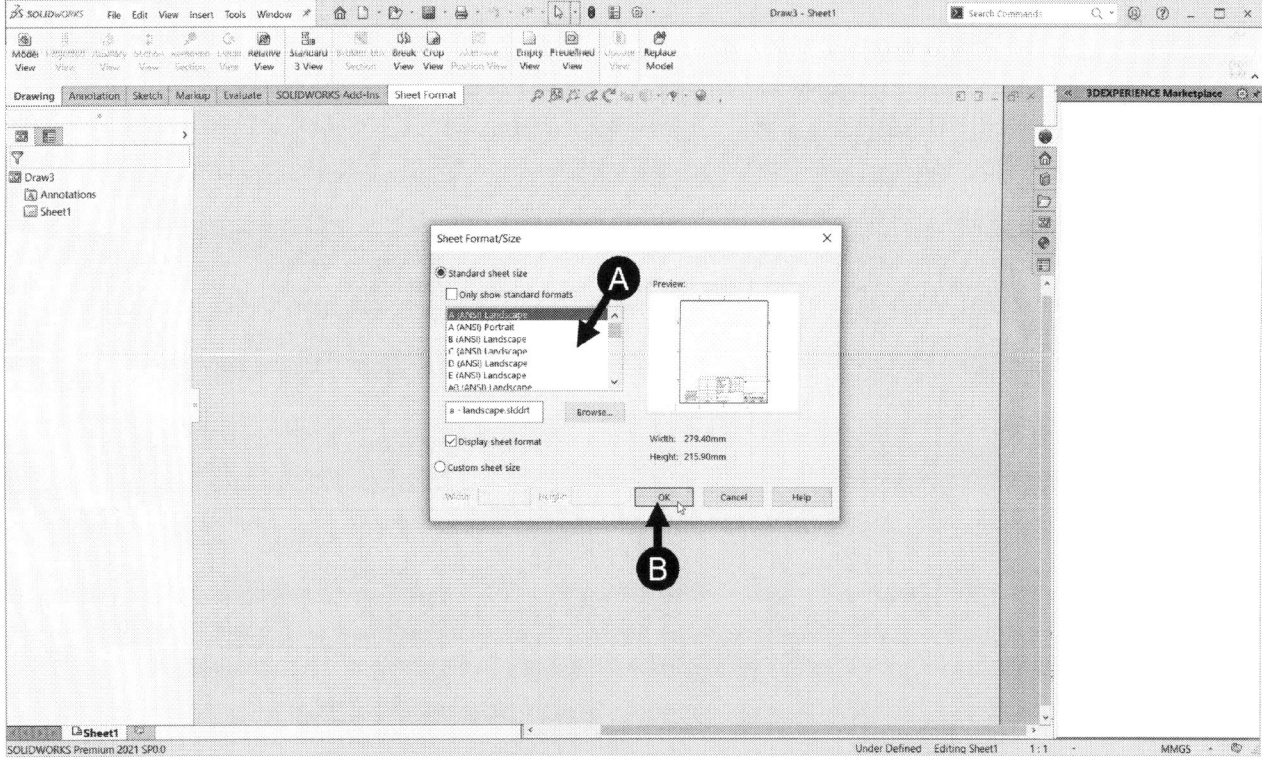

> Select the required sheet format from the **Sheet Format/Size** dialog box, as shown above.
> Next, press on the **OK** button to display the drawing sheet with **View Palette** task pane, as shown.

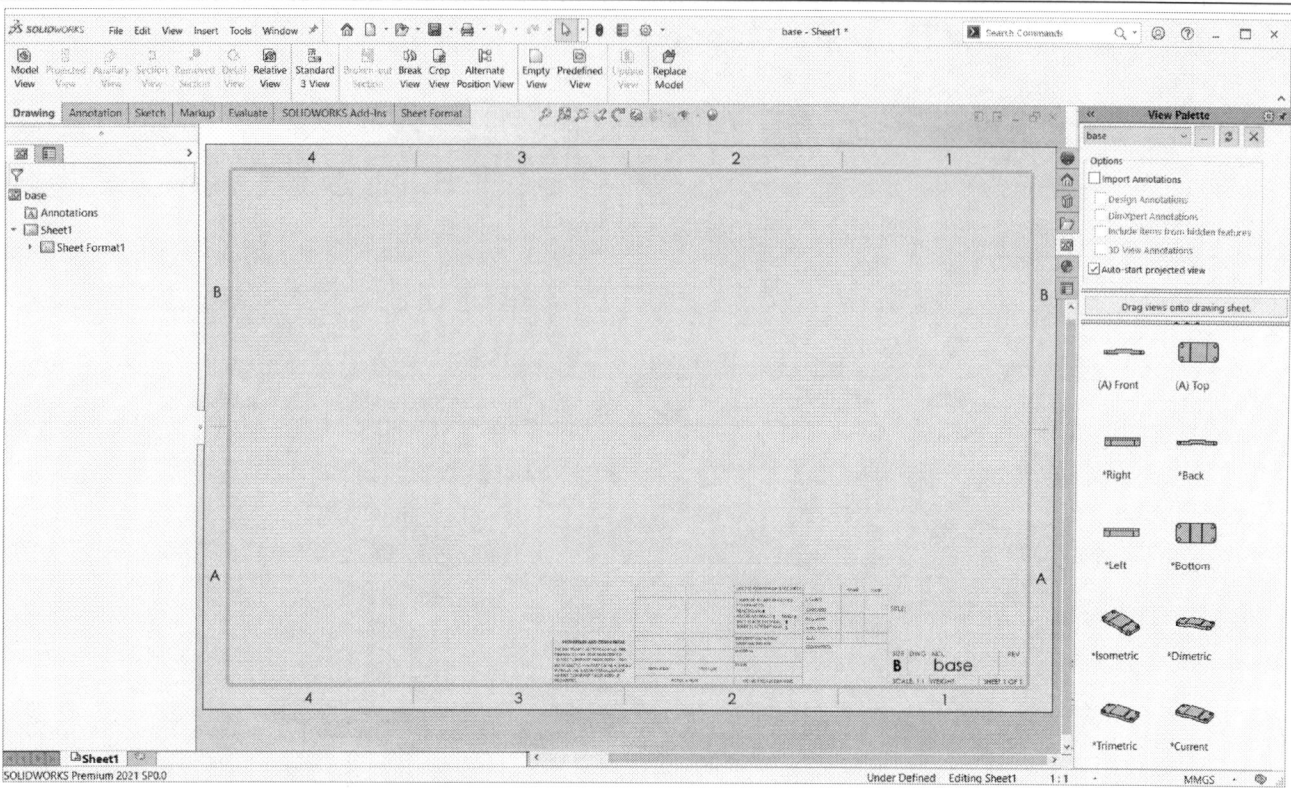

➢ Now you can simply drag the required view from the **View Palette** task pane and place it in the drawing sheet, as shown.

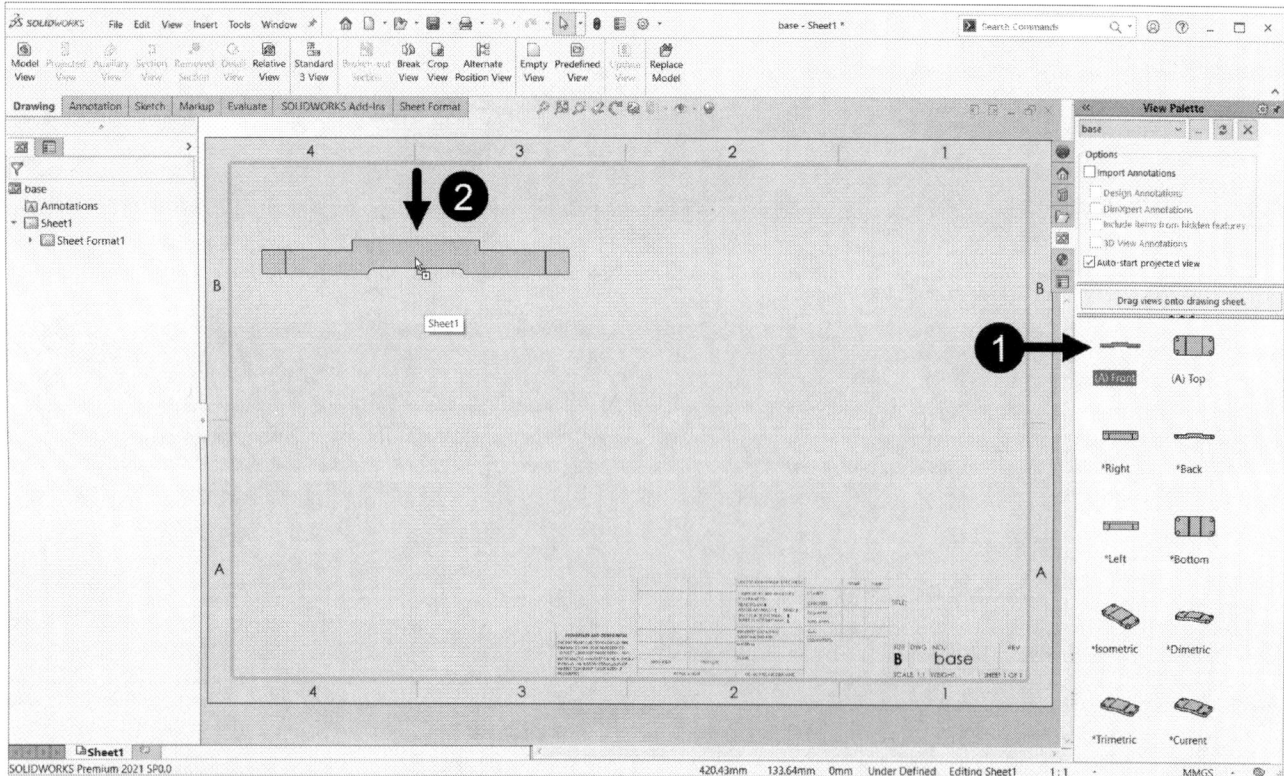

➢ After placing any required view, the **Projected View** dialog box get displayed. Also, you can place other projected views by moving the cursor and clicking at the respective locations, as shown.

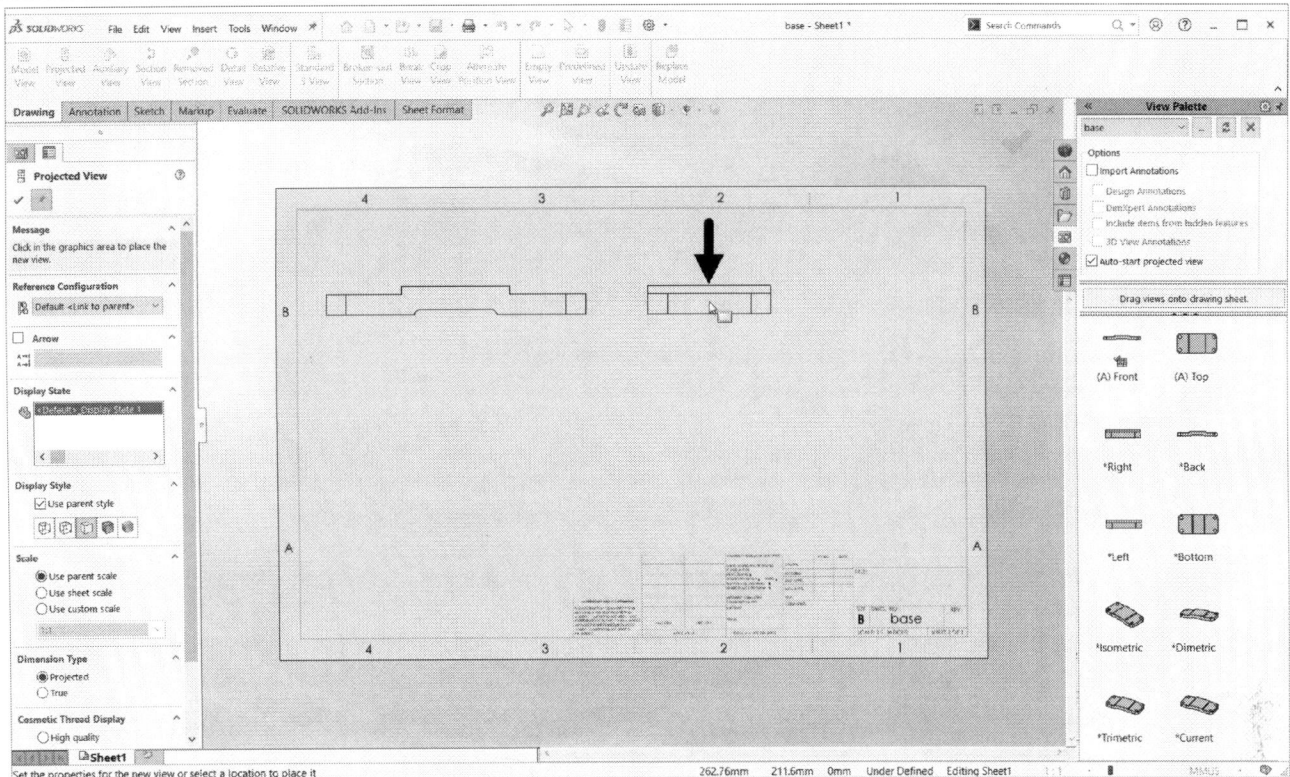

Generating Standard Views

The **Standard 3 View** tool is used to generate standard views i.e. Top, Front, and Side view of a 3D model or assembly in the drawing sheet of the Drawing Environment.

➢ Click on the **Standard 3 View** button from the **View Layout CommandManager** to display the **Standard 3 View** PropertyManager, as shown.
➢ Click on the **Browse** button of the PropertyManger to display the **Open** window, as shown.
➢ Browse to the required file and double click on it to generate it's all standard views in the drawing sheet automatically, as shown.

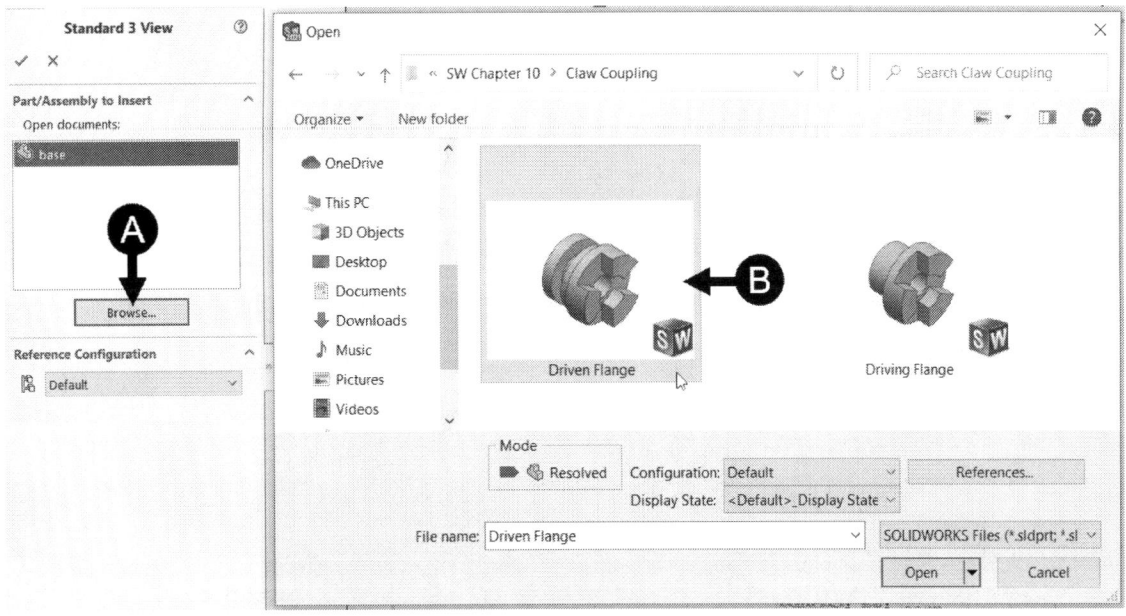

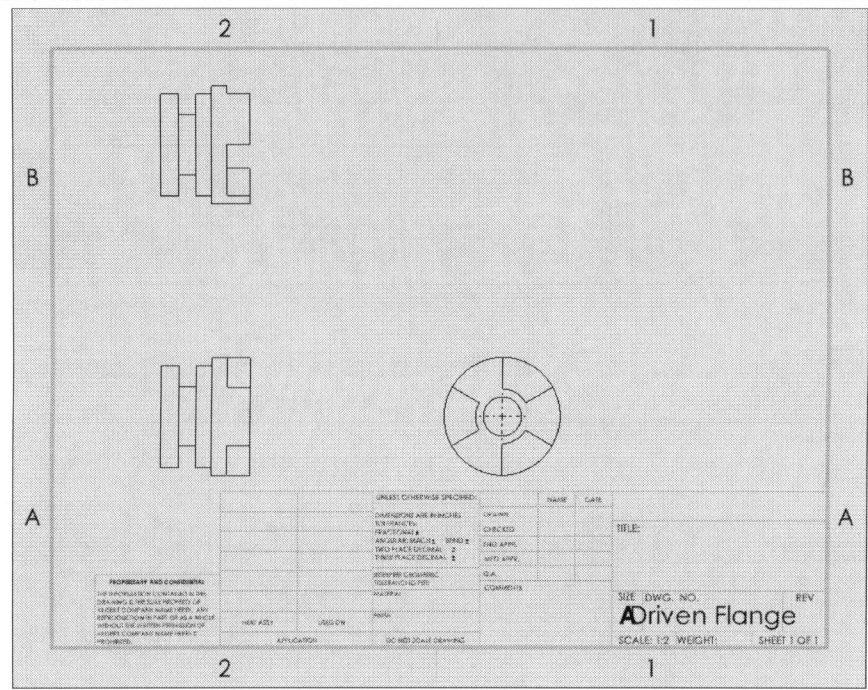

- To change properties of any view, click on it to display the **Drawing View PropertyManager**, as shown.
- Next, select the required options from the PropertyManager, as shown

  The options in this PropertyManager are discussed further in this chapter.

To move or change the locations of the views in the drawing sheet, you can select the main view and drag the cursor, the other views will also move accordingly, as shown. The other two views can be moved in only one direction if you move them separately.

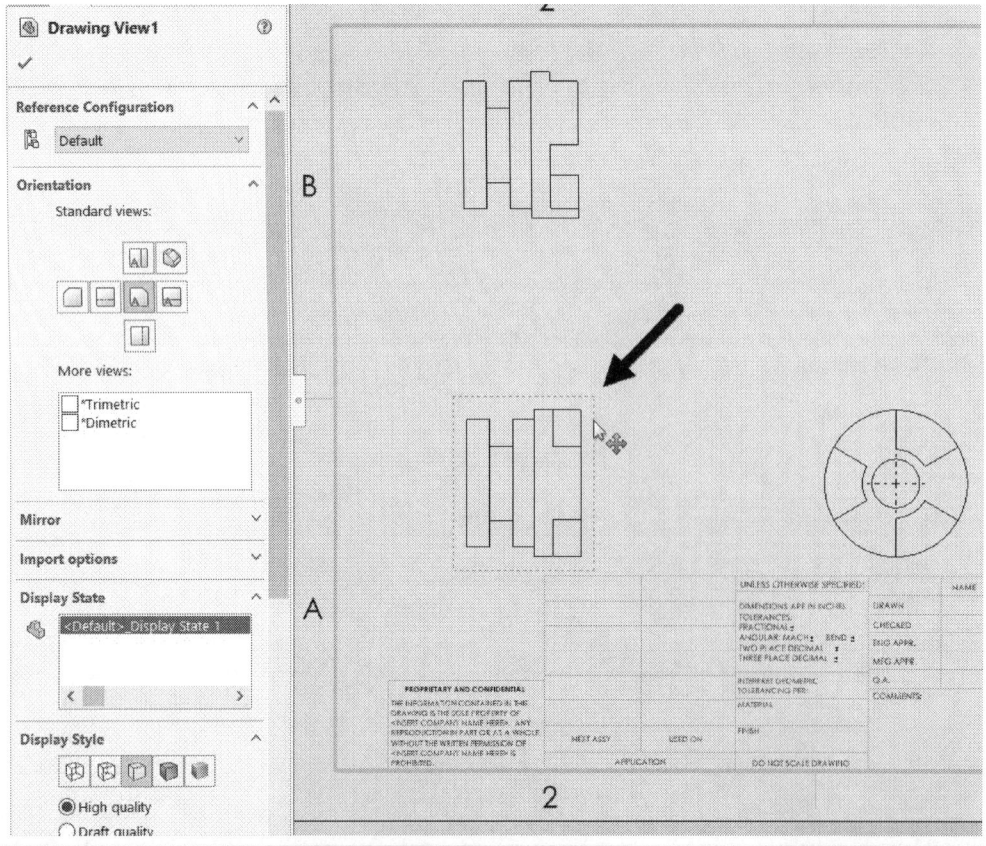

Generating Model View

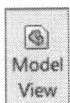

The **Model View** tool is used to create the first or base view in the drawing sheet of the Drawing Environment. You can then generate other projection views from it.

> Click on the **Model View** button from the **View Layout CommandManager** to display the **Model View PropertyManager**, as shown.
> Click on the **Browse** button of the PropertyManger to display the **Open** window, as shown.
> Browse to the required file from the **Open** window and double click on it to generate its base view, as shown.

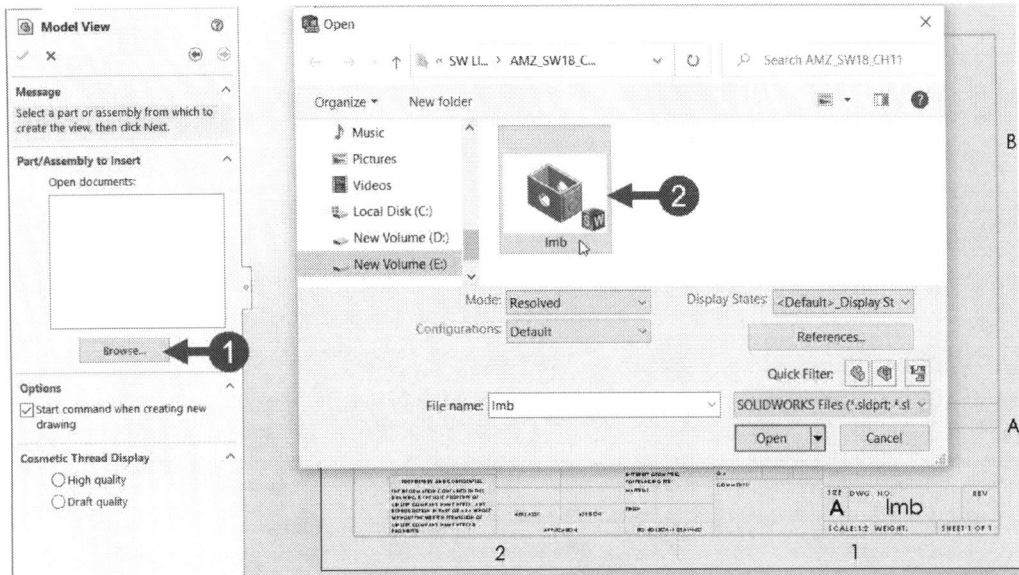

> You can click in the drawing sheet to place the base view, as shown.

  Note that if you select the **Preview** check box of the **Model View PropertyManager**, then the preview of the selected file gets visible.

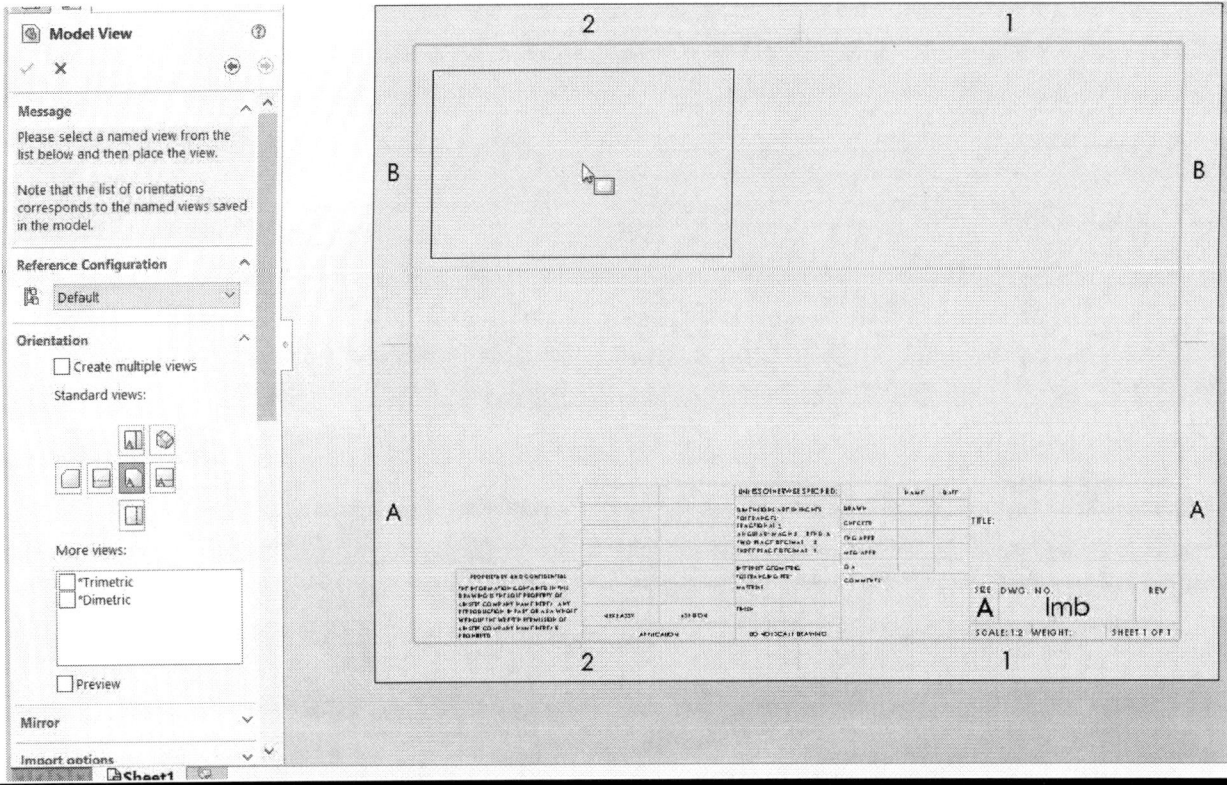

Drawings and Views

You can select the required orientation, display style and other parameters from the PropertyManager. Some of them are discussed next.

To change Orientation of Drawing View (View Type)

To change the view orientation of the drawing view:

➢ Select the required button under **Orientation** rollout to change view orientation, as shown.
➢ Select the **Preview** checkbox to display the preview of view selected, as shown.

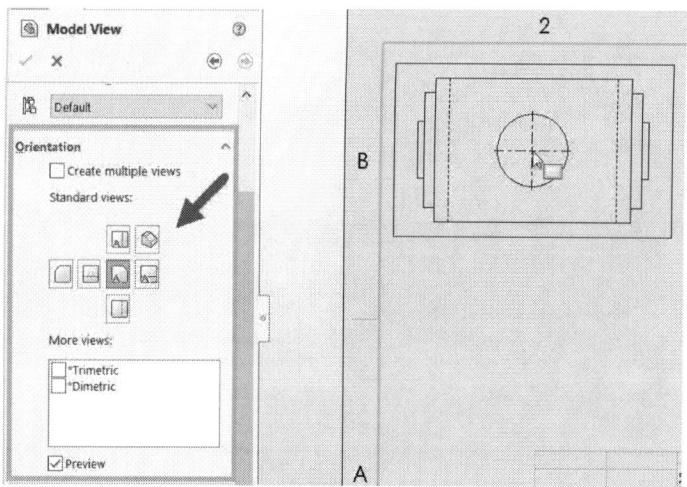

To change Display Style

To change the display style of the drawing view, select the required button under **Display Style** rollout, as shown.

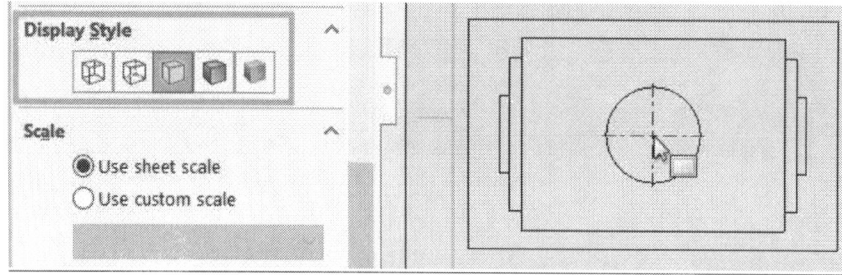

To change Scale value

To change the scale value (size) of the drawing view:

➢ Select the **Use custom scale** radio button under **Scale** rollout, as shown.
➢ Next, select the required option from the dropdown list under it, as shown.

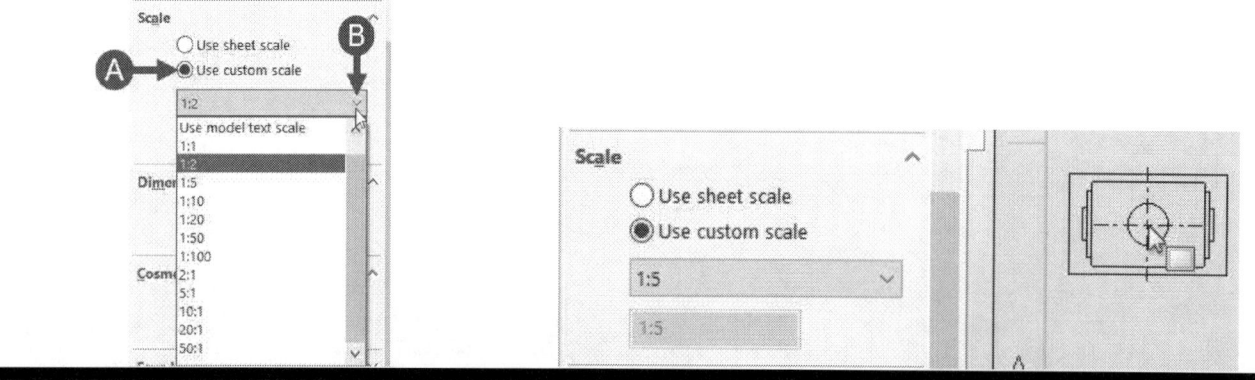

Projected view

After creating the base view in the drawing sheet of drawing environment, you can generate different Orthographic/projection views from it. To generate the projection views from the base view, follow the steps:

- Click on the **Projected View** button from the **View Layout CommandManager** to display the **Projected View PropertyManger**, as shown.
- Move the cursor upto some distance from the model in the drawing sheet to display the projected view, as shown.
- Next, click at the required loclation in the drawing sheet to place the projected view generated, as shown.

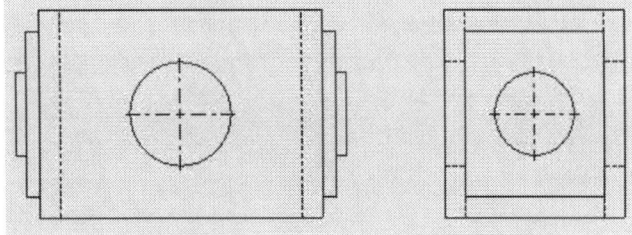

Similarly you can generate other projected views in the drawing sheet also, as shown.

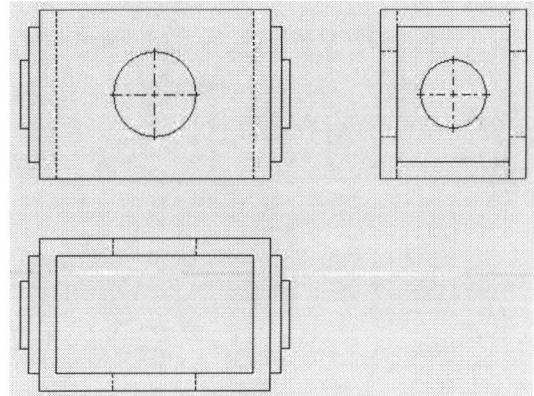

To change display style of any of the projected view.

- Click over the required projected view to display **Drawing View** PropertyManager, as shown.
- Select the required option from the **Display Style** rollout, as shown.

  Similarly you can make other changes to the drawing views also, if required.

- Click on the ✓ **Close dialog** button of the PropertyManager to apply changes and exit it.

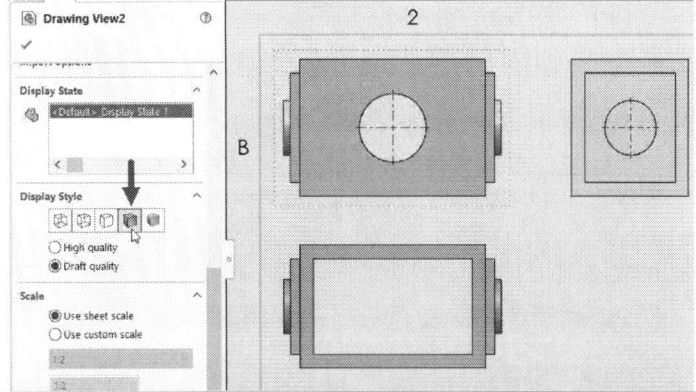

Drawings and Views

Auxiliary view

To display the Auxiliary view of the drawing view.

➢ Click on the **Auxiliary View** button from the **View Layout CommandManager** to display the **Auxiliary View PropertyManger**, as shown.
➢ Click on the inclined line from the drawing view to display preview of Auxiliary view, as shown.
➢ Selected the required options from the PropertyManager.
➢ Move the cursor up to some distance in inclined direction to place the Auxiliary view generated, as shown.
➢ Click on the ✓ **Close dialog** button of the PropertyManager to exit it.

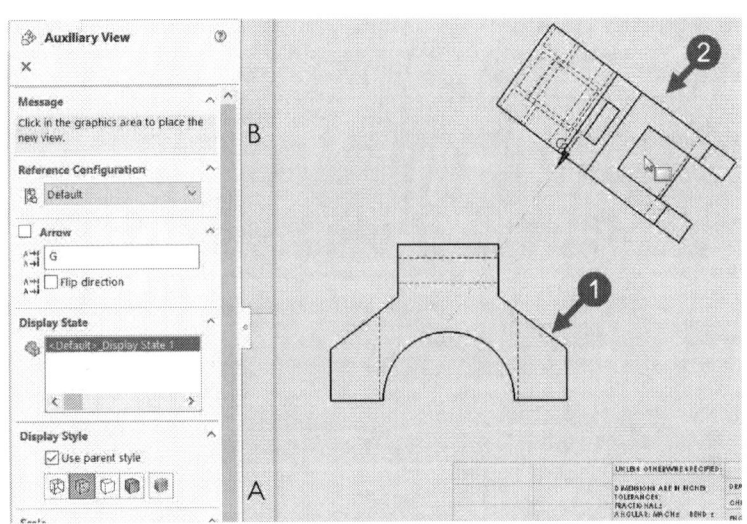
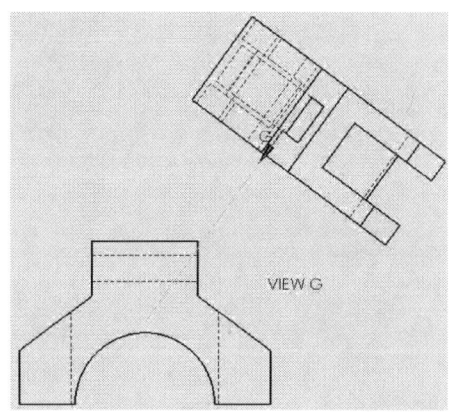

Section View

This tool is used to create section view of the drawing view by cutting it with the section line or section plane.

➢ Click on the **Section View** button from the **View Layout CommandManager** to display the **Section View Assist PropertyManger**, as shown.
➢ Click on the required button under **Cutting Line** rollout of the PropertyManager, as shown.
➢ Next click to define the position of the cutting line, as shown.
➢ Now, click on the **OK** button of the toolbar displayed, as shown.
➢ Move the cursor up to some distance and click to place the generated section view, as shown.
➢ Click on the ✓ **Close dialog** button of the PropertyManager to exit it.

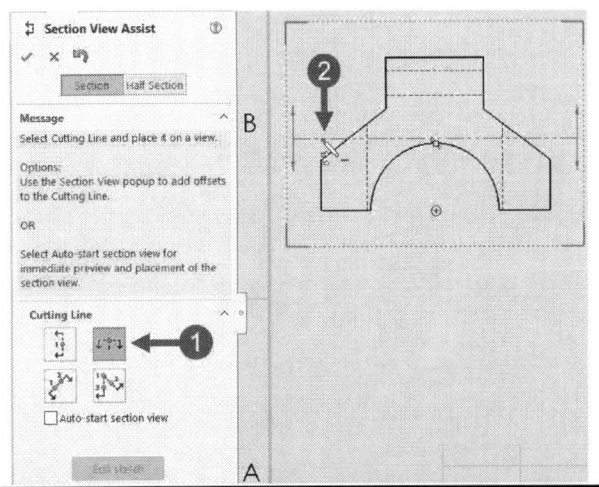
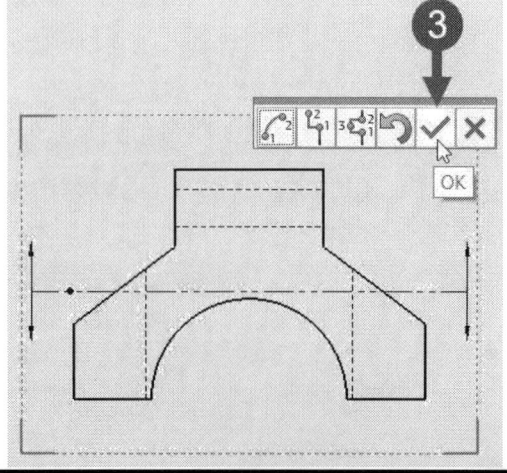

Drawings and Views

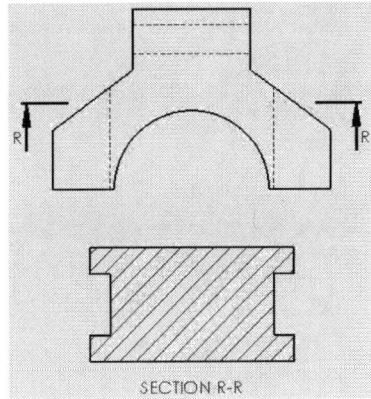

Detail view

This tool is used to enlarge a portion of a drawing view or entire drawing view contaning features which are difficult to see, you can use detailed view to zoom it. To generate the detailed view of any existing drawing view.

➤ Click on the **Detail View** button from the **View Layout CommandManager** to display the **Detail View PropertyManger**, as shown.
➤ Click on the drawing view to define center point.
➤ Move the cursor up to some distance and click to define diameter of circle and display the preview of generated detailed view, as shown.
➤ Next move the cursor up to some distance and place the generated detailed view, as shown.

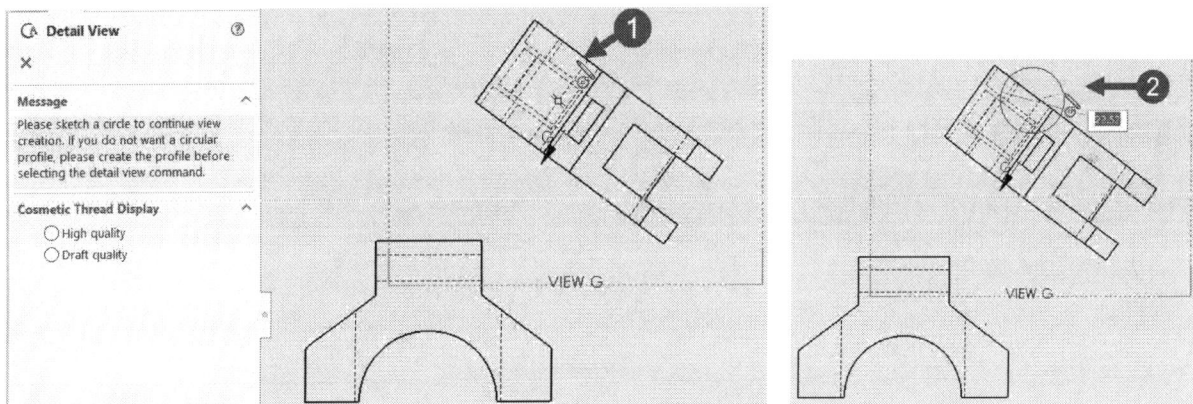

➤ Select the required options from the PropertyManager if required, as shown.

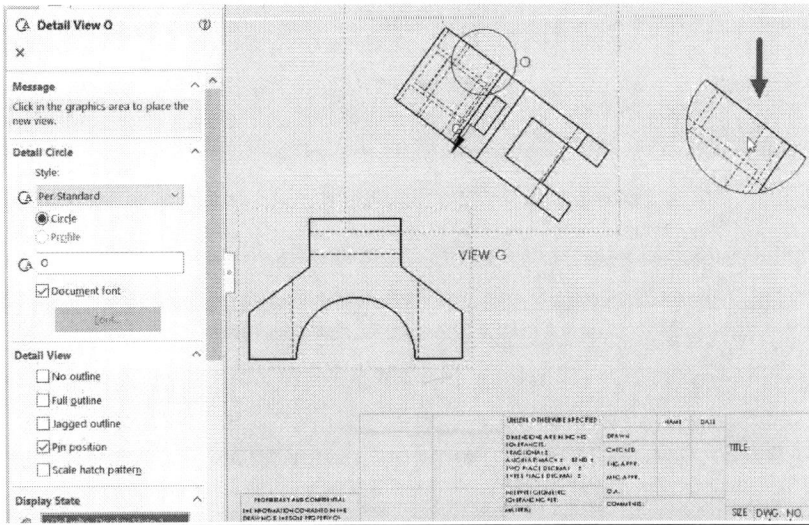

Drawings and Views

11-13

➤ Click on the ✓ **Close dialog** button of the PropertyManager to exit it.

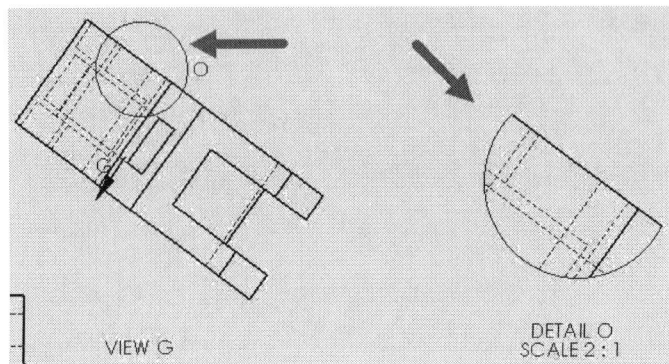

 Broken-out Section

To create a broken out section of a view:

➤ Click on the **Broken-out Section** button from the **View Layout CommandManager** to activate it.
➤ Draw a spline over required portion of the view, as shown.
➤ Next click on the **OK** button of the **Broken-out Section PropertyManger** to exit it and display the broken-out section of the view, as shown.

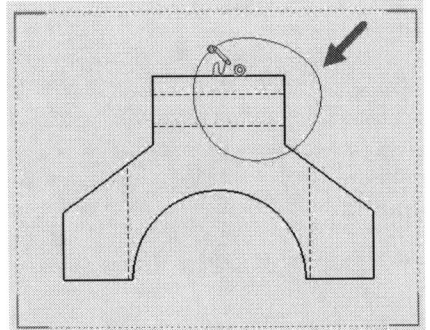 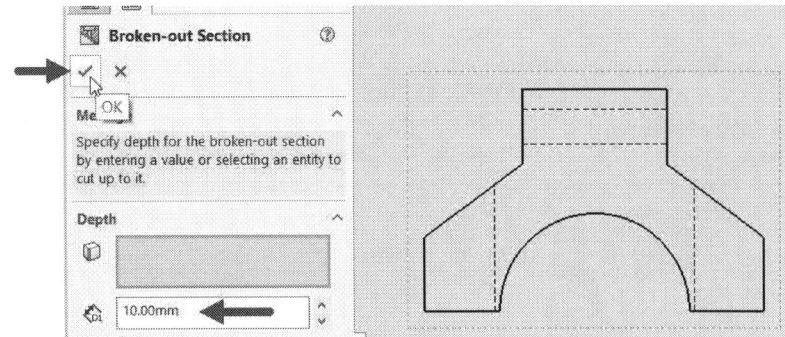

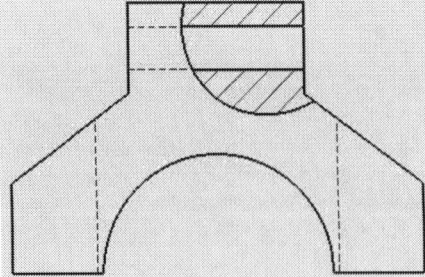

 Break

This tool is used to remove some portion of view whose length to width ratio will be very high and display it.

➤ Click on the **Break** button from the **View Layout CommandManager** to activate it and display the **Break View PropertyManager**, as shown.
➤ Select the required options and enter required value in the PropertyManager, as shown.
➤ Click to define two break lines with the required gap between each other, as shown.
➤ Next click on the **OK** button of the **Broken-out Section PropertyManger** to exit it and display the broken-out section of the view, as shown.

Drawings and Views 11-14

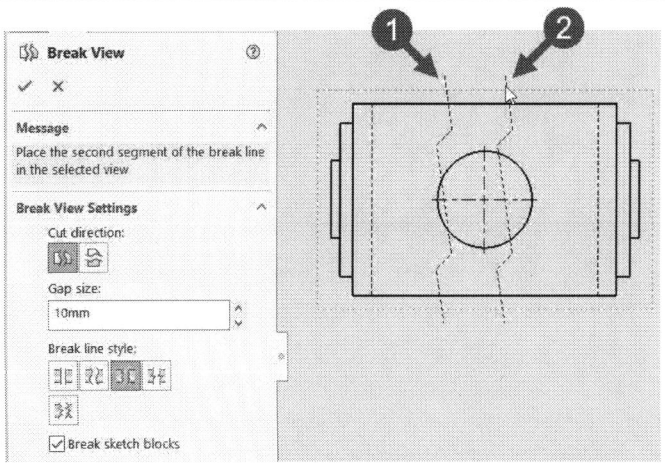 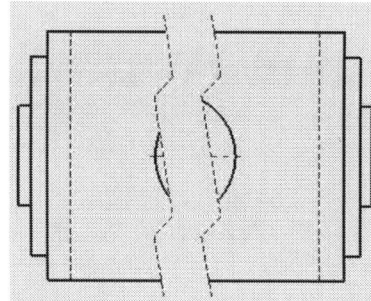

Generating the Drawing View of an Exploded Assembly

To generate the drawing view of an exploded assembly.

➢ Import an assembly file in the drawing sheet in isometric view as discussed earlier, as shown.
➢ Right click on it to display the shortcut menu, as shown.
➢ Select the **Show In Exploded State** option from the shortcut menu to display its exploded view, as shown.

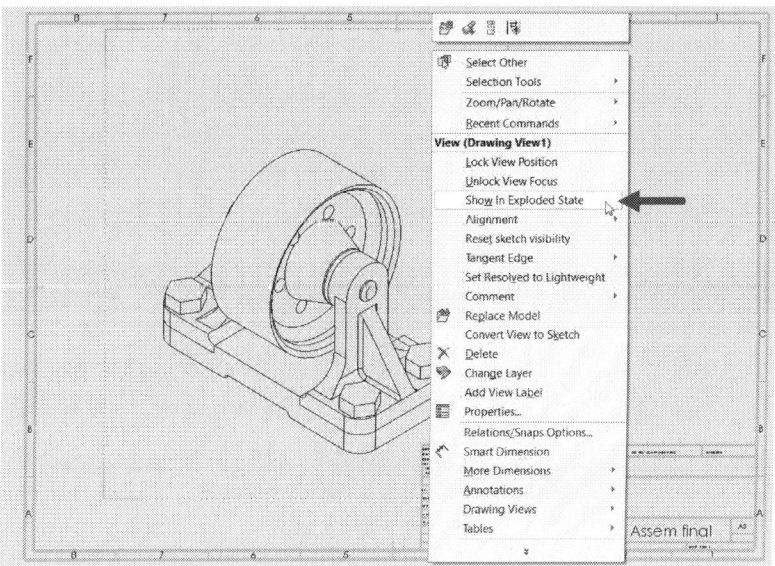 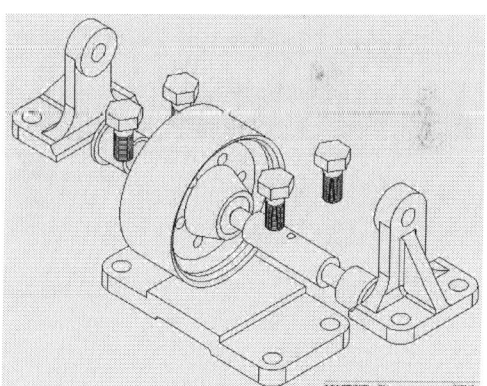

Generating Bill of Material

To generate bill of material:

➢ Click on **Tables > Bill of Materials** option from **Annotation CommandManager** to display **Bill of Materials PropertyManger**, as shown.
➢ Click on the drawing view in the drawing sheet, all options of PropertyManager get visible, as shown.
➢ Next you can select the required options of PropertyManager, if required.
➢ Click on the **OK** button of PropertyManager to exit it and display the bill of material attached with cursor, as shown.

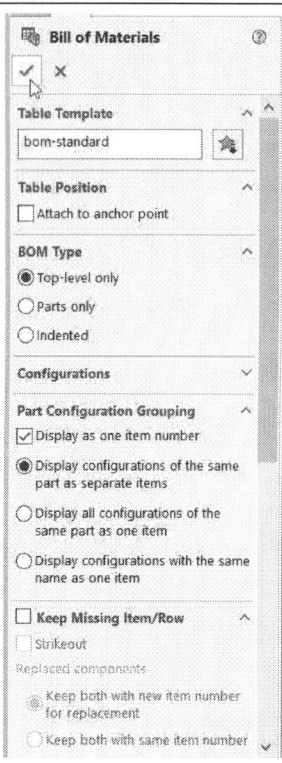

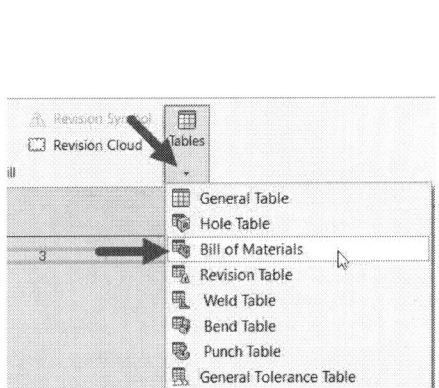
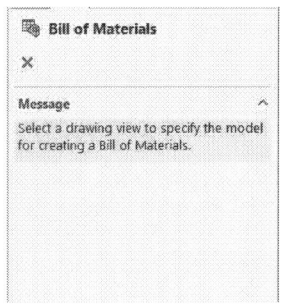

➢ Next click at the required location of drawing sheet to place it, as shown.

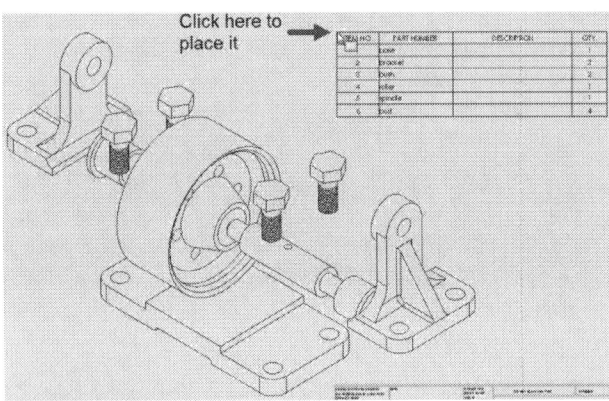
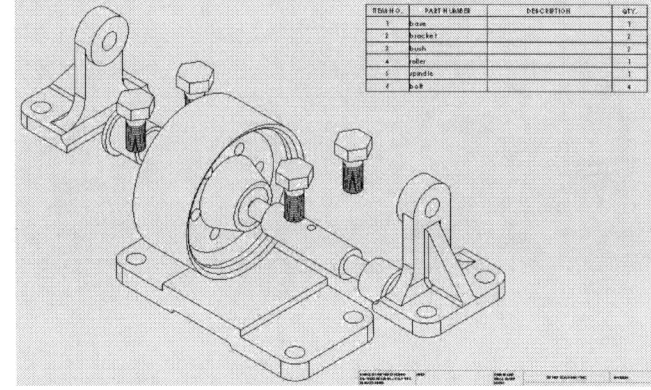

Adding Balloons

The **Balloon** tool is used to add balloons to the components available in the drawing sheet. To apply dimensions to the drawing view.

➢ Click on **Balloons** [Balloon] button of **Annotation CommandManager** to display **Balloon PropertyManger**, as shown.
➢ Select the required option and enter the required values in their respective edit boxes of the PropertyManager, as shown,
➢ Click on any component, the balloon gets attached with it, as shown.
➢ Next move the cursor up to some distance and click to place the balloon attached with it.

Drawings and Views   11-16

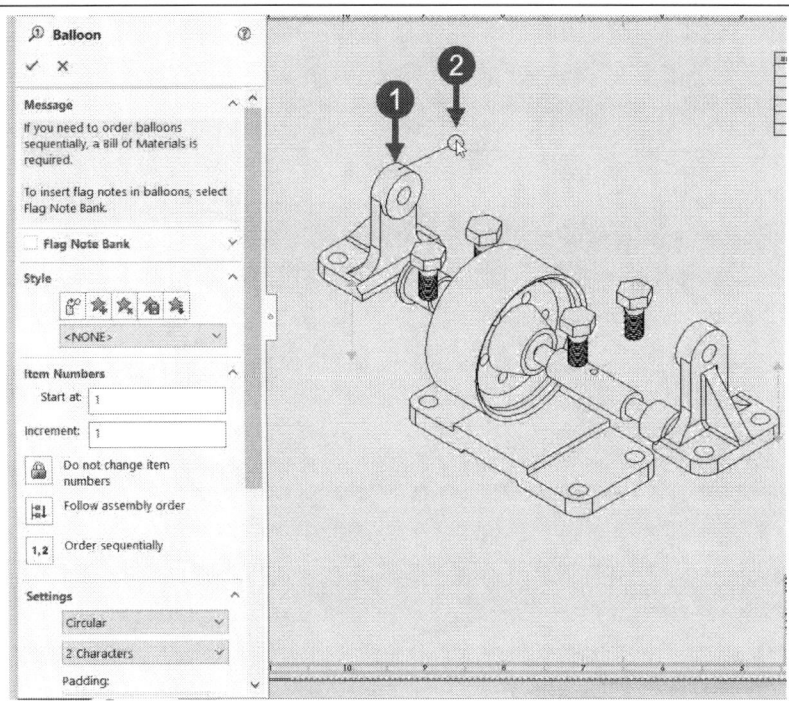
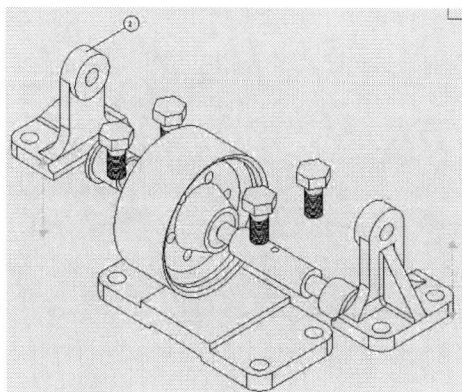

> Similarly, you can add balloons with other components also, as shown.
> Click on the **OK** button of the PropertyManager to exit it and display the balloons added, as shown.

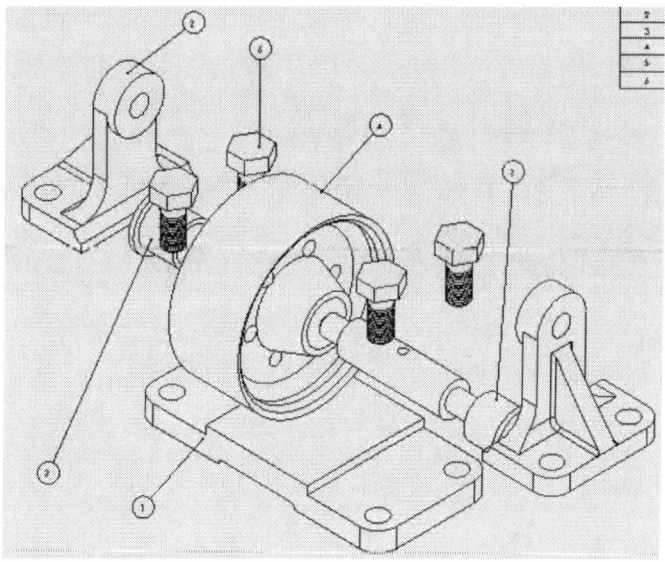

Adding Balloons Using Auto Balloon Tool

The **Auto Balloon** tool is used to add balloons to the components automatically.

> Click on **Auto Balloons** button of **Annotation CommandManager** to display **Auto Balloon PropertyManger**, as shown.
> Select the required option and enter the required values in their respective edit boxes of the PropertyManager, as shown,
> Click on the drawing view to display the preview of automatically generated balloons, as shown.
  You can still select any other option from the PropertyManager, as shown.
> Click on the **OK** button of the PropertyManager to exit it and display the automatically generated balloons added, as shown.

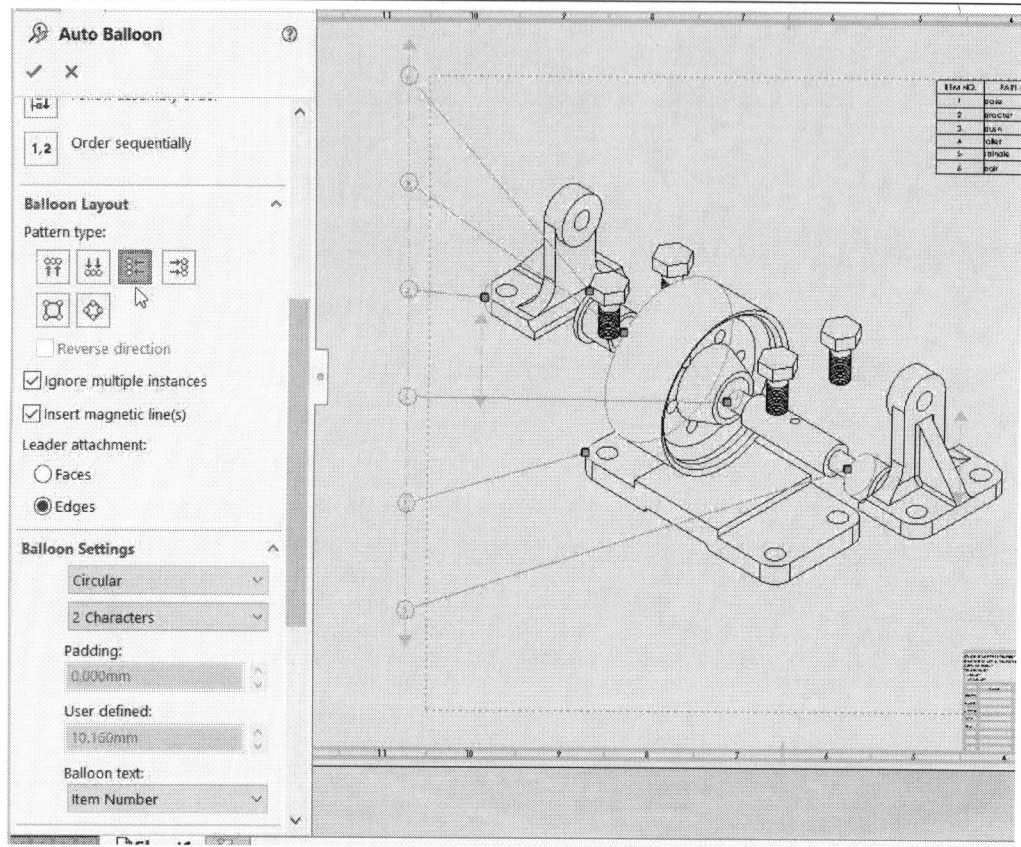

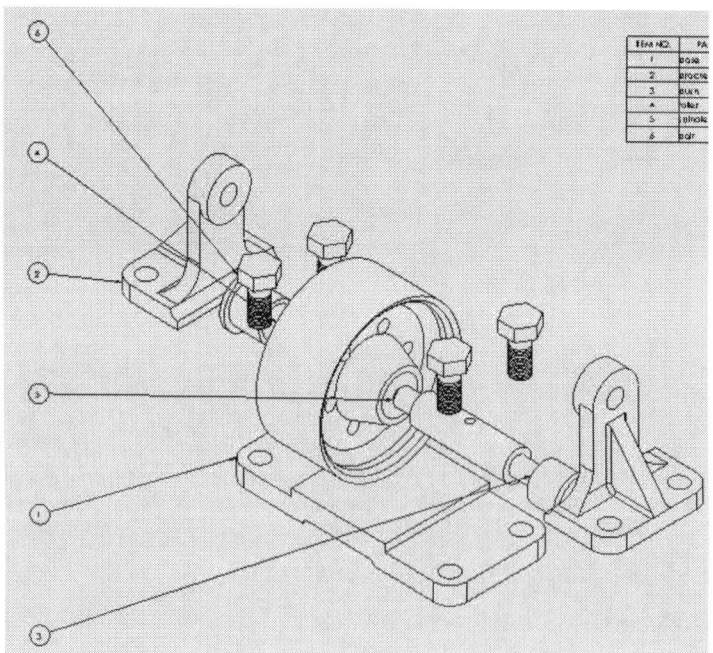

Customize the Title Block

You can edit and customize the Title Block by entering the required details or design parameters, as per your requirements.

> Right click over the **Sheet Format** from the **FeatureManager Design Tree** to display the shortcut menu, as shown.

> Select the **Edit Sheet Format** option from the shortcut menu to make the title block editable, as shown.

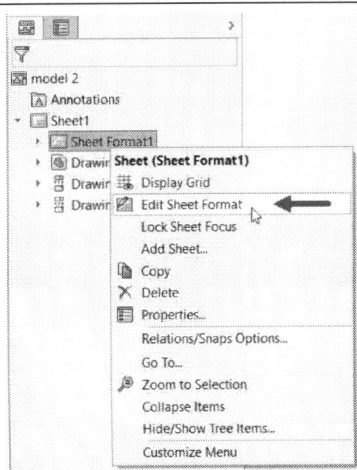
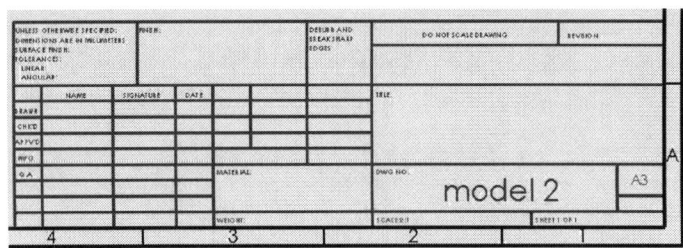

- Now double click on any box and enter the required details in it, as shown.
- Click on the **OK** button of the **Note PropertyManager** displayed, to exit it and apply the changes, as shown.

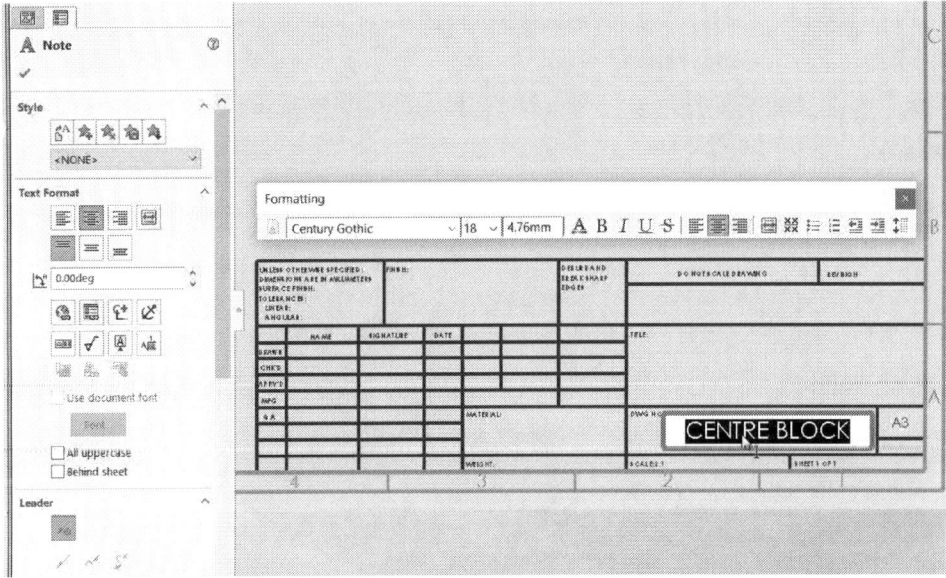

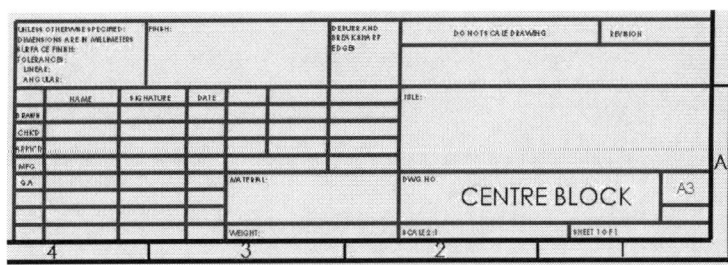

Similarly, you can edit and enter required details in other boxes of the title block also.

- To remove any unwanted line, you can simply select it and press the **Delete** key to remove it, as shown.

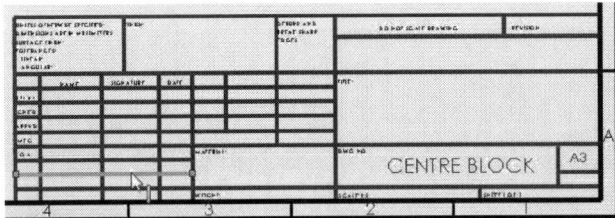
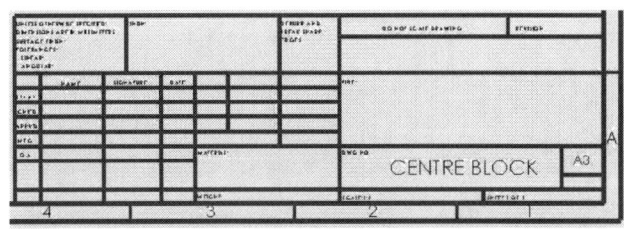

Drawings and Views

11-19

➤ Now click on the **Return** button on the top right corner of the drawing area to return to the drawing sheet with modified title block, as shown.

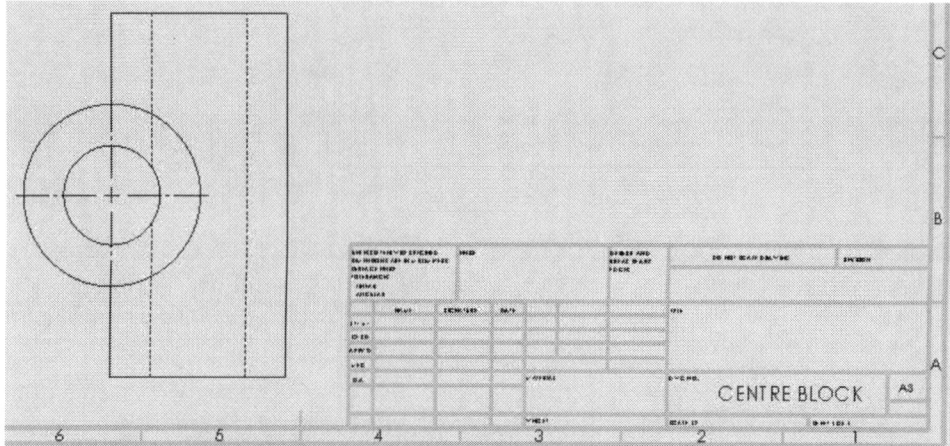

Applying Dimensions to the Drawing View

The option available in the **Smart Dimension** drop down of **Annotation CommandManager** can be used to apply dimensions to the drawing views in the Drawing Environment. The use of these options is same as discussed in the previous chapters.

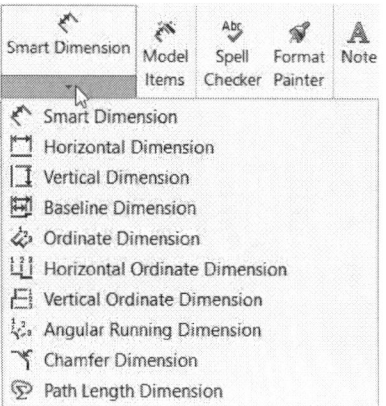

Generate Dimensions of the Drawing View

The **Model Items** button is used to import all the dimensions in the drawing view, that you have applied to the model in the Part Environment.

➤ Click on the **Model Items** button from the **Annotation CommandManager** to display the **Model Items PropertyManager**, as shown.
➤ Select the **Entire model** option from the Source drop down of the PropertyManager, as shown.
➤ Select the other required options of the PropertyManager.
➤ Now click on the **OK** button of the PropertyManager to generate dimensions, as shown.
  For the better visibility of dimensions, you can slightly move and rearrange them one by move.

SolidWorks 2021 - Step-By-Step Guide

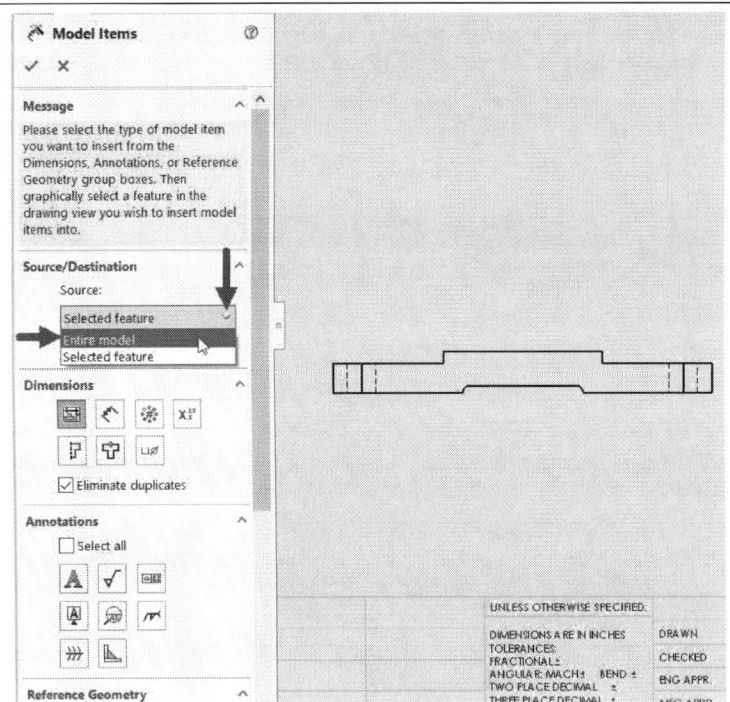

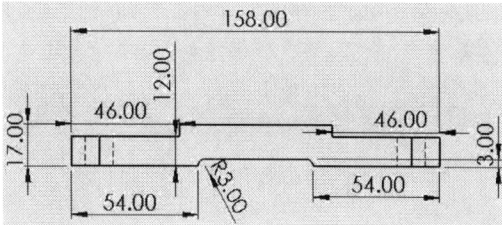

Drawings and Views

11-21

Examples:

Example 1

In this example, you will create 2D drawing of the parts shown below.

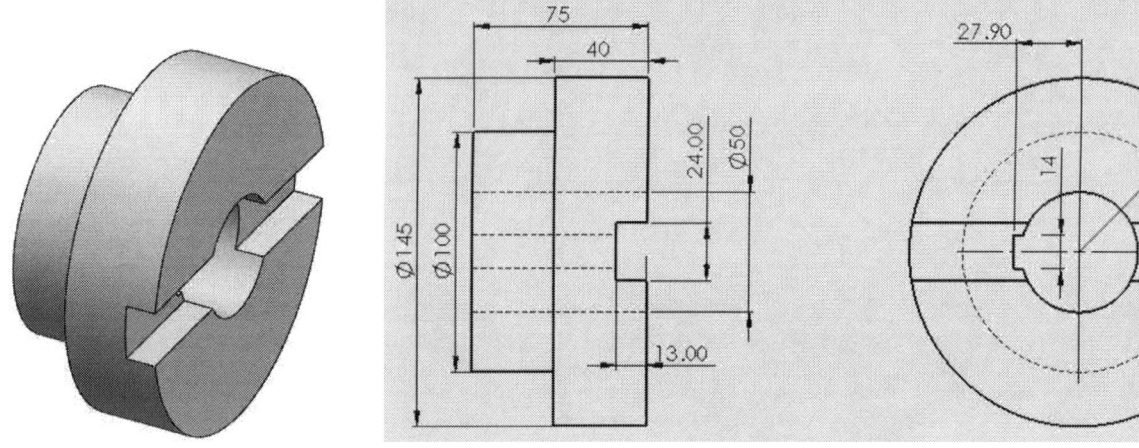

- Start SolidWorks 2021 by clicking the SolidWorks 2021 icon on your desktop.
- Click on the **Drawing** button from the **Welcome – SolidWorks 2021** dialog box displayed to enter in the Drawing Environment, as shown.
- Double click on the **A3 (ANSI) Landscape** from the **Sheet Format/Size** dialog box to select it, as shown.

Note that you need to select the **Only show standard formats** check box to display all sheet size formats, as shown.

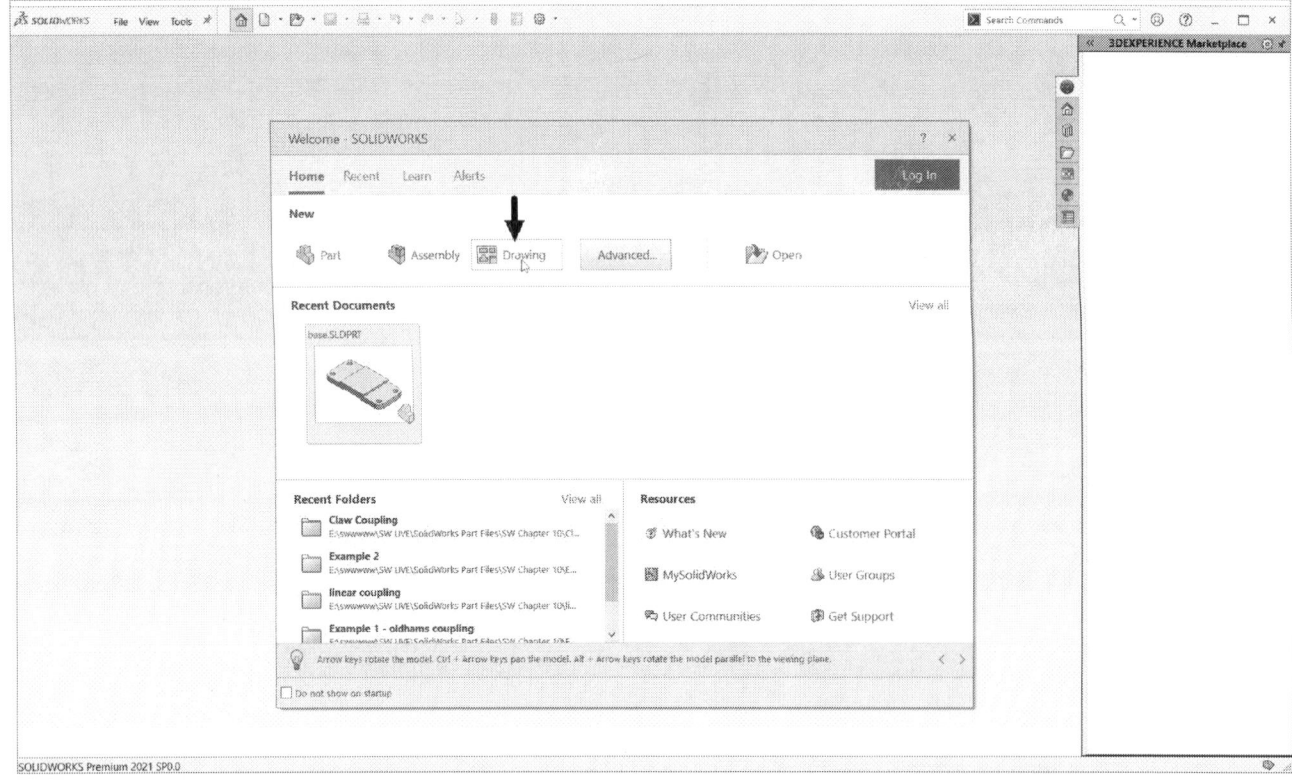

SolidWorks 2021 - Step-By-Step Guide

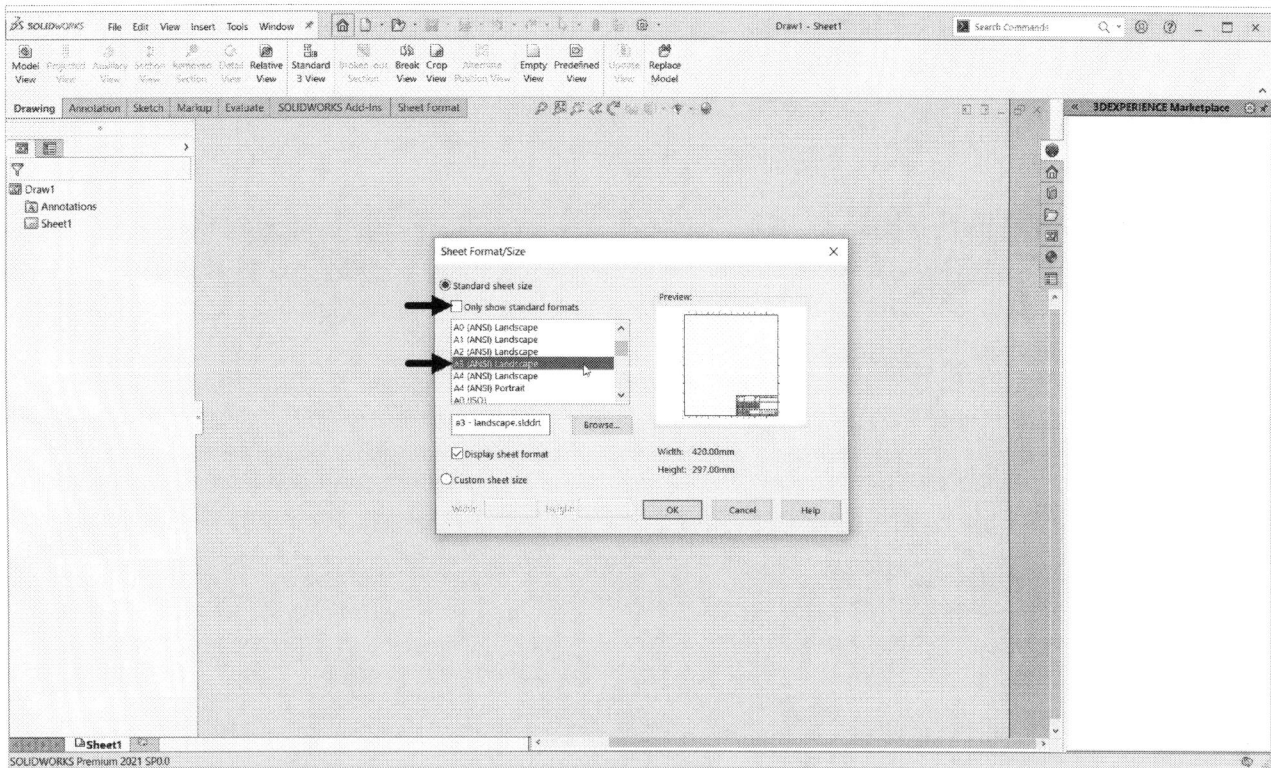

➢ Now, click on the **Browse** button of the **Model View PropertyManager** displayed with the drawing sheet in the Drawing Environment, as shown.

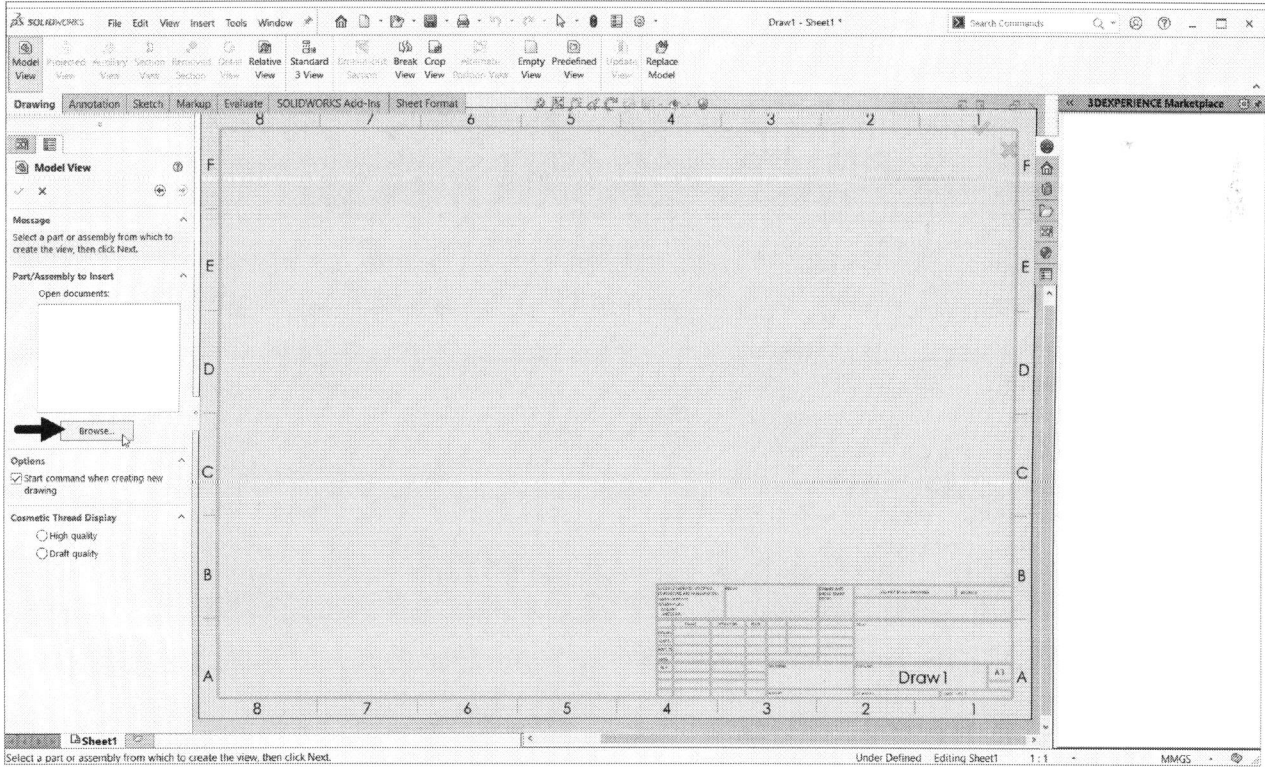

➢ Browse to the folder containing parts created in chapter 10 from the **Open** window displayed, as shown.
➢ Double click on the **flange** file to generate its base view, as shown.
➢ Select the **Preview** checkbox from the **Model view PropertyManager** to display the preview of selected file, as shown.

Drawings and Views   11-23

➤ Click in the drawing sheet to place the base view of the selected file, a shown

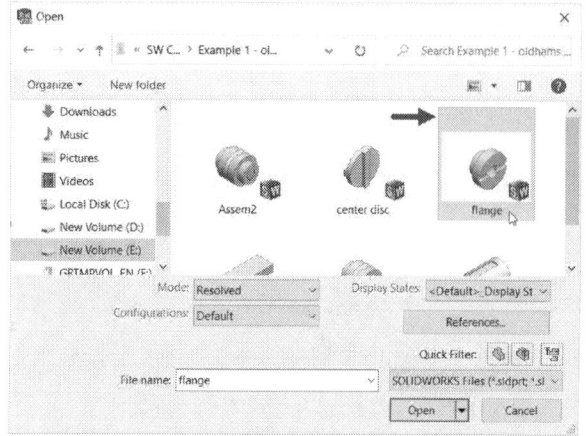 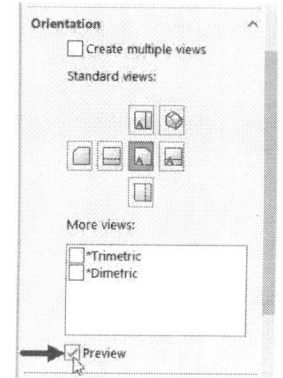 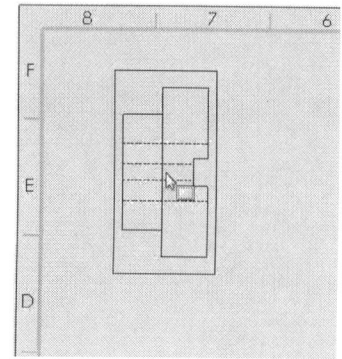

➤ Move the cursor up to some distance in right direction and click to place its Projected View, as shown.
➤ Similarly, you can place another Projected view in downward direction, as shown.

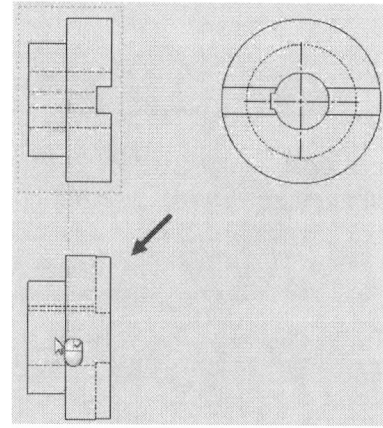 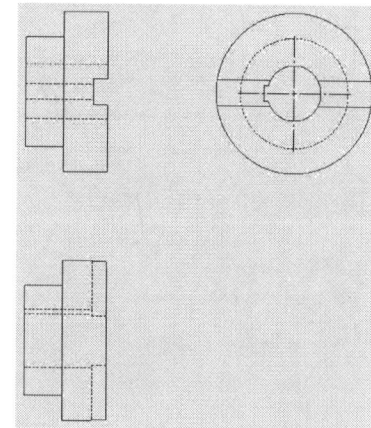

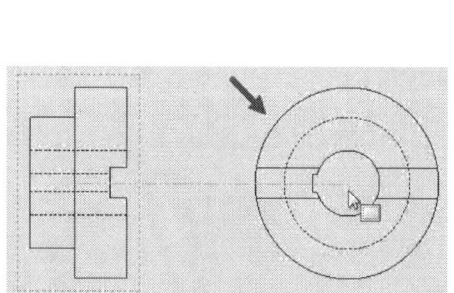

➤ Now select the **Model Items** button from the **Annotation CommandManager** to display the **Model Items PropertyManager**, as shown.
➤ Select the **Entire model** from the **Source** drop down list of the PropertyManager, as shown.
➤ Now select the base model and then click on the **OK** button the PropertyManager to exit it and display the dimensions, as shown.

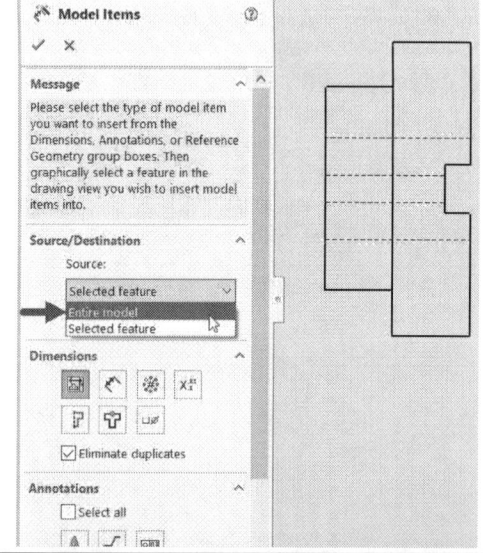 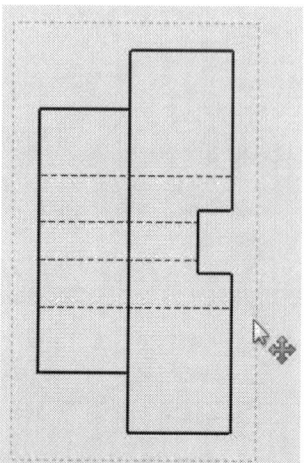 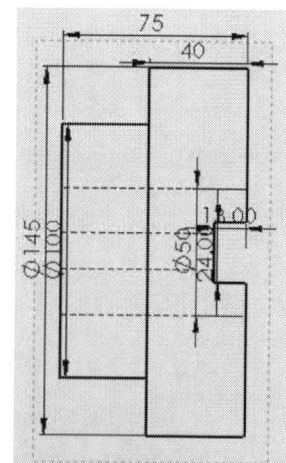

Drawings and Views

Note that as the dimension generated are overlapping each other so you need to move and relocate/rearrange them properly, as shown.

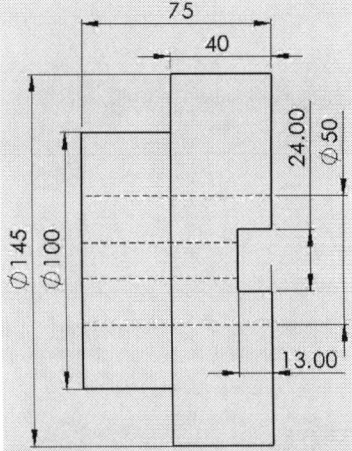

➢ Similarly, generate and rearrange the dimensions of projected view on right, as shown.

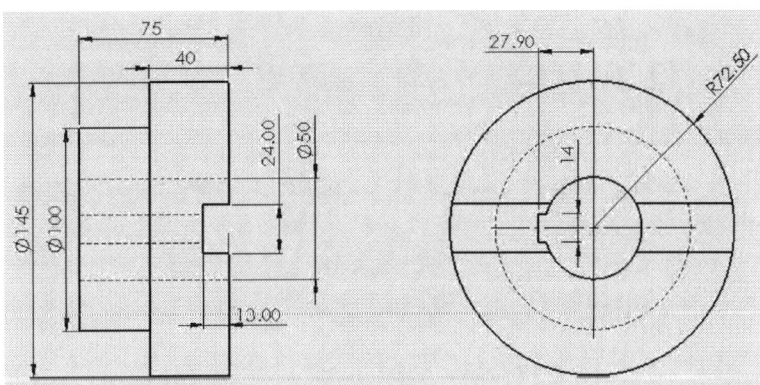

➢ Click on the **Save (Ctrl+S)** button from the Menu Bar to display the **Save As** dialog box.
➢ Next browse to the folder of chapter 5 and enter name **ch11-exam01** in the **File name** edit box.
➢ Click on the **Save** button from the dialog box to save the file.
➢ Now enter the **Close** ☒ button from the upper right corner to close it.

Questions:

1. Which tool is used to create base view of the drawing file and how?
2. How can you generate standard view of any selected file?
3. How can you scale any drawing view in the drawing sheet?
4. How can we generate auxiliary view of a model?
5. How can you edit the sheet size?
6. How can you create section view of any drawing view?
7. What is the use of **Detail view** tool?
8. How to generate the drawing view of an exploded assembly?
9. How can you use **Break** and **Broken-out Section** tools used?
10. How can you generate bill of material in drawing sheet?

Exercises:

Exercise 1

Create this part and then create its orthographic views. Add dimensions and annotations to the drawing.

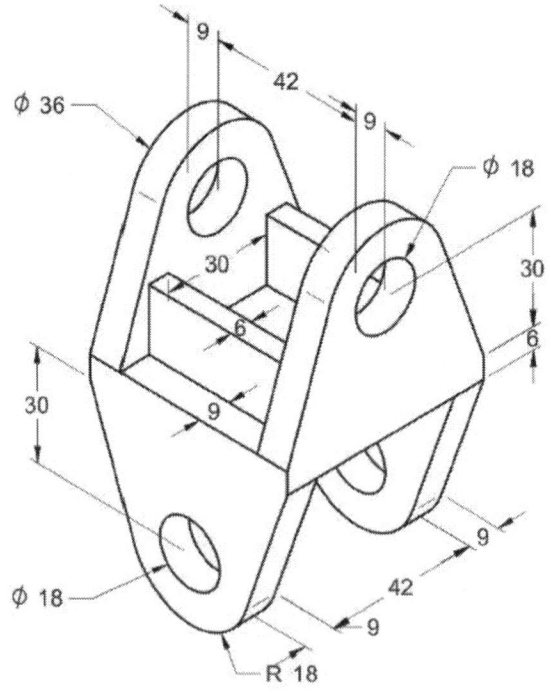

Exercise 2

Create this part and then create its orthographic views and an auxiliary view. Add dimensions and annotations to the drawing.

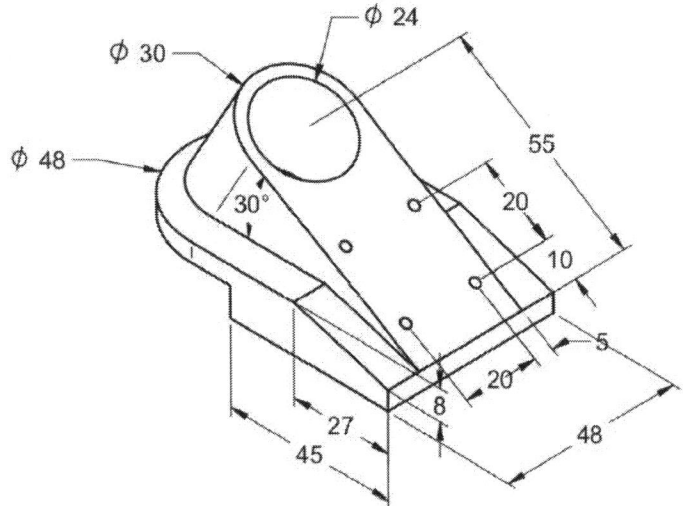

Chapter No: 12 Sheet Metal Design

Sheet metal is a component having uniform thickness. When we bend or unbend then length of thickness will change. You can make sheet metal parts by bending and forming flat sheets of metal. In SolidWorks, Sheetmetal parts can be folded and unfolded enabling you to show them in the flat pattern as well as their bent-up state. There are two ways to design Sheetmetal parts in SolidWorks. Either you can start the Sheetmetal part from scratch using Sheetmetal tools throughout the design process or you can design it as a regular solid part and later convert it to a Sheetmetal part. Most commonly, you design sheet-metal parts in Sheetmetal environment from the beginning. In this chapter, you will learn some of the mostly used tools.

The main topics covered in this chapter are:

- ❖ Starting a Sheetmetal Part
- ❖ Flat
- ❖ Flange
- ❖ Boundary Blend
- ❖ Solid model to Sheet metal component

Before creating a Sheet metal part file, you need to display the **Sheet Metal** tab with all the tool used in creating a Sheetmetal component. By default, the **Sheet Metal** tab might not be visible in the SolidWorks drawing environment. To start sheetmetal part file, you need to display all the tools used in creating it. Note that by doing same, you can toggle between the visibilities of tabs.

> Enter in the Part Environment.
> Next right-click over the tabs to display the shortcut menu, as shown
> Select the **Sheet Metal** option to display the **Sheet Metal** tab with all the tools used in creating sheet metal part file, as shown.

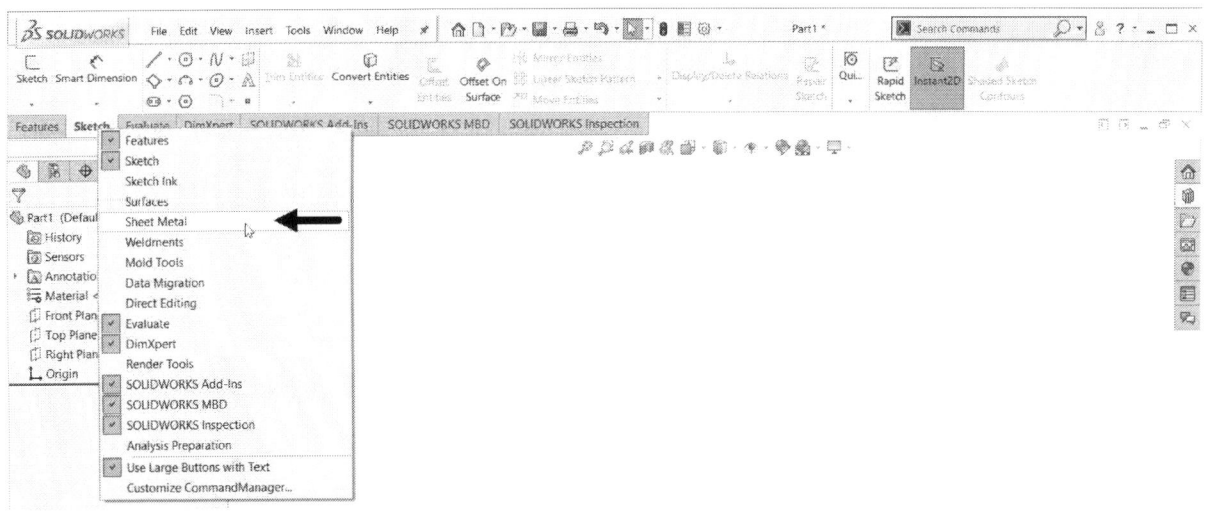

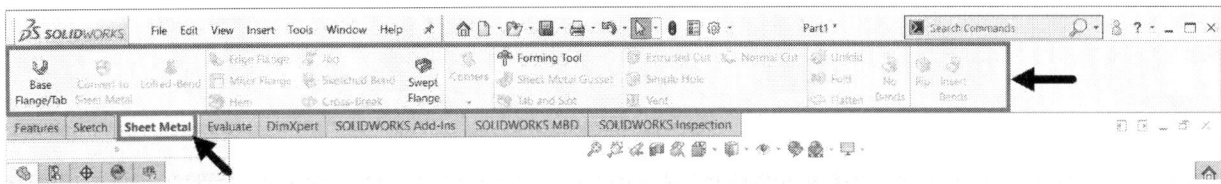

Starting a Sheetmetal Part File

To create a base feature/flange for sheet metal component, follow the steps given next.

➢ Click on the **Base Flange/Tab** button from the **Sheet Metal CommandManager** to enter in the sketching environment.

➢ Select the required plane and draw the sketch over it, as shown.

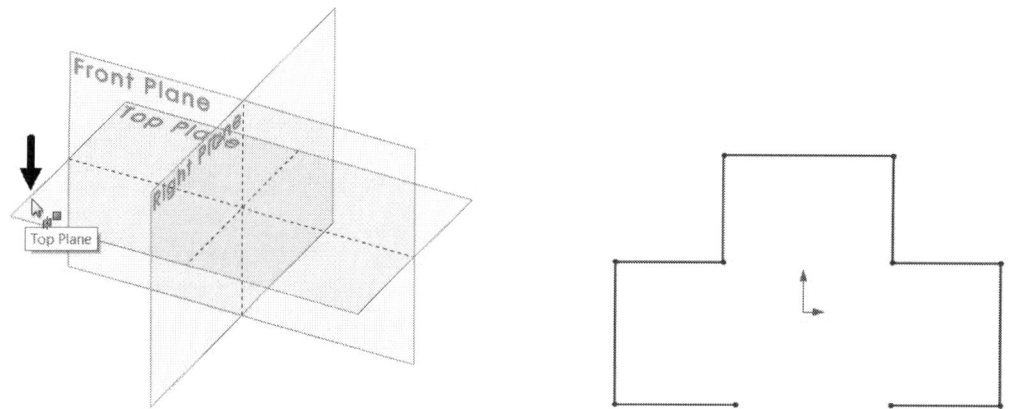

➢ Exit from the Sketch environment to display the preview of the base flange along with the **Base Flange PropertyManager**, as shown.

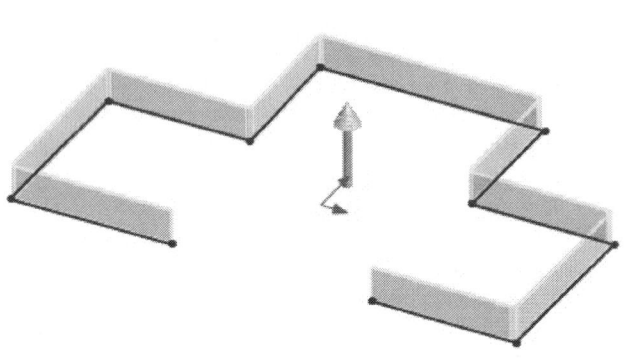
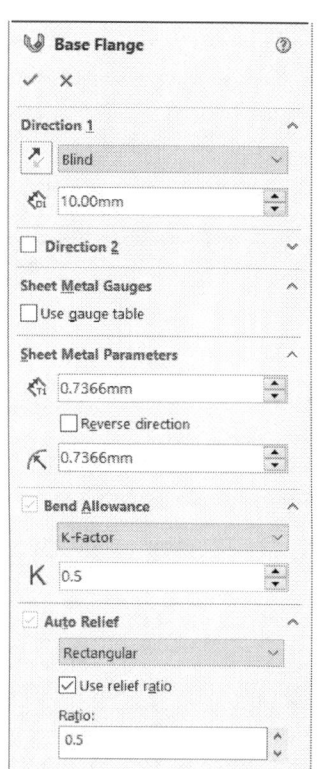

The options in this PropertyManager are discussed below:

Direction 1/Direction 2

The options in this rollout are used to define the length of flange in direction 1 and direction 2. Note that these rollouts will get displayed only if the sketch of base flange will be open.

Sheet Metal Gauges Rollout

The **Sheet Metal Gauges** rollout enables you to select any default gauge tables or browse to user defined gauge table to create the sheet metal parts. To display and use the options in this rollout, follow the steps:

- Select the **Use gauge table** checkbox to display options in this rollout, as shown.
- Next, you can select the required default gauge tables from the **Select Table** drop down list, as shown.
- You can also click on the **Browse** button in this rollout to browse and select the user defined gauge table, if required.

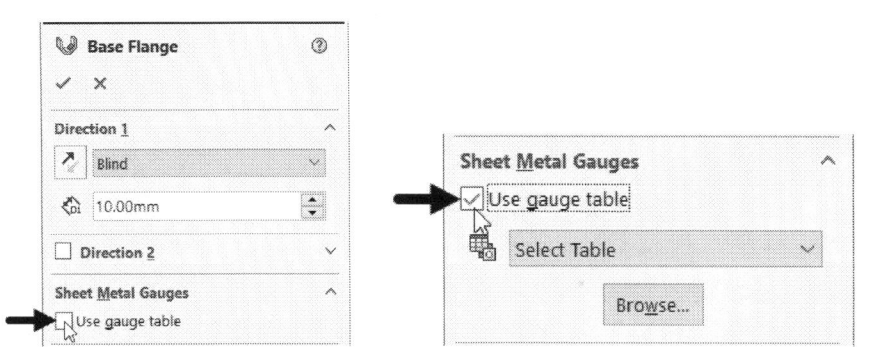
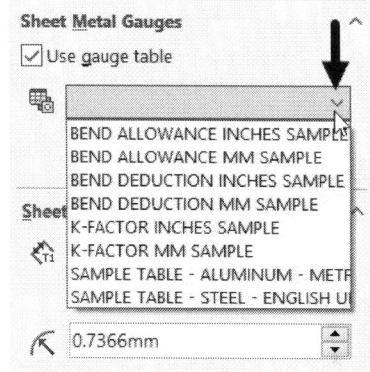

Sheet Metal Parameters Rollout

The options in this rollout are used to define thickness and bend radius of the sheet, as discussed below:

- The **Thickness** spinner is used to define the thickness of the sheet.
- The **Reverse direction** check box is used to flip the direction of material added to the base flange.
- The **Bend Radius** spinner is used to define the bend radius of the base flange. Note that this spinner will not be available if the sketch of the base flange is closed.

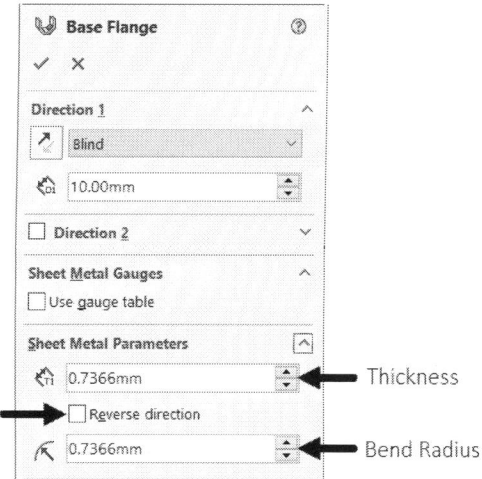

Bend Allowance Rollout

The options in the **Bend Allowance Type** drop-down list of this rollout are used to define the bend allowance for all bends in the sheet metal component. These options get highlighted only after selecting the **Override default parameters** check box, discussed next:

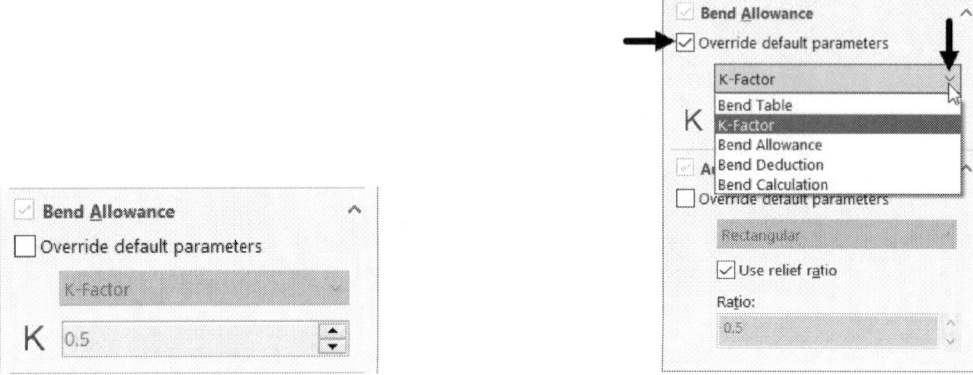

Bend Table

The **Bend Table** option is selected to define the bending allowance by selecting the required bend table from the **Bend Table** drop-down list below it, as shown. You can also click on the **Browse** button to browse the location of the folder and select the user defined bending table, as shown. If you have saved a user-defined bending table file that is created in Microsoft Excel.

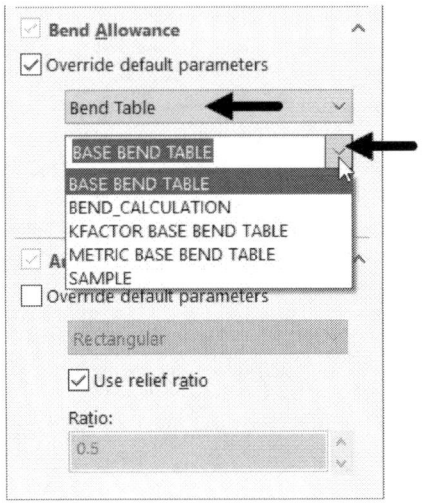
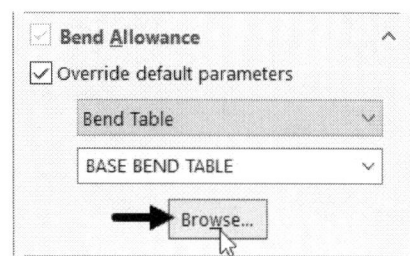
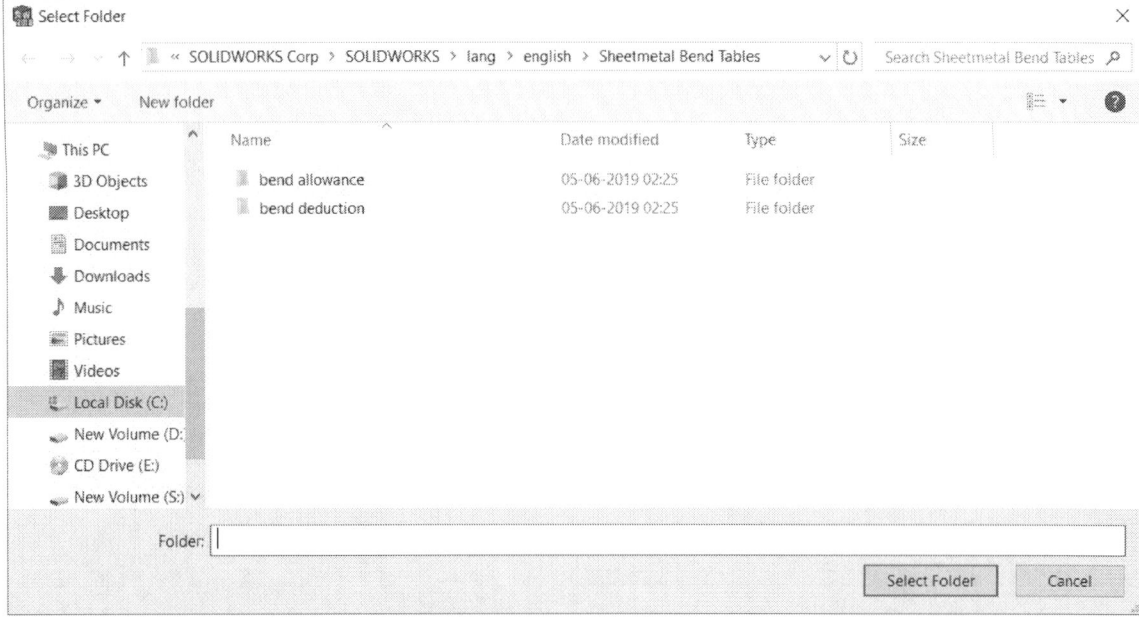

Sheet Metal Design

K-Factor

The **K-Factor** is the ratio of the distance between the inner face of the sheet and the neutral sheet to the thickness of the sheet, as shown. Next, you can enter the required value for the **K-Factor** in the **K-Factor** spinner displayed, after selecting it, as shown.

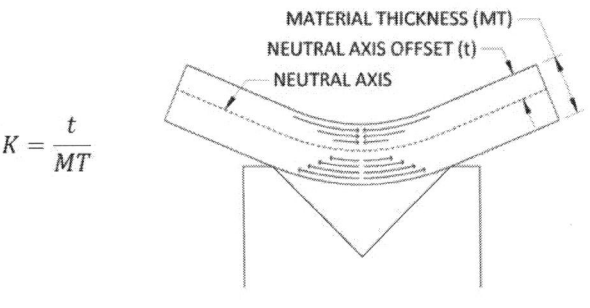

$$K = \frac{t}{MT}$$

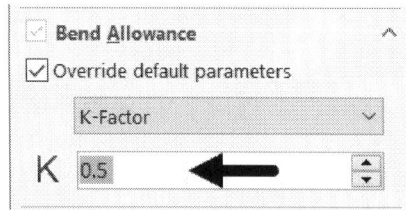

Bend Allowance

The **Bend Allowance** is the arc length of the bend as measured along the neutral axis of the material that you are using, as shown. Next, you can enter the required **Bend Allowance** value in the **Bend Allowance** spinner displayed, after selecting it.

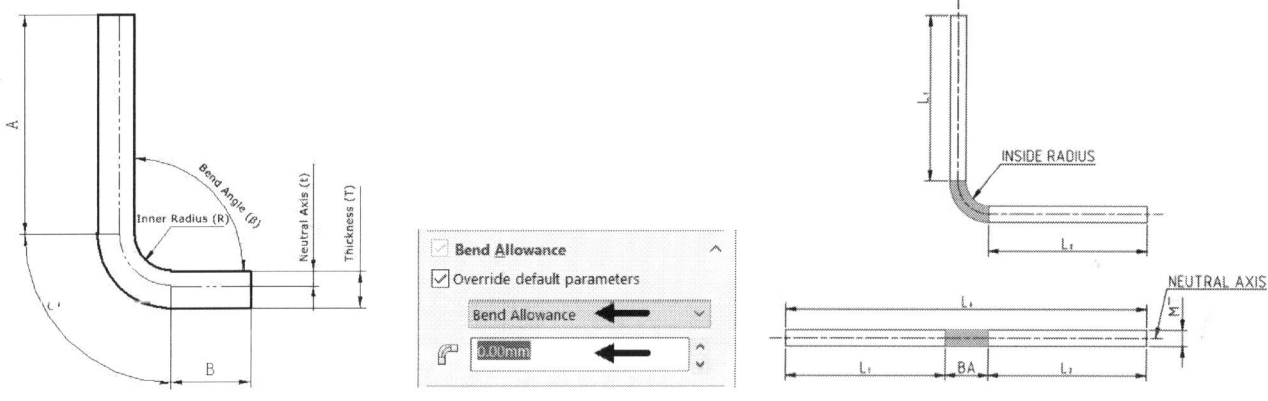

$$BA = A\,\frac{\pi}{180}\,(R + KT)$$

BA - Bend Allowance
A - bend Angle in deg
R - inside bend radius in m
K - constant
T - material thickness in m

Bend Deduction

The **Bend Deduction** is the amount the Sheet metal that will stretch when bent as measured from the outside edges of bend. Also, the **bend deduction** is the difference between the Bend Allowance and twice the outside setback, as shown.

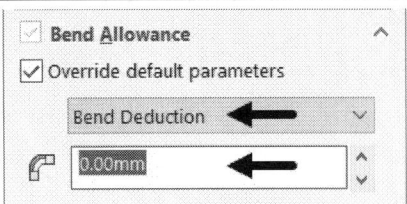

$$BD = 2(R + T) \tan \frac{A}{2} - BA$$

BD - Bend Deduction
R - inside bend radius in m
T - material thickness in m
A - bend angle in deg
BA - Bend Allowance

Bend Calculation

The **Bend Calculation** is selected to calculate the bending allowance by selecting/using the required bend table from the **Bend Table** drop-down list, as shown. You can also click on the **Browse** button to browse the location of folder and select the user defined bending table, as shown.

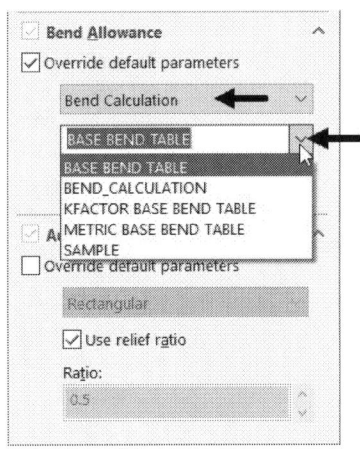
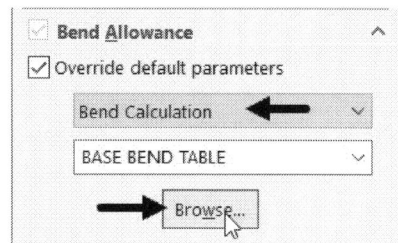

Auto Relief Rollout

This rollout is used to define the relief in the sheet metal component. To avoid tearing of the sheet while bending, the reliefs are provided. These options get highlighted only, after selecting the **Override default parameters** check box, discussed next:

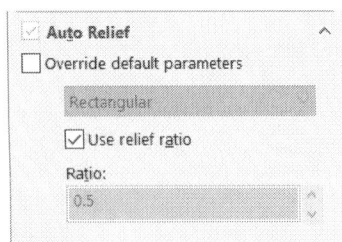
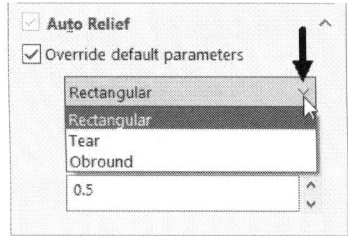

Auto Relief Type

This drop-down list is used to define the type of relief that you need to define to the base flange. There are three types of reliefs available in this drop-down list: **Rectangular**, **Tear**, and **Obround**. You can enter the required relief ratio value in the **Relief Ratio** spinner displayed after selecting the **Rectangular** and **Obround** option, as shown above.

To create Base flange, follow the steps:

> Select the **Base Flange/Tab** button from the **Sheet Metal CommandManager** and select the required plane to enter in the Sketching environment, as shown.

➢ Next, using the sketching tool available in the **Sketch CommandManager**, draw the sketch for the base flange, as shown.

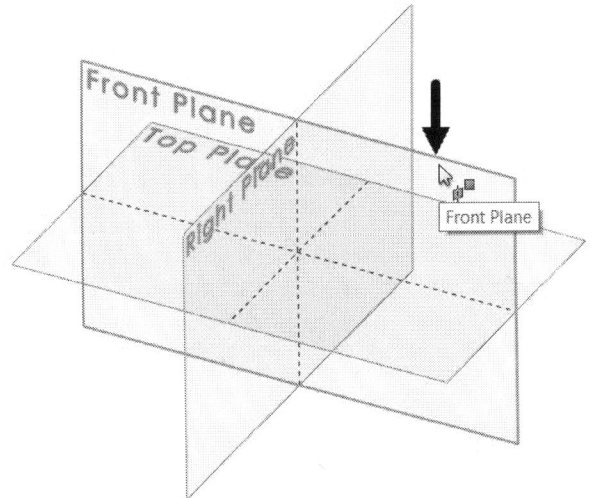
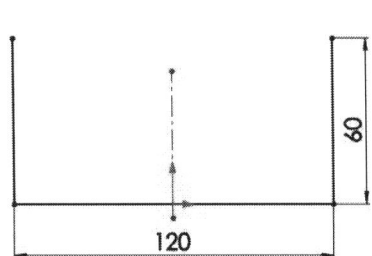

➢ Exit from the Sketching environment to display preview of the base flange along with the **Base Flange PropertyManager**, as shown.

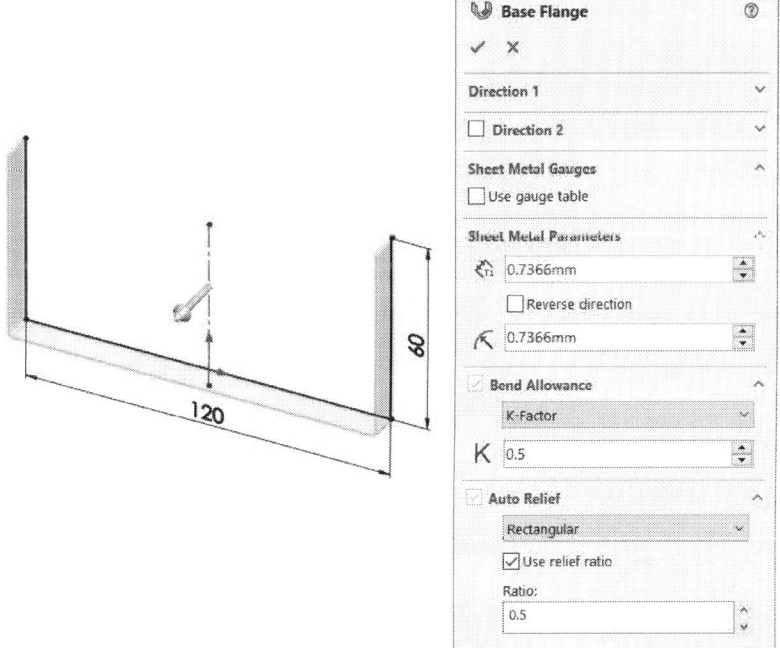

➢ Enter the required values in the edit boxes of PropertyManager and select the required options available in it, as discussed earlier and as shown.

You can also adjust the depth of base flange by dragging the handle attached with it, as shown.

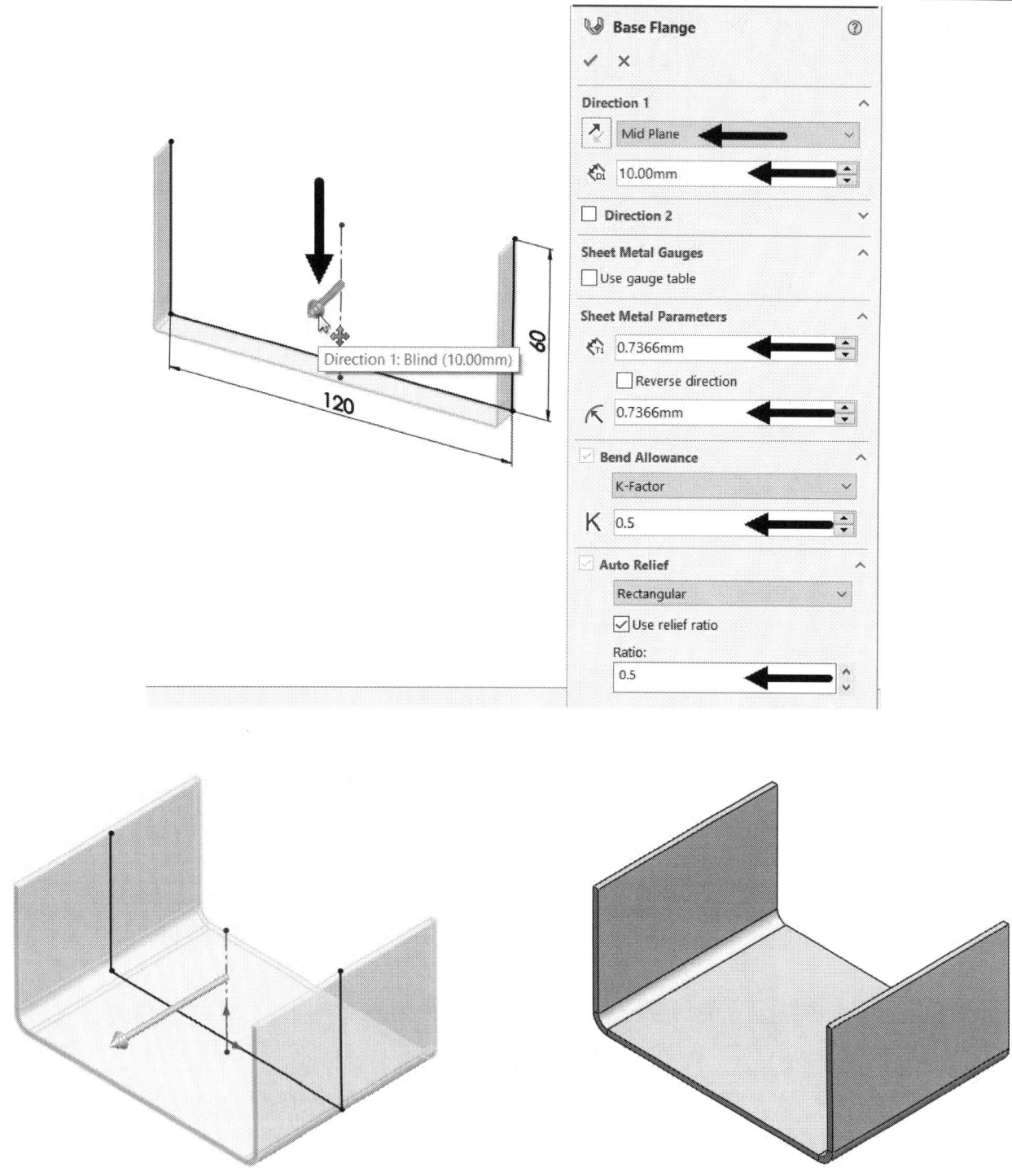

Note that you can also draw the sketch in the Sketching environment and then select the **Base Flange** tool from the **Sheet Metal CommandManager** to create a base flange for a sheet metal component.

Below you can see base flange created from the open sketch with single sketch entity and multiple sketch entities, as shown.

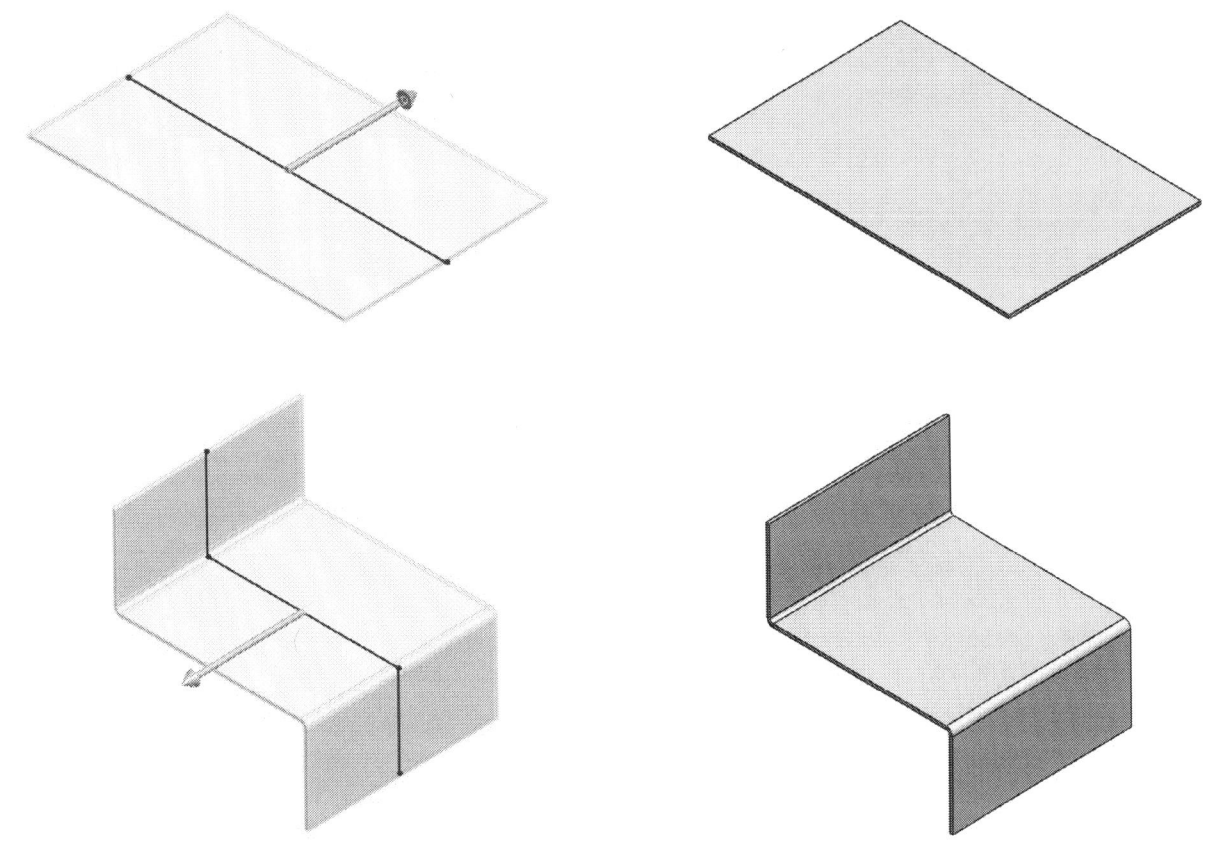

Base flange created from the close sketches, as shown.

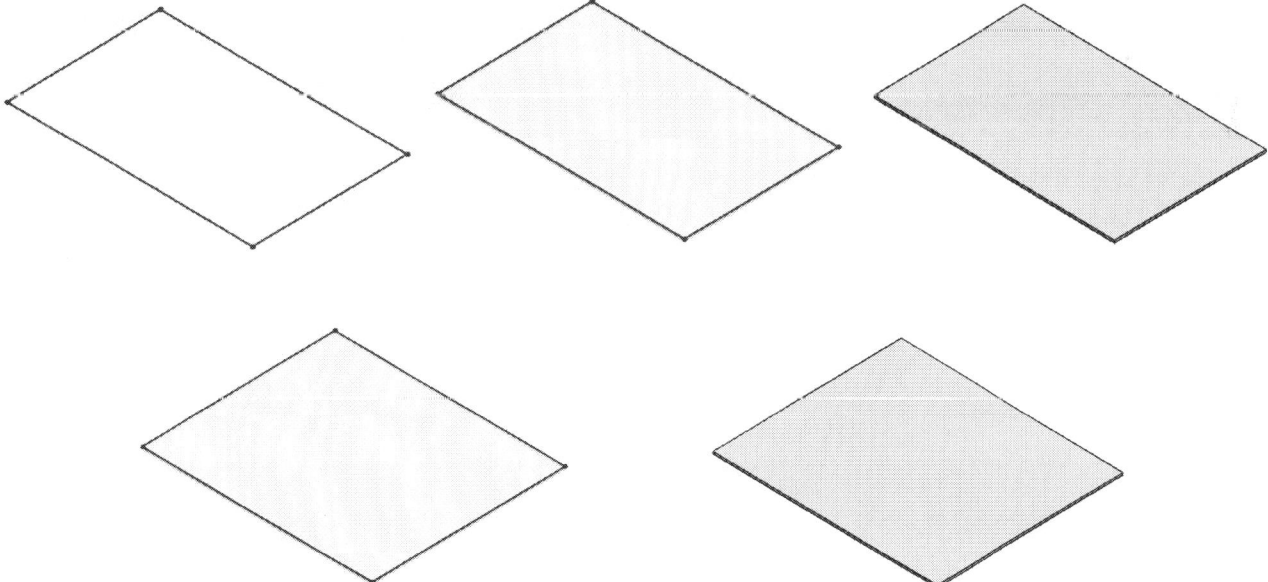

Convert to Sheet Metal

This tool is used to convert a solid model into a sheetmetal component. To do so, follow the steps:

- Create a solid model in **Part** mode, as shown.
- Select the Convert to Sheet Metal button from the **Sheet Metal CommandManager** to activate it and display the **Convert To Sheet Metal PropertyManager**, as shown.

➤ Now select the surface that you want to keep fixed, as shown.

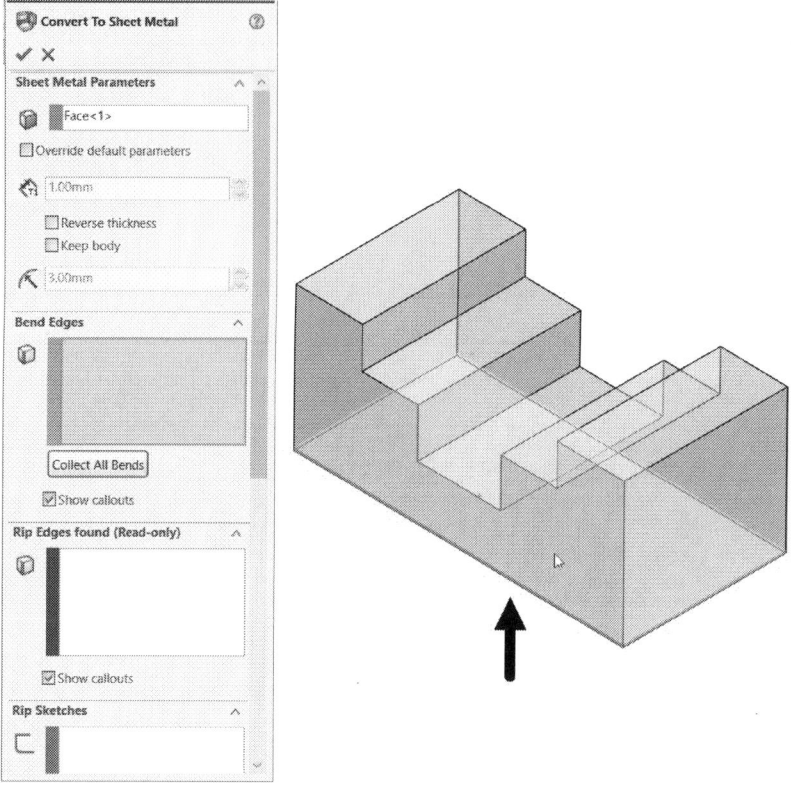

➤ Adjust the required sheet thickness and the radius of the bend using the **Sheet thickness** and **Default radius for bends** spinners of the PropertyManager.

➤ Select the **Reverse thickness** check box from the **Sheet Metal Parameter**s rollout to flip the direction of sheet metal thickness, if required.

➤ Now select the edges of the selected face, as shown.

Note that while selecting the bend edges, the corresponding rip edges get selected automatically, as shown.

➤ To change the bend radius of the edges individually, click over the attached callouts and enter the required values in it, as shown.

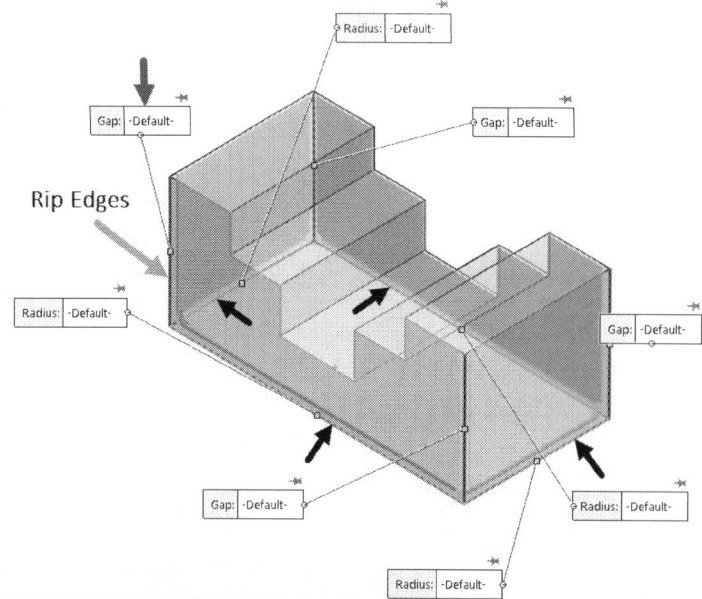

➤ Now click on the ✓ OK button of the **Convert To Sheet Metal PropertyManager** to display the converted solid model into Sheet Metal component, as shown.

The **Rip Sketches** rollout is used to define a required rip by selecting a 2D or 3D sketch. The **Default gap for all rips** spinner in the **Corner Defaults** rollout is used to specify the required rip width. And the **Default overlap ratio for all rips** spinner is used to adjust the material length for **Overlap** and **Underlap** rips.

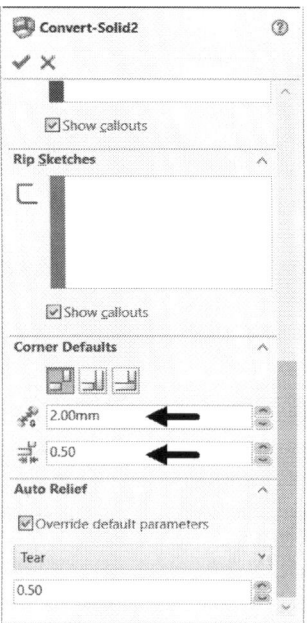

➤ Click on the **Flatten** button from the **Sheet Metal CommandManager** to display the flat pattern of the sheet metal component, as shown.

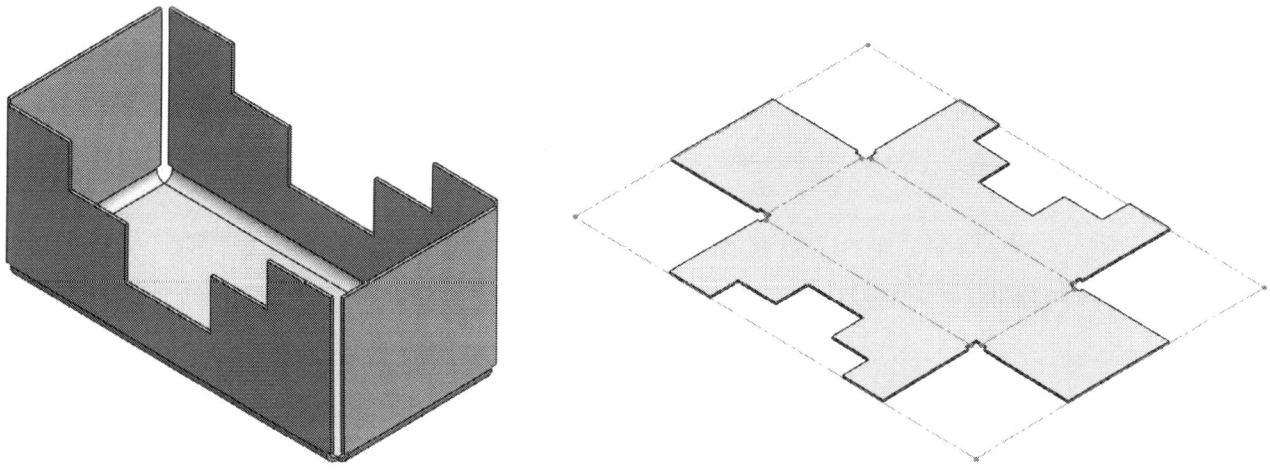

Lofted Bend

This tool is used to create a sheet metal component by connecting two open sketches created on two different planes. The steps to create a lofted feature are explained below:

➤ Draw two different sketches on two different planes, as shown.
➤ Select the **Lofted-Bend** tool from the **Sheet Metal CommandManager** to display **Lofted Bends PropertyManager**, as shown.

Sheet Metal Design 12-11

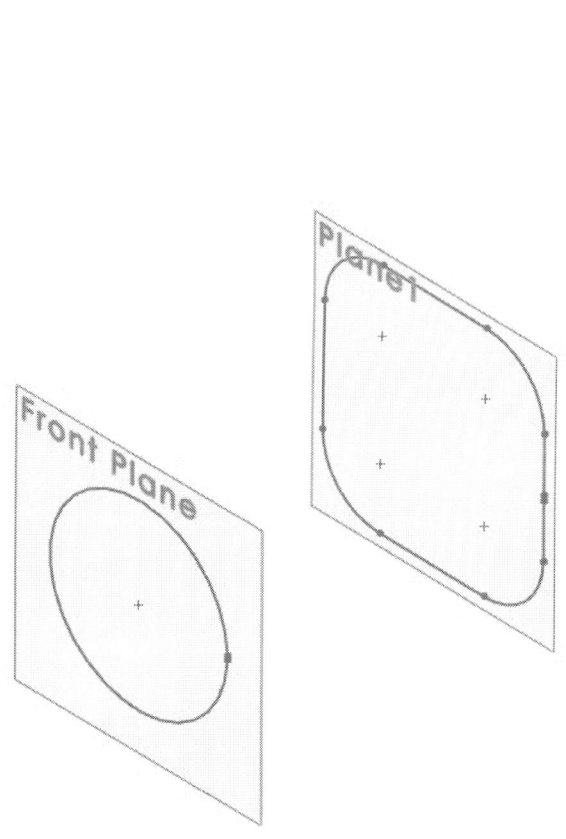 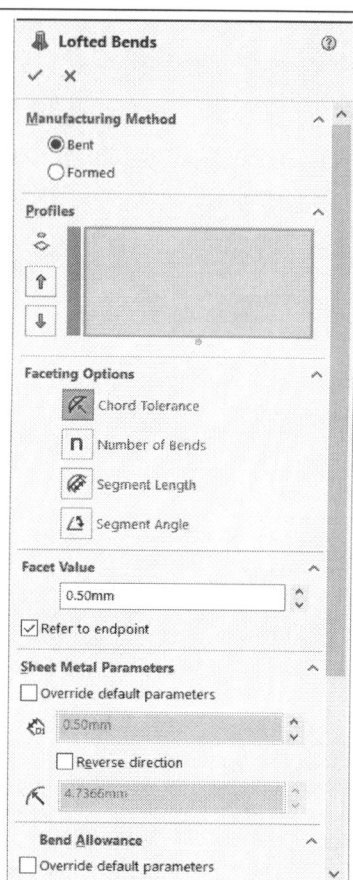

➢ Click on both sketch or sketch entities one by one to display the lofted feature, as shown.

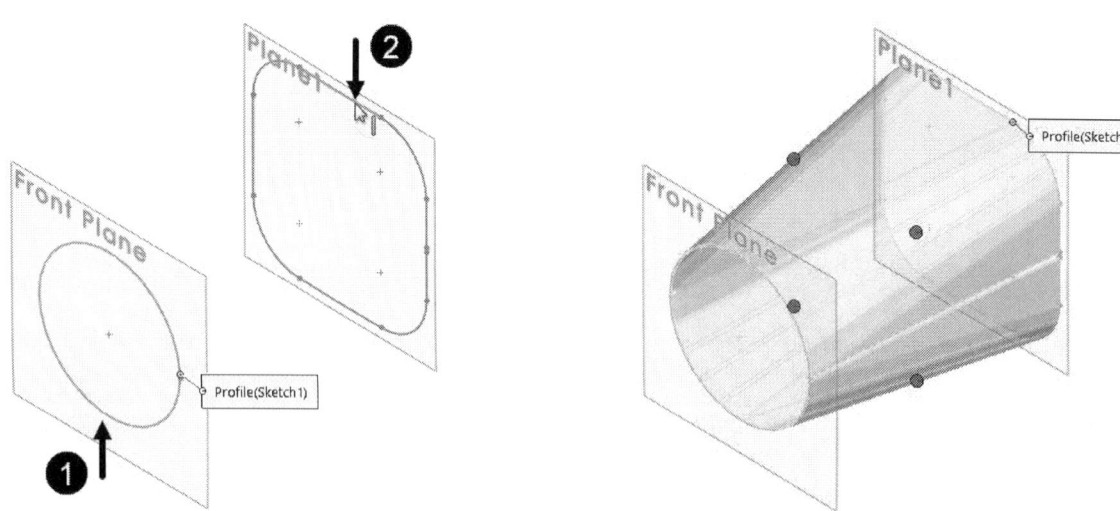

➢ Select the **Override default parameters** check box under Sheet Metal Parameters rollout of the PropertyManager to highlight option under it, as shown.
➢ Now you can adjust/enter the required sheet thickness and Bend radius values in their respective spinners, if required and as shown.
➢ You can select the **Reverse direction** check box to flip its direction, if required.
➢ Now click on the **OK** button from the PropertyManager to exit it and display the lofted feature created, as shown.

Sheet Metal Design

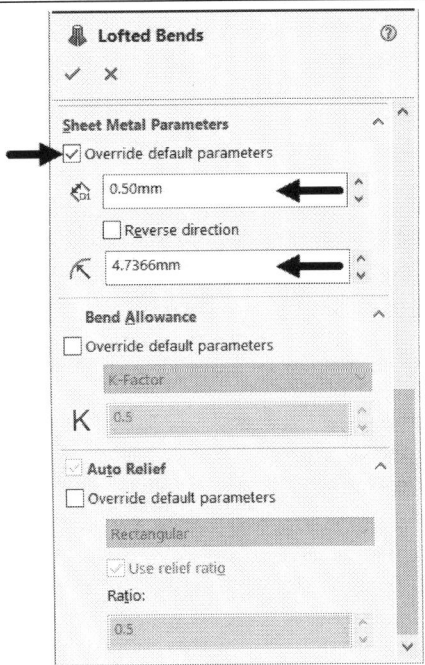 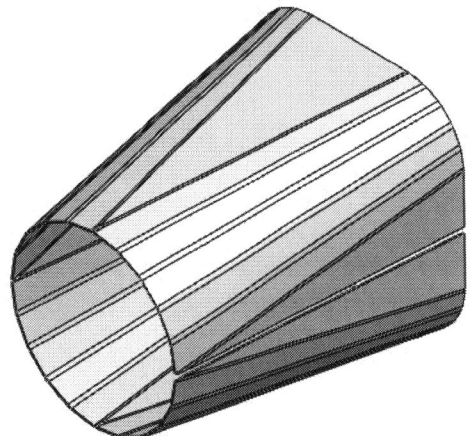

Similarly, you can create a Lofted sheet metal component by selecting the **Formed** radio button in the **Lofted Bends PropertyManager**, as shown.

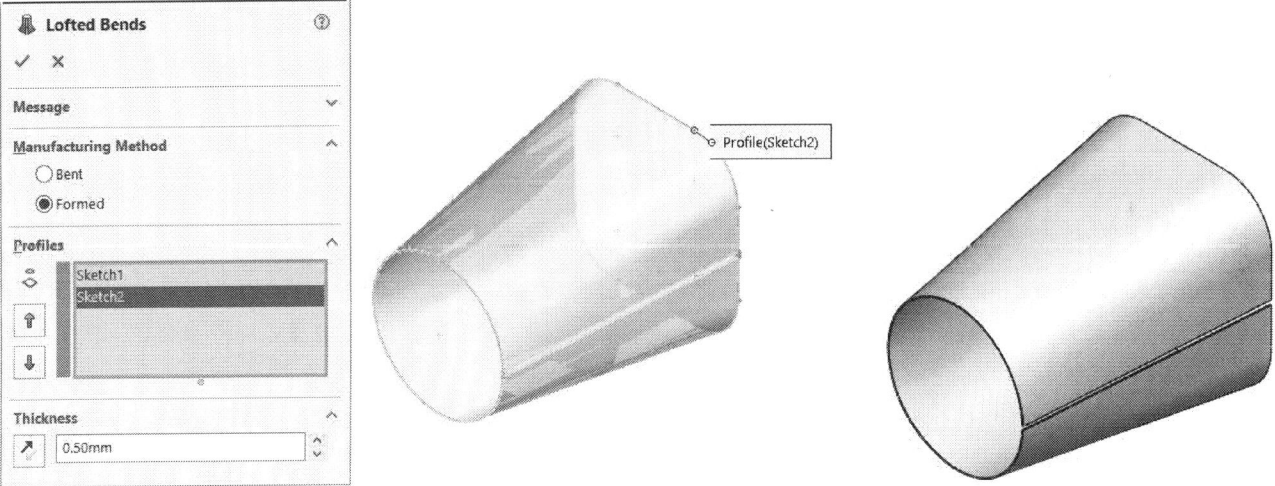

Edge Flange

This tool is used to create a flange/bent wall at an angle by selecting the edge of base flange or existing flange. To create an Edge Flange, follow the steps:

> First create a base feature or primary wall of sheetmetal as discussed earlier, and as shown below.
> Next, select the **Edge Flange** tool from the **Sheet Metal CommandManager** to activate it and display the **Edge-Flange PropertyManager**, as shown.

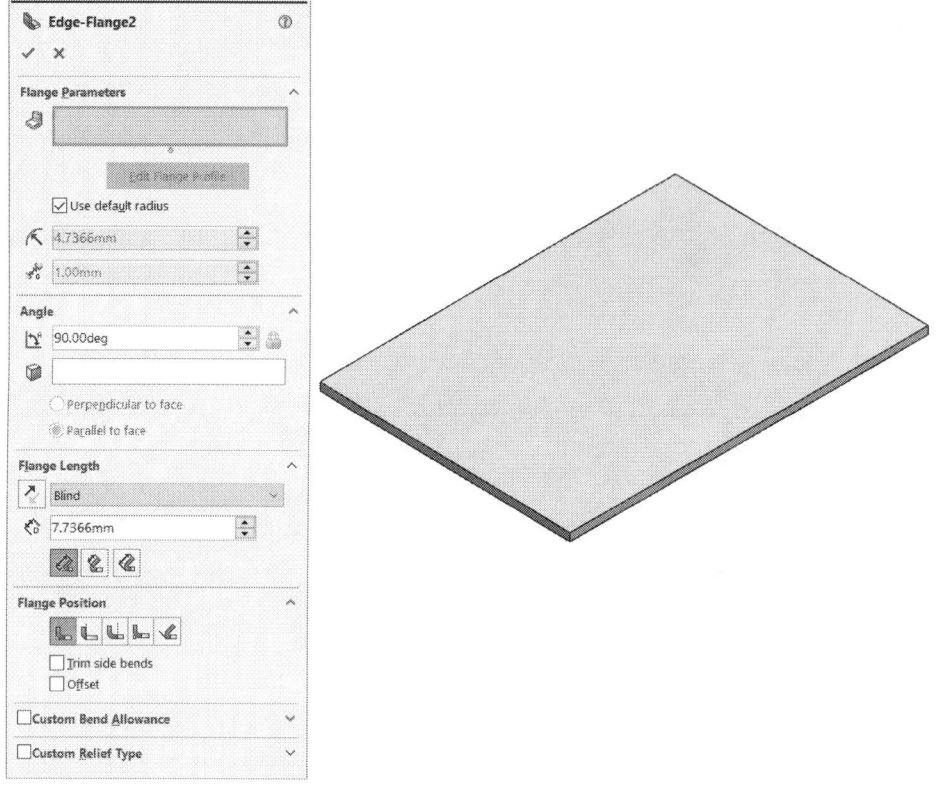

- Select the edge of the base model to display preview of the Edge Flange feature along it, as shown.

  Note that, while moving the cursor upto some distance; the length of edge flange feature will change accordingly.

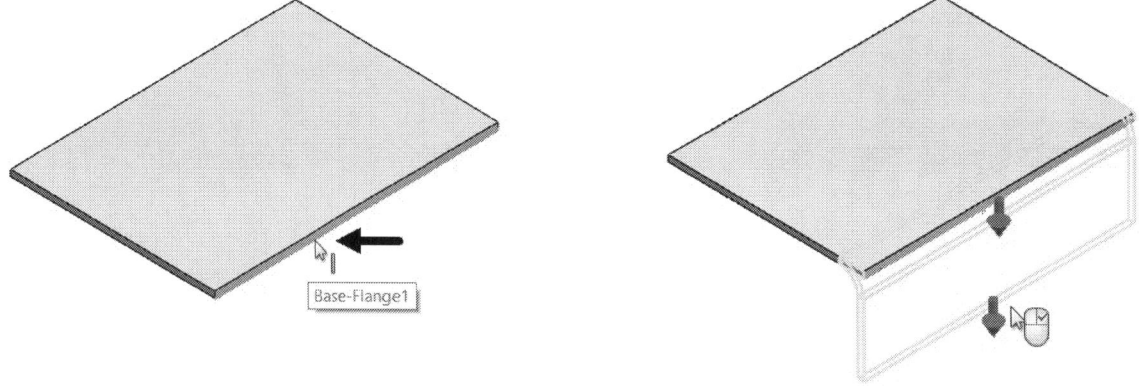

- Now click at the required location to display the Edge Flange feature, as shown.

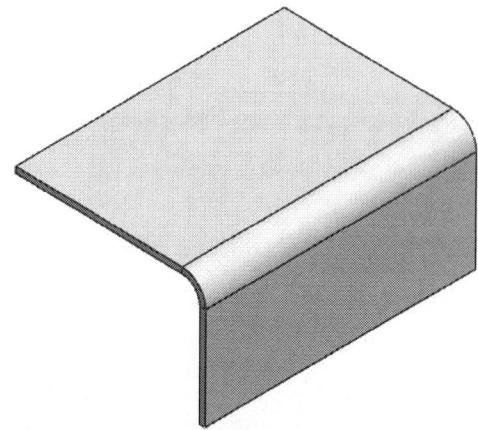

The options in the **Edge-Flange PropertyManager** are discussed next.

Flange Parameters Rollout
The options in this rollout are used to specify the edge used for creating the edge flange, its bend radius and profile of the edge flange. These options are discussed next:

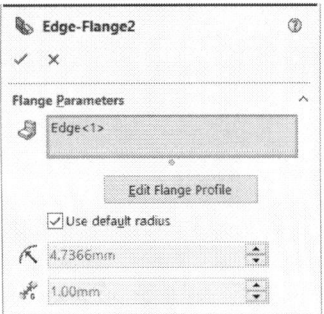

- **Edge:** This selection box is used to select the edge/edges to create the edge flange.

- **Edge Flange Profile:** This button is selected to edit the profile of the edge flange.

- **Use default radius:** This checkbox is selected to use the default radius. To enter the user defined values, deselect it and enter the required values in the respective edit boxes.

- **Bend Radius:** You can enter/adjust the required bend radius values in this spinner.

- **Gap distance:** You can enter/adjust the required profile of the edge flange, as shown.

Angle Rollout
The options in this rollout is used to specify the angle of the flange, by entering the required angle value between 0 to 180 degrees in the spinner, as shown. After selecting the face, you can set the Parallel or Perpendicular relation for the Flange angle, by selecting their respective radio buttons, as shown.

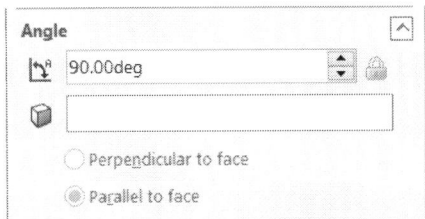 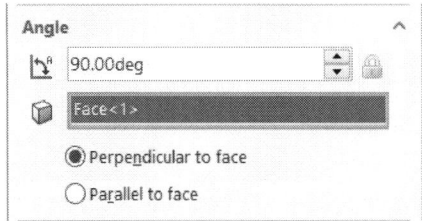

Note that if you select **Up To Edge and Merge** option from the **Length End Condition** drop-down list, the **Flange Angle** spinner get locked, as shown. You need to click on the 🔒 button to unlock it and then enter the required value in it, as shown.

Sheet Metal Design

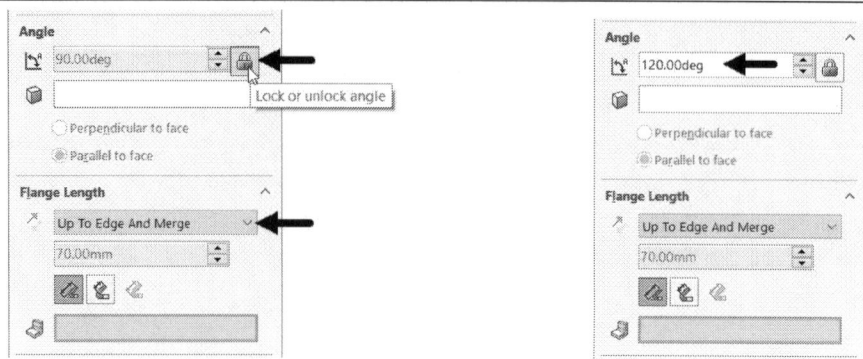

Flange Length Rollout
This options in this rollout are used to define the length of the flange. Some of the options in this rollout are same as discussed earlier and other options are discussed next.

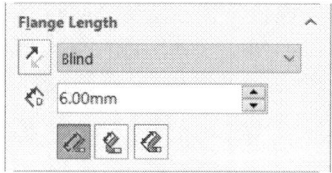

 Outer Virtual Sharp

This button is selected to define the length of the flange from the outer virtual intersection point/sharp. Which is an imaginary vertex by extending the tangent lines virtually from the outer radius of the bend, as shown below.

 Inner Virtual Sharp

This button is selected to define the length of the flange from the inner intersection point/sharp. Which is an imaginary vertex by extending the tangent lines virtually from the inner radius of the bend, as shown.

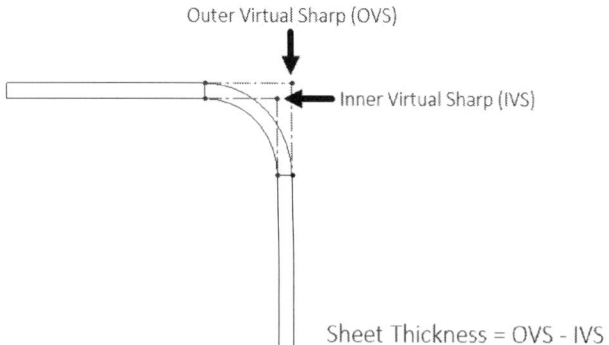

Tangent Blend

This button is used to define the length of the flange from the imaginary line created by extending the tangent line from the outer radius of the blend and parallel to the edge at end of the flange created. The Tangent Blend is valid for bends that are greater than 90 degrees.

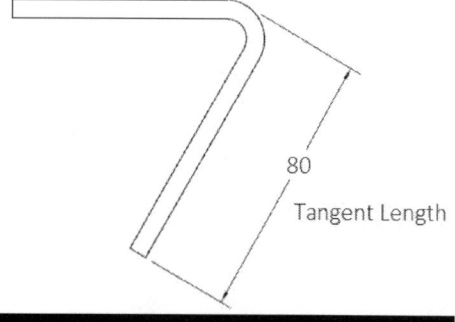

Sheet Metal Design

Flange Position Rollout

The options in this rollout is used to define the position of the flange on an edge. The options in this rollout are discussed next.

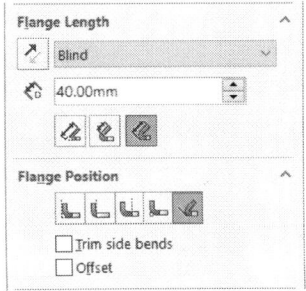

Material Inside
This button is selected to create the edge flange so that the material of the flange or bend lies inside the maximum limit of sheet, as shown.

Material Outside
This button is selected to create the edge flange so that the material of the flange or bend lies outside the maximum limit of sheet, as shown.

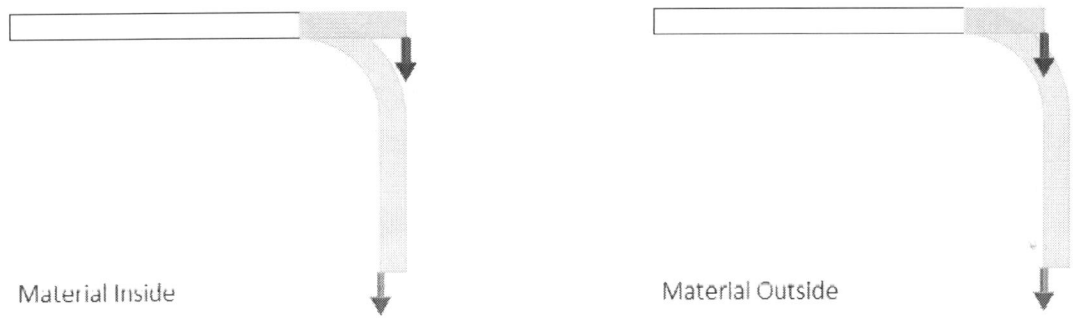

Bend Outside
This button is selected to create the edge flange so that the bending of sheet starts from the end point of maximum limit of the sheet, as shown.

Bend from Virtual Sharp
This button is selected to create the edge flange so that the bending of sheet starts from the virtual sharp, as shown. end point of maximum limit of the sheet, as shown.

Note that the position of the flange depends upon the selection of **Outer Virtual Sharp** button, **Inner Virtual Sharp** button, or **Tangent Bend** button.

Sheet Metal Design

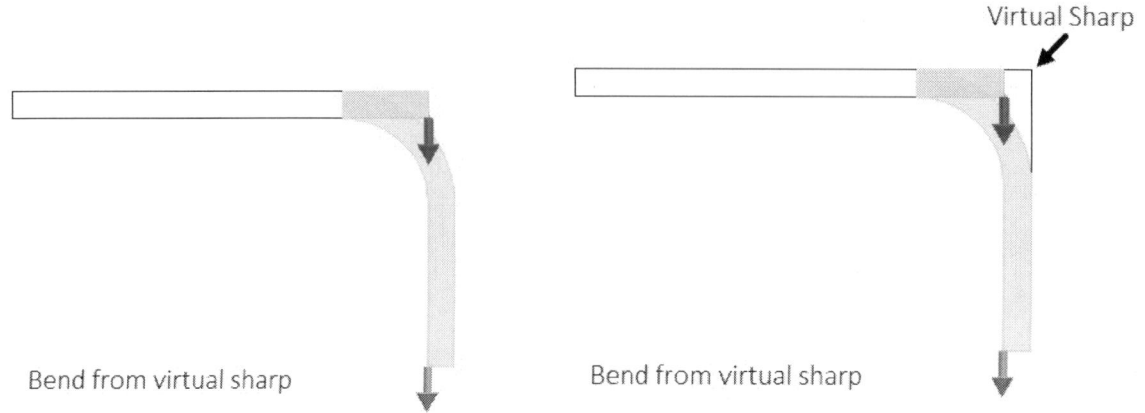

Bend from virtual sharp   Bend from virtual sharp

Tangent to Bend
This button is selected to create the edge flange so that the material of the flange lies tangent to the maximum limit of the sheet, as shown. Note that this option is only valid for bend angle 90 degree or above it.

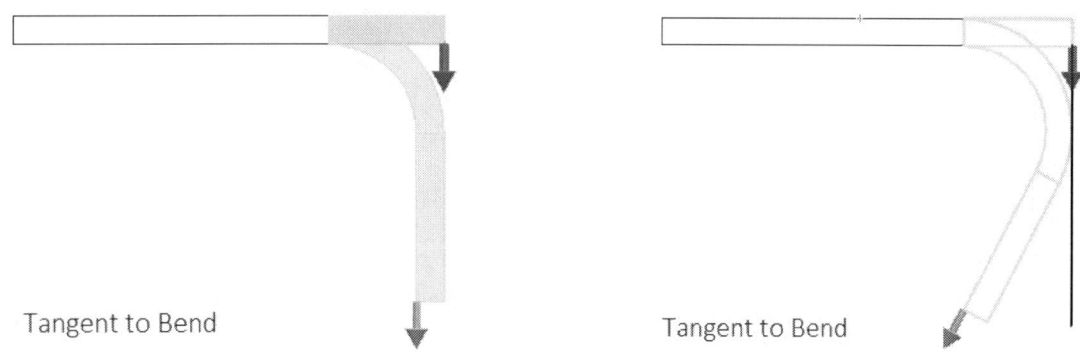

Tangent to Bend   Tangent to Bend

Tangent side bends
This checkbox is selected to trim extra material in its nearby bend, as shown. Note that the cut that trims the nearby bends get automatically resized and cannot be edited.

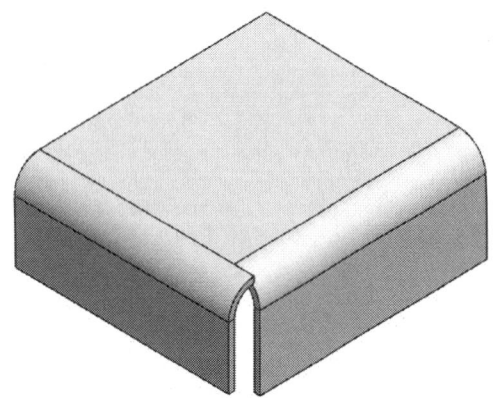 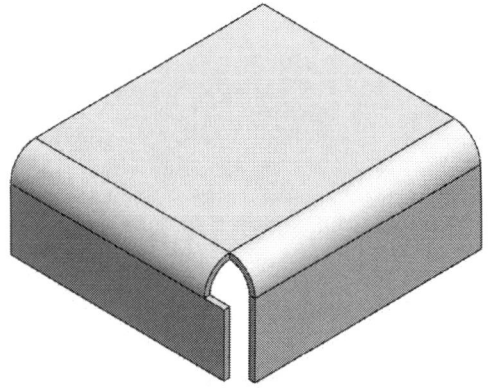

Trim side bend cleared   Trim side bends selected

Offset
This check box is selected to create an edge flange at an offset distance from the selected edge, as shown. After selecting this check box, you can select the required option from the **Offset End Condition** drop-down list and enter the required offset distance in the **Offset Distance** spinner displayed. The **Reverse Direction** button is used to change the direction of offset.

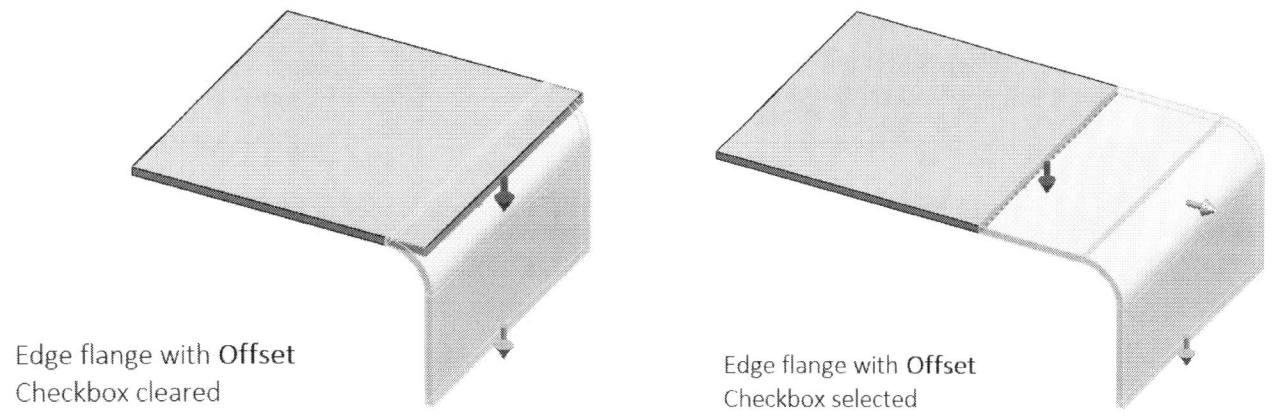

Edge flange with **Offset** Checkbox cleared

Edge flange with **Offset** Checkbox selected

Custom Bend Allowance Rollout

The options in this rollout is used to define the type and value for bend allowance. To display options in this rollout, select the **Custom Bend Allowance** check box, as shown.

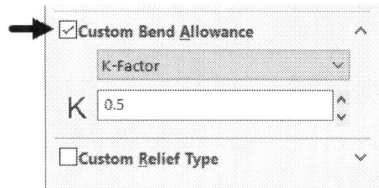

Custom Relief Type Rollout

The options in this rollout is used to add relief cuts and then select the type of relief cuts. To display options in this rollout, select the **Custom Relief Type** check box, as shown.

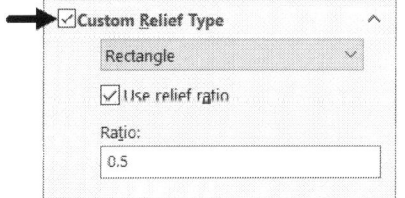
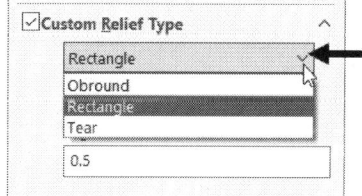

Obround

The **Obround** option in the **Relief Type** drop-down list is used to add the relief in such a way that the edges of the relief merging with the sheet are rounded. To create Obround relief, follow the steps.

> Select the **Obround** option from the **Relief Type** drop-down list.
> Select the **Use relief ratio** check box if it is not selected by default.
> Enter the required value in the **Ratio** edit box to display preview of Obround relief, as shown.

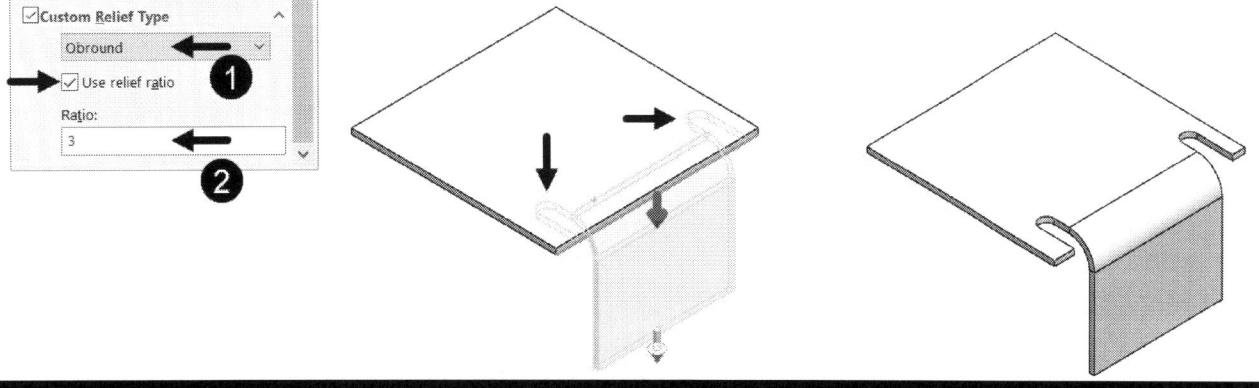

Sheet Metal Design

To modify the relief, you can deselect the **Use relief ratio** check box to display the **Relief Width** and **Relief Depth** spinners, as shown. Next, enter the required values in both to display preview of obround relief, as shown.

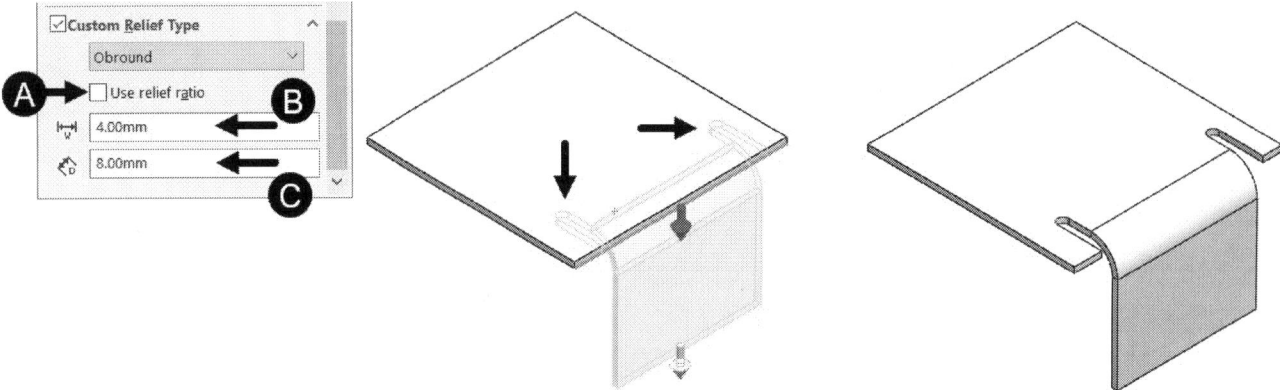

Rectangle

The **Rectangle** option in the **Relief Type** drop-down list is used to add the relief in such a way that the edges of the relief merging with the sheet are rectangle. To create Rectangle relief, follow the steps.

> Select the **Rectangle** option from the **Relief Type** drop-down list.
> Select the **Use relief ratio** check box if it is not selected by default.
> Enter the required value in the **Ratio** edit box to display preview of Rectangle relief, as shown.

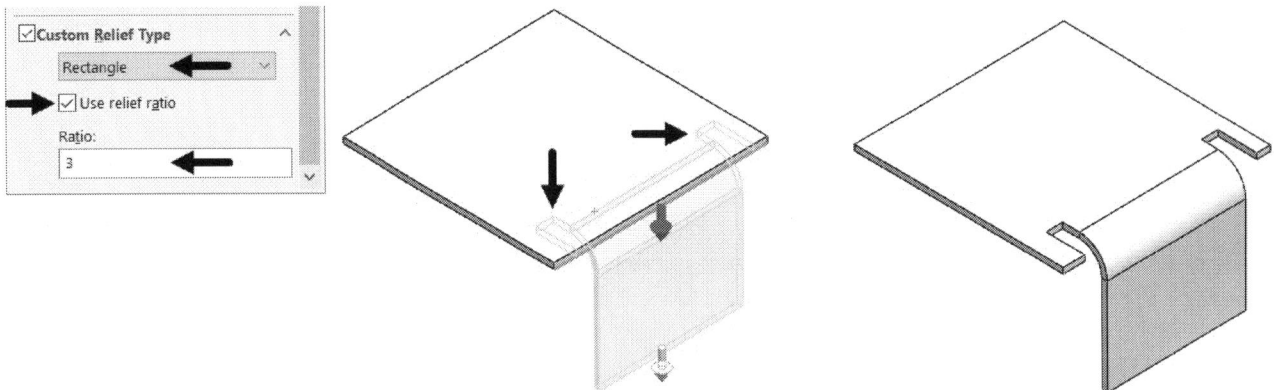

To modify the relief, you can deselect the **Use relief ratio** check box to display the **Relief Width** and **Relief Depth** spinners, as shown. Next, enter the required values in both to display preview of obround relief, as shown.

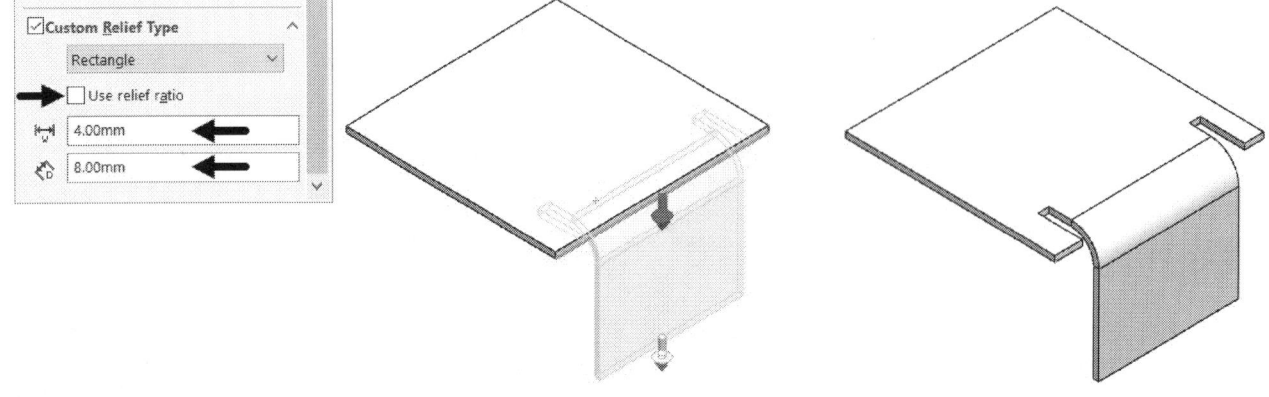

Tear

The **Tear** option in the **Relief Type** drop-down list is used to add the relief in such a way that it will tear the sheet in order to accommodate the bending of sheet. To create Tear relief, follow the steps.

> Select the **Tear** option from the **Relief Type** drop-down list.
> Select the **Rip** button if it is not selected by default to display preview of Tear relief, as shown.

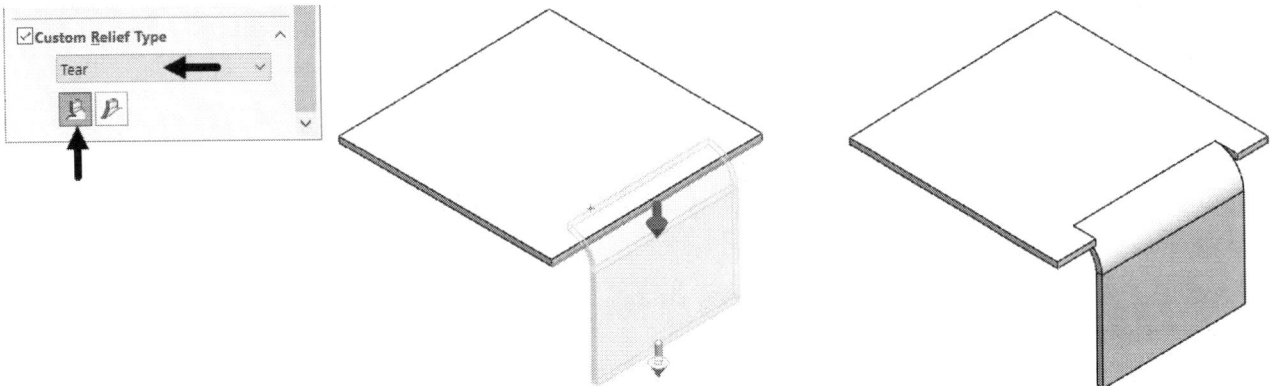

Now select the **Extend** button to extend the outer faces of the bend to the outer face of the sheet on which you create the edge flange, as shown.

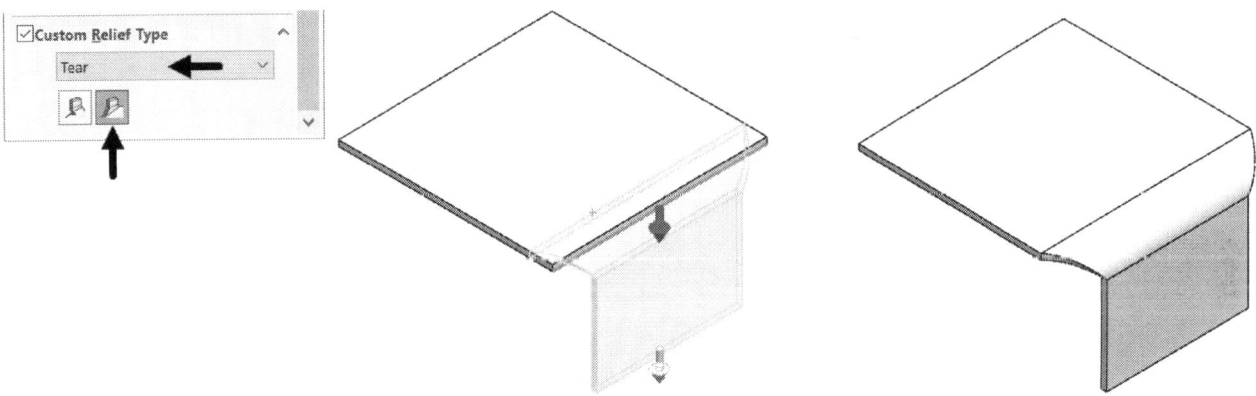

Miter Flange

This tool is used to create a series of flanges along the edge/edges of a sheet metal component.

> Select the **Miter Flange** tool from the **Sheet Metal CommandManager** to activate it. A message to select a plane, planar face, or an edge get displayed, as shown.

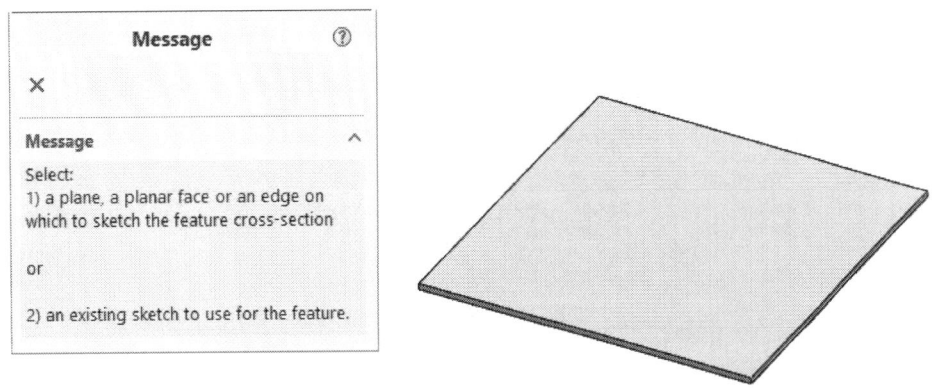

- Select an edge along which you which you want to draw the sketch and enter in the Sketching environment, as shown.

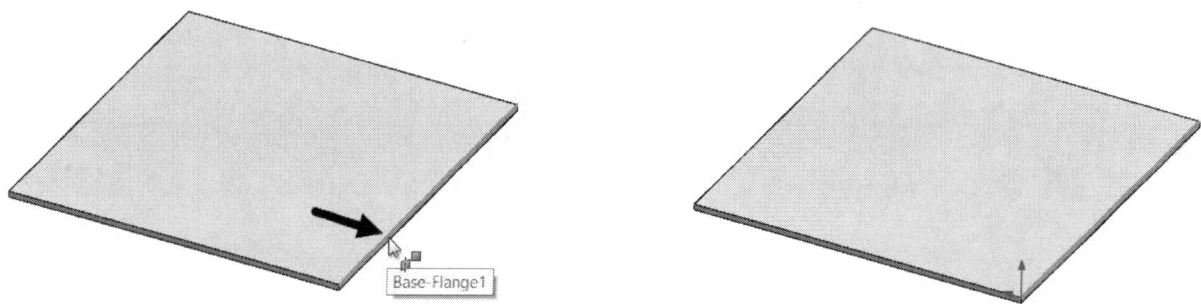

- Press the **Ctrl+8** key of keyboard to make sketching plane parallel to the screen.
- Now draw a sketch, as shown.

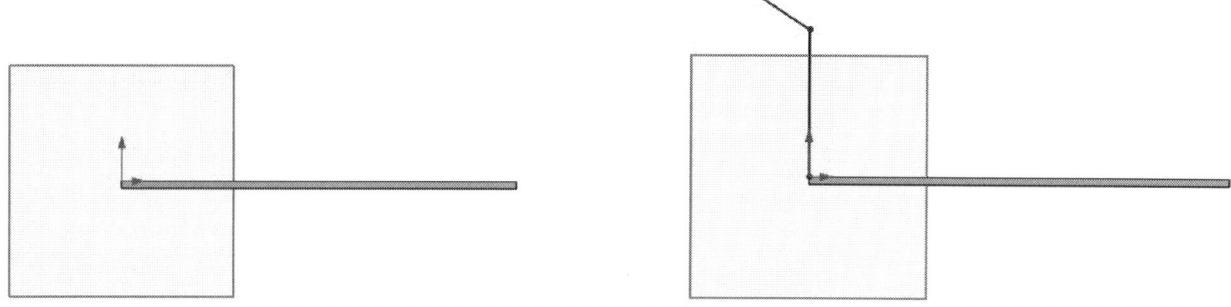

- Exit from the Sketching Environment to display the preview of Miter Flange along with **Miter Flange PropertyManager,** as shown.

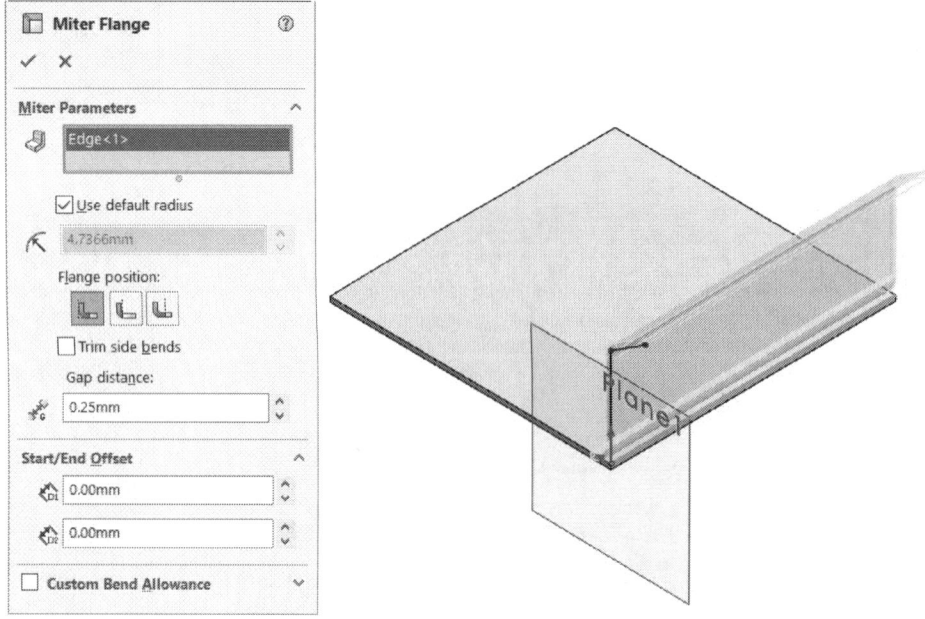

- Select other edges to display preview of Miter Flange along all selected edges, as shown.

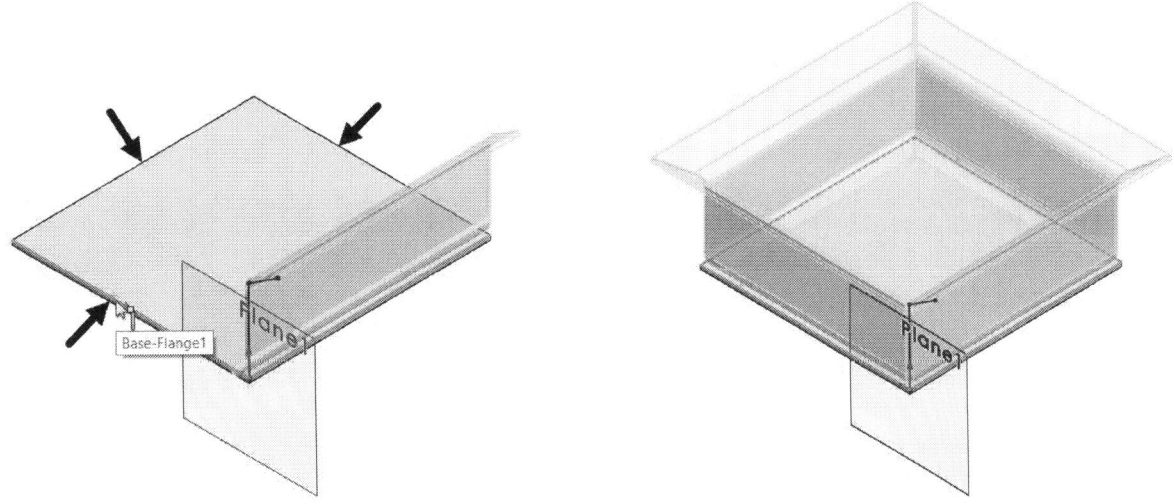

➢ Click on the **OK** button of the PropertyManager to exit it and display the Sheet Metal component with Meter Flange feature, as shown.

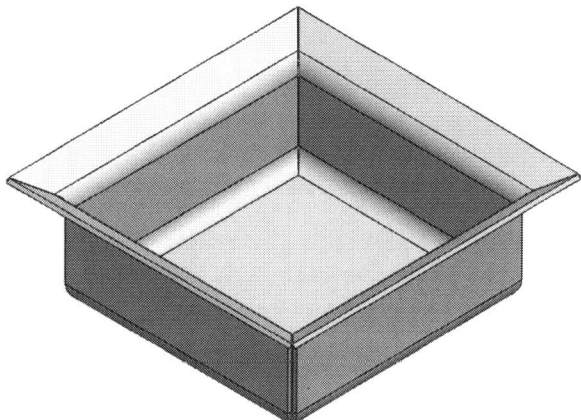

The use of options in this PropertyManager is same as discussed in **Edge Flange PropertyManager**, previously in this chapter. You can enter the required values or use these options, if required.

o   Below is the Miter Flange with the modified Rip distance by using the **Rip Gap** spinner of the **Edge Flange** PropertyManager, as shown.

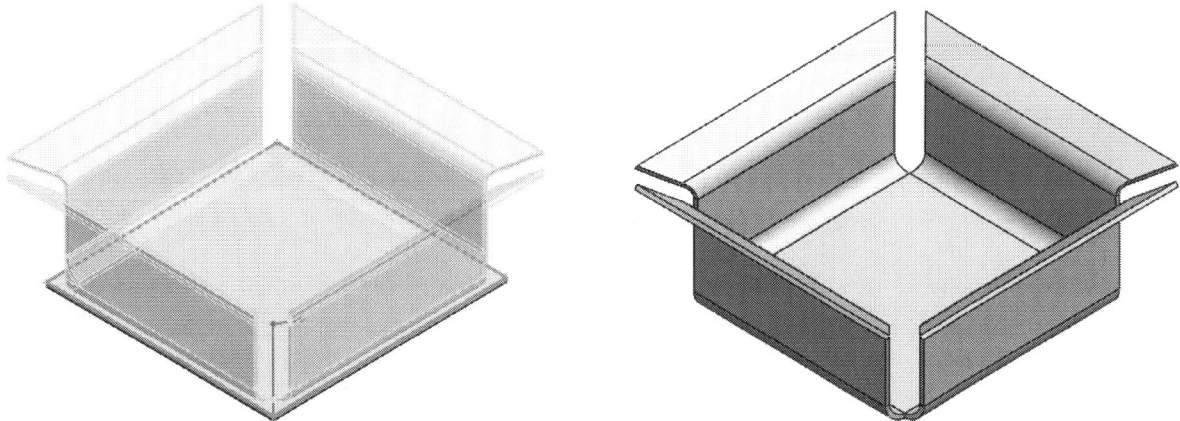

o   Below are the Miter Flange created on a single or multiple edge with offset distances from both sides, as shown. By using the spinners in the **Start/End Offset** rollout of the PropertyManager.

Sheet Metal Design

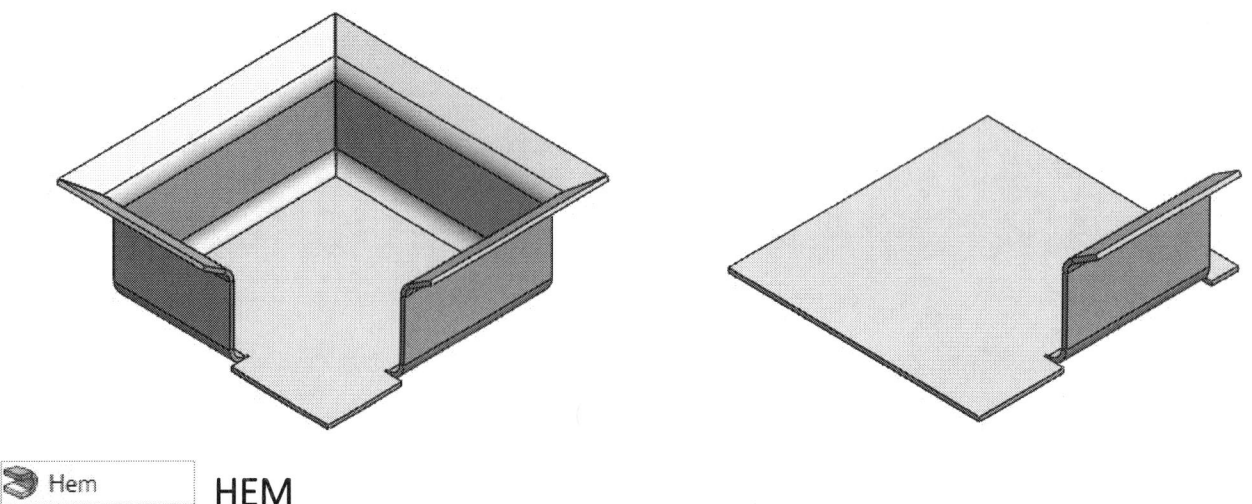

HEM

Hemming is the process of removing the sharp edges of a sheet metal component by bending them, to hide burrs, rough edges, and improve appearance. It also helps in joining two sheet metal components. To create a hem feature on a sheet metal part, follow the steps:

> Select the **Hem** tool from the **Sheet Metal CommandManager** to activate it and display the Hem PropertyManager, as shown.
> Select the edge of a flat surface to display preview of a hem feature along it with the default settings, as shown.

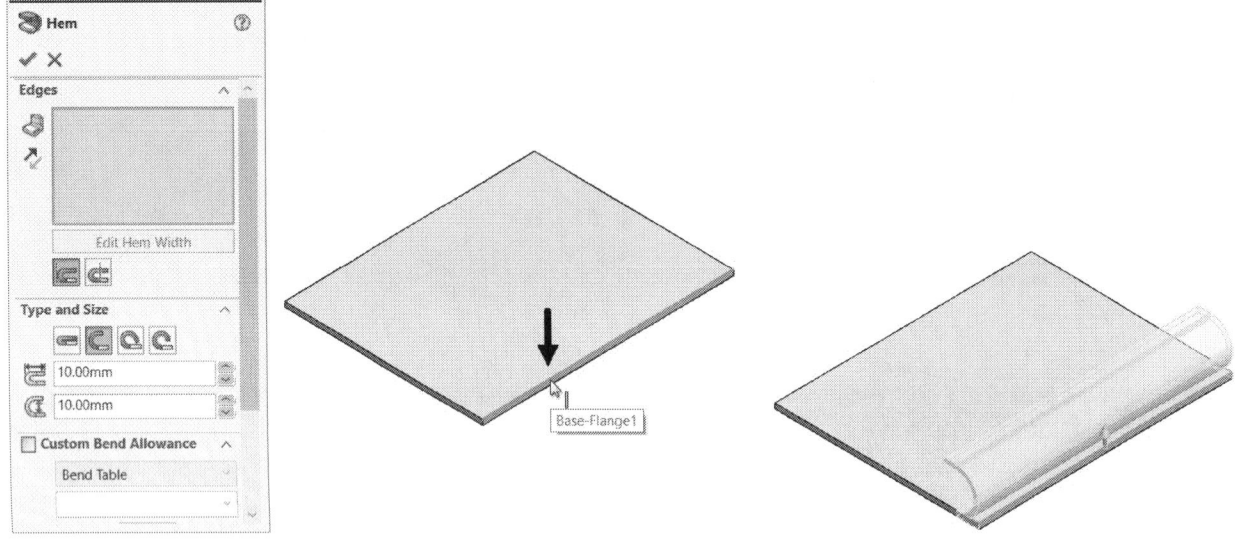

> You can click on the **Reverse Direction** button from the **Edges** rollout to toggle between the direction of hem feature, if required, as shown.

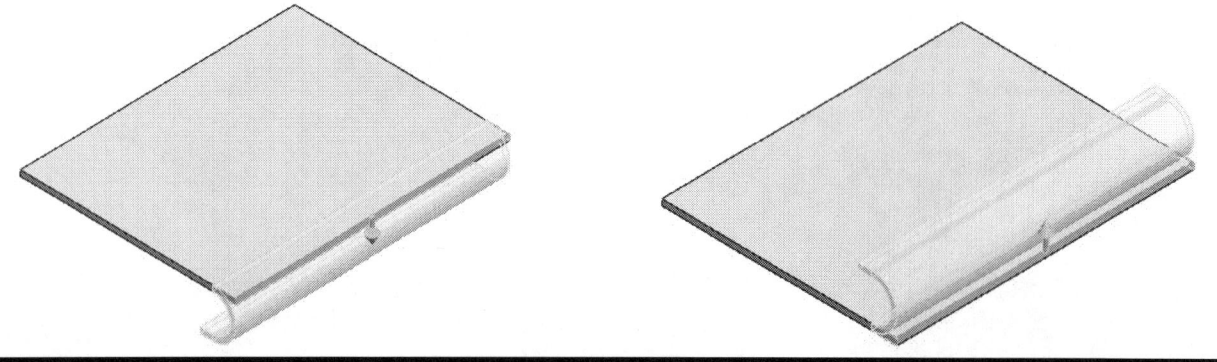

Sheet Metal Design

- The **Bend Inside** and **Bend Outside** button in the **Edges** rollout and selected to define, where to add the material.

  - The **Bend Inside** button is selected by default and the bend of the hem feature gets created inside the size/limit of the sheet, as shown.

  - By clicking on the **Bend Outside** button, the bend of the hem feature gets started, outside the size/limit of the sheet, as shown.

Hem with Bend Inside   Hem with Bend Outside

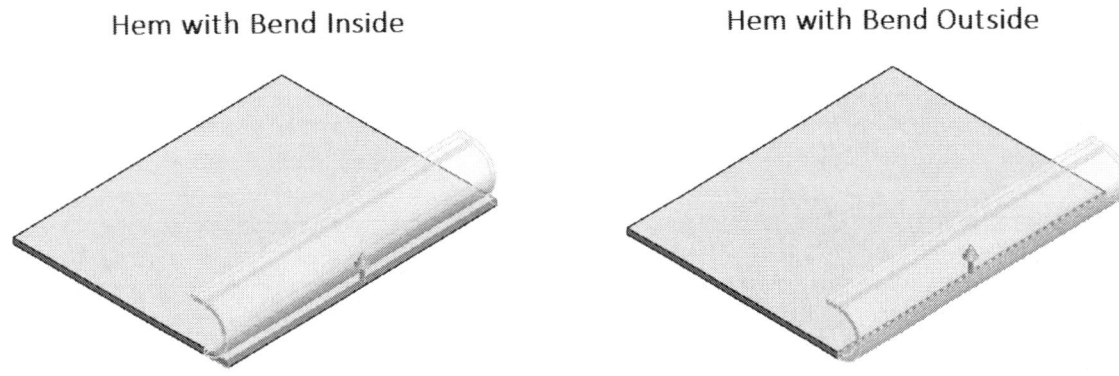

- The options in the **Type and Size** rollout are used to define the type and size of the hem.

  - By selecting the **Close** or **Open** button from **Type and Size** rollout, you can create close hem and open hem features, as shown.

Close Hem   Open Hem

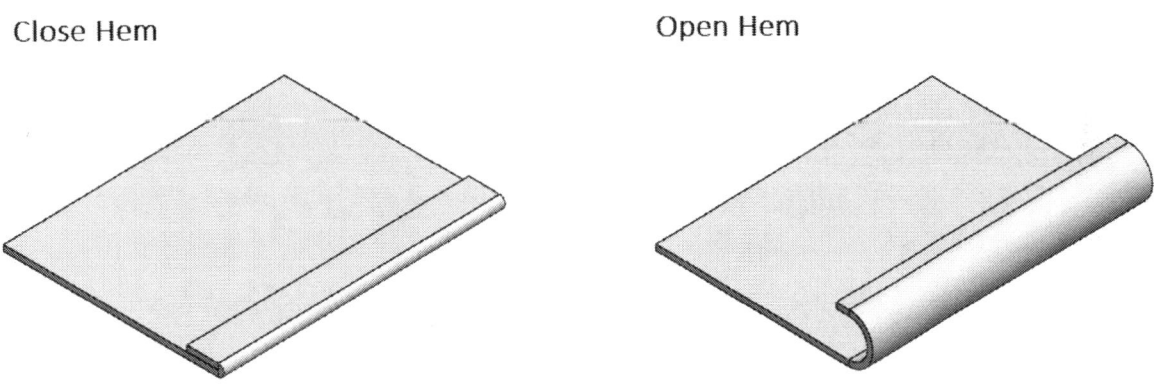

  - By selecting the **Tear Drop** or **Rolled** button, you can create the below shown hem features.

Tear Drop Hem   Rolled Hem

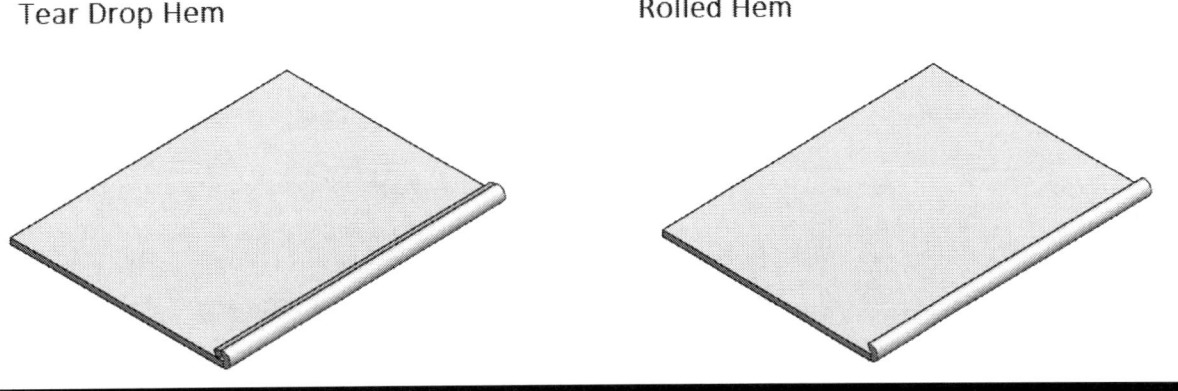

- After selecting the above Hem Types, you can enter the required values in their respective spinners displayed below them, as discussed below.

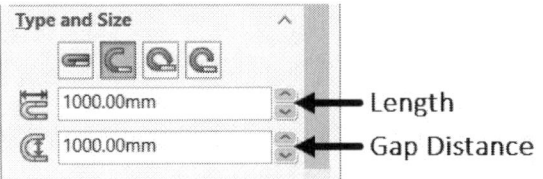
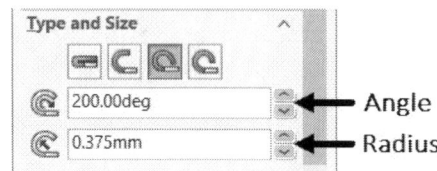

- **Length** spinner displays after selecting the **Closed** or **Open** hem
- **Gap Distance** spinner displays after selecting the **Open** hem
- **Angle** spinner displays after selecting the **Tear Drop** or **Rolled** hem
- **Radius** spinner displays after selecting the **Tear Drop** or **Rolled** hem

- If you select multiple edges, intersecting each other, Mitered corners get automatically added to it, as shown below.
- Also, the **Miter Gap** spinner under **Miter Gap** rollout get displayed in the PropertyManager, as shown. You can enter/adjust required values in it, as shown.

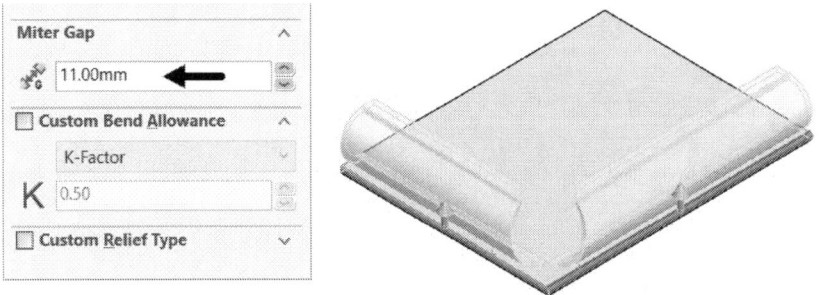

- If you want to use something other than the default bend allowance, you can select the **Custom Bend Allowance** checkbox and then select the required allowance type. And enter its required values, as shown.

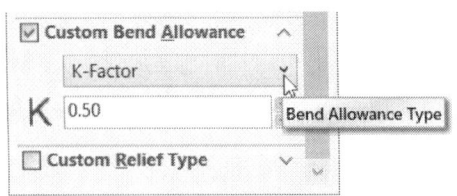
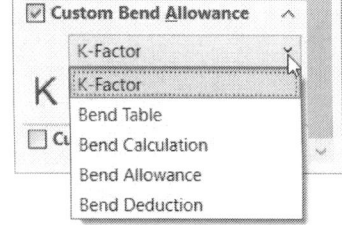

- To add relief cuts, you can select the **Custom Relief Type** checkbox and then select the required type of relief cut from the **Custom Relief Type** drop-down list, as shown.

  - If you select **Tear** option from the **Custom Relief Type** drop-down list, then you need to select the **Rip** and **Extend** buttons below it, as shown.

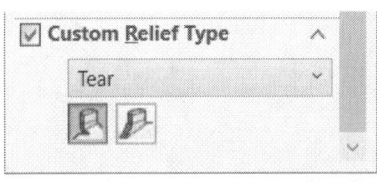
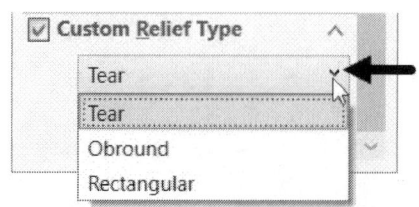

Sheet Metal Design

- If you select **Obround** or **Rectangular** option from the **Custom Relief Type** drop-down list and then after selecting the **Use Relief Ratio** check box, you need to set a value for Ratio, as shown.

    While as if you deselect it, you need to set values for **Relief Width** and **Relief Depth**, as shown.

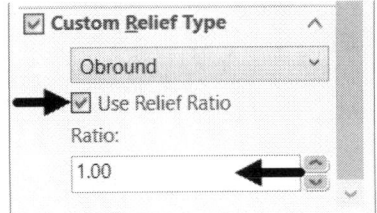 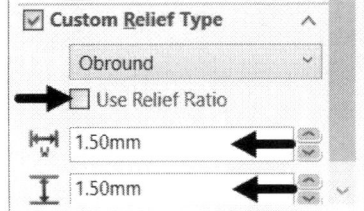

 Jog

This tool is used to create two bends in a sheet metal component by using a sketched line. The sketch must contain only one line and it is not necessary for line to be horizontal or vertical. Also, it is not necessary to keep the length of the bend line equal to the length of faces you are bending. To create a Jog feature on a sheet metal part, follow the steps:

➢ Click on the **Jog** tool from the **Sheet Metal CommandManager** to activate it and display the PropertyManager with a message, as shown.
➢ Click on the planar face of the sheet metal part to draw sketch of bending line over it, as shown.

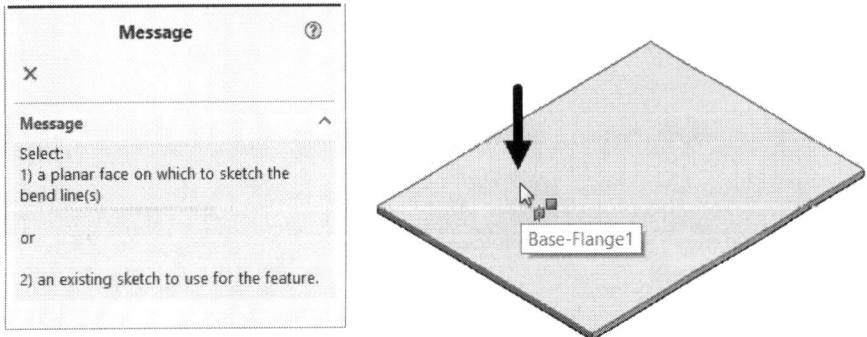

➢ Press the **Ctrl + 8** keys from the keyboard to make sketching plane parallel to screen and draw the sketch, as shown.

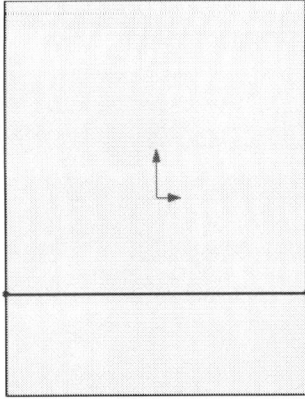

➢ Exit from the sketch to display the **Jog PropertyManager**, as shown.

Sheet Metal Design

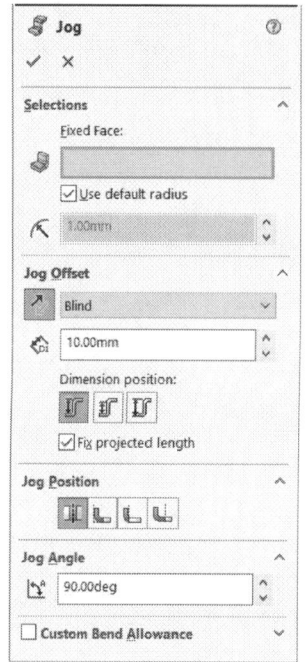 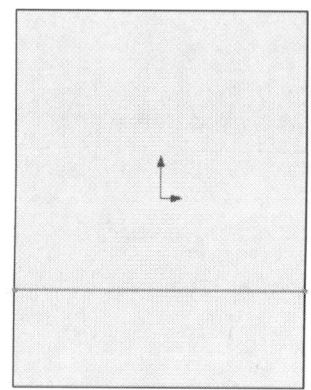

- Now click on one of the planar faces to make it a fixed face and display the preview of jog feature, as shown.

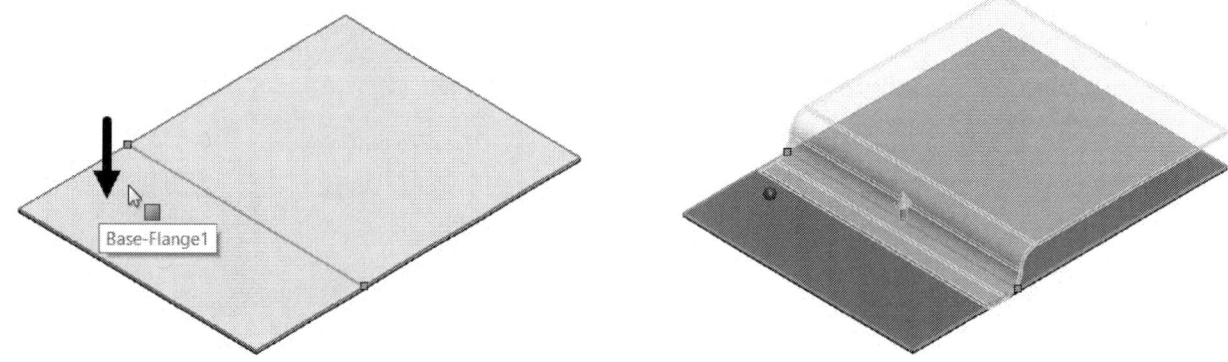

- To change the bend radius, deselect the **Use default radius** checkbox under the **Selections** rollout and then enter/adjust the required values in the respective spinner bellow it, as shown.

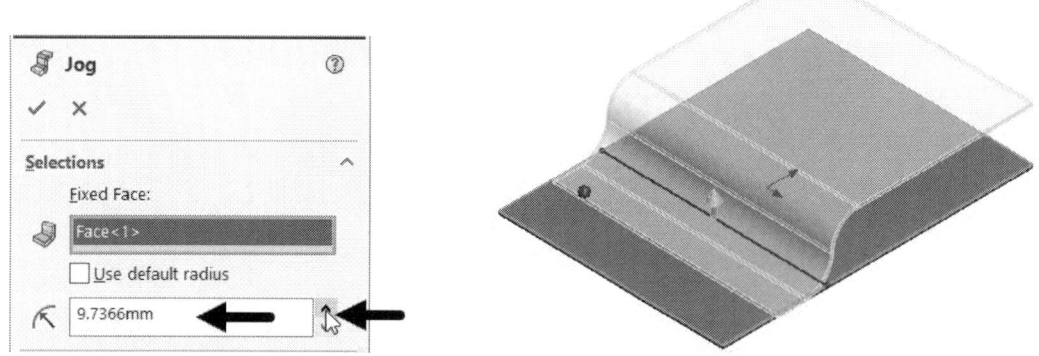

- By default, the **Blind** option is selected in the **End Condition** drop-down list under **Jog Offset** rollout of the PropertyManager, as shown.
- You can enter the required offset distance in the **Offset Distance** spinner below it, as shown.

- You can flip the direction of jog feature by clicking on the ↗ **Reverse Direction** button, if required.
- You can select the **Outside Offset**, **Inside Offset**, or **Overall Dimension** under the **Dimension position** for the required dimension positioning, as shown.
- To stay the same length for the face of the jog, select the **Fix projected length** checkbox, if it is not selected.

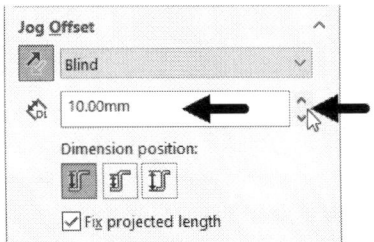

- Now for Jog positioning, you can select the required option from the **Jog Position** rollout: **Bend Centerline**, **Material Inside**, **Material Outside**, or **Bend Outside**, as shown.
- Enter or adjust the required Jog angle value in the **Jog Angle** spinner, as shown.
- You can select the **Custom Bend Allowance** checkbox and set the required allowance type and value, to use something other than the default bend allowance.

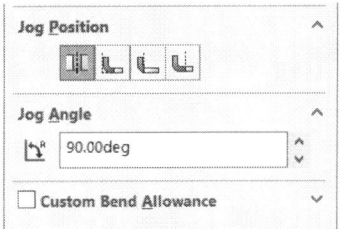

- Click on the ✓ **OK** button of the PropertyManager to exit it and display the sheet metal component with Jog feature, as shown.

  Note that, you need to click on the **OK** button of the **SolidWorks** message box, if displayed.

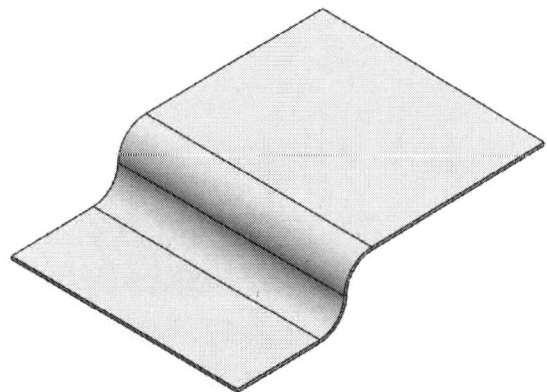

Sketched Bend

This tool is used to create a bend by using a bending line, created on the flat surface of the Sheet. To create a Sketched Bend, follow the steps:

- Click on the **Sketched Bend** tool from the **Sheet Metal CommandManager** to activate it and display the PropertyManager with a message, as shown.

- Click on the planar face of the sheet metal part to draw sketch of bending line over it, as shown.
- Press the **Ctrl + 8** keys from the keyboard to make sketching plane parallel to screen and draw the sketch, as shown.

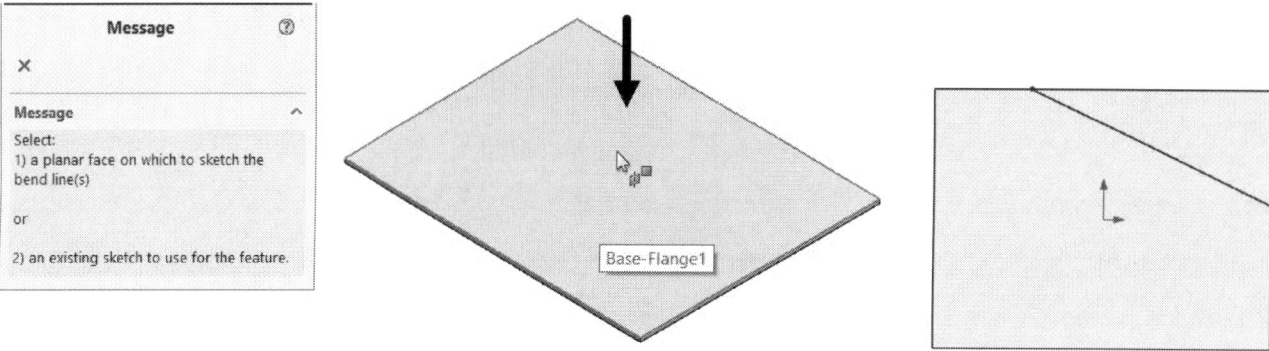

- Exit from the sketch to display the **Sketched Bend PropertyManager**, as shown.
- Click on the left area of the sheet to select it as the fix face and display the preview of Sketched Bend feature, as shown.

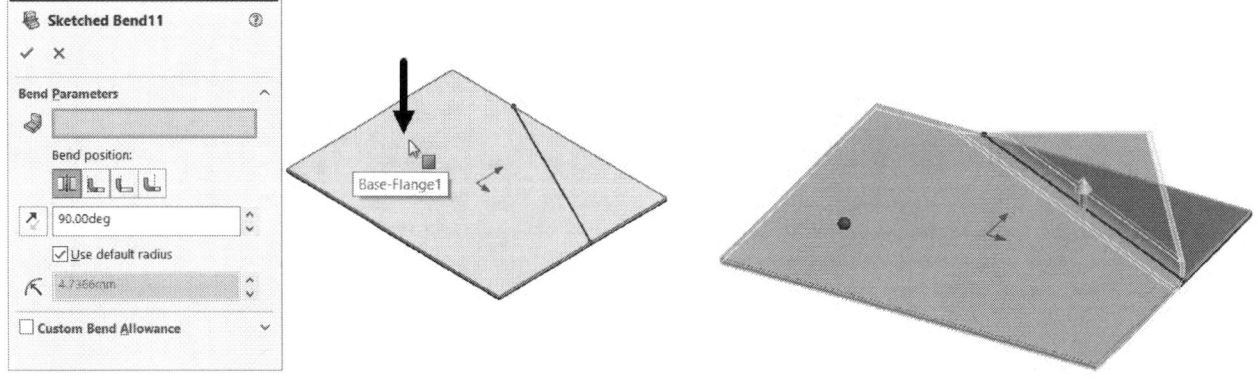

The use of options in this PropertyManager is same, as discussed earlier in this chapter. You can select the required options and enter the required bend angle value in the respective spinner, if required.

- Click on the ✓ OK button of the PropertyManager to exit it and display the sheet metal component with Sketched Bend feature, as shown.

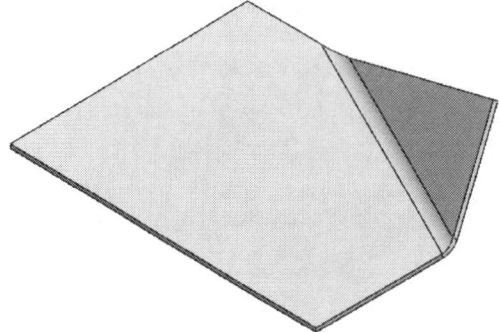

Cross-Break

This tool is used to add a graphical representation of a cross break to a sheet metal component. In HVAC or duct works, the cross breaks are used to stiffen sheet metal. To create a Cross Break to a sheet metal component, follow the steps:

- Click on the **Cross-Break** button from the **Sheet Metal CommandManager** to activate it and display the **Cross Break PropertyManager** with a message, as shown.
- Click on the Flat surface to display preview of Cross Break over it, as shown.

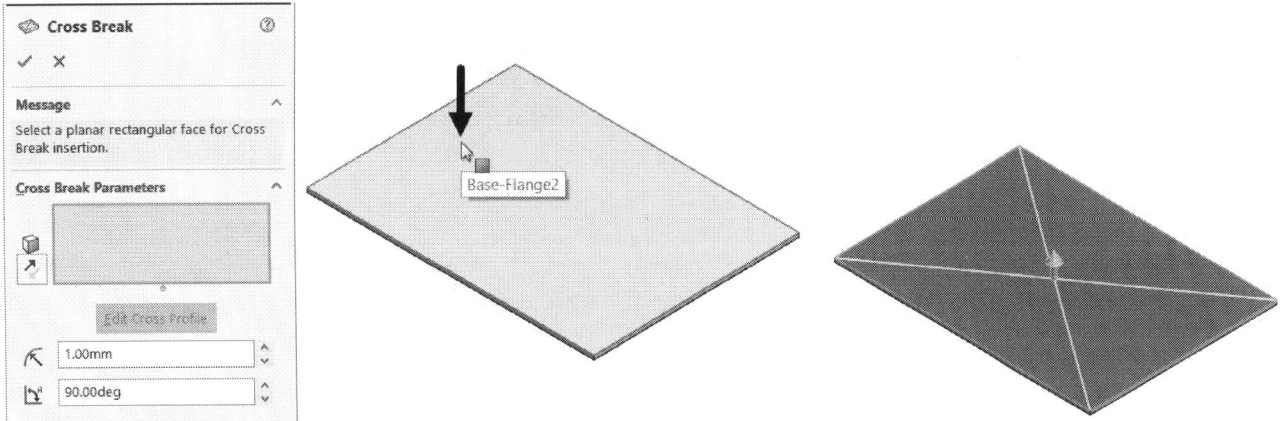

- Enter the required Break Radius and Break Angles values in their respective edit boxes, as shown.

  You can click on the **Edit Cross Profile** button to modify the cross-break sketch. To move the points that define the sketch, as shown.

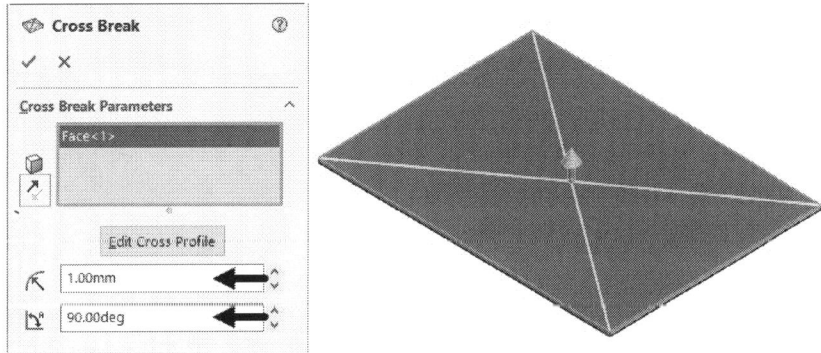

- Next, click on the ✓ **OK** button of the PropertyManager to display the Sheet with Cross-Break feature, as shown.

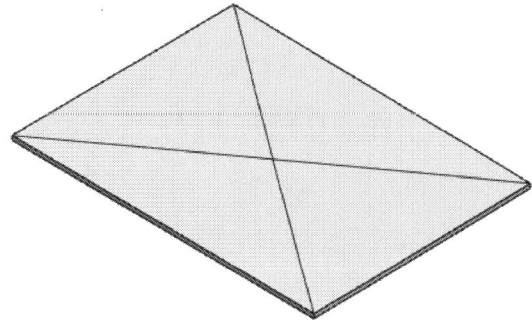

Swept Flange

The use of this tool is similar to the **Sweep** tool, discussed earlier in this book. You need to create a profile of open sketch to create a sheet metal component with Swept Flange feature. You can use sketch or series of existing sheet metal component edges as path. Also, this tool is used to create compound bends in sheet metal components. To create a Swept Flange to a sheet metal component, follow the steps:

Sheet Metal Design

➤ Draw an open sketch along any edge of sheet metal component, as shown.

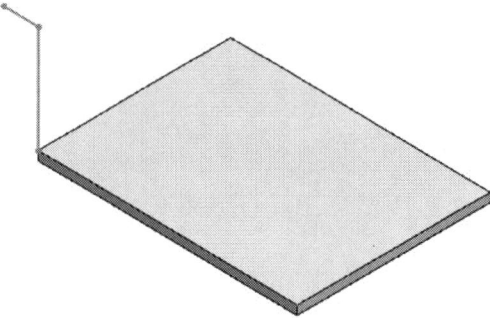

➤ Next, select the **Swept Flange** tool from the **Sheet Metal CommandManager** to display **Swept Flange PropertyManager**, as shown.

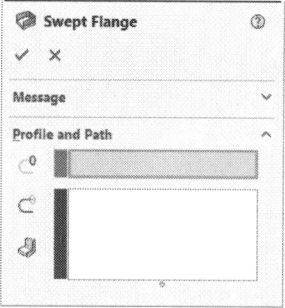

➤ Select the profile sketch first and then select the edges as path sketch to display preview of swept flange feature, as shown.

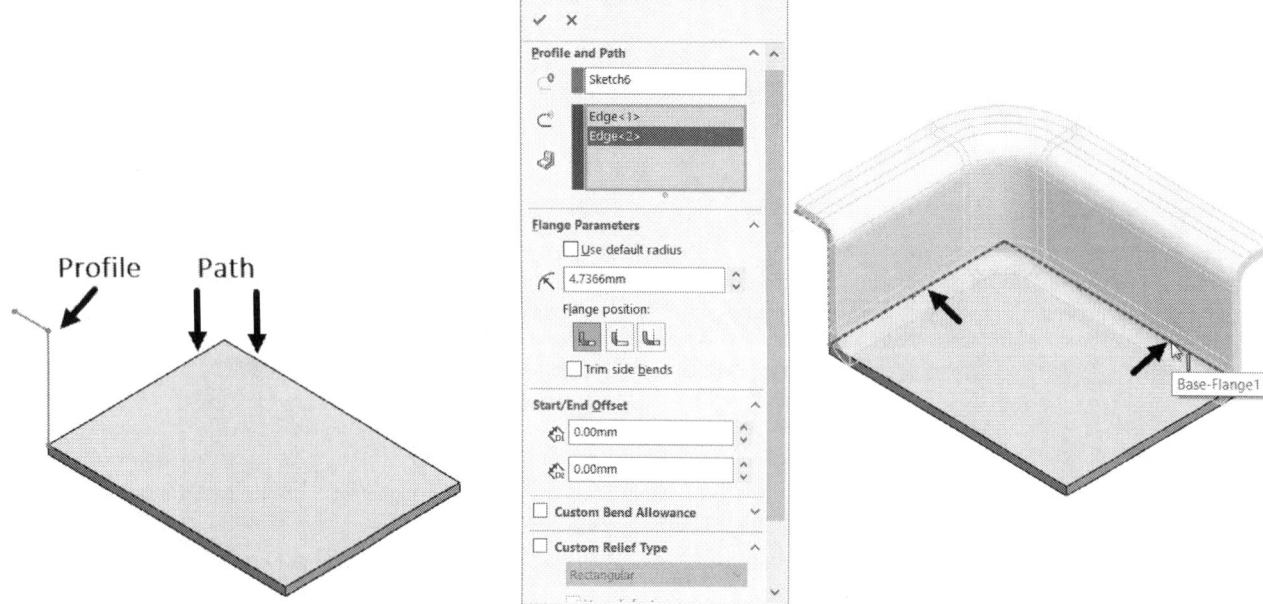

The use of option in this PropertyManager is same as already discussed in this chapter. You can use the required options and enter the required values in various spinners, if required.

➤ Now click on the **OK** ✓ button of the PropertyManager to display sheetmetal component with **Swept Flange** feature, as shown.

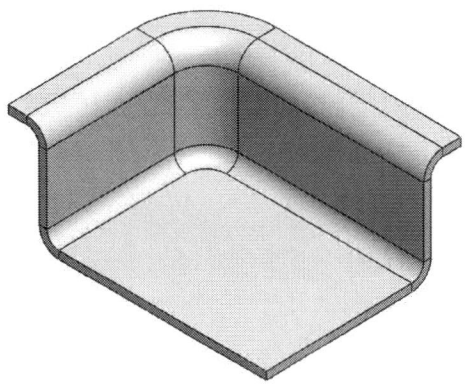

Note that, while creating the flat pattern, the chamfers or fillets on the bend region of the Swept Flange will not appear. And for flat pattern, the software calculates a linear calculation.

Corners

The options in this flyout list are used to close the gap between corners, created while creating the edge flanges. The options are shown and discussed below:

Closed Corner

To close the gap using this **Closed Corner** option, follow the steps:

➢ Select the **Closed Corner** option from the **Corners** flyout to display the **Closed Corner PropertyManager**, as shown.
➢ Select the required planar face or edge that you want to extend and display the preview, as shown

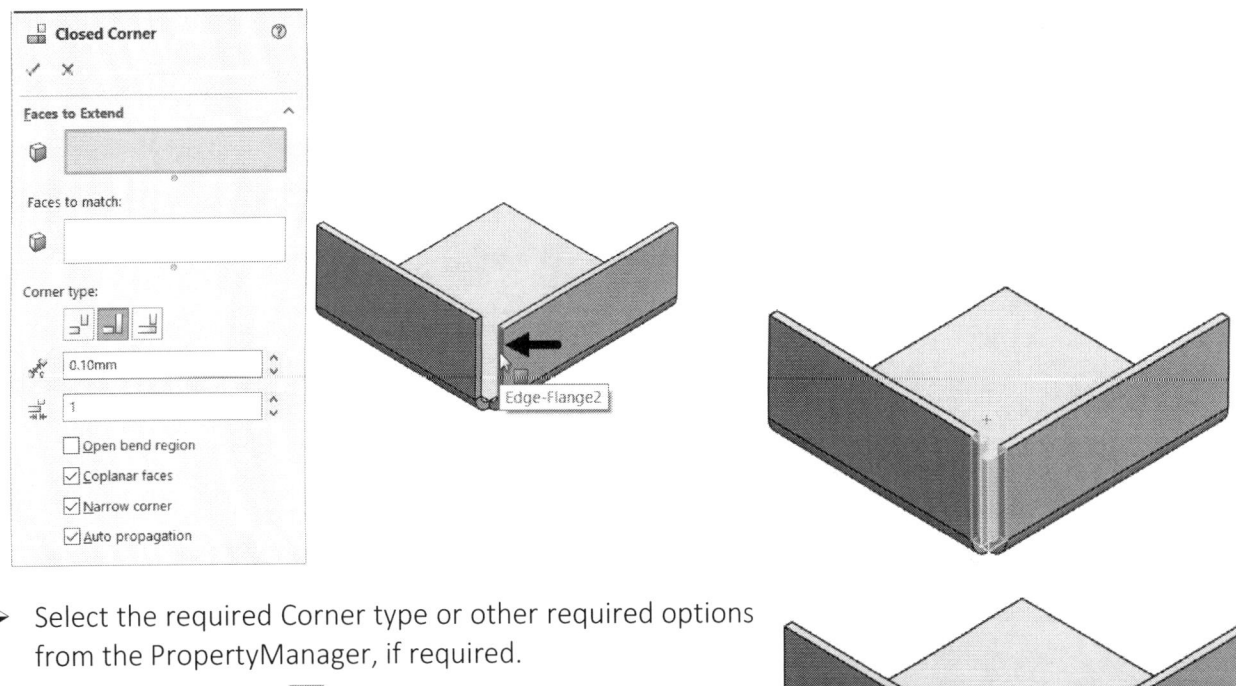

➢ Select the required Corner type or other required options from the PropertyManager, if required.
➢ Next click on the **OK** button of the PropertyManager to display sheetmetal component with Closed Corner feature, as shown.

Sheet Metal Design

Welded Corner

This option is used to add a weld bead at the corners of the folded sheet metal component to close the gap. To apply Welded Corner, follow the steps:

> Select the **Welded Corner** option from the **Corners** flyout to display the **Welded Corner PropertyManager**, as shown.
> Click on the side planar face to be welded and display the preview of Welded Corner, as shown.

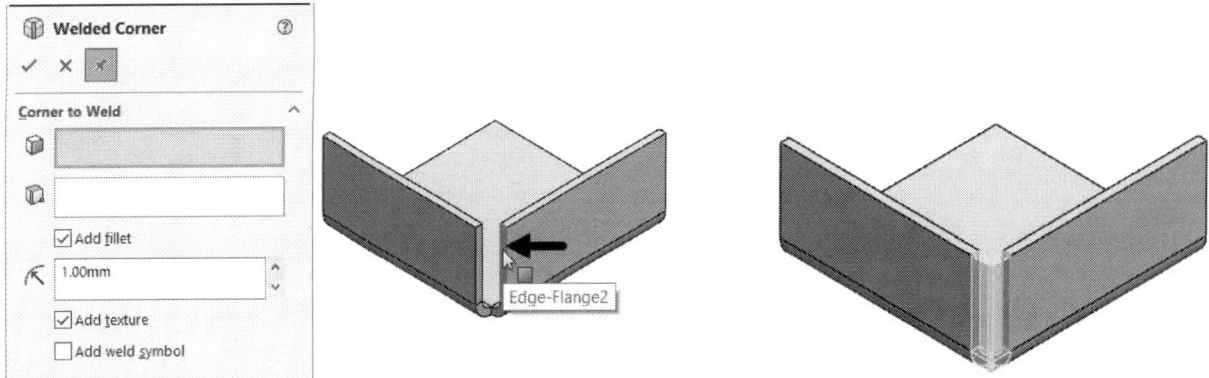

> Select the required options from the PropertyManager, if required.
> Next click on the OK ✓ button of the PropertyManager to display sheetmetal component with Welded Corner feature, as shown.

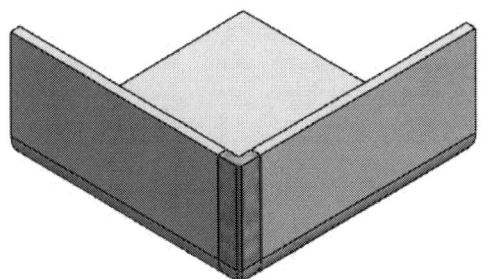

Break-Corner/Corner-Trim

This option is used to break the edges of the sheet metal component by creating fillets or chamfers. To do so, follow the steps:

> Select the **Break-Corner/Corner-Trim** option from the **Corners** flyout to display the **Break Corner PropertyManager**, as shown.
> Click on the respective edges or flange faces to break and display the preview of Break Corner by chamfer, as shown.

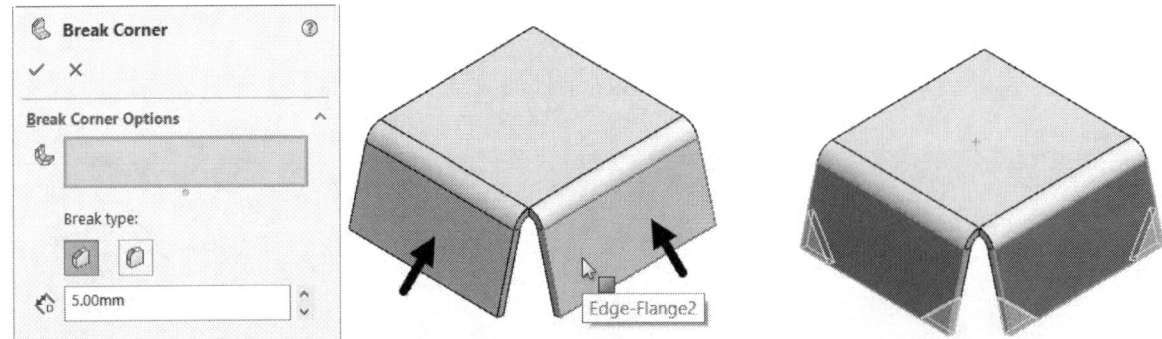

Sheet Metal Design

- As the **Chamfer** button is selected by default, you can enter or adjust the required distance value in the **Distance** spinner, as shown above.
- Next, click on the **OK** button of the PropertyManager to display sheetmetal component with Break Corners as chamfer, as shown.

Similarly, you can break corners as fillet, as shown. By selecting the **Fillet** option of PropertyManager and by entering the required radius value in **Radius** spinner.

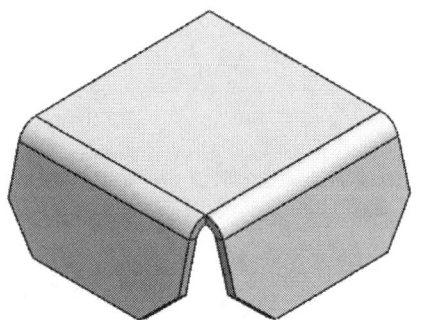 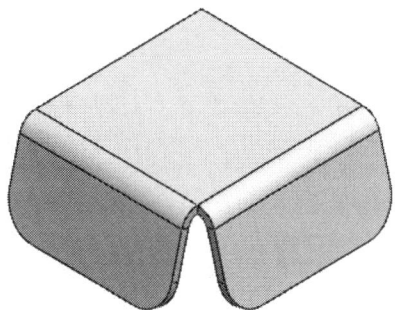

 **Corner Relief**

This tool is used to apply the bend relief at the corners of the sheet metal components. To do so, follow the steps:

- Select the **Corner Relief** option from the **Corners** flyout to display the **Corner Relief** PropertyManager, as shown.
- Click on the **Collect all corners** button to display the preview of Corner Relief and display other option in the PropertyManager, as shown.

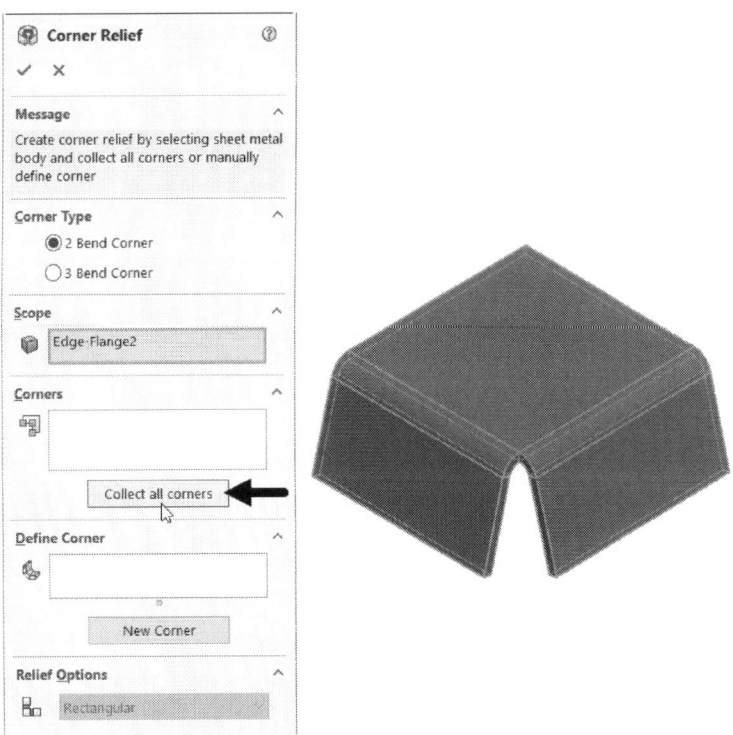

Sheet Metal Design

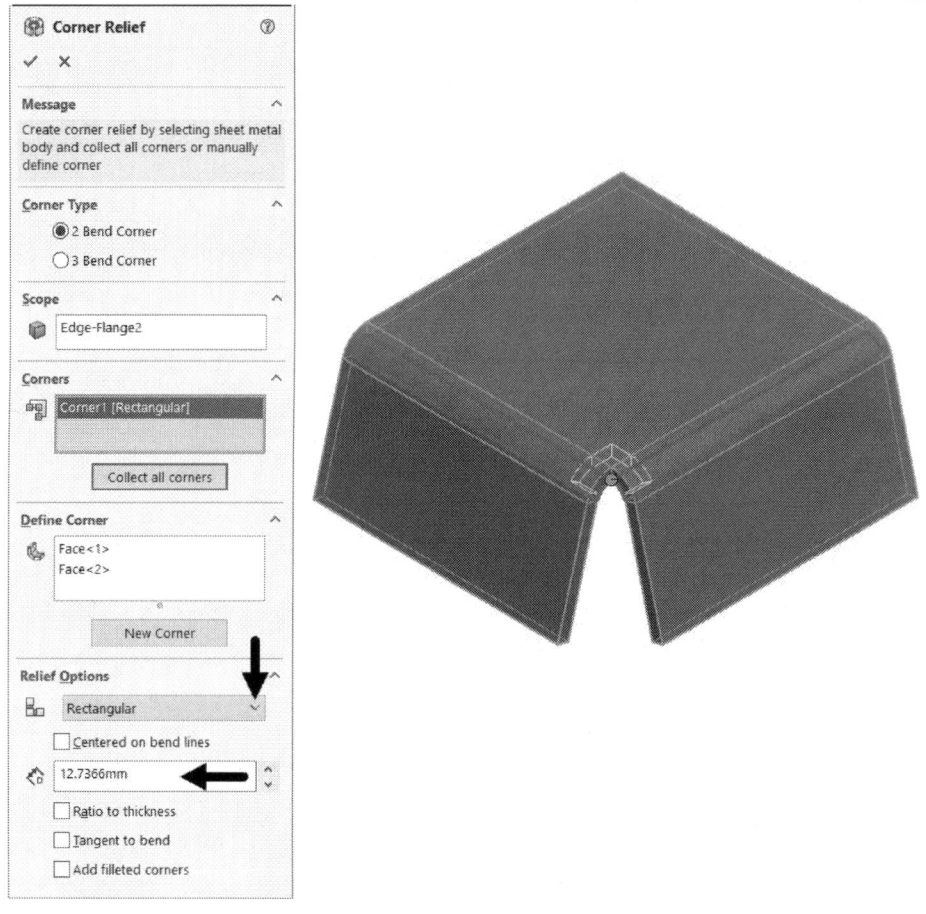

- Next, select the **Rectangular** option as the Relief type and enter the required value in the **Slot Length** spinner of the **Relief Options** rollout, as shown above.
- Now, click on the **OK** button of the PropertyManager to display sheetmetal component with Corner Relief, as shown.

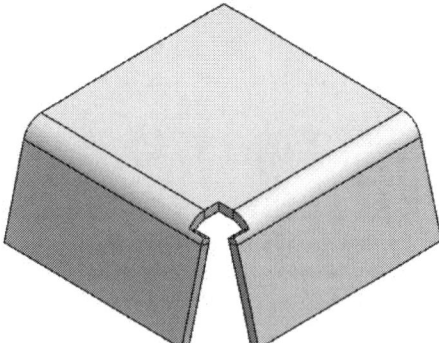

Similarly, you can create other types of corner reliefs by selecting the required Relief type from the **Relief Options** rollout of the PropertyManager, as shown. And enter the required values in their respective spinners.

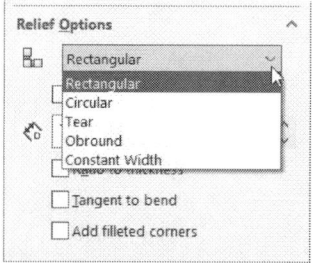

 ## Sheet Metal Gusset

This tool is used to create gussets, which is same like a rib feature, discussed earlier in this book. To strengthen the sheet metal component. To do so, follow the steps:

> Select the **Sheet Metal Gusset** tool from the **Sheet Metal CommandManager** to display the **Sheet Metal Gusset PropertyManager**, as shown.
> Select the two planar faces one by one to display preview of Sheet Metal Gusset feature, as shown.
> Select the required options and adjust the required parameters in the PropertyManager for the gusset feature, as shown.

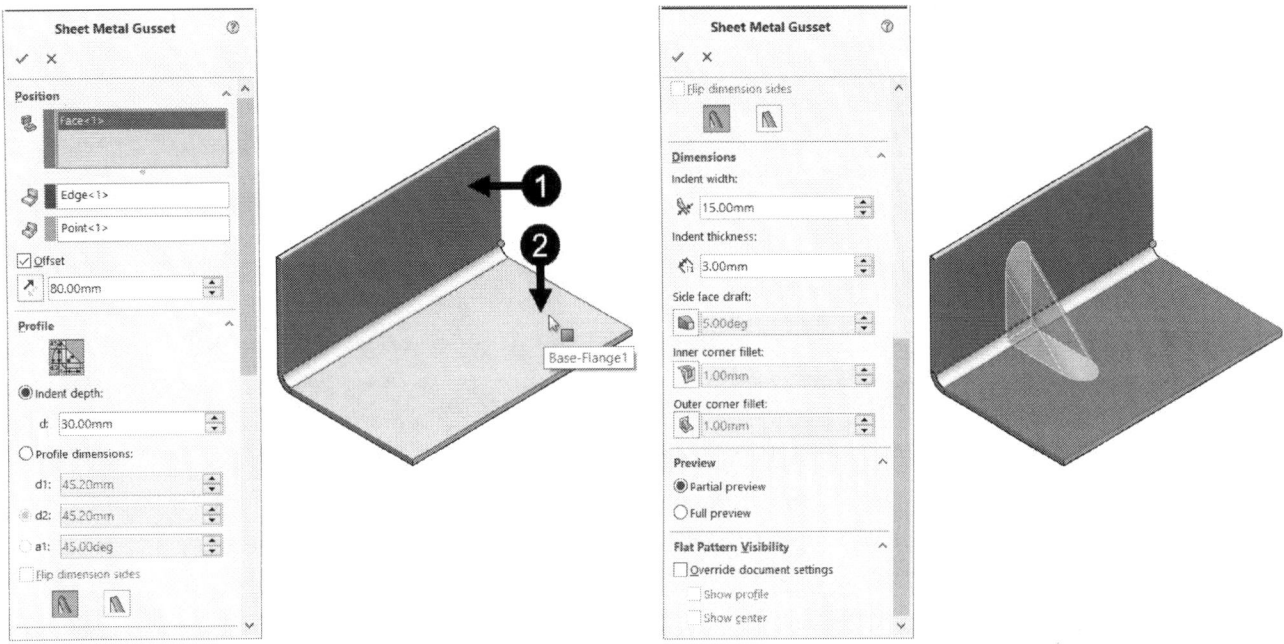

> Next, click on the **OK** button of the PropertyManager to display sheetmetal gusset feature, as shown.

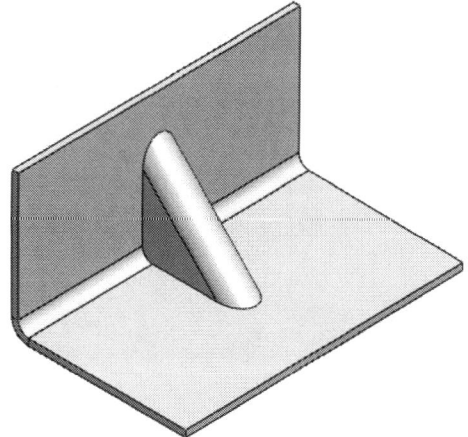

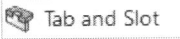 ## Tab and Slot

This tool is used to interlock two bodies by creating tabs on one body and slots on another body. To do so, follow the steps:

> Select the **Tab and Slot** tool from the **Sheet Metal CommandManager** to display the **Tab and Slot PropertyManager**, as shown.

Sheet Metal Design

- Select the edge for tabs and then select the corresponding face for slots to display preview of Tab and Slot feature, as shown.

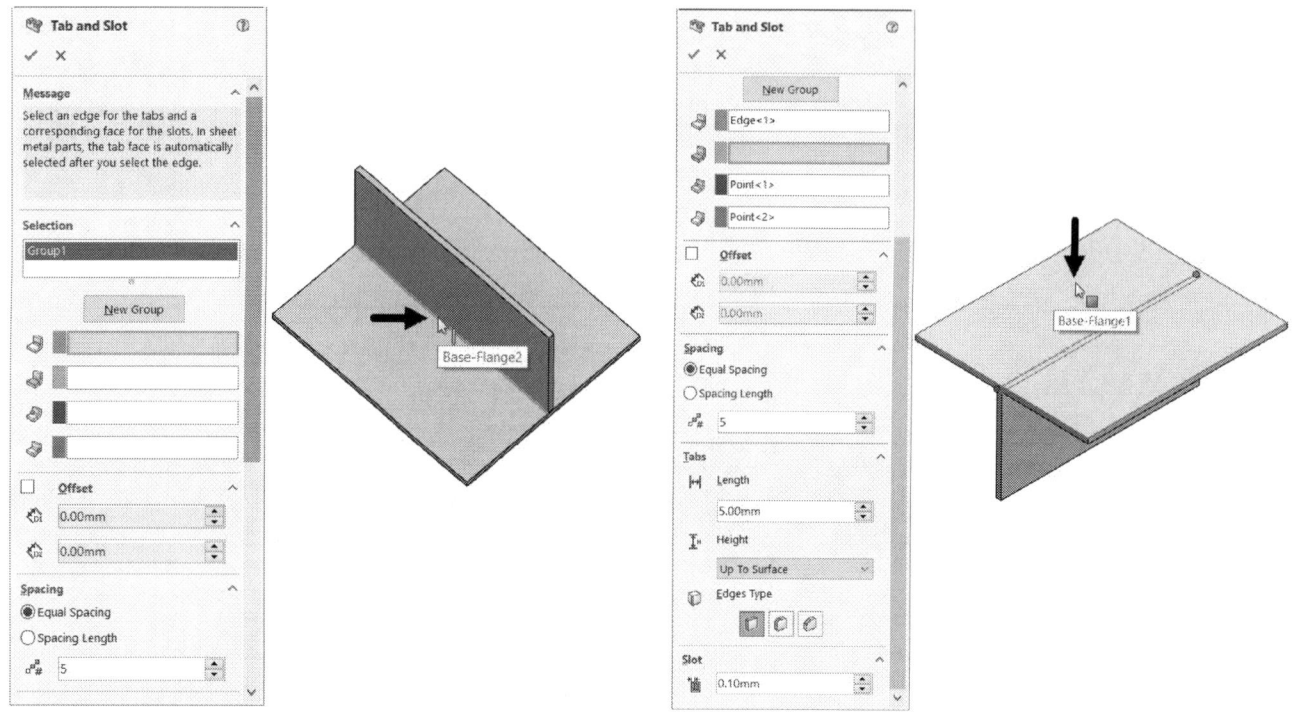

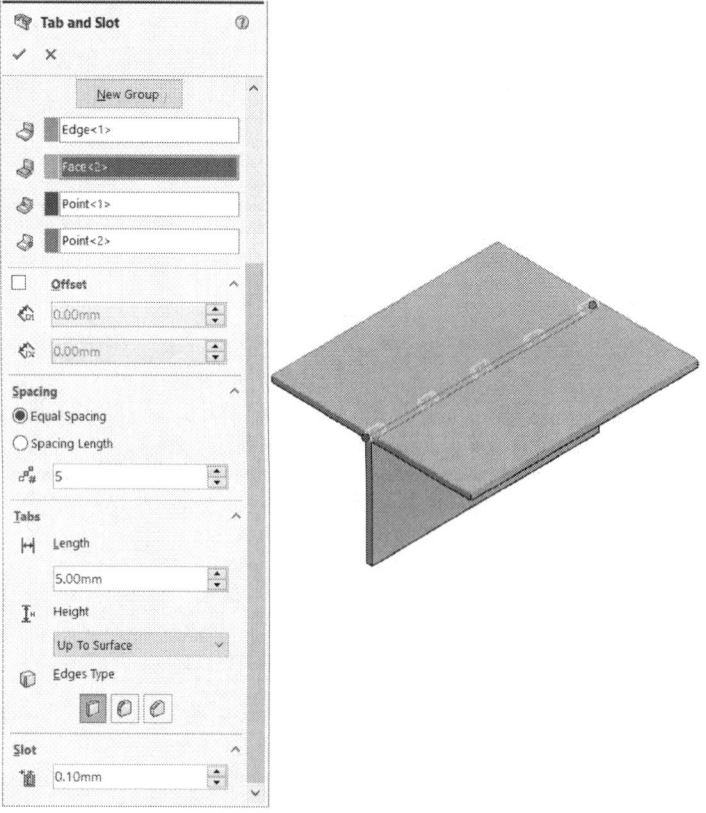

- Select the required options and adjust the required parameters in the PropertyManager, if required.
- Next, click on the OK button of the PropertyManager to display sheet metal component with Tab and Slot feature, as shown.

Sheet Metal Design

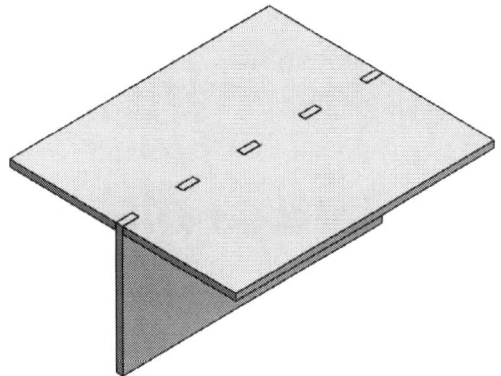

 Extruded Cut

This tool is used to create cuts on the planar faces of the sheetmetal components. And, the procedure to use this tool is similar to use of Extruded Cut tool for cutting in solid models, discussed earlier in this book. To do so, follow the steps:

- Select the **Extruded Cut** tool from the **Sheet Metal CommandManager** to display the **Extrude PropertyManager**, as shown.
- Click on the planar face to enter in the sketching plane and draw the sketch, as shown.

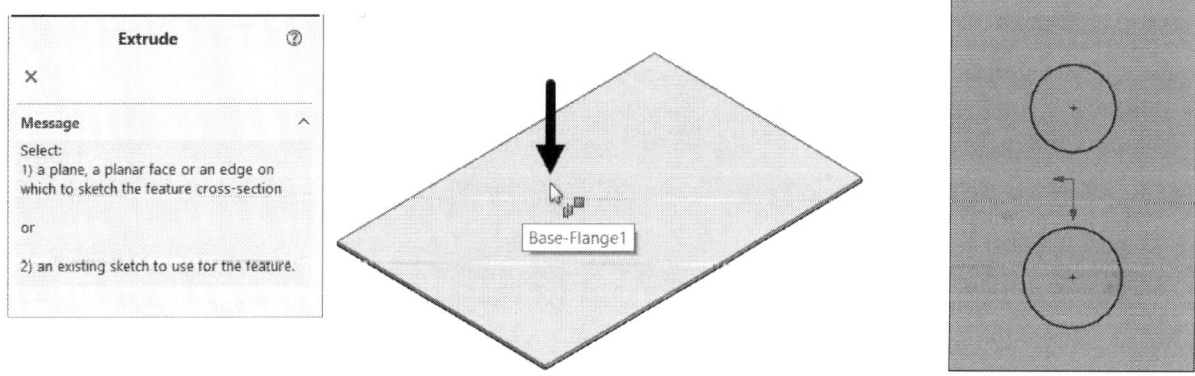

- Now click on the **Exit Sketch** button of the **Sketch CommandManager** to exit from Sketching Environment and display the preview of Extruded Cut feature, along with **Cut-Extruded PropertyManager**, as shown.

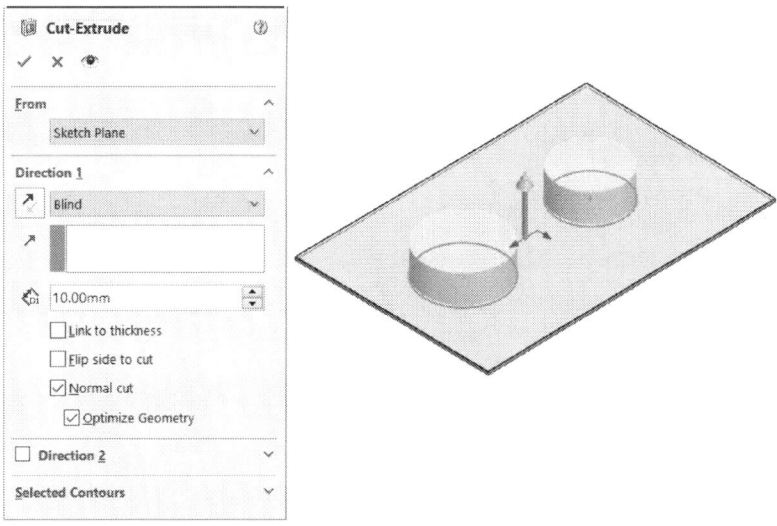

Sheet Metal Design

➤ Next, select the **Link to thickness** checkbox to adjust the depth value for the Extruded Cut feature, with respect to the sheet thickness, as shown.

The **Normal cut** check box is used for the bent sheet metal components. And the use of other options in the PropertyManager is same, as discussed earlier in this book.

➤ Next, click on the **OK** ✓ button of the PropertyManager to display sheet metal component with Extruded Cut feature, as shown.

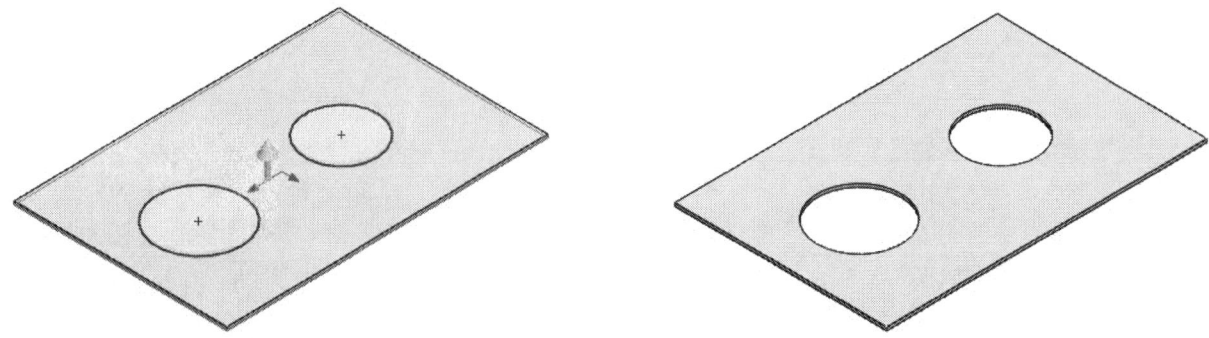

Simple Hole

This tool is used to create a simple hole on the planar faces of the sheetmetal components. And, the procedure to use this tool is similar to Simple Hole tool for creating hole in solid models, discussed earlier in this book. To do so, follow the steps:

➤ Select the **Simple Hole** tool from the **Sheet Metal CommandManager** to display the **Hole PropertyManager**, as shown.

➤ Click on the planar face of the sheet metal component to place and display the preview of simple hole feature, as shown.

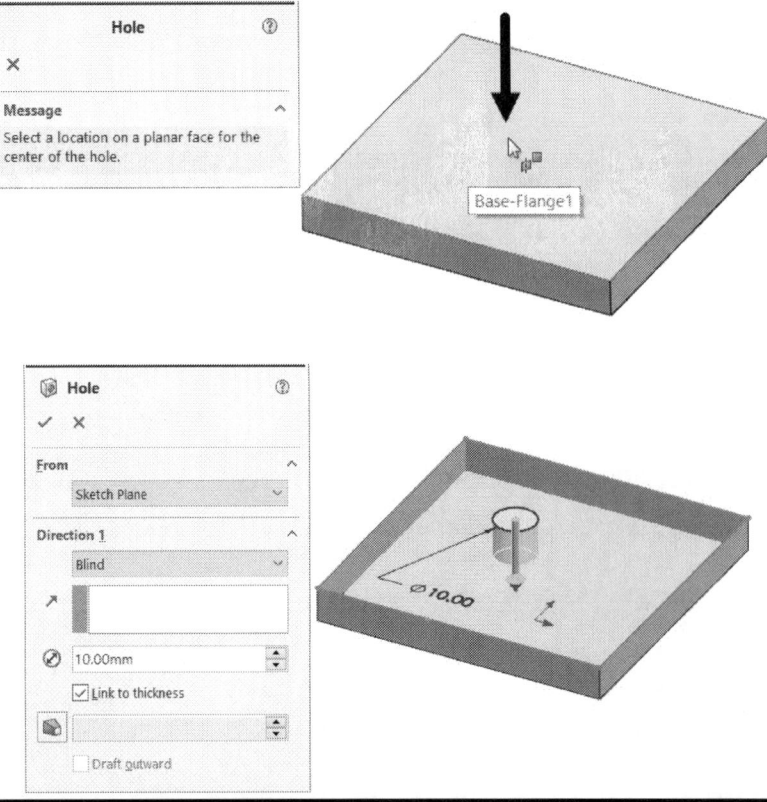

Sheet Metal Design   12-40

The options in this PropertyManager gets visible and use of these options is same, as discussed earlier in this book. You can select the required options, as per your requirements.

➤ Next, click on the **OK** ✓ button of the PropertyManager to display sheet metal component with Simple Hole feature, as shown.

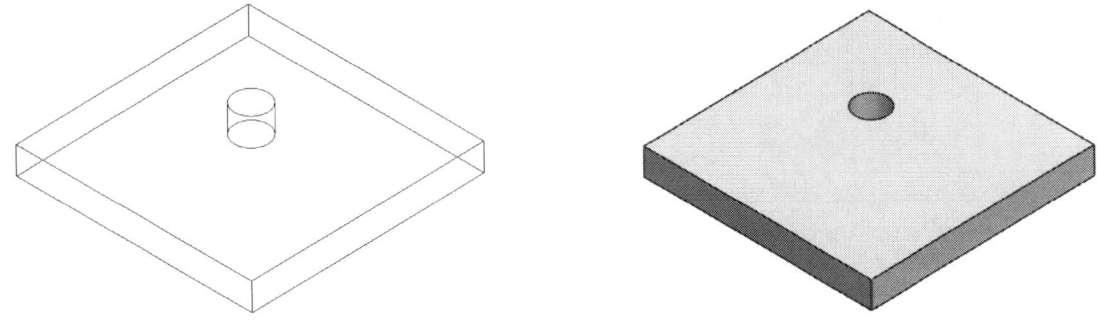

Vent

This tool is used to create vents in a sheetmetal component. To create vents, follow the steps:

➤ Draw a sketch for the vent feature on the planar surface, as shown.

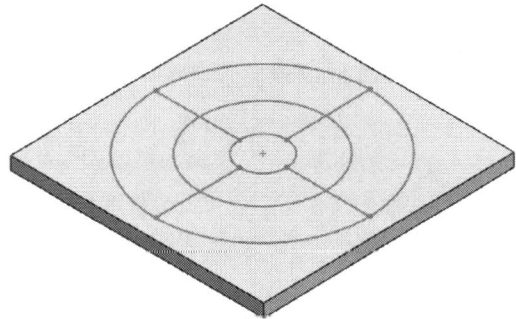

➤ Select the **Vent** tool from the **Sheet Metal CommandManager** to display the **Vent PropertyManager**, as shown.
➤ Select the outer edge of the sketch to display the partial preview of vent feature, as shown.

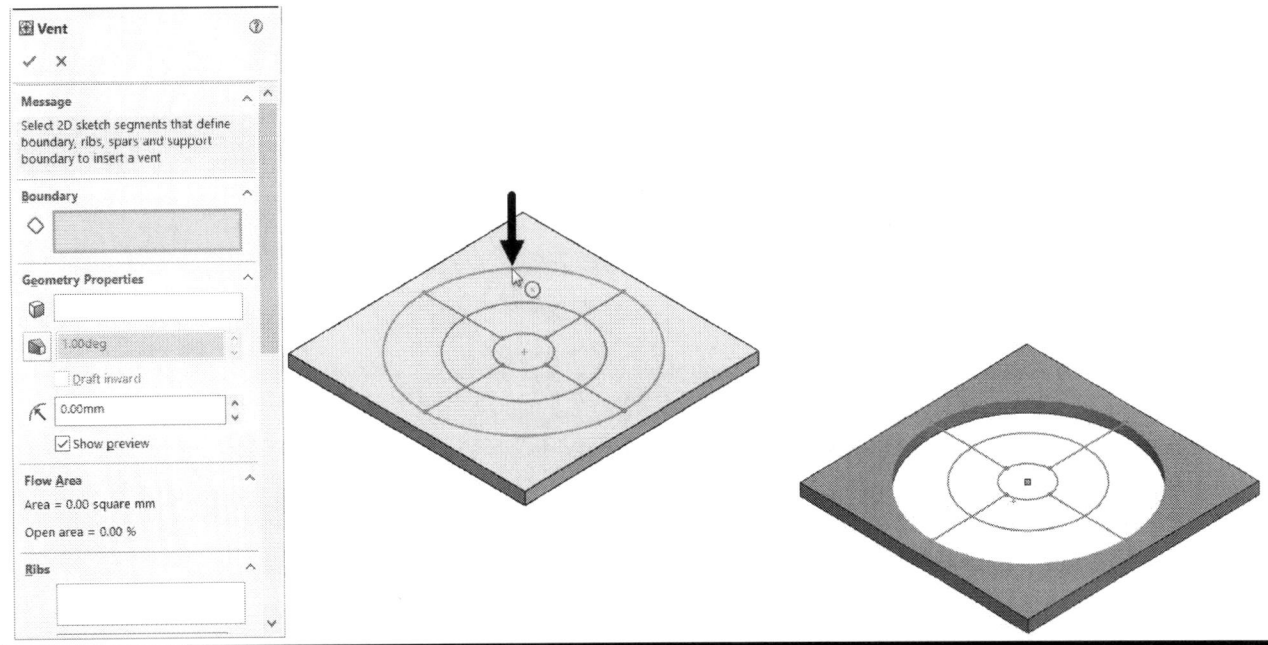

- Next click in the **Ribs** selection box and then select the sketch entities for ribs to display preview of ribs, as shown.
- Now, click in the **Spars** selection box and select the sketch entities for Spars also, as shown.

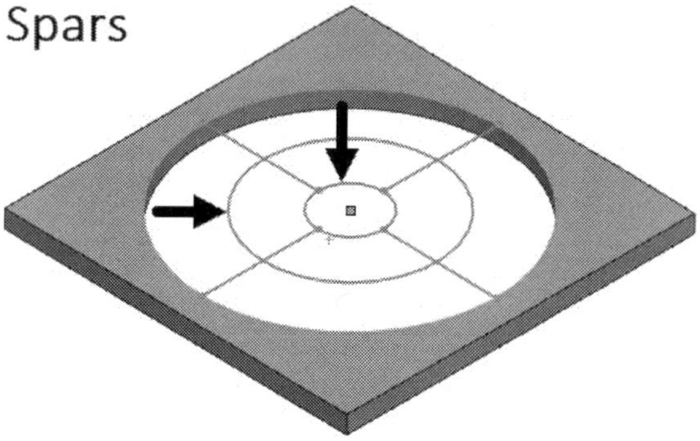

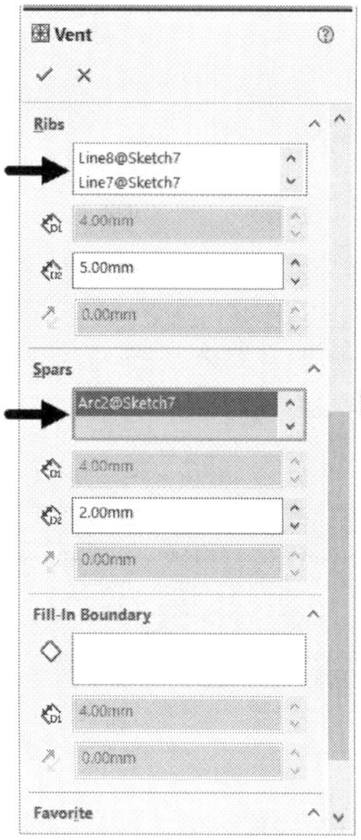

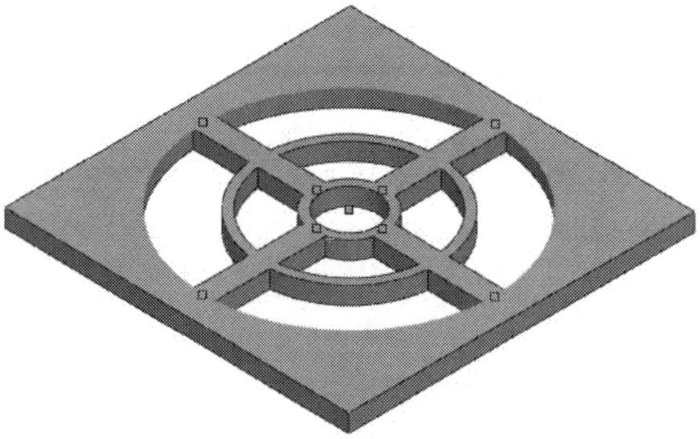

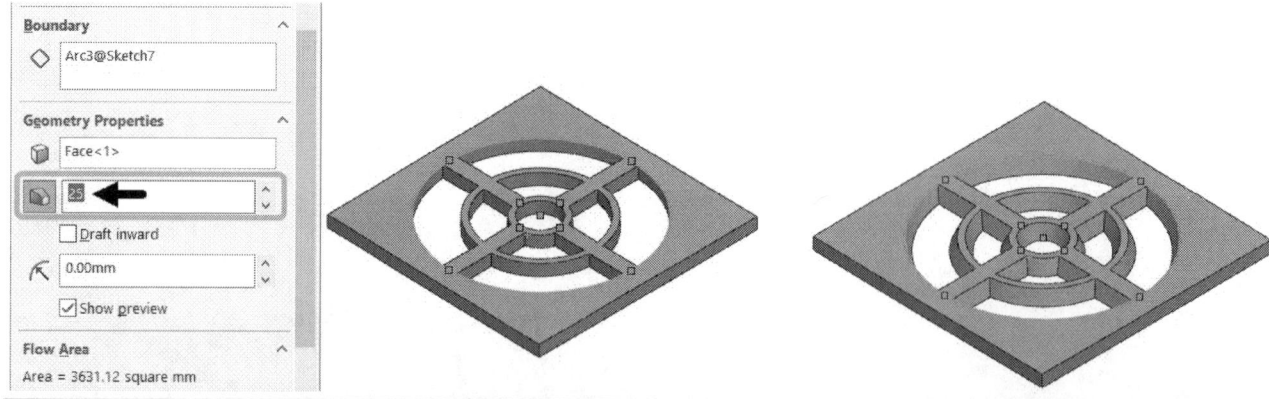

- You can enter the required values for depth, width & offset from surface of ribs & spares in their respective spinners of the PropertyManager, if required.
- You can also change draft angle by clicking on the **Draft On/Off** button under **Geometry Properties** rollout and enter the required Draft angle values in the respective spinner, as shown.

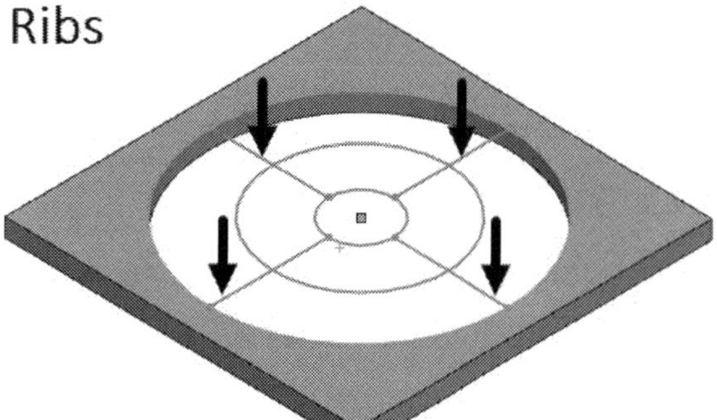

Sheet Metal Design

- Next you can select other options and enter required values in the PropertyManager, if required.
- Next, click on the OK ✓ button of the PropertyManager to display sheet metal component with Vent feature, as shown.

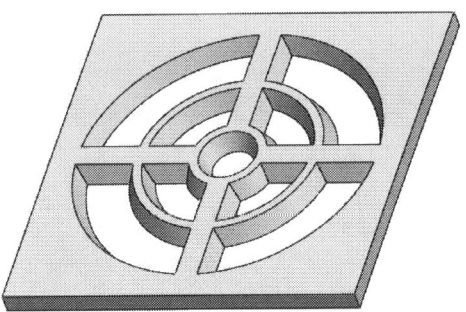

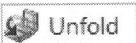 **Unfold Tool**

This tool is used to flatten/unfold selected bend/bends or all the bends of the sheet metal component.

- Select the **Unfold** tool from the **Sheet Metal CommandManager** to display the **Unfold PropertyManager**, as shown.
- Click on one of the planar faces to select it as the fixed face, as shown.
- Now select the bends that you want to flatten one by one, as shown.

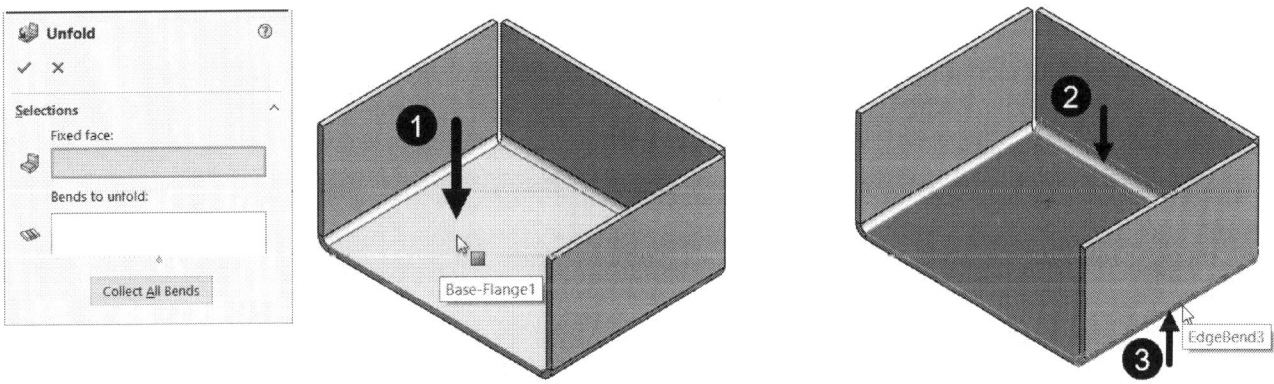

- Now click on the **OK** button of the PropertyManager to display the sheet metal component with flatten surfaces, as shown.

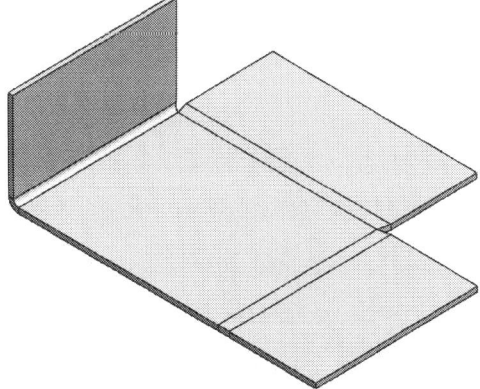

Note that, if you select the **Collect All Bends** button of the PropertyManager, the system will select all bends automatically, as shown. And you can then flatten/unfold all of them together, as shown.

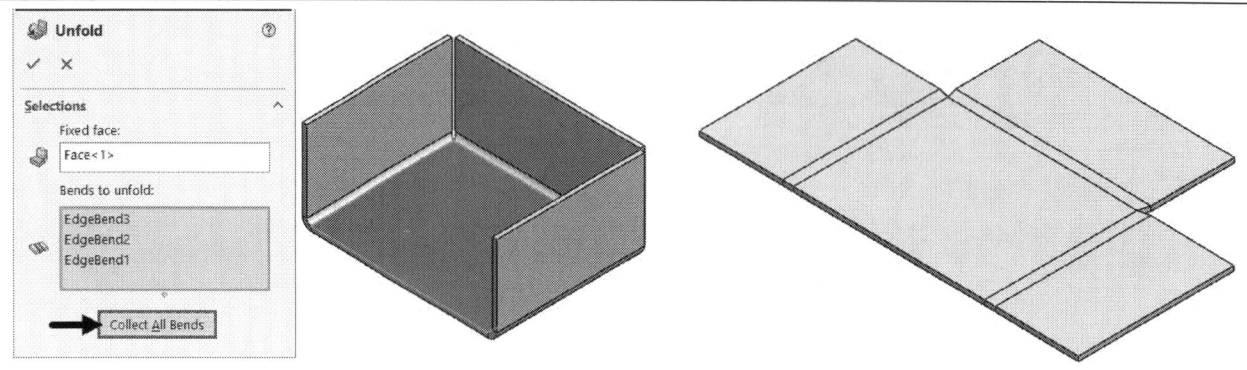

 **Fold Tool**

This tool is used to return the selected unfolded bend/bends of the sheet metal component to its folded state.

➤ Select the **Fold** tool from the **Sheet Metal CommandManager** to display the **Fold PropertyManager**, as shown.
➤ Next, as the fixed surface have got selected automatically, select the unfolded bends that you want to bend, as shown.

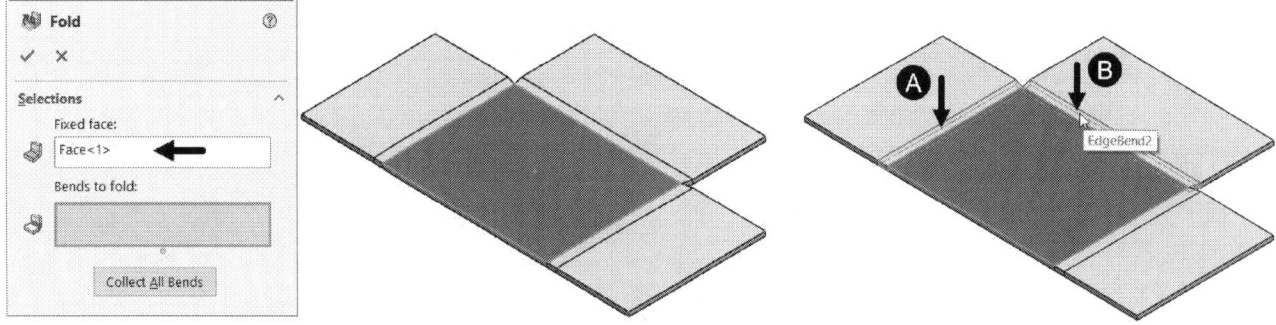

➤ Now click on the **OK** button of the PropertyManager to display the sheet metal component with bends, as shown.

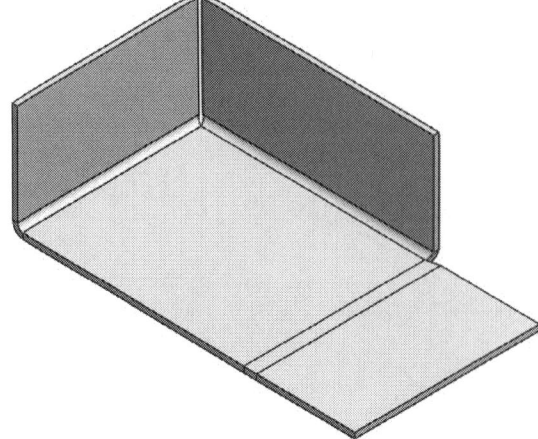

Note that, if you select the **Collect All Bends** button of the PropertyManager, the system will select all flatten bends automatically, as shown. And you can then bend/fold all of them together, as shown.

Sheet Metal Design

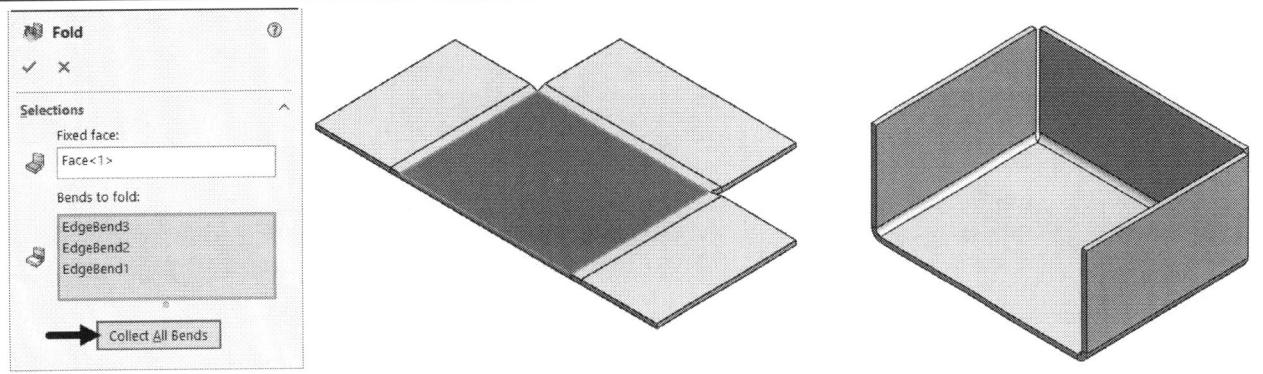

Note that the **Unfold** and **Fold** tools are very useful while adding a cut across a bend of sheet metal component. By following the below given steps:

- First flatten the bend or bends of the sheet metal component, using the **Unfold** tool.
- Next, add a cut.
- And then using the **Fold** tool you can return the bend/bends to its folded state.

 Flatten Tool

This tool is used to create the Flat Pattern the sheet metal component. The flat pattern is mainly used in the machine shop or tool room to define the size of sheet used and the shape of the sheet needed before bending.

- Select the **Flatten** tool from the **Sheet Metal CommandManager** to display the Flat Pattern of sheet metal component, as shown.

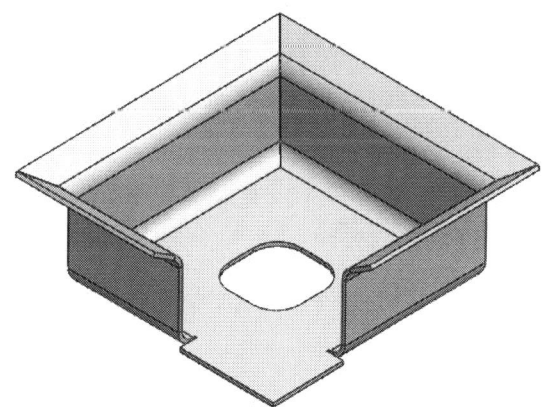 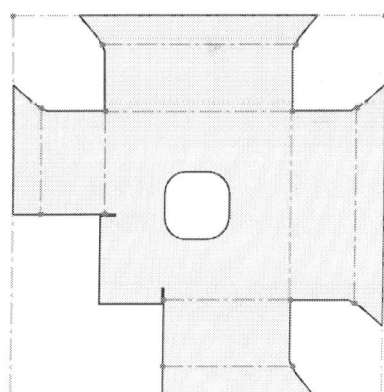

- To edit the Flat Pattern, right click over **Flat-Pattern1** from the **FeatureManager Design Tree** to display the pop-up toolbar, as shown.
- Next, click on the **Edit Feature** option of the toolbar to display the **Flat-Pattern PropertyManager**, as shown.
- Next you can select the required options from the PropertyManager.

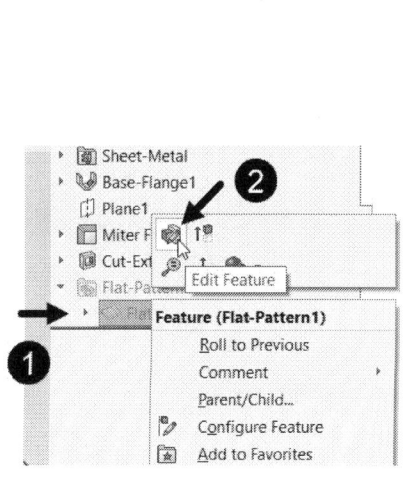
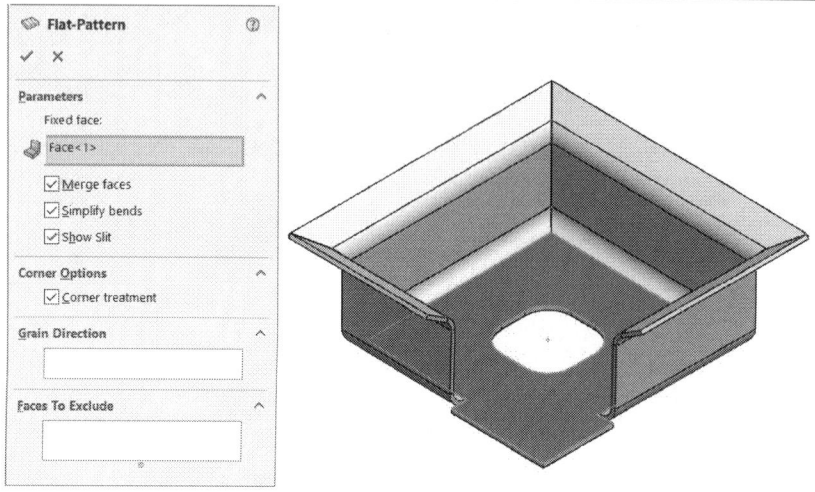

The options in the **Flat-Pattern PropertyManager** are discussed next:

Fixed face
The **Fixed face** is selected to define the face that will be fixed while opening the sheet to create the flat pattern.

Merge faces
This check box is selected to merge the faces that are planar and coincident in the Flat Pattern. After selecting it, the lines in the bend regions will not get visible.

Simply bends
This check box is selected to straighten curved edges in the Flat Pattern. By deselecting it, complex edges remain in the Flat Pattern.

Show Slit
This check box is selected to show slits that are added for some corner relief features.

Corner Options
The **corner treatment** check box in the **Corner Options** rollout is selected to apply smooth edges in the Flat Pattern.

Grain Direction
The selection box under this rollout is use to select an edge or line.

Faces To Exclude
The selection box under this rollout is used to select any faces in the drawing area that you do not want in the Flat Pattern, when they interfere with bends. You should select the Front or Back of each face that you want to exclude.

To preview the flat pattern of a Sheet Metal component:

> Right click over the ⬙ Flat-Pattern from the **FeatureManager Design Tree** to display the shortcut menu, as shown.

Sheet Metal Design

➤ Next select the **Toggle flat display** option of the shortcut menu to display the preview of Flat Pattern, as shown.

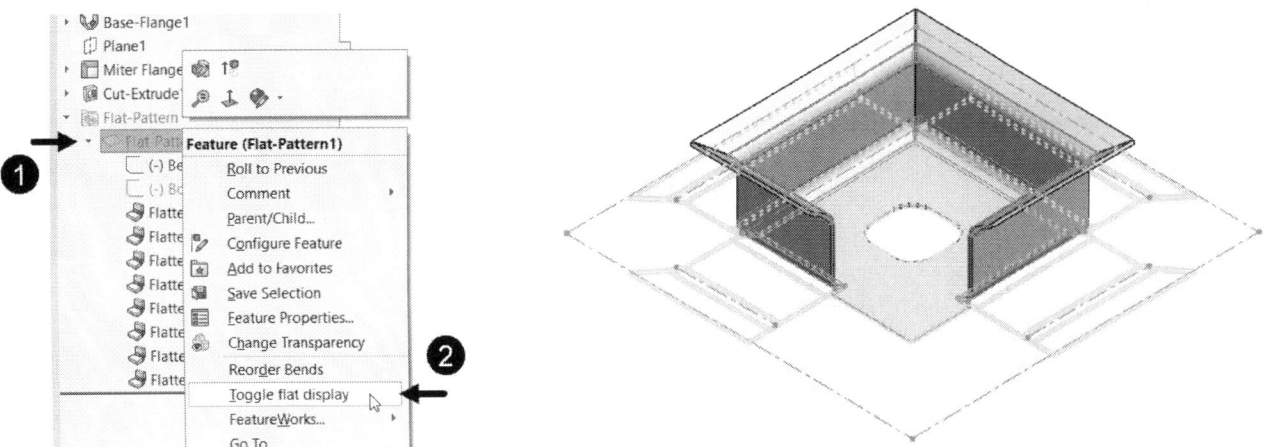

 Rip Tool

This tool is used to add a gap between the edges of a shelled solid part before converting it into a Sheet Metal.

➤ First create a shelled solid part, as shown.
➤ Select the **Rip** tool from the **Sheet Metal CommandManager** to display the **Rip PropertyManager**, as shown.
➤ Next select the edges one by one, as shown.
➤ Enter the require Rip gap value in the respective selection box of the PropertyManager.
➤ Now click on the **OK** button of the PropertyManager to display the solid part with Rip feature, as shown.

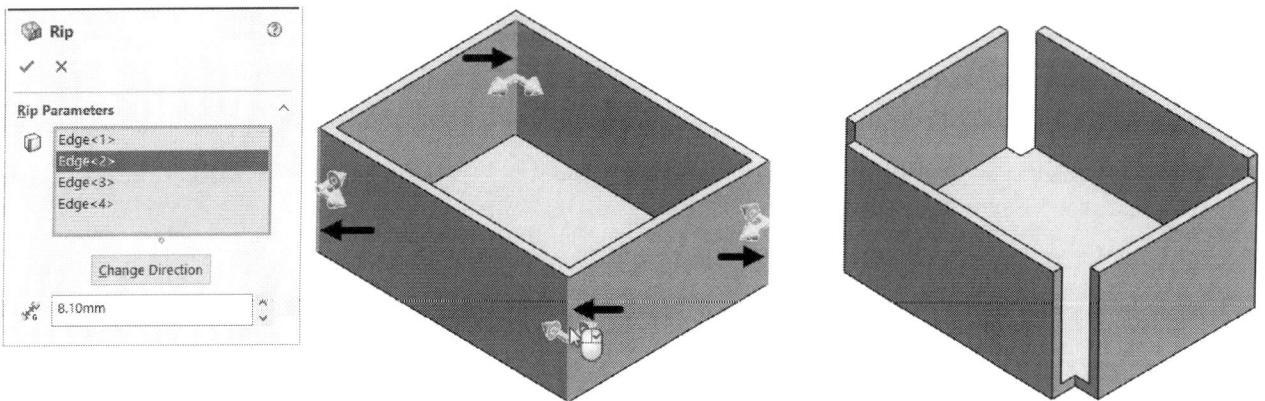

Insert Bends Tool

This tool is used to add bend to the part component to convert it into the sheet metal component. To do so, follow the steps:

➤ First create a solid part, as shown.
➤ Select the **Insert Bends** tool from the **Sheet Metal CommandManager** to display the **Bends PropertyManager**, as shown.
➤ Click on the top surface of the part model and click on the **OK** button of the **SOLIDWORKS** message box, as shown.

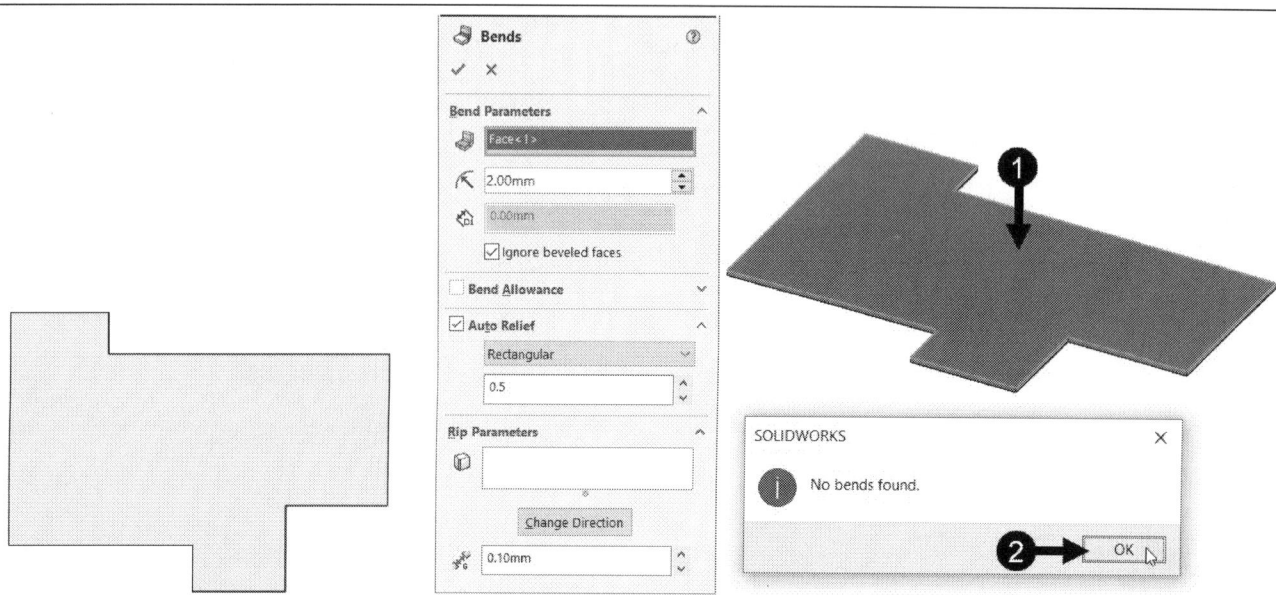

- Click on the **Flat-Sketch** under the **Process-Bends** node of the **FeatureManager Design Tree** to display the pop-up toolbar, as shown.
- Next, select the **Edit Sketch** option to enter in the Sketching environment and draw the sketch as shown.

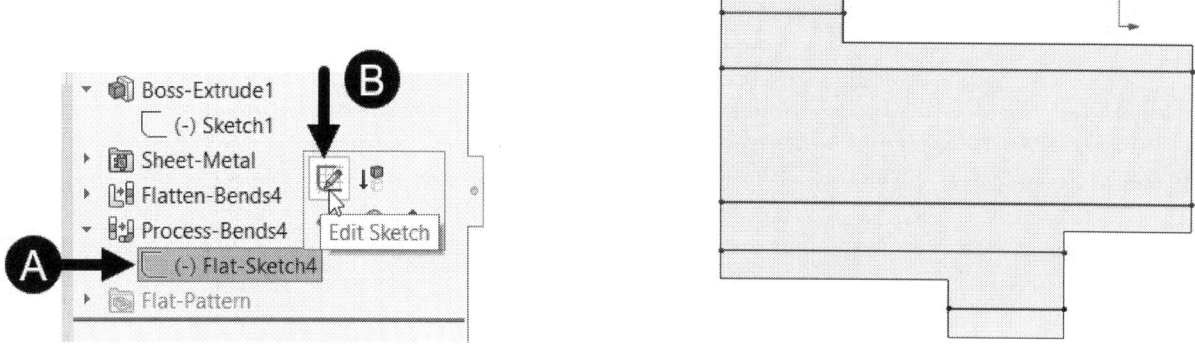

- Now exit from the Sketching environment to display the sheet metal component with bends along the recently drawn bending lines, as shown.

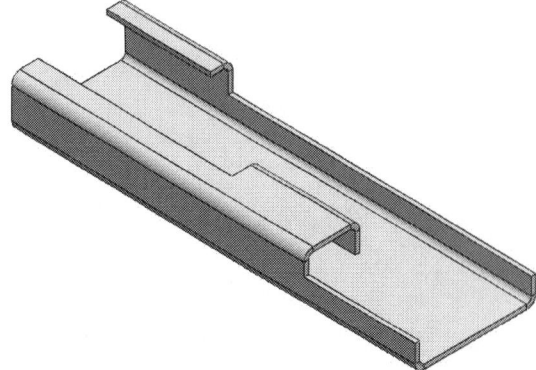

Note that these bend features will also get visible under the **Process-Bends** node of the **FeatureManager Design Tree**, as shown.

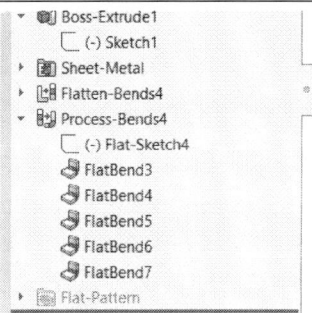

No Bends Tool

This tool is used to straighten the bends of the sheet metal component that are created from a solid part, as discussed above. You can simply select the **No Bends** tool from the **Sheet Metal CommandManager** to display the part model without any bends, as shown.

Note that this tool works as the toggle button and you can click on the **No Bends** tool again to roll back to the sheet metal component with bends. Alternatively, you can also use the rollback bar from the **FeatureManager Design Tree** to toggle between visibility of bends, as shown.

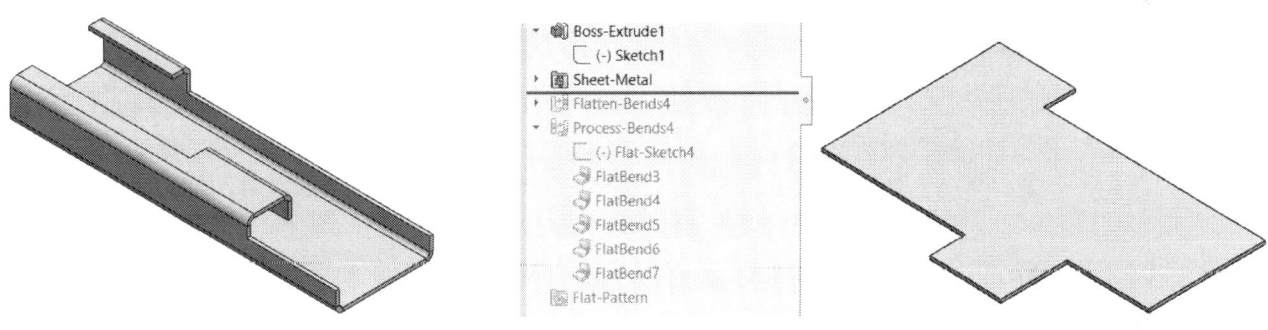

Questions:

1. Which button is selected to create base feature for Sheet Metal?
2. What is the use of **Tab and Slot** tool?
3. Which tool is use to flatten the Sheetmetal part model?
4. How can we use **Swept Flange** tool?
5. Which tool is used to straighten the bends of the sheet metal component?
6. What is the use of **Hem** tool?
7. How can we use **Miter Flange** tool?
8. Which tool is used to convert a solid model into sheet metal component?

Chapter 13: Surface Design

SolidWorks surface tools can be used to create complex models/geometries using various standard tools like Extruded, Revolved, Swept, Lofted and so on. Surface models are used in automobile, aerospace, and plastic industries. The use of these tools is same as discussed earlier, the only difference is for creating a surface model, you need to select the required Surface button from the **Surfaces CommandManager**. In this chapter, you learn the basics of surfacing tools that are commonly used.

The main topics covered in this chapter are:

- Use of some standard tools for creating surface model
- Extruded Surface
- Revolved Surface
- Swept Surface
- Lofted Surface
- Boundary Surface
- Filled Surface
- Freeform
- Planar Surface
- Offset Surface
- Ruled Surface
- Surface Flatten
- Fillet
- Surface Editing Tools

Before creating a Surface model, you need to display the **Surfaces** tab with all the tool used in creating a Surface model. By default, the **Surfaces** tab might not be visible in the SolidWorks drawing environment. To start Surface model, you need to display all the tools used in creating it. Note that you can toggle between the visibilities of tabs similarly, as discussed in previous chapter.

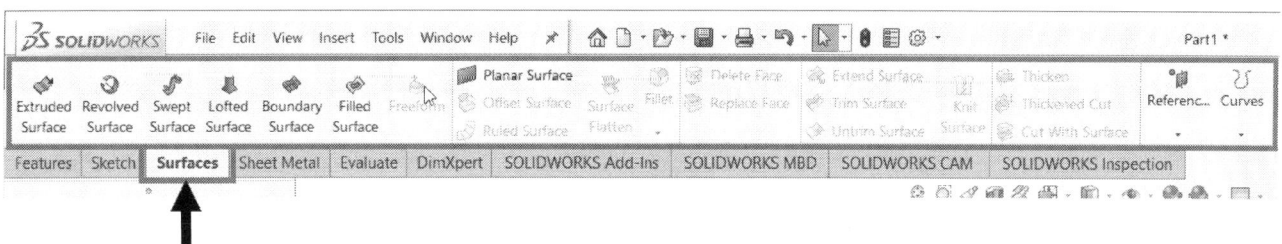

The use of some of the tools in **Surface** tab is almost same as discussed in previous chapters.

 Extruded Surface

This tool is used to create an extruded surface model, by selecting an open or close sketch. To create an extruded surface model using this tool, follow the steps.

- Draw the open or close sketch first, as shown.

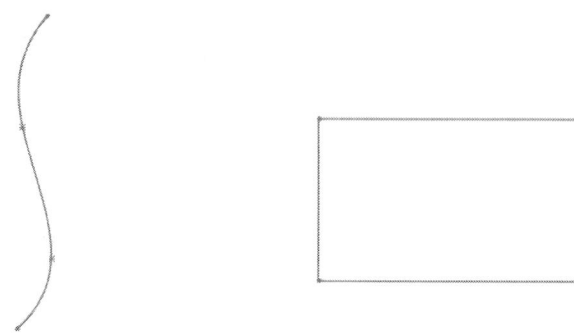

- Select the **Extruded Surface** tool from the **Surfaces CommandManager** to display **Surface-Extrude PropertyManager**, as shown.
- Click on the open sketches first to display preview of surface model, as shown.
- Next, click in the **Selected Contours** box of the PropertyManager and then click on the close sketch to display preview of another surface model, as shown

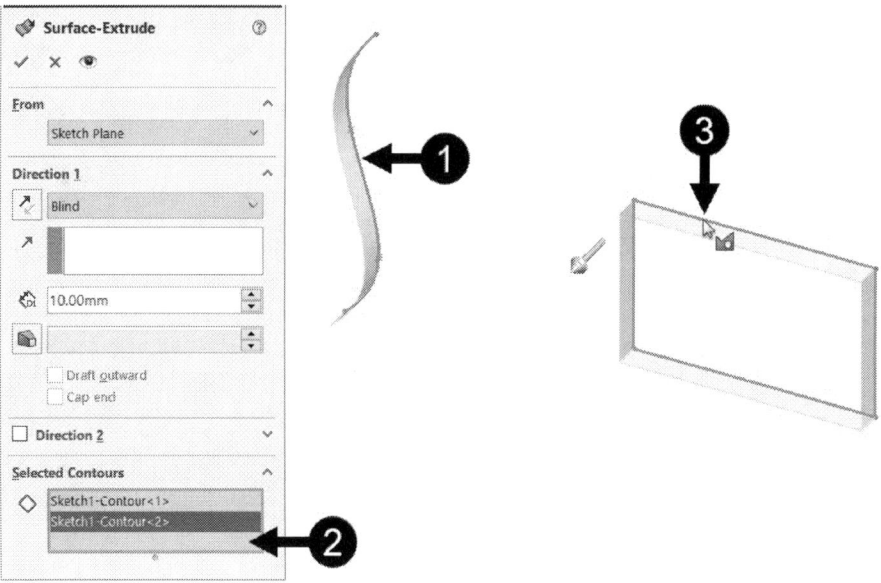

The use of options in this PropertyManager is same as of **Boss-Extrude PropertyManager** as discussed earlier in chapter no 5 of this book. You can select the required options and enter the required values in it, as per your requirements.

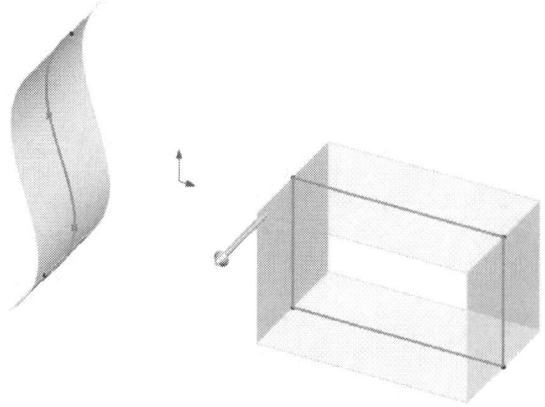

- Click on the OK button of the PropertyManager to apply changes and display the Extruded surface model, as shown.

Note: You can select the **Cap end** check box under **Direction 1** rollout of the PropertyManager to toggle between a solid model and a surface model (for close sketches), as shown.

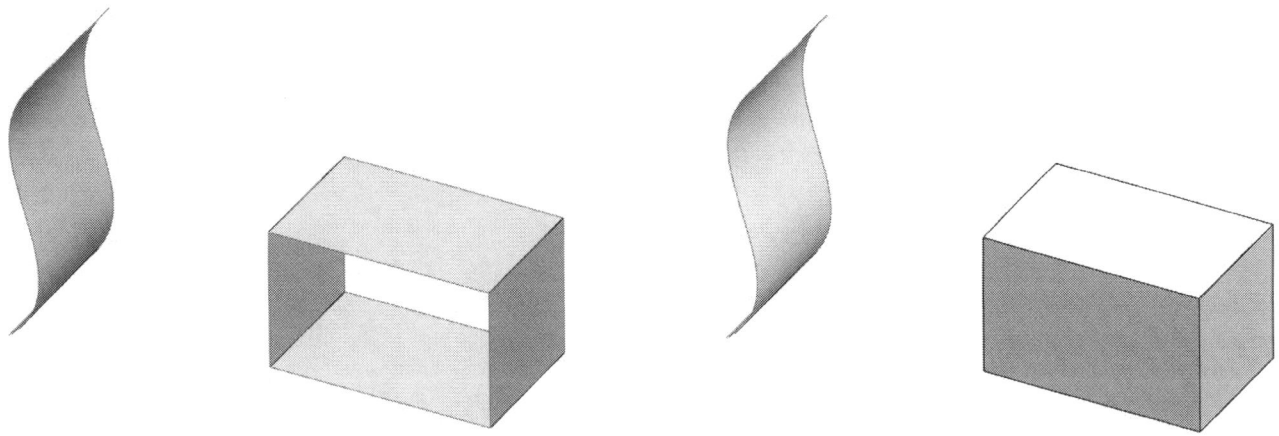

Revolved Surface

This tool is used to create a Revolved surface model by revolving an open or close sketch, along an axis. To create a revolved surface model using this tool, follow the steps.

- Draw the sketch with a centerline, as shown.
- Select the **Revolved Surface** tool from the **Surfaces CommandManager** to display **Revolve PropertyManager**, as shown.
- Click on the center axis to display preview of Revolve surface model along it, as shown.

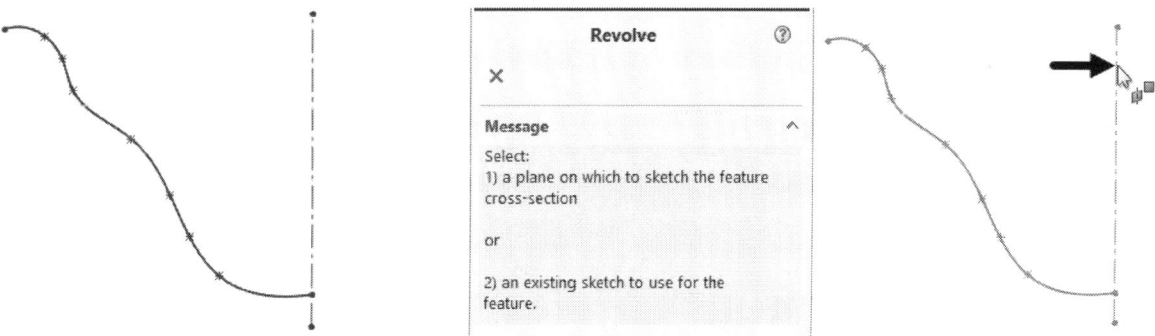

The PropertyManager get modified and the use of options in this PropertyManager is same as of **Revolve PropertyManager** as discussed earlier in chapter no 5 of this book. You can select the required options and enter the required values in it, as per your requirements.

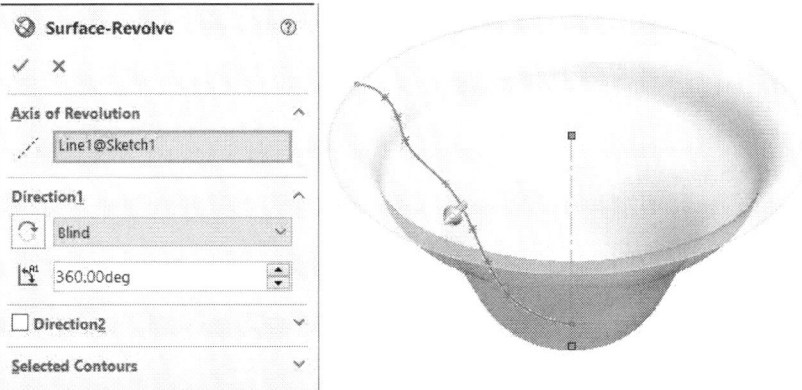

- Click on the  button of the PropertyManager to apply changes and display the Revolved surface model, as shown.

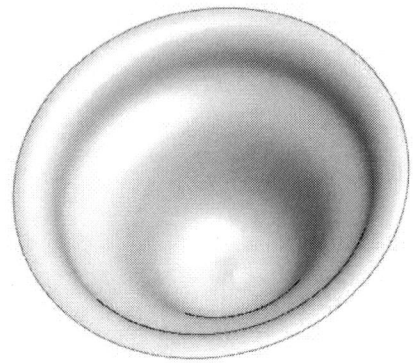

Swept Surface

This tool is used to create a Swept surface model by sweeping an open or close sketch/profile, along a path. The steps to create a Swept Surface model are explained below:

- Draw the sketch for path on **Top** plane, as shown.

- Now, create a perpendicular plane along one of the endpoints of the above sketch, as shown.
- Next, draw another sketch for profile over it, as shown.

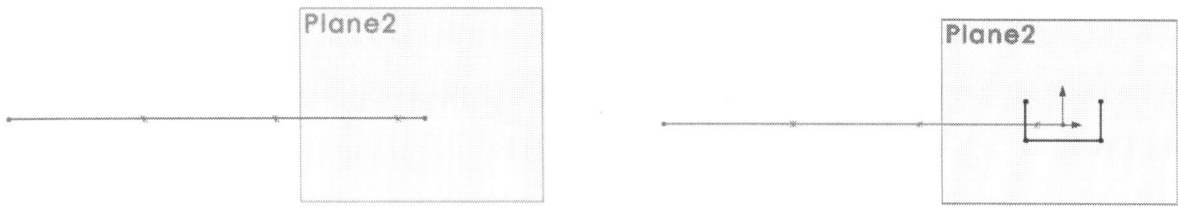

- Select the **Swept Surface** tool from the **Surfaces CommandManager** to display **Surface-Sweep PropertyManager**, as shown.
- Now, select the Profile and Path sketch one by one to display the preview of Swept Surface feature, as shown.

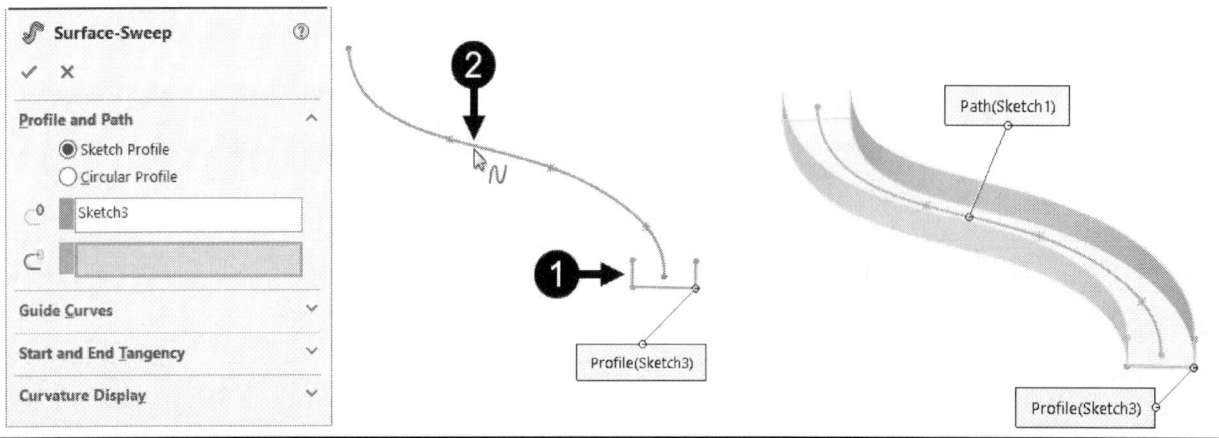

The use of options in this PropertyManager is same as of **Sweep PropertyManager** as discussed in chapter no 8. You can select the required options and enter the required values in it, if required.

> Click on the ✓ button of the PropertyManager to apply changes and display the Swept surface model, as shown.

 **Lofted Surface**

This tool is used to create a Loft surface model by connecting two or more sketches created on different planes. The steps to create a lofted surface model are explained below:

> Draw three sketches on three different planes, as shown.

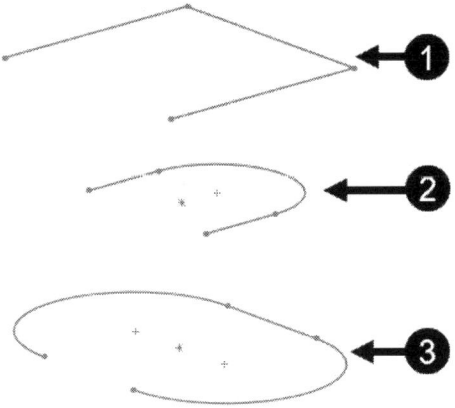

> Select the **Lofted Surface** tool from the **Surfaces CommandManager** to display **Surface-Loft PropertyManager**, as shown.
> Now, select the sketches one by one to display the preview of Swept Surface feature, as shown.

The use of options in this PropertyManager is same as of **Loft PropertyManager** as discussed in chapter no 8. You can select the required options and enter the required values in it, if required.

> Click on the ✓ button of the PropertyManager to apply changes and display the Lofted surface model, as shown.

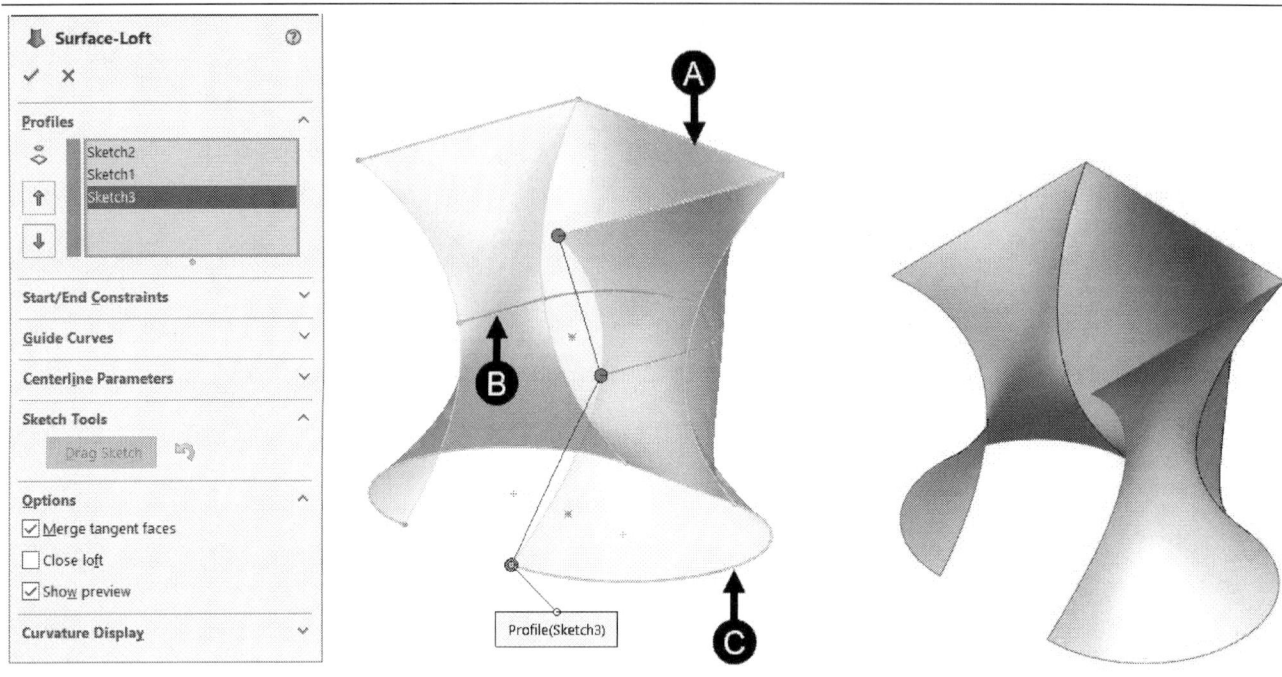

Boundary Surface

Boundary Surface This tool is used to create surfaces that can be tangent or curvature continuous in both directions. This tools also works as Lofted surface tool but this tool delivers a higher quality results as compared to other. The steps to use this tool are explained below:

➢ Draw the sketches on two different planes, as shown.

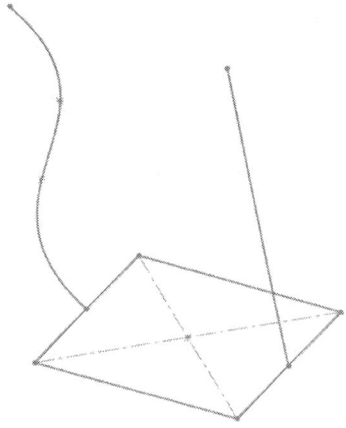

➢ Select the **Boundary Surface** tool from the **Surfaces CommandManager** to display **Boundary-Surface PropertyManager**, as shown.
➢ Now click on one of the sketch entities of first sketch, as shown.
➢ Now, click on the ![icon] **Select Open Loop** button of the **SelectionManager** displayed and then click on the **OK** button to select it, as shown.
➢ Similarly select another open sketch entity to display the preview of Boundary surface feature along the both selected open sketch entities, as shown.

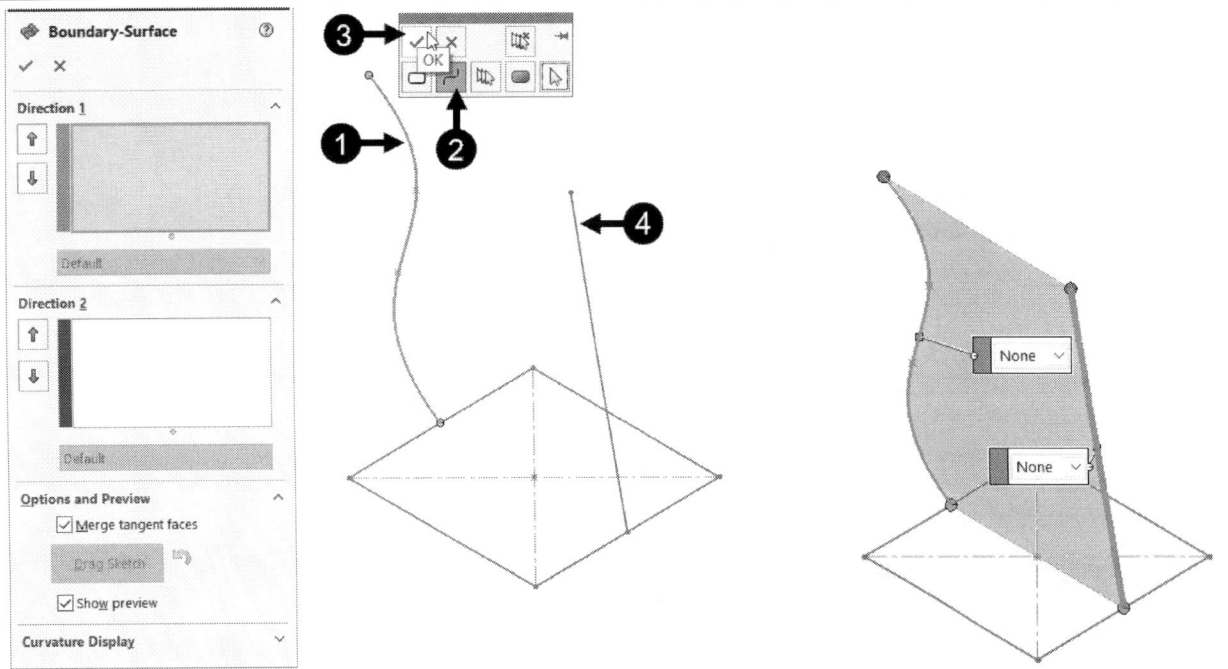

- Now click in the box under **Direction 2** rollout and then select another sketch to display preview of Boundary surface feature along it, as shown.

  The use of options in this PropertyManager is same as of **Boundary PropertyManager** as discussed in chapter no 8. You can select the required options and enter the required values in it, if required.

- Click on the ✓ button of the PropertyManager to apply changes and display the Boundary surface model, as shown.

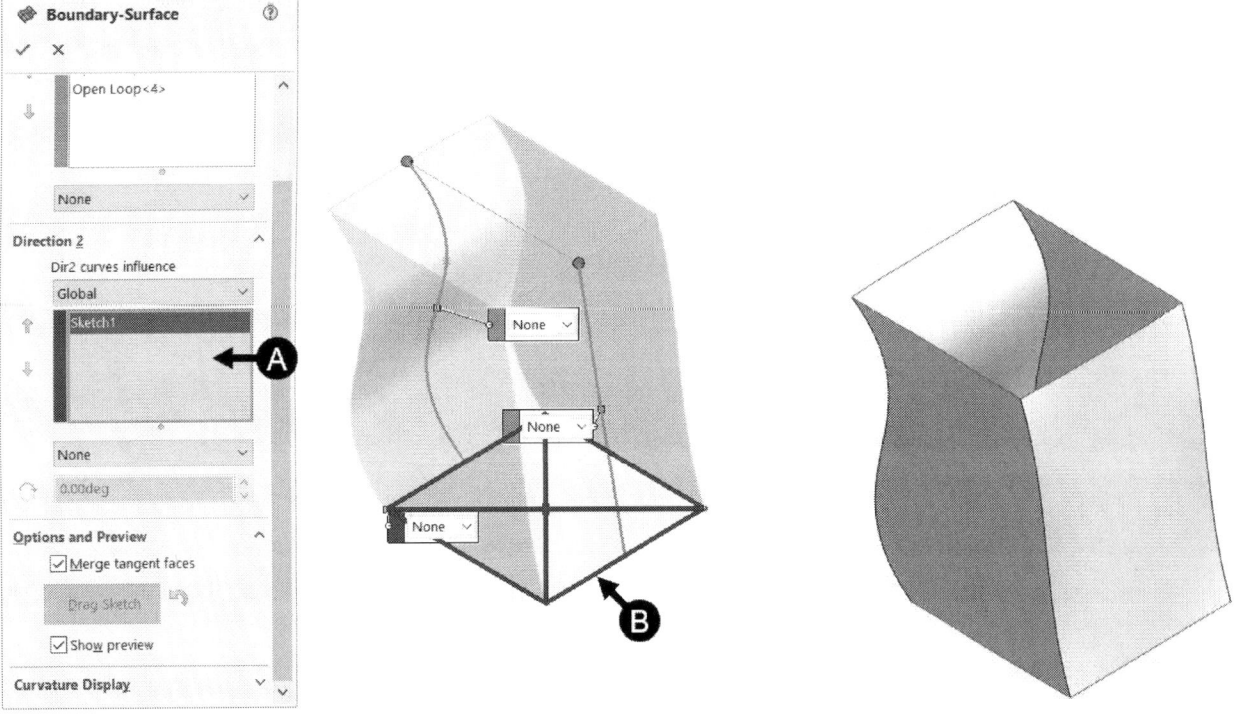

Surface Design   13-7

Filled Surface

This tool is used to construct a surface patch to fill the gap in a surface model by selecting the edges, sketches or curves. The steps to use this tool are explained below:

➢ Create a surface model, as shown.

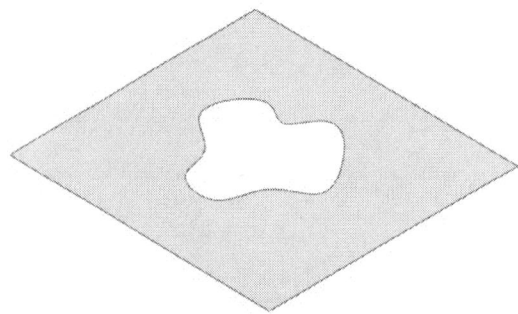

➢ Select the **Filled Surface** tool from the **Surfaces CommandManager** to display **Fill Surface PropertyManager**, as shown.
➢ Now select the boundaries of the area to create the surface patch along it and display preview of Filled surface, as shown.

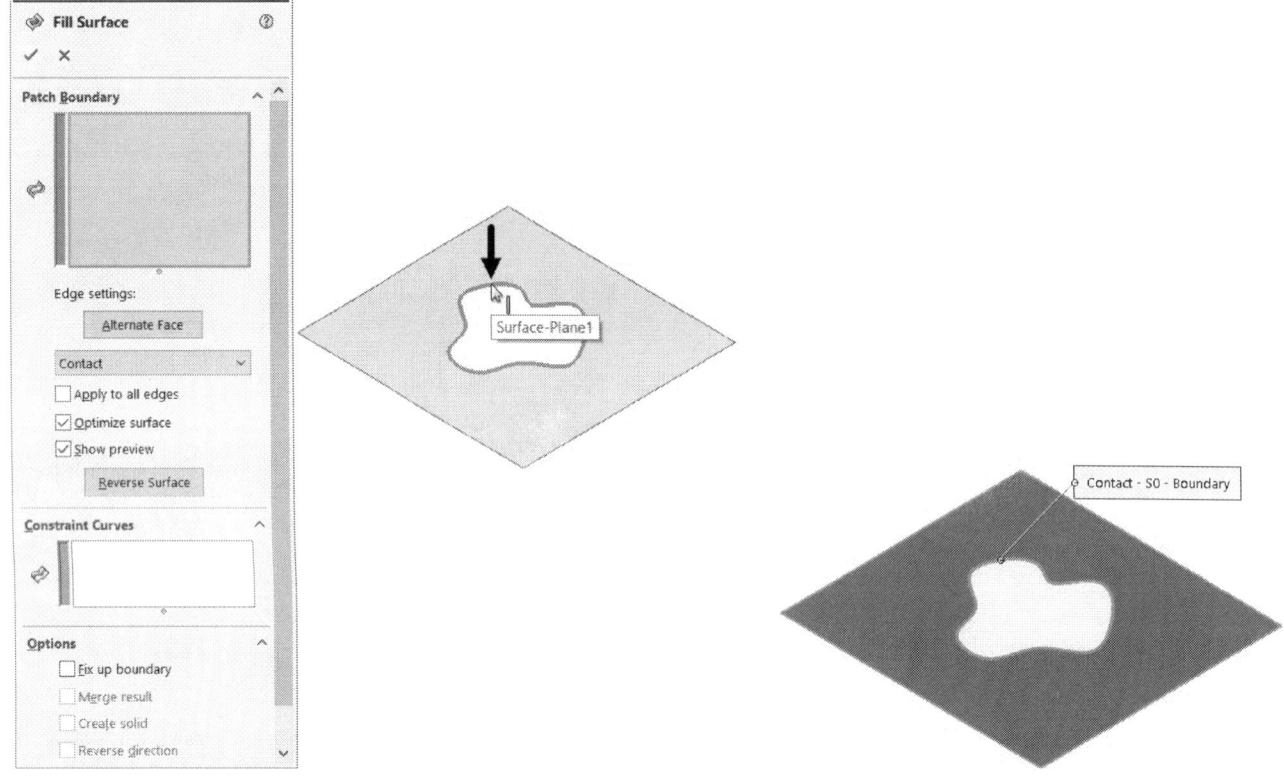

➢ Click on the ✓ button of the PropertyManager to apply changes and display the Filled surface model, as shown.

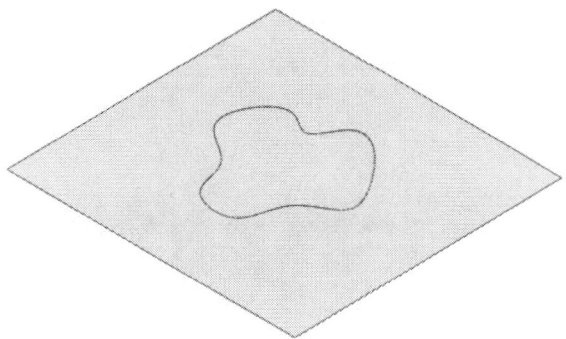

Freeform

Freeform — This tool is used to modify the faces of surface model by freely deforming it by pulling various control points placed in it. The steps to use this tool are explained below:

➤ Create a surface model, as shown.

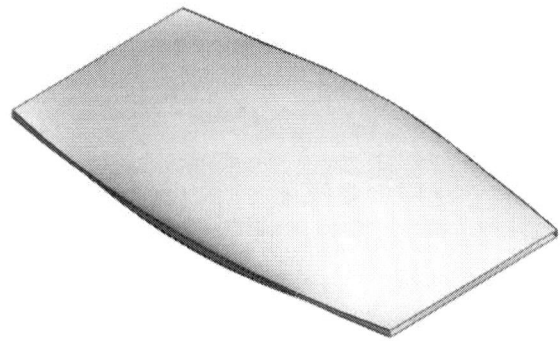

➤ Select the **Freeform** tool from the **Surfaces CommandManager** to display **Freeform PropertyManager**, as shown.
➤ Select the surface that you want to modify/deform, as shown.

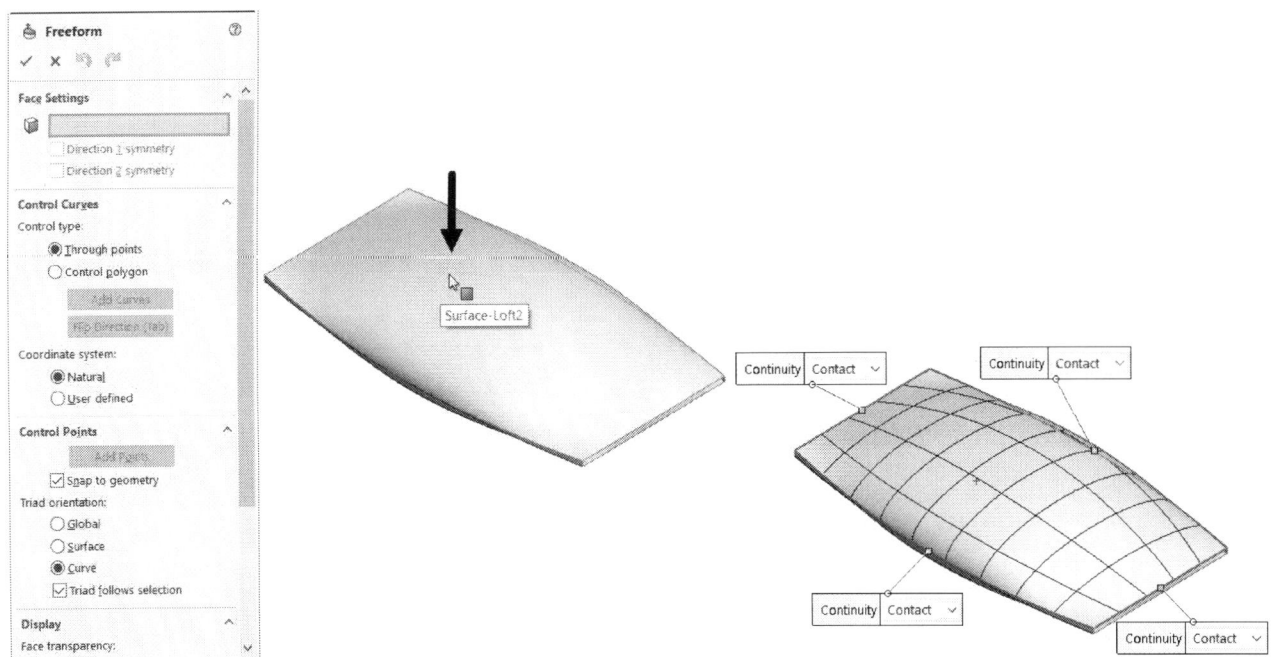

➤ Now, click on the **Add Curves** button under the **Control Curves** rollout of the PropertyManager.
➤ Click on the selected surface to place curve/curves over it, to deform its face, as shown.

Surface Design

➢ Click on the **Add Curves** button to exit it.

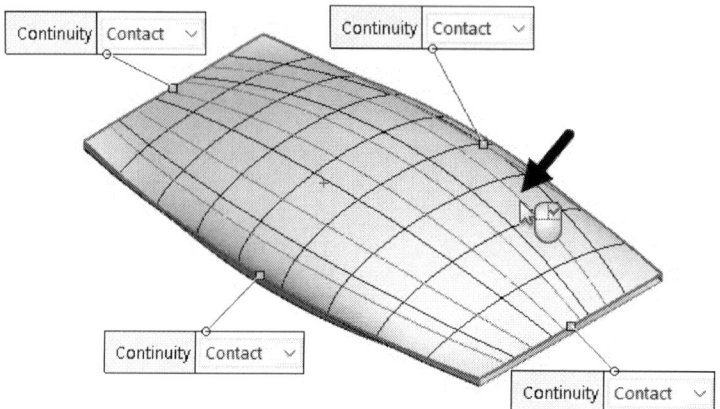

➢ Next, click on the **Add Points** button from the **Control Points** rollout.
➢ Click on the previously placed control curves and place the control points over it, as shown.

Similarly, place the control point on all curves and placing more numbers of control points makes it easy while deformation the surface and keeping accuracy.

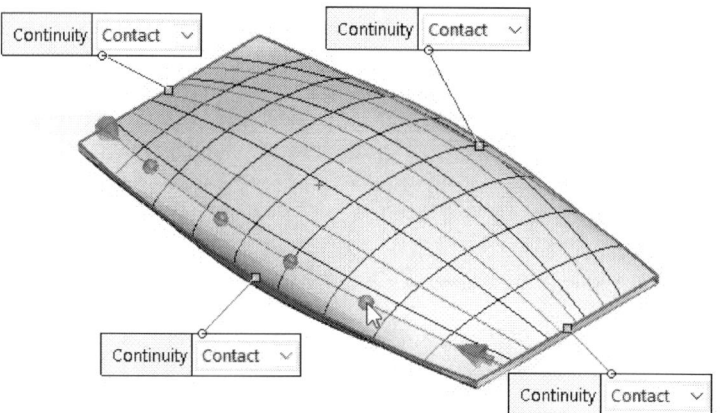

➢ Click on the **Add Points** button again to exit it.
➢ Now click on the control curves to highlight control point placed over it, as shown.
➢ Select and drag the control points to deform the surface, as shown.

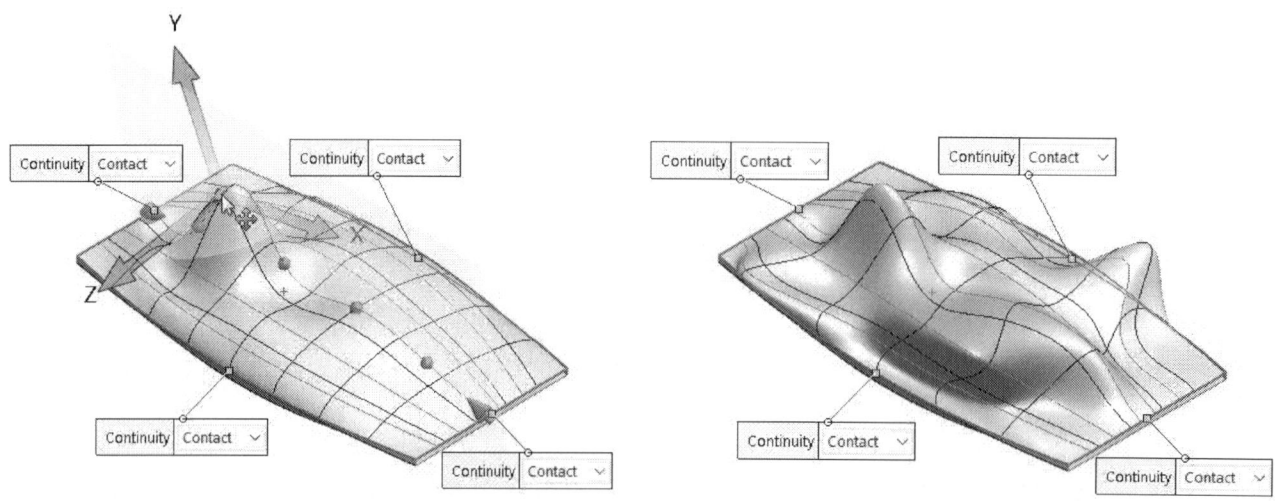

➢ Click on the ✓ button of the PropertyManager to apply changes and display the deformed model, as shown.

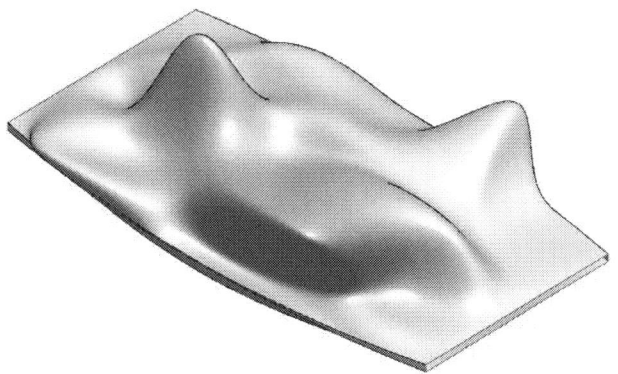

Planar Surface

This tool is used to construct a planar patch to fill the gap among surfaces, by selecting the edges, sketches or curves. The steps to use this tool are explained below:

➢ Select the **Planar Surface** tool from the **Surfaces CommandManager** to display **Planar Surface PropertyManager**, as shown.
➢ Now select the boundaries/edges of the surface model to display preview of Planar surface, as shown.

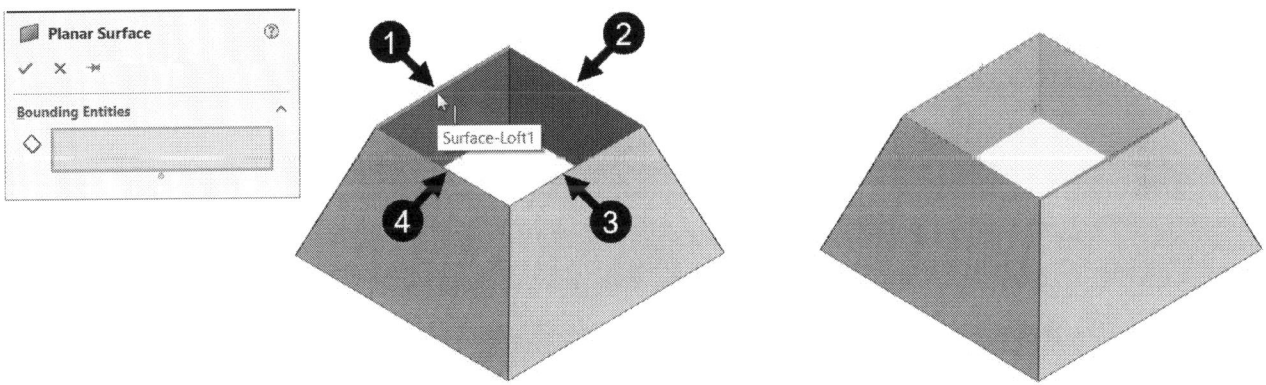

➢ Click on the ✓ button of the PropertyManager to apply changes and display the surface model with Planar surface, as shown.

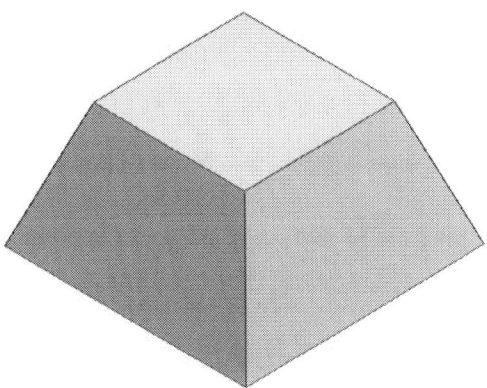

Surface Design

Offset Surface

This tool is used to create a surface at an offset distance, from the selected surface/face. The steps to use this tool are explained below:

> Select the **Offset Surface** tool from the **Surfaces CommandManager** to display **Offset Surface PropertyManager**, as shown.
> Now click on the required surface to display preview of Offset surface along it, with the default distance entered in the PropertyManager, as shown.

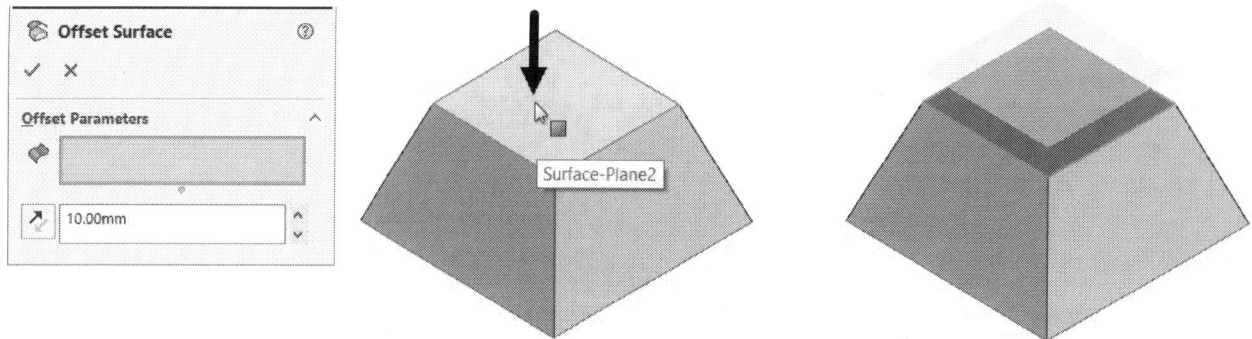

> Enter the required distance in the **Offset Distance** spinner of the PropertyManager, if required.
> Now click on the ✓ button of the PropertyManager to apply changes and display the surface model with Offset surface, as shown.

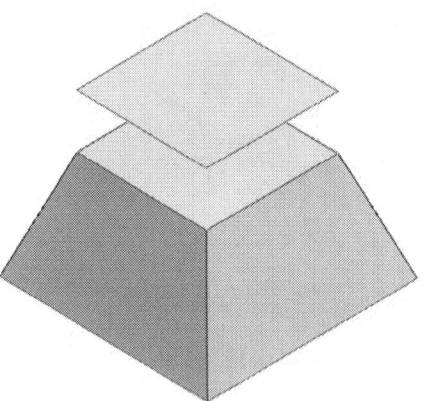

Ruled Surface

This tool is used to select the edges of the surface model to create surfaces that extend out in the specified direction from it. The steps to use this tool are explained below:

> Select the **Ruled Surface** tool from the **Surfaces CommandManager** to display **Ruled Surface PropertyManager**, as shown.
> Select one of the edges of the surface model to display preview of Ruled surface along it, as shown.

Note that as the **Tangent to Surface** radio button under the **Type** rollout is selected by default thus the preview of the Radial surface gets displayed accordingly.

- Similarly select other edges of top surface of solid model to display Ruled surfaces along all selected edges, as shown.
- You can enter the required distance in the **Distance** spinner under **Distance/Direction** rollout of the PropertyManager, as shown.

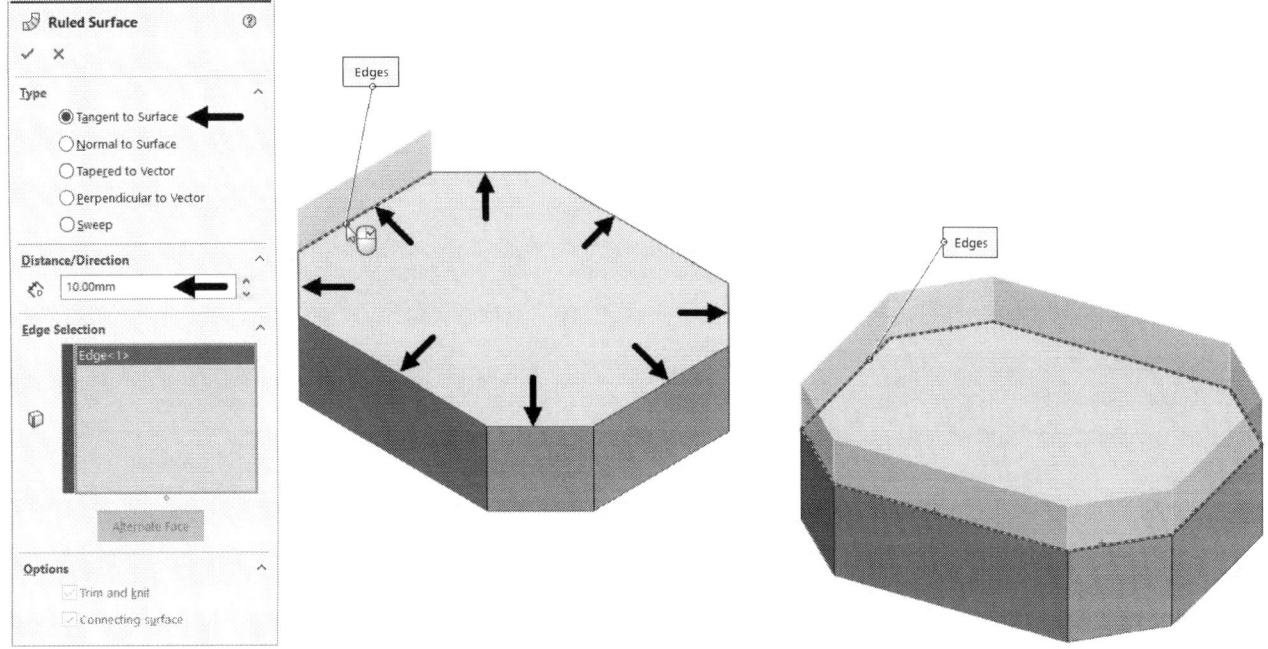

- Now click on the ✓ button of the PropertyManager to apply changes and display the surface model with Ruled surfaces, as shown.

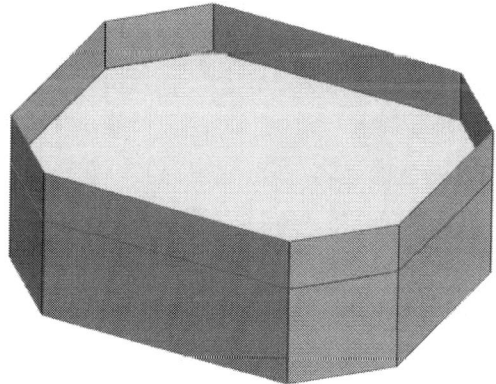

Similarly, you can create other Radial surfaces by selecting the other radio buttons under **Type** rollout, shown below one by one:

- By selecting the **Normal to Surface** radio button. Use the ↗ **Reverse Direction** button, if required, as shown.

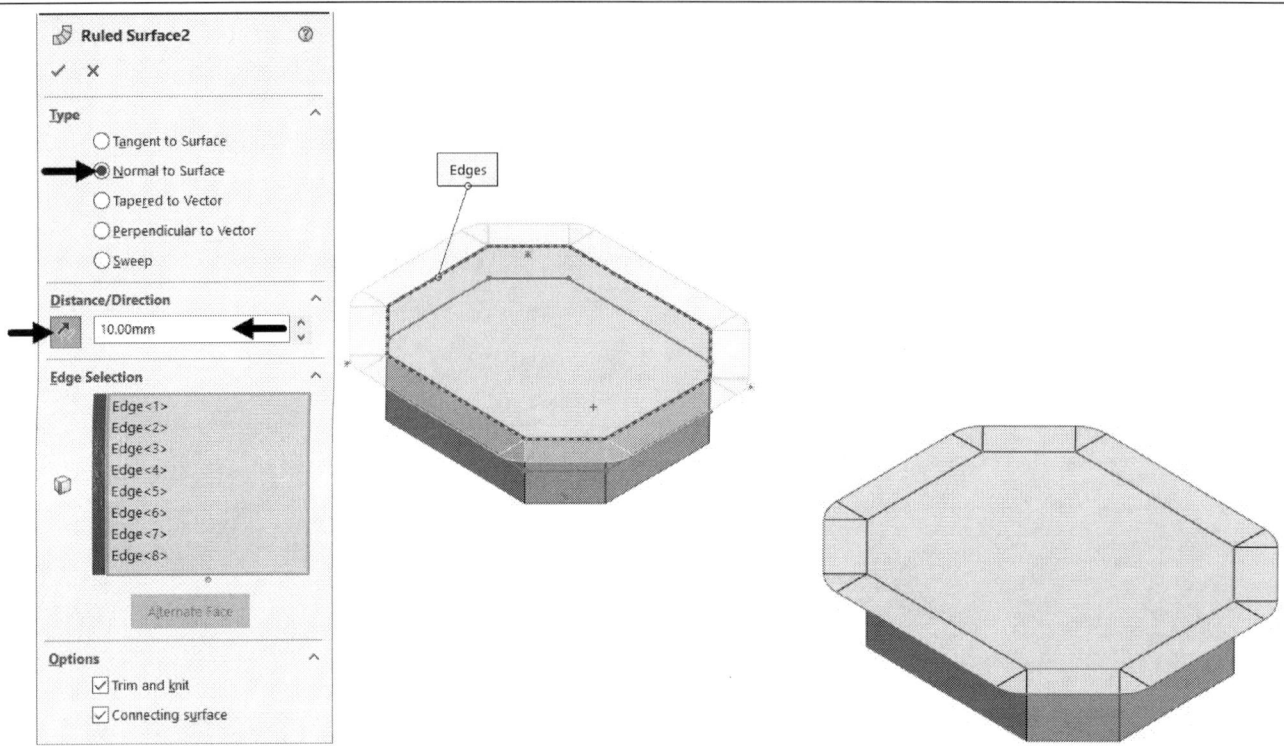

- By selecting the **Tapered to Vector** radio button. Here, you need to define the edge as Reference vector and enter the required angle in the **Angle** spinner also, as shown.

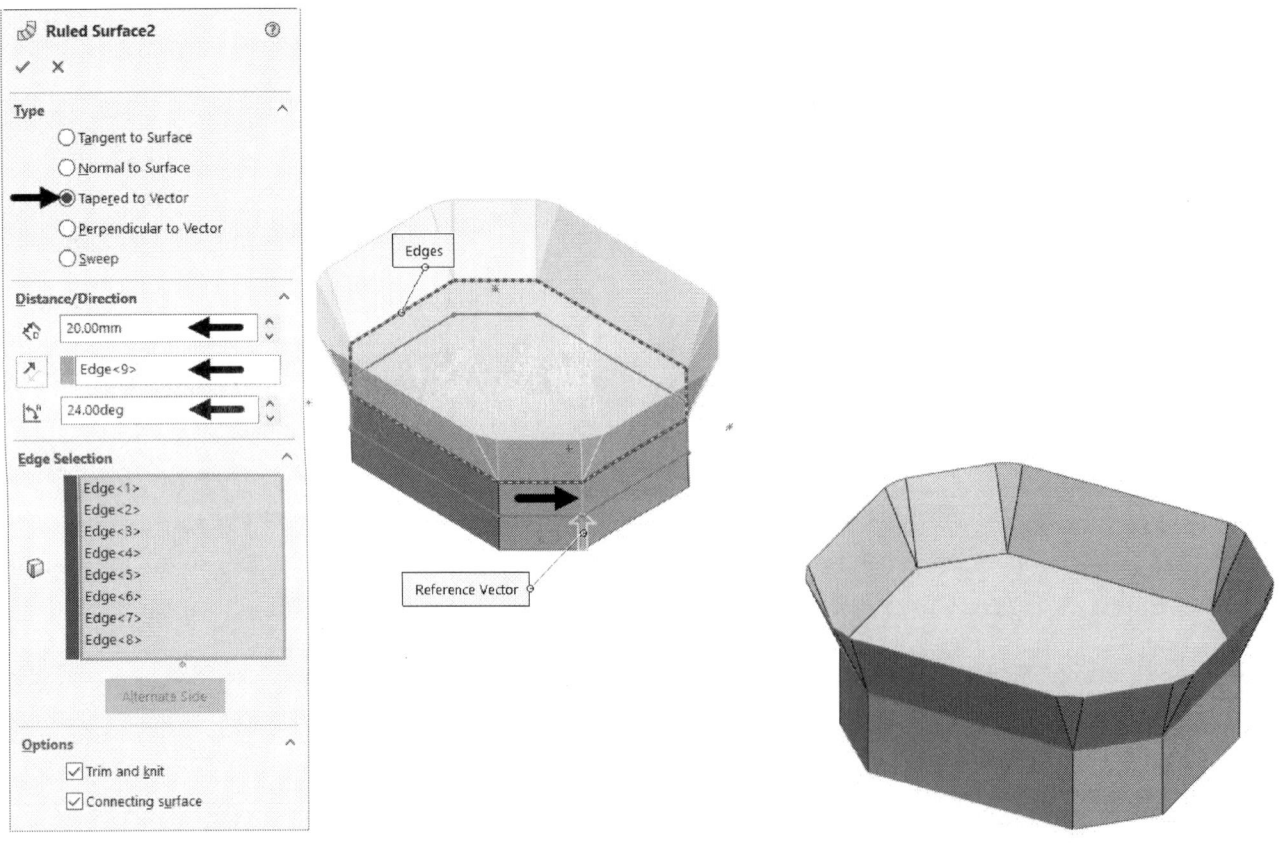

- By selecting the **Perpendicular to Vector** radio button. You need to define the edge here also, as shown.

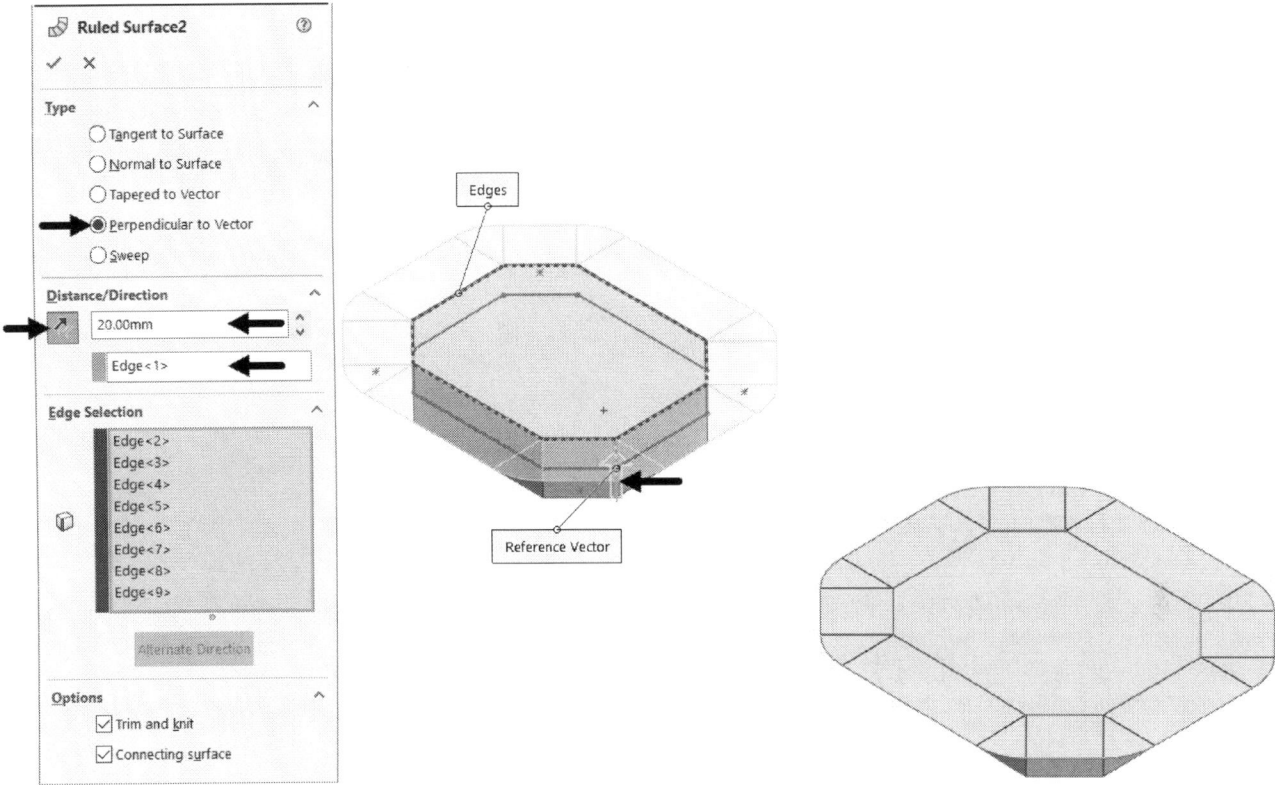

- By selecting the **Sweep** radio button. You need to define the edge here also, as shown.

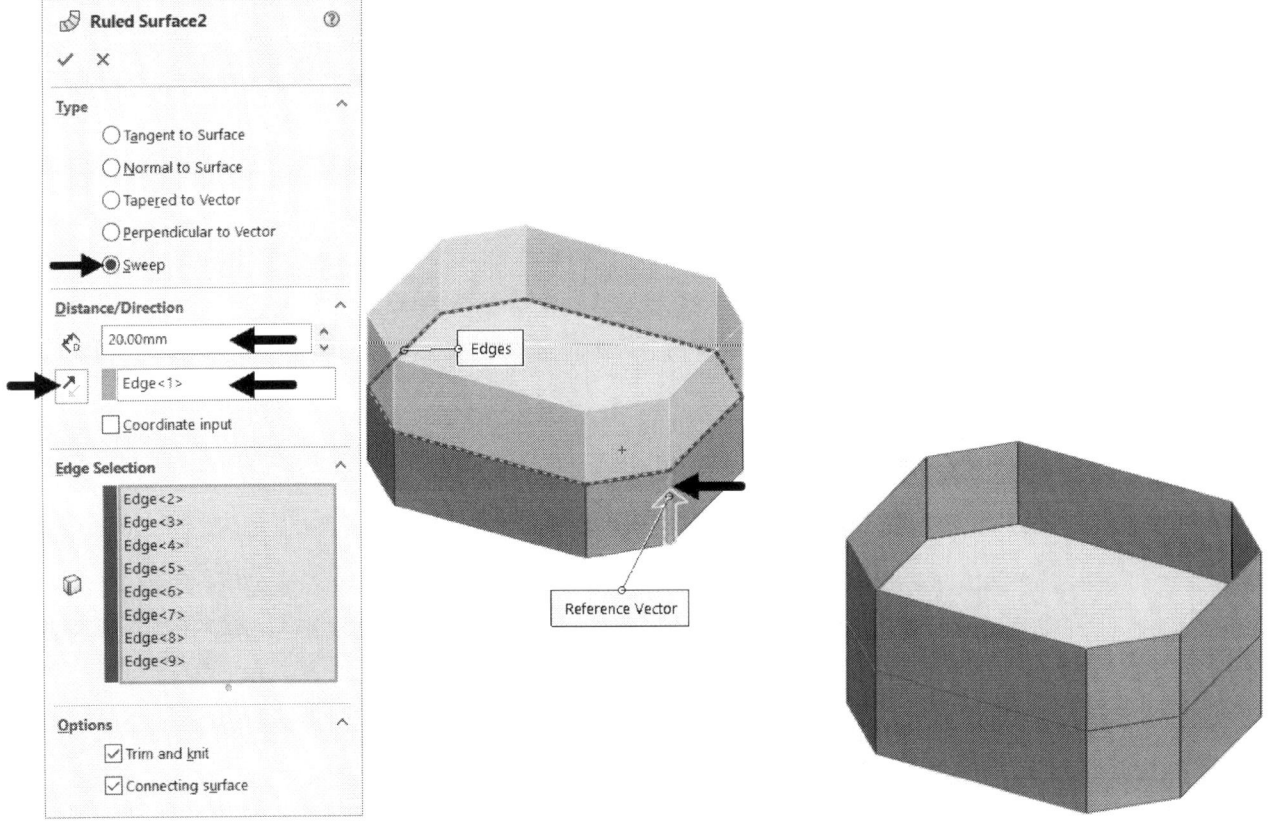

Surface Flatten

This tool is used to flat the surface or set of surfaces to avoid deformation of some surfaces and faces when flattened. The steps to use this tool are explained below:

➢ Select the **Surface Flatten** tool from the **Surfaces CommandManager** to display **Flatten PropertyManager**, as shown.
➢ Click on the surface of the model that you want flatten, as shown.
➢ Now, click in another selection box of the PropertyManager and then select the vertex point or vertex of the surface model to display preview of Flatten surface, as shown.

The **Relief Cuts** check box is selected to apply relief in the surface.

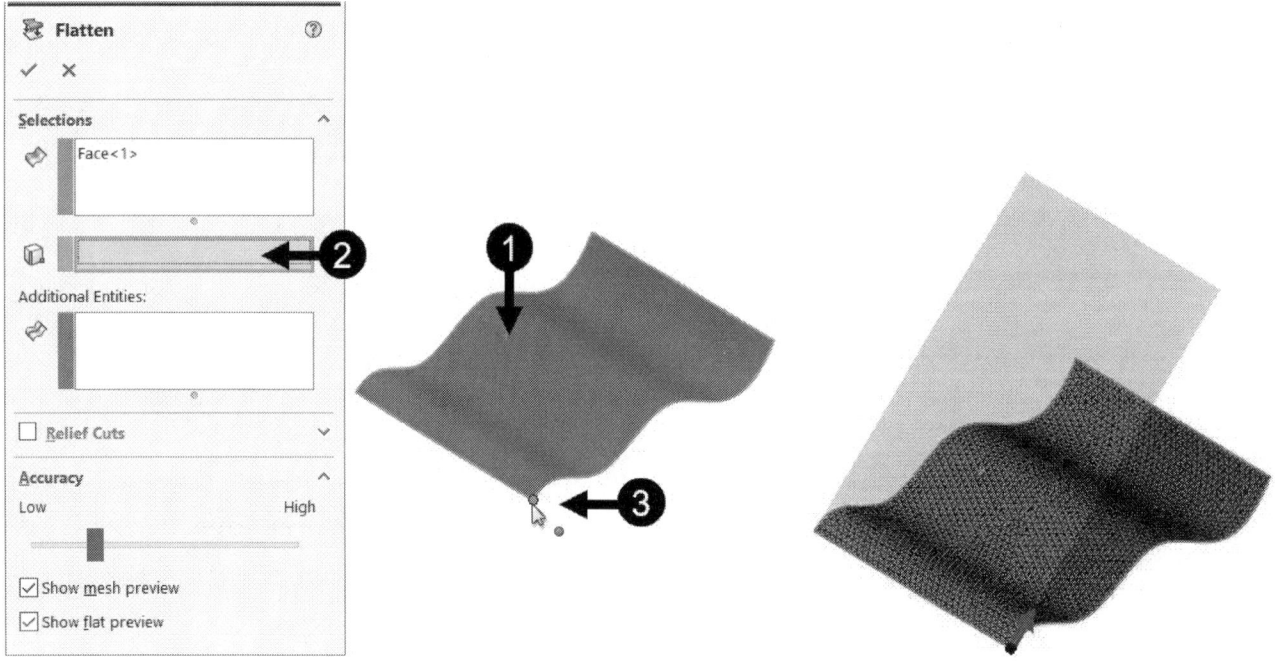

➢ Now click on the ✓ button of the PropertyManager to apply changes and display the surface model with Flatten surface, as shown.

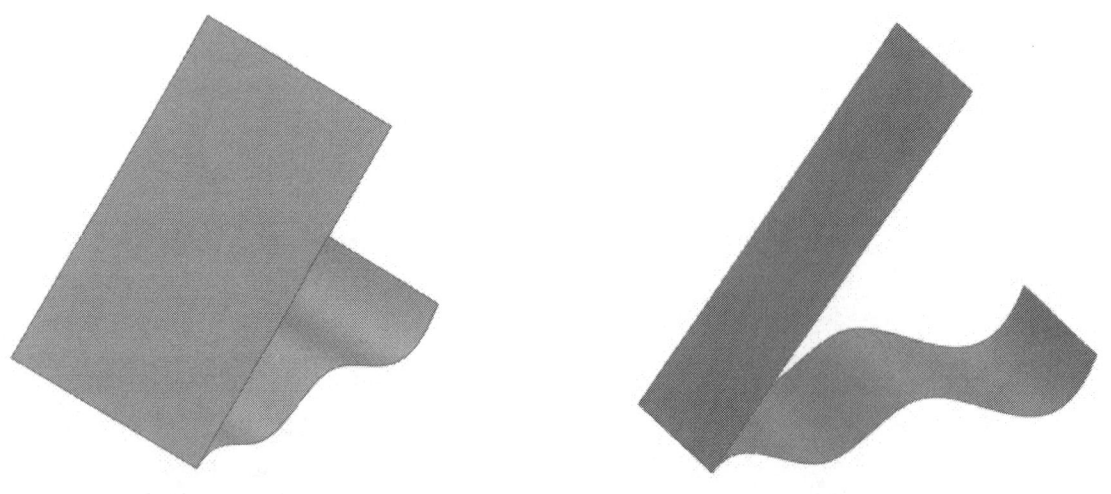

Fillet

 This tool is used to fillet the sharp corner of the surface model. The steps to use this tool are explained below:

- Select the **Fillet** tool from the **Surfaces CommandManager** to display **Fillet PropertyManager**, as shown.
- Select the required edge to display preview of Filleted edge with fillet radius attached with it, as shown.

Note that the preview of the fillet feature gets visible only if you select the **Partial preview** radio button under **Items To Fillet** rollout of the PropertyManager, as shown.

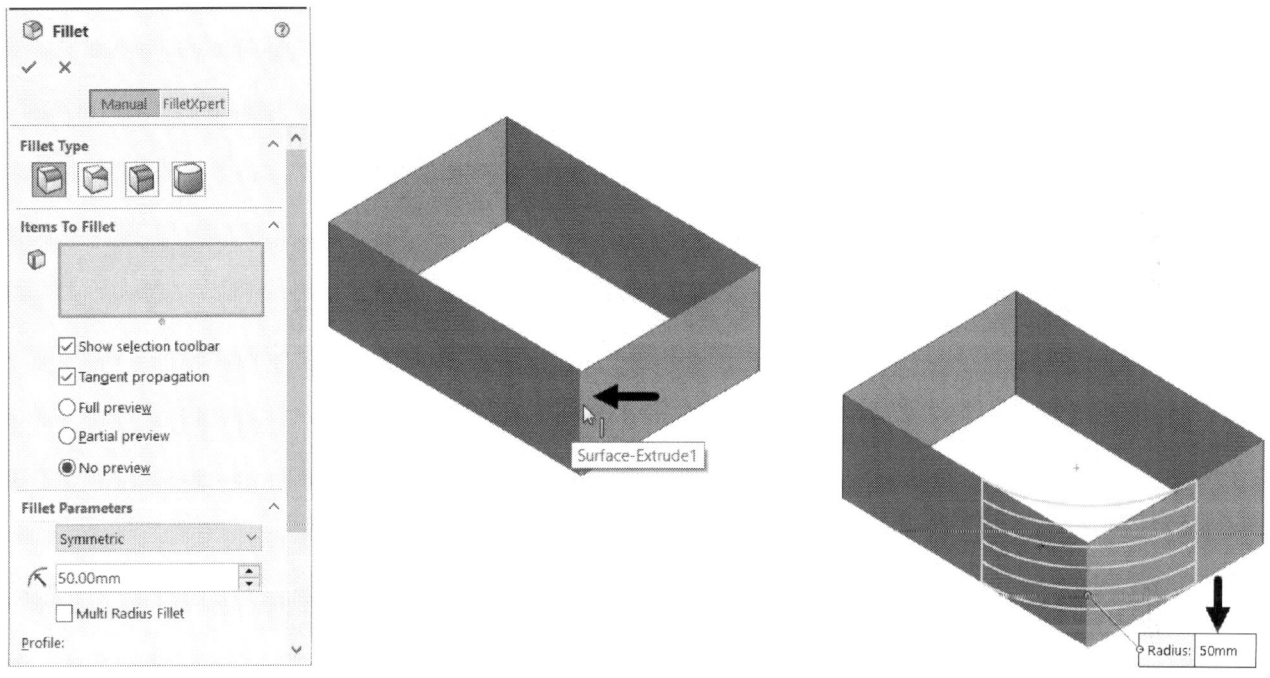

The use of options in this PropertyManager is almost same as discussed in **Fillet PropertyManager** in chapter 9.

- Now click on the ✓ button of the PropertyManager to apply changes and display the surface model with Filleted edge, as shown.

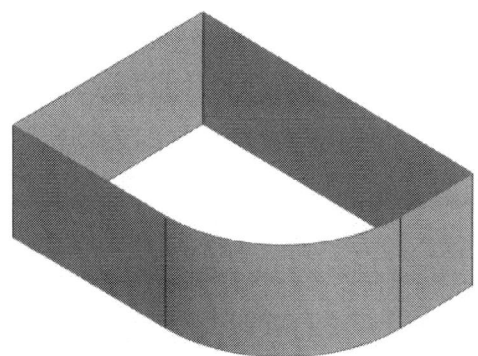

Surface Editing Tools

After creating the Surface model, there are few tools that are used in editing the Surface model. These tools are discussed one by one below:

Delete Face

This tool is used to remove the face/faces of solid and surface model. The steps to use this tool are explained below:

> Select the **Delete Face** tool from the **Surfaces CommandManager** to display **DeleteFace PropertyManager**, as shown.
> Next, select the **Delete** radio button under **Options** rollout of the PropertyManager, as shown.
> Click on the faces to be removed, as shown.

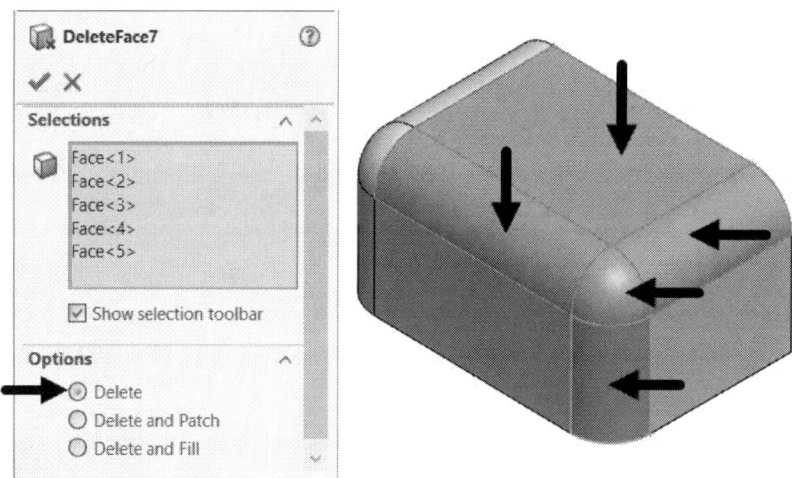

> Now click on the ✓ button of the PropertyManager to apply changes and display the surface model with deleted faces, as shown.

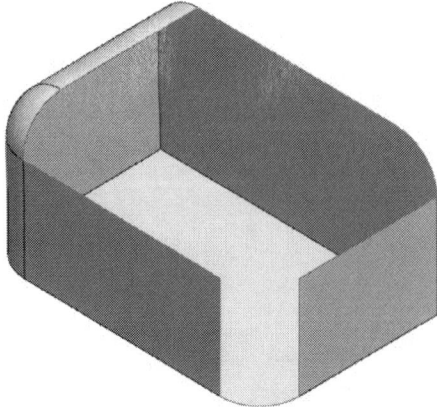

Similarly, you can remove faces by using the **Delete and Patch** & **Delete and Fill** radio buttons under **Options** rollout, as shown. For both, you can select the **Show preview** button to display its preview.

❖ By selecting the **Delete and Patch** radio buttons, the selected faces get removed and adjoining faces get patched to form an unbroken surface, as shown.

Surface Design

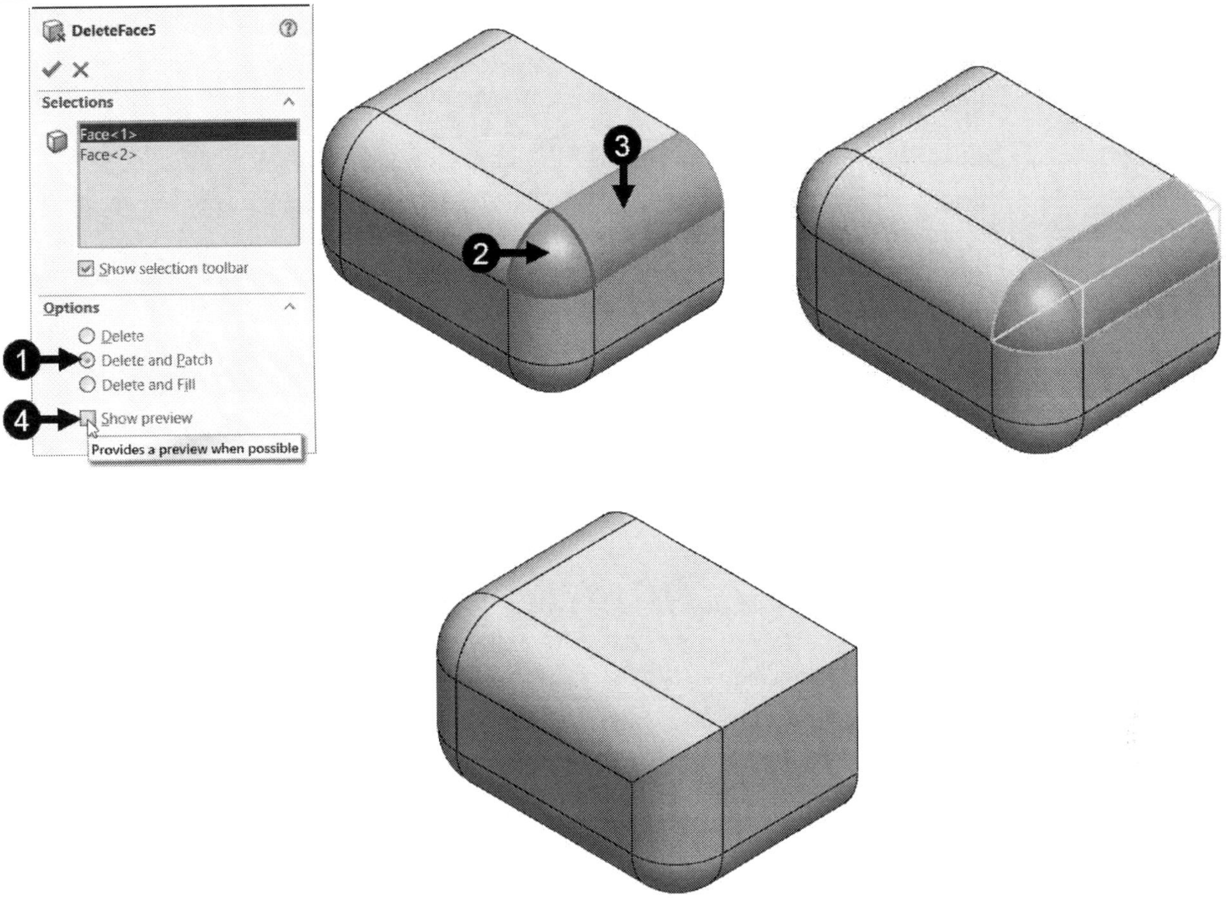

❖ By selecting the **Delete and Fill** radio buttons (without selecting **Tangent Fill** check box below it) the faces are deleted and covered by a single unbroken surface, as shown.

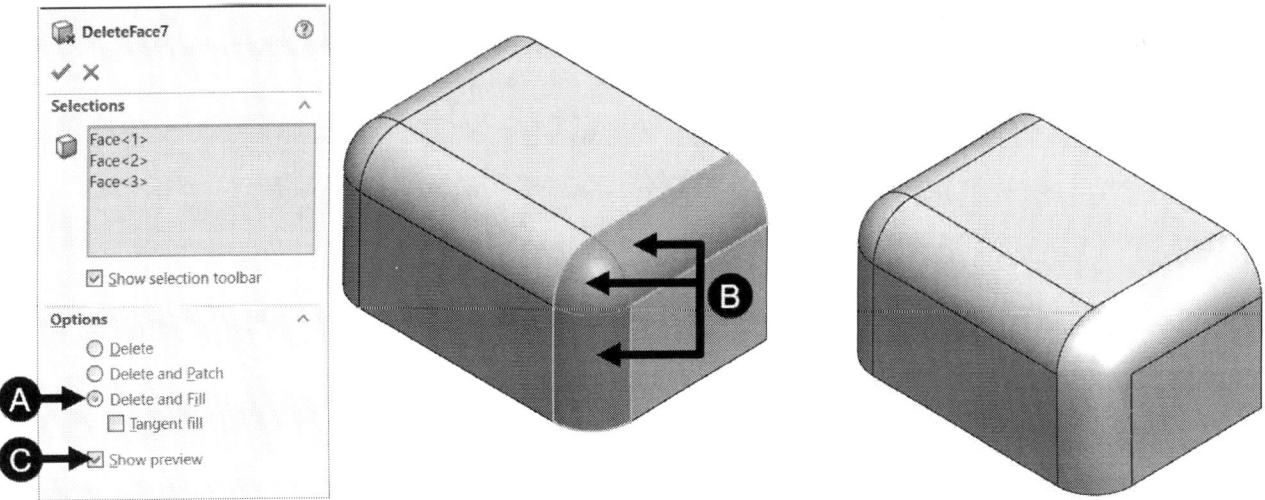

Note that, if you select the **Tangent fill** check box, the deleted faces are covered/filled by tangent edges, as shown.

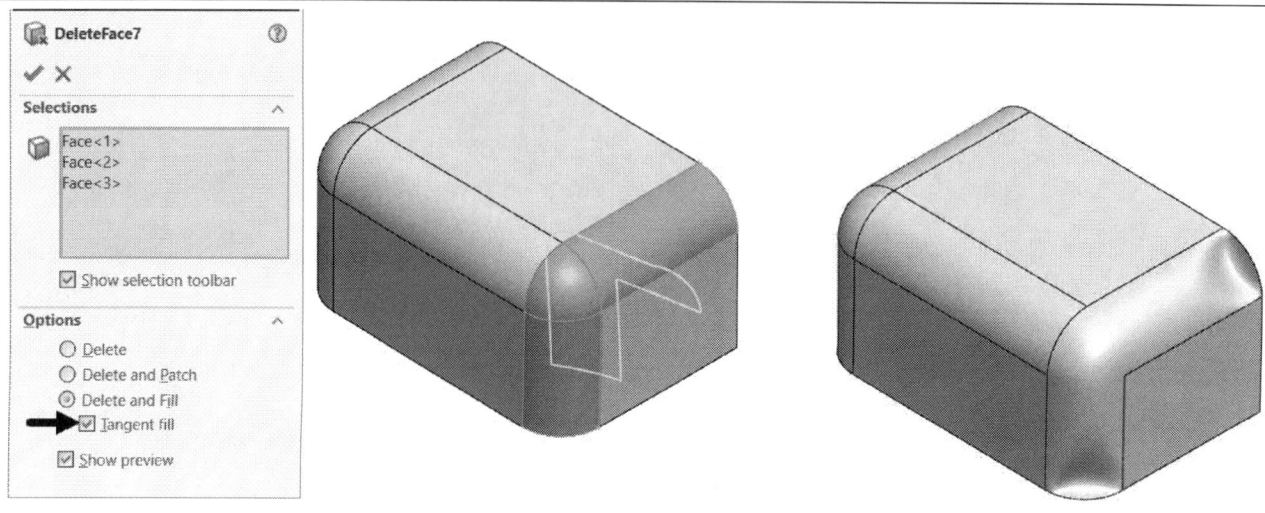

Replace Face

This tool is used to replace faces of a surface or solid model with new surface model. The steps to use this tool are explained below:

> Select the **Replace Face** tool from the **Surfaces CommandManager** to display **Replace Face PropertyManager**, as shown.
> Click on the face to be replaced, as shown.
> Next click in the second selection box of the PropertyManager and then click on another surface, as shown.

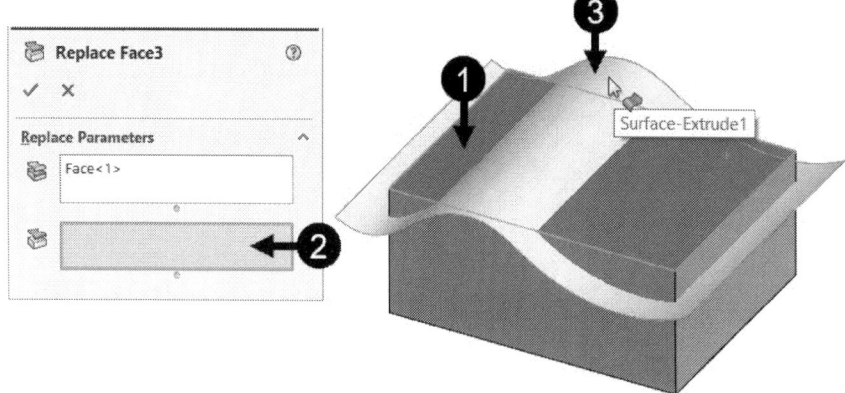

> Now click on the ✓ button of the PropertyManager to apply changes and display the model with replaced surface, as shown.

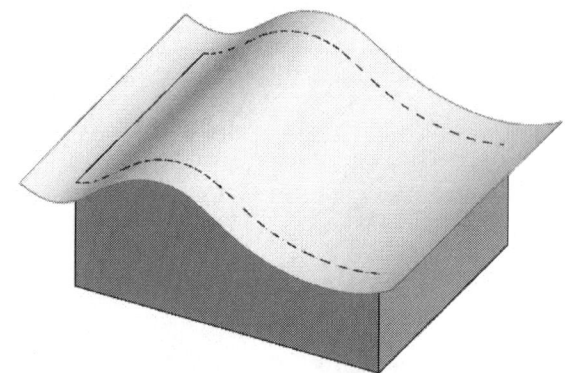

Surface Design

Extend Surface

This tool is used to extend edge/edges or face of a surface model. The steps to use this tool are discussed below:

- Select the **Extend** tool from the **Surfaces CommandManager** to display **Extend Surface PropertyManager**, as shown.
- Select the edge to be extended and display its preview, as shown.
- Select the **Distance** radio button under **End Condition** rollout, if it is not selected, as shown.

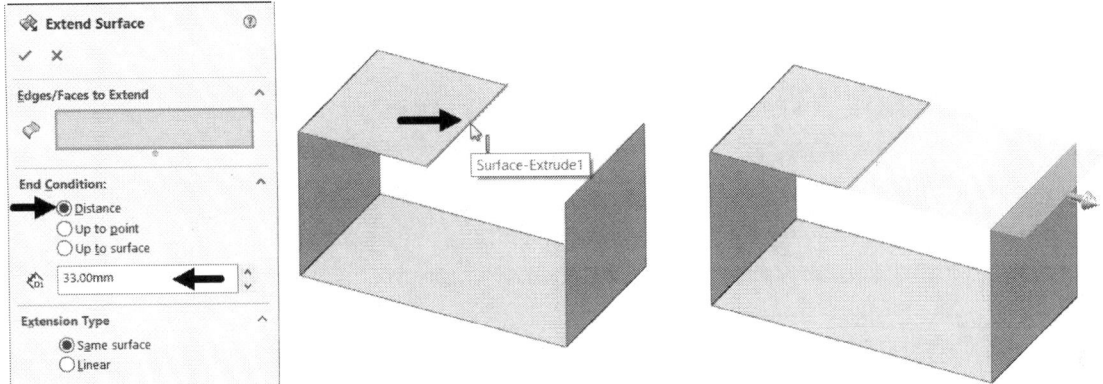

- You can enter the required distance value in the **Distance** spinner to extend it upto the required distance, as shown above.
- Now click on the 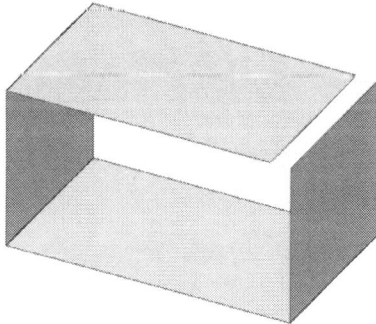 button of the PropertyManager to apply changes and display the model with extended surface, as shown.

Similarly, you can extend any surface upto the selected vertex/point by selecting the **Up to point** button of the PropertyManager and then selecting target point of the surface model, as shown.

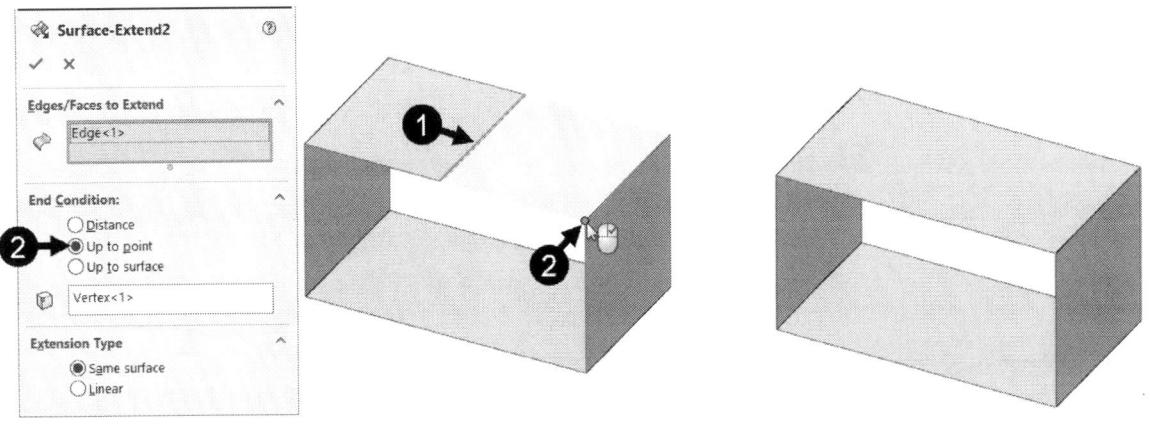

Surface Design

13-21

Also, you can extend the surface upto the selected surface by selecting the **Up to surface** radio button of the PropertyManager and then selecting target surface of the surface model, as shown.

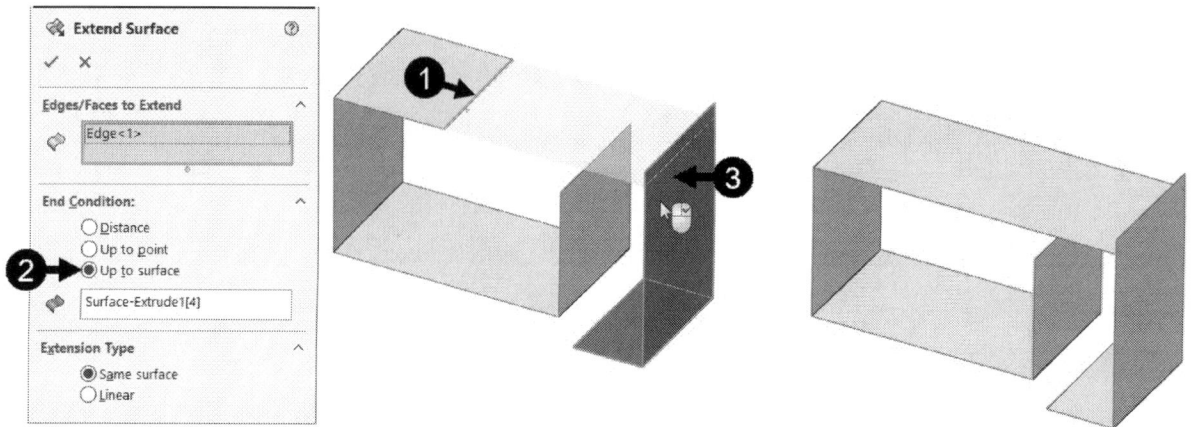

 **Trim Surface**

This tool is used to trim the unwanted or intersecting portion of the surfaces by using a surface, sketch, or plane as a trim tool. The steps to use this tool are discussed below:

- Select the **Trim Surface** tool from the **Surfaces CommandManager** to display **Trim Surface PropertyManager**, as shown.
- Select the surface to select it as the trim tool, as shown.

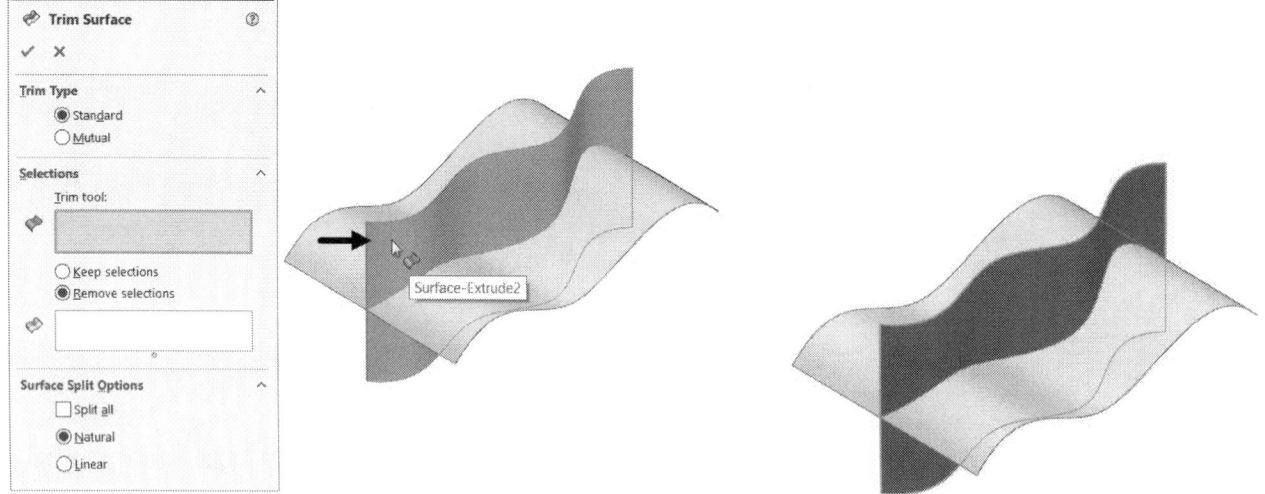

- Now click on the required side of the surface that you want to trim/remove, as shown.

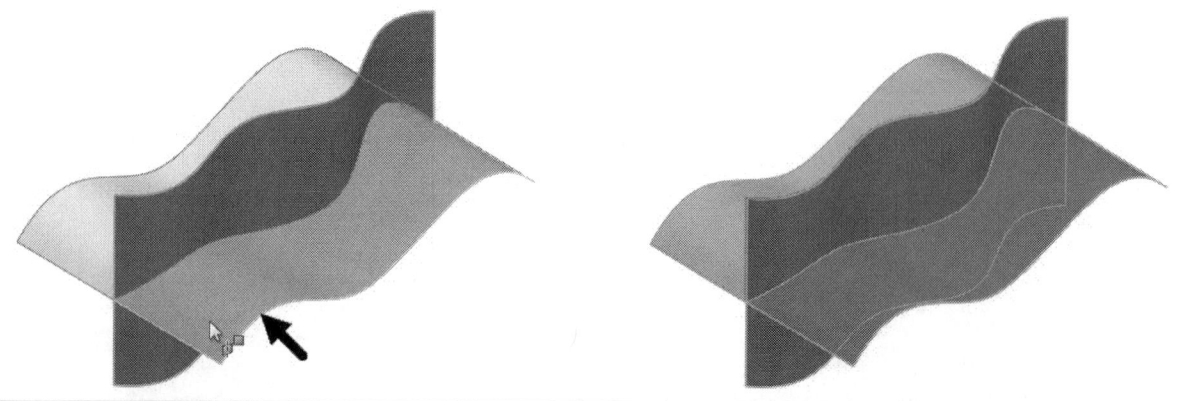

➤ Now click on the ☑ button of the PropertyManager to apply changes and display the model with trimmed surface, as shown.

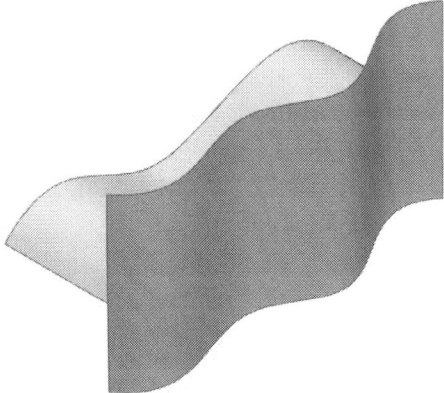

You can also trim multiple surfaces by selecting multiple surfaces as trim tool, as discussed below:

➤ Select the **Trim Surface** tool from the **Surfaces CommandManager** to display **Trim Surface PropertyManager**, as shown.
➤ Select the **Mutual** radio button and then click on the surfaces to select both as trim tools, as shown.

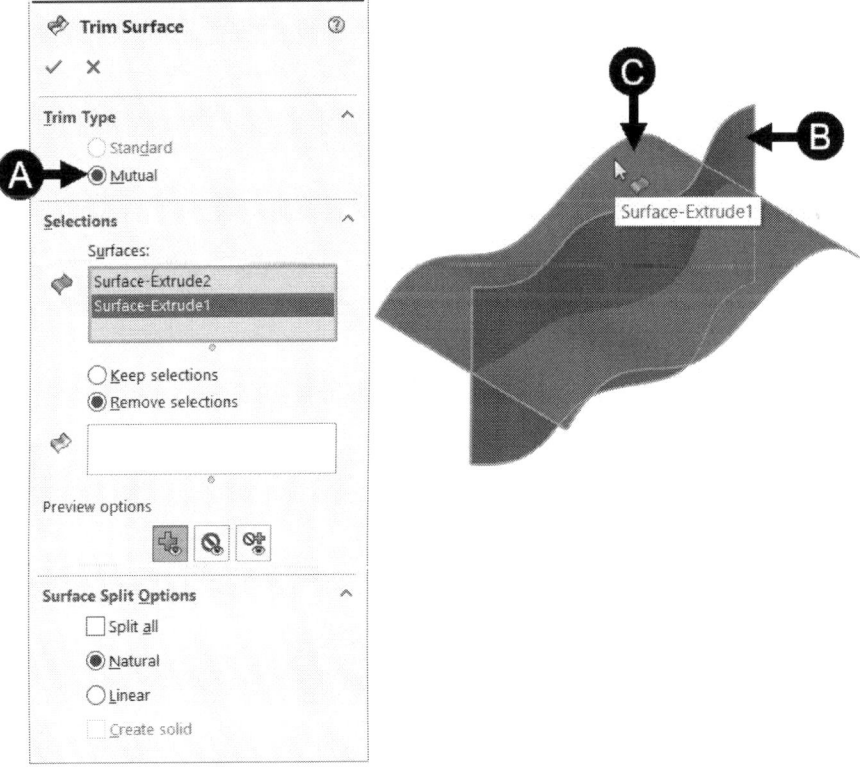

➤ Now click in another selection box of the PropertyManager and click on the required sides of surface to be removed and display preview of removed surfaces, as shown.

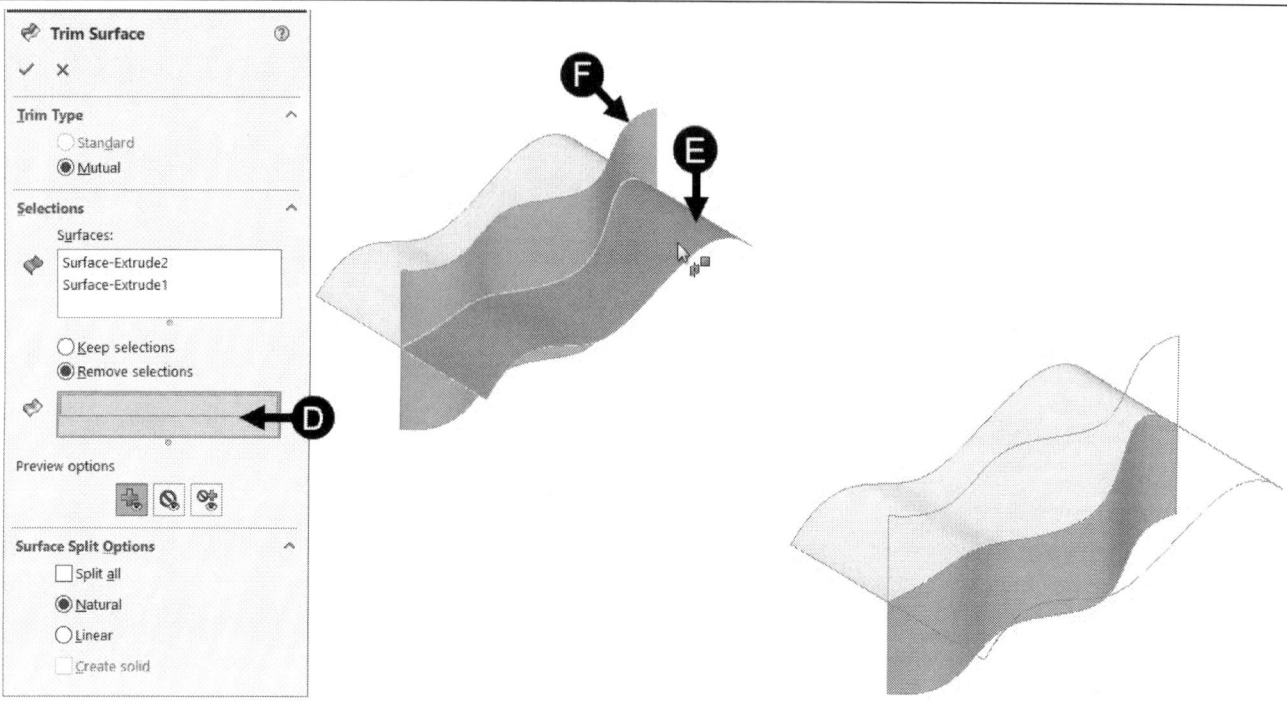

Note that the buttons under **Preview options** area of **Selections** rollout are used to toggle between visibilities of preview of trimmed portions of surfaces.

➤ Now click on the ✓ button of the PropertyManager to apply changes and display the model with trimmed surfaces, as shown.

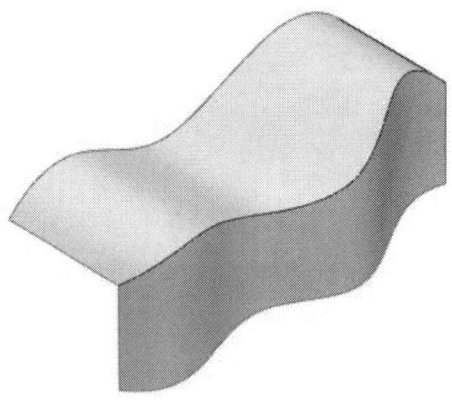

Untrim Surface

This tool is used to patch the trimmed gaps like holes and other cuts in a surface model, by extending an existing surface along its natural boundaries. The steps to use this tool are discussed below:

➤ Select the **Untrim Surface** tool from the **Surfaces CommandManager** to display **Untrim Surface PropertyManager**, as shown.

➤ Click on the surface to untrim the trimmed gaps and display the preview of utrimmed surface, as shown.

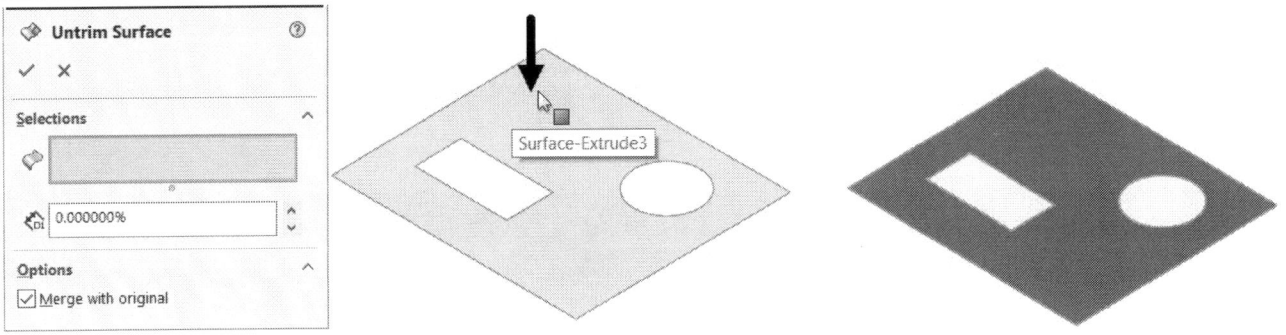

> Now click on the ✓ button of the PropertyManager to apply changes and display the model with untrimmed surfaces, as shown.

Knit Surface

This tool is used to combine two or more faces and surfaces into single surface. The steps to use this tool are discussed below:

> Select the **Knit Surface** tool from the **Surfaces CommandManager** to display **Knit Surface PropertyManager**, as shown.
> Click on both surfaces one by one to select both, as shown.

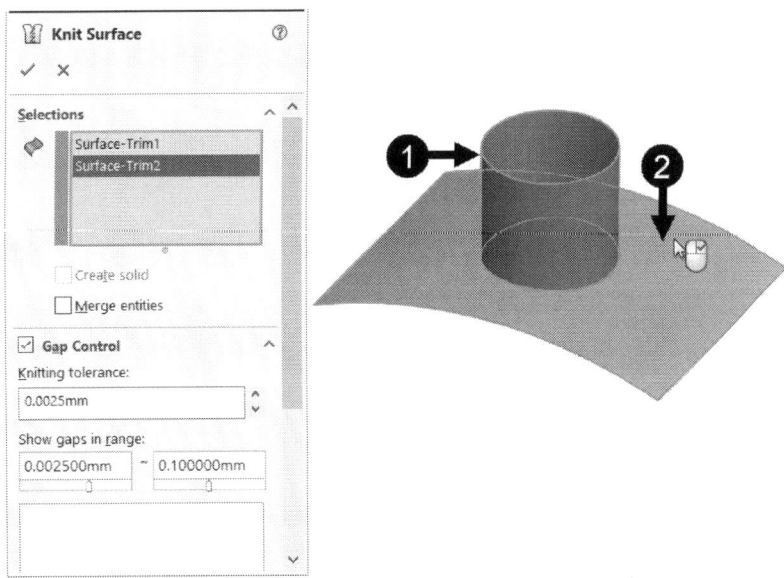

> Now click on the ✓ button of the PropertyManager to apply changes and display the Knit surfaces, as shown.

Also, the **Surface-Knit** feature get displayed in the **FeatureManager Design Tree**, as shown.

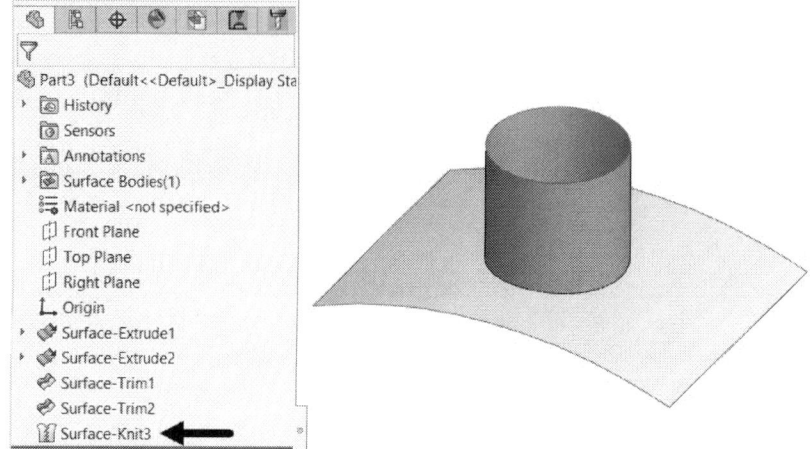

 **Thicken Surface**

This tool is used to increase thickness of surface/surfaces of the surface model. The steps to use this tool are discussed below:

➢ Select the **Thicken** tool from the **Surfaces CommandManager** to display **Thicken PropertyManager**, as shown.

➢ Click on surface to display preview of thicken surfaces, as shown.

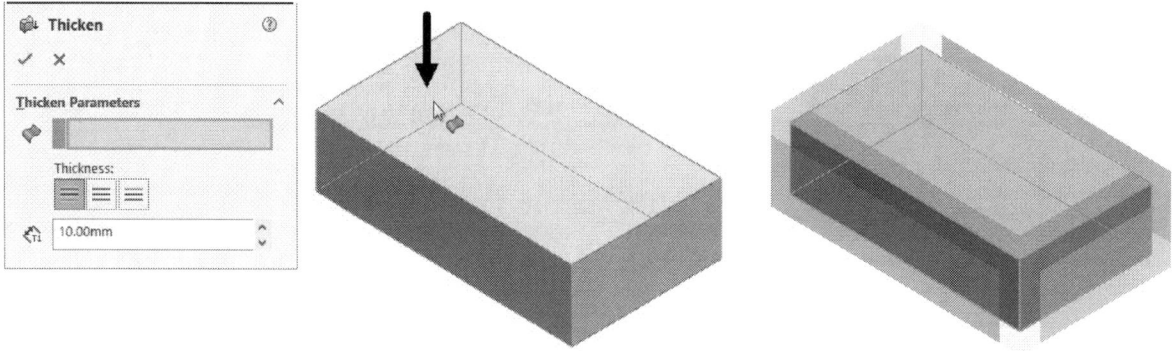

➢ You can enter the required thickness in the **Thickness** spinner and select the required Thickness option from the PropertyManager, as shown above.

➢ Now click on the ✓ button of the PropertyManager to apply changes and display the surface model with Thicken surfaces, as shown.

Thicken Cut

This tool is used to thicken a surface to cut a solid model and create multiple parts. The steps to use this tool are discussed below:

➤ Select the **Thicken Cut** tool from the **Surfaces CommandManager** to display **Cut-Thicken PropertyManager**, as shown.

➤ Click on the surface to be thickened and display preview of thickened surfaces, as shown.

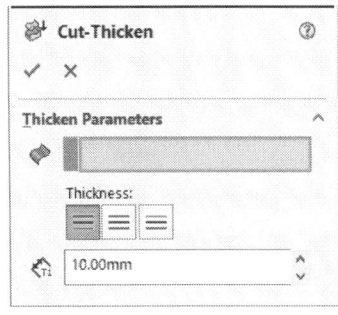 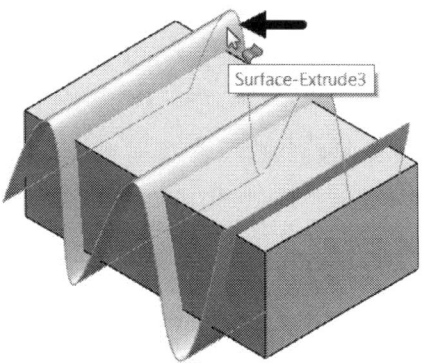 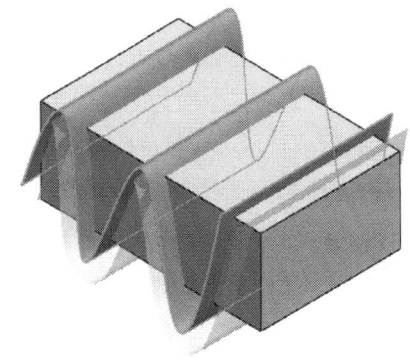

➤ Enter the required thickness in the **Thickness** spinner and select the required Thickness option from the PropertyManager, as shown above.

➤ Now click on the ✓ button of the PropertyManager and select **OK** button of the **Bodies to Keep** dialog box displayed to apply changes and display the Surface model with Thicken Cut feature, as shown.

Note that you can also keep the required bodies only by selecting the **Selected bodies** radio button under **Bodies** rollout of the **Bodies to Keep** dialog box and select the required bodies.

 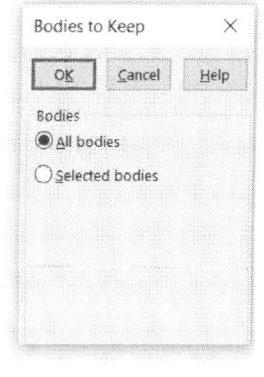 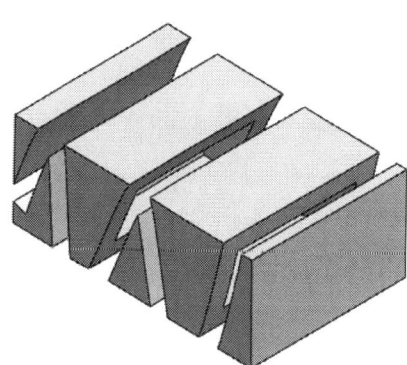

Cut With Surface

This tool is used to cut a solid model by removing material in the shape of selected surface as the cutting tool. The steps to use this tool are discussed below:

➤ Select the **Cut With Surface** tool from the **Surfaces CommandManager** to display **SurfaceCut PropertyManager**, as shown.

➤ Click on the surface to be used as cutting tool for solids, as shown.

➢ Next click on the ✓ button of the PropertyManager to apply changes and display the solid model with cutting surfaces, as shown.

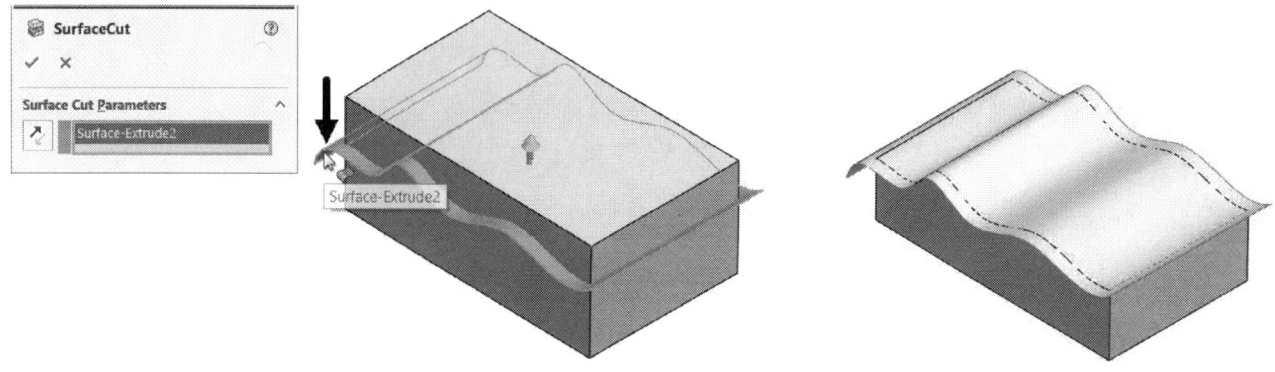

Questions:

1. Which tool is used to fill the gap in Surface model?
2. Which tools is used to trim unwanted portion of surfaces and how?
3. Which tools is used to increase thickness of a surface model and how?
4. Which tool is used to patch the trimmed gaps in the surface model and how?
5. What is the use of **Planar Surface** tool?
6. Which tool is used to flat the surface?
7. Which tool is used to combine multiple faces or surfaces in a single surface?
8. What is the use of **Ruled Surface** tool?

Exercises:

Exercise 1

Create the model shown next.

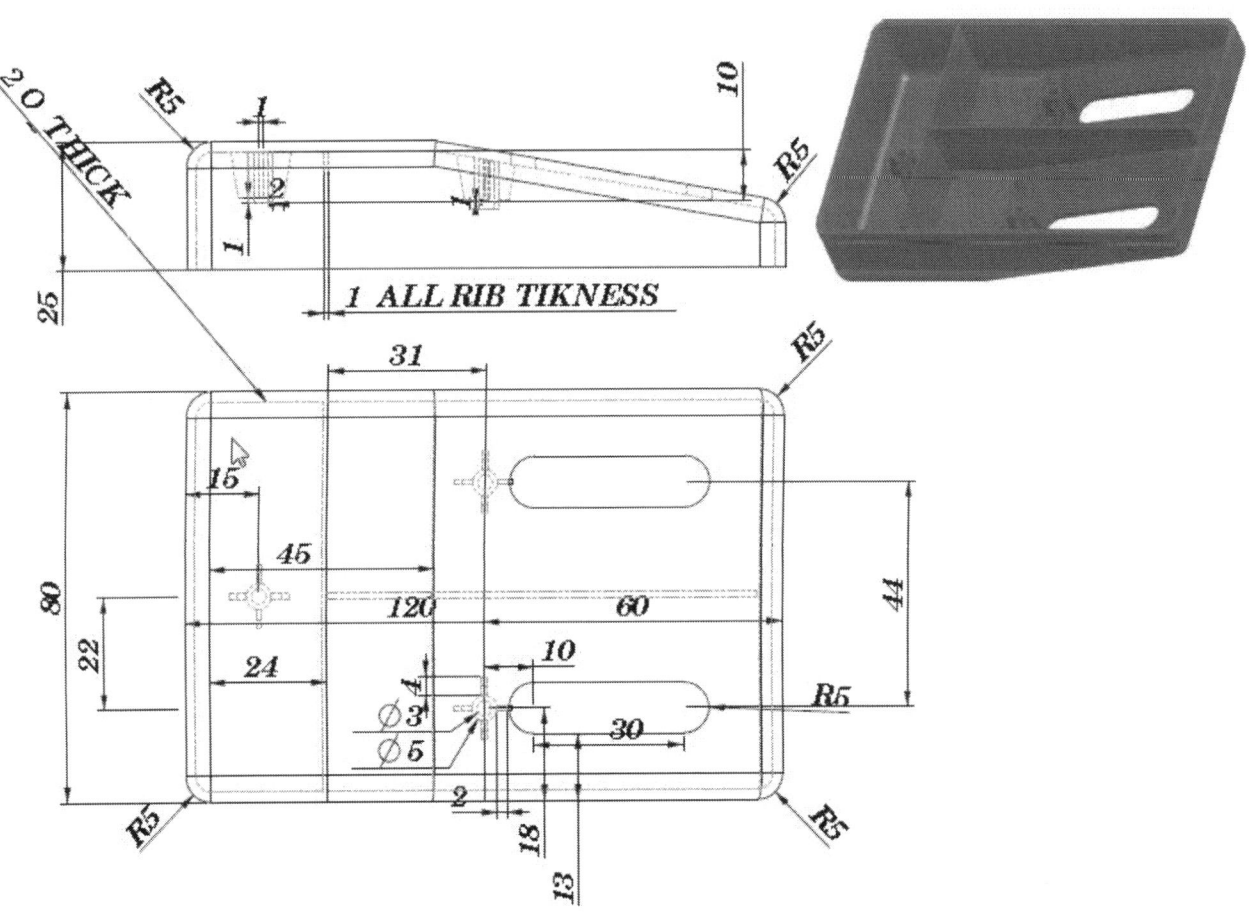

Surface Design

Index

3

3 Point Arc 2-17, 2-24
3 Point Center Rectangle tool 2-15
3 Point Corner Rectangle tool 2-14

A

Add Curves button 13-9
Add Points button 13-10
Add Relation option 4-6
Add Relations PropertyManager 4-6
Add Tab 9-17
Add/Finish Mate button 10-5
Advanced Mates rollout 10-9
Aligned 10-13
Angle radio button 2-5
Angle Mate 10-8
Angle Rollout 12-15
Angle spinner 5-18, 6-6, 10-8, 12-26, 13-14
Angle-distance 3-3
Angle-distance radio button 3-4
Annotation CommandManager 1-11, 11-15
Anti-Aligned 10-13
Apply Scene button 2-36, 10-18
Arc PropertyManager 2-16
Arc Tool 2-16
As sketched radio button 2-4
At angle button 6-6
Attach Radii selection box 9-14
Auto Balloons button 11-17
Auto Balloon PropertyManger 11-17
Auto Relief Rollout 12-6
Auto Relief Type 12-6
Automatic Mate 10-4
Auxiliary View button 11-12
Auxiliary View PropertyManger 11-12
Axis of Revolution option 5-18
Axis PropertyManager 6-11
Axis tool 6-10

B

Balloon PropertyManger 11-16
Balloon tool 11-16
Base Flange PropertyManager 12-2
Base Flange tool 12-8
Base Flange/Tab button 12-2, 12-6
Begin Assembly PropertyManager 10-1, 10-18
Bend Allowance 12-5
Bend Allowance Rollout 12-3
Bend Allowance spinner 12-5
Bend Calculation 12-6
Bend Deduction 12-5
Bend from Virtual Sharp 12-17
Bend Inside button 12-25
Bend Outside 12-17, 12-25, 12-29
Bend Outside button 12-25
Bend Radius spinner 12-3
Bend Table drop-down list 12-4, 12-6
Bend Table option 12-4
Bends PropertyManager 12-17
Bi-directional 3-14
Bill of Materials option 11-15
Bill of Materials PropertyManger 11-15
Blind 5-4, 5-12, 12-28
Bodies rollout 13-27
Bodies to Keep dialog box 13-27
Boss-Extrude PropertyManager 5-1
Boundary Boss/Base tool 8-13
Boundary Cut tool 8-15
Boundary PropertyManager 8-13
Boundary Surface tool 13-6
Boundary-Cut PropertyManager 8-15
Boundary-Surface PropertyManager 13-6
Break Alignment option 4-4
Break button 11-14
Break Corner PropertyManager 12-34
Break View PropertyManager 11-14
Break-Corner/Corner-Trim option 12-34
Broken-out Section button 11-14
Broken-out Section PropertyManger 11-14

C

Center Face Set selection box	9-15
Center of Mass tool	6-18
Center Rectangle tool	2-14, 4-22
Centerline tool	2-7, 2-42
Centerpoint Arc Slot tool	2-25
Centerpoint Arc Tool	2-16, 4-29
Centerpoint Straight Slot	2-23
Chamfer button	12-35
Chamfer Method drop-down	9-23
Chamfer PropertyManager	9-20
Chamfer tool	9-20
Change tab	9-18
Choose Font dialog box	2-38, 3-12
Circle flyout	2-8
Circle PropertyManager	2-8, 2-9
Circle Tool	2-8
Circle Type rollout	2-9
Circular Pattern option	7-15, 8-20
Circular Pattern PropertyManager	3-19
Circular Profile radio button	8-5
Circular Sketch Pattern option	3-19
CirPattern PropertyManager	7-15, 8-20
Closed Corner option	12-33
Closed Corner PropertyManager	12-33
Coincident	4-10
Coincident button	4-10
Coincident constraint	10-6
Collect All Bends button	12-43, 12-44
Collect all corners button	12-35
Collinear	4-8
Collinear button	4-8
CommandManager	1-8
Concentric	4-11
Concentric button	4-11
Concentric Mate	10-7
Conic PropertyManager	2-21
Conic tool	2-21
Construction geometry	3-15
Control Curves rollout	13-9
Control Points rollout	13-10
Convert Entities button	3-10
Convert Entities PropertyManager	3-10
Convert Entities tool	3-10
Convert To Sheet Metal PropertyManager	12-9
Coordinate System tool	6-14
Copy Entities tool	3-24
Copy PropertyManager	3-24
Coradial button	4-12
Corner button	3-7
Corner Defaults rollout	12-11
Corner Options rollout	12-46
Corner Relief option	12-35
Corner Relief PropertyManager	12-35
Corner tab	9-19
Corners flyout	12-33
Counterbore button	7-4
Counterbore Slot button	7-10
Countersink button	7-9
Cross Break PropertyManager	7-31
Cross-Break button	7-31
CrvPattern PropertyManager	7-16
Curve Driven Pattern option	7-16
Curves selection box	8-13
Custom Bend Allowance checkbox	12-19, 12-26, 12-29
Custom Relief Type checkbox	12-19, 12-26
Custom Relief Type drop-down list	12-26
Custom sheet size radio button	11-4
Cut With Surface tool	13-27
Cut-Extrude PropertyManager	5-10
Cut-Extruded PropertyManager	12-39
Cut-Loft PropertyManager	8-12
Cut-Sweep PropertyManager	8-5
Cut-Thicken PropertyManager	13-27
Cutting Line rollout	11-12
Cylindrical/Conical Face option	6-12

D

Deboss button	9-8
Default gap for all rips spinner	12-11
Default overlap ratio for all rips spinner	12-11
Default radius for bends spinners	12-10
Delete and Fill radio button	13-18
Delete and Patch radio button	13-18
Delete Face tool	13-18
Delete radio button	13-18
DeleteFace PropertyManager	13-18
Depth Spinner	5-4, 5-7
Detail View button	11-13
Detail View PropertyManger	11-13
Dimension position	12-29

Dimension PropertyManager	2-37
Direction 1 Angle spinners	3-4
Direction of Extrusion	5-6
Display Style flyout	6-7
Display Style rollout	11-10
Distance 1 and Distance 2 spinners	3-5
Distance Distance button	9-21
Distance mate	10-8
Distance radio button	13-21
Distance spinner	10-8, 12-35, 13-13, 13-21
Distance-distance radio button	3-4
Draft Angle spinner	5-7, 5-16, 9-4
Draft On/Off	5-7, 5-16, 12-42
Draft PropertyManager	9-3
Draft tool	9-3
DraftXpert PropertyManager	9-3
Drawing button	11-1, 11-22
Drawing View PropertyManager	11-8, 11-11

E

Edge Flange Profile	12-15
Edge Flange PropertyManager	12-13
Edge Flange tool	12-13
Edges rollout	12-24
Edit Circular Pattern option	3-21
Edit Cross Profile button	12-31
Edit Feature button	7-8, 7-14
Edit Feature option	12-45
Edit Linear Pattern option	3-21
Edit Sheet Format option	11-18
Edit Sketch option	12-48
Ellipse Property Manager	2-19
Ellipse Tool	2-18
End Condition	5-3, 5-12
End Condition Rollout	7-7, 13-21
Entire model option	11-20
Equal relation	4-9
Equal button	4-9
Equal distance check box	3-5
Exit Sketch button	2-39
Explode PropertyManager	10-14
Exploded View button	10-14
Extend Entities tool	3-9
Extend Surface PropertyManager	13-21
Extend tool	13-21
Extrude Boss/Base tool	5-1
Extruded Cut tool	5-10, 12-39
Extruded Surface tool	13-2
Extrusion direction buttons	9-2

F

Face Face button	9-23
Face Fillet button	9-15
Face for Wrap Sketch area	9-7
Face Set 1 selection box	9-15
Face Set 2 selection box	9-15
Faces To Exclude	12-46
Far Side Countersink Angle spinners	7-8
Far Side Countersink Diameter spinner	7-8
FeatureManager Design Tree	1-11
Fill Surface PropertyManager	13-8
Filled Surface tool	13-8
Fillet option	12-35
Fillet PropertyManager	8-24, 9-11, 13-17
Fillet tool	9-11, 13-17
FilletXpert	9-16
Fit	7-7
Fix	4-12, 10-8
Fix button	4-12
Fix option	10-8
Fixed face	12-46
Flange Angle spinner	12-15
Flange Length Rollout	12-16
Flange Parameters Rollout	12-15
Flange Position Rollout	12-17
Flat-Pattern	12-45
Flat-Pattern PropertyManager	12-46
Flat-Sketch	12-48
Flatten PropertyManager	13-16
Flatten tool	12-45
Flip Mate Alignment	10-6, 10-20
Fold PropertyManager	12-44
Fold tool	12-44
Font button	2-38
For construction	2-5, 2-7, 2-9
For Corners & From Midpoints	2-13
Freeform PropertyManager	13-9
Freeform tool	13-9
Full Round Fillet button	9-15

G

Gap distance 12-15, 12-26
Grain Direction 12-46
Graphics toolbar 6-1
Guide Curves box 8-10

H

Head Clearance spinner 7-8
Hem PropertyManager 12-24
Hem tool 12-24
Hide/Show Items drop-down 6-1
Hide/Show Items flyout 2-34, 4-7
Hole button 7-9
Hole PropertyManager 7-1, 12-40
Hole Specification PropertyManager 7-3, 7-4, 8-24
Hole Specifications rollout 7-7
Hole Type rollout 7-3, 7-6, 7-9
Hole Wizard tool 7-3
Horizontal 2-5, 4-6
Horizontal button 4-6
Horizontal Dimension 2-30, 4-2
Horizontal Ordinate Dimension 4-4
Horizontal relation 4-6

I

Infinite length 2-6
Inner Virtual Sharp 12-16
Inner Virtual Sharp button 12-17
Insert Bends tool 12-47
Insert Components button 10-2
Insert Line PropertyManager 2-4, 2-36
Insert Spline Point option 2-11
Inside Offset 12-29
Intersection 4-11, 6-17
Intersection option 6-17
Intersection button 4-11
Items To Fillet rollout 13-17

J

Jog Angle spinner 12-29
Jog PropertyManager 27
Jog tool 12-27

K

K- Factor spinner 12-5
K-Factor 12-5
Knit Surface PropertyManager 13-25

L

Line button 2-3
Line tool 2-3
Linear Pattern flyout 7-13
Linear Pattern PropertyManager 3-18, 3-21, 7-13, 8-25, 10-36
Linear Pattern tool 7-13
Linear Sketch Pattern button 3-18
Linear/Linear Coupler button 10-12
Link to thickness checkbox 12-40
Lock mate 10-7
Loft PropertyManager 8-7, 8-9
Lofted Bends PropertyManager 12-11, 12-13
Lofted Boss/Base tool 8-7, 8-12
Lofted Cut tool 8-12
Lofted Surface tool 13-5
LPattern Pattern Feature 7-14

M

Mass Properties tool 6-18
Mate Alignment portion 10-13
Mate PropertyManager 10-4
Mate tool 10-4
Material Inside 12-17, 12-29
Material Outside 12-17, 12-29
Menu Bar 1-8
Merge button 4-13
Merge faces 12-46
Merge result 5-7
Mid Plane 5-6, 5-15
Midpoint 4-11
Midpoint button 4-11
Midpoint line 2-6
Midpoint Line tool 2-7
Mirror Entities tool 3-16
Mirror PropertyManager 3-16, 7-11, 8-26
Mirror tool 7-11, 9-9
Miter Flange PropertyManager 12-22
Miter Flange tool 12-21

Miter Gap rollout 12-26
Miter Gap spinner 12-26
Model Items button 11-20
Model Items PropertyManager 11-20
Model View PropertyManager 11-3, 11-9
Model View tool 11-9
Modify dialog box 1-13
Modify edit box 2-28, 2-30
Move Entities tool 3-22
Move PropertyManager 3-23
Mutual radio button 13-23

N

Near side countersink 7-8
Near Side Countersink Angle spinners 7-8
Near Side Countersink Diameter spinner 7-8
Neutral radio button 9-4
New icon 1-1
New button 1-5, 2-1, 10-1, 11-1
New Drawing Part/Assembly option 11-5
New SOLIDWORKS Document dialog box 1-1, 1-5, 2-1
New tool 1-5
No Bends tool 12-49
Normal cut check box 12-40
Normal To Profile option 8-10, 8-15
Normal to Surface radio button 13-13
Note PropertyManager 11-19
Number of Instances selection box 9-14
Number of planes to create spinner 6-3

O

Obround option 12-6, 12-19
Offset 5-3, 5-5, 5-11, 12-18
Offset Distance spinner 6-3, 12-18, 12-28, 13-12
Offset Distance edit box 3-13
Offset End Condition 12-18
Offset Entities PropertyManager 3-13
Offset Entities tool 3-13
Offset Face button 9-22
Offset From Surface 5-5, 5-14
Offset Surface PropertyManager 13-12
Offset Surface tool 13-12
One Line/Edge/Axis option 6-11
Open button 1-7, 12-25
Open dialog box 1-7, 10-19

Options button 1-11
Options rollout 7-8
Ordinate Dimension 4-4
Orientation rollout 2-4, 11-10
Outer Virtual Sharp button 12-16, 12-17
Outside Offset 12-29
Overall Dimension 12-29
Overlap rip 12-11
Override default parameters check box 12-3, 12-6, 12-12

P

Parabola PropertyManager 2-20
Parabola tool 2-19
Parallel 4-8
Parallel button 4-8, 6-9, 10-6
Parallel Mate 10-6
Parallel Plane 6-8
Parallelogram tool 2-15
Part button 1-1, 1-5, 2-1
Partial Ellipse tool 2-19
Partial preview radio button 13-17
Path Length Dimension option 4-5
Path Length PropertyManager 4-5
Path Mate button 10-11
Pattern tools 7-13
Perimeter Circle Tool 2-9
Perpendicular button 4-8
Perpendicular Constraint 4-8
Perpendicular mate 10-7
Perpendicular to Vector radio button 13-15
Plain White option 2-36
Planar Surface PropertyManager 13-11
Planar Surface tool 13-11
Plane At An Angle 6-6
Plane PropertyManager 6-3, 6-6, 8-17, 8-26
Plane Through Selected Points 6-5
Point tool 2-27
Point and Face/Plane option 6-13
Point PropertyManager 2-27
Point tool 2-27
Polygon PropertyManager 2-25
Polygon tool 2-25
Power trim button 3-6
Preview options area 13-24
Process-Bends node 12-48

Profile Center button 10-9
Profile Twist drop down list 8-4
Projected View button 11-11
Projected View dialog box 11-6
Projected View PropertyManger 11-11
Projection option 6-17

Q

Quick Access toolbar 1-5

R

Radius spinner 9-14, 12-26
Rectangle flyout 2-13
Rectangle PropertyManager 2-13
Rectangle tool 2-13
Rectangular option 12-27, 12-36
Reference Geometry tool 6-2
Relief Depth 12-20, 12-27
Relief Depth spinner 12-20
Relief Options rollout 12-36
Relief Ratio spinner 12-6
Relief Type drop-down list12-19, 12-20, 12-21, 12-26
Relief Width 12-20, 12-27
Relief Width spinner 12-20
Replace Face PropertyManager 13-20
Replace Face tool 13-20
Return button 11-20
Reverse Direction .5-3, 5-17, 5-19, 5-23, 12-3, 12-12, 12-29, 13-13
Reverse direction check box 12-3, 12-12
Revolve PropertyManager 5-17, 13-3
Revolve tool 5-17
Revolved boss/base tool 5-17
Revolved Cut tool 5-20
Revolved Surface tool 13-3
Rib PropertyManager 9-1
Rib tool 9-1
Rib1 PropertyManager 9-1
Ribs selection box 12-42
Rip and Extend option 12-26
Rip Gap spinner 12-23
Rip PropertyManager 12-47
Rip Sketches rollout 12-11
Rip tool 12-47
Rolled button 12-25

Rotate Entities tool 3-24
Rotate PropertyManager 3-24
Ruled Surface PropertyManager 13-12
Ruled Surface tool 13-12

S

Save As dialog box 1-7
Save button 1-7
Scale Entities tool 3-25
Scale PropertyManager 3-26
Scale rollout 11-10
Scibe button 9-8
Section View Assist PropertyManger 11-12
Section View button 11-12
Select chain 3-14
Select Open Loop button 8-11, 13-6
Select Table drop down list 12-3
Selected bodies radio button 13-27
Selected Contours 5-8
Selected Contours box 5-8
SelectionManager 13-6
Selections rollout 12-28, 13-24
Sheet Format 11-1, 11-3
Sheet Format/Size dialog box 11-1
Sheet Metal CommandManager 1-9
Sheet Metal Gauges rollout 12-3
Sheet Metal Gusset PropertyManager 12-37
Sheet Metal Gusset tool 12-37
Sheet Metal option 1-10, 12-1
Sheet Metal Parameters rollout 12-3
Sheet Metal tab 1-10, 12-1
Sheet Properties dialog box 11-4
Sheet tab 11-4
Sheet thickness 12-10
Shell PropertyManager 9-5
Shell tool 9-5
Show custom sizing 7-7
Show In Exploded State option 11-15
Show preview check box 9-5
Show Slit 12-46
Side Face Set 1 selection box 9-15
Simple Hole tool 7-1, 12-40
Simply bends 12-46
Size 7-7
Sketch button 2-2, 2-36
Sketch Chamfer option 3-3

Sketch Chamfer PropertyManager	3-3
Sketch Driven Pattern option	7-17
Sketch Driven Pattern PropertyManager	7-17
Sketch Fillet tool	3-1
Sketch Fillet PropertyManager	3-1
Sketch Plane	5-2, 5-11
Sketch Profile radio button	8-4
Sketch tool	2-2
Sketched Bend PropertyManager	12-30
Sketched Bend tool	12-29
Slot Length spinner	12-36
Slot PropertyManager	2-22
Smart Dimension button	2-28, 4-1
Smart Dimension flyout	2-27, 4-1
Smart Dimension tool	2-28, 2-30
Solid Profile radio button	8-6
SOLIDWORKS message box	5-18
Spars selection box	12-42
Specify Twist Value option	8-4
Spline flyout	2-10
Spline Tool	2-10
Standard 3 View button	11-7
Standard 3 View PropertyManager	11-7
Standard drop-down list	7-6
Start constraint and End constraint drop-down list	8-9
Start constraint drop-down list	8-10
Start/End Constraints rollout	8-9
Straight Slot tool	2-22
Stretch Entities	3-27
Stretch PropertyManager	3-27
Stretch tool	3-27
Surface Flatten tool	13-16
Surface tab	13-1
Surface/Face/Plane	5-2, 5-11
SurfaceCut PropertyManager	13-27
Surface-Extrude PropertyManager	13-2
Surface-Loft PropertyManager	13-5
Surface-Sweep PropertyManager	13-4
Sweep Boss/Base tool	8-3
Sweep PropertyManager	8-2
Sweep radio button	13-15
Sweep tool	12-31
Swept Boss/Base tool	8-1
Swept Cut button	8-4
Swept Cut tool	8-4
Swept Flange PropertyManager	12-32
Swept Flange tool	12-32
Swept Surface tool	13-4
Symmetric	4-12, 10-10
Symmetric button	4-12, 10-10
System Options dialog box	1-11

T

Tab and Slot PropertyManager	12-37
Tab and Slot tool	12-37
Tangent	4-9
Tangent button	4-9
Tangent Arc	2-17, 5-27
Tangent Bend button	12-17
Tangent Blend	12-16
Tangent Fill check box	13-19
Tangent Mate	10-7
Tangent Plane	6-7
Tangent side bends	12-18
Tangent to Bend	12-18
Tangent to Surface radio button	13-12
Tapered to Vector radio button	13-14
Tear Drop button	12-25
Tear option	12-21
Text tool	3-11
Thicken Cut tool	13-27
Thicken PropertyManager	13-26
Thicken tool	13-26
Thickness button	9-2
Thickness spinner	9-5, 9-7, 12-3, 13-26
Thin Feature	5-8
Thin Feature checkbox	5-18
Through All	5-4, 5-13
Toggle flat display option	12-47
Trim Entities tool	3-6
Trim Away Inside button	3-8
Trim Away Outside button	3-8
Trim PropertyManager	3-6
Trim Surface PropertyManager	13-22
Trim Surface tool	13-22
Trim to closest button	3-9
Two Planes	6-12
Two Points/Vertices option	6-12
Type and Size rollout	12-25
Type rollout	13-12
Types of Draft rollout	9-4

U

Under Head Countersink Angle spinners 7-8
Underlap rip 12-11
Unfold PropertyManager 12-43
Unfold tool 12-43
Unit Precision drop-down 2-37
Units and Dimension Standard dialog box 1-6
Untrim Surface PropertyManager 13-24
Untrim Surface tool 13-24
Up To Body 5-6, 5-14
Up To Edge and Merge option 12-15
Up To Next 5-4, 5-13
Up To Surface 5-5, 5-14
Up To Vertex 5-5, 5-13
Use custom scale radio button 11-10
Use default radius 12-15
Use default radius checkbox 12-28
Use gauge table checkbox 12-3
Use relief ratio check box 12-19, 12-20
Use Relief Ratio check box 12-27

V

Variable Size Fillet button 9-13
Vent PropertyManager 12-41
Vent tool 12-41
Vertex 5-2, 5-11, 9-21
Vertex button 9-21
Vertical 2-5, 4-7
Vertical button 4-7
Vertical Dimension 4-3
Vertical Dimension option 4-3
Vertical Ordinate Dimension 4-5
View (Heads-Up) Toolbar 1-8
View Layout CommandManager 1-11
View Palette task pane 11-5
View Sketch Dimensions 2-34, 3-2
View Sketch Relations 4-7

W

Welded Corner option 12-34
Welded Corner PropertyManager 12-34
Width button 10-11
Wireframe mode 6-7
Wrap Parameters rollout 9-7
Wrap PropertyManager 9-7
Wrap tool 9-7
Wrap Type and Wrap Method rollout 9-7

Made in United States
Orlando, FL
23 July 2024

49396758R00235